VOICE
OF THE
7TH
ANGEL

VOICE
OF THE
7TH
ANGEL

THE END IS NOT YET

---

by
Andrew Contreras

SANTA FE

Sunstone books may be purchased for educational, business, or sales promotional use. For information please write: Special Markets Department, Sunstone Press, P.O. Box 2321, Santa Fe, New Mexico 87504-2321.

FIRST EDITION

10 9 8 7 6 5 4 3 2 1

Library of Congress Cataloging-in-Publication Data:
Contreras, Andrew, 1950–
    Voice of the 7th angel : the end is not yet / by Andrew Contreras.—1st ed.
        p. cm.
    ISBN: 0-86534-310-1
    1. End of the world—Biblical teaching. 2. Bible—Prophecies—End of the world.
I. Title: Voice of the seventh angel. II. Title.

BS649.E63 C66 1999
236'.9—dc21   99-059029

Published by SUNSTONE PRESS
            Post Office Box 2321
            Santa Fe, NM 87504-2321 / USA
            (505) 988-4418 / *orders only* (800) 243-5644
            FAX (505) 988-1025
            www.sunstonepress.com

CONTENTS

Preface—9

Acknowledgments—12

Introduction—13

1 The Voices—17
• Lots of Leading Voices Shall Proliferate
• The Seventh Angel
• The "Blessed Hope" — Any Day Now?
• 20/20 Blindness
• Crafty Rap of the Rapturists
• What's the Difference?

2 Sorting Out the Facts—37
• Time to Turn Back? or Get Off the Tour Bus?
• Strong Medicine for Rapture Syndrome/Pious Paranoia
• Tribulation or Indignation?
• Thief in the Night?
• Which Thief?!
• Secret New Facts Revealed to The Lamb

3 The Signposts—62
• Detour — The Museum of Religious Imperialism
• "Peace and Safety?" — or, Wars and Rumors of Wars?
• Famines, Diseases, & Earthquakes Widespread
• New Age Birth Pangs and Woes of Mother Earth
• Preview: The Birth of JOY
• Quick — Take Your Pick

4 New World Order Options—93
• Zion & the New World Order Paradox
• The World Order of the Beast
• New World Order of Cinderella — Glass Slipper of Mystery Babylon
• Signpost of The Last 7 Years — The Worldwide Week of the Beast

5 Not Yet—118
- The End Is Not By and By
- Hate First
- Love as Cold as Ice
- The Iconoclasts of 21st Century Idolatry
- Small or Great, Rich or Poor, Believer or Heathen

6 "Ye Shall Not Die...Ye Shall Be As Gods!"—148
- When You See the Abomination...
- The "Kanaph" Invasion — The Aliens Are Coming
- Hi-tech Synthetic God

7 The Fundamental Dread—173
- Past is Prologue
- Great Tribulation Politics and Power Struggles
- Politics of Persecution
- Great but Short, yet All-Inclusive Tribulation
- Holy Incest? Holy Whoredom? — or Wholly Arrogance and Fear?

8 Gates of Hell Prevail—193
- Prevailing Over That Which Prevails
- Who Overcomes Who?
- Beyond Flesh
- The Goyim, or the Goyim?
- Shadow of the Chosen Faith
- Key to the Contradiction
- Gates of Hades Endnote

9 Marvel, or Revolt?—217
- Dire Straits
- Elijah and the Revolution
- Mind-Benders and Marvels
- The "Universal" Allure and The Race Against Time
- Prepare the Way of the "Maestro of Marvels"

10 Messiah Mistake—242
- "Son of Man" or "Man of Sin?"
- "Falling Away?" Apostasy? — A Premier Sign of the Times
- Occupy: as in Occupant, or as in Occupation?
- Oops! (Don't Be Mistaken)

11 The Sieve of Vanity—267
- Immediately When?
- Galactic Blackout — Power, Gloom, and Fright
- Blood Flood — The Vintage of Earth Matures
- Armageddon Hosts "Gog" Convention and Vulture Banquet
- Finally, Truth Distilled From Muddy (or perhaps Bloody) Waters

12 Seven Last Plagues—298
- The Wrath Of God
- Hailstones, Skyscrapers, and Bombshelters
- Babylon, or New Jerusalem?

13 Figs & Generation Finále—322
- Fig-uratively Speaking
- This Generation Shall Not Pass
- God's Name in the Center of the World

14 Tell Us When—341
- Kingdom-Come Ideology
- Hosanna Hearts and the Barabbas Factor
- The Acceptable Year-Acceptable Witness Link
- Priorities in Order
- It's Different Now

15 Ten Virgins—367
- Five Wise, Five Foolish
- Unique Circumstances Demand Unique Responses
- Key to Readiness
- Christi-any-way-you-want-it
- The Marturéo Complex

Endnotes—389

PREFACE

Openly stated here at the outset, and as the reader will surely gather out of the body of this work, a very deliberate effort is made to starkly challenge, with maximal austerity, the mainstream beliefs of traditional and neo-traditional "believers," particularly of Christian namesake. This is done out of *"necessity"* in a deliberate effort to force the reader away from any majority-held opinions, interpretations and perspectives on Biblical teachings and spiritual subjects, prophecy topics in particular.

A political proverb passed on to me quite a number of years ago, originating with a sage whose name I never learned, but with whose wisdom I instinctively identified almost instantly upon its birth in my ear, provides the rationale for this approach. That poignant proverb helped to foster in me a healthy sense of skepticism that has remained a faithful companion of mine to this very day. I have employed the principle it embodies in the challenges I pose throughout this book. And though the "tough love" approach taken in presenting my theme may at times seem harsh or unkind, even at best, it is nonetheless in love that I have offered my absolute best to the search for Truth, hoping that the wisdom of my trusty proverb might assist me to be a blessing to all who venture to read my ravings and join me in the quest.

For all I know, my little proverb was probably born from the womb of the Holy Bible itself; for it most certainly resembles, just as a daughter her mother, the teaching of the Master with respect to political majority dynamics. You may already by familiar with it too:

"The majority is always wrong."

ACKNOWLEDGMENTS

Many thanks and a huge debt of gratitude are due to those on earth who have made this work possible and supported me in its fulfillment, especially my family and friends.

First, to my dad and mom, Casimiro and Amalia (Casey and Molly to most), who provided the bulk of the material blessings that made my studies and manuscripting a tactical possibility. Not only so, but they encouraged and reinforced my efforts consistently from start to finish with unceasing patience, faith and moral support. They have been God's loving angels to me throughout my entire life.

Another set of angels—my "kids," Gabe, Glory, Xavier and Andrea—have likewise been pillars of strength, agents of inspiration and indispensable spiritual sounding boards of priceless feedback throughout the entire writing process. Their precious sacrifices of time, funds and personal attendance to the needs of our home to keep it (and me) all propped up and running smoothly, while I neglected to even eat sometimes, are an integral part of this "labor of love." (God, they're all great cooks, and kind critics too!) Wading through my early manuscripts and then later revisions to bounce back their hearty input and honest critique kept me in touch with Planet Earth.

My dear friends, Ann, Marquita and Eli have been as good as family in the fanning of my flame. They have little idea, I think, how greatly they contributed to the final product and the inspiration to complete it.

Lastly, but certainly not in the least, kudos to Jim Smith of Sunstone Press and to his great professional staff for the amazing miracle they churned out by producing this book in less than two handfuls of weeks.

And, no thanks great enough can I offer to our incomparable CREATOR in heaven for the opportunity to make this offering to His people. If it indeed contributes ultimately to His greater glory, I will be eternally overflowing with joyous thanks for that miracle of miracles. It will have been another one of His.

INTRODUCTION

Entitled "Voice of the 7th Angel," and highlighting the finality of the seventh and last voice of the angels of the Apocalypse, this book renders a definitive, and unpopular, statement about the much talked-about "End of the World." In its pages, the prevailing vogue of weak and watered down mainstream beliefs about the end times are seriously challenged. They are exposed for their frivolity and fantasy, and rocked to their fickle foundations in a courageous search for the "elusive" truth—one that fraudulent fables of Rapture cannot dispel— a truth revealing that *The End is not yet!*

A burgeoning plethora of modern-day prophecy "experts" and scholars of Bible texts have all raised their assorted voices to expound on their "illuminated" understandings of the ancient scriptures that detail the visions of the Prophets concerning the Time of The End. Yet, a hazy shadow of uncertainty and a thick fog of confusion hovers tenaciously over this sorely misunderstood subject— thanks to all the overflowing hype, of the best-selling type, and to blind devotion to an ill-founded "Christian" tradition of misguided narrow-mindedness. Lacking most in the spiritual bankruptcy of our times, and evident in the popularized expositions of today's Bible prophecy experts, is a sense of *courage* in the quest for truth.

This book's frank study of the very same Scriptures that seem to lead to conflicting conclusions by the various prophecy experts of notoriety examines not only the differing and deviant conclusions of these leading voices but the reason for the conflict. The unadulterated teachings of the Scriptures are the guiding light of each of the chapters herein. That light dispels the popular hype cultivated and promoted by such works as those authored by Hal Lindsey (of *The Late Great Planet Earth* fame, *Apocalypse Code*, and others) as well as by numerous other authors and television personalities, too numerous to name, who subscribe to and nourish Rapture dogmas based on escapist eschatologies. The deep-seated dreads that drive the embracing of such contrived doctrines, which are in direct conflict with the truth, are confronted with almost brutal honesty as we learn from our study that the end cannot possibly be yet, nor at any random unexpected moment!

Nor will we see the birth of the "New World Order" without experiencing the travail! The best-selling purveyors of Rapture-mania have indeed rightly perceived many of the "signs of the times" as per the prophets of the Bible; yet they remain heavily deluded about the times of the signs! This hard-hitting examination of the prophetic texts and related biblical teachings reveals that Second Coming buffs and expectant "rapturophiles" have a great deal of "hard labor" ahead of them before the "baby" of their "blessed hope" is ever delivered. There shall be no spiritual caesarean section or anesthetic relief from the dreaded Great Tribulation spoken of by the prophets, which they clearly state will precede the New Age of Messiah.

Indeed, a "New Age" is about to dawn upon the world of mankind, as so many modern-day prophets are loudly heralding; I too affirm we are definitely treading the threshold of a New World Order. But, sadly, the darkest hour ever known to humanity—the final hour of travail immediately preceding the emergence of the NWO—remains desperately dim in the uncertain light of the array of flickering prophetic "candles" now feebly blowing in the wind, though they abound across the landscape of our generation. This book reveals what fuels the fickle flames of the great majority of today's best-selling Christian "prophets," and it projects a bold and blazing light on the *actual* perspective provided to us by the ancient prophets of the Bible regarding the coming New Age with which our planet is so pregnant.

As the "controversy of Jerusalem" continues to swell and threaten the peace and stability of the entire globe, so does the infamous emergence and rise of the ambitious demigod Antichrist—seeking to exploit humanity and the resources of Earth to establish a planetary fortress for galactic domination (headquartered in Jerusalem)—become an even more clear and present reality. The literal and symbolic significance of Jerusalem and how Christians may, or may not, be connected is well documented within the pages of the *"Voice of the 7th Angel."*

And for the spiritually minded, at last, the facts are unearthed—Christians are neither the root of the New Age Jerusalem, nor the trunk, nor a separate new tree unto themselves. Just as they share a common root with their Jewish mother, so they also share a common destiny with her (both the bitter and the sweet) as the *Daughter* of Jerusalem.

Discussion of the New World Order, the dynamics and the principal powers which charge that competitive conflict for global domination, is also visited at one of the "stops" in what this author has termed a "tour" of the Prophetic Landscape authentically painted for us by the ancient Prophets of the Hebrew Scriptures. This is a tour which promises, and fulfills its pledge, to take us off the worn-out beaten paths of the popular, best-selling tour lines of the mainstream to the rugged, but realistic sites of genuinely raw and veritable, non-commercial prophetic exploration. Thanks for joining the tour, and please fasten your seat belts!

1

SO MANY VOICES

And the angel which I saw stand upon the sea and upon the earth lifted up
his hand to heaven, and sware by him that liveth for ever and ever,
who created heaven, and the things that therein are, and the earth, and the
things that therein are, and the sea, and the things which are therein,
that there should be time no longer:
But in the days of the voice of the seventh angel,
when he shall begin to sound, the mystery of God should be finished,
as he hath declared to his servants the prophets.
The Book of Revelation, chapter 10, verses 5-7.

Everywhere it seems there are voices resounding the theme of the end of the age, the time of the end, and the last days. There's a lot of talk these days of a New Age and a New World Order. We hear so many thoughts and theories about what the coming new millennium will bring. So many voices, views, and versions of what the future holds in store fill the air! So many, many differing opinions and conflicting ideas abound, even among so-called experts on the prophetic texts dealing with these themes! Is the end of the world at hand? Are we in the last generation?

Well, treading the threshold of the 21st century now, ours is truly a most extraordinary hour of history. Not to be compared with, yet not exactly strange, it is a thoroughly unique and absolutely unparalleled day and age, especially in light of the dramatic changes that have swept through our world in the last 100 years—not to mention the last 20 or 30—with the inconceivable yet to come!

I comment that it isn't really so strange, because the more I dig into the historic writings of the Hebrews the more it becomes evident that they possessed some uncanny foreknowledge of exactly how the future would flower and what fruit it would bring forth. (A particularly salient example of this is visited in chapter 13 about the "fig tree.") Mysterious as it may be, that pre-written history is fulfilling itself. And although history repeating itself is an all too common thread throughout the tapestry of time, Hebrew history alike, I actually did mean to say fulfilling itself, playing itself out as an almost foregone conclusion.

I find that the headline developments of this astonishing, and now quickly passing century were written thousands of years ago in long anticipation of the very times in which we live. A study of the writings of now long-dead Hebrew seers, which will be our focus throughout these pages, not only reveals where we presently are on their documented prophetic timetable, but what is next on the itinerary for the near future—not exactly a fearless prospect, I must admit. Ancient prophecies have predicted our current predicament quite precisely. Most widely familiar are those of the most notable prophet of all: *Yeshua Ha'Mashiach* as he's known to the Hebrews, *Christo Iesous* to the Greeks, and to English speakers, *Jesus Christ*. His prophetic testimony, on record in the pages of the New Testament, describes the developing conditions of our modern world with uncanny, and even frightening accuracy.

Our purpose in this book is to embark on a tour of various prophetic texts which have been well preserved and passed on to us from ancient Hebrew sources, some dating back well over 3,000 years. My endeavor as your guide is to stop at as many of the major points of interest that will serve to compose an accurate and comprehensive picture of the end-time landscape as foretold by these ancients.

It is my fervent conviction that, taken together, there is nothing confusing, contradictory or conflicting in their many separate writings; but rather, aside from the as yet sealed portions, there lies a very clear, and highly-coordinated vision of *future history* safely preserved in their phenomenal prophetic chronicles—just waiting for our discovery and amazement. Some sights may excite you, others may frighten you; but if our tour of them doesn't shatter whatever trace of complacency may have crept into your life, then I will have indeed failed in my literary endeavor.

We shall examine the order, as well as the nature of end-time developments foretold by the numerous Hebrew prophets of the Old and New Testaments of the Bible; special focus will be directed to the prophecies given by Christ.

Bear in mind, these are not voices of clairvoyants from recent issues of the *National Enquirer*, or of contemporary diviners like Jean Dixon, or of other twentieth century psychics or seers like Edgar Cayce or George Orwell, or even of Renaissance prophets like Nostradamus not yet even 500 years old. The voices I will echo in this book are nothing less than eminently ancient. The most recent ones are now over 1900 years old. And beyond any mere coincidence, all of those voices—some dating back 3,500 years—sang in complete chorus.

The state of affairs actually prevailing in this day and age was forecast most clearly by the Lead Voice in the chorus, as we shall see.

Lots of Leading Voices Shall Proliferate

And as he sat upon the mount of Olives, the disciples came unto him privately, saying, Tell us, when shall these things be? and what shall be the sign of thy coming, and of the end of the world? And Jesus answered and said unto them, Take heed that no man deceive you. For many shall come in my name, saying, I am Christ; and shall deceive many. . . . And many false prophets shall rise, and shall deceive many. . . . For there shall arise false Christs, and false prophets, and shall shew great signs and wonders; insomuch that, if it were possible, they shall deceive the very elect. Behold, I have told you before.—Matthew 24:3-5, 11 & 24-25

It is largely because of the increasing perplexity and global distress that prevails in our world as we approach the year 2000, that so many voices are raised to cry for reason, trying to make sense of things, and to find direction and purpose. In this contemporary climate of confusion, disorientation and rapid-fire change, the soil is fertile for the proliferation of prophets, saviors, deliverers and messiahs. Their doctrines and persuasions, theories and visions, and the teeming voices of these multitudes of "answer-men" abound. They're everywhere!

From political panderers to evangelical vendors, *everybody* has "the solution" and claims to know the answer. All of them will lead you out of your distress to a better place, supposedly.

Whether it be Bill Clinton, Gloria Steinem, Fidel Castro, Mikhail Gorbachev, David Koresh, Kofi Annan, Margaret Thatcher, Henry Kissinger, Yasser Arafat, Yitzhak Rabin, Nelson Mandela, Pope John Paul II, Indira Gandhi, Shimon Peres, John Hagee, Mao Tse-tung, John Dewey, Caspar Weinberger, Chuck Missler, Bill Bennett, Ayatola Khomeni, Hal Lindsay, Billy Graham, Mary Anne Williamson, Louis Farrakhan, Benjamin Netanyahu or now Ehud Barak, they all have "the answer"—some probably more than others. There is no intent to deride any of the illustrious figures just mentioned, but only to give some inkling of the myriad assortment of would-be answer-men-and-women prominent in our time who believe they have (or have had) ideas and agendas worthy of mass acceptance and adherence.

The trouble is, how do you sort through so many voices for a transcendent truth that really resolves the old mystery: "What in the world is going on in this life, and exactly what *are* we doing here?" Which voices satisfactorily answer the questions: "Where are we going? What's it all about? What should we believe? Are there any absolutes? Is there a right or wrong way? Will it all ever make sense? Will things just simply continue spiraling ever faster in the direction they are headed now? Will it ever end?"

As King Solomon pondered, "What is the conclusion of the whole matter?"

The Seventh Angel

Well, let us take comfort in the voice of the Seventh Angel. For when he shall begin to sound, the Scriptures tell us, then *"time shall be no longer"* and *"the mystery of God shall be finished."* The tangled mess of all the ages will be unwound. The truth will be completely manifest. The confusion will be dispelled. The lies and the liars will be exposed. Deceit and corruption will be halted forever.

Retribution will then be meted out to each of the world's vile leaders—of whatever brand—including the multitude of false Christs and false prophets who misled and seduced the masses into the predatory snare of the Soul Slayer. The travesties of mankind shall be terminated. The oppressors and exploiters, opportunists and extortioners, sorcerers (evil chemists & druggists), "dogs" (practicing wanton incontinence), whoremongers (sex/lust merchants), all liars and deceiving propagandists (commercial, educational, governmental, or religious), and all God-hating blasphemers will pay their dues.

The earth will be cleaned up. Those who destroyed the earth will be destroyed.[1] The weapons of war will be incinerated and war abolished.[2] The New Earth Order of Messiah will be established.[3] Earth will be inherited by the meek and the poor, who will be its prime ministers, governors, judges, and law enforcement agents.[4] Love, liberty, peace, goodness, and harmlessness will be the law of the New Earth Order.[5] Under the direction of the Supreme Prince of Peace, the Earth, its people, and all its inhabitants (animals too) and resources will be managed the way they were meant to be since the beginning.[6] This momentous occurrence is referred to by orthodox Jews as the Coming of Messiah and by most Christians as the Second Coming of Christ.

Could this scenario be any time soon?

The "Blessed Hope"—Any Day Now?

Some voices regularly proclaim its advent any day! Some not only declare that the day is immediately imminent, but have actually forged desperate dogmas to that effect—to which they unswervingly adhere, and even expect that their disciples swear to the same in order to be accepted in their religious circles. It is truly dismaying to note that a great many of these mistaken dogmatists actually sell these artificially contrived doctrines to desperate hopefuls in the public marketplace for monetary gain (via books and magazines, audio and video cassettes, television and radio programs, conferences, etc.). Surely, you have also heard their voices, perhaps having caught a drift of their mass media preachings on radio or TV now and then, or even read their books or checked out their videos and tapes.

Actually, a good number of these folks are completely sincere, especially the sheep of these folds. And herein is a major tragedy in the making; because, unfortunately, sincerity does not translate directly into being right. In fact, being unwittingly deceived, tricked, or simply ignorant, only to find out later that we were wrong in our position—though absolutely sincere—is a condition we have all experienced and can relate to. In this case, however, the stakes are sobering and serious, actually a life-and-death matter, as we'll examine shortly. And further, these deathly risky doctrines go beyond being innocently mistaken. Artificially contrived in essence, they are diabolical departures from truth, arrived at by turning a blind eye to Scriptural facts. Such dogmas actually ensnare souls in a lethal, lukewarm complacency that can only lead to taking the infamous *"mark of the beast,"* as we shall explore shortly.

Many have hastily formulated foolhardy (and completely unrealistic) endtime doctrines that emphasize the *"blessed hope"* of *"looking for Messiah's coming"* as *the central theme* of last-generation religion—often with reckless disregard for the purposeful lifestyle that precedes any such hope.[7]

Ignoring what the full nature of His Coming signifies, in terms of the preconditions surrounding this event, they handily, and perilously, dismiss very crucial aspects of it that do not suit their taste. Such over-anxious anticipants fit perfectly the description the prophet Amos gave of their brand of belief in chapter 5 of his book: *"Woe unto you that desire the day of the LORD! to what end is it for you? the day of the LORD is darkness, and not light. As if a man did flee from a lion, and a bear met him; or went into the house, and leaned his hand on the wall, and a serpent bit him. Shall not the day of the LORD be darkness, and not light? even very dark, and no brightness in it?"* A little later, it will become more clearly understood why for so many folks the blessed hope will not be as blessed as they anticipate.

Christ Himself qualified the advent of the "blessed hope" in these words from the Gospel according to Matthew, chapter 24, verses 32-34: *"Now learn a parable of the fig tree; When his branch is yet tender, and putteth forth leaves, ye know that summer is nigh: So likewise ye, when ye shall see all these things, know that it is near, even at the doors. Verily I say unto you, This generation shall not pass, till **all these things** be fulfilled."* Referring here specifically to His return to Earth from His extraterrestrial domain bringing restoration and salvation—this time in awesome power and magnificence at the end of the age—He made it clear that a *whole set* of circumstances and events would need to take place before the doors would burst open at His arrival. As we shall view for ourselves on one of the upcoming prophetic tour stops, this most *definitely includes* the "historic marker" known as the *Great Tribulation*.

The volumes of prophecy speaking of the latter days indicate that the advent of the New Earth Order of Messiah **is indeed** about to burst open the doors. The commentary and analysis in this essay is focused on this theme of the coming of that Great Day of God Almighty and its advent being relatively imminent; yet, although in agreement that it is certainly *close at hand*, this spectacular event definitely *cannot occur within the next seven years* (as of date of this writing). The signs which we are presently seeing, and will continue to witness with increasing frequency, are sign posts on the latter-day highway, indicating that our destination—the destiny of this very generation—is right around the corner. Again, this destiny is prophesied to occur all within the same generation that witnesses the *entire set* of endtime signs provided by Messiah passing before its view.

The timing of this event and the "historic markers" that signal its arrival, which even now casts its shadow across our thresholds, will be the object of our study tour. The following chapters deal with what the Last Generation can expect to experience before it concludes.

For the sake of injecting a sense of realism commensurate with current events and contemporary circumstances and developments, we shall also engage in some hypothetical speculation about the prophetic future. As a reader, you will, of course, have to judge as to any likelihood that it may be inspired (as we all wait to see just how everything plays out). That is, an attempt is made to present a clear vision of what is yet to come, based on personal revelation and one man's individual understanding of the prophecies. However, each reader will have to rely personally on the witness of the Spirit of Truth to determine whether this voice is an inspired oracle or just another one of the "many." Is it merely one to be recycled like last week's grocery store tabloid; or might it perhaps "baptize you with fire" to leave you clinging to nothing but absolutely the most significant things in life? It shouldn't be long before the answer is evident.

One thing that shall be unequivocally echoed within these chapters is that all these signs to be covered shall come to pass within one generation, which we have already referred to above as the Last Generation. The major historic marker in this regard is visited in detail in the chapter entitled *"Figs and Generation Finále."* Of course, understanding that a generation is not a fixed number of years and varies, depending on life spans and average longevity of the generational members, leaves us with an imprecise range to consider when concerned with timing. Nonetheless, it does impose a definite limit on how long things can be stretched out before coming to a conclusion. And even with modern medical advancements, still the average life span is reported (by CBS Evening News, 9/11/97) to be at its all-time high in the USA at 76.1 years. Of course, it was reported 3,500 years ago by Moses in the Psalms to average between 70-80.[8]

Even if only ten or twelve years yet remain for this generation, like the pregnancy of a woman in her latter weeks, they will probably seem terribly protracted because of the expectancy, *and* because of the swelling burden of trouble that we shall all experience in these last years. That small number is really not many years at all—which most of us over forty are keenly conscious of. Yet, in view of the trouble to come, the divine act promised of "shortening those days" will without doubt be tremendously welcomed by the time of our post-Tribulation deliverance.[9] (Much more on this in later chapters.)

Christ Yeshua spoke of this coming time of trouble as an *"hour of temp-*

tation, which shall come upon all the world, to try them that dwell upon the earth." (Revelation 3:10) He foretold it to be a season of *"great tribulation, such as was not since the beginning of the world to this time, no, nor ever shall be." (Matthew 24:21)* The great prophet Daniel described it as *"a time of trouble, such as never was since there was a nation." (Daniel 12:1)* In the book of the Apocalypse, Apostle John foresaw and was told of this same *"great tribulation, out of which came . . . a great multitude which no man could number." (Revelation 7:9-14)* And, Apostle Paul literally characterized the coming day of the Lord *"as travail upon a woman with child." (1 Thessalonians 5:3)*

We shall also return to this key passage of Paul's letter to the Thessalonians again later. It has great significance in sorting out the type and nature of the events connected with the Day of The Lord—about which there is great misunderstanding and confusion, particularly among most mainstream Christians. This metaphor of the *pregnant woman* going into painful and hard labor is seen often in the holy Hebrew Scriptures related to the birth of the Global Messianic Order. Additionally, since another prophetic feature is directly associated with this pregnancy, let's not forget to take note that the other key sign of the times the apostle posted in this same passage is that the prevailing irony of the day would be the clamor of *"peace and safety!"*

20/20 Blindness (Having Eyes, They See Not)

Besides due to being uninformed or ill-informed, the most fundamental causes of confusion in spiritual and prophetic matters are rooted in misplaced priorities and/or a lack of willingness to accept the truth. In the case of prophecy regarding the latter days, the time of the end and the Day of The Lord, a *great deal of confusion* prevails among Bible "scholars" and Christians. Differences and debate focusing on some *very critical issues* about end-time events (among other things) seriously plague the Christian community. Perhaps getting to the root of the problem will reveal why.

It is a fact that all of us are carnal and subject to temptations and weaknesses universally common to everyone.[10] Christ taught that, though *"the spirit indeed is ready/willing"* to meet challenge and difficulty, *"the flesh is weak." (Mark 14:38 & Matthew 26:41)* Therefore, He repeatedly admonished us to watch and pray lest we enter into temptation by that weakness. Apostle Paul likewise, pointed out later that, indeed, we are all *"men of like passions," (Acts 14:15)* that is, subject to the same weaknesses and temptations.

What are those passions, temptations and weaknesses? The same as those that resulted in Eve and Adam falling into error: *"And when the woman saw that the tree was good for food, and that it was pleasant to the eyes, and a tree to be desired to make one wise, she took of the fruit thereof, and did eat, and gave also unto her husband with her; and he did eat." (Genesis 3:6)*

The apostle John reiterated these weaknesses and passions in the following admonition: *"Love not the world, neither the things that are in the world. If any man love the world, the love of the Father is not in him. For all that is in the world, the lust of the flesh, and the lust of the eyes, and the pride of life, is not of the Father, but is of the world. And the world passeth away, and the lust thereof: but he that doeth the will of God abideth for ever." (I John 2:15-17)*

These sweeping weaknesses of the human family are common to and cross all cultures, races, ages, and genders. Very basically, they are, as John clearly articulated them in his second epistle: 1) *immediate desires of the flesh*, especially pleasurable gratification, as well as avoidance of pain; 2) *all that the eyes find attractive and alluring* beyond ourselves, which is most often coveted for possessing or consuming; and 3) *pride*, or aggrandizement and exaltation of self as the ultimate end.

The Scriptures of the Hebrews (which will be our exclusive purview in this book) detail the history of their people and their struggles with these very issues. Unlike every other national history book—unrealistically patriotic and overly glorifying of their respective nations, beyond reliability—Bible scriptures hide nothing, not even the wrongs and sins of the very People of the Book. They provide accounts of their greatest heroes grappling with and being overcome by these very same difficulties. Even the most notable were not immune. In fact, most often, these common weaknesses consumed the Jewish people in general like a malignant cancer and eventually destroyed them. *"Now all these things happened unto them for ensamples: and they are written for our admonition, upon whom the ends of the world are come." (1 Corinthians 10:11)*

It is truly a tragedy that so many lives and so much martyred blood was shed that these Scriptures might be passed faithfully on to us, such that we might benefit from their history, as well as their guidance into the future; for, history keeps repeating itself and the future remains a dim, uncertain vision through the eyes of the repeaters.

Christianity, originating as a sect of Judaism, inherited the great legacy of these holy writings and the tremendous wealth of their indispensable lessons. Yet, confusion about them and lack of understanding plagues the majority of Christians and cripples their churches; all of it with roots in the age-old weaknesses we have just outlined, which are all so clearly articulated in those very Scriptures as invaluable history lessons. A close examination of the situation reveals that it's not due so much to an ignorance of the writings, and the lessons and principles they convey, but to an outright disregard for them—the same old historic pattern![11]

Why should the people of God, who were destined, according to Moses, to be the head and not the tail (Deuteronomy 28:13), end up confusedly chasing their tails? Very simply because, for the most part (and as the Holy Scriptures teach), their priorities are all misplaced. As Christ and all the Prophets taught, everything is a matter of *values*. What you value dominates your life and determines your destiny. *"For where your treasure is, there will your heart be also." (Matthew 6:21)* And, what you place first in the order of your pursuits defines what your values are. Conflicting, jumbled, or distorted values make for similar belief systems.

The principle has long been established by Messiah that those individuals who are pure in heart *"shall see God." (Matthew 5:8)* In the same sermon and along the same vein, Christ also taught that if your eye is *"single,"* focused on the value of laying up treasures in heaven, rather than on earth, your whole body will be *"full of light."*[12] *That* is what comprises the quality and state of being *"pure in heart"*.

Contrary to the clouded and shallow notions of sin often impressed upon us by misguided Christians, Jesus did *not* teach purity as *"Thou shalt not eat, nor drink, nor enjoy beauty, nor have any carnal pleasure."* Rather, he simply taught that all of those joys of life are *secondary* to caring for the well-being and happiness of your neighbor (as much as your own!)—which is actually an integral part of loving God first with all your heart, soul, mind, and strength.

In terms of His principal concern—values—He taught that the primary order of our existence is to *"seek first the kingdom of God and His righteousness." (Matthew 6:33)* In those terms, purity is a matter of singleness of purpose and devotion, much more than some supposed and highly elusive moral rectitude (of or by carnal measure).

In fact, Christ insisted that such manner of moral righteousness is actually quite *insufficient* to save anyone at all. It is highlighted poignantly in His admonition to His disciples in the "Sermon on the Mount" with reference to the exemplary uprightness of the scribes and Pharisees of that time: *"For I say unto you, That except your righteousness shall exceed the righteousness of the scribes and Pharisees, ye shall in no case enter into the kingdom of heaven." (Matthew 5:20)* According to Jesus, the renown zeal of the scribes and Pharisees to uphold the law of righteousness, with all of its precepts of morality, was not enough to gain them entrance into the kingdom of righteousness.[13] We see in this proclamation that He was obviously referring to another more profound level of goodness, one which reaches beyond the enumeration of all the "thou-shalts" and "shalt-nots."

The principle of purity in heart definitely requires re-examination in this different light. Indeed, only a few short verses later in the discourse, He outlined the formula quite lucidly.

The purity to which He referred is the whole subject of the portion of the Sermon on the Mount contained in chapter 6 of the book of Matthew. Yeshua (as I prefer to call Him) plainly taught there that public image and the personal appearance of holiness is a thoroughly self-serving objective and its own reward in and of itself. No other benefit did He impute to such a moral endeavor; and in fact, He insisted that one's morality and fasting from indulgences of the flesh be a private matter of secret concern between the person and his God, including one's good deeds.

Instead, in this epic teaching, He turned all attention to the magnificent Father and His kingdom, His design, His will, His glory, our dependency on Him; and also to our human propensity to trespass into temptation and evil, and the crucial need for the all-important *forgiveness and reconciliation* for which He stands. Yeshua went on to conclude in this "sermon" that the sole endeavor of a man's life should be to seek first the kingdom of God and *His* righteousness—not our own!

In other words, no righteousness of any sort was to take priority over that which belongs to God and His perfect purpose for creation. Pursuing *that purpose* was taught as what the sole and all-consuming quest of our lives should be.

The essential moral issue of primordial concern, according to Christ, is whether we are divided in our devotion or ill-focused on any other quest. He taught that it is a travesty of truth and a defiance of God-ordained propriety to attempt to be a servant or slave of two masters. In any such faulty endeavor, He declared that one's eye is not *focused* (or, *"single,"* as He put it) but, instead, *"evil."* Therein is the core and cause of true immorality. The Lord's final analysis of that unrighteous human condition is that the entire being is consequently rendered thoroughly immoral, or *"full of darkness!"*

The "light of life" was revealed by Jesus to be a matter of total absorption with performing the will of His Father and fulfilling His desire for the Creation—establishment of His utopian kingdom. To "see God" is to understand this principle and fulfill it. Being pure in heart is being pure in purpose. Morality arises inherently out of this purposeful singularity of devotion to seeking *God's kingdom* for the sake of *His* righteousness; not in seeking one's own righteousness for the sake of self-aggrandizement.

Gratifying self-centered lusts in this world—the root and fruit of self-aggrandizement—is the driving motivation which absorbs the ungodly humans who lack clear vision for the magnificence of God's intent and purpose.[14] Such pursuits rob men of the light of life and engulf them in pervasive darkness. It is in the light of this Messianic perspective that we begin to touch on the cause of so much confusion among so many "Christians" and "churches," among whom, the quest for personal morality often becomes the all-consuming internal beacon or grand guiding spotlight, which effectively blinds them to the selfless truth. And the truth is, you cannot serve God and mammon! If you believe you can seek the kingdom of God while also pursuing materialism—no matter how morally pure you may think yourself to be—your eye is evil and you are deceived through and through.

So, with respect to an illuminated understanding of the Bible, its laws and its prophets, how can compromising Christians possibly hope to know the truth or be blessed with the correct deciphering of it, when they reject its most basic principles of faith in God (as those we have just seen stipulated within some of its most revered pages)? Their very own biblical tenets of faith, which they consentingly attribute to Him as the source, declare that their entire persons, when devoted to more than one master, can only be full of obscurity! To further compound their predicament (according to Matthew 6:23), they blindly go about even qualifying their darkened state of being as one of "enlightenment!" They claim to have the light!—and to *be* the "light of the world!"

How can they pretend that such a dim, impure condition of duality could lead to seeing God (who is The Truth)? The prerequisite for true enlightenment is a pure heart, not one plagued with the darkness of shared or dual devotion! And, how can you trust that someone who serves mammon (material gain), or tries to serve *both* mammon *and* God (Matthew 6:24), can possibly know what they are talking about, or has any real light in their life? According to Messiah, such trust is the formula for disaster; for, *"If the blind lead the blind, both shall fall into the ditch." (Matthew 15:14)*

This highly uncompromising perspective on values and priorities is presented to point up the fact that, as was said earlier, some very critical issues, which have become matters of debate and difference, really should not be unclear or of any controversy whatsoever to any who have eyes to see and ears to hear. But, a person's priorities and values will either clarify or cloud that individual's perspective and ability to understand.

To those who do "watch and pray"—that is, keep diligently focused, alert and spiritually in tune—understanding the precepts, principles and teachings of the Bible is pretty uncomplicated. It is actually quite difficult to get confused when the right channel is finely tuned in.[15] However, watching and praying in today's "fundamentalist" circles often easily becomes nothing more than a shallow exercise in vain religiosity and hypocritical self-deception. Going through the motions, without a heart for truth, in an effort to superficially justify oneself, without truly paying the price of unfeigned love of God (i.e., forsaking the pursuit of mammon), is an all-too-common contemporary phenomenon. Christ too, in His day, was most certainly beset by these very same types of religious people who affirmed they loved God, but yet in practice despised His Word and Principles, and *"loved darkness, rather than light."*[16]

Ye hypocrites, well did Esaias prophesy of you, saying, This people draweth nigh unto me with their mouth, and honoureth me with their lips; but their heart is far from me. But in vain they do worship me, teaching for doctrines the commandments of men.—Yeshua quoting Isaiah in Matthew 15:7-9.

In such cases, the supposed praying watchers are blinded, and their very prayers are in vain.[17] For, as Solomon affirmed, whosoever turns away his ear from hearing the precepts and direction of The Father is not only in darkness, but *"even his prayer shall be abomination." (Proverbs 28:9)* Rather than practicing the *"pure religion . . . undefiled before God and the Father"* about which the apostle James taught in the first chapter of his epistle,[18] too often, those who cannot divorce themselves from mammon contrive *man-made doctrines* to justify their lukewarm half-heartedness. In that fashion, many fundamentalists fundamentally deny the Christ and God whom they honor merely with their mouths and lips while teaching and preaching human schemings which they fraudulently present as divine.

The foregoing, admittedly, are strong allegations. Even insinuations of such a scathing sort merit substantiation and a more penetrating look at this phenomenon and its implications, especially in terms of our objective of establishing some facts about the prophetic biblical picture of the endtime. A true and correct understanding of the prophetic facts are, as I see it, absolutely critical to passing "the great test" and a matter of life and death; otherwise why bother to write a book about it?

The Crafty Rap of the Rapturists

Some major doctrinal issues that need to be challenged for their fragile and fickle foundation in fantasy, as well as for the disastrous implications of subscribing to such utterly false notions, begin with the folly of believing in some supposed "rapture" of the believers prior to any experience of Tribulation. Those who do subscribe to this fanciful flight of the imagination believe that Messiah could appear *at any moment* to retrieve His "Bride" from off the earth. This teaching is known as the doctrine of "imminency." That is, according to this particular interpretation of prophecy, the second coming of Christ is *immediately* imminent and could happen *any day* to snatch the Church (metaphorically referred to in the Bible as the Bride of Christ)[19] out of the plagues which will befall the earth in the final days of this age. Maybe you've seen the bumper stickers and T-shirts, or heard the believers proclaiming that they could vanish at any moment, also advising you to be prepared, lest you be one of those "left behind."

Well, as with any other type of truly effective (i.e., persuasive) untruth or deceit, there is some degree of truth blended into it by which the lie is made to have credibility. For such a doctrine to appear to have enough validity to be worthy of belief, it is necessary to borrow scraps of truth from the "real thing" to sew on to the artificial one in order to give it resemblance to the original and to patch the obvious holes in it. In the process of such laborious crafting, the real thing is nearly destroyed and supplanted by the contrived one. Such is the case with this particular patchwork doctrine of rapturism, which is actually nothing more than a hastily stitched together cloak of religious delusion and nothing less than a virtually criminal and practically unforgivable contrivance. Adding to the seriousness of the matter, this lukewarm dogma runs rampant as a very widely accepted teaching and belief among the great majority of today's "fundamentalist" Christians, especially in America.[20]

You see, because Christians have become so mammonized and materialistic, they have become dull in their senses. They are, therefore, easily led and misled by those who can successfully exploit their weaknesses (the temptations earlier discussed and more well-detailed later). Those who promise them rapturous escape from Tribulation readily capture their affection, allegiance and followership. Such clever synthesizers of pseudo salvations also subtly convince the unwitting sheep that they're special people (**the** Bride of Christ) bestowed with special graces and understanding, especially because they are subscribers to such masterful teachings by such "knowledgeable scholars."[21]

And of course, these very knowledgeable *false Christs* (or, *pseudo anointed ones,* as per the ancient Greek language manuscripts) *and false prophets* are especially skilled at stitching together the bits and pieces that have been cut out of the original truth so as to fabricate a particularly *palatable replica.* That degraded replica coincidentally matches all the carnal qualities of Eve's and Adam's Edenic snare, being: *"good for food"* (appealing to fleshly taste); *"pleasant to the eyes"* (pleasing to the mind and imagination); and, a fruit to be desired *"to make one wise"* (conferring or bestowing exaltedness upon its partakers).

The pseudo shepherds dare not expose the sheep to the sharp, uncompromising, unadulterated voice of *truth* in the sacred Scriptures, especially those scriptures that teach there *is* a price to pay and a heavy **cost** attached to following the teaching of Christ. Instead, they cunningly craft candied promises assuring them peace and safety, rapture and escape from tribulation. Such tactful strategies, of course, serve well in maintaining followerships and flocks of fleece-bearing devotees seduced by placating voices. But what say the Scriptures in this regard?

Thus saith the LORD of hosts, Hearken not unto the words of the prophets that prophesy unto you: they make you vain: they speak a vision of their own heart, and not out of the mouth of the LORD. They say still unto them that despise me, The LORD hath said, Ye shall have peace; and they say unto every one that walketh after the imagination of his own heart, No evil shall come upon you.—Jeremiah 23:16-17.

All the sinners of my people shall die by the sword, which say, The evil shall not overtake nor prevent us.—Amos 9:10.

And mine hand shall be upon the prophets that see vanity, and that divine lies:

they shall not be in the assembly of my people, neither shall they be written in the writing of the house of Israel, neither shall they enter into the land of Israel; and ye shall know that I am the Lord GOD. Because, even because they have seduced my people, saying, Peace; and there was no peace.—Ezekiel 13:9-10.

For when they shall say, Peace and safety; then sudden destruction cometh upon them, as travail upon a woman with child; and they shall not escape.— 1 Thessalonians 5:3.

These skillful diviners of false visions employ their wily craftiness to fabricate what Apostle Peter called *"cunningly devised fables"* that have no connection with reality, treacherously twisted and warped fictions invented to suit the weaknesses of the flesh.[22] And beyond being lured by the lust of the flesh with the proverbial sweet bread of deceit (Proverbs 20:17)—namely, the pleasant, promising visions of pre-tribulation rapture into the sky—they and their followers are actually convinced that they are "one-up" on the rest of the world. They are wholly persuaded that they are in a privileged class which possesses a special understanding, an esoteric knowledge that makes them a *select group* not subject to what the rest of us will have to go through[23]— namely, a universal *"hour of temptation, which shall come upon **all the world**, to try them that dwell upon the earth."* (Revelation 3:10)

What's the Difference?

This "hour of temptation" highlighted by Yeshua in the Apocalypse is the crux of the matter—especially in terms of being truly and positively prepared (in practice) for its eventuality; rather than being foolishly duped into the damnation of believing we won't even have to face it, and thus not preparing adequately for it, if at all. Being conned that they are to be exempted from it is the stumbling stone that trips up so many would-be fundamentalist Bible-believers of this last generation into a headlong fall into delusion; a duped downfall that leaves them doggedly insisting that they actually see the light and understand the truth about the imminent future of the world, about their own destiny and the prophetic word. Well, the truth about this impending "hour" shall be the matter which will divide the sheep from the goats, and the wheat from the chaff in the last days.

This subject of supreme *trial* is at the *heart* of the apocalyptic confusion *and* the related debate. And, it will be the soul of damnation to those who swallow the perilous fundamentalist poison that is being dispensed to opiate the fear and anxiety that tribulation evokes in those who seek so desperately to save their lives. For *"Whosoever shall seek to save his life shall lose it; and whosoever shall lose his life shall preserve it." (Luke 17:33)* Seeking to save oneself from tribulation and trial, though a quite natural tendency, is an uncommitted, unconvinced and unbelieving basis upon which to seek truth and spiritual preservation.

Precisely because the pursuit to preserve our lives on this planet is generally such a natural inclination and becomes such a universal human obsession is the reason why so few enter into the gates of true life. As Christ so aptly exhorted:

Enter ye in at the strait gate: for wide is the gate, and broad is the way, that leadeth to destruction, and many there be which go in thereat: Because strait is the gate, and narrow is the way, which leadeth unto life, and few there be that find it. Beware of false prophets, which come to you in sheep's clothing, but inwardly they are ravening wolves."—Matthew 7:13-15.

Over the years, I have gathered that coming to a knowledge and understanding of the truth is a relatively rare human experience. Plainly, the pursuit of transcendent truth is certainly not the primary or preoccupying quest which drives the race of majority humankind. I have witnessed that the pursuits and preoccupations of my fellow men and women on earth, largely speaking, revolve around a highly self-centered quest to maximize the satisfaction of and benefit to all that is concerned with one of the most unenduring elements of all—the human flesh. Yet, truth testifies that there is no enduring substance to life in this dimension and negates the supreme importance that is universally (almost) attached to that carnal endeavor.

The loudest, strongest, predominant voices which prevail on Planet Earth are those promoting carnal, worldly achievement and denying a transcendent truth. Those worldly voices harmonize in one consolidated voice: that of the Established Order, the utterly vain world system of devotion to consumerism, covetousness, possessiveness, grandiosity and to all other carnal priorities and self-centered values of an all-too-temporal quality. Together, these powerful voices—which provide the everyday programming for the average human child and reduce him to an unenlightened animal of expediency—resound out of the same carnal obscurity which long ago echoed in the classic philosophical darkness voiced by Pontius Pilate in the 1st century of the Common Era. Before conceding to the crucifixion of the brightest light of truth the world has ever known, Pilate excused himself with the shallow rationalization, *"What is truth?"*

This was not a question posed to the unjustly condemned Prince of Life for an answer. It was, instead, the cynical expression of Pilate's own resignation to a condemned life of patently dubious meaning and void of true purpose, which only an acceptance of truth could remedy. At that point, Pilate did not care for an answer; but instead spoke for all the rest of humanity in offering the condoning voice of absolution for turning away from truth to embrace carnal expediency.

Pilate flunked his "hour of temptation" by dismissing the Voice of Truth which witnessed to a kingdom that was *"not of this world"* for which Christ was willing to lay down his life; sadly, the "holy people" also failed. The religious folks of that day who waited for the "blessed hope" of the kingdom, many of whom had just a few days earlier lifted up their voices crying, *"Hosanna in the highest"* and hailing Him as King, now just as loudly denied Him, demanding His crucifixion and voicing their affection for the established order of the day crying, *"We have no king but Caesar!"*

The age-old conflict of *the flesh versus the spirit* rages on. The flesh demands its kingdom of self-satisfaction *now*. Immediacy is a primary concern. The spirit alone is able to relate to a kingdom of life beyond death that transcends the temporal—and terminal—world. Only the spirit is able to deny the demands of the flesh for immediate gratification. The truth of life can only be grasped by the spirit; and the flesh, unable to see, hear, touch, or comprehend anything beyond the present, and demanding here-and-now satisfaction, rejects and refuses any such transcendent reality. At the same time, the spirit of truth counters and opposes absolute commitment to the lust of the flesh and its narrow focus upon itself. In this conflict, only the spirit can endure and emerge victorious from the critical "hour of trial" to which I have been alluding.

Absorbed entirely with itself, the flesh cannot bear the trial and tribulation of that "hour," nor even the thought of it. Sacrifice, suffering, pain and death (deterioration and/or destruction of the flesh) are the dreaded and hated enemies of the carnal being. So are they the dread of religions which pander to the lusts of the flesh. It is this dread which prompts even those who profess a faith in Christ—who so willing laid down his life[24] to certify His transcendent teachings—to so dogmatically disqualify themselves from the Great Tribulation and misconstrue its intent and value.

Christianity, as a philosophy of life which exalts the preeminence of the spirit as the ultimate reality, is a teaching and religion of denial of self and subordination of the flesh to the supremacy of the spirit. As such, any voice or strange twist of doctrine which promises exemption from tribulation in favor of sparing the flesh from trial is highly suspect for heresy. None of the voices of the Bible's prophets taught any form of absorption with the carnal things of this world, but rather, an overarching commitment to the priorities and values of God's realm; and, that it is indeed incumbent upon each of us to demonstrate our affection for the values of the one over the other through testing and trial. Hence, life is such as it is: replete with temptation, trial and tribulation. Our choices in the heat of the test determine our fitness for the kingdom of God and an eternally enduring life in it.

Christ taught, *"It is the spirit that quickeneth [the essential substance of life]; the flesh profiteth nothing: the words that I speak unto you, they are spirit, and they are life."* *(John 6:63)* Saint Paul later explained to the Corinthians, *"The natural man receiveth not the things of the Spirit of God: for they are foolishness unto him: neither can he know them, because they are spiritually discerned."* *(1 Corinthians 2:14)* And to the Romans, Paul exhorted that being carnally minded (ruled by the flesh) would strip a person of life and place him or her in a mortal condition of hostile opposition to The Creator.[25]

Bible doctrine is clear—setting one's affection on things of earth, rather than on the higher substance of the next, eternally enduring dimension, is actually a suicidal embrace of absolute vanity and profound darkness.[26] Moreover, in that spiritual darkness of preferring fleshly temporal values over spiritual realities is where delusion and confusion abound!

In that environment where flesh is favored over spirit, false prophets, pimping what appeals to the flesh, flourish and proliferate. That very condition of seeking to preserve the world-based welfare of the flesh is what engenders so much difficulty understanding the spirit-based teachings of the Bible—and its prophecies. All authentic prophets of the Great Spirit[27] teach a detesting and repudiation of earthly idols and bring the light of enduring values to the hearts and minds of men.

The profession of religious faith, sainthood, or prophethood while yet secretly idolizing mammon, is a vain and feigned attempt to simulate "en-

Proclaimers of visions are of several types: political, financial, scientific, divine, etc.

All accounted for, the flood of their many voices deluges our lives with mixes of feelings: hope and despair; excitement and apprehension; sometimes optimism and occasionally cynicism; and yes, even fear as well as fascination. Everyone has a stake—however small sometimes—in the future.

The future and predicting what it holds in store is even big business these days. Beside religious soothsayers divining the future and increasingly turning prophets into profits, there are the lucrative psychic hotlines, tons of seminars, books, tapes and other related, fashionable consumer lures proferred by the New Agers; and we can hardly omit the stock market and futures options, statistical computer modeling, etcetera; and even weather forecasting is a big bucks enterprise nowadays. But, for all the competing endeavors at fortune-telling, whether high tech or low, none really pin down the future with much of any certainty.

If anything at all is certain and can be generally agreed upon by the perplexed members of this harried generation, regardless of which prophets we listen to or believe, it is that *uncertainty* and *dramatic change* frame and characterize most all our expectations for the 21st century.

Whatever the brand of future-tellers, their visions are, at best, generally laced with a great deat of educated guesswork, and precious few are genuine psychic phenomenon or really reliable prophecy. Not to except myself, I too have injected some of my own personal theorizings into the views presented in this book. But overall, as previously noted, the prophecy explorations of this study are an excursion into age-old writings that will take us back 20 centuries, and even more than 3000 years in some cases, to probe and survey the oracles of the ancient Hebrew "clairvoyants" for clues they offer about this future day in which we live, as well as that one into which we must soon pass.

My primary intention is not so much to establish the crediblity of these biblical oracles, which only eventual fulfillment of their prophecies can do, but more to help insure their voices are heard clearly among the myriad of others—and not drowned out *or watered down!* Moreover, I endeavor to do so in an arena outside and free of any association with all the trappings of establishment religion, its suffocating organizationalism, holier-than-thou denominationalism and excessively narrow dogmatism. The objective is to examine the visions of the Hebrew prophets without any mainstream or "cultic" bias imposed upon them, stemming from any of the various sectarian doctrinal dogmas that commonly prevail.

I expect that you should assess the contents of this presentation rigorously for whatever possible factual quality it might embody and then render your own judgment. As the case is made, each reader shall need to sort the plausible from the implausible, the credible from the incredible, and the fact from the fiction. Most of all, I hope to familiarize each of you with the selected words of the Prophets (provided by extensive endnotes and excerpted citations) which will help you reflect on their veracity in terms of their applicability to the world of today.

All pretenses aside, I must state for the record that unbiased I am not; for I possess many personal biases, and like practically all of us, have been influenced by many voices and teachers in my lifetime. Those influences and biases are certainly reflected in this book, and my opinions are, of course, woven in throughout. However, the influence, voices, and visions which prevail herein originate to an overwhelming degree from the Holy Scriptures of the TaNaKh (called the "Old Testament" by Christians)[1] and the New Testament of the Bible (only rarely accepted by Jews). The often unique interpretations of these scriptures which I express in these pages is either inspired by the Spirit of Truth, or not. Again, each reader must discern and discriminate in that regard for her- or himself.

My most notable bias, which will be evident and even conspicuous throughout these chapters, is that I have been completely convinced the writers of both the TaNaKh and the New Testament were divinely inspired. In addition, I also believe that, though their writings and language are often idiomatic, frequently laced with symbolism and sprinkled with parable and allegory, most often *they actually meant exactly what they said.* That is, they intended to be understood at face value. And so, comprehending their words is often just a matter of adjusting to their manner of speech *and seeking* to properly decipher the meanings of their figurative language. In the final analysis, my most fervent hope for this "tour" is that we shall actually be able to *hear the voices of the Prophets* (and accurately glimpse the visions they convey) as they echo down through the ages to be reverberated in these pages now many, many centuries later.

The previous chapter attempted to illustrate and establish that *hearing (and seeing)*—actually comprehending the messages and signals that reach our minds—can be a tainted process resulting in corruption of the message.

Signals and data can, as we all know, be distorted, contaminated or corrupted in the communication process. It is in the reception process, however, where they are most often either completely misunderstood or distorted—"purity of heart" being the critical determinant. At the reception point is where they are frequently filtered and converted into editted messages which become more *selectively agreeable* to the individual ear. (Most honest folks admit to the cafeteria principle of learning and opinion forming: namely, chosing to hear only what we want to hear.)

As promised and as honestly as possible, we shall endeavor to take up in this chapter the facts in the Scriptures that pertain to two major prophetic events which absolutely cannot bear misreading or misinterpretation. These two future events are hugely different in nature and yet so enormously and frequently confused in most circles where attention is paid to Bible prophecy. Surely though, as we progress into our study tour, it should become obvious to the seekers of truth (folks without cafeteria ears and escapist agendas) that these two momentous times are **not** one and the same, nor are they concurrent or overlapping in any way.

It should also become clear, as we reach the conclusion of our tour of the ancient prophetic landscape, why even coming across this information should concern us; and why most folks would rather not hear about it at all; and why others of us can hardly wait for these events to play out.

Time to Turn Back? or Perhaps to Get Off the Tour Bus?

Please stick with me as we begin to sort things out. It is necessary to present some background narrative in order to proceed with the tour and es-tablish some facts.

There does exist quite a sizeable camp of prophecy aficionados among the numerous Christian sects and factions (both mainstream and otherwise) who profess a high regard for the teachings and prophecies of the ancient Hebrews. I have already stated that, as a direct outgrowth of the Judaism of the Hebrews, Christianity has also naturally inherited their ancient sacred writings and, in general, places a great deal of ostensible reverence on the words of their prophets. At least this is what is professed and what *should* actually be the case. The fundamentalists, in particular, pride themselves in their literalist interpretations, beliefs and views on those scriptures.

However, rife among these various factions of self-proclaimed "Bible-believers" are a particularly unauthentic *and uneasy* number (a very sizeable lot, actually) who are really *quite uncomfortable* with the plain truth. This lot has decidedly arranged to filter and remake the words of the sacred Scriptures into more pleasing "truths." In the process, they've divined quite novel doctrines which are now being popularly sung to a *distinctly different tune* than the *original* one composed by the holy prophets they so outwardly "revere."

Please humor me a little as we "tune in" to a choice "melody" of theirs in the following allegorical parody which typifies the modern carefree "tunes" to which they "dance" so mirthfully. A favorite "hymn" of this contemporary choir of comfort—which I shall fictitiously entitle *"Flight of Fancy"* (or alternately, *"Rapture Reverie"*)—is chorused with a refrain borrowed from a very well known and highly respected Hebrew of the New Testament era. The chorus is misappropriated from one of Apostle Paul's epistles to the Thessalonians and will serve to highlight a perfect example of the fundamental fakery that masquerades as fundamentalism in our latter-day world.

The lyrics of this suppositious song of salvation, especially as regards their prophetic beliefs, constitute the core of this choir's ill-founded endtime doctrines. The words of the chorus are taken from chapter 5, verse 9, of the first epistle to the saints of Thessalonica (1Th.5:9). The gleeful chorus goes:

> *"God hath not appointed us to wrath,*
> *but to obtain salvation by our Lord Jesus Christ."*

The following verse from the Apocalypse is also craftily woven into the lyrics of this revisionist rendition of the ancient prophetic anthem. It too is misapplied (by a forced misinterpretation) to reinforce the errant theme of the modern twist on an old faithful melody:

> *"Because thou hast kept the word of my patience,*
> *I also will keep thee from the hour of temptation,*
> *which shall come upon all the world,*
> *to try them that dwell upon the earth." (Revelation 3:10)*

These verses, among others, are liberally misread and misconstrued to contrive and rationalize a fundamentally flawed and contradictory notion—now become doctrine—which is all too popular among supposed fundamentalist Bible-believers.

That doctrine holds that believers are allegedly promised an *escape from tribulation,* referring in particular to the Great Tribulation (discussed in much more detail in the pages following). The escape is known by a more and more popularized term—the "Rapture"—which you may have already been familiar with. The "hosanna choirs" who sing this *"Rapture Reverie"* are known, for the sake of quick classification of their doctrine, as Pre-Tribulation Rapturists.

This "song" of theirs (by which I satirize their escapist doctrine) serves purposefully to comfort the ranks of the *fearful* and to assure the congregations of the *uncommitted* that the *"hour of temptation"*—intended specifically to try *"all the world"*—shall supposedly *not befall them!*

At this point, if you haven't jumped off already, you may be wondering whether you caught the right bus or even care to continue the tour we're supposed to be embarking upon. I imagine you may be asking, "What does any of this have to do with me? Who cares whether the Christians are confused about their eschatologies? Just where is this prophecy tour leading, anyway? Can't we just skip this detour into the doctrinal debates of the flakey fundamentalists and compromising Christians?"

Well, your point is well taken, if you do happen to be thinking that all of this has nothing to do with you; because, it just might not be of any consequence to you personally. But again, please bear with me. There is a method to my madness.

Let me at least establish the fact that it is the Christians who are most preoccupied with and applied to the study of the endtime prophecies of the Hebrews. They, more than practically any other group, are most adamant that the prophecies of the end times are being fulfilled in this generation. They, more than any others, are raising the flag and vocalizing the belief that we have entered the last generation and that the end of the world is near. They, more than any other people, claim to have detailed knowledge of the events of the future and just how they will play out, both in terms of the specific nature of anticipated future developments as well as the sequence in which they will occur and what the final outcome will be. They, above all others, claim to possess unerring inside information of a divine source which is so sure to come to pass that they are willing to lay down their lives for its veracity!

(Are they, really!?—Actually, despite the dubious depth of devotion most of them demonstrate here in the West, a few truly are and **do** make such dire sacrifices; although, this holds true almost entirely in the totalitarian countries of Asia and Africa, particularly Islamic and Communist regimes where tribulation already goes hand-in-hand with faith in Christ. Nevertheless, again I ask, are they, really?)

Well, as time draws on, especially as we transition more fully into the new millennium, I guarantee that all of us will hear and read even more (surely not less) of the eschatologies of the Christians. Already, these themes of theirs widely paint and splash our collective consciousness with their rumors of the end of the world and the coming of Christ Messiah. Popular movies and prime time television programs already capitalize enormously on endtimes dooms-day themes heralded by Christians. So, to be able to separate the hype and the nonsense from the facts seems to me to be of great worth to practically every-one (who cares at all, of course), Christian or otherwise. Again, whether you may be person of faith (in the Bible) or not, either way, most assuredly, you will hear more and more about these endtime themes as time goes by.

So, if you are interested in the least, perhaps you will consider staying on this bus for a couple more chapters to see exactly where this study tour might be headed. Jump ahead, if you wish; but, just try not to miss the hottest points of interest on the itinerary (e.g., the next chapter).

Back now to the *Rapture Reverie* theme song from the Christian soundtrack to their Hollywood-style production of *"The End Times:"*

The fact is—and *this* they do have correct—according to the Scriptures, believers are *not* appointed to *wrath*. They're absolutely right on this score. Wrath is not a part of the destiny of the saints.[2] And, yes, the saints are to be kept during the hour of temptation, or the Great Tribulation as it may be. The trouble is, the facts in both these (quite distinct) scriptural cases are definitely misinterpreted, misunderstood, misapplied, confused and mismatched by these rapturists in the dreamy doctrines of their idealized world of salvation rev-erie. Something's wrong when facts cannot be faced for what they really are!

In that world of forced fiction, where the forcing of facts into clothes that do not fit outranks the finding of facts in their naked beauty, they deliberately ignore the enormous difference between the implications of "wrath" as op-posed to "tribulation." They dress them both alike, as though they were identi-cal twins, only with different names. And then, for heaven's sake (really for the sake of convenience), they proceed to disown them both altogether, not want-ing to have anything to do with either one of them—ultimately leaving them on the Jews' doorstep for adoption (as we learn more about in chapters 7 & 8).

Strong Medicine for Rapture Syndrome (Pious Paranoia)

Well, when not caught up in their reveries, a sort of tribulation phobia grips the rapturists. It has driven them to a paranoid schizophrenia in which their unstable dual mentality concocts delusional misinterpretations of Scripture that make them feel pious and persecuted (when often neither is the case). At the same time, so fearful of persecution are they that they feel compelled to embrace fictitious pre-tribulation rapture doctrines, fancying to be saved from the worst of it all, the final trial. In their world of fear, delusion and shakey commitment, Great Tribulation is generically lumped together with the Wrath of God as something just as horrifying and unendurable. That is, to speak of the Great Tribulation in those Christian circles is to toss up the same red flag as the word "wrath" also does.

They know the Scriptures clearly assure that the believers are not appointed to wrath; but they also ought to know the same scriptures plainly promise every devout disciple a dose of tribulation and persecution.[3] Yet, being perfectly aware of how dreadful it is foretold to be, they refuse to accept that they are appointed to the greatest of all tribulations. So frightening is it to them that the uncommitted half of their double hearts frantically grasps at straws of sheer fiction, which they desperately imagine may save them from drowning in that which they so intently dread. In this case, the flimsy straws come in the form of cowardly misinterpretations of facts.

According to the tenets of rapturemania, being kept from the hour of temptation is interpreted as being delivered from the horror of Great Tribulation, mistaken for God's wrath. This, they say, happens by means of the "snatching away" of the saints in the mystical event they endearingly term the *"Rapture."*

This term, borrowed from the Latin versions of the New Testament, is not found in the authorized English versions and is otherwise more authoritatively known as the (aerial) *"gathering together"* of the saints, or the *"catching up together"* into the sky of the called-out ones. The Greek manuscripts employ the term *harpázo*, which conveys a meaning more akin to a snatching up or away, seizing, or plucking out of something.

The occasion of this snatching away, or plucking of the people of God out of the earthly realm, will most assuredly be nothing less than rapturous, and is indeed a comforting assurance;[4] but the fictitious fantasy which they attach to this salvation event is not in the nature of it; rather, it is in the timing of it, as well as in its purpose, which they also mistake.

The pre-tribulation rapturists contend vehemently that it is intended to provide them an escape from the frightful hour of Tribulation and, therefore, occurs *before* the onset of that time of trial. This, they argue, is what is inferred by the promise that they will be *"kept from the hour of temptation."* They mistakenly allege this particular promise to indicate they will be taken away, or rapturously snatched out of this worldwide trial period (which we noted above is confused with the time of God's wrath). This pet verse of theirs from Revelation 3 (already quoted, and presented in its context below) is just one of several consistenty misused to justify their misinterpretation of all the pertinent scriptures on this topic of the ultimate and universal trial and tribulation to come.

(Again, please try to hang in with me over this rocky stretch of road through all the semantics and proof-texting—and with patience at my pontificating.)

In their typically less than courageous perspective on the Holy Scriptures, they have erringly neglected to take note that the term *keep* denotes more exactly (from the Greek *teréo*) *to guard by keeping an eye on, watch over, take care of, preserve, attend to carefully.* Not by any stretch of meaning is it implied or to be assumed that that should be accomplished by removal, extraction, or sparing from hazard or adversity.

To make the meaning of "keep" even more emminently clear—and to the shame and deserved embarassment of these anxious rapturists "caught up" in their fantasies of flying away to escape the Great Tribulation—the same word, *teréo*, appears earlier in the very same verse to declare the Lord's rationale for *keeping* these saints from the worldwide hour of temptation. The meaning, even without the aid of Greek manuscripts and dictionaries, is perfectly clear. For your convenience, the passage under review is provided below:..

And to the angel of the church in Philadelphia write . . . I know thy works . . . for thou hast a little strength, and hast kept my word, and hast not denied my name. . . . Because thou hast kept the word of my patience, I also will keep thee from the hour of temptation, which shall come upon all the world, to try them that dwell upon the earth. Behold, I come quickly: hold that fast which thou hast, that no man take thy crown. Him that overcometh will I make a pillar in the temple of my God, and he shall go no more out: and I will write upon him the name of my God, and the name of the city of my God, which is new Jerusalem, which cometh down out of heaven from my God: and I will write upon him my new name. He that hath an ear, let him hear what the

Precisely because these *faithful overcomers* addressed above have **not** allowed His words to *escape* preservation, or to be *spared from* their careful attendance to them, or to be *snatched out* of their repertoire of consistent observation, He too promises in commensurate fashion to preserve them in His jealous personal care. Because they have kept His word in patience, and not succumbed to the *hosanna syndrome*,[5] He promises to royally reward their patience, *not* to exempt them from the trial which is to come upon *"all the world, to try them that dwell upon the earth."*

In this passage, the terms *try* and *temptation* are mother and daughter. From the early Greek manuscripts they are *"peirázo"* and *"peirasmos,"* meaning (in the case of *try*) to put to the test or trial, to examine, scrutinze; and (in the case of *temptation*) a putting to the proof, especially by adversity, affliction, or trouble.

Therefore, to deliver the believers out of that global trial would (by simple logic) make it impossible for them to "overcome" in that very hour of proving and putting to the test. It would also be a flagrant contradiction of Christ's express wishes for His disciples, outlined in a solemn prayer to the Father for them: *"I pray not that thou shouldest take them out of the world, but that thou shouldest keep [teréo] them from the evil." (John 17:15)* Here again, the Greek word *teréo* is translated as "keep" to signify **preservation**. From the context here too, "keep" *obviously* suggests no hint whatsoever of deliverance by removal, sparing, or escape from the tempation and trial, other than by preservation in the midst and in the face of it.

Now for some more "exciting" semantic facts, which are as grossly overlooked and glossed over as the very scriptures in which they're found.

Tribulation or Indignation?

As has been posed in the earlier sections, there is actually a broad and gaping difference between the *hour of temptation* (tribulation) and *wrath* (indignation). Any alert student of the Bible (with functional eyes and ears)[6] understands well the unified concept of temptation and tribulation, which has absolutely nothing to do with the wrath or indignation of God.

Consider the following sample collection of Bible excerpts regarding tribulation which make it quite clear that the people of God are promised, and should expect, and even be glad of tribulation:

Remember the word that I said unto you, The servant is not greater than his lord. If they have persecuted me, they will also persecute you; if they have kept my saying, they will keep yours also (John 15:20.). . . . And ye shall be hated of all men for my name's sake: but he that shall endure unto the end, the same shall be saved (Mark 13:13). . . . He that received the seed into stony places, the same is he that heareth the word, and anon with joy receiveth it; yet hath he not root in himself, but endureth for a while: for when tribulation or persecution ariseth because of the word, by and by he is offended (Matthew 13:20-21). . . . Blessed are they which are persecuted for righteousness' sake: for theirs is the kingdom of heaven (Matthew 5:10.). . . . These things I have spoken unto you, that in me ye might have peace. In the world ye shall have tribulation: but be of good cheer; I have overcome the world (John 16:33).—Christ Yeshua

My brethren, count it all joy when ye fall into divers temptations; knowing this, that the trying of your faith worketh patience. But let patience have her perfect work, that ye may be perfect and entire, wanting nothing.—James 1:2-4.

And not only so, but we glory in tribulations also: knowing that tribulation worketh patience (Romans 5:3). . . . For verily, when we were with you, we told you before that we should suffer tribulation; even as it came to pass, and ye know (1Thessalonians 3:4). . . . [After being stoned to death (as his assailants thought) in Lystra, Apostle Paul defiantly returned there] confirming the souls of the disciples, and exhorting them to continue in the faith . . . [declaring] that we must through much tribulation enter into the kingdom of God (Acts 14:22). . . . So that we ourselves glory in you in the churches of God for your patience and faith in all your persecutions and tribulations that ye endure: Which is a manifest token of the righteous judgment of God, that ye may be counted worthy of the kingdom of God, for which ye also suffer (II Thessalonians 1:4-5).—Apostle Paul

The word "tribulation" in the New Testament of the Bible is translated from the Greek, *thlipsis*, meaning *pressure* (literally or figuratively). The other forms this same Greek word takes in the English New Testament are *afflicted, affliction, anguish, burdened, persecution,* and *trouble.* Defining it similarly,

Webster's dictionary provides the root-word derivation for "tribulation," through Middle English, French and Latin, as a word with a base meaning equivalent to *pressure,* or *oppression*. And, in the collection of excerpts cited above, we see the clear connection between the pressure of tribulation and the oppression of persecution, as well as between the trial of one's faith and patience.

On the other hand, let us now examine the concept of *indignation*. To quote the Webster dictionary, indignation is *"anger aroused by something unjust, unworthy, or mean."*

The Great Day of God Almighty, besides marking the restoration of His sovereignty over the earth and the restoration of Earth to His original design (paradise), is marked by a precursory period of indignation, wrath, vengeance and judgment aroused by wicked humans. This period of wrath is spoken about throughout the holy writings of nearly all the Hebrew prophets from Moses to Malachi, and on up to the beloved John. It is a day of jealous indignation in which The Almighty Creator obliterates the idolatrous superstructures and city systems of man, along with wicked, egotistical man himself (and his ally, the Beast), and then recovers possession of Earth and its people.

The great day of the LORD is near, it is near, and hasteth greatly, even the voice of the day of the LORD: the mighty man shall cry there bitterly. That day is a day of wrath, a day of trouble and distress, a day of wasteness and desolation, a day of darkness and gloominess, a day of clouds and thick darkness, a day of the trumpet and alarm against the fenced cities, and against the high towers. And I will bring distress upon men, that they shall walk like blind men, because they have sinned against the LORD: and their blood shall be poured out as dust, and their flesh as the dung. Neither their silver nor their gold shall be able to deliver them in the day of the LORD's wrath; but the whole land shall be devoured by the fire of his jealousy: for he shall make even a speedy riddance of all them that dwell in the land.—Zephaniah 1:14-18. Therefore wait ye upon me, saith the LORD, until the day that I rise up to the prey: for my determination is to gather the nations, that I may assemble the kingdoms, to pour upon them mine indignation, even all my fierce anger: for all the earth shall be devoured with the fire of my jealousy.—Zephaniah 3:8.

Come near, ye nations, to hear; and hearken, ye people: let the earth hear, and all that is therein; the world, and all things that come forth of it. For the indignation of the LORD is upon all nations, and his fury upon all their armies: he hath utterly destroyed them, he hath delivered them to the slaughter. . . . For it is the day of the LORD's vengeance, and the year of recompences for the controversy of Zion.—Isaiah 34:1-2, 8.

This day of the LORD's vengeance, described above, is also the day of His annihilating wrath. It is that day foretold when YHWH judges the nations of the world to rid the planet of the evil usurpers of Earth who by wicked devices have expropriated His world for self-glorifying purposes and thereby utterly defiled the planet.

However, tribulation, on the first hand, is always a precursor to wrath and vengeance. Tribulation occurs as a cleansing and purging mechanism. It serves to flush impurities and undesirable attributes or properties from things of value. In short, tribulation is a sorting out process intended to purge out the undesirable from the desirable, the bad from the good, the unworthy from the worthy. Plagues on the world in general, as well as on individuals in particular, and any other sorts of afflictions or troubles associated with tribulation, are nothing more than a means of testing, cleansing, purging and refining in order to distill, disentangle and separate the fine from the crude and the pure from the gross.

Almost sixty different references can be found scattered throughout the Bible on this concept of trial and tribulation for exactly the purpose outlined above. And although some degree of destruction and loss often occurs in the trial process, it cannot be compared with the ravages of annihilation that are implicit in the phases of indignation and vengeance connected with the coming Great Day of God Almighty. In fact, a proper response (*i.e.,* repentance) to the afflictions of tribulation actually deters wrath and quiets indignation.

Consider only a few more especially salient references to trial and tribulation from the prophets of the Bible:

When thou art in tribulation, and all these things are come upon thee, even in the latter days, if thou turn to the LORD thy God, and shalt be obedient unto his voice; (For the LORD thy God is a merciful God;) he will not forsake thee, neither destroy thee, nor forget the covenant of thy fathers which he sware unto them.—Moses, Deuteronomy 4:30-31

Many shall be purified, and made white, and tried; but the wicked shall do

wickedly: and none of the wicked shall understand; but the wise shall under-
stand (Daniel 12:10). . . . And some of them of understanding shall fall, to try
them, and to purge, and to make them white, even to the time of the end:
because it is yet for a time appointed (Daniel 11:35).—the prophet Daniel

Beloved, think it not strange concerning the fiery trial which is to try you, as
though some strange thing happened unto you: But rejoice, inasmuch as ye
are partakers of Christ's sufferings; that, when his glory shall be revealed, ye
may be glad also with exceeding joy (1 Peter 4:12-13). . . .That the trial of
your faith, being much more precious than of gold that perisheth, though it be
tried with fire, might be found unto praise and honour and glory at the ap-
pearing of Jesus Christ: Whom having not seen, ye love; in whom, though
now ye see him not, yet believing, ye rejoice with joy unspeakable and full of
glory: Receiving the end of your faith, even the salvation of your souls (1
Peter 1:7-9).—Apostle Peter

Blessed is the man that endureth temptation: for when he is tried, he shall
receive the crown of life, which the Lord hath promised to them that love
him.—James 1:12

For thou, O God, hast proved us: thou hast tried us, as silver is tried.—King
David, Psalms 66:10

Therefore thus saith the LORD of hosts, Behold, I will melt them, and try
them; for how shall I do for the daughter of my people?—Jeremiah 9:7

Every man's work shall be made manifest: for the day shall declare it, be-
cause it shall be revealed by fire; and the fire shall try every man's work of
what sort it is.—Paul, 1 Corinthians 3:13

And I will bring the third part through the fire, and will refine them as silver
is refined, and will try them as gold is tried: they shall call on my name, and
I will hear them: I will say, It is my people: and they shall say, The LORD is
my God.—Zechariah 13:9

Behold, I have refined thee, but not with silver; I have chosen thee in the
furnace of affliction.—Isaiah 48:10

To establish you, and to comfort you concerning your faith: That no man should be moved by these afflictions: for yourselves know that we are appointed thereunto. For verily, when we were with you, we told you before that we should suffer tribulation; even as it came to pass, and ye know.—Paul, 1Thessalonians 3:2-4

Now, in light of so many references to the promise of testing and proving, ask yourself, "How could so many professed believers of the Bible be convinced that they should escape the coming Great Tribulation of all time?"

Thief in the Night?

Contrary to any mistaken impression that might be gathered from the subtitle of this book, there is no denying the truth of a certain *imminency* associated with the coming of the Messiah and the Great Day of God Almighty. That sense of imminency is indeed repeatedly stressed in Bible Scripture. And of course, Messiah Himself strongly affirmed during His first visit to earth that no man knew the day or the hour of His return.

Imminency, however, should not be confused with surprise (from failure to discern either the times or the seasons). You see, the time of the end—the Day of the LORD—is broken into distinct seasons: the pre-tribulation season, moving toward absolute apostasy; the season of Great Tribulation, brought about as a consequence of pervasive apostasy; the swift season of wrath, indignation, and vegeance to strip Satan and his secular children from their destructive dominion of Earth; immediately followed thereafter by the season of establishment of paradise over the whole earth under the peaceful reign of Messiah which will endure 1000 years.

On more than one occasion, Yeshua's disciples, as well as others, pressed Him to reveal the time when His world government would be established. On one of those occasions shortly before His betrayal, arrest and crucifixion, they urged Him, *"Tell us, when shall these things be? and what shall be the sign of thy coming, and of the end of he world?"* (Matthew 24:3) His reply was, *"Of that day and that hour knoweth no man, no, not the angels which are in heaven, neither the Son, but the Father. Take ye heed, watch and pray: for ye know not when the time is."* (Mark 13:32-33)

Then again, at the conclusion of His forty-day post-resurrection sojourn with them in His hyperphysical body—just prior to His ascension and disappearance through the clouded atmosphere into hyperspace—they pressed Him anew. And again, He answered their anxious inquiry with essentially the same exhortation: *"And he said unto them, It is not for you to know the times or the seasons, which the Father hath put in his own power." (Acts 1:7)*

Bear in mind, the Messianic Order of Peace and Prosperity has been the supreme hope of all ages among the Hebrews. Therefore, it is no wonder that having discovered their Prince they now were so impatient to see His world-wide kingdom established. The time was just not fully come.[7]

Despite all the urgings upon Him to reveal a specific time when the Great Day of Mashiach would dawn, the graphics He consistently sketched about that day were largely colored with *indefiniteness* and *unexpectedness*. His most weighty strokes were in these two hues and shades, rather than in the tint and tone of imminency which has come to be cast over His teachings by later remakes. Even the subsequent (second generation) visions sketched by His original followers were true to the original. The tinge of imminency seems to have been splashed on sometime thereafter.

Because this issue is so central to achieving clarity about this upcoming Great Day of The Prince of Peace, the following compilation of quotations is provided to help establish the amount of stress that has been placed in the Scriptures on impressing the idea of indefiniteness and unexpectedness, *as opposed to so much supposed imminency.* Careful reading of these and other related Scriptures on this topic definitely does not reflect the any-moment idea as much as it does the desire of The Father to have total discretion about timing in the fulfilling of His own purposes:

Behold, I come as a thief. Blessed is he that watcheth, and keepeth his garments, lest he walk naked, and they see his shame.—Christ, Revelation 16:15.

But of that day and that hour knoweth no man, no, not the angels which are in heaven, neither the Son, but the Father. Take ye heed, watch and pray: for ye know not when the time is. For the Son of man is as a man taking a far journey [far from any suggestion of imminency, I might add], who left his house, and gave authority to his servants, and to every man his work, and commanded the porter to watch. Watch ye therefore: for ye know not when the master of the house cometh, at even, or at midnight, or at the cockcrowing, or in the morning: Lest coming suddenly he find you sleeping. And what I say unto you I say unto all, Watch.—Christ, Mark 13:32-37

Watch therefore: for ye know not what hour your Lord doth come. But know this, that if the goodman of the house had known in what watch the thief would come, he would have watched, and would not have suffered his house to be broken up. Therefore [Likewise, in the Greek] be ye also ready: for in such an hour as ye think not the Son of man cometh.—Christ Yeshua, Matthew 24:42-44

The day of the Lord will come as a thief in the night; in the which the heavens shall pass away with a great noise, and the elements shall melt with fervent heat, the earth also and the works that are therein shall be burned up.—2 Peter 3:10.

For yourselves know perfectly that the day of the Lord so cometh as a thief in the night.—Paul, 1 Thessalonians 5:2.

Remember therefore how thou hast received and heard, and hold fast, and repent. If therefore thou shalt not watch, I will come on thee as a thief, and thou shalt not know what hour I will come upon thee.—Christ, Revelation 3:3.

The scriptures quoted above, ironically enough, form the hub of this very popular doctrine of imminency among the mainstream Christian sects who say that Messiah could sneak up and appear at any unexpected moment. Yet, **where** in these verses—which they so regularly and widely use to substantiate this dogma—are we supposed to gather the supposed sense of imminency so emphatically stressed by the any-moment cult?

Good thieves, we should note, know the vast difference between mere surprise and the much more critical element of **vulnerability**. Surprise is not the issue being stressed in these admonitions; falling into a state of vulnerability is. And, most vulnerable of all conditions is the fantasy world of intoxication with mammon.

Let us, for the moment, set aside any concerns about the chronic and typical misreading of the Scriptures that underlie this doctrine to examine the main rationale provided by the imminency cult for subscribing to this belief.

What we find is that it is regularly stressed that believers must be somehow prodded so as to maintain devout and ever-faithful lifestyles right up to the final moment of the "thief's" arrival. It is taught by these particular sects that, because Jesus could come at any time, it is therefore that much more imperative that we diligently strive to maintain our state of preparedness and fulfill our Christian calling (while there remains time yet to do so). And, to abide in such a state of preparedness, they reason, takes on a particularly fresh sense of urgency when the Lord's arrival might come at any moment.

Very sensible reasoning—it would appear—especially if it's clear what the Christian calling consists of. An earlier section of the previous chapter, entitled "20/20 Blindness," begins to explore the fogginess that obscures an understanding of that calling. So, even if it were true that Yeshua could come at any moment of any day, do we know what it is that He would hope to find us engaged in?

It is evident in the Scriptures that Christ's concern about the conditions (apostasy vs. faithfulness) that He knew would prevail among His subjects upon His future return was almost dire. Otherwise, He would not have devoted so many of His discussions to that topic and stressed so repeatedly the importance of *watching* and *praying*. The parable Jesus told in the Gospel of Luke (18:1-8) on this principle of unrelenting faithfulness and vigilance reveals an anxiety He felt about those future conditions. In concluding the parable, He raises the issue, *"When the Son of man cometh, shall he find faith on the earth?"* (It is plain to me that it was certainly a well-founded preoccupation.)

And, at least in this respect, the imminency doctrinaires are not so far off. Their rationale definitely possesses a certain merit: namely, the good sense of urging a constant vigilant faithfulness, which of course is the principle established in the numerous passages of Scripture we are considering now. Yeshua Himself obviously knew the value of maintaining a sense of uncertainty regarding the day of His return so as to keep His disciples on their toes and diligently engaged in preparation of His kingdom. People do tend to fall off to sleep when they are relaxed, or to get caught in the tide of worldliness, when they are not striving against it. Most everyone is familiar with the common expression, "When the cat's away, the mice will play." So, there is no argument that the importance of being ready is the flame that is being fanned by this vigorous and repeated instruction to vigilance.

But let's take another look at these and some other related scriptures (which I promised in an earlier section to come back to) in terms of the thief notion. Since that metaphor is used so often, there must be more to it than simply the element of surprise. After all, the tone of the thief scriptures cited above implies plainly "the thief" *will not come as a thief* to those who maintain a state of readiness. They, nor their houses, nor their goods will be in jeopardy. In fact, the literal phrasing of more than one of those citations makes it clear beyond any debate that the children of God are **not** to be subject to that element of surprise—if they have not gone to sleep and have eyes to see (1 Thessalonians 5:4-6).

On top of those, we shall examine prophetic scripture with our own eyes which states plain as day that Messiah *cannot come at any moment!*

These scriptures will show that the very same dogmatists who have married the notion of Christ coming at any moment are really the ones who will get caught with their proverbial pants down. They shall be most vulnerable to the thief. They in particular shall suffer the most tragic loss to this thief who comes *"at an hour when [they] think not!" (Luke 12:40)* Which is exactly the point!—*"such an hour as ye think not!" (Matt.12:44)* Remember, they think He can come at any hour; and they certainly think that He will not delay until after the Tribulation.

To expect Jesus at any moment is to discard half of the Book of Revelation—which the cult of the tribulation escapists fruitlessly struggle to even begin to understand anyway (though they so confidently affirm to). Even the very first verse of the Book of the Revelation escapes them! Eyes to see and a heart to understand will notice from that first verse that Jesus Christ Himself *learned something that He previously did not know*, at least not fully.

Secret New Facts Revealed to The Lamb

While on earth, both before his death and after His resurrection, He declared that not even *He* knew the exact day or the hour when all would be fulfilled (as quoted above from the Gospel of Mark and repeated in Matthew 24:36). This fact remained true for all practical purposes until about 90 C.E.[8] when the Book of Revelation, or the Apocalyse, was written by the apostle John. Contrary to the misleading book headings at the top of chapter one of Revelation in some publications of the Holy Bible, the Book of Revelation is *not* the revelation of St. John the Divine! Rather, verse one declares the prophecy to be *"the revelation of Jesus Christ, which God gave unto Him, to shew unto His servants things which must shortly come to pass."* Obviously, these were things that Yeshua was unable to show unto His servants while he was yet present with them before leaving earth at His ascension almost 60 years prior.

Now though, after having suffered being sacrificed as the Lamb of God (see Revelation chapter 5), He was found worthy to break open the seals of the seven-sealed book of revelation (actually a roll or scroll of the ancient type). This scroll-book sealed with seven seals is mistakenly referred to by many so-called prophecy experts and scholars as a book of the *future*. Whereas, in reality it provides a revelatory overview of *all the ages*, and then brings into particular focus the view of *the end* of those ages, which is its primary emphasis. Though it is an extensive study of its own, which we will not fully have opportunity to explore in this treatise, for the time being let us condense some of its major features in order to stick with the current topic.

One of those major features is the specific outlay of times and seasons it contains. Times which previously had been unknown even to Christ Himself before this revelation were subsequently—after Yeshua's crucifixion and resurrection—revealed quite specifically to Him in terms of even a countdown of *days*. Not only so, but the countdown is provided in two other corroborating formats as well, additionally enumerating corresponding periods of time in *both months and years*.

The first six seals of this special scroll cover the general dynamics of earthly affairs all the way through the entire course of earth's history to the coming of the Great Day of the Wrath of God. It's the opening of the sixth which discloses details of that final Day wherein YHWH at last annihilates the wicked constructs of revolting, rebellious men who have achieved nothing more than oppression, murder and war (esp. victimizing the vulnerable righteous and poor) during their decadent dominion of Planet Earth.

The seventh portion of the sealed Revelation—just as in the development of the plot of many books and movies—is a *flashback* to focus on a particular period of history that most concerns the Writer of this Script, God Almighty. In the first six sealed revelations, He laid out His general overview and provided sufficient background to then jump back to fully develop *the theme of importance*—the conclusion of man's day, and the coming of His own. This, as we have noted, is what was of such keen interest to the early followers of Yeshua the Lamb, particularly in terms of exactly *when*.

Consistent with the other New Testament prophets, the Apocalypse does not fail to reiterate and refresh us on the notion of "the thief." In it, at least two direct mentions of Messiah coming *as a thief* are made. Those two references found in chapters 3 and 16 were quoted in the list provided earlier above. Both have tremendous significance in resolving the meaning of the thief concept in its fullest sense. Both involve vigilance and hanging on to something precious that should not be lost, lest the losers thereof should be overcome with shame (and probably grief). Now, besides unexpectedness or taking advantage of vulnerability, isn't that which a thief specializes in, more particularly, the forcible taking of another's property?

It seems the key word is *"as."* In other words, this is how it will *seem* to the "victims" whom he surprises. In reality, The Creator is simply coming to reclaim what was His to begin with and which was merely consigned or commissioned to mankind for enhancement, safekeeping and enjoyment.[9] After thousands of years of the general dynamics of Revelation chapter 6, however—during which time man has converted himself into a vile self-proclaimed god and rejected the status of entrusted steward of the earth, in favor of being the exploitive and abusive expropriator of Earth and her resources—now he feels that the earth is his to do with as he pleases. Now that he has arrived at the degree of mastery that has rendered it possible for him to destroy that earth by the diabolical creations of his own hands, he seems to think that The Creator can be defied and denied His right to the planet made by His own hand. Well, to the thieves He will viewed as a thief.[10]

And to those who align themselves with thieves, will He also appear as a thief—in more ways than one! Revelation 16:15 (quoted earlier) is a reference that is found couched in a passage describing the final preparations for the vengeance of the "thief" upon the real thieves.[11] In this passage, He gathers together *"the kings of the earth and of the whole world . . . to the battle of that great day of God Almighty . . . into a place called . . . Armageddon."* Here is where they—the kings of the earth and *the beast*—gather together *"to make war against Him [the Lamb] that sat on the horse, and against his army"*[12] in final defense of their theft of the earth against its reclamation by the rightful owner, who Himself comes "as a thief!" These Armageddon forces are headed up by *the Beast* (a.k.a. the Antichrist), the consummate pirate, who will even attempt to steal the name and place of God.[13] (This thief will steal your soul, if you are fooled by his marvels and take his *mark* in order to participate in his "magnificent" New World Order.)

Those who espouse the any-moment doctrine of escapism and believe that their thief-in-the-night-messiah will come to steal them away into the clouds of heaven before they are confronted with having to deal with the real thief are already victims of a thief. In their self-induced state of sleep/darkness, they are already subjects of a theft that has robbed them of their vision, their understanding,[14] as well as their sense of urgency about being ready. For, how can they claim or believe themselves to be ready for the coming of the

Son of man (Jesus) coming *"in such an hour as ye think not."*

It is at that time, unexpectedly faced with either taking the mark or not, that they will have to endure that which they desired so desperately to escape and take the *only appropriate stand* (which they squeamishly avoided, claiming Jesus would return first). And if they do, all the mammon they worked so hard for over the years—houses, cars, furnishings, businesses, bank accounts, toys and accessories—will all be stripped from them as a contribution to the socialist New World Establishment of The Beast.

And, if they fail to watch and pray that they might *escape the cares of this life*,[25] then as was mentioned in an earlier paragraph, they shall suffer the vengeance of the *other thief* for their alignment with the agenda of this new Robin Hood by taking his mark. This will be supremely tragic, since the prophets we have been citing have made the message so perfectly clear: It is only *those who do not watch* that the calamity of the thief will vex (Revelation 3:3, quoted earlier above). And, for all that the any-moment Christians insist that they possess the light of understanding on the allegory of the thief, it is shamefully ironic that they are so blind to scriptures that contradict—back to back in the very same passages that they reference about the thief—the very notion they conclude from those scriptures. How true it is that a divided allegiance (the evil eye of Yeshua's exposition on serving two masters) only fills your whole being with *darkness* (the perfect condition for the stealth of a thief, incidentally).

Now, to conlude this section with the fulfillment of one of my promises, let's revisit the perfect example of self-induced blindness to passages of prophecy which are plainly unambiguous. To Apostle Paul, as he outrightly states in this passage we are about to review, the topic of this study (of the thief notion) was so explicitly exempt from debate and dispute that he even felt his letter on the subject was an unnecessary reiteration. Thank God, though, that he was given to reaffirmation:

But of the times and the seasons, brethren, ye have no need that I write unto you. For yourselves know perfectly that the day of the Lord so cometh as a thief in the night. For when they shall say, Peace and safety; then sudden destruction cometh upon them, as travail upon a woman with child; and they shall not escape. But ye, brethren, are not in darkness, that that day should overtake you as a thief. Ye are all the children of light, and the children of the day: we are not of the night, nor of darkness. Therefore let us not sleep, as do others; but let us watch and be sober. For they that sleep sleep in the night; and they that be drunken are drunken in the night. But let us, who are of the day, be sober, putting on the breastplate of faith and love; and for an helmet, the hope of salvation. For God hath not appointed us to wrath, but to obtain salvation by our Lord Jesus Christ.—1 Thessalonians 5:1-9

In a matter of only nine verses he summarized the essence of our whole discussion. Of course the day of the Lord will come as a thief in the night. But to whom will he appear in such a manner, bringing sudden destruction upon them? To those who proclaim "Peace and safety!"

Do you see any substantial difference between that cry and "Rapture, rapture and no tribulation," which the escapist cults call the "blessed hope?"

The particularly profound feature of this passage is its unmistakable inference that though it is as obvious as a pregnant woman that there will be eventual *travail* at the end of that pregnancy, yet the prevailing clamor will be "Peace and safety"; or perhaps otherwise phrased, "No troubles for us—we'll be safe in the sky!" The fallacy of this fanciful attitude will not serve the fans of this fantasy well, however. For it is unequivocal that *"they shall not escape!"*—no matter how adamantly they affirm their safety. Equally as profound in this passage is the starkly lucid declaration that the brethren, as children of light and of the day, are not in any kind of darkness that that Day should overtake *them* as a thief. Yet the imminency cult persists.

And finally, as though grasping at any possible last straws to salvage their drowning eschatologies and their dreams of being spared tribulation, they redefine the word "wrath" in verse nine to conveniently accomodate their completely erroneous and shallow notions that they, as supposed brethren, are not appointed to "that terrible Great Tribulation."[26]

Isn't time the facts are faced up to? The world needs to see a testimony of Christian courage, not fundamentalist cowardice and thievery of truth!

3

THE SIGNPOSTS

Let them bring them forth, and show us what shall happen:
let them show the former things, what they be,
that we may consider them, and know the latter end of them;
or declare us things for to come.
Show the things that are to come hereafter,
that we may know that ye are gods:
yea, do good, or do evil, that we may be dismayed, and behold it together.
Isaiah 41:22-23

Our tour of the prophetic oracles of the Hebrews moves ahead now, if you didn't jump off the bus at our last stop when the flaming-hot fact sheets were handed out. Our itinerary will take us to several more of the major markers along the wandering route "back to the future," all pointing to the time of the end and the future Day of God Almighty.

Going back to view the age-old record of the apocalyptic signs posted so long ago should prove to be a veritable baptism of fire. Studying the writings in preparation for this book has, frankly, scalded my tail and left my eyebrows singed. Our fiery tour through the Scriptures is certain to be the scorching enemy of complacency, lethargy, and mediocrity, all of which should vanish in smoke by the end of the tour, as should any thought of banking on an extended future on this increasingly cursed planet.

Signposts which mark the end of the age, the end of Earth's domination by wicked men, truly abound throughout the prophetic scriptures of the Jews. And, although this essay may not seek to identify them all, I endeavor to highlight the most significant of them. Special attention will be focused on the signs posted by Jesus from key passages in the New Testament, especially the chapters in Matthew's, Mark's and Luke's gospels which deal particularly with end-of-the-age prophesies. Of course, as the Old and New Testaments together have consistently proven to make up an integrated whole, extensive reference will be made to the many other prophets (from both eras) who all together support a tightly unified "big picture" of the looming End (as well as of the Restoration).

But, before we proceed, please allow me a quick detour into a side street that I feel cannot be justifiably bypassed. To do so would be like visiting a foreign country without ever meeting any of its people. And this detour is, in fact, exactly for that purpose, to make sure the people of the Book which we shall be touring in our study don't get hastily passed over, and especially, not trampled over.

There is so much that qualifies as tragic in the subject matter I have undertaken—history, our modern world, its imminent end, and the Scriptures that define all that human experience—that I almost cringe at having to so repeatedly use the words *tragedy, tragic* and *tragically*. Yet, I persist; and I find no other. By now too, you have surely also noted my conspicuous lack of grace in my treatment of all that which I consider to be disgraceful and wrong. Well, notwithstanding my hesitation, my proposed detour at this time involves delving into *more* tragedy and disgrace.

The purpose of it all, as with practically the whole volume of this book, is to set things straight—as early on as possible, in this case—before losing our bearings even as we embark!

As we proceed, it is extremely important keep in mind that the teachings and writings of the prophets which shall be referenced throughout these pages are directed primarily to The People of the Book (as they are often called), being the bearers and also the subjects and objects of those prophesies. In cases when prophesies are directed at some *other* group or body of people, the identities are quite specifically named.

This is important to remember in sorting out the confusion about what applies to whom in the prophecies; particularly when considering the questionable interpretations of the self-denominated Christians who espouse *tribulation escapism* and other elitist doctrines which covet spiritual or religious privilege.

Detour to The Museum of Religious Imperialism

Tell us, when shall these things be? and what shall be the sign when all these things shall be fulfilled? And Jesus answering them began to say, Take heed

---

63

lest any man deceive you: For many shall come in my name, saying, I am [the way, the truth, and the life]; and shall deceive many.—Christ, Mark 13:4-6

The tragedy is this: A sort of "Christian" imperialism (for lack of a better term) has ravaged the theological landscape of our world for nearly 1700 years; actually, "Gentile" imperialism perpetrated in the name of Christ more accurately describes it. The wake of this sweeping disgrace has left the world with nothing but mountainous heaps of devastated doctrinal rubble to sort through for mere clues about the Truth (which, in fact, consists of a whole *set of unified truths* as can be found in the holy scriptures of the Hebrews). These truths once stood tall upon solid foundations as sound social landmarks and benchmarks before they were shamefully toppled in the (ongoing) "take-over"—and subsequent make-over.

By imperialism I refer to what is so apparent today in the ongoing power struggle to maintain religious-theological hegemony by the so-called Christians—really, the *gentile* Christians. (Here I go again!) Well, the very strength of the take-over is evident in the fact that Christianity has, for centuries now, come to be regarded as a gentile movement, a gentile faith, a gentile religion, when nothing could be further from the truth!

All taken into account, the long and the short of it is that they—nominal, usually self-proclaimed Christians—now presume to possess *the torch* of divinely inspired dogma. Thus they presumptuously think to tell the whole world how the Hebrew Scriptures are to be interpreted and understood.

By means of interpretational aggression upon a scriptural domain that was not theirs to begin with, they have severely overstepped in their self-serving assertion to have taken over the light of the world. (The aggression consists in their efforts to *force uninspired interpretations* on the Scriptures.) By sheer force of numbers, really, they have essentially commandeered the Scriptures of the Hebrews and continue to hold a centuries-old corner on how they are to be interpreted. And by sheer strength of long tradition, they maintain their warped-by-time doctrines to be "hi-fidelity" dogma, virtually "unerring" and absolutely "irrefutable." Thereby, they effectively establish their *own* preeminent "holiness" and autocratic authority.

Somewhat more mildly, Saul (Apostle Paul) characterizes it as *"a zeal of God, but not according to knowledge. For they being ignorant of God's righteousness, and going about to establish their own righteousness, have not submitted themselves unto the righteousness of God." (Romans 10:2-3)*

As we progress into our study, it will become very apparent just how self-serving this imperialistic aggression is. And though the "'fundamentalists" are among the most guilty, they are by no means the only religious imperialists to perpetrate the presumptuousness that Apostle Peter called "private interpretation." *"Knowing this first,"* he said, *"that no prophecy of the scripture is of any private interpretation. For the prophecy came not in old time by the will of man: but holy men of God spake as they were moved by the Holy Ghost. (2 Peter 1:20-21)* However, I suppose the imperialist religious mentality is that if you assemble enough of a "Christian" mob who wills to agree on an acceptable interpretation, then it's no longer "private."

And now, as a matter of course, you have many denominational cults evolving to vie for "the torch." Only, what mostly evolves, in fact, is not holier and holier denominations possessing more and more refined truth, but often just more varieties of greater or lesser heresies and apostasies (which is why Christians are always calling for revival and renewal).

Lurking in the shadows of all this "Christianity" is the Dark Force, the dynamic activity of an invisible agent who is unrelenting in his campaign to squelch the truth and divide and conquer the land for himself. He is intent, and thus far very successful, in defeating the will of YHWH from being *"done in earth as it is in heaven."* This Evil Dynamic must displace or be displaced. Therefore, the establishment of the kingdom of heaven on earth "cannot be permitted" because he will have no place there, especially not as Lord. Hence, we have an explanation for this continued and sustained imperialist aggression upon the true meaning of the Scriptures—with every denominational Tom, Dick and Harry Christ(ian) jumping in on the assault with their own private interpretations—and that, of course, is *divide and conquer!*

All the confusion that persists about scriptural, theological, and prophetic matters is related to the divisive element of PRIDE, the adoration and exaltation of *self* (frequently a group, national, or denominational phenomenon), the diametric opposite of selfless love. But let's not detour into that exposé quite yet, lest we veer too far off our main course. *Let's get on with getting to know the People of the Book.*

In terms of detours, the ones I would really hope to steer you away from are the common heretical departures from the intent of the Sacred Scriptures, including the tragic turning away from the sworn object of the Holy Book. The popular heresies to which I refer frequently pose that the People of the Book have been categorically *cast off* and *substituted* by new peoples. These newly favored souls now, by the sheer whim and pretentious fancy of some of them, claim to have replaced the originals as the new objects of the Immutable Promises (i.e., YHWH's irrevocable covenants—please see footnote).[1] Most blatantly, these fallacious doctrines prevail among non-Jewish Christians who blindly follow generally accepted teachings without responsibly challenging their veracity against the Book itself.

A great number of religious imperialists presume to have been dubbed the new-and-improved "spiritual Israel," a "new testament brand" of People of the Book, who profess themselves to be separately classed as *distinct* and *above* the original, supposedly "fallen" People.

But all the mumbo jumbo aside, very simply, the point is that there is only *one* ethnic group of people that can rightly be referred to as the People of the Book, whether New Testament era or "Old." And, for the most part, the Scriptures are addressed *to and for them.* Although, included among them are those (Gentiles) who align themselves with the People and become grafted into their root, or tree trunk as it may be—which is to say, they *become one with* them, *not distinct* or apart from them!

The great prophet Isaiah expressly proclaimed that Gentiles (non-Jews) are welcomed to **join** themselves to The Root and take **equal** hold of the covenant made to Abraham and his seed. He made it clear that they shall also participate on the same level with the chosen seed in the holy mountain of Messiah's kingdom upon earth (in the land of Canaan, now mistakenly called Palestine). However, we see that, without debate, the Scriptures he penned specify only *one* unified gathering of the "outcasts of Israel" which also **includes** *"others . . . beside those"* outcasts.

Note that the passage I reference from Isaiah begins with a *ban* against imposing any distinction or separation between Gentile and Jew both devoted to the same LORD:

Neither let the son of the stranger [Heb. nekár = foreigner, non-Hebrew alien], that hath joined himself to the LORD, speak, saying, The·LORD hath utterly separated me from his people: neither let the eunuch say, Behold, I am a dry tree. For thus saith the LORD unto the eunuchs that keep my sabbaths, and choose the things that please me, and take hold of my covenant; even unto them will I give in mine house and within my walls a place and a name better than of sons and of daughters: I will give them an everlasting name, that shall not be cut off. Also the sons of the stranger, that join themselves to the

LORD, to serve him, and to love the name of the LORD, to be his servants, every one that keepeth the sabbath from polluting it, and taketh hold of my covenant; even them will I bring to my holy mountain, and make them joyful in my house of prayer: their burnt offerings and their sacrifices shall be accepted upon mine altar; for mine house shall be called an house of prayer for all people. The Lord GOD which gathereth the outcasts of Israel saith, Yet will I gather others to him, beside those [Israelites] that are gathered unto him.—Isaiah 56:3-8

No amount of craftiness or cunning revisionism can change what is written—nor to whom, nor for whom—although clever efforts have succeeded in "rewriting" the Book by means of *creative interpretation*. These imaginative interpretations are nothing short of flagrant departures from the stated truth of the Scriptures.

And just as signs of the time abound in our day, so do such heresies, which amount to nothing less than the foretold *apostasies* we were admonished to expect (*another sign* of the times, which we shall probe more deeply later). As we saw in the quotation from the apostle Mark heading up this section, Jesus headed up His own discourse on the signs of the endtimes with a forecast of exactly *this* most characteristic sign: *many* specious aggressors taking over the landscape in the name of the Anointed One (Christos in Greek), *denominating themselves* as the way, the truth, and the life—and deceiving huge masses!

As we explore the prophetic signs, it is important to be aware that many of them do apply to the world in general, speaking to its prevailing conditions and its common future. However, many of the predictions we shall study are specifically addressing the People of the Book, often in relation to the surrounding world. Remember, though, that one inherently straightforward characteristic of the Bible is that it requires precious little interpretation to gather who it is directed at. In nearly all cases, it tells you, if you follow the text carefully.

The essence of this cautionary note is this: Many creative interpretations of the Book endeavor to create a convenient system of re-classification whereby certain people must endure and overcome severe adversity (e.g., Great Tribulation), while others escape; certain souls are favored and privileged, while others are cursed and ill-favored. The resultant system is not just a bogus artificial contrivance, but it is very subtle, confusing, and makes the understanding of the scriptures a neurotic endeavor; thanks to those that simply cannot accept the truth for what it plainly is.

Very simply, the People of the Book are those belonging to the basic ethnic group of those who actually wrote the Book (as a divine oracle) With rare exceptions, they were all Hebrews, or Jews as they have more commonly come to be known. Their religion, or spiritual-theological philosophy, is commonly known as Judaism, after the generally faithful religious practice of the favored tribe of Judah (from which the term "Jew" is derived).

Christianity, in the purest sense of the word, began as nothing other than a sect, offshoot, or branch of Judaism. Such that, Christianity—in the strictest terms—is a Jewish religion, or belief system, begun by Jews, named after a Jew, originally dominated almost entirely by Jews, and spread by Jews. There is absolutely nothing un-Jewish or non-Jewish about it, except its alien proselytes. Please understand, the Jews (supplemented by their Gentile proselytes) are the People of the Book.[2]

Yet the foreign, Gentile converts (proselytes), which eventually grew to outnumber and dominate the population of the (very Judaistic) Christian faith, have, in the process, come to despise the Jewish roots and nature of Christianity. They have not been satisfied to have been included, or grafted into the tree of Judaism and Israel; but now exalt themselves in conceit against the natural, or original branches, as the "new-and-improved People of the Book."[3] We have seen this haughty, presumptuous attitude reflected in the pages of history all too often even to find room to do justice on the subject here in this book.[4] It persistently pervades even today's world of post-Dark Ages "enlightenment."

Very tragically, the anti-Semitic disease of envy has resulted in innumerable centuries of hateful persecution of this people. Untold horror and holocaust has been perpetrated upon them in this century alone, and more is yet to come in the near future. (No wonder the "Christians" persist in distancing themselves from these supposed "children of wrath!")[5]

This disgraceful phenomenon of self-righteous discrimination between The People and the supposed "People"—as well as *against* The People—is quite conspicuous in the "fundamentalist" interpretations of the (Jewish) Scriptures, which we shall be further exploring. Sad to say, Gentile theologians of today's overwhelmingly Gentile-populated Christianity, you will find, even proudly insist that the Christian Church is a *Gentile entity*. In their staggering confusion, they have twisted the truth to concoct a delusional, discriminatory theology which relegates a distinct high honor of church-hood upon themselves, while denying that the *Jews* are **the** actual *selected, elected, and sanctified ekklesia of Yahweh* (esp. those devout in the faith).

To clarify some terminology, the word "church," used in most English translations of the New Testament to refer to the corps of believers, is actually a **very** distant relative of the original term used by the writers of the New Testament to refer to the people of God, the chosen or *called-out ones*, the People of the Book.

The original Greek manuscripts employed the term *"ekklesia"*—a compound word denoting a *calling out of,* or *calling forth from*—to refer to those individuals or people separated out from generic humanity to observe specially the purposes of the Creator GOD in their lifestyles. Many of you may be familiar with the terms "ecclesiastic" or "ecclesiastical," which more apparently bear resemblance to the original word used in the ancient Greek copies of the Bible. Even these words, however, have suffered considerable erosion in meaning in that they are simply references to clergymen and church-related affairs. Which, without careful attention to the root meaning, leave us still without much light on the subject.

To the vast majority of folks, the mention of church immediately evokes images of *buildings* with steeples, or spired cathedrals, temples and chapels, as well as perhaps the assemblies and congregations of church-goers who may frequent them;[6] but seldom, if ever, synagogues. Sad to say, even "synagogue" in the original use of the word (Gk. *sunagogé*) did not refer to a building, but actually means *a gathering, assembly, or congregation* in the Greek. So that, in their true sense, neither churches nor synagogues refer whatsoever to buildings or places, but to *people*.

Still, there is a significant difference between *sunagogé* and *ekklesia*. And, it is absolutely not, except in the most corrupted sense, that one refers to Jewish assemblies, while the other to Christian assemblies or congregations. The word *ekklesia* (mistranslated "church"), meaning neither a building or congregation, literally denotes those **people called out** of the mundane vanity of the established world order to pursue the establishment of the Kingdom and righteous order of YHWH.[7]

Be not mistaken, at the outset of this primeval calling out, it was the Hebrews, or *Jews*, who comprised this *"Church!"* Since the time of Abraham,[8] through the time of Moses,[9] Joshua, the Judges, David and the other kings of Israel, and on through the time of Yeshua Ha'Mashiach and His Disciples,[10] and then their disciples, both before the Common Era as well as at its outset, the Church was overwhelmingly made up of Hebrews, or Jews. The *Gentile bias* imposed upon things Christian is a latter-day perversion that is perpetuated by the same theological blindness which that unfounded bias fosters and promotes.

Our corrupted lingual customs—based on religious prejudice and arrogance, and pseudo-spiritual elitism—give us to understand that synagogues are anti-Christian institutions, and that churches are non-Jewish, Gentile institutions. These notions, which are perpetuated particularly by (ignorant) Christians, and acquiesced to by seriously wounded Jews, are thorough travesties of the truth!

It is out of this concern that I have taken the time, at this point in our tour, to make sure that you are on the right bus! This tour will not trek down the well-worn routes of centuries of misinterpretation, misconceptions, mischaracterization, or misapplication and misuse of sacred teachings. We can trust that (mis-)guided tour to the popular tour lines, whose buses provide prophetic panoramas skewed through rose-colored windows (or assorted other shades and tints) and follow the worn, narrow ruts of the old traditional beaten paths—along which the Truth has been so severely trampled that its real blossom and fruit is never seen, but merely fantasized as part of a dogma (fable really) based on imagination.

At any rate, now that you know that you are not on a "church" bus, you may even be more anxious to get off, or perhaps more encouraged to go on. I hope heartily for the latter.

"Peace and Safety?"—or, Wars and Rumors of Wars?

One major signpost, at which we shall stop a while to survey the landscape, really seems more of a *billboard* these days! It has already been mentioned in passing in the foregoing chapters. Our modern world is one of widespread, chronic, and highly devastating conflicts (particularly with the advent of high-energy explosives used in conventional weapons, not to speak of the "unconventional" weapons of mass destruction). This condition of pervasive conflict that characterizes this century in particular is precisely what prompts the very broad and deep longing for peace and security felt the world over.

The elusive search for peace and the famine for safety and security is not at all a localized phenomenon. It's a global concern, and nothing less than the key word of the day—"peace with security"—especially in international affairs, and more especially in the Middle East and Israel.

Not a day goes by that we do not hear of wars and rumors of wars, peace negotiations, UN peace-keeping missions, cease-fires, disarmament, border clashes, some coup d'état or toppling of a regime by armed insurgency, ethnic tensions, international tensions, "intifadas" and jihads, race clashes, genocides, massacres, retaliations, hostages, kidnappings, urban bombings, terror attacks, militias, or some insurgent activity by some extremists guerrilla or liberation front throughout the world somewhere. Television brings it home to us *everyday*, unless we opt for *The Simpsons*.

Fact: Wars—A total of 72 armed conflicts worldwide in 1995 were reported by CBN's *Newswatch*. Only 2 months into 1996, there were reports of conflicts flaring in Spain, France, Bosnia, the Koreas, China-Taiwan, Russia-Chechnya, Greece, Turkey, Israel, Sri Lanka, Philippines, 3 different regions of Mexico alone, Guatemala, El Salvador, Ecuador, Peru, Venezuela, Bolivia, and S. Africa. Fact: The U.S. spent nearly $6.6 billion between 1992-1995 to support U.N. peacekeeping missions in Haiti, Somalia, Rwanda, and Bosnia. Fact: According to *Encyclopaedia Britannica*, more than 200 wars have been fought throughout the globe since World War I. Peter Jennings of ABC's *World News Tonight* reported (on 10/10/98) that 25 major armed conflicts raged in 1997, and most recently (summer 1999), in his weekly "The Century" segments reported on the 70 million deaths that resulted from WWII alone.

Even in the "land of the free," the only way to be free of the disturbing of our peace by the continual onslaught of this daily news is to intoxicate ourselves with drugs (legal or illegal), or on television entertainment, or some other multimedia amusement (e.g., the computerized type), or on another great favorite addiction—shop-till-you-drop consumerism.

In all actuality though, peace and security, even in the mighty USA, is really nothing more than a rapidly fading illusion. To wit, consider the fear and insecurity evoked by the bombings of the World Trade Center and the Oklahoma City federal building; or by frequent urban gang wars and ever-brewing racial tensions threatening a repeat of the 1992 Los Angeles Riot; how about satchel-sized portable nuclear weapons or the very real threat of anthrax or VX-type chemical weapons in the hands of any of the many rabid enemies of the USA?

A recent edition of PBS's *Frontline* (October 13, 1998), entitled "Plague Wars," flooded our living rooms with even more fright and insecurity at the horror of what it documented as the alleged ongoing research at Russia's Sverdlovsk biological weapons research facility. Despite mutually signed treaty bans, plague horrors of absolutely apocalyptic dimensions (beyond the imagination!) lurk in the shadows of secrecy and cover-up, continuing to be developed for use as offensive weapons against "free-world" enemies. Even our American Disneyland-ish daydreams are now haunted by the ominous, rapidly rising shadows of endtime nightmares.

This century alone has already seen the scale of **two World Wars**, much less a multitude of others—among them, the ones we are all most familiar with, such as Korea, Vietnam, Arab-Israel, Iran-Iraq, Britain-Argentina, Afghanistan-USSR, Chechnya-Russia, Persian Gulf, and Bosnia. Most folks already know that Christ predicted an era of pervasive conflict in the time of the end, before the day when He would come with great power and glory.

Shortly before His crucifixion, He left us with these telling words for the future: *"Ye shall hear of wars and rumours of wars: see that ye be not troubled: for all these things must come to pass, but the end is not yet." (Matthew 24:6)* The parallel account by Luke in his Gospel reads, *"But when ye shall hear of wars and commotions, be not terrified: for these things must first come to pass; but the end is not by and by." (Luke 21:9)* The amplified meaning of the word "commotions" (as translated from the Greek *"akatastasia"*) is more at *instability and disorder*. This prophesy has aptly described the history of the world over the centuries, and today's increasingly troubled world manifests little positive change or hope for contradicting its veracity. In fact, both the former League of Nations and the UN, created to avert any subsequent world wars, have proven pathetically ineffectual at cultivating any real tranquillity in the world's soil of constant upheaval and turmoil; and worst of all, *"the end"* still *"is not by and by."*

Wars and rumors of war are to be the order of the day in the time of the end, according to the prophesies. But, in highlighting this disturbing signpost as a major milestone on the last leg of the road to the end of the age, it seems Christ is also advising a measure of serenity in the face of such terrifying and distressful calamity. He calls for composure against premature anxiety; for, as He goes on to state, this is *not the definitive omen* signaling the final hour of the end of the age; but indeed, more of the same, in addition to other forms of even more intense travail, is yet to come, He said.

Continuing on in this passage to expand on this particular sign, He elaborated on the ravaging conflicts of our day by predicting the exact nature of so many of our modern tensions—racial clashes. Examine and analyze the basis for the armed clashes and conflicts that have been pointed out in the preceding fact box. You will notice that from Mexico to Bosnia, and Israel to Rwanda, that the bloodshed and tension is tied to race and ethnicity—or, *"éthnos epí éthnos"*, as Jesus put it.

Translated from the early Greek manuscripts of the New Testament into English, we read, *"For nation [éthnos, or ethnic group] shall rise against [epí] nation [éthnos], and kingdom against kingdom: and there shall be famines, and pestilences, and earthquakes, in divers places. All these are the beginning of sorrows."* (Matthew 24:7-8) So, not only are countries or nation-states rising up against each other (kingdom vs. kingdom), but *within* sovereign states—as we've seen even in Canada, the USA, and Mexico— serious and often bloody tensions flare between ethnic groups. Far from the utopian dream of a united world free of class struggle and racial strife, we see our world plagued more and more with reinvigorated ethnocentrism mixed with renewed intolerance, envy, and struggles for dominance and power (the deadly formulas for racial and civil wars, all based on the ingredients of egotistical, vengeful, hateful pride).

Famines, Diseases, & Earthquakes Widespread

As for the famines, pestilences (diseases and plagues), and earthquakes foretold by The Prophet in the passage quoted above, they too are commonly becoming almost ordinary, everyday occurrences throughout our modern world. In fact, as the sensibilities of the average citizen grows ever-more dull, they have become so ordinary that only those who suffer them really *feel* their impact.

> **Fact: Famines**—The World Health Organization estimates that only 1/3 of the world's population of 5,750,000,000 is well-fed, while 1/3 is under-fed, and **1/3 is starving**; 200 people die of starvation every 10 minutes; and, over 4 million will die of hunger this year (1996).

Fact: Pestilences—The following is a press release from the World Health Organization taken from the Internet:

INFECTIOUS DISEASES KILL OVER 17 MILLION PEOPLE A YEAR: W.H.O. WARNS OF GLOBAL CRISIS

Nearly 50,000 men, women and children are dying every day from infectious diseases [18m per year]; many of these diseases could be prevented or cured for as little as a single dollar per head, the World Health Organization says in The World Health Report 1996, published [January 1997]. At least 30 new diseases have emerged in the last 20 years and now together threaten the health of hundreds of millions of people. For many of these diseases, there is no treatment, cure or vaccine.

"We are standing on the brink of a global crisis in infectious diseases. No country is safe from them. No country can any longer afford to ignore their threat," the Director-General of WHO, Dr. Hiroshi Nakajima, says in the report. The report warns that some major diseases, such as cholera, malaria and tuberculosis are making a deadly comeback in many parts of the world, despite being preventable or treatable. At the same time, many new and highly infectious diseases such as HIV/AIDS and the notorious Ebola haemorrhagic fever - both of which are incurable - are emerging to pose additional threats. Fears are growing over a possible food-chain link between bovine spongiform encephalopathy ("mad cow disease") and a variant of the incurable Creutzfeldt-Jakob disease, due to an infectious agent that attacks the human brain.

Meanwhile, antibiotics and other life-saving drugs used against many diseases are rapidly losing their effectiveness as bacteria and other microbes develop resistance to them. For example, doctors worldwide are losing some of the most useful and affordable antibiotics against the two principal bacteria which cause pneumonia, the major cause of death in children.

The World Health Report 1996 - Fighting Disease, Fostering Development, published by WHO, states that infectious diseases are the world's leading cause of premature death. Of about 52 million deaths from all causes in 1995, more than 17 million were due to infectious diseases, including about 9 million deaths in young children. Up to half the world's population of 5.72 billion are at risk of many endemic diseases. In addition, millions of people are developing cancers as a direct result of preventable infections by bacteria and viruses, the report says.

And for those who may have missed the *Frontline* edition of "Plague Wars" by PBS, which I made reference to in the previous section, there are Pandora's Boxes (vials, actually, warheads and the like) already bursting at the seams with the most heinous and horrifying diseases imaginable. Many are bio-engineered for superior virility, contagiousness, and resiliency against modern medical defenses, making them impossible to contain by vaccination or with antibiotics. Released into the air or water in any or perhaps various key points of deployment, these weapons could—and most likely will—result in the terrifying *"pestilences in divers places"* which Jesus also earmarked as a major sign of the times.

Then there is the matter of the recent dramatic rise in seismic activity across the planet. Among the dreadful series of sure signs of the end of the age foretold by the crucified Christ are the frequent quakes that now rock our world on a repeated and ever more regular basis.

Fact: Earthquakes—In an article entitled, "Earth Online", by Alexandra Witze, in the April 1996 issue of Earth Magazine, discussing the *"huge number of quakes"* for which there is late breaking news available on the Internet through the Worldwide Web site of the National Earthquake Information Center in Golden, Colorado, the author points out that the huge list must be culled. Due the huge number of frequent earthquakes, quakes below 3.5 in the mainland U.S. are not even listed, and those below 5.5 are culled from the world-wide list. Earth Magazine reported on 55 quakes around the world of *6.4 magnitude or higher throughout 1995* alone. Any of these magnitudes are potential killer quakes, depending on where they are centered. The Kobe quake (mag. 6.8) in Japan killed at least 4,400 people, and the Sahkalin Island quake (mag. 7.0) in Russia killed 1,700 in 1995. The quake centered in Izmit, Turkey on August 17, 1999 that killed at least 14,000, left 600,000 without shelter, and caused an estimated $10 billion in damage was of magnitude 7.4. (A magnitude 8.0 on the Richter scale is 10 times stronger than a 7.0 and 100 times stronger than a 6.0.) One of the largest quakes on record occurred in Alaska in 1964. At magnitude 9.2 it was 140 times stronger than the Kobe quake by Richter measurements.

Of even more recent origin (September, 1999), let me share follow-up information on the unprecedented frequency of earthquakes shaking our late 20th century planet, which comes to us from a separate source. (Incidentally, the latest breaking news, now only five weeks following the massive Izmit quake in Turkey, is that of three more major quakes; one rocking the ancient city of Athens where at least 101 just died in a crushing 5.9 temblor; another in Taiwan, 90 miles south of the capital, 7.6 by Richter measure, that has killed more than 2,100; now followed by another Mexican quake centered in Oaxaca measuring 7.5 killing at least 29 and causing terror in their capital 250 miles north where the 1985 rocker killed nearly 10,000. The count is 4 major quakes causing severe damage in only 6 weeks! This doesn't count the dozens of other major tremors in the last 3 months that haven't made the news because they didn't affect major population centers.)

Following the massive quake in Turkey earlier in the week, on the August 20, 1999 edition of *CBS Telenoticias*, correspondent Carlos Botifol provided a report on what he called the "wave of tremors worldwide." In that television news broadcast he interviewed seismic activity analyst Hugo Rico of the California Institute of Technology. Mr. Rico said that "a mapping of the numerous points throughout the globe where violent movements of the earth's crust have occurred since Tuesday's quake in Turkey would light up the globe like a Christmas tree." He stated that there had been 20 quakes greater than 4.0 on the Richter scale that week alone; 7 of them were felt on the same day as the Izmit quake in Peru, China, Cyprus, Vancouver, as well as elsewhere in Turkey; 4 occurred on Wednesday in California (south and central), New Zealand, Peru and Chile; on Thursday, the borders of Ecuador-Peru and Armenia-Azerbaijan-Iran, as well Tajikistan and Turkey again, experienced shaking; and on Friday, tremors rolled through Costa Rica and Idaho. Rico went so far as to dismiss that week's series of quakes as *nothing unusual* and predicted that the following week would more than likely produce about he same number of tremors.

Earthquakes 6.5 or Greater Or Causing Significant Death or Damage		
1900-1969	48 earthquakes	*Average:* 6 per decade
1970-1989	33 earthquakes	*Average:* 17 per decade
Jan.-July 1990	10 earthquakes	*Average:* 10 per 6 months (200 per decade)
July 1990-Oct. 1992	133 earthquakes	*Average:* 4.93 per month (600 per decade)

Source: Energy, Mines and Resources Canada

Yet, though all these signs become so widespread and devastating, which they will continue to do as foretold, both in intensity and frequency—just as the labor pains of a woman in child-bearing—they are still only the *beginning of sorrows,* according to the prophecy. (The actual Greek word from which "sorrows" was translated is *odín,* meaning a pang or throe, esp. as in child-bearing.)

This conspicuous global pregnancy has long since begun to show its swelling signs of the times. And, all the overspreading talk of peace can no longer conceal the swollen world conditions that promise major throes of imminent trouble and tribulation. In fact, the amplitude of all the flowing rhetoric of peace and the draping prattle of security, which we hear so much of on a daily basis, is now nearly the biggest sign itself; much as a maternity dress serves to announce the pregnancy, more than to conceal it.

New Age Birth Pangs and Woes of Mother Earth

What happens next?—Something that "Christians" dread the most. So dreaded is the thought of it that the great majority of fundamentalist Christians have concocted elaborate theories about "raptures" and "snatchings away" intended to assure themselves of escape *before* this next crucial period of time to follow. The *"beginning of sorrows"* will eventually give way to the dire and imminent full-scale sorrows of *hard labor,* a short time foretold by Christ during which *Great Tribulation* would prevail.

It is an intense, though brief, period of time when love wears so perilously thin at all levels that only a substitute facade of politically correct socialist concern and care will remain to take its place.

Even *"natural affection"* among families shall collapse to brutal levels of betrayal. Already we see the shadows of the looming unspeakable Evil darkening our horizons. The chill of it permeates the air even here in "the home of the brave" where divorce, abandonment, sexual abuse, and other forms of violent abuse and betrayal pervade our culture and all its institutions from the school house to the White House. If it's not child abuse, it's parent abuse, or elder abuse, or spousal abuse, or teacher abuse, or intern abuse. If it's not teen (& now even pre-teen) school-house shootings and juvenile murders and massacres, it's Presidential aides and Cabinet members committing "suicide" or getting "killed in plane crashes." Brotherly and neighborly love, and good will between people in general, has in our days hideously transformed from the average decency of Dr. Jekyll to the raging evil nature of Mr. Hyde.

Modern 20th century society has swiftly decayed into an environment where no one can be trusted, no one keeps their word, and deceit and lying are now *the custom!* Governments and presidents; merchants and advertisers; even the healthcare industry and families have not escaped; religionists too; employers and employees; you name it, they all do it, all the time!

The only "goodness" we have come to expect as customary is the exploitive serving of purely selfish concerns—which often masquerades as benevolence, concern, care, public service or social welfare. And, as if we just don't have enough of this masquerade of goodness, the New World Order advocates are promising us an even more righteous costume party which will feign a truly grandiose **facade of godliness**, completely humanistic and hollow, and denying the only true source and possibility of it.

The omens are everywhere. A failure to recognize them only testifies to the effectiveness of the subtle strategy of mankind's evil Adversary.

But, as the present sweeping trend already ominously portends, the liberating laws of God are soon to be summarily rejected and abandoned as politically incorrect. Gradually displacing them is the humanist secularism of the New World Order of the "Evolved-Illuminated Homo Sapiens" (ha!) where self-righteous Big-Brother ideology is embraced and YHWH God is disdained and His teachings ridiculed. This bogus "New World Order" on our thresholds, a version of which was touted by former President George Bush, is symbolized by John the Revelator in the Apocalypse (chapter 17) as a mysterious Whore-on-the-back-of-the-Dragon symbiote, which finally breaks down into conflict.

The Novus Ordo Seclorum, or "New Worldly Order" proclaimed on the US dollar bill is already aggressively posturing itself to fulfill the worst of Bible prophecy. During the coming global regime of the imminent new secular order of the ages, *"enduring unto the end"* as a devoted worshipper of God will be a feat of overcoming and victory in itself; and, according to the words of Christ, will also determine the salvation, preservation, and deliverance of one's soul. It will be a twisted era of consummate Big Brother perversity in which the genuinely good people of earth will be reckoned and declared enemies of The State.

The success of the neo-pagan, secular hedonists of the Western World, and especially of the USA, in repressing, denigrating and eradicating the values and principles of godliness *as taught by the Bible*, casts a tell-tale shadow of the looming figure that is yet to darken the entire world. An order has emerged over the last century that is rapidly fulfilling the vision of the Apostle Paul in his discourse on the "perilous times" of the last days:

This know also, that in the last days perilous times shall come. For men shall be lovers of their own selves, covetous, boasters, proud, blasphemers, disobedient to parents, unthankful, unholy, without natural affection, trucebreakers, false accusers, incontinent [no self-control], fierce, despisers of those that are good, traitors, heady, high-minded, lovers of pleasures more than lovers of God; having a form of godliness, but denying the power thereof: from such turn away.—2 Timothy 3:1-5

The word "fierce" in this passage should also have been highlighted in bold print, since the Greek *"chalepoi"* (translated "perilous") connotes *fury and ferocity*, attesting to the violent temperament and character of the generation of the last days.

More and more each year (weekly almost) in our increasingly degenerate world, the general decency and civility of by-gone years is being displaced by the growing violence, viciousness, terror and ruthlessness which is overrunning our weakened nations throughout the globe. In the battle for the soul of Earth, Godlessness has come to prevail—i.e., pervasive luciferian lawlessness and lovelessness—as the nations self-righteously abandon any affinity for Judeo-Christian morality. Repeated fits of intense international pain and anguish constantly become more frequent and sustained, subsiding only briefly before recurring again or shifting to new places in the bowels of our global society.

Paradoxically—in an attempt to gain acceptance—the coming new worldly order, yet to fully emerge, will advance its hollow *"form of godliness"* by mimicking godly principles, such as: justice, equity, inclusion and tolerance (for all but the resistance elements, of course); care for the poor and disadvantaged; redistribution of wealth and a better standard of living "for all"; crime-fighting and a return to law & order; civility and human rights advocacy; and especially unity, security and peace. Even pan-religious activity will be promoted for a brief period in the name of peace, brotherhood and unification.

It will be a fairly good show. But it will be very brief—about three-and-half years—until the Abomination of Desolation occurs. The world will then be cast into the last 42 months of unrelenting travail, as the authentic New World Order (of Messiah) painfully traverses the birth canal to its dramatic emergence on planet Earth in full glory. (Much more detail is offered in the following chapters on this "Abomination," spoken of by Daniel the prophet back in the 6th century BCE)

What follows the arrival of the Abomination, and its relatively peaceful prelude, is described by the prophet Daniel as *"a time of trouble such as never was since there was a nation even to that same time. . . . " (Dan.12:1)* Jeremiah likewise spoke of this same time: *"Ask ye now, and see whether a man doth travail with child? wherefore do I see every man with his hands on his loins, as a woman in travail, and all faces are turned into paleness? Alas! for that day is great, so that none is like it: it is even the time of Jacob's trouble; but he shall be saved out of it." (Jer.30:6-7)*

In the cosmic rivalry for domination of Planet Earth, "Jacob" is caught in the middle. Indeed, in several chapters, Daniel too implicates the "holy people" (as do also the other Prophets) as bearing the brunt of the travail. Yet, as a glimmering light at the end of the tunnel, Daniel extends the same assurance of hope which we see given by Jeremiah; in the continuation of the verse cited above from chapter 12, the prophecy promises: *"And at that time thy people shall be delivered, every one that shall be found written in the book."* The titanic wrestling for possession of God's earth involves, as a central game piece, the city of Jerusalem, the holy land and the chosen people (*"Jacob"*) associated with it.[11]

The ancient old-testament signposts most indicative of the closure of the age of man are those signaling the ultimate battle for Jerusalem. Designated as *"the city of the great king,"* it is destined as capital of the great Prince of the genuine New World Order of Peace who will rule from Zion at the finale, and it is there that the global controversy finally centers. The birth of this **truly new** world, however, will not occur until after 3½ years of intense travail, trouble and tribulation as "the Beast" attempts to preempt its coming with a specious new world order of his own. As we shall learn from the prophecies yet to be studied, he jealously covets Jerusalem as his capital where *"he shall plant the tabernacles of his palace . . . in the glorious holy mountain. . . . "*

"Yet he shall come to his end, and none shall help him." (Dan.11:45)

Preview: The Birth of JOY

A woman when she is in travail hath sorrow, because her hour is come: but as soon as she is delivered of the child, she remembereth no more the anguish, for joy that a man is born into the world.—Christ Yeshua, John 16:21

Jumping way ahead in our prophecy tour, a sneak preview of "the end of it all" (as Peter put it in the fourth chapter of his first epistle) reveals that, though the birthing travail will be almost unimaginably intense, it will come to an abrupt conclusion in short order. Then, after the great shaking of heaven and earth which the prophet Haggai foretold, at last, *"the desire of all nations shall come." (Hag.2:7)*

As Daniel put it (above), not very long after the capture of *"the glorious holy mountain"* by the Beast, the Wicked Prince to come, *"yet he shall come to his end"* and there shall be no salvation to prevent his final doom. John the Revelator says that, even before the utter annihilation of his allied Armageddon legions, the Beast will be taken alive, along with his chief spokesman and technician of marvels, to be *"cast alive into a lake of fire burning with brimstone." (Rev.19:19-21)* His confused armies will then be squashed like grapes and *"the kingdoms of this world . . . become the kingdoms of our Lord and of His Christ; and He shall reign for ever and ever." (Rev.11:15)*

The first phase of that everlasting rule of joy is spoken of only briefly in chapter 20 of the Apocalypse as a period of 1000 years during which "the Dragon" is incarcerated in the "bottomless pit"—probably referring to some nether "wormhole" where he is kept captive, suspended in time and space, perhaps the same "stargate" by which he invaded Earth to begin with. In any event, this phase of the Kingdom of God constitutes the "Restoration," or *"the times of restitution of all things, which,"* according to Peter in Acts chapter 3 (v.21), *"God hath spoken by the mouth of all His holy prophets since the world began."* This will be a period on Earth when, for the first time since the Serpent appeared in Eden, the deceitful, egotistical influence of the Devil will be abolished and his agenda eradicated; this future day is called *"the times of refreshing"* by Peter, and commonly labeled "The Millennium" or the Millennial Reign of Messiah (Christ), when Peter prophesies that GOD will *"send Jesus Christ." (Acts 3:19-20)*

John actually elaborates much more (in Revelation 21 & 22) on the final phase of the Kingdom of God, New Jerusalem, the supreme "Mother Ship" which he foresees *"descending out of Heaven from God"* to the Earth. However, John at least outlines the first phase in a few verses of Revelation 20; briefly, he tells of a period of shared rule and dominion by the saints and martyrs who are resurrected to preside and officiate with Christ during The Millennium. Again, this first stage is what is called the Restoration to which Peter alluded as the theme of such broad popularity to *"all the holy prophets."*

Indeed, the restoration has been, and still is, of enormous interest to believing Jews and to many millions of Gentile converts around the world who also wait for the Kingdom of God with all-consuming expectation. And without a doubt, the Prophets had much to say about this Great Day of God Almighty when the poor, meek, persecuted and preyed upon will be raised from their graves to have things set straight on their behalf.

John says, *"And I saw thrones, and they sat upon them, and judgment was given unto them: and I saw the souls of them that were beheaded for the witness of Jesus, and for the word of God, and which had not worshipped the beast, neither his image, neither had received his mark upon their foreheads, or in their hands; and they lived and reigned with Christ a thousand years. But the rest of the dead lived not again until the thousand years were finished. This is the first resurrection. Blessed and holy is he that hath part in the first resurrection: on such the second death hath no power, but they shall be priests of God and of Christ, and shall reign with him a thousand years."* (Revelation 20:4-6)

Jesus said, *"Blessed are the poor in spirit: for theirs is the kingdom of heaven. Blessed are they that mourn: for they shall be comforted. Blessed are the meek: for they shall inherit the earth. Blessed are they which do hunger and thirst after righteousness: for they shall be filled. Blessed are the merciful: for they shall obtain mercy. Blessed are the pure in heart: for they shall see God. Blessed are the peacemakers: for they shall be called the children of God. Blessed are they which are persecuted for righteousness' sake: for theirs is the kingdom of heaven."* (Matthew 5:3-10)

(And to address another popular "private interpretation," which devises separate destinies for Jews and Gentiles—one earthly and one "heavenly"— it helps to read on. For, despite the gainsaying of the rapturists and other elitists who say the earthly Restoration is strictly for the Jews, while they themselves will supposedly bask in the glories of a non-earthly, heavenly destiny, Jesus contradicts them! Note that in the same "Sermon on the Mount" which we have just excerpted, He doesn't teach His disciples to pray, "Father, take us to your heavenly kingdom," but instead, *"Thy kingdom come. Thy will be done in earth, as it is in heaven."—Matt.6:10)*

God's will shall be done on Earth when His heavenly world order, His Kingdom, is established on this planet by Messiah, the King **of kings** (who shall jointly rule and reign with the Prince of Peace in The Millennium).[12] To help establish what that Heavenly Will is and what that thousand years can be expected to bring, I have compiled the following rather lengthy list of verses from several of the Prophets. I trust you will be inspired by them, as I have been.

Remember, the Prophets and all the enlightened Hebrews understood that death was only a temporal condition, which they called "sleep." They knew, as Job affirmed, *"Though after my skin worms destroy this body, yet in my flesh shall I see God." (Job 19:26)* David likewise concurred, *"Therefore my heart is glad, and my glory rejoiceth: my flesh also shall rest in hope. For thou wilt not leave my soul in [the grave, Heb. she'ol]; neither wilt thou suffer thine Holy One to see corruption." (Ps.16:9-10)* He added in the next Psalm, *"As for me, I will behold thy face in righteousness: I shall be satisfied, when I awake, with thy likeness." (Ps.17:15)* Isaiah testified, *"Thy dead men shall live, together with my dead body shall they arise. Awake and sing, ye that dwell in dust: for thy dew is as the dew of herbs, and the earth shall cast out the dead." (Isa.26:19)*

Thus, the following verses of promise were taken to mean life in the flesh would one day be restored—in the *"regeneration"*—as an everlasting condition where these beautiful promises would be fulfilled *on earth* to resurrected flesh-and-bone humans. The resurrected Yeshua, you remember, partook of a broiled fish and of a honeycomb to attest to His quite human restoration. (Luke 24:39) *"A spirit hath not flesh and bones, as ye see me have,"* was His response to the initial fright His disciples showed at His reappearance after crucifixion and burial. (Luke 24:42)

And so, I take these verses completely literally; for I'm not of the camp of Christians who, as one of my mentors used to say, are so heavenly minded they're no earthly good! In line with the great and godly founding fathers of America and their advocacy of *"life, liberty and the pursuit of happiness,"* I entitle them *"The Divine Design—A Blueprint for Utopia"*:

Life (true and everlasting)—Thou wilt shew me the path of life: in thy presence is fulness of joy; at thy right hand there are pleasures for evermore. (David, Psalm 16:11)

If they obey and serve him, they shall spend their days in prosperity, and their years in pleasures. (Job 36:11) They shall be abundantly satisfied with the fatness of thy house; and thou shalt make them drink of the river of thy pleasures. (David, Psalm 36:8) I am come that they might have life, and that they might have it more abundantly. (Messiah, John 10:10) If then God so clothe the grass, which is to day in the field, and to morrow is cast into the oven; how much more will he clothe you, O ye of little faith? And seek not ye what ye shall eat, or what ye shall drink, neither be ye of doubtful mind. For all these things do the nations of the world seek after: and your Father knoweth that ye have need of these things. But rather seek ye the kingdom of God; and all these things shall be added unto you. Fear not, little flock; for it is your Father's good pleasure to give you the kingdom. (Yeshua, Luke 12:28-32)

Liberty—*The Spirit of the Lord is upon me, because he hath anointed me to preach the gospel to the poor; he hath sent me to heal the brokenhearted, to preach deliverance to the captives, and recovering of sight to the blind, to set at liberty them that are bruised. (Messiah, Luke 4:18 & Isaiah 61:1) And ye shall hallow the fiftieth year, and proclaim liberty throughout all the land unto all the inhabitants thereof: it shall be a jubilee unto you. (Moses, Leviticus 25:10) Is not this the fast that I have chosen? to loose the bands of wickedness, to undo the heavy burdens, and to let the oppressed go free, and that ye break every yoke? (Isaiah 58:6) Now the Lord is that Spirit: and where the Spirit of the Lord is, there is liberty. (Paul, 2 Corinthians 3:17)*

And I will walk at liberty: for I seek thy precepts. (David, Psalm 119:45) For, brethren, ye have been called unto liberty; only use not liberty for an occasion to the flesh, but by love serve one another. (Paul, Galatians 5:13) And ye shall know the truth, and the truth shall make you free. . . . Verily, verily, I say unto you, Whosoever committeth sin is the servant of sin. . . . If the Son therefore shall make you free, ye shall be free indeed. (Jesus, John 8:32-36) Because the creature itself also shall be delivered from the bondage of corruption into the glorious liberty of the children of God. (Paul, Romans 8:21)

Pursuit of Happiness—*Thou wilt shew me the path of life: in thy presence is fulness of joy; at thy right hand there are pleasures for evermore. (David, Psalm 16:11) Happy is that people, that is in such a case: yea, happy is that people, whose God is the LORD. (Psalm 144:15) And he brought forth his people with joy, and his chosen with gladness: (Psalm 105:43) For God giveth to a man that is good in his sight wisdom, and knowledge, and joy: but to the sinner he giveth travail, to gather and to heap up, that he may give to him that is good before God. (Solomon, Ecclesiastes 2:26) The meek also shall increase their joy in the LORD, and the poor among men shall rejoice in the Holy One of Israel. (Isaiah 29:19)*

For ye shall go out with joy, and be led forth with peace: the mountains and the hills shall break forth before you into singing, and all the trees of the field shall clap their hands. (Isaiah 55:12) Therefore the redeemed of the LORD shall return, and come with singing unto Zion; and everlasting joy shall be upon their head: they shall obtain gladness and joy; and sorrow and mourning shall flee away. (Isaiah 51:11)

Also the sons of the stranger, that join themselves to the LORD, to serve him, and to love the name of the LORD, to be his servants, every one that keepeth the sabbath from polluting it, and taketh hold of my covenant; Even them will I bring to my holy mountain, and make them joyful in my house of prayer: their burnt offerings and their sacrifices shall be accepted upon mine altar; for mine house shall be called an house of prayer for all people. (Isaiah 56:6-7) I will also clothe her priests with salvation: and her saints shall shout aloud for joy. (Psalm 132:16) He that keepeth the law, happy is he. (Solomon, Proverbs 29:18)

And the angel said unto them, Fear not: for, behold, I bring you good tidings of great joy, which shall be to all people. (Luke 2:10) Let the heavens rejoice, and let the earth be glad; let the sea roar, and the fulness thereof. Let the field be joyful, and all that is therein: then shall all the trees of the wood rejoice. Before the LORD: for he cometh, for he cometh to judge the earth: he shall judge the world with righteousness, and the people with his truth. (Psalm 96:11-13) O let the nations be glad and sing for joy: for thou shalt judge the people righteously, and govern the nations upon earth. (Psalm 67:4)

Now the God of hope fill you with all joy and peace in believing, that ye may abound in hope, through the power of the Holy Ghost. (Paul, Romans 15:13) I will see you again, and your heart shall rejoice, and your joy no man taketh from you. (Messiah, John 16:22) And these things write we unto you, that your joy may be full. (I John 1:4) If ye keep my commandments, ye shall abide in my love; even as I have kept my Father's commandments, and abide in his love. These things have I spoken unto you, that my joy might remain in you, and that your joy might be full. (Messiah, John 15:10-11) If ye know these things, happy are ye if ye do them. (Messiah, John 13:17) Well done, thou good and faithful servant: thou hast been faithful over a few things, I will make thee ruler over many things: enter thou into the joy of thy lord. (Messiah, Matthew 25:21)

Now unto him that is able to keep you from falling, and to present you faultless before the presence of his glory with exceeding joy, to the only wise God our Saviour, be glory and majesty, dominion and power, both now and ever. Amen. (Jude 1:24-25)

The great joy so eloquently set forth in these immortal promises have their root in the central one of them all—the promised restoration of Jerusalem, *"the city of the great king,"* this time as the *"joy of the whole earth."* *(Ps. 48:2)*

Over 2700 years ago, both Micah and his great contemporary, Isaiah, prophesied of the day when Jerusalem would serve as the capital of a worldwide reign of unending peace:

In the last days it shall come to pass, that the mountain of the house of the LORD shall be established in the top of the mountains, and it shall be exalted above the hills; and people shall flow unto it. And many nations shall come, and say, Come, and let us go up to the mountain of the LORD, and to the house of the God of Jacob; and he will teach us of his ways, and we will walk in his paths: for the law shall go forth of Zion, and the word of the LORD from Jerusalem. And he shall judge among many people, and rebuke strong nations afar off; and they shall beat their swords into plowshares, and their spears into pruninghooks: nation shall not lift up a sword against nation, neither shall they learn war any more. But they shall sit every man under his vine and under his fig tree; and none shall make them afraid: for the mouth of the LORD of hosts hath spoken it.—Micah 4:1-4

Isaiah, in almost identical wording in chapter 2 of his book, declared that *"all nations"* shall flow into this supreme *"mountain."*

Much later in chapter 65 of Isaiah, where the Divine Voice promises a total ban on any form of destruction or harmfulness all throughout His "holy mountain," He decrees that even the animals will enjoy a world of peace where the one-time predators will "feed together" on herbs along with their former prey. He also decrees renewed longevity for the human race, many of whom survive the wrathful day of God's vengeance to help repopulate the earth; at a hundred years old, a human will still be a child. (See Isaiah 65:18-25.)

True freedom based on absolute and inviolable property rights will be the law, where *"they shall build houses, and inhabit them: and they shall plant vineyards, and eat the fruit of them. They shall not build, and another in-*

habit; they shall not plant, and another eat: for as the days of a tree are the days of my people, and mine elect shall long enjoy the work of their hands. They shall not labour in vain, nor bring forth for trouble; for they are the seed of the blessed of the LORD, and their offspring with them." Exploitation, oppression, opportunism, unjust taxation and all other forms of economic violence—and every form of violence altogether—will be banished forever.

Conditions of that sort would truly be a cause for joy worldwide. It's by reason of the above that this same prophecy of Isaiah bids us, *"Be ye glad and rejoice for ever in that which I create: for, behold, I create Jerusalem a rejoicing, and her people a joy. And I will rejoice in Jerusalem, and joy in my people: and the voice of weeping shall be no more heard in her, nor the voice of crying."*

In the century after Isaiah, the prophet Jeremiah also confirmed that Jerusalem would be the capital of that worldwide joy when the perverse ideologies of evil men no longer prevail: *"At that time they shall call Jerusalem the throne of the LORD; and all the nations shall be gathered unto it, to the name of the LORD, to Jerusalem: neither shall they walk any more after the imagination of their evil heart. (Jer.3:17)* As King David said in the Psalms, *"the city of the great king"* shall one day be no longer a burdensome bone of contention, as it is today, but *"the joy of the whole earth." (Ps.48:2)*

Isaiah said the "Great King" would resolve all the world's ills with wonderful wisdom and understanding, and bring righteousness, equity and peace— at last, and for ever!

And the spirit of the LORD shall rest upon him, the spirit of wisdom and understanding, the spirit of counsel and might, the spirit of knowledge and of the fear of the LORD; and shall make him of quick understanding in the fear of the LORD: and he shall not judge after the sight of his eyes, neither reprove after the hearing of his ears: But with righteousness shall he judge the poor, and reprove with equity for the meek of the earth: and he shall smite the earth with the rod of his mouth, and with the breath of his lips shall he slay the wicked. And righteousness shall be the girdle of his loins, and faithfulness the girdle of his reins.

The wolf also shall dwell with the lamb, and the leopard shall lie down with the kid; and the calf and the young lion and the fatling together; and a little child shall lead them. And the cow and the bear shall feed; their young ones shall lie down together: and the lion shall eat straw like the ox. And the sucking child shall play on the hole of the asp, and the weaned child shall put his hand on the cockatrice' den. They shall not hurt nor destroy in all my holy mountain: for the earth shall be full of the knowledge of the LORD, as the waters cover the sea . . . and his rest shall be glorious.—Isaiah 11:1-10

For unto us a child is born, unto us a son is given: and the government shall be upon his shoulder: and his name shall be called Wonderful, Counsellor, The mighty God, The everlasting Father, The Prince of Peace. Of the increase of his government and peace there shall be no end, upon the throne of David, and upon his kingdom, to order it, and to establish it with judgment and with justice from henceforth even for ever. The zeal of the LORD of hosts will perform this.—Isaiah 9:6-7

Quick—Take Your Pick

And this gospel of the kingdom shall be preached in all the world for a witness unto all nations; and then shall the end come.—Matthew 24:14

As I attempted to show earlier, you will find in reading them that the Scriptures of the Holy Bible are replete with the promise of paradise—one that is free of all curse, corruption, covetousness, violence, liars, fraud, stealth and cover-ups, imperialistic politics, profiteering extortioners, opportunists, oppressors, evil chemists, destructive sciences, and selfish lust. Peace, pleasure, and joy will be the order of the day in the coming utopian order of Messiah; and love will be the law of the land.[13] *"Beloved, let us love one another: for love is of God; and every one that loveth is born of God, and knoweth God. He that loveth not knoweth not God; for God is love." (I John 4:7-8)*

The impending annihilation of the corrupt systems and evil established orders of men, foretold by the Prophets, will make way for the implementation of the Plan of God to restore the earth to the conditions which were originally intended. At last, the will of The Creator will be done on earth and have its fulfillment in the coming of the Theocratic Civilization of God on Earth, a kingdom unlike anything found on earth today.[14]

The Prophets make it so clear that the Kingdom of God will be incredibly splendid and magnificent. Referred to by them as a great mountain or high hill topping all others, this Civilization will dominate and bring all other surviving nations and cultures under tribute to its law of love, harmlessness, freedom, justice, peace and security. Such idealistic features of an earthly existence may strike you as appealing, I don't know; but they are at the heart of the "good message" denoted by the Old English word *gospel*. On the other hand, maybe you personally don't consider them such good news; or maybe *"this gospel of the kingdom"* sounds nice, but seems like just a lot of "pie in the sky" to you.

Well, I admit, the other option (the Luciferian scheme, to be substantially detailed and studied in the following chapters) is naturally much easier to subscribe to, since its (temporal) manifestation can be seen, tasted, touched, and consumed on a daily basis in our present physical state of being—which many feel is all we've got. The Prince of Peace, however, strongly proclaimed some uncommonly *good news*, the "gospel" of another kingdom, another order, a distinctly different arrangement than that which currently prevails on earth; and it verily does take a measure of *faith* to subscribe to it. His future worldwide civilization will be ordered according to the good will of The Father, which, as we saw evidenced, is for life, liberty, and happiness in the genuine and enduring sense—free of destructive egotistical lusts, which, contrary to popular belief, is not all we've got to choose from.

The empty, terminal consumer lust of the present earth order, now under the Evil Seducer who appeals to instant gratification and fear of death, is not the only option, although conventional worldly "wisdom" declares it so. The bogus notion that *that* is all there is has been convincingly negated by the Hebrews (& others) and even proven by them as hollow; only, modern skeptics refuse to believe their testimony. (I suppose they are afraid to "throw their lives away" by believing such "preposterous claims" as that one of their crucified prophets *arose from the dead*, and that others heard from GOD and had the future revealed to them in detail.) According to worldly tenets, "seizing the day" as an hedge against an "uncertain" and "unlikely" future (esp. a "forever" one) is of more "certain" value than capturing the moment as an investment in a "supposed" unending future life "which only fools waste their lives believing in."

And so, a "logical" skepticism about the existence of God—i.e., casting away faith—is touted by the seculars as the "sensible thing to do" in "making the most out of life" before dying. That popular "prudent" perspective and a subconscious, yet pervasive, fear of death drives people into the waiting arms of the Author of Perdition, the god of *the dead*. Selfishness and its byproducts of death and destruction are the trademark products of this god's egotistical mentality and motivations. His myopic "wisdom," wrote the apostle James, *"descendeth not from above, but is earthly, sensual, devilish." (James 3:15)* It destroys the nobility of man and renders him a dead animal with nothing but lust to redeem his vain existence from perdition.

Whereas, Messiah—who said He had *"not come to destroy men's lives, but to save them"*—affirmed that GOD *"is not the God of the dead, but the God of the living." (Luke 9:56 & Mark 12:27)* In like manner, Ezekiel was told to earnestly appeal to the wayward, death-bound house of Israel with this plea: *"Say unto them, As I live, saith the Lord GOD, I have no pleasure in the death of the wicked; but that the wicked turn from his way and live: turn ye, turn ye from your evil ways; for why will ye die, O house of Israel? (Ezek. 33:11)*

Which, then, shall your choice be—the Righteous Civilization of YHWH (presided by The Prince of Peace and based on sacrificial love as the key to life), or the kingdoms of this world (master-minded by the god of the dead and based on covetous lust as the only logical complement to death)? Strange, isn't it, that the choice could be so hard to make. As usual in these matters, it's all a question of faith; and that is usually a matter of values, preferences and priorities.

Where does your faith lie? What do you choose to believe and value? Have you been blindly convinced by the blasphemers that there is no God and, therefore, nothing beyond this temporal "life" that is swiftly ticking away? Or, are your eyes open to the profound nature of LIFE, which testifies loudly and clearly to the existence and power of a benevolent Creator who longs to be recognized and appreciated? I speak of the same GOD recognized and worshipped by each of the prophets quoted in this book, The One who promised and intended (according to those prophets) that a paradise be established on Earth for the eternal enjoyment and pleasure of the children of The Creator. He is The One who, far in advance, posted the prophetic signs of the times we have been reviewing on this study tour in order that you might be persuaded (by their divine accuracy) to choose faith in **life** (everlasting).

Although the wine of the consumer establishment satisfies quickly and produces an almost immediate high, its instant intoxication is really a lethal lie which only mimics life in a cruel counterfeit of joy.[15] I, along with the Prophets, plead with you to disavow the vast covetous majority obsessed with the materialist cares of this system and the deceitfulness of worldly prosperity, and who are in denial of the promises and power of the Almighty Creator. Commit to discovering and cherishing the truth about the design of Creation and the purpose of existence—found in the eminently good message of the New World Order of GOD!

The Prophets' divine testimony to the truth about the Kingdom of God is credible, hopeful, and our only salvation. Don't be discouraged, disillusioned or drawn away from faith in their prophetic witness by sensual Western Christians and their First World materialist mentality. The prideful, self-centered Babylonish churches of the West have become corrupted by mammon, arrogant in the abundance of their prosperity, divisive in their doctrinal competition to be "holier than thou," and insensitive to the sweeping hopelessness and suffering in the world. These conditions, among others, have effectively castrated the virility of their witness, virtually annulled their commissioned ambassadorship, and practically thwarted, or at least served to nullify the testimonies of Christ and the Prophets.

Rather than faithful and loyal embassies to attract, gather, shelter, and nourish hopeful immigrant citizenry into the of Kingdom of God, our churches have become squabbling heirs, pridefully striving for position and power,[16] consumed with arrogant assertion of their cultist preeminence (each claiming some special corner on the truth), and divisively engaged in denominational self-aggrandizement; all of which has distorted the truth beyond recognition and left the world thoroughly disenchanted with the God of the Bible and the Kingdom for which He stands.

As we shall see in a later chapter, the essential measure of Western churches' emissarial efforts in relation to their actual ability—considering their enormous wealth of resources—reflects a dismally low ratio of accomplishment; so much so, that, relatively speaking, it ranks as a practical failure. The *"gospel of the kingdom'"* is not being **effectively** *"preached in all the world for a witness to all nations"* as it should be, neither in terms of extent or with respect to a full and true representation. As Isaiah once alluded, the mission has essentially been aborted and resulted in nothing but "hot air."[17]

To compensate for and rectify that miserable shortcoming, the task of advancing and promoting the message of the Global Civilization of Christ throughout the world will evidently have to be completed by supernatural means, as prophesied in Revelation chapter 14. The LORD be thanked, too, that two highly prominent prophets are yet to appear on the world scene to help set the record straight as faithful witnesses also of this same *"everlasting* gospel" of God's New World Order—namely, *"the hour of HIS judgment."* These two potent witnesses will be world famous, as we shall see in a later chapter; and they'll be joined by countless multitudes of regular folks throughout the world, even in the extreme adversity of the Great Tribulation, to offer the same witness and proclaim the same hope, the same message embodied in the *"everlasting good-spell"* which at the last is proclaimed in every corner of the globe by the supernatural flying messenger spoken of in the Apocalypse.[18]

And so, to conclude this chapter, let us note that one of the definitive signs of the times marking the close of the confused age of secular humankind is that the proclamation of gospel of the New World Order of YHWH will be witnessed by all nations, *"and then shall the end come."*

Implicit in that far-reaching witness is **choice**; and all nations must needs have theirs; we all should, *and we do* immediately upon hearing of the heavenly option. It is then incumbent upon us all to make the wisest choice possible, before our personal end comes.

And as always, please be advised that there are many corrupt trees bearing corrupt fruit. Your heart, mind, and soul too will suffer corruption, if you carelessly partake of pseudo-sanctimonious doctrines of sanctioned assimilation into the Babylonish world order.[19] Be it Egypt, Assyria, Babylon, Persia, Greece, Rome, Europe or America, they are all the establishment glories of worldly men borne up by the mentorship, transcendent domination, and the underlying demagogic dynamic of the Great Red Dragon.[20] But, by this record, I hereby witness to the words of the Prophets who themselves gave testimony to another more Excellent Option which is not of this world and which renounces both the Dragon and the Order of the Whore. More on this to follow.

And if it seem evil unto you to serve the LORD, choose you this day whom ye will serve . . . but as for me and my house, we will serve the LORD. . . . God forbid that we should forsake the LORD, to serve other gods.—Joshua 24:15-16

4

NEW WORLD ORDER OPTIONS

How art thou fallen from heaven, O Lucifer, son of the morning!
how art thou cut down to the ground, which didst weaken the nations!
For thou hast said in thine heart, I will ascend into heaven,
I will exalt my throne above the stars of God:
I will sit also upon the mount of the congregation, in the sides of the north:
I will ascend above the heights of the clouds; I will be like the most High.
Yet thou shalt be brought down to hell, to the sides of the pit.
They that see thee shall narrowly look upon thee, and consider thee,
saying,
Is this the man that made the earth to tremble,
that did shake kingdoms; that made the world as a wilderness,
and destroyed the cities thereof; that opened not the house of his prisoners?
Isaiah 14:12-17

The term "New World Order" is tossed about rather freely these days; I too make use of it liberally throughout the pages of this book. Yet, it is really a concept that remains pretty amorphous and abstract for most of us.

On the basis of what I have studied and been able to learn about the usual secular application of the term, images are conjured up in my mind of a global system—political, economic and sociological—wherein the numerous things that divide people into competing and conflictive groups will one day be conquered and dissolved. The ostensible objective, as I gather, seems to be that of a unified international order of cooperation and peace; which all sounds quite nice on the surface. But what if the goal of the globalists, or whoever is engineering this trendy concept, is different than what it appears? What if there lies something horribly insidious at the roots of all the talk of the New World Order?

Well, perhaps the Prophets may be able to help dispel some confusion on this score. Part of the purposeful ploy of the Dark Force (identified in last chapter) is to create enough confusion—that is, maintain enough obscurity—so as to strip the bewildered masses of Earth of any rational defense against what can otherwise be discerned as a Satanic Strategy of domination. It's an age-old tactic to effectively paralyze and disable victims into a position of utter vulnerability, leaving them easily overwhelmed and at the manipulative mercy of the cunning strategist. But to simplify the New World Order concept, hopefully, let us consider the three basic World Orders spoken of by the Hebrew prophets we've undertaken to study.

Zion & the New World Order Paradox

First, the ultimate and supreme world order at the hub of all Hebrew history and tradition, both past and future, is the World Order of Zion, the "darling virgin" of YHWH. According to all their prophets, at the end of the age of cursed man, it is to finally prevail on earth over all other dominions, under the rule of the Almighty Prince of Peace, the Anointed One of God the Father; we previewed this in the last chapter. However, the Hebrew prophets spoke definitively about two other global establishments vying for domination in the transcendant scheme of world history. John the Revelator in particular, writer of the Apocalyse, nailed the three competitors down for critical review and analysis. He also concurred with his antecedant Hebrew colleagues that New Jerusalem, the mated Bride of Messiah (allegorically speaking), would constitute the ultimate (and genuinely New) World Order of all Earth, with Zion as its capital.

John speaks eloquently of this Bride in several chapters of Revelation (12, 20-22, and briefly in 19). In chapter 12, she is seen as a great heavenly wonder—a pregnant woman clothed with the sun, the moon under her feet, and a crown of twelve stars upon her head. Then moving from allegory to real substance, we see in the later chapters that he attempts to describe an actual civilization.

In its final form, this civilization he described, the "great holy city" where God Himself dwells,[1] eventually requires a remake or refabrication of the earth to accommodate it, with a huge bejeweled (pyramidal?) city as its centerpiece. This city, called New Jerusalem, is a superstructure made of transparent gold, lying 1400 miles square, and 1400 high on a side. (Probably of the same geometric design mimicked in the great pyramids of Egypt.) The very last page of the Bible, in the very last chapter describing this city, records an open invitation to all humanity to immigrate to this magnificent heavenly civilization, an *entirely new* world order:

And the Spirit and the bride say, Come. And let him that heareth say, Come. And let him that is athirst come. And whosoever will, let him take the water of life freely.—Revelation 22:17

Aside from the fabulous superstructure that houses this civilization, the major focus in these chapters of the Apocalypse noted above is on the **people and personalities** who make it up, and the nature of its **culture**. The rather mysterious characterization and personification of it as a *living entity*—a woman and bride wedded to God Himself—stresses the nature of it as a knit-together unit of personalities loving and caring for one another with intimate, interdependent, intersustaining, mutually serving interrelations. God serves us, we serve Him, and all serve each other in love in the worship of the God of Love (*Who is the Temple* in this city without a temple).[2] At last, His righteous Will is realized and accomplished in all its fullness, glory and purity by willing humans brought into Oneness.[3]

Nevertheless, during this secular age of earth before her ultimate triumph, the Bride is persecuted and warred against, as John relates so graphically throughout the Apocalypse. This occurs with particular severity during the last 1260 days of oppressive beastly history noted in chapter 12 and 13 of the Revelation. During those last three-and-a-half years, the world order of The Beast—the basic, underlying arch-competitor of this divine order called the Bride of Christ and New Jerusalem—desperately attempts to completely crush and obliterate the essential elements of the Messiah's kingdom; namely, the living stones of New Jerusalem.[4]

Though the success of this beastly world order (already on our horizon) will be sweeping in the short run, it is nonetheless limited, and its efforts futile in the long run. Ultimately, it meets its own crushing devastation in an all-out war of the worlds as it attempts to engage Almighty God with its 21st century weaponry at the battle of Armageddon, intending to prevent the establishment of the world order of Christ and His Bride.

The World Order of the Beast

The *Beast* is a term applied in the Apocalypse and elsewhere in the Holy Scriptures to an ungodly entity that is fundamentally inhuman; and thus, menacing, without conscience, and driven by baser motivations and lusts of a essentially animal character. (In biblical terms, or spiritually speaking, individual people who forsake godliness to be driven by base natural lusts are also called beasts.)[5]

Prophetically, the term is applied to three key entities: (1) *the coming Antichrist* (as the son of perdition, son of Satan, and final demagogue-turned-autocrat of Earth's last world empire); (2) *the spirit of evil itself* (Satan, formerly Lucifer, the Serpent, the Dragon, the Destroyer, Apollyon, Abaddon, the Devil); and finally, in terms of material manifestation on earth, (3) *the iniquitous political world order of Satan* (manifest in various eras throughout history by the hegemonies of the assorted world empires that have arisen to exert their ungodly power and influence over mankind).

All together in complement, these beasts are referred to in the Apocalypse by the crowning title of the *"Great Red Dragon"* having seven blasphemous, crowned heads, the last of which finally sprouts ten horns. The heads are symbolic of the seven major world empires. This includes the ultimate formation of the seventh and final world empire, a coalition of 10 endtime nations under the beastly political leadership of the Antichrist, next to arise. The spiritual leadership, inspiration and power embodied throughout it all is that of Lucifer himself. It is in chapter 12 (and in 13) of the book of Revelation that John introduces us to the world order of *"the Devil"* in his figurative description of a *"great red dragon, having seven heads and ten horns, and seven crowns upon his heads." (Rev.12:3)*

As mentioned a bit earlier, it is in this chapter of the Apocalypse that the arch-rivalry and fundamental war between good and evil is typified in the persecutory hostility of the Dragon against the Bride. The world order of the Dragon has continually strived to defeat the establishment of the Kingdom and Will of God on earth. This was the central aim of the Devil in masterminding the assassination of its crucified King; and has likewise been his key purpose in directing the age-old, on-going campaign to destroy the Bride (those devoted to taking up their own crosses daily in loyalty to their King and His coming world order). Chapter 13 of Revelation goes into even more dire detail about the Dragon's relentless endtime war on the saints and against God.

This mysterious dragon continually metamorphoses throughout history, manifesting himself by serially raising each one of his various heads defiantly decked with names of blasphemy. From the Pharaohs to the Caesars, the sovereigns of these grand empires assumed unto themselves the status of living gods.

At the last, the Dragon's final head sprouts ten horns each bearing a crown (symbolizing ten endtime nations) which bestow all their political authority and military and economic might unto The Beast (earthly offspring of the Dragon). This beast (the *"son of perdition"*) will be the "incarnation" of the ever-so-subtle Serpent who promised Godhead to Adam and Eve back in the beginning; this time the same blasphemous promise will be to all of 21st century humanity on a worldwide scale. How will he achieve this global hoax and hoodwinking of the last generation? By luring it around his own powerful, internationally exalted person and the high-science apparatus of the "living image" to be made in his likeness, which everyone will ultimately be obliged to worship!

The highly alluring (& captivating) tactic to be employed in the ensnaring of the world into this new order of the Beast will be *vicarious greatness*. This is the trusty lure that so easily captures the affections of nearly all of us simple folks—greatness by association. It's the "I-touched-him" or "I-know-him" syndrome—the same complex that makes people feel special about shaking a president's hand or being photographed with him; about being personally invited to an "attended" fundraiser or to the White House, or perhaps being selected as an intern; like the special honor of receiving a presidential award, or otherwise rubbing elbows with high dignities. People are always quick to hitch their wagons to a rising star, if it means they too might somehow be carried to new heights by association with the star. Thus, by joining together to serve, worship, and glorify the Beast, we thereby glorify ourselves. (More on this in later chapters, esp. 6, 9 & 10.)

The entire 13th chapter of Revelation is dedicated to this Beast and the details of his New World Order, which will involve a lofty Hitlerian-style allure eventually ratcheted up into a regime of severe neo-fascism. According to the prophet Daniel, predecessor of John by 600 years, three of the final ten governments that comprise the core "axis powers" of this new world order will be overrun and forcibly reined into the camp of the Beast. Great cunning and might (and magic) characterize this coming, dreadful "fourth Reich" under an all-new, crowing bestial "führer" of wonders.

Key passages in chapter 17 and 19 of Revelation provide additional detail about this global government and its marvellous leader. Essentially, this human Beast literally incarnates and epitomizes the age-old ambition of Satan to *be God*. And at the last, though only very briefly, the Devil actually achieves this counterfeit status for a 42-month period as the Premier of the Worldwide Secular Order of Planet Earth (the pinnacle accomplishment of the great scarlet serpent, who is the actual dynamic power working in and through this anti-Christ).

As stated above, complimentary prophecies dealing with this Antichrist are given both in the Apocalypse and in the book of Daniel. Six hundred years before John, Daniel recorded revelations about this blasphemous beast in passages of chapters 7, 8, 9, 11, and 12 of his book. The apostle Paul too, in the time of John, also contributed some key detail to the profile. But it was Jesus who drew the focus on this *"abomination"* as an especially significant sign that would mark the beginning of the end. Pointing us back to read about the *"abomination of desolation spoken of by Daniel the prophet,"* (Mat. 24:15) He indicated three-and-a-half years of Great Tribulation would prevail under the world order of the Beast just prior His own coming at the end of the age. The reading of Daniel and also of Revelation establishes this conclusion, among other important features of the future.

The sum of these oracles, however, according to a careful reading of them and contrary to the superstitious surmisings of the great majority of fundamentalist and other Christian Bible prophecy "experts," does not add up to the uniting of all the world's religions under this dragonish new order, as the experts imagine, at least not for long. Rather, it will be the abolishing of all religions and the institution of the global adoration of only one god! That god, the Prophets have said, will be a man—empowered and begotten of Satan—through whom the Devil accomplishes his age-old ambition to dethrone YHWH (Yahweh) and take His place.

A new age is indeed about to spring forth for *"a little season"* in which self-adoring Lucifer will finally be able take his "rightful" place as the author of a better planetary ideology. By his new standard, YHWH (of the Bible) shall be debased as a "vain, tyrannical, uncaring egotist," undeserving of the "superstitious" worship of humans, and publically demoted to His "proper place" as "just another" of the many gods of ancient "mythology." The objective of this blasphemous Luciferian ideology is to completely demerit YHWH; thereby, the Devil can then advance his own candidacy as God of Earth and achieve his long-desired goal to be acknowledged as the Most High and Mighty One![6] His campaign for this office will flatteringly lure egotistical humans to join the Devil in his new credo—the worship of Me!

Once inaugurated, the Wicked Imam will wield untold forms of power of which we can only now speculate (and do, in later chapters). Nothwithstanding his own uncanny powers and might, he will encounter nearly invincible opposition in the form of two endtime prophets of GOD who arise on YHWH's behalf.

Empowered by GOD, this world renowned duo of YHWH will command the powers of nature to combat and counter the agenda of the Beast who will be unable to squelch the evidence and power of their witness until the very end. Efforts by the Beast to assassinate them will meet with no success until the last few days before the zero hour. Their defense against attackers will be some form of heat flash, energy beam, or fireball "spoken" from their mouths at the speed of thought, which literally consumes would-be assassins. After 42 months of their challenge to his regime, the Antichrist finally overcomes and kills them, only to shortly have to face the One whom they served. The awsome spiritual and technological might of the Beast will be a pathetic candle flame in a hurricane when he next meets the Almighty!

In the face of the troublesome witness of YHWH's phenomenal "flame-throwing" duo, the Antichrist will convince the people of earth that Jah is nothing more than a rogue, hostile extraterrestrial bent on the forceful take-over of Earth.[7] The Beast will persuade the world that they must join him and his planetary liberation front in solidarity against the subjugation of humanity to a hostile alien empire where, by his measure, individual sovereignty and *"human rights and freedoms must be relinquished to the tyranny of YHWH."* The two witnesses will finally be killed as infiltrating alien invaders.

Through all this the Antichrist will fraudulently pose as liberator and savior of planet Earth. Will he get your vote? Will you wear his mark and cultic number like Americans flaunt bumper stickers for their politicians of choice? (More on this in a later chapter, entitled "Messiah Mistake.")

New World Order of "Cinderella"—Glass Slipper of Mystery Babylon

On top of the Dragon dynamic, the Apocalypse poses the image of a "third" world order, a great and mighty, materialist city system of superpower category, both militarily, economically, and technologically. According to John, it is in this mega-metropolitan establishment that we find responsibility for the blood of prophets, saints, and "all that were slain upon the earth." This particular world order is described as a MYSTERY, a wonder, a marvel, and a great whore—THE MOTHER OF HARLOTS AND ABOMINATIONS OF THE EARTH—succintly labeled BABYLON. Chapters 17 and 18 of the Apocalypse are dedicated to the description, analysis, and decoding of the symbolism related to this Great Whore. (Though she is 3rd in the order of our study, in worldly political terms, rather than Third World, she is the First World oppressor of the Third and due to be overthrown by them in the end.)

This whorish establishment maintains a distinctive, symbiotic relationship with the Dragon, almost until the very end of her history, when she finally meets her violent overthrow and demise. The vision of this garish woman, whom John sees in his vision riding upon the *"scarlet coloured beast, full of names of blasphemy, having seven heads and ten horns"* effectively "blows" John's mind for the magnitude of the spectacle.

Though it is truly difficult to imagine exactly how awe-inspiring it must have been, nonetheless, when the encryption code is cracked, the written record still offers an awesome and even staggering perspective of our planet's socio-political dynamics. Without some familiarity with the Hebrew Scriptures, however, the symbolism can seem nothing but a mystifying abstraction of bizarre graphics. The master key to even beginning to comprehend the pictograph of these two chapters on the Great Whore lies in the writings of the TaNaKh, or as some dismissingly call it, the "Old" Testament.

An attentive student of the so-called Old Testament immediately recognizes the "encrypted" language used to describe this metropolitan system, and readily understands that *whoredom* is "code" language for spiritual adultery. The ancient language of love by which the Creator refers and relates to His beloved human creatures in the Old Testament (& in the New) reveals an intense desire to maintain a devoted conjugal relationship of love with His people, as a deeply devoted husband with an equally faithful wife. In that same sense, it is explicitly pronounced in those writings that wandering from that commited relationship is an act of whorish infidelity.[8]

But, as with so many other ill-conceived biblical interpretations, the fundamentalist and not-so-literal Christians alike have practiced circus-worthy contortionism to attempt to make this allegorical city system fit their ill-illuminated perspectives of the world.[9] Without detouring into the unprofitable maze of their various twisted interpretations, suffice it to say that, generally, most view this "great whore" as a *false religious system* also blended with some obvious economic prowess (as per the extensive characterization of it in chapter 18 of the Revelation). Some of the most *classically erroneous interpretations* have even ventured to tag the Roman Catholic Church as this BABYLON.

Ironically though, even in the dark "light" of these twisted twilight interpretations—originating out of the shadowy regions of dual devotions—there can be seen the outline of a certain truth obscurely illuminated. Yet, because of the prevailing shadows of night in that region of half-heartedness and dual loyalties, the full truth is not wholly revealed; and so, creative (and often deluded) imaginations kick in and run amuck.

Honest and good hearted folk, without any self-serving agenda other than to simply seek the truth, readily recognize it in its simplicity. Even the elaborate symbolism used in the painting of the picture of this mysterious whore doesn't effectively hide it. It's easy to see that the only "religious" aspect of this super-city *"which reigneth over the kings of the earth" (Rev.17:18)* is in the excessive materialism and obsession with mammon that pervades it. As even the faint glimmer of twilight reveals, *it is indeed* a system of worship that the Apocalypse is describing—the very same alternate system of devotion which Christ referred to in His "Sermon on the Mount." (Please see earlier study in opening chapter, under section entitled "20/20 Blindness.")

Christ Yeshua, in the direct manner used with His Disciples, clearly defined the world to them as a choice between only two religions (not the pantheistic variety many theologians flailing attribute to this allegory on Babylon). He identified them categorically as either that of singularly serving God (as His Bride does), or alternately, serving mammon (as the Gentile idolators do). (See Matthew 6:19-33)

Now, in terms of this domineering allegorical Whore called Babylon the Great, the question must be raised, "What is it exactly that reigns over the kings of the earth?"

The clear answer: *covetousness!*—the lust for wealth, power, and material glory. That, without question, is the Bible story of history and mankind's age-old, overriding obsession, as well as his basic metropolitan religion![10]

Archaeology too, in its quest to uncover the civilizations of the past, reveals and confirms this truism practically above all else. The stones of history speak loudly of the tireless strivings by ancient men for **self-glorification**— through the construction of lush palaces, tombs, temples, hanging gardens, skyscraping towers and glamorous cities to mark their imperialist places in history.[11] Each empire, striving to outdo and overrule the others, eventually left behind the grand, crumbling structures by which they all attempted to reflect, flaunt, and immortalize their glories—pyramids, palaces, pantheons, coliseums, massive stone relief works and statues, and archives detailing their military might, prowess, conquests, and spoils. The greatness of any ancient civilization always seems to be measured by their materialist achievements.

And in our own day and age, it almost goes without saying to note that nearly every contemporary society on earth measures its success against that of the greatest city system on the planet today, each of them coveting her prosperity and might.

The trademark glories of every worldly civilization, past and present, are their *riches* and the superstructures (buildings & cities) and armies financed by that wealth. To enlarge and defend their bottomless appetites for power, wealth, and glory—and their grand metropolises based on those greedy, materialist values—the ancient imperialists amassed and instituted blood-wringing armies and military machines. And by these armed forces, the oppressors found it profitable to conquer, victimize, and ravage other peoples, often peace-loving societies, which they "needed" to subjugate and spoil so as to finance the aggrandizement of their own nationalist glories.

This criminal barbarism was, typically, accomplished by regularly employing aggravated violence to accrue more and more wealth, territory, and ill-gotten possessions. (Native Americans and Mexicans, among numerous other indigenous peoples around the globe victimized by the Europeans, know how this agenda works.) And often, the subjugated peoples provided not only the finances and materials but also the coerced labor to build those cities and "civilizations." (In our modern world, particularly since the abolition of African-American slavery, this is done more indirectly, insidiously and deceitfully in the form of wage slavery, exploitive taxation, currency devaluations, and even more egregiously by *pittance slavery in Third World sweatshops*; modern agendas of *economic subjugation* constitute more peaceful and insidious forms of violence, known as *economic violence*. As the Bible says, it is possible *"by peace"* and *"craft"* to *"destroy many."—Dan.8:25*)

(Now, with respect to the richest, most powerful city-system in today's world, does any of this ring familiar? If not, please read chapters 17 & 18 of Revelation provided for your convenience at the conclusion of this chapter. Perhaps you too may conclude that, "under the influence" of her wine, it can be awfully difficult, if not impossible, to discern or grasp truth.)

According to the perspective of the Hebrew prophets, materialism/covet-ousness has driven and corrupted mankind into idolatry since the dawn of time. The original humans, for starters, were not satisfied even in the utopian beginnings of the Garden of Eden with the joyous nakedness of being clothed solely with freedom, beauty, and glorious natural surroundings. As the ac-count goes, they needed to *accessorize*; and, ashamed that their primitive skill level could only produce crude creations of fig leaves sewn together, they felt it necessary to hide themselves from the Father of nature when He stumbled onto their new entrepreneurial venture to become *"as [decorated] gods."*

Well, their crude beginnings to decorate themselves with the material vestments and creations of their own hands and human designs soon gave way to full blown self-adoration. It wasn't terribly long before the first child to be born to this first couple—on the now corrupted planet—developed the technology to establish the first city, and then named it after his own "spit-ting" image.[12]

To me, it becomes supremely easy to see what John the Revelator re-vealed in his exposé on the Great Whore—the New World Order of 20th Cen-tury BABYLON (in her epitome). "Cinderalla's glass slipper" fits her per-fectly well. And, although Cinderella's "sisters" (or perhaps in this case, daugh-ters) all covetously feign to squeeze into that shoe, it is exclusively tailored to the MOTHER OF HARLOTS AND ABOMINATIONS OF THE EARTH.

Throughout the world, all we see these days is an international, or pan-national effort to emulate the splendid success of the MOTHER metropolis—the epitome of all great city systems—except among those who *"hate the whore."* And even among those who regularly resist her, denounce her, dem-onstrate against her, and beratingly burn her flag in envious effigy, nonethe-less, the lust for *"the wine of her fornication"* rages out of control there too as large segments of their populations crave to emulate and partake of her ob-scene indulgences and liberalisms.

Every nation on earth, coveting to imbide liberally of her *"golden cup,"* seems to inexorably shackle themselves to her addictive cosmopolitanism.[13]

We see all nations now moving toward market-driven economies (of the supposedly "free-market" type, yet dominated by the global-class financiers);[14] all lured by profit into "privatization" of industry (with mostly foreign invest-ment by the merchandising giants of the world, primarily from guess-where, and with loaned foreign capital—which the ASEAN nations are finding will only enslave them to the IMF and the World Bank); many establishing and operating their own get-rich-quick stock markets, promoting Western-style consumerism, and aggressively pursuing the quest to trade freely with the opulent West (and perhaps one day enjoy "most-favored-nation" trading status); all increasingly arming and militarizing their countries (e.g., the alarming, new Latin-American arms race; or the African escalation; how about the Asian subcontinent nuclear race) against what—their own "freed" populations? Let us not forget to mention the nearly universal dependence and adoring adoption of Western-style medical technologies.[15]

And despite all the obvious signs that *"Babylon the great is fallen, is fallen,"* the credo of the Whore is that, without faded glory, she maintains her regal, superpower status; in like manner, she persistently vouches that her matrimonial "IN-GOD-WE-TRUST" covenant remains in effect; and quite deludely, she insists proudly that she is so mighty and well established that nothing can undo her.

How much she hath glorified herself, and lived deliciously, so much torment and sorrow give her: for she saith in her heart, I sit a queen, and am no widow, and shall see no sorrow.—Revelation 18:7

All of the above telltale characteristics of the Great Whore are outlined by John in the Book of Revelation. And indeed, the shocking truth about this BABYLON exposed by John is more than most folks can bear, particulary First World Westerners! Their materialistic mindsets cannot even stand to contemplate its profound implications.

It so thoroughly undermines the foundations of their very lifestyles that their subconscious defense mechanisms block out any painful exposure to the brilliant spotlight of this revelation. Long accustomed to the twilight of *whorish infidelity* to the Divine Commitment of singularly loving God with all their heart (which they only lipservice), their darkened eyes quickly and automatically turn away at the mere glimpse of its disclosure of their two-timing adultery. Absolutely unwilling to see that they have become one with such a depraved system,(cf. footnote 13) they try to project the light of John's revelation away from themselves and upon the "false religious practices" of others, condemning others as wayward and harlotrous while regarding themselves as faithful and true.[16]

Caution! Taking up the spotlight of this prophetic testimony in disclosure of the Whore and her lovers is to literally hazard one's life for the sake of truth! It provokes far more wrath than taking away the bottle from the wino, the smack from the junkie, or the acetaminophen from the American (or worse yet, his oil and gasoline!). Not only can the addicts of covetousness not cope with forfeiture of their intoxicating "high," they typically oppose any deprivation of it, often in convulsive fits of withdrawal. Any who venture to confront or uncover the awful truth of BABYLON'S agenda, or to oppose it, are frequently met with severe reactionary rage and virulent violence, either blatant or covert.

Be it a lone, daring prophet, or even a whole nation who might oppose her mammonistic politics and avaricious agenda—or even a "backward" village of natives in the way of her industrial/mercantile advance—any impeding of her greedy imperialistic commercialism is to invite bloodshed and murder upon yourself. Peering behind the propaganda reveals that when they're not outright "politically-justified" military actions against "totalitarianism or communism," the killings and carnage are often the surreptitious work of her backstage henchmen, murderous marionettes who commit fornication with her.

And I saw the woman drunken with the blood of the saints, and with the blood of the martyrs of Jesus: and when I saw her, I wondered with great admiration [marvelled in astonishment]. . . . And in her was found the blood of prophets, and of saints, and of all that were slain upon the earth.—Revelation 17:6 & 18:24

This patent yet hidden truth is, of course, a large part of the reason why the endtime coalition of the ten nation-states under the Beast *"shall hate the whore."* They have witnessed and tasted firsthand of her cold-blooded conceit and cruel self-serving atrocities. Her determination to remain firmly seated in the dominant position and role of queen over all the earth compels her to engage in *widespread bloodshed* of the prophets who expose her, the saints who counteract and defy her agenda, and of the innocent victims of all her murderous efforts to advance that agenda *"upon many waters"*—all to protect her national and egoistic international interests.[17] All of this hidden mystery is profiled for us in plain sight, as they say, in the coded passages of the Apocalypse to which we have referred in this section.

One of the primary reasons why the obvious truth about BABYLON is not readily apparent to most Bible students has also already been studied in this and a previous chapter. It's basically a matter of (psychological) denial—unwillingness to accept the truth, because of the lifestyle adjustment it demands. In verses 4-8 of Revelation 18, John poignantly summarizes the issue, including the dreaded divine mandate and the fateful destiny of this opulent city system (and those entrenched in it), which is so unthinkable to those who so dearly love it:

And I heard another voice from heaven, saying, Come out of her, my people, that ye be not partakers of her sins, and that ye receive not of her plagues. For her sins have reached unto heaven, and God hath remembered her iniquities. . . . How much she hath glorified herself, and lived deliciously, so much torment and sorrow give her: for she saith in her heart, I sit a queen, and am no widow, and shall see no sorrow. Therefore shall her plagues come in one day, death, and mourning, and famine; and she shall be utterly burned with fire: for strong is the Lord God who judgeth her. (Revelation 18:4-8)

In other words, just as the great majority of Jews taken into captivity in the era of the Babylonian diaspora (6th century BCE) declined to return to the promised land and opted to remain settled there—having grown so comfortable, attached, and assimilated into the whorish material paganism there—so, the subjects of today's BABYLON cannot forsake the delicious *"pleasures of sin for a season." (Hebrews 11:24-27)*

Only precious few can cope with the recognition that, spiritually speaking, *"Babylon the great is fallen, is fallen, and is become the habitation of devils, and the hold of every foul spirit, and a cage of every unclean and hateful bird" (Rev.18:2)*, (although, one 24-hour period of TV viewing in the land of the "boob tube" will exemplify the fitting reality of this graphic description). Especially not thinkable is that *"in one hour so great riches [will] come to nought"*; nor is the thought that *"with violence shall that great city Babylon be thrown down, and . . . be found no more at all." (Revelation 18:21)* These are considered as absolutely unthinkable and unacceptable utterances to be applied to "the greatest metropolitan establishment on earth."

"Oh, that refers to Rome, or the Vatican, or to Saddam Hussein's reconstruction of ancient Babylon in Iraq," they say. And of course, the dismissing denial prevalent among BABYLON lovers is only strengthened when they pause to contemplate the "limited" lifestyle options: I mean, all things con-

sidered, "Where would we all go . . . and what else would we do, if we were to **come out of her?**"

Well, before leaving this scandalous (and "outrageous") perspective of 20th century BABYLON—and without attempting to *fully* expose the awful truth of it, which would take an entire volume of its own—let us complete the profile in cursory fashion by listing the other Revelation traits of this whorish new world order that sits so oppressively upon so many peoples.

According to Revelation 17:1, she sits *"upon many waters"*: *"And [the angel] said unto [John], The waters which thou sawest, where the whore sitteth, are peoples, and multitudes, and nations, and tongues [language groups]. (Rev.17:15) And the inhabitants of the earth have been made drunk ["stoned" and deluded] with the wine of her fornication [the delicious by-product of international relations with her]." (Rev.17:2);* for it is with HER that *"the kings of the earth have committed fornication [despite their first obligations to the welfare of their own citizens whom they consistently rip-off and defraud]" (Rev.17:2),* as well as having also hooked their own nations on the seductive *"golden cup in her hand full of abominations and filthiness of her fornication."* She holds the gold, and by that monetary control oppresses and rules over the international arena of humanity.

Her land is "paved with streets of gold," it is said; and she holds out the cup of "golden opportunities," the unbridled democratic freedom to wallow drunkenly in all the prosperity money can buy and also to partake of any imaginable libertarian style of life made possible thereby and contained therein. Those humanist liberties range from plain pagan hedonism to university and elementary school curriculum-promoted sodomy, to court-protected Satanism and child sacrifice at legally sanctioned clinics; let's not overlook the lucrative opportunities in the ever-growing covert black (and often only grey) market traffic in narcotics, arms and other contraband, including high technology to enemy nations, all of which has burgeoned unabatedly under liberalist "democratic" banners. ("Just don't get caught—especially invading our turf" seems to be the cardinal rule.)

Mingled among the assorted abominations swishing deep inside this filthy cup are no doubt the infamous international political and economic subversion tactics (already hinted at) used to preserve dominance, power and protected prosperity (i.e., the buying and selling of nations, and souls of men).[18] After all, the paving material for those streets of gold has to come from somewhere.

Her luxurious shopping malls and department store emporiums fail for floor space to display all the fine clothing and luxurious merchandise. *"And the woman was arrayed in purple and scarlet colour, and decked with gold and precious stones and pearls, having a golden cup in her hand full of abominations and filthiness of her fornication (Rev.17:4). . . . Alas, alas, that great city, that was clothed in fine linen, and purple, and scarlet, and decked with gold, and precious stones, and pearls!" (Rev.18:16)*

The "purple and scarlet color" designation speaks of the expensive colors worn by reigning royalty in ancient times, when those dyes involved a costly production process and could only be afforded by royalty—such as the purple Roman robe used to mock the condemned "King of the Jews." Yet now, with the development of synthesized dyes by Western chemists, the land has been flooded with color. Formerly reserved for wealthy nobility, such color is now royally enjoyed by the "common folk" in a world (First World, that is) where millions live as kings and queens, princes and princesses, and where even teenagers own their own luxurious chariots, which even Solomon, Pharaoh, or Caesar would have awed at! Purple and scarlet denote the ruling dominance of the West's superpower hegemony over the kings of the earth, namely, other governments and their respective nations. (Incidentally, these colors, when study is made of "purple," are those hoisted high on banners to which much allegiance is sworn for, and which are often burned in disdain of, our allegorical Cinderella.)

Beneath the reigning whore, the dynamic force bearing up and carrying her is really the Great Red Dragon, who will, one day soon, violently turn to cast her off and devastate her: *"And the ten horns which thou sawest upon the beast, these shall hate the whore, and shall make her desolate and naked, and shall eat her flesh, and burn her with fire. For God hath put in their hearts to fulfil his will, and to agree, and give their kingdom unto the beast, until the words of God shall be fulfilled. And the woman which thou sawest is that great city, which reigneth over the kings of the earth." (Rev.17:16-18)*

The avid ambition of the Dragon to be singularly worshipped as God will compel him to abolish all other forms of devotion and idolatry, including the adulterous pursuit of the lavish prosperity, opulence, materialism, and consumerism of BABYLON. He will banish the political, cultural, and religious liberalism of this mammon-based world order from his own, and will tolerate no other gods before him—no longer even the god of mammon! From the smallest Harry Homeless to the biggest Mr. Mike Rosoft Gates, every soul on earth will be compelled to revere, venerate, adore and pay homage to the Beast of the 666.

Once the Beast successfully ravages and devastates the Whore, his audacious megalomania will soar defiantly into the heavens when finally he dares to engage the "intergalactic" Lord of all the Universe (the Lamb, turned Lion at this point). His ultimate act of self-exaltation and blasphemy, in the very last hour of the age of cursed man, will be to successfully rally the nations of Earth to join him in his heavily-armed, high-tech military resistance to the establishment of the Kingdom of Almighty God on this planet, the New Order of the Lamb: *"And the ten horns which thou sawest are ten kings, which have received no kingdom as yet; but receive power as kings one hour with the beast. These have one mind, and shall give their power and strength unto the beast. These shall make war with the Lamb, and the Lamb shall overcome them: for he is Lord of lords, and King of kings . . ." (Rev.17:12-14)* No vestige of victory against the mighty Whore, however, will transfer in the least to his grandiose challenge of the Almighty Lamb.

Even the task of overthrowing the reigning superpower of BABYLON will not be an easy one (as Saddam Hussein foolishly miscalculated). For she is described as not only *"that great city"* (6 times), but *"Babylon, that mighty city!" (Rev.18:10)* Yet, her sweeping destruction will be devastatingly swift, and leave the multinational merchants "weeping, mourning, wailing, and casting dust on their heads," or perhaps casting their heads *into the dust* by jumping out of their high-rise corporation and bank buildings! *"For in one hour is [her] judgment come. And the merchants of the earth shall weep and mourn over her; for no man buyeth their merchandise any more." (Rev.18:10-11)* No more lucrative market for their Made-in-Korea, Made-in-Taiwan, Made-in-China, Made-in-Japan, Made-in-Thailand, Made-in-The Philippines, Made-in-Germany, Made-in-Mexico, Made-in-Malaysia, Made-in-Singapore, Made-in-Indonesia, Made-in-Brazil, Made-in-Spain, Made-in-Sri Lanka, Made-in-India, Made-in-France, Made-in-Sweden, Made-in-Italy merchandise, etc.

"The merchants . . . which were made rich by her, shall stand afar off for the fear of her torment, weeping and wailing, and saying, Alas, alas, that great city, that was clothed in fine linen, and purple, and scarlet, and decked with gold, and precious stones, and pearls! For in one hour so great riches is come to nought."—Revelation 18:15-17

Not only do the manufacturers and merchants of all the luxurious consumer goods and other exports/imports weep and wail, but the traffickers (ocean-going freight companies, like the giant COSCO) also break down in utter anguish: *"And every shipmaster, and all the company in ships, and sailors, and as many as trade by sea, stood afar off, and cried when they saw the smoke of her burning, saying, What city is like unto this great city! And they cast dust on their heads, and cried, weeping and wailing, saying, Alas, alas, that great city, wherein were made rich all that had ships in the sea by reason of her costliness [particularly labor, which is why low-cost imports are so profitable]! for in one hour is she made desolate." (Revelation 18:17-20)*

Only one "Cinderella" could fit this shoe size. Suddenly, the injunction to exit from out of these sinister, bloody shoes and footsteps begins to take on keener significance. For, to linger for the sake of the delicious lifestyle she affords is to suicidally sentence oneself to the verdict of a double volume of horror and torment.

For her sins have reached unto heaven, and God hath remembered her iniquities. Reward her even as she rewarded you, and double unto her double according to her works: in the cup which she hath filled fill to her double. How much she hath glorified herself, and lived deliciously, so much torment and sorrow give her: for she saith in her heart, I sit a queen, and am no widow, and shall see no sorrow. Therefore shall her plagues come in one day, death, and mourning, and famine; and she shall be utterly burned with fire: for strong is the Lord God who judgeth her. And the kings of the earth, who have committed fornication and lived deliciously with her, shall bewail her, and lament for her, when they shall see the smoke of her burning, standing afar off for the fear of her torment, saying, Alas, alas, that great city Babylon, that mighty city! for in one hour is thy judgment come.—Revelation 18:5-10

One hour?! Utterly burned with fire!! Transpiring in *one day!* Well, the advent of nuclear weapons removes the mystery from any speculation about how such sweeping destruction by fire could be accomplished so swiftly. With an enlightened understanding of the radical perspectives of the sacred Scriptures, the taste for *"the wine of the wrath of her fornication"* should rapidly sour for those who take the Bible seriously! The lusty appeal of Satan's lure— *"all the kingdoms of the world and the glory of them"*—suddenly lacks its luster in the light of Revelation chapters 17 and 18, wouldn't you say?

Signpost of The Last 7 Years—The Worldwide Week of the Beast

The endtime emergence of these entities of transcendant spiritual significance—that is, these three competing world orders, each vying to become the
ultimate New World Order[19]—is highlighted in the Scriptures by what is virtually the most important prophetic signpost of all: *a great multinational peace
treaty.* It is at this major "crossroads" on the endtime expressway where the
marker of the *last 7 years* is posted. This crucial signpost brings the entire
history of man to a focal point and finale. At this point is where the theocratic
quality of Zionism, the indulgent idolatry of liberalist Babylonism, and the
anti-God Dragonism of bestial man-worship all meet in the olympic arena of
peaceful global contest.

According to the prophet Daniel (c. 538 BCE), in the final (70th prophetic) week of the desolations and transgression that are determined upon
the "holy city" and people of Daniel (the Jews), there shall arise a notorious
"prince of the covenant" before the end of it all. This amazing leader instantly becomes world famous for the role he plays in negotiating a landmark
international agreement which ostensibly results in the long-sought-after "peace
with security" discussed earlier.

*And he [the prince of "the covenant"] shall confirm the covenant with many
for one week [Hebrew "shabuwa" = 7 years]: and in the midst of the week he
shall cause the sacrifice and the oblation to cease, and for the overspreading
of abominations he shall make it desolate, even until the consummation, and
that determined shall be poured upon the desolate.—Daniel 9:27*

The above verse from the book of the prophet Daniel is a very key scripture to the understanding of the nature and order of end-time events. We will
revisit this passage again later to explore the depth of its implications; for
indeed, in the *"midst of the week"* (3½ years into the last 7) he breaks the
covenant, causing the renewed Jewish worship *"to cease"*; then the infamous
"abomination" appearing in Jerusalem sends stunning shock waves of *"desolation"* around the world. But for the time being, permit it to be asserted that
the *confirmation of this covenant* will be the **dawn** (or nightfall, more fit-
tingly) of the coming era of the short-lived, global secular order of the Beast,
as well as constitute the "baptism" or "anointing" of this bogus "Premier of

Peace" who will shortly thereafter claim title to the entire world.

In answer to the persistent, desperate cries of the Godless world for peace, security and order, a preeminent demagogue, a spurious messiah, will arise to lead the world into the 21st century. This emergent world ruler, who we have already referred to in this chapter as The Beast, will be the classic wolf in sheep's clothing, to quickly turn autocratic and totalitarian. His rhetoric and guise will be advocacy of international order, morality, justice, and a new social ethic, all in the name of transcendent humanism and peace. His intent—to subjugate, dominate and ultimately glorify himself as the "supreme being"; and as such, to mandate universal worship of his personality as embodied in the electronic, 24-hour-a-day, living image made in his likeness and utilized to captivate the populations of earth by their love of technology (as our "saving grace").

According to the prophecies, this Demagogue Extraordinaire of the New Worldly Order will come in *peaceably* upon the wealthiest and most prosperous (*"fattest,"* oil-laden) places of the Middle-eastern domain (*"province"*) and achieve hegemony (*"the kingdom"*); and *"by peace shall destroy many."* (Dan.8:25)

Daniel writes, there shall arise *"a vile person, to whom they shall not give the honour of the kingdom: but he shall come in peaceably, and obtain the kingdom by flatteries [smooth Marxist-style promises]. And with the arms of a flood shall they be overflown [completely overpowered] from before him, and shall be broken [crushed—speaking of a sweeping conquest utilizing a massive acquisition of armaments by the vile prince]; yea, also [or, namely] the prince of the covenant. And after the league made with him he shall work deceitfully: for he shall come up, and shall become strong with a small people. He shall enter peaceably even upon the fattest places of the province; and he shall do that which his fathers have not done, nor his fathers' fathers; he shall scatter among them the prey, and spoil, and riches [socialist redistribution of wealth, definitely not an emirish or sultanish ideology]: yea, and he shall forecast his devices against the strongholds [publicly advertise his strategy against the dominant powers], even for a time."* (Daniel 11:21-24)

For the first half of the *"shabuwa"* spoken of in Daniel 9:27, quoted above, a sufficient state of peace and security shall be accomplished to allow for the people of Israel to re-institute daily sacrifice and offerings of the Old Testament type in Jerusalem; this will involve animals sacrificed in atonement for sin, as peace offerings, etc. Almost certainly, it will also involve a temple or tabernacle of some sort, even if temporary or provisional—and an altar, at least—**on the holy site of the Temple Mount in Jerusalem**, where the Islamic Dome of the Rock now rests. Imagine that possibility! If you thought that was a dead custom relegated to the annals of ancient history which you only read about, just wait and see.

At present, the tensions and conflict over the highly controversial religious claims to Jerusalem and the Temple Mount—by both Jews and Muslims—are an enormous obstacle to any such Judaic practice ever occuring under the current circumstances and prevailing political climate. An absolute political miracle must occur before the climate could change sufficiently to favor any peaceful repossession by the Jews of the Temple Mount compound, where the "daily sacrifice" would needs be centered, and over which **another** Arab-Israeli war is **already brewing**. Somehow, the prince of the covenant will successfully intervene to facilitate the resolution of the **controversy of Jerusalem** (by a 7-year pact). Moreover, he will do so in such a manner that the Jews will feel adequately reassured about their ancient claims to the holy site to actually revive the sacrificial ritual there soon after the implementation of the pact.

Peace and *safety* (security) will be the buzz words marking this historic crossroads; but only to herald a very short-lived phenomenon, unfortunately. Peace will be experienced in very transitory fashion, and only as an isolated and scattered phenomenon. For, the Red Horse of Revelation chapter 6 will gallop rough-shod from region to region fulfilling its age-old purpose of "taking peace from the earth" and causing men to "kill one another." In fact, the tragic irony of these last days is that the only thing louder than the rhetoric and cries for peace will be the noise of war.

It is said that the understanding of the 70-week Prophecy of Daniel is the key to the understanding of all endtime prophecy. Though that is somewhat of an exaggerated statement, nonetheless, it is central to pinning down the 2520-day countdown to the zero-hour of the end of the age. The study of only four verses from Daniel chapter 9 (verses 24-27) is quite intricate and merits a deep study that is not fully presented here in this thesis due to space and the difficult but important task of keeping with the central theme. We have only touched in cursory fashion upon certain aspects of the whole prophecy. Those aspects treated by this discourse are those that focus pri-

---

marily on the final 70th week of the prophecy. Apology is due for glossing over this short passage from Daniel, without an adequate explanation and analysis of the details that lead to the conclusions which support the assertions presented herein about the last "week." Many good studies from various sources all concur that the final *shabuwa* of Daniel's prophecy represents the concluding era of man's secular history. God willing, the complete study may be presented in a future publication. In the meantime, please avail yourself of a study already in publication which analyzes the incredible and marvelous intricacies of this passage.[20] A passage which precisely predicted, more than 500 years in advance, with astonishing accuracy, the events related to the first visit of Messiah to the earth, including the exact day of His presentation to Israel as their King (April 6, 32 CE). This amazing prophecy also incorporated the fact that he would be subsequently *executed*, despite His guiltlessness, in atonement for the transgressions of all humankind.

The seven-year "week" of the Beast will be the last season of the dominion of wicked man upon the earth—so wicked, in this case, that even the term "beast" hardly does him or his order justice. His first-phase appearance may be disarming as he dons his sheepy fleece of peacemaker, but the second half of the week will be bloody, tyrannical and totalitarian. His new world order will be the crown jewel of all the woes the world has ever seen!

Supplemental

Though the following excerpts merit much deeper study to reveal their shocking potentcy, they're provided at this point to quickly identify the establishment dynamic that has captivated the majority of the world's poplulation. For now, notice the references to consumerism, mercantilism, and opulent materialism (and the stupefying addiction to it) which, as its prominent features, mark this allegorical city system built on blood, violence, and oppression; not to mention its pervasive corruption and infestation by despicable inhabitants of morbid and predatory motivation. This conceited queen of kingdoms also believes herself to be protected and invincible.

And there came one of the seven angels which had the seven vials, and talked with me, saying unto me, Come hither; I will shew unto thee the judgment of the great whore that sitteth upon many waters: with whom the kings of the earth have committed fornication, and the inhabitants of the earth have been made drunk with the wine of her fornication.

So he carried me away in the spirit into the wilderness: and I saw a woman sit upon a scarlet coloured beast, full of names of blasphemy, having seven heads and ten horns. And the woman was arrayed in purple and scarlet colour, and decked with gold and precious stones and pearls, having a golden cup in her hand full of abominations and filthiness of her fornication: and upon her forehead was a name written, MYSTERY, BABYLON THE GREAT, THE MOTHER OF HARLOTS AND ABOMINATIONS OF THE EARTH. And I saw the woman drunken with the blood of the saints, and with the blood of the martyrs of Jesus: and when I saw her, I wondered with great admiration.

And the angel said unto me, Wherefore didst thou marvel? I will tell thee the mystery of the woman, and of the beast that carrieth her, which hath the seven heads and ten horns.

The beast that thou sawest was, and is not; and shall ascend out of the bottomless pit, and go into perdition: and they that dwell on the earth shall wonder, whose names were not written in the book of life from the foundation of the world, when they behold the beast that was, and is not, and yet is.

And here is the mind which hath wisdom. The seven heads are seven mountains, on which the woman sitteth. And there are seven kings: five are fallen, and one is, and the other is not yet come; and when he cometh, he must continue a short space.

And the beast that was, and is not, even he is the eighth, and is of the seven, and goeth into perdition. And the ten horns which thou sawest are ten kings, which have received no kingdom as yet; but receive power as kings one hour with the beast. These have one mind, and shall give their power and strength unto the beast. These shall make war with the Lamb, and the Lamb shall overcome them: for he is Lord of lords, and King of kings: and they that are with him are called, and chosen, and faithful.

And he saith unto me, The waters which thou sawest, where the whore sitteth, are peoples, and multitudes, and nations, and tongues.

And the ten horns which thou sawest upon the beast, these shall hate the whore, and shall make her desolate and naked, and shall eat her flesh, and burn her with fire. For God hath put in their hearts to fulfil his will, and to agree, and give their kingdom unto the beast, until the words of God shall be fulfilled.

And the woman which thou sawest is that great city, which reigneth over the kings of the earth.

REVELATION CHAPTER 18

And after these things I saw another angel come down from heaven, having great power; and the earth was lightened with his glory. And he cried mightily with a strong voice, saying, Babylon the great is fallen, is fallen, and is become the habitation of devils, and the hold of every foul spirit, and a cage of every unclean and hateful bird. For all nations have drunk of the wine of the wrath of her fornication, and the kings of the earth have committed fornication with her, and the merchants of the earth are waxed rich through the abundance of her delicacies.

And I heard another voice from heaven, saying, Come out of her, my people, that ye be not partakers of her sins, and that ye receive not of her plagues. For her sins have reached unto heaven, and God hath remembered her iniquities. Reward her even as she rewarded you, and double unto her double according to her works: in the cup which she hath filled fill to her double. How much she hath glorified herself, and lived deliciously, so much torment and sorrow give her: for she saith in her heart, I sit a queen, and am no widow, and shall see no sorrow. Therefore shall her plagues come in one day, death, and mourning, and famine; and she shall be utterly burned with fire: for strong is the Lord God who judgeth her.

And the kings of the earth, who have committed fornication and lived deliciously with her, shall bewail her, and lament for her, when they shall see the smoke of her burning, standing afar off for the fear of her torment, saying, Alas, alas, that great city Babylon, that mighty city! for in one hour is thy judgment come.

And the merchants of the earth shall weep and mourn over her; for no man buyeth their merchandise any more: The merchandise of gold, and silver, and precious stones, and of pearls, and fine linen, and purple, and silk, and scarlet, and all thyine wood, and all manner vessels of ivory, and all manner vessels of most precious wood, and of brass, and iron, and marble, *and cinnamon, and odours, and ointments, and frankincense, and wine, and oil, and fine flour, and wheat, and beasts, and sheep, and horses, and chariots, and slaves, and souls [actually bodies & perhaps body parts] of men. And the fruits that thy soul lusted after are departed from thee, and all things which were dainty and goodly are departed from thee, and thou shalt find them no more at all.*

The merchants of these things, which were made rich by her, shall stand afar off for the fear of her torment, weeping and wailing, and saying, Alas, alas, that great city, that was clothed in fine linen, and purple, and scarlet, and decked with gold, and precious stones, and pearls! For in one hour so great riches is come to nought.

And every shipmaster, and all the company in ships, and sailors, and as many as trade by sea, stood afar off, and cried when they saw the smoke of her burning, saying, What city is like unto this great city! And they cast dust on their heads, and cried, weeping and wailing, saying, Alas, alas, that great city, wherein were made rich all that had ships in the sea by reason of her costliness [labor costs highest in all the world]! for in one hour is she made desolate.

Rejoice over her, thou heaven, and ye holy apostles and prophets; for God hath avenged you on her. And a mighty angel took up a stone like a great millstone, and cast it into the sea, saying, Thus with violence shall that great city Babylon be thrown down, and shall be found no more at all. And the voice of harpers, and musicians, and of pipers, and trumpeters, shall be heard no more at all in thee; and no craftsman, of whatsoever craft he be, shall be found any more in thee; and the sound of a millstone shall be heard no more at all in thee; and the light of a candle shall shine no more at all in thee; and the voice of the bridegroom and of the bride shall be heard no more at all in thee: for thy merchants were the great men of the earth; for by thy sorceries were all nations deceived.

And in her was found the blood of prophets, and of saints, and of all that were slain upon the earth.

5

NOT YET

Let no man deceive you by any means: for that day shall not come,
except there come a falling away first, and that man of sin be revealed,
the son of perdition;
Who opposeth and exalteth himself above all that is called God,
or that is worshipped; so that he as God sitteth in the temple of God,
shewing himself that he is God.
II Thessalonians 2:2-4

As anxious as many of us may be for the whole Dragon-Whore world scene to come to a conclusion, *the end will definitely not be yet.* Absolutely not! There is no way the end can come, until the stage has been fully set and every crucial act has been played out, or until the fat lady sings, as they say. And so, what does it matter, anyway?

Well, to the broad population of 20th century Earth, it doesn't matter at all. But then, I don't imagine that you, especially at this point in our literary journey, are just any old Jane, or Joe Citizen. You must care. Or, at least you are still open enough to proceed with honest curiosity. So let's explore why it matters.

Being ready for the things that are to come upon the world in the next few years is absolutely no laughing matter, and it's certainly nothing to get *rapture-ous* about. From a readiness standpoint, it entails a great deal more than the unwitting Christians of the mainstream have even cared to contemplate (seriously). As we've learned, their "blessed hope" consists of the expectation that they will be sparingly raptured away at any moment; or at least, in the "nick of time," anyway. Some television prophecy programs even string their audiences on with the weekly closing salutation, "Unless the Lord comes in the next seven days, we'll see you again next week." These are the same folks who think to leave behind their books and tapes and other prophecy productions to guide us through the dark hours of the Great Tribulation after they're gone. Think again!

Overly anxious Christians, possessed with the pseudo-preparatory notion of *imminence* (as explored in Chapters 1 & 2), love to imagine that their troubles will soon suddenly dissolve without further ado. And with "good" reason. After all, there's not a single expectant mother on earth who relishes the idea of suffering through the inevitable labor and pain of giving birth. Nonetheless, the "blessed hope" they are so obsessed with will in no way be prematurely precipitated in the least; not by any amount of wishful thinking or creative twisting of the Scriptures can this labor be induced. And there is no *cesarean section* that can be performed in this pregnancy to spare the feeble or the squeamish of their tribulation.

Thoroughly acquainted with the weakness of men's human flesh and their anxious hope for an end to affliction, Jesus forewarned his followers, *"The days will come, when ye shall desire to see one of the days of the Son of man, and ye shall not see it. . . . Whosoever shall seek to save his life shall lose it; and whosoever shall lose his life shall preserve it." (Luke 17:22-33)*

For now, though, let's turn our focus to the rest of the endtime world.

In this same passage just quoted from Luke 17, Messiah went on to also foretell the future state of the last generation by giving a "big picture" that described what their general activities would be. Now nearly 2000 years old, these prophecies Christ gave regarding the endtime societies of the world characterized them very succinctly—*carrying on routinely as ever*. Of all the possible scenarios that could have been imagined to evolve after thousands of years of history and development of civilization, what Yeshua predicted was a time when essentially the same old human routines would invariably prevail—until the very day of doom, He said.

And indeed, what do we see after two millennia? We see a global society blindly believing that the future holds enough promise of security to persistently pursue the deep-rutted, age-old pattern of the world and proceeding as though nothing at all could possibly be wrong with our "modern" lifestyles or practices. As if in a hypnotic trance which disconnects them from the brutal reality of the world's wickedness, we see nations thoroughly and unwaveringly indulged in the very same carnal, material routine that the mundane societies of Noah's day and Lot's day also were (nominal religious folk included). In both those cases, sensing no need for drastic change, they carried on mindlessly after their carnal human instincts until the very day of their wholesale doom and demise.

And as it was in the days of Noe, so shall it be also in the days of the Son of man. They did eat, they drank, they married wives, they were given in marriage, until the day that Noe entered into the ark, and the flood came, and destroyed them all. Likewise also as it was in the days of Lot; they did eat, they drank, they bought, they sold, they planted, they builded; but the same day that Lot went out of Sodom it rained fire and brimstone from heaven, and destroyed them all. Even thus shall it be in the day when the Son of man is revealed.—Luke 17:26-30

Let me note that nothing particularly sinful is indicated about the activities listed in this prophecy. Those pursuits are, after all, normal and acceptable activities, generally speaking. The only indictment here is that they maintained an unwavering course of obsessive self-indulgence, without any regard for their exceedingly corrupt condition. Nor was any effort made to rectify that course until, at last, their "Titanics" suddenly slammed the fateful "iceberg" of their catastrophic demise.

Based on familiarity with the societal conditions in the days of Noah and Lot, the suggestion is that, despite being *consumed with violence* and *totally enthralled with evil conceptions* (as in Noah's day—see Genesis 6), nothing substantial was done to reverse the course. Instead, those societies simply immersed themselves in the baser "instincts" of humanity. Lot, of course, was a citizen of Sodom, which had been so completely consumed by their own prosperity that in their *"pride, fullness of bread, and abundance of idleness"* (and hoarding from the poor) they fell a lusting after *"strange flesh." (Ezekiel 16:49 & Jude 1:7)* Both those ancient societies were no doubt infected with the very same forms of depravity, as some others in history; certainly, it matches closely what we see exploding today right before our own eyes.

The real essence of Christ's prophecy here is that, very simply, no revising or reforming of that same old routine pursuit of mindless materialism will take place among the societies of the endtime world, despite the signs of the times! To use the dreaded "r" word, no *repentance* will find its way into the lives of the last generation. Rather, in persistently pagan, carnal fashion they were foreseen striving hard as ever to maintain the Godless established order of mammon. In fact, we are witnessing humanity trying with greater impulse than ever to maximize their carnal prosperity and to realize the consummate secular order of all ages, based on nothing other than material gain, the love of money, the lust of the flesh, and the outright denial of the principles of Godliness—nothing new!

Meanwhile, opposition to the corrupt humanism of these apostate pagan societies is faithfully maintained by devout dissidents; and they have their work long-since assigned and cut out for them.[1] And as The Master did, so too do His loyal followers denounce such faithless materialist lifestyles fraught with futility and corruption. True also to His teachings, they likewise shall consequently be classified as "subversive, religious extremists."[2] For, what they boldly proclaim is an imminent end to the fabulous folly of the "New World Order"; and at the same time defiantly expose the beastly Führer of the "Fourth Reich," the fiendish fraud embodied as its heroic man-god who is to emerge on the world scene at the outset of the last 7 years.

The allegiance of these committed "subversives" is faithfully pledged to Yeshua, the Prince of Peace, to the Order and Rule of Alpha and Omega, the Holy Civilization of YHWH, the eternal city of El Shaddai, the New Jerusalem of Jah—the Kingdom of Adonai. And what is so easy to dodge now by the compromising class of believer must eventually become a solid commitment to a vigorous campaign of opposition to the global luciferian agenda. Either that, or as with Hitler, the deafening silence of compromise will amount to a hailing shout of condoning approval; only this time, conceding to the mark of the final Führer will damn your soul!

At the debut of the specious peace-and-prosperity-proclaiming *"prince of the covenant"* spoken of by the prophet Daniel, the curtain will fall on the final act of stage-play Christianity; then the crosses that have so long been laid down as pews to spectate from must be taken up again.

The End Is Not By and By

Before much longer, the cost of remaining true to the calling of Christ—to "proclaim and exemplify the kingdom of God in every corner of the world, for a witness unto all nations"—will make present day Christianity in the USA seem like a cartoon show. Swelling hatred and spite will eventually explode against consecrated non-conformists.[3] Their crime?—renunciation of institutionalized idolatry (mammon worship) and the worship of man/self, especially their firm refusal to take and bear the mark of the globalist regime of dear Big Brother. Soon, their uncompromising rejection of the Godless systems and ideologies of man, rooted in his liaison with the Dragon, will result in a relentless, worldwide campaign to repress and eradicate them.

Supposed escape from this Tribulation scenario is nothing other than the "American Revised Standard" version of the so-called "blessed hope" preached by the heretical rapturists. The preemptory appeal of that "blessed escape" notion is precisely what Jesus himself preempted by his admonition quoted earlier that *"The days will come, when ye shall desire to see one of the days of the Son of man, and ye shall not see it. . . . Whosoever shall seek to save his life shall lose it; and whosoever shall lose his life shall preserve it."* (Luke 17:22-33) Blinded by conformist, seeking-to-save-their-lives doctrines, the light of Christ's version of Christianity remains overwhelmingly obscured to them.

This variety of piety prefers the security of the bushel basket of conformity over the high-risk exposure of blowing in the wind atop the "candlestick" to which Christ referred.[1(please revisit)] But when the mark is issued, conformity to Establishment materialism, the *traditional hiding place* of the half-hearted, will no longer provide any cover or camouflage. At that point, either they will abandon their beloved lifestyles of holy harlotry to, at last, serve God with all their heart and soul, or they must sell out completely to mammon and take the mark.[4] The number of the Beast will be *the only escape* the cowardly and the covetous will find from the persecutory wrath of the Dragon and the attendant era of Great Tribulation.[5]

This blessed hope we hear the fundamentalists rave about so much in connection with their pre-tribulation escape into the sky is nothing less than the fanciful C-section mentioned at the beginning of this chapter. To them, the blessed hope is being surgically excised (spiritually speaking) from having to face up squarely to their unpopular and politically incorrect calling, especially during the most trying time of all history. And no wonder. . . .

Endtime societies will finally trade-in the primitive brutality of today's ethnic cleansing for the very latest model of societal purification, *cultural cleansing* of the "politically incorrect." In fact, this coming global campaign against the "reactionary religious right" becomes the personal vendetta of the blasphemous, beastly Big Brother of the New Secular Order who literally wages a war of extermination on these resistance elements—known in the Bible as believers, saints, disciples, the elect, the remnant, the servants and chosen people of God.[6] Jesus is quoted identically in no less than three separate Gospels by Matthew, Mark and Luke as promising that all men and all nations would hate these endtime separatists.

Then shall they deliver you up to be afflicted, and shall kill you: and ye shall be hated of all nations for my name's sake. And then shall many [erstwhile believers] be offended, and shall betray one another, and shall hate one another.—Matthew 24:9-10

And ye shall be betrayed both by parents, and brethren, and kinsfolks, and friends; and some of you shall they cause to be put to death. And ye shall be hated of all men for my name's sake.—Luke 21:16-17

Now [just as in Orwell's "1984"] the brother shall betray the brother to death, and the father the son; and children shall rise up against their parents, and shall cause them to be put to death. And ye shall be hated of all men for my name's sake: but he that shall endure unto the end, the same shall be saved.— Mark 13:12-13

Apostasy and The Last 7 Years

This sweeping hate campaign of repression, promised by the prophets, reflects the consummation of another key sign of the times—*the apostasy,* specifically foretold by the Apostle Paul. Apostasy, though already rampant in the swelling pagan societies of the secular world, as well as in varying degrees among so many professing "faith communities," becomes full-blown as the persecution of the politically incorrect loyalists to Christ intensifies during the Last Seven Years.[7] As a matter of fact, this prophetic period of apostasy is best described as a *sifting period* wherein loyalties and allegiances will be definitively selected and sworn. The loves and hates of all men will be unfurled as they choose and fly their true colors. And, today's banner of loving both God and mammon will not be one of the options!

This show of true colors begins to conclusively divide the sheep from the goats. And, while the faithful remnant of true sheep weather the storm, the "goatly" lovers of mammon flee the torment into the arms of BABYLON for refuge. Not only so, but the religious goats (pseudo God-lovers) turn to butt, betray, trample and gore the sheep in their increasingly more eager defection to the (ever more uni-cultural) new world order of *anti-God, humanist materialism.*[8]

The tolerant multicultural character of BABYLON (where all are welcomed to worship whatever individual gods they please in her temple of Mammon) reverts to a uni-cultural (bigoted, hypocritical) intolerance of dissidents who denounce the obscene materialist culture of the Whore, as well as the holier-than-thou socialist materialism of the Beast. The *politically-correct apostasy*, like the flight of a foreboding comet, is already in full view and soon to reach its "perihelion" as it signals (in omen) the rise of this boastful, blaspheming Beast and butcher, who ultimately proclaims himself to be God.

Now we beseech you, brethren, by the coming of our Lord Jesus Christ, and by our gathering together unto him, that ye be not soon shaken in mind, or be troubled, neither by spirit, nor by word, nor by letter as from us, as that the day of Christ is at hand. Let no man deceive you by any means: for that day shall not come, except there come a falling away [Gk., apostasia] first, and that man of sin be revealed, the son of perdition; who opposeth and exalteth himself above all that is called God, or that is worshipped; so that he as God sitteth in the temple of God, shewing himself that he is God.—II Thessalonians 2:1-4.

Almost 600 years before Paul penned this prophetic alert to the believers in Thessalonica, the prophet Daniel (c. 534 BCE) foresaw the rise of this same cunning, boastful beast who starts out as a "little horn"—meaning, a relatively small-scale leader of lesser prominence.

I considered the horns ["horns" symbolically representing political leaders and powers], and, behold, there came up among them another little horn, before whom there were three of the first [10] horns plucked up by the roots: and, behold, in this horn [were] eyes like the eyes of man, and a mouth speaking great things. . . . I beheld then because of the voice of the great words which the horn spake: I beheld even till the beast was slain, and his body destroyed, and given to the burning flame. . . . I beheld, and the same horn made war with the saints, and prevailed against them. . . . And he shall speak great words against the most High, and shall wear out the saints of the most High, and think to change times and laws: and they shall be given into his hand until a time and times and the dividing of time [3½ yr.].—Daniel 7:8, 11, 21, & 25 (see also 7:24).

In about 90 CE (or AD, as some prefer), the Apostle John, in the Book of Revelation, spoke of the *same horn* and also echoed Daniel's characterization of the horn as a *beast.*

And they worshipped the dragon which gave power unto the beast: and they worshipped the beast, saying, Who is like unto the beast? who is able to make war with him? And there was given unto him a mouth speaking great things and blasphemies; and power was given unto him to continue forty and two months. And he opened his mouth in blasphemy against God, to blaspheme his name, and his tabernacle, and them that dwell in heaven. And it was given unto him to make war with the saints, and to overcome them: and power was given him over all kindreds, and tongues, and nations. And all that dwell upon the earth shall worship him, whose names are not written in the book of life of the Lamb slain from the foundation of the world.—Revelation 13:4-8.

Under this worldwide regime of the blasphemous little horn who is acclaimed as God, the prayers by many churches for "revival" *will be answered.* True Christianity—of the 1st century type, marked by *affliction, persecution, tribulation* and authentic passion—will finally be revived.

This scenario, demanding do-or-die devotion, is *the dread* of today's First World, Western, bourgeois Christians, who fantasize about being "raptured" into the sky to save their skins *before* the advent of this era. These poor souls go to desperate lengths to *"wrest the scriptures, to their own destruction,"* exactly as Apostle Peter cautioned in his second epistle when speaking of the trouble some unseasoned and vacillating people have in sorting out the truth in Paul's writings concerning the coming of the Lord.[9]

Hate First

Then shall they deliver you up to be afflicted, and shall kill you: and ye shall be hated of all nations for my name's sake.—Matthew 24:9.

As outlined in the preceding paragraphs, the stage is even now being set for the coming hateful war of persecution and extermination of the followers of God. The rationale is already being incrementally established in gradual, subtle, and yet, systematic ways. Deliberate and determined efforts are continually being made in societies around the world, particularly in the mass media, to cast Bible believers negatively in perverse and undesirable shades. Capitalizing on the rank hypocrisy of so many nominal Christians, virtually all Christians are sweepingly characterized as regressive, backward adherents of an outmoded religiosity that contradicts and defies the values of New Age, Enlightened Humanism.

Christ-lovers and theocratic, worshippers of God are constantly and systematically denigrated as undesirable elements who pose a hindrance to the evolution of "progressive," pro-choice, humanist-based, self-determined social and economic "democracy." When not attacked physically for their faith, as is presently the case in numerous countries around the world in both Hemispheres, they are attacked by the propaganda machines (print and broadcast media) in a relentless campaign to drown them in a flood of lies and mischaracterizations.[10]

As each day passes, it becomes easier and easier to understand how Christ's prophesy that his peace-and-truth-loving followers would be *"hated of all nations"* can so readily become such a widespread and global phenomenon. Especially with the recent advent of worldwide mass media communications (of the instantaneous electronic variety), the frightening power now exists, and is already being utilized, to sway billions of people on every continent—and, in an ever more vile world of evil-mindedness, sad to say, this is overwhelmingly for evil purposes. A global climate of hate can now be easily incited by the mass power brokers with the media at their fingertips, who desire to push an agenda of thought control and manipulation for their personal advantage and aggrandizement. Vilification campaigns against any select group of "undesirables" can now be accomplished with summary ease and virtually instantaneous facility.

Those who are awake know that public opinion is now a direct result of the mind-altering information selectively fed to the unwitting audiences of the mass media. Politically undesirable elements (i.e., nonconformists to the establishment agenda) can now be swiftly ostracized and spitefully targeted for public hate by the awesome mind-control apparatus of the heavily biased mass media—thus, vicious reprisals in the name of "law & order," such as the infamous massacre at Waco, Texas can be perpetrated with impunity. And, in terms of subtle selectivity and bias, question: why is it that the hundreds of arsons (let alone the bombings) of church buildings over the last few years haven't sparked the nationwide outcry for hate-crimes legislation that the (unconscionable) attacks on homosexuals and abortions clinics has?

Consider the vengeful bias so woefully evident among of some of our most well-known American establishment news sources. Grounded in their own specious "patriotisms" and opinionated hatred of dissidents opposed to the mainstream political, social, and philosophical ideologies by which they personally happen to swear (and swell their bank accounts), they target those of different affections with their spiteful, inflammatory rhetoric via the platform of their daily, so-called "news" programs. As a prime example, the long-time anchor man of a major network evening news broadcast loves to repetitiously invoke bigoted terminology, which he liberally reiterates with brain-washing and mind-conditioning frequency in reference to groups he capriciously wishes to brand as worthless and vile. Pretentiously presuming to be the ultimate patriots, these shapers of public opinion (such as this television news "filter") exploit their mass media advantage to manipulate unwitting audiences into salivating at their command (in true Pavlovian style) against what are hypocritically labeled *"hate groups."*

That sort of Big Brother bigotry is epidemic in mass media circles *today.* Yet, it's only the larval stage of what those mediums are to become—launch pads of barrages of murderous, hateful slander campaigns against the holy conscientious objectors to the reprehensible and heinous systems that are rapidly evolving to tyrannize the unwitting victims of the New Age. One thing you can bank on, such establishment-oriented machinations will never herald the Kingdom of God and the New Jerusalem Order of Messiah, much less defend or advocate for those who do. The Establishment is the establishment. Their first love is the status quo, and more and more money, power and glory. Whoever does not conform or submit to their dictated program, is systematically crushed beneath the wheel of their money-driven machine with a barbaric might-makes-right vengeance. (Do you dare oppose or expose them?)

What exactly is behind this hate campaign? Well, beyond mere human wickedness, the Holy Prophets tell of an alien invading force which has occupied the earth for millennia. They describe a dynamic that has driven the building of man's empires and city-systems since before the "great" civilization of the Pharaohs, the same force that, out of jealous rebellion and hatred for the Almighty Creator and GOD of all the galaxies, has strived to *undo the design of creation* since the beginning. And the key objective?—to supplant it with a *substitute system* that diverts man from linkage with the Creator and His intention for the creation; one that, in the end, would actually glorify this covetous, competing force *as God!*

The driving motive in this campaign is manifest in the strategy employed by this demonic alien invader. It's the same psychology with which he has seduced nearly all the inhabitants of Earth—his *own* perverse psychology. This evil luciferian alien must rule Earth to fulfill his ambition. Any element of devotion to YHWH (Yahweh),[11] the Creator, must be systematically eliminated to facilitate his domination of Earth, and thus, his own egomania. All opposition to this agenda must be crushed and extinguished.

Subtle Stratagem, Tactical Terror, Ungodly Goal

To carry out the ancient alien plot and fully accomplish the time-limited task (with time running out) requires the ability to sway billions of people to cooperate with the anti-God, envy-rooted scheme. Unifying earth's millions to assent and conspire in this evil plot, of course, begins (like Hitler) with *capturing the minds*—by way of appeal to the aspirations, passions, cravings, ambitions, and fascinations—of those masses. Such human entrapment has been no outstanding challenge for this shape-shifting alien who first appeared in the fascinating form of a psychic, whispering (perhaps telepathic) reptile, as hinted by the Hebrew text.

Wasting no time in sinking his piercing, barbed hook into his unwitting victims, his very first communication with humans (in Eden) was deliberately to incite *covetousness and envy*.[12] Getting them to subscribe to his psychology and adopt his own mentality meant he could now also successfully manipulate them at will by luring them along with the promise of personal aggrandizement: *"You can be great!"*; or in his own words, *"Ye shall be as gods."* But of course what he was really getting at was "I will make you great, if you will make me great." Again his own words later reveal his driving motivation: *"All these things will I give thee (the kingdoms of the world and the glory of them), if thou wilt fall down and worship me." (Matthew 4:8-9)*

From the beginning, his cunning approach was to raise issue with the level of contentment with "merely" human status by bringing Eve's and Adam's attention to what they didn't have, as opposed to all that they did enjoy. Having captured their audience, he then went on to provoke them to envy by insisting that God had lied to them as part of a "selfish scheme" to *deprive them* of access to the resources they had at their fingertips which would effectively "raise" their standard of existence to that of *gods*.[13]

The very same subtle stratagem provides the dynamic psychology that drives today's materialist societies of the world, propelling them along the guided path to the ultimate blasphemy. In only a few short years now, the well-conditioned, well-prepped masses of the coming 21st century—already psychologically subdued and enslaved—will fall down as his avowed adorers and worship this wicked alien, believing he will be their key and gateway to glory and godship.

What is his bait?—the essential accessories for any god: *knowledge* and the *power* to attain grandeur; for as even popular wisdom concedes, knowledge is power.

This pervasive, lingering force is described in chapters 12 and 17 of the Apocalypse as a *"great red dragon, having seven heads and ten horns, and seven crowns upon his heads . . . full of names of blasphemy . . . which was, is not, and yet is."* This Dragon, according to the Scriptures is the ages-old master-mind and dynamic force behind the anti-God systems of humanity. *"Anti,"* actually meaning *"opposite to"* or *"instead of"* in the Greek, very appropriately reflects how man's systems have somehow always shunted the knowledge of God by substituting assorted *other forms of synthetic gods*; the Serpent's intention, of course, being to distract men from recognition of the True and Ultimate God of Creation and His Plan and Purpose.

In the course of history, the Dragon has not been particularly discriminate about the forms of gods he seduces people into worshipping—whether cows, calves, bulls, cats, objects in the heavens, men, women, money, stone items, wood items, or more recently, electronic items—not *until the final days* of his tenure on earth, that is. Any variety of idol throughout time has temporarily sufficed and served his substitutionary purpose; until at long last, he shall successfully achieve his ultimate aim of being personally worshipped worldwide as the "supreme and only God."[14]

You may regard this prospect as entirely unlikely, if not impossible, in this age of modern human enlightenment, science, and logical empiricism. Modern men arrogantly regard themselves as too enlightened and sophisticated to worship gods and idols.

Does this haughty "enlightened sophistication" account for the modern infatuations with Emmy Awards, Oscars, Grammies, Heismans, Olympic Golds, Miss Americas; as well as for packed stadiums at World Series games, Super Bowls, World Cups, NBA championships, or full-house matches at Madison Square Gardens, et cetera, in which their gods "earn" multimillions per year; and not least of all, how about for the inconceivably massive audiences that worship the "living" electronic images of their gods on television for an incredible 49 hours a week (average per household in the USA)!?

Are these devotions any more sophisticated than those of the Romans, or the Greeks, or the Egyptians and Babylonians! (At least they were sentient enough to worship the supernatural.) And lest we overlook one of the most fanatical of all idolatrous rites, have any of you been to a rock concert with the "kids" lately to sample the maniacal adoration of the exalted gods of modern "music" (too often, not musical at all) who tickle their ears and sing them "tunes" they love to hear! Well, the "Pied Piper" of all pied pipers will shortly call us all to dance!

At that time, anyone who refuses to dance, who resists or denounces his imposition of institutional idolatry as the standard "tune" of global devotion and social purpose will be targeted for attack and elimination as a seditious and subversive rebel element. During those final days, just like Christ in His day, those who do not bow down to the Establishment and who pledge allegiance to another order—of justice, peace, righteousness, mercy and love under the God of Abraham, Isaac, and Jacob—will be indicted as malefactors and criminal elements. Either you worship the image of this exciting new god of high technology miracles, or you literally run for your life.

In the final years and months, the Dragon hastens to speed the implementation of his egotistical agenda, because he knows he has only a short time to "get it together."[15] He steps up his campaign to incarnately rule the world outright and to capture the *worship of the entire world's population* in the persona of the bombastic "little horn," also called "the beast"—"that man of sin . . . the son of perdition . . . that Wicked . . . whom the Lord shall consume and destroy at His coming." (See Revelation, chapters 12 & 13, and II Thessalonians, chapter 2.) All other forms of worship will be abruptly annulled. The only legitimate religion shall then be the worship of an **image** made to the beast.

An hi-tech image which is brought to "life" will have the power to speak and identify for "termination" any and all individuals on earth who refuse to worship this beast and his 'living' image. A very real possibility, certainly not beyond imagination in our times, is that this image may be a computerized bionic android, a biomechanical clone composite, or even some type of holographic image (also computer-operated, of course), created in the image of the grand Caliph of the New World Order.

As a crucial and integral part of this new world order of high technology, a marking will be implemented to brand every citizen of this diabolical global system as a loyal subject of the new "egalitarian" regime. Refusal to receive this unifying mark or to worship the beast and his image will not only represent a violation of the international law of this new establishment and classify the conscientious objectors as treasonous subversives, but will also preclude the dissidents from any participation in the economics of routine daily life. To conscientiously object and reject the mark will mean starvation and total exclusion from system services, and of course, *fugitive status* as a wanted outlaw!

Christians too, regardless of their persistent cowardly denial of the Scriptural facts, will not escape this day by means of any rapture of any sort. (Those *leaving behind* video tapes, books, and other "salvation" materials ought not delude themselves; because, their illusions of rapture are the only things they will be leaving behind!)

The slogan "love it or leave it" perfectly describes the choice that will need to be made by every soul who lives to see the day being outlined here. Those who refuse to love it will earn that already popularized label, mentioned earlier, commonly used by the news media. Lately, we have all heard it over the air waves being frequently spewed like venom from the mouth of snakes in reference to those who have no love for the Establishment agenda.

Back in the sixties, anti-establishment sympathizers were called "commies," "Marxists," "socialists," and sometimes plain old "dirty hippies." Today they're **"hate groups!"** (vis-à-vis "the religious right")—itself a hate-inciting term all-inclusively used now to "mark" anti-tyranny and anti-establishment objectors of almost any stripe. As suggested, one need only tune in to the daily television news broadcasts to get a regular dose of just such bigoted, hateful epithets used to demonize and categorize politically incorrect dissidents, who do not bow down to the "sanctity" of the "State."

Social pressure to isolate, ostracize and punish non-worshippers of the Establishment is now an organized *international endeavor*, by the way. The Anti-Terrorism Summit convened by the Mubarak administration in Egypt on March 13, 1996 attended by 28 states is just such an example. Another, as recently as December 2, 1997, this time in Buenos Aires, Argentina, constituted the inauguration of the First International Congress on Terrorism. At this 3-day gathering, experts from the USA, Israel, and Argentina urged the international community to redouble their efforts to eradicate "terrorism."

Obviously, no one likes or wants terrorism; but, like the term "hate groups," most often it's a matter of the pot calling the kettle black. I mean, look who's calling who a terrorist, or a hate monger.

When the Establishment terrorizes enemies with cruise missiles, it's classified a legitimate act of war and a "surgical strike" against an "aggressor state" or a "terrorist cell." But when popular liberation fronts strike out at aggression, such as at that of the Algerian establishment with its military-backed cancellation of the 1992 general elections—when democratic victory by the Islamic opposition party was evident—that then is conveniently and hypocritically called "terrorism." What do you suppose the Boston Tea Party, the Boston Riots, the Minutemen, the Continental Army, the Siege of Boston, and the subsequent American Revolution would have been called by today's International Congress on Terrorism? (According to the Establishment, "might makes right," remember?)

In the New Global State, any refusal to bow down to its authoritarian might shall be grounds for arrest and apprehension, man-hunt, imprisonment, and *confiscation of all goods and property*—and not least of all, execution. In that extreme environment of totalitarian social control, one need not be a terrorist at all to be equally ranked among them as *"sympathizers"* (as some will certainly declare me to be after reading this book). It is, after all, a matter of sympathies; that is, either love God and serve Him, or embrace the Establishment agenda. (An interesting side note about the coming new global Establishment of the Beast, which should provide the astute with a clue about its power base and cultural origins, is that *beheading* will be a common sentence for convicted *state infidels* who dissent and reject this wanna-be new world order and its bogus messiah.)[16]

For those "religious-right extremists" who espouse a Higher Power of earth and heaven, the penalty will be death, persecution, torturous abuse, ridicule, scorn and ostracism. As pointed out, the precedents being set for *these* veritable crimes of hate are already well on their way to fiendishly full flowering and maturation in this very generation. The poisonous, evil fruit of anti-God man-worship is ripening even now for harvesting and voracious savoring by the lovers of The Lie *and* its Originator. They, in order to validate their beloved Lie, must discredit, condemn, persecute and even murder the witnesses of the Truth so as to snuff out their light, which exposes the wickedness of the haters of God. It's is an old tactic of all such murderers, practiced since time immemorial against all who stood for truth, from righteous Abel to Dr. Martin Luther King Jr., and most notably against the Lamb of God Himself. Accordingly, those who will not bow to the supremacy of the glorious

Luciferian Establishment to come "must all die."[17]

The satanic strategy, of course, is to eliminate all opposition to the final fulfillment of the grand global agenda of *self*-validation, *self*-actualization, *self*-aggrandizement and *self*-glorification. Which agenda is, ultimately, nothing more (nor less) than **the** age-old desire and will of the Dragon, at last incarnate. And, to deny the Old Serpent (a.k.a. the Devil and Satan)[18] his lust for power and glory is to evoke his bigoted, hateful wrath and invite his cold-blooded, murderous aggression.

His blood has always run cold; most frightening though, is that his frigid venom seems to be rapidly poisoning the veins of the whole world.

Love as Cold as Ice

And because iniquity shall abound, the love of many shall wax cold.—Matthew 24:12.

This know also, that in the last days perilous times shall come. For men shall be lovers of their own selves, covetous, boasters, proud, blasphemers, disobedient to parents, unthankful, unholy, without natural affection, trucebreakers, false accusers, incontinent, fierce, despisers of those that are good, traitors, heady, highminded, lovers of pleasures more than lovers of God; having a form of godliness, but denying the power thereof: from such turn away.—2 Timothy 3:1-4 & 13.

And even as they did not like to retain God in their knowledge, God gave them over to a reprobate mind, to do those things which are not convenient; being filled with all unrighteousness, fornication, wickedness, covetousness, maliciousness; full of envy, murder, debate, deceit, malignity; whisperers, backbiters, haters of God, despiteful, proud, boasters, inventors of evil things, disobedient to parents, without understanding, covenantbreakers, without natural affection, implacable, unmerciful: Who knowing the judgment of God, that they which commit such things are worthy of death, not only do the same, but have pleasure in them that do them.—Romans 1:28-32

The frost-bitten state of "natural affection" in this day and age stands as another of the woeful signs of the bone-chilling times in which we live. Even the one-time greatest nation on earth has demonstrated in this last generation the utter corruption of its once-exemplary social structure, particularly in the well-documented phenomenon known popularly as "the breakdown of the family."

Natural affection refers to the tenderhearted affection of kindred (esp. near kin) one for another. Need we iterate in this essay (with the ghastly statistics) the heinous and horrifying trends, brought home to us nearly everyday now via our newspapers and television sets, of the increasing acts of cold-heartedness, neglect, abandonment, abuse, murder, torture, and other senseless perpetrations of violence that now seem to permeate every level of our society!? A terrifying number of these acts are committed against defenseless infants and children, as well as our elderly population, much less simply between children and parents, husbands and wives.

Anyone not disturbed to their very foundations with these waxing statistics and reports of this "breakdown" or, perhaps more appropriately, *meltdown* of our society's nuclear core, is himself a victim of the *"love of many waxing cold."* This trend, as has been documented in the USA, has roots in the cause Apostle Paul precisely identified in his epistle to the Romans (1:28): *"And even as they did not like to retain God in their knowledge, God gave them over to a reprobate mind, to do those things which are not convenient."*

Prior to 1962 in the USA, crime, delinquency, and social erosion was statistically flat, that is, relatively stable, and in some cases even declining, such as with the divorce rate. However, since that year—when the Supreme Court outlawed prayer and Bible reading in America's public schools—the social indicators have either skyrocketed or plummeted (as with literacy and SAT scores) off the charts! The "meltdown" has resulted in the USA now leading the world in violent crime, divorce, voluntary abortion, illicit drug use (with all its related implications), not to mention leading the industrialized world in teen pregnancy, and fatherless children!

FACT: Since the landmark Supreme Court decision banning prayer and Bible reading in the public schools of the USA, effective with 1962-63 school year, the increasing lack of moral restraint among its population is overwhelmingly evident in the key social indicators. Almost immediately, the number of violent crimes jumped dramatically, so that by 1990 the rate of offenses multiplied by 794% (practically 8 times!) over the 1962 rate. (Again, the pre-1962 era showed a relatively stable rate.) Divorces, which had been declining since the late 40s, multiplied to 417% over the 1962 rate by 1983. The average current rate of the brutal extinction of infant lives before birth now hovers near 1.5 million per year, with approximately 32 million casualties in this unjustified war against the innocent over the last 30-some years. Single-parent families—i.e., children involuntarily stripped of holistic family life—increased to 160% by 1990. Unmarried couples cohabiting without formal commitment to family multiplied by a staggering 536% by 1989. Birth rates for high school girls, ages 15-19, shot up 553% by 1987; the same increase also documented in girls 10-14 years of age. By 1975, sexually transmitted disease jumped 226% in the same age group, and 257% for ages 10-14. Pre-marital sex among 16 year olds jumped 365% by 1980, among 17 year olds 271% by 1981, 208% by 1982 for aged 18, and vaulted to 1000% by 1987 for 15 year olds. Each of these statistical indicators reveals a drastic decrease in selfless love and concern for others as taught by the religious principles outlawed by the Supreme Court in 1962.[19]

When natural affection breaks down, as it obviously is in today's world, trust dissolves into *insecurity and fear*, which rise then to levels where people desperately seek some sort of savior, a hero—something to believe in. And since God no longer ranks as a candidate, no longer is officially welcomed in the public square (particularly in government), no longer part of the formative process of the human character in our public educational institutions, consequently, our options for viable saviors is limited. These days it boils down to who has the biggest voice and carries the biggest stick.

As in Orwell's *1984*, "Big Brother" seems to be the only one we can "trust" to look after our welfare and "best interests." He seems to be the only hero out there. Blind as we are, we fail to see that the same dynamic that is responsible for the general fear, insecurity, and distrust which we "enjoy"— and for the proscription of the Holy Scriptures and their principles from public life—is the very power to which we commit our souls for "safekeeping." Oh, what irony! What folly! What complacent blindness! What lust-manipulated mentalities!

Both in the Scripture quotations above and in a previous section, it has been pointed out that the Holy oracles predicted that last-day societies would be *"without natural affection . . . despisers of those that are good (godly),"* and *"haters of God."* And also that, in those pleasure-oriented societies, *"evil men and seducers"* with an agenda of deceit would proliferate and endeavor to redefine the meaning of righteousness, or *"godliness"* as the prophets often called it. Well, what's with all the deceit, the spite for God, and the waning of natural affection? Why the pervasive deterioration of the fabric of decency in our world?

Most critical thinkers have already pinned it down—*covetousness!* characterized by unscrupulous lust and selfishness. Some of the usual forms it takes are greed, unjust gain, theft and robbery. Sometimes it's exercised by outright force and violent seizure, or often by subtlety and cunning; but it has become widespread and pervasive, whether perpetrated by a government agency such as the IRS, a private corporation such as the Federal Reserve, a deceitful purveyor of goods or services, a cheating employee, or the local neighborhood sex offender.[20] In one form or another, it is one of the primary driving forces behind the established world order of ungodly/secular men, regardless of which era or generation is under consideration, although the last generation is predicted to be particularly rife of it.

In ancient times, the prophet Jeremiah very aptly concluded that this was the universal cancer of his own people, which drove them to lie, cheat and exploit—or, deal falsely, as he summed it up. According to him, every one of his people (from the least to the leaders) were pathologically obsessed by it, including the religious folks.[21] Sound familiar?

Webster defines covetousness as "an inordinate desire for wealth or possessions or for another's possessions." The Holy Bible calls it lust and envy, as well as *the root of all evil,* and the source of most all wars.

But they that will be rich fall into temptation and a snare, and into many foolish and hurtful lusts, which drown men in destruction and perdition. For the love of money is the root of all evil: which while some coveted after, they have erred from the faith, and pierced themselves through with many sorrows.—1 Timothy 6:9-10.

From whence come wars and fightings among you? come they not hence, even of your lusts that war in your members? Ye lust, and have not: ye kill, and desire to have, and cannot obtain: ye fight and war, yet ye have not, because ye ask not. Ye ask, and receive not, because ye ask amiss, that ye may consume it upon your lusts. Ye adulterers and adulteresses, know ye not that the friendship of the world is enmity with God? whosoever therefore will be a friend of the world is the enemy of God. Do ye think that the scripture saith in vain, The spirit that dwelleth in us lusteth to envy?—James 4:1-5.

It is covetousness that separates men from God and distinguishes the societies of the established world order from the people of God. Covetousness (excessive and often insatiable lust) reduces people to spiritual adulterers and adulteresses discontent with simple godliness and plenty from the hand of the Creator. Covetousness versus the True Values of YHWH—love of God and each other—draws the line between the friends of the world and the friends of God.[22]

Covetousness drives men to seek other gods that cater to their insatiable lusts and to worship strange gods that condone and promote envy, theft, robbery, violence, hatred, war, murder, blasphemy, and idolatry. Indeed, the inspired insight of the apostle Paul moved him to classify the practice of covetousness as *idolatry*.[23] Covetousness is self-worship, the *crowning idolatry*, and at the core of all other idol worship. Worship of idols is obviously practiced for the sake of getting something from the idol to satisfy selfish lusts. Covetousness is what *leads to the breakdown* of natural affection; because it is nothing less than the consummate manifestation of plain old *selfishness*, so typical of the Me Generation of our days!

The "breakdown of natural affection" and the "love of many waxing cold" are the *sisters of doom!* When these cold-blooded sisters are seen cavorting hand-in-hand down the streets of the new secular order, the apostasy will have blossomed, and the fruit of violence and hate will soon ripen for harvest.[24] Remove YHWH from the public life of our endtime societies, and the result will be pervasive violence and *"only evil continually,"* just as in the days before the Flood! (Genesis 6:5-7 & Luke 17:26)

The Iconoclasts of 21st Century Idolatry

Lest I be thought to overstate the evil of covetousness, let us recall that it was at the root of the vicious and brutal torture and murder of Jesus Christ. The chief priests and the elders (rulers) of Israel sought his execution because of envy. Even Pontius Pilate, the Roman governor at that time, knew that was their motivation.[25] These selfsame envious leaders are quoted in the Gospel of John as voicing serious agitation at Christ's sweeping influence on the general public, because they perceived it as threatening to undermine the status quo;[26] and of course, the status quo was (and still is) founded in materialism. From the initial jeering and scoffing of Christ for His teaching against mammon, these big-name religionists—who were no less consumed with covetousness than anyone else[27]—eventually became the loudest voices demanding His crucifixion.[28]

The rejection and subsequent murderous execution of Christ was nothing more than the desperate effort of self-serving materialists to maintain the established order and to preserve their stake in it—which they clearly loved more than God. A similar high-profile assassination will occur in the very last days, only a few days before the voice of the seventh angel declares *the end of the wicked establishments of depraved men.*[29] Two iconoclasts we've talked a little about in earlier chapters will be the new targets.

Two witnesses dressed in sackcloth testifying against the sinister hedonism of New Age idolatry will "plague" the self-absorbed secular societies of the last generation.[30] Various attempts to silence and to kill these two prophets will be made, without success, until the end of their 1,260-day activity. Apparently headquartered in Jerusalem, they will finally be assassinated there and lie unburied in the streets for 3½ days; the only funerary service or memorial they will be afforded is a global festival of glee to celebrate their assassination. All around the world and only hours then till doomsday, people of the new international order of 666 will make merry, send gifts to one another, and *party* over the killing of these two prophets who tormented them during the three-and-a-half-year regime of Big Brother.

And I will give power unto my two witnesses, and they shall prophesy a thousand two hundred and threescore days, clothed in sackcloth. . . . And if any man will hurt them, fire proceedeth out of their mouth, and devoureth their enemies: and if any man will hurt them, he must in this manner be killed. These have power to shut heaven, that it rain not in the days of their prophecy: and have power over waters to turn them to blood, and to smite the earth with all plagues, as often as they will.

And when they shall have finished their testimony, the beast that ascendeth out of the bottomless pit shall make war against them, and shall overcome them, and kill them. And their dead bodies shall lie in the street of the great city, which spiritually is called Sodom and Egypt, where also our Lord was crucified. And they of the people and kindreds and tongues and nations shall see their dead bodies three days and an half, and shall not suffer their dead bodies to be put in graves. And they that dwell upon the earth shall rejoice over them, and make merry, and shall send gifts one to another; because these two prophets tormented them that dwelt on the earth.

And after three days and an half the Spirit of life from God entered into them, and they stood upon their feet; and great fear fell upon them which saw them. And they heard a great voice from heaven saying unto them, Come up hither. And they ascended up to heaven in a cloud; and their enemies beheld them. And the same hour was there a great earthquake, and the tenth part of the city fell, and in the earthquake were slain of men seven thousand: and the remnant were affrighted, and gave glory to the God of heaven. The second woe is past; and, behold, the third woe cometh quickly.

And the seventh angel sounded; and there were great voices in heaven, saying, The kingdoms of this world are become the kingdoms of our Lord, and of his Christ; and he shall reign for ever and ever. And the four and twenty elders, which sat before God on their seats, fell upon their faces, and worshipped God, saying, We give thee thanks, O Lord God Almighty, which art, and wast, and art to come; because thou hast taken to thee thy great power, and hast reigned.

And the nations were angry, and thy wrath is come, and the time of the dead, that they should be judged, and that thou shouldest give reward unto thy servants the prophets, and to the saints, and them that fear thy name, small and great; and shouldest destroy them which destroy the earth.—Revelation 11:3-18.

My purpose in highlighting the activities and fate of these two uncompromising iconoclasts is manifold. First, it's to establish that, as Jesus specified, the end shall not come until the job is done. An effective witness for *"the gospel of the kingdom"* which He proclaimed must first be accomplished on a worldwide scale even in the face of the Beast and his 666 regime; and Christians shall not be relieved of their duty just because they want to quit early and go home.

Secondly, it's important to understand what the job of shedding the light the Gospel entails—above all, a firm renunciation of conformity to the wicked world orders of men and Satan, not only in word and in tongue, but in deed and in truth.[31] This is plainly symbolized by the totally unfashionable garb worn by the two witnesses, which in itself proclaims a blaring rejection of the materialist values of our proud endtime societies in favor of the humility of worldly poverty and faith through self-denial.[32] Moreover, when it's not compromised for self-serving convenience, the task of being the light of the world is a miserable one that involves provoking antipathy and persecution over the "torment" that light causes in the dark hedonist world of selfish people.[33] Witnessing on behalf of the Kingdom of God involves hazarding your life for it, and no true believer is above that expectation.[34]

Thirdly, even in the face of the amazing power and miraculous proofs supporting these fire-breathing witnesses of YHWH, we will see the hardened, apostate societies of the last generation refuse repentance and decidedly turn to fully hate God and everything connected with Him. This will become wholly manifest in their spiteful rejection of the two sackclothed prophets and their glee at the violent quashing of them in the end. But let's not skip over the fine-print story beneath the big, bold headlines: namely, 3½ years of a concerted state-citizen "cleansing" campaign to identify and exterminate all the other holy "vermin" worldwide who sympathize with the witnesses in sackcloth and likewise bear testimony to a Kingdom that is quite apart from this wicked world establishment.

All of this information is crucial for anyone who believes they may live on into the new millennium. It was all provided by the Prophets for purposes of briefing us on what to expect and, hence, what to prepare for. Understanding the facts about what is to transpire is critical to our decision about how to plan to live and prepare for the magnitude of such earth-shaking events. Additionally, it is for our firm assurance that, as these things begin to come to pass, we might recognize that the Prophecies are utterly true and faithful, and thus, wholly to be counted on for complete fulfillment!

Realistically, the prospects for the Great Travail yet to come in prelude to the birth of the incomparable Kingdom of God on earth is grim, period! Part of our ability to brace ourselves to endure it lies in the positive, unshakable guarantee we have that the ordeal is limited to a brief and calculable span of time that will end with the rapturous coming of the *"desire of all nations"*— the utopia of Messiah, *"the blessed hope."* Understanding what leads up to this fabulous event and what must occur in fulfillment of the prophecies is priceless information that should help us *"endure unto the end,"* as Jesus said we'd be expected to do, all the while being completely assured that the sacrifice of our lives and *"the sufferings of this present time are not worthy to be compared with the glory which shall be revealed in us." (Paul, Rom.8:18)*

If we are wakeful and "watching and praying"—being aware and sensitive in spirit—we simply cannot fail to see the stage being set for the final blasphemy and terror of the regime of Big Brother. A later chapter, "Messiah

Mistake," delves even deeper into "the apostasy," or "falling away," which is already priming the world for Brother Beast; but our focus here is on the very apparent signs of the times so readily evidenced by the daily news, as well as by so much of the rest of our daily experience. For so many of us, our personal daily lives seem to be catching up with the even more dire daily news which reflects a world scene in which people everywhere are waxing colder and colder in terms of human love and natural affection. Pervasive maliciousness, greed, strife, envy, hate, perversity and brutality characterize the frigid social climate of the exceedingly violent world in which we "live."

Increasingly, we see the scenario painted by the Prophets matching up perfectly with the actual picture of modern-day life, the *"perilous times"* of the *"last days"* which Paul detailed in his second epistle to Timothy (quoted in previous section). Poignantly leading off the description of these times which he so accurately foresaw, he wrote: *"For men shall be lovers of their own selves, covetous . . ."* The list went on, of course, to describe a high-minded, blaspheming, unholy society thoroughly wrapped up in itself, void of natural affection and self-restraint, obsessed with self-gratification, and marked by ferocity and rank animosity and malice. Is it only me alarmed at the tempo and character of this prophesied trend toward unrestrained covetousness?

Even the poor, who are promised to be first when the first of this world shall be last,[35] are increasingly infected with the worship of these devils of covetousness and envy that I've been zeroing-in on. Again, merely keeping up with a decent daily news source reveals the extent of the epidemic. On a daily basis now, we see the less fortunate of the developing world "driven" to resort to violence in striving to achieve a par existence with those in the First World who prosper so lavishly. (And I'm not talking about poverty characterized by desperate, starving abjection, which would perhaps offer justifiable cause.) Protests, demonstrations, armed conflicts, and bloodshed occur *daily* in some part of the world or another over merely *perceived* economic injustice. One need only peer over the fence into Latin America (try CBS's *Telenoticias*) for ample evidence of this assertion. Until the standard of living reaches the intoxicating levels of luxury in which Mama Babylon wallows, the unrest will not cease—nor even then![36]

Don't misunderstand me, institutionally assured poverty imposed by greed-ridden governments who exploit and oppress their peoples is equally contemptible. Theft is theft, altogether abhorred by YHWH, and is even more abominable when it's institutional. Establishment greed cannot help but infect its poor victims with envy and covetousness, eventually spawning unrest, uprising and protest, which invariably spills over into violence and even Marxist revolt. The innumerable cases of this phenomenon occurring in this century alone are staggering and remain a daily, ongoing bane to this generation from Asia, to Africa, to Latin America. The depravity, destruction, aggression and bloodshed across the globe due to institutionalized covetousness and envy is one of the grimmest signs of our times.

The more the mentality of covetousness prevails across the planet, the more frigid the love in the world becomes. The more impassioned people become with riches and things, the more distant they slip away from virtue and godliness. Suddenly, in just this very climate, as Apostle Paul admonished, in some perverted way, *gain becomes godliness*.[37] And, the worst feature of this rampant condition is that so few escape its powerful grip and alluring seduction. All too frequently, the iniquity that accompanies the lust for money consumes even would-be Bible-believers, who, via their own Bible teachings, inherit a generous legacy of abundant exhortations against the love-smothering *"love of money."*

The bitter closing days of the last, loveless generation will see ice-cold betrayals even of next of kin—and between "fellow" Christians, as well—over the addiction to materialism and the love of the Babylonish Establishment and all its delicacies.[38] In fact, this phenomenon marks the most tragic aspect of the period of time encapsulated within the very last few years of the Dragon's planetary domination. I regard it as tragic, because so many multitudes of supposed Christians and faith communities will show their true colors as nothing more than loyalty to dollar-sign idolatry, the love of mammon; recalling Paul's endtime prophecy to Timothy, really *"lovers of pleasures more than lovers of God."*

Rather than holding true to the iconoclast call of Christ (i.e., to *"reprove the world of sin"*),[39] and effectively demonstrating to the world the sole values of any real consequence,[40] very sadly, they have been sucked into adopting the ways of the world.[41]

All—Small or Great, Rich or Poor, Christian or Pagan

Those who claim to be followers of the Mashiach of Bethlehem affirm by very virtue of the fact that they take his name unto themselves that they fully accept and practice the teachings of this man of love, forgiveness, and renunciation of material gain. Jesus' singular expectation of his followers was that in identical fashion to His own they continue true to His mission.[42] As stated in the beginning of this chapter, adherents of His faith are supposed to be bearers of "the light," so that all the world might know the way of truth, even to the laying down of our lives for this sake. Instead, the lifestyles of the great majority of nominal believers are nothing but a mockery of the teachings of Christ and a profaning of the name they nonchalantly adopt.[43]

Such profane, shallow love—really disguising an internalized penchant for worldly values—is decried by the prophet Ezekiel: *"And they come unto thee as the people cometh,"* he said, *"and they sit before thee as my people, and they hear thy words, but they will not do them: for with their mouth they shew much love, but their heart goeth after their covetousness." (Ezek. 33:31)*

Much more severely yet, Apostle Peter condemned such covetous religious teaching and practice as the damnable, lying heresies of pernicious phony preachers who are actually highly injurious to the cause of Christ.[44] Through an appeal to covetousness, they lure people like assets into their "holy corporations" (some call them "partnerships") which they then "trade" on the religious "stock market" (esp. on TV) in an attempt to attract even more "investments" into their filthy-lucre-driven enterprises to stimulate more growth and greater profits (donations) in the competing sectarian marketplace.

But, the whole unholy charade will not go on much longer. According to Jesus, all that hot lip service of love will turn to freezing icicles of bitter betrayal—to the homicidal extreme—even of family members who refuse the pressure of the selfish mainstream materialists to *take the mark* of economic prosperity and survival and who take a stand for the way of faith, patience, truth and love of God. Covetous Cain will soon rise up again to slay righteous Abel when he sees that God has rejected his me-first religious hypocrisy of bringing a half-hearted offering that was not of the first and finest of his fruits, which he held back for himself. (Genesis 4) Like Cain, who put off his offering to the end, it will soon be too little and too late to find acceptance.

Almost two thousand years ago, the book of Revelation predicted that all the world would wonder after a Godless "beast" that would unify the earth under one global system of economics. (And, like Americans and the Clinton-Lewinsky scandal, it's the economy that truly matters and effectively blinds us to the character of its purveyor.) That system, which is already under development, is currently racing to its final form with practically all the technology completed for facilitating its implementation. In fact, the advertisements for the introductory prototypes are on television here in the USA almost daily. England and Australia are among the countries that have already initiated the early mechanics of the full-scale system yet to be imposed. This system which is rapidly coming together involves a number and a mark issued to every human on planet Earth.[45]

Without this mark, groceries or gasoline cannot be purchased, bills cannot be paid, paychecks cannot be cashed or even collected, services cannot be rendered or paid for, emergency medical treatment or any such like service cannot be acquired, and any and all other transactions involving monetary exchanges will be entirely un-negotiable! That's the word!

What does this mean? It means the global establishment will make it totally impossible for anyone to participate in routine daily life involving the supply of goods and services without taking a number and/or a marking that signifies a person's commitment to the system. This means the usual pursuits of life in all mainstream international societies will suddenly take on a new twist. Every soul must either sell out to the system, or get out! Everyone either takes the Beast's Mark or his Number to prosper in the new regime, or they do as Messiah taught—*"forsake all"* and become a hated disciple of Christ without possessions. (Luke 14:33) What will you do? How committed are you to the secular system of materialistic pursuits? It's all a matter of values.

For the great, complacent majority who are already sold out to the intoxicating consumer convenience of life in the secular world, their values are established and that decision seems to be a given. There is no question but what material security will be the primary factor in the choice of the covetous majority of the human race when they're faced with the mandate to convert to the 666 number system of the Mark. Of course, there's that one other little incentive, already mentioned, which makes it quite easy to conclude that there will be nearly universal participation: refusing the mark will be a capital violation of international law. Indeed, the one legislative decree that supersedes all others in the bizarre scenario prophesied for the last-days is the order that every human must revere the Beast (who institutes the 666 economy) by worshipping his living image—for which the penalty of refusal is death.

This is the same beast that has been under extensive discussion in previous sections; a "human" beast with an inhuman master, who incarnates an ancient agenda of self-realization, demanding the worship of himself by the entire human race. The stage is being set and the scheme is already approaching its final phases; and, unless you're not human, you'll have to play it out to the end. (Anyone who tells you differently is a pernicious false prophet probably trying to *"make merchandise of you"* out of financial interest in your persuasion, or perhaps to glory in your followership.)

Christian or otherwise, you will be faced with the wondrous, worldwide, hi-tech system of the Antichrist, his Mark, his Image, his despicable self-righteous blasphemy, his planetary cultural cleansing mandate, and his totalitarian economy. "Christian" or not, you will have to exercise your sovereign decision-making authority to sell your soul, or not. This is the central theme around which the final drama will revolve. This is the test and trial so feared and dreaded by the community of people who already know this prophetic scenario is soon to unfold—and seek escape from it. It is under these dire circumstances that the values and priorities of every man and woman will be manifest, Christians not exempted.[46]

Great Tribulation is the term that best describes this *"hour of temptation, which shall come upon all the world, to try them that dwell upon the earth."* *(Rev.3:10)* At that time, the words of the prophet Daniel regarding the *"time of the end"* shall be fulfilled: *"Many shall be purified, and made white, and tried; but the wicked shall do wickedly: and none of the wicked shall understand; but the wise shall understand." (Dan.12:10)* It is then that so-called mystical concepts, such as the *"washing of one's robes in the blood of the Lamb"* will be ever so clearly comprehended. Those who understand the concept will endure and emerge "out of great tribulation" having made their robes white thereby, not those who rapturously escape![47]

Fatefully though, the choices we have been contemplating here (between mammon & God, really) are already being made today and everyday. Who and what each of us loves is on trial daily. Only, the trial is "trifling" now as compared to when the furnace begins to blast as we approach the final end of the age. This is undoubtedly the period of (future) history Christ was making reference to in Matthew 24, Mark 13, Luke 17, and Luke 21—all passages about the end of the age. He said:

Then shall they deliver you up to be afflicted, and shall kill you: and ye shall be hated of all nations for my name's sake. And then shall many be offended, and shall betray one another, and shall hate one another. And many false prophets shall rise, and shall deceive many. And because iniquity shall abound, the love of many shall wax cold. But he that shall endure unto the end, the same shall be saved. And this gospel of the kingdom shall be preached in all the world for a witness unto all nations; and then shall the end come.—Matthew 24:9-14

But take heed to yourselves: for they shall deliver you up to councils; and in the synagogues ye shall be beaten: and ye shall be brought before rulers and kings for my sake, for a testimony against them. And the gospel must first be published among all nations. But when they shall lead you, and deliver you up, take no thought beforehand what ye shall speak, neither do ye premeditate: but whatsoever shall be given you in that hour, that speak ye: for it is not ye that speak, but the Holy Ghost. Now the brother shall betray the brother to death, and the father the son; and children shall rise up against their parents, and shall cause them to be put to death. And ye shall be hated of all men for my name's sake: but he that shall endure unto the end, the same shall be saved.—Mark 13:9-13

Whosoever shall seek to save his life shall lose it; and whosoever shall lose his life shall preserve it.—Luke 17:33

And ye shall be betrayed both by parents, and brethren, and kinsfolks, and friends; and some of you shall they cause to be put to death. And ye shall be hated of all men for my name's sake. But there shall not an hair of your head perish. In your patience possess ye your souls.—Luke 21:16-19

Not everyone will pass the test of true love, faith, and patience. Many, preferring to continue to compromise and conform for fear of losing their possessions and material security will forsake the Rapture-based Hosanna "faith" they once served so lavishly with their lips. Many, fearing reprisal for belief in God, or for giving haven, or being suspected of harboring, or being related or even associated with "religious extremists" (the New Age's "most-wanted"), will even betray their own family members to the officials of the new global State, crying "Crucify them!" or maybe, "Off with their heads!" Bounty and reward will motivate plenty of "crime-stoppers" calls too, I'm sure. Many of these betrayals will probably occur out of envious hatred, like that of Cain who was denied the rapture of acceptance by God. In any event, this dreadful scenario will come to pass *before any blessed hope of rapture* ever occurs—*"In your patience possess ye your souls."*

Unable to hide anymore behind religious pretenses, the uncloaked lovers of mammon will prove the absolute veracity of the principles taught by Christ, which they beforetime denied: *"No man can serve two masters . . . either he will hate the one, and love the other; or else he will hold to the one, and despise the other (Mat.6:24)."* The wheat will finally be separated from the chaff, the silver from the dross, the wicked from the just, and the real lovers of God from the woolly, religion-cloaked profaners who in actuality despise Him.[48]

No dubious or ambiguous allegiances or affections, as those that now persist among "faith communities," will continue when the mark is implemented. The New Secular Order will demand absolute allegiance to the Order and the Imam of the New International State. In the coming new world order, to confess to being a Christian or subscriber to His Gospel will, of necessity, mean *committed, unequivocal scorning of secular materialism and the forsaking of mammon at the cost of your life!*

That presently scarce brand of Christian will be universally hated by establishment relatives, friends, and people of all nations *for the sake of that gospel*; namely, the *good news* that this temporal Order of Covetousness will be annihilated in short order to the clear the way for the eternal Righteous Order of Messiah. Subscribing to *that gospel* of the Kingdom will render you an enemy and outlaw of the State, and any veneer of religion previously sported as an opiate for an uncommitted conscience will be quickly melted away and disintegrate, along with the pseudo gospel of the "rapture."

As we have reflected on already, the Establishment has *no love* for those who do not conform to it, and severely represses those who expose the truth about the secular agenda (denial of God for the sake of immediate gratification of selfish lusts with impunity). With whom will you side—the haters or the hated?

"He that shall endure unto the end, the same shall be saved."—Matthew 24:13

"Nevertheless when the Son of man cometh, shall he find faith on the earth?"—Luke 18:8

6

"YE SHALL NOT DIE . . . YE SHALL BE AS GODS"

Of the fruit of the tree which is in the midst of the garden,
God hath said, Ye shall not eat of it, neither shall ye touch it, lest ye die.
And the serpent said unto the woman, Ye shall not surely die:
For God doth know that in the day ye eat thereof,
then your eyes shall be opened, and ye shall be as gods . . .
Genesis Chapter 3

For those of us stricken by the Eve Syndrome, our greatest dream shall perhaps very soon be fulfilled. We shall be as gods! The last three-and-one-half years of man's depraved history will be distinguished by the secular gospel of self-actualization. This final, brief chapter of man's iniquitous dominion of Earth will be earmarked by a *knowledge explosion* and the ultimate in *self-worship*, not to mention the love of *rah*.[1]

Besides being brief, however, it will also be stormy—a time of great tribulation. The struggle to actualize the age-old desire to "have it all" takes on a furious character, a maniacal quality. Time is short, and the serpentine Alien knows it; the pace to implement his evil agenda will need to be stepped up dramatically as time runs out.

According to the prophet Daniel, the key move to be made in order to hasten the execution of the Serpent's grand design is to "baptize and anoint" his "human" agent. Fairly extensive mention has already been made of this bestial agent (esp. in the previous chapter). Among several titles used, we have referred to him in popular terms as the Antichrist, and particularly as the vile *"Beast"* spoken of by the prophets John (of the Apocalypse) and Daniel. The earliest clue given as to his identity is provided for us by Daniel (c. 550 BCE). Crucial information provided in his prophecy facilitates the discerning of who this nefarious agent will be when he appears (seven years before the

d). That info comes in the form of Daniel's reference to him as *"the prince*

covenant" and in his noting that the grand debut of this prince will be

shall *"confirm the covenant with many for one week."*

is "prince" *confirms* "the covenant," the countdown to the zero

d our notorious agent is effectively anointed to fulfill his des-

world as one planetary society in pursuit of evolutionary

e strategy, of course, will be to hastily herd the citizens

to a stampede to deify themselves as gods; this they

their glorious new Vicar, who will be idolized for

human spirit.

many" will be lauded as a supreme achieve-

for mankind; not just "world class," but

g, where any and all earthly hurdles

ooperation! *"At last,"* he'll pro-

nary destiny to reach beyond

w, peacefully unified, noth-

king our aspirations be-

em, he'll declare the

d for the gods, are

complish by

of earth,

plish-

ar-

al
ded
eath
educ-
e then,
orphose
y.
touch, and
totally unto
thus become
ER us!). In the
piece of his New
Mother Ship—to
enticity of the Pre-

the entire world must
onstruction of a "living
he demon-become-God-
e persuaded that they are
verence to the Premier Pon-
human (and thus self-) exal-
ip, and glorify Satan himself!
e new, consummate idolatry of
hall be thine!"—avows the bearer
Eves of this New Age of Enlight-
7 & Genesis 3:5)
however, will be the fact that not all
subscribe to his human-demon hybrid
de theater of this dramatic endeavor to
image of the vile producer of this dam-

nip)
e allure

will be more than Earth's duped masses can resist. Coveting to be gods in their own right, they'll be led by their lust to follow him whithersoever he leads them—all the way to the worship of the Serpent himself!

Naturally, he will not be presented or viewed as Satanic, but as wonderfully Luciferian; Lucifer, of course, being the *light-bearer*, the *"bright, morning star"* of the New Dawn, the new Age of Enlightenment. The world, newly "enlightened" by the *Luciferian intellect* and the explosion of technologic advancement, will esteem itself (urged on by the Serpent) to have transcen to the threshold of deity. The promised conquest of aging, disease, and will obsess the last generation, who will be readily captivated by these tive assurances from the extraordinary "prince of the covenant." H during the last half of his seven-year notoriety, will virtually metam into the *acclaimed supreme deity* of the societies of the 21st centu

During that final phase, to satisfy the people's need to see, feel, the Beast shall assimilate the transdimensional Satanic Forc himself to be bodily imbued with the essence of its power, an "God With Us, Among Us, and In Us" (and especially OV meantime, his prime minister, the miracle-manifesting mouth World Order, will likewise be endowed with power from th call down fire from heaven, and thereby certify the auth mier Paramount of the New Age of Power and Glory.[2]

This minister of techno-marvels will mandate that worship the Beast, particularly by the creation and c image" (detailed later in this chapter) in honor to and-deliverer-of-mankind. By so doing they will b really honoring themselves, vicariously, through re tiff of Global Paganism. *In their vicarious act of* tation, they shall in every *actuality* exalt, worsh The Devil will be the power and *essence* of th the New Age of 21st Century HUMANITY!

"If thou therefore wilt worship me, ALL of "light and knowledge" to the ego-struc enment—"Ye shall be as gods!" (Luke

To the dour dismay of the Serpent the people of earth will entertain or blasphemy. In the darkened worldw remake reality in the conception an of who this nefarious agent will be when he appears (seven years before the end). That info comes in the form of Daniel's reference to him as *"the prince of the covenant"* and in his noting that the grand debut of this prince will be when he shall *"confirm the covenant with many for one week."*

Once this "prince" *confirms* "the covenant," the countdown to the zero hour begins, and our notorious agent is effectively anointed to fulfill his destiny of uniting the world as one planetary society in pursuit of evolutionary humanist godhead. The strategy, of course, will be to hastily herd the citizens of the nations of earth into a stampede to deify themselves as gods; this they will endeavor to do through their glorious new Vicar, who will be idolized for his remarkable elevation of the human spirit.

The landmark *"covenant with many"* will be lauded as a supreme achievement for humanity, one gigantic step for mankind; not just "world class," but a step into the inter-galactic class of being, where any and all earthly hurdles can now be surmounted through peaceful cooperation! *"At last,"* he'll proclaim, *"humanity has arrived at their evolutionary destiny to reach beyond where primitive men have not gone before! . . . Now, peacefully unified, nothing shall be impossible to us!"* Charismatically sparking our aspirations beyond the moon and Mars, or our own mere solar system, he'll declare the galaxy to be within our grasp: *"The heavens, once reserved for the gods, are now ours for the taking!"*

The real end goal of the Serpent, which he purposes to accomplish by means of all the mass euphoria he shall inspire among the peoples of earth, will be to set himself up as the *Supreme Being*. To facilitate this accomplishment, he will invoke the aid of a powerful spokesperson, a prophet of marvels, the prime-minister-to-be of the soon-to-come Global Federation of Earth. It will be the purpose of this orator of unearthly faculty to rouse the public awe and captivate the veneration and worship of the masses of earth on behalf of the Serpent. The Serpent, of course, himself being an alien of otherworldly essence, requires a human entity, an agent by which to realize and fulfill his diabolical intent—which is where the Beast comes in. The Beast, as we have noted, is a man chosen by the Serpent through which this evil alien incarnates and realizes his ancient goal of deposing YHWH from the realms of earth to supersede Him as the Premier Deity of the galaxy.

Promising the people of Earth that his nexus with the advanced extraterrestrial powers of the Transdimensional Intellect (aboard the Mother Ship) can transform and empower all humanity to achieve immortality, the allure will be more than Earth's duped masses can resist. Coveting to be gods in their own right, they'll be led by their lust to follow him whithersoever he leads them—all the way to the worship of the Serpent himself!

Naturally, he will not be presented or viewed as Satanic, but as wonderfully Luciferian; Lucifer, of course, being the *light-bearer*, the *"bright, morning star"* of the New Dawn, the new Age of Enlightenment. The world, newly "enlightened" by the *Luciferian intellect* and the explosion of technological advancement, will esteem itself (urged on by the Serpent) to have transcended to the threshold of deity. The promised conquest of aging, disease, and death will obsess the last generation, who will be readily captivated by these seductive assurances from the extraordinary "prince of the covenant." He then, during the last half of his seven-year notoriety, will virtually metamorphose into the *acclaimed supreme deity* of the societies of the 21st century.

During that final phase, to satisfy the people's need to see, touch, and feel, the Beast shall assimilate the transdimensional Satanic Force totally unto himself to be bodily imbued with the essence of its power, and thus become "God With Us, Among Us, and In Us" (and especially OVER us!). In the meantime, his prime minister, the miracle-manifesting mouthpiece of his New World Order, will likewise be endowed with power from the Mother Ship—to call down fire from heaven, and thereby certify the authenticity of the Premier Paramount of the New Age of Power and Glory.[2]

This minister of techno-marvels will mandate that the entire world must worship the Beast, particularly by the creation and construction of a "living image" (detailed later in this chapter) in honor to the demon-become-God-and-deliverer-of-mankind. By so doing they will be persuaded that they are really honoring themselves, vicariously, through reverence to the Premier Pontiff of Global Paganism. In their vicarious act of human (and thus self-) exaltation, they shall in every actuality exalt, worship, and glorify Satan himself! The Devil will be the power and essence of the new, consummate idolatry of the New Age of 21st Century HUMANITY!

"If thou therefore wilt worship me, ALL shall be thine!"—avows the bearer of "light and knowledge" to the ego-struck Eves of this New Age of Enlightenment—*"Ye shall be as gods!" (Luke 4:7 & Genesis 3:5)*

To the dour dismay of the Serpent, however, will be the fact that not all the people of earth will entertain or subscribe to his human-demon hybrid blasphemy. In the darkened worldwide theater of this dramatic endeavor to remake reality in the conception and image of the vile producer of this damnable fiction will be the glaring torches of those in the audience who will defiantly disrupt this movie-magic to expose the diabolical plot. All will not go smoothly for the devious protagonist and his planetary cast of billions of adoring humans during the course of this unfolding drama; for not all will worship and confirm the Beast as God.

Quite to the contrary, strong opposition will mount against him and his insidious plot. (It is precisely for this sake that this book is written—to arm and truly prepare that counter force of resistance and opposition.)

And the third angel followed . . . saying with a loud voice, If any man worship the beast and his image, and receive his mark in his forehead, or in his hand, the same shall drink of the wine of the wrath of God, which is poured out without mixture into the cup of his indignation; and he shall be tormented with fire and brimstone in the presence of the holy angels, and in the presence of the Lamb: And the smoke of their torment ascendeth up for ever and ever: and they have no rest day nor night, who worship the beast and his image, and whosoever receiveth the mark of his name. Here is the patience of the saints: here are they that keep the commandments of God, and the faith of Jesus.—Revelation 14:9-12

The patience and faith of those that keep the commandments of God will carry them through this consummately dark period of the last seven years, and particularly the last 3½ stormy years of Great Tribulation. Those who are prepared to endure and are determined to renounce the materialist agenda of the humanist, anti-God, idolatrous order of the Serpent must either flee to refuge in the wilderness, or brave martyrdom as active "resistance elements" in the forbidding urban environments of Big Brother.

Otherwise, in order to remain securely ensconced in the mammon-based global Establishment of planet Earth, you will need to worship the image of the Beast and receive his mark, number, or name in your right hand or forehead. This will be the only shelter from the all-seeing, all-knowing Big Brother of the fully blossomed, fully ripened planetary dominion of Satan. Forget the lying delusions of the "Christians" who proclaim salvation by the "rapture." That damnable doctrine of the fundamentalist false prophets is in heretical contradiction to the *patience and faith* of those who indeed *keep the commandments!*

Babylonish Christianity will be rocked by frightful shock waves, which will shatter the dreamy complacency of the "rapturophiles." Seven years before the end, the unveiling of the *"prince of the covenant"* (at the historic moment of covenant confirmation) will place the compromising nominal faith communities in the supremely uncomfortable position of having to immediately stand to expose this demonic fraud; or to sink deeper into their dream state of denial.

Their present sworn denial of the Scriptural facts—especially the fact that all saints shall be subject to Great Tribulation, without exception—will then begin to haunt them with lingering dread that their foolish idolatries and love of mammon must now, at last, be forsaken. Either that, or they will hunker down even more deeply in their delusion that "Jeezus" will show up at any minute to rapture them; stubbornly persisting meanwhile in simply biding their time in the same old idolatrous denial of Christ that woefully now characterizes their tenacious clinging to their materialism. In all cases, seeing the Beast with their own eyes will catalyze them one way or the other, either into greater delusion and denial, or into a fiery baptism of repentance!

Even more shattering to the Christo-mammonism of the great majority of lip-service believers will be the approach of the *midnight hour* at the midpoint of the *final "shabuwa."* Then panic will grip both halves of the hearts of the "mediocris-tians!" Having never fully committed themselves to washing their filthy-lucre-soiled robes in the blood of the Lamb, and suddenly without any greenbacks to finance their dual devotion, their dreaded day of reckoning will have arrived. No more only slightly blood-tinted Christian garb, dyed or patterned with the camouflaging color of *money.* (Indeed, cash shall then be no more.) Then, we must either *wash* our robes in the Lamb's blood, and thoroughly purify ourselves from the world (of mammon),[3] or take the mark of the Beast in order to preserve our lives and material security. The pretense will finally be over. We shall either fear and worship God, or fear and worship the image of Big Brother!

It is in *"the midst of the week,"* according to the prophecy of Daniel that this *"abomination of desolation"* occurs. At that point, all "superstitious religious practice" will be ceased by the Prince of the Covenant (now the Covenant-breaker), and strictly sole obeisance to him will be permitted throughout the world. Then the full-scale war with the dissident saints—loyal to the testimony and faith of Christ—explodes.

"Then shall be great tribulation, such as was not since the beginning of the

world unto this time, no, nor ever shall be."—Yeshua Ha'Mashiach

When Ye Shall See the Abomination . . .

The scenario summarized above surrounds the most critical development of all history and all Biblical prophecy. It is the most consequential sign of signs that the end of all things is at hand.

Let no man deceive you by any means: for that day shall not come, except there come a falling away first, and that man of sin be revealed, the son of perdition; who opposeth and exalteth himself above all that is called God, or that is worshipped; so that he as God sitteth in the temple of God, shewing himself that he is God . . . (II Thessalonians 2:3-4)

What makes this prophetic sign so significant? It is accompanied by very well defined, unmistakable chronological information. The prophets spoke of this event attaching explicit and very specific terms regarding its timing.

Let's resume our prophetic excursion into the future with a quick review of the signs given by the most important of the oracles, Messiah Himself.

In His thorough and detailed endtime discourse to his disciples, recorded both in Matthew 24 and Mark 13, often called the Olivet Discourse by scholars, Yeshua nails down the answer to their original and central query: *"What shall be the sign of thy coming and of the end of the world?"* After describing broadly the conditions they (i.e., the future heirs of their discipleship tradition) would encounter at that time, and the state in which the world would be found in its final hours, He punctuated and accentuated the chronology of endtime developments with a direct reference to the words of the prophet Daniel. It is at this point in the discourse that Yeshua addresses the question with a specific when-then sign that implicates a time element:

When ye therefore shall see the abomination of desolation, spoken of by Daniel the prophet, stand in the holy place, (whoso readeth, let him understand:) . . . then shall be great tribulation, such as was not since the beginning of the world to this time, no, nor ever shall be. And except those days should be shortened, there should no flesh be saved: but for the elect's sake those days shall be shortened. . . . Immediately after the tribulation of those days shall the sun be darkened, and the moon shall not give her light, and the stars shall *fall from heaven, and the powers of the heavens shall be shaken: And **then** shall appear the sign of the Son of man in heaven: and **then** shall all the tribes of the earth mourn, and they shall see the Son of man coming in the clouds of heaven with power and great glory. And he shall send his angels with a great sound of a trumpet, and they shall gather together his elect from the four winds, from one end of heaven to the other.—Matthew 24:15-31*

The time element included here (by association) comes from the prophecy of Daniel regarding the *"abomination of desolation,"* mentioned three times in the book of Daniel in exactly those terms.[4]

As already briefly stated, the final "hour" of secular history will be a "shortened" period of three-and-one-half years marked by the abomination of desolation standing in "the holy place" or "the sanctuary of strength . . . where it ought not."[5] The length of time for this critical period in history is well established in the Scriptures, leaving no doubt about the exact term of its duration.

Both chapters 9 and 12 of the book of Daniel provide corroborating references to this same future period of time, and spell out its length. In chapter 12, the period is actually numbered in days. In chapter 9, the period is defined as one half of a "shabuwa," a commonly used Hebrew term for a period of seven days or seven years, depending on the context.

The Hebrews marked the passage of time, both of days and years, in shabuwas and sabbaths. That is, just as seven days made up a *shabuwa (one week)* ending with the sabbath day, so did seven years make up a shabuwa also ending with a sabbath, a sabbatical year wherein the land was allowed to rest for the entire seventh year. The best example of *shabuwa* being used to define a period of seven years is found in Genesis, chapter 29, where Jacob served Laban an *additional shabuwa* to obtain his other daughter Rachel as his second wife. Most of our English versions of the book of Daniel employ the word "week" to translate this one-word term that applies in Hebrew (or Aramaic) to a multiple of seven.[6]

Thus we read in chapter 9 of Daniel that a covenant is confirmed for *"one week" (one shabuwa).* Then, in the midst of the week, an apparent reversal occurs of the extraordinary developments which follow the celebrated ratification of this renowned seven-year treaty or accord—the most notorious of those developments being *animal sacrifice* in Jerusalem! This ancient rite is revived a little more than 8 months after the confirming of the covenant.

The subsequent reversal—revocation and termination of the practice—comes after nearly 34 months of daily sacrifices, when the prince of the covenant intervenes to call it off. This reversal of circumstances which occurs *"in the midst of the week"* (3½ years into it) is directly related to the *"overspreading of abominations"* that causes *"desolation"* in Jerusalem and the sanctuary until the end of that "week."

In all three verses from the book of Daniel which make specific reference to the abomination of desolation, each of them connect it with a taking away, or a causing to cease of the *daily sacrifice.* (See footnote 4.) It is the very first mention of the abomination (in Dan.9:27) which also connects the covenant to a revival of daily animal sacrifice. This daily sacrifice will evidently be of the same type that was instituted among the Hebrews in Exodus 29 and Numbers 28 involving a lamb sacrificed both in the morning and in the evening at the door of the tabernacle (a large pavilion-style tent serving as a mobile sanctuary before the days of the Temple construction).

The suggestion in Daniel 9:27 is that the accord, pact, or treaty may be preexisting and already negotiated, drafted, and perhaps even signed at the time of its *"ratification"* by the prince of the covenant. This "prince" is the same character I've dubbed with various descriptive titles in previous pages. Here he emerges as a powerful political figure that is central to the multilateral *ratification of the accord* by his masterful rallying of a multitude of parties to its firm implementation. Most notable is that, as part of the implementation of this treaty,[7] there is afforded to the Jews (to whom the prophecy is directed)[8] the opportunity to revive the ancient priestly rite of the daily sacrifice at the door of the tabernacle or temple.

It strikes me of great interest to take note that proposing seven-year plans has become a rather popular practice of late in the political arenas of the '90s; this one, however, should be easily distinguished from the many others by its geographical focus. It will center on the "holy city" of Jerusalem, about which there is considerable and continual controversy in our time.[9] In fact, hardly a day goes by now that this controversy is not brought to our attention via the daily news media.

One of the most recent major flare-ups of conflict in the region (September 1996) has produced the worst violence in 30 years; and "the beat goes on" to date. A very cunning and persuasive figure will he be who successfully engineers a resolution to this nagging distress. Though it be brief in duration, it will, nonetheless, be a highly remarkable achievement; for peace, as everybody knows, does not come easily in this part of the world.

Alert Israel-watchers most likely will not miss the ratification of *this* particular seven-year accord. Also not to be overlooked, and something that's pretty much common knowledge to those who tune in keenly to current events and developments there, is that determined efforts and powerful strides have been made to renew temple worship in Jerusalem according to the ancient pattern gone out of practice nearly 2,000 years ago! Directly connected with this is that *serious plans have already been undertaken to reconstruct another temple* on the same site as the previous two, both of which, each in their era, suffered complete destruction.

Led by Gershon Salomon, a former Israeli army officer of Six-day War fame, a group known in short as "The Temple Mount Faithful" has already sought in 1991 to obtain permit from the government to lay a cornerstone on the temple mount (Mt. Moriah) in Jerusalem. Permit was denied because of the tense political situation that prevails, aggravated by the fact that the site is already occupied by the oldest Islamic shrine in the world, Qubbat As-Sakhrah (also called the Mosque of Omar, or commonly, The Dome of the Rock) in addition to Al Aqsa mosque, another smaller sanctuary on the same site. It is hard to imagine that the pact under consideration here will not somehow address the resolution of this enormously controversial issue so politically and emotionally-charged.

One thing for certain, though, is that, after a little more than eight months of the confirming of the "holy" covenant, the daily sacrifice will begin. Again, the prophet Daniel provides us with the detailed chronology of this major milestone on the last stretch of the road to the grand finale.

Then I heard one saint speaking, and another saint said unto that certain saint which spake, How long shall be the vision concerning the daily sacrifice, and the transgression of desolation, to give both the sanctuary and the host [of God's people] to be trodden under foot? And he said unto me, Unto two thousand and three hundred days; then shall the sanctuary be cleansed.—Daniel 8:13-14

We know this to be a reference to the last 2,300 days of secular history; because, as shown in earlier paragraphs and related footnotes, the era of the *"transgression of desolation"* is the final phase to occur immediately after the cessation of the daily sacrifice, and immediately before the appearing of the sign of the Son of man coming in the clouds of heaven. Then, of course, the despoiled sanctuary shall be cleansed and the reign of Antichrist quashed.

On the ancient Jewish calendar, seven years—the proposed length of the covenant and the final period allotted for completion and "consummation" of the Seventy-week Prophecy of Daniel—is equivalent to 2,520 days. Therefore, since the *combined period* allocated to the fulfillment of the revived daily sacrifice *and* the subsequent transgression of desolation (until its termination) is given as 2,300 days, obviously the daily sacrifice does not begin immediately at the commencement of the seven-year covenant. At least 220 initial days of the 2,520 remain unoccupied by these two principal features of the 70th and final "week" of Daniel (9:24-27).

Naturally, once the covenant is confirmed, opening the way for renewal of this temple-based pattern of worship, a period of time will be required to complete the necessary preparations for initiation of the sacrificial rite. The primary requisite will be insistence on the siting, as well as the attachment of the rite to *a sanctuary* built on the sacred site, whether it's provisional (as in the case of the Mosaic tabernacle) or a fixed structure which would probably require more time to erect. And so, it is quite easy to follow the logic that leads to the understanding of where the first 220 "missing" days have gone.

Since we know from Daniel chapter 12 (verse 11, see footnote 4) that the duration of time from the removal and curtailment of the sacrifice until the end is 1,290 days, then we know the sacrifice will only be performed for 1,010 days (or between 33-34 months). Simple math tells us that if the total time allotted to both the sacrifice and the abomination is 2,300 days (until the end), and only 1,290 days remain after the sacrifice is abolished, then 1,010 days is to be the duration of the animal sacrifice in Jerusalem; while the 1,290 days is the allotted time for the desolation perpetrated by Antichrist.

The Last 7 Years

To summarize the timeline of the final seven-years and its sequence of events, we begin with the confirming of the holy covenant by the soon-to-emerge, charismatic champion of world peace and unification. This starts the seven-year countdown. Subsequently, the Jews in Israel procure sufficient peace and security to complete preparations for daily animal sacrifice and building of a temple. After about eight months, the sacrificial worship begins. The daily sacrifice continues for nearly three years, short a couple months, until the ingenious engineer of the covenant ratification betrays and revokes the agreement in order to implement his own Great Secular Agenda (denouncing the divisive, obsolete "theological superstitions of antiquity," particularly those of the "regressive" Jews and Christians).

At the mid-point of the seven-year accord, this potent, new political superstar, with the broad support of his cultural allies (non-Western) and seduced masses of flattered constituents, forcefully intervenes and abolishes the new temple worship involving sacrificial lamb offerings. Within a month's time, the holy place is sacrilegiously occupied by Antichrist, the Jews driven out, and the abomination of desolation set up.

Formerly the sanctuary of worship to YHWH, the temple site on the holy mount (Moriah) in Jerusalem is converted into the global headquarters or palatial compound of the demonic hero of the new global order.[10] The newly established secular regime constitutes the integration and unification of international politics, economics, and "religion" under the autocratic rule of the newly acclaimed world premier who seizes power by astonishing, overwhelming supernatural powers and forces, and who is subsequently hailed the supreme being.[11]

Evidently, at the mid-point or sometime during the first half of the covenant period, in what develops as an multinational military power-grab led by the erstwhile chief negotiator and champion of the peace accord ratification (now leader of an international coup), the Antichrist champion suffers a mortal wound—whether by assassination or a military strike is not clear. However, by some amazing means, the slain rhetorical demagogue and political strong man is then miraculously healed of a mortal wound incurred from an assault with a deadly weapon.[12]

Seizing upon a phenomenal recovery and resurrection from death, he proclaims himself a living marvel of God-like proportions; and the people of the world (amazed by the miracle of his healing) assent en masse and acknowledge him as a representation of human attainment to godhood. All of this will more than likely be propelled by claims of contact and alliance with "extraterrestrials," who provide the source of the healing technology (as well as other technologies, esp. of weapons class).[13]

With renewed vigor to his rhetoric, he praises the gods of science, technology and armaments. By his account, our technological prowess and stunning advancements in science toward unlocking of the secrets of the universe prove the "truth" of the Serpent's assertion in the garden of Eden that "God is a liar!" For now, we have arrived at the capability of defying death and validating the claim made by the subtle Serpent that we *"shall not surely die"* by partaking of the forbidden fruit of knowledge and discovery of the profound scientific secrets of the universe; but rather, we "shall be equal with God" as a result of tapping the fountain of knowledge, and by the mastery it endows us with.

At last, by his account, we shall have arrived at competitive status with all other civilizations of higher intelligence in the universe that have also attained to this knowledge.[14] *"After all,"* I imagine him boastfully affirming, *"Gods and angels are nothing more than intergalactic beings that have attained greater intelligence and knowledge in advance of our own. Now, however, we have finally evolved to become equal to them; and in fact, by our new mastery we shall defy any invasive incursion against our planetary sovereignty and defend Earth from foreign domination by alien forces of extraterrestrial origins (especially the so-called Christ!)."*[15]

Every corner of the earth—soon to be completely linked with electrically powered, audio-visual, electronic communications devices (television/computer monitors and perhaps bionic implants)[16] —will witness his grandiose orations,[17] probably not much different than the following:

"We are all gods and there is no limit to our potential. . . . There is no God, but Us. . . . We are God, and you are God, and I am God! . . . Together we are all One God.[18] *I will lead you so that together we shall all be God, as I am. . . . All power is at our fingertips; but we must unite to achieve our potential. . . . Our salvation/survival can only be a product of our total unity to apply ourselves and all our resources to the resolution of the problems of our planet. . . . Our technological mastery must be fully harnessed to empower us to conquer all evil and to defend ourselves from all enemies—beginning with the religious superstitions of ignorance. . . .*

"The ignorance fostered by mystical beliefs and faith in false notions of supernatural spiritual powers must be eradicated for the sake of our planetary preservation and advancement. . . . The so-called supernatural is now within our reach. . . . The gifted prophets, saints, and mystic figures of the past were merely enlightened humans who realized their own potential or visitors to Earth from extraterrestrial civilizations of higher intelligence and advanced technologies, which thus caused us to wonder, revere, and worship in our ignorant awe. . . . We must no longer remain the captives of primitive religious hoaxes and fraudulent, barbaric theologies that divide and fracture

our global society. . . . These superstitions debilitate our potential and stymie
our advancement toward a global civilization of a United Earth. . . .

    "Together, in me, with me, you too can be God. . . . Behold my victory
over death. . . . We possess the power of the gods. . . . There is no other power,
there is no other God. . . . And now you see that I am God and am bestowed
with the Power of God by the Collective Genius I embody on behalf of You
All. . . . Our shared common enemies are ignorance, superstition, and divi-
sion. . . . These enemies must be vanquished and eradicated from our planet,
or we shall perish as a race unable to meet the challenges of the 21st century,
both in terms of environmental cataclysm, as well as intergalactic alien threat.
. . . We must unite!. . . . All opposition must be quashed. . . . All isolationist or
autonomist interests by nationalists, religious separatists, or sovereignty-seek-
ing individualists must be subjugated under the One-world State of Planet
Earth which I embody, or Earth itself shall be conquered by rogue forces of
extraplanetary origins. . . . Even now agents of such forces advancing the
rogue Christ invasion have infiltrated Earth and seek to consume and domi-
nate our planet by sedition, terror, aggression and tyranny. . . ."

    Such a scenario as portrayed above is strictly conjectural, but certainly
not outside prophetic probability, nor altogether without Scriptural bases (depending on one's scope of vision, whether narrow or unlimited). Your own
individual study under inspiration of God may reveal much greater insight
than what may be contained in this unconventional, though still finite perspective; I am simply sharing how I imagine the plot will unfold.[19]

The "Kanáph" Invasion—The Aliens Are Coming

    By now, it is probably quite obvious that the perspective conveyed in this
book views certain Biblical prophecies with what might be regarded as a quasi
"science fiction" outlook. Indeed, it is extremely difficult (for me) to read the
Bible records and its prophecies without visualizing extraterrestrial aliens from
outer space, UFOs, technologically advanced civilizations in other worlds,
cosmic conflicts between powerful intergalactic Forces (Dark vs. Good), and
so on. A considerable portion of the Biblical narrative describes just these
types of subject matter.

    I also believe my particular views spring, in large part, from the influ-
ences of the times in which we live, an era marked by stunning advancements
in science and technology, far beyond, to our knowledge, what Earth has ever

witnessed in all its recorded history. Moreover, "science fiction" is perhaps not even quite the most accurate term by which to describe the outlook I embrace and present herein; for, what I see in the Holy Scriptures I hardly regard as fiction by any stretch; and certainly, it seems more and more as each day passes that one-time *science fiction* is regularly transformed into *actual reality* in our daily lives!

In any event, our day and age is unarguably saturated with sci-fi themes and images. Most of them project a vision of the future filled with advanced machines and high technology to serve our every whim and fancy, a world where nothing is any longer considered impossible, given enough time and money devoted toward fulfillment of our dreams and visions. However, as so much of what was fictional only a few years ago becomes a reality before our eyes—more and more so all the time—none of it should at all surprise us, really. The Bible long ago declared that the time of the end would be characterized by a *marked increase* in knowledge.

But thou, O Daniel, shut up the words, and seal the book, even to the time of the end: many shall run to and fro, and knowledge shall be increased.—Daniel 12:4

Here the translators hardly did Daniel's prophecy justice in their choice of words. Clearly, knowledge *should increase* with time! The word "increase," however, was translated from the Hebrew *rabáh* [רבה], meaning *to become great, many, much, numerous,* or *to multiply.* So, to have been consistent with at least 74 other instances of the usage of *rabáh* in the Scriptures—including the Genesis account of creation where the creatures were commanded to *"be fruitful, and multiply, and fill"* the earth—the translators could have utilized the world *"multiplied"* to have given a more profound (and accurate) meaning to the prophecy. Notwithstanding, let it suffice to be said that only a blind and deaf person cannot grasp how profound this prophecy is; everybody's intensely aware that we live in the highly touted *Information Age* in which everything of appeal has become *"hi-tech."*

Everyone agrees, this amazing era into which we happen to have been born is unquestionably characterized by a staggering multiplication of knowledge. Bear in mind that in the last year alone (1997) *numerous* mind-boggling scientific advancements have been announced, which not so long ago—only a few mere decades—were considered merely fanciful prospects only *imagined* by "science fiction" writers and visionaries.

Anti-gravity machines are *now operational* (albeit of limited power), able to suspend objects weightlessly. Hand-held human sensor devices have been developed, able to detect a human being in darkness or in hiding at a distance of 200 yards via the magnetic impulse generated by the human heartbeat; another (hand-held) utilizes miniaturized radar-generating circuitry to detect humans (or other objects) through as much as 2 feet of solid concrete. Existing electromagnetic ray guns are in the process of being miniaturized for easy portability; one targeted use is for law enforcement agents to disable getaway vehicles and stolen cars, etcetera, by paralyzing the electrical system of the vehicle. Micro mechanisms consisting of cogs, gears, and levers (etc.) are etched out of silicon wafers and used to build microscopic machines invisible to the human eye. Entire laboratories contained in microchips are now being manufactured, capable of performing 10,000 analytical experiments at one time, making some entire conventional medical and chemical labs obsolete.

And of course, in the fields of genetics, microbiology, and other biotechnologies, knowledge is literally exploding! Take, as one big example—among numerous other biotech developments related to genetic engineering and manipulation—human cloning, now not a fantasy, but a moral, ethical, and legal controversy on Capitol Hill, both in Congress and the White House, where regulatory measures are currently being debated in a race to anticipate the misuse of the *presently available* and very real technology. (A ban on human cloning is presently in effect.) On similar cutting-edge fronts, geneticists can now produce bananas genetically engineered to produce the protein substances that are used to inoculate against polio (for one); so that immunization is accomplished by simply eating a banana. "Pharming" is a new word coined to refer to the genetic engineering of "designer cow clones" which are genetically altered to produce milk containing specific proteins that are really human medicines.[20]

Ready to compete with the divine, a new Miracle Healer has already emerged on Planet Earth, able even to reverse the age-old human scourges of *blindness* and *deafness!* We know this wonder worker by the 20th century title *High Technology.* Neuroprosthetics is the technology of electronic devices replacing failed or non-functional human organs and limbs. Reminiscent of TV's "Six Million Dollar Man," the term *bionics* is a suitable synonym for discussions of recent phenomenal developments in this field of technology which were only fantasy a few years ago in the era of the "Bionic Man." Recent news reports, which some of you may have seen, have featured the announcement of "bionic cures" for incurable conditions that Christ Jesus became renowned for undoing by some miraculous ability.

In May of 1998, *cochlear implants* were announced via a popular television news broadcast as an experimental fix for deafness. This tiny device implanted in the ear and connected to the auditory nerve leading to the brain translates sound into the electrical impulses the brain needs to understand sound. The interviewed recipient of one of these miracle devices said she is now able to understand 96% of a telephone conversation.[21]

In the same segment, reporter Gina Smith covered the development of *neurochips* by a team of scientists at Cal Tech; these combine computer chips *with living brain cells*. Their goal is to eventually develop neurochips that can be inserted into the human brain bridging the broken connections responsible for paralysis, memory loss, as well as other sensory problems. In the words of Ms. Smith, "Such technology isn't likely in the near term; then again, 20 years ago, few scientists believed that technology like that helping [the cochlear implant recipient] hear again would even be possible in their lifetimes."

Only months later in November, more late-breaking bionic news reached our living rooms—computer chip manufacturing technology now promises hope for curing blindness! This microscopic-realm technology has produced a "bionic eye." As explained by reporter James Walker, thousands (4-5,000) of microscopic solar cells are implanted onto a silicon chip (about the size of brad nail head) that would then be implanted in the back of the eye and send electrical impulses through the optic nerve to the brain, allowing the blind to see again. Trials with animals have already reportedly been successful, and in the next two years tests in people will tell whether this "miracle" can correct human blindness.[22]

On this same evening, Peter Jennings led off ABC's *World News Tonight* with "remarkable scientific news . . . of tremendous implications" which he felt some people might find "frightening." The report was on the recent success by scientists at growing *stem cells* in the laboratory, those basic embryonic cells with the peculiar ability to grow into any type of human tissue— bone, brain, blood, heart, eye, liver, etcetera—when so triggered by normal biological processes.

In this report on what Jennings said some people are likening to "finding the holy grail of biology," claims were related from researchers in Maryland and at Wisconsin University that they are learning how to "turn the cells on" to grow into just the type of human tissue they want (for grafting and organ repairs, etc.).[23] The ultimate potential, of course, is to grow complete organs for transplant. "The complication," according to reporter James Walker, "is that that the cells come from human embryos, either from fertilized eggs stored at fertility clinics or from abortions" considered by Congress as "already human beings" in legislation which currently bars federal funding for such research.

And I could go on and on, were this the major theme of this essay. I have not included the Hubble Telescope discoveries, the new X-ray telescope launched by the shuttle mission commanded by the first woman ever, and many others, the multitude of which have all been publicly announced to us in recent months via the daily news media (let alone that which is still kept secret). As everyone readily acknowledges, we are presently dealing with a literal *knowledge explosion!* (If only the public in general could also acknowledge that the Bible, in some "uncanny" way, foresaw this very historic moment in time some 2,600 years ago, and placed it squarely in the *"time of the end!"*)

All of this is capped by serious contemplation of contact with technologically-advanced extraterrestrial beings—another of those science fiction hopes of modern man, on which he has invested multibillions over the last 40-50 years in various SETI (Search for Extra-Terrestrial Intelligence) programs.

Seriously dismissing any and *all fiction* related to the possibility of making such contact, exobiology, the search for extraterrestrial life, has taken on quite a sober aspect in recent days. Once relegated almost entirely to the realm of science fiction, the notion that we are not alone in the universe has been heavily popularized by very serious scientists, such as the late astrophysicist Carl Sagan (d. Dec. 20, 1996), to such an extent that a great majority of us now strongly believe in the possibility that other life exists outside of earth. This particular non-fiction is, of course, no big news to Bible students. The Bible has always testified of this truth and, in fact, provides clear account of past instances of extraterrestrial contact in ancient times, and predicts reoccurrence of that phenomenon.[24]

In this regard, awesome developments in just the past year (1997)—whether fictional or not is hard to say—have taken place which make one shudder at the possibilities. At considerable risk to retention of their credibility, major news media have (at least) reported on a recent mass sighting of a huge unidentified flying object over Phoenix, Arizona.[25] Thousands of citizens in the Phoenix area testify, including policemen and air traffic control tower personnel (according to reports), to having witnessed the silent passage overhead of a lighted craft of such enormous dimensions that it was reckoned to have been unlike anything of earthly origin.

Again, this is not particularly alarming to students of the sacred Hebrew Scriptures, having been told well in advance to expect such phenomena, with such alerts as, *"Fearful sights and great signs shall there be from heaven (Luke 21:11)."* Which brings us to the *kanáph invasion.*

Though Hollywood has very faithfully and aggressively helped to prepare the way of the Beast—that is, to prepare the public for his arrival by its *special effects* and movie magic—still an element of incredulity lingers like an early morning fog veiling the landscape. For instance, the report of the Phoenix UFO sighting, remains a big question mark for many of us. According to the prophets, however, the *abomination of desolation* shall one day soon rapidly melt away the fog. And when it clears, the world will wonder in astonishment—to the point of *worship!*

The arrival of this abomination, according to the glimpse of it I glean from the prophecies of Daniel, shall leave us as awestruck as a visit to the city of Hiroshima would have in the days immediately following the devastating drop of the atom bomb there in 1945. Desolation of that sort (if you can even imagine the sight; I have only seen photos) is what is conveyed by the meaning of the word *shamém*, the Hebrew word which the English translators evidently felt the word "desolate" (or desolation) best represented. *Shamém* denotes a sense of devastation that leaves one *stunned, stupefied, astonished,* and also *appalled.*

Beyond even that, and seemingly encrypted in the Hebrew wording used to announce the appearance of the "abomination" (in Dan.9:27), is the phrase *"kanáph shiquwtsiym"*—describing the initial desolation. It was translated as *"the overspreading of abominations."* Interestingly enough, and consistent with the highly probable hypothesis I embrace that the Antichrist Beast will be connected with and empowered by extraterrestrials—namely, the Alien of all aliens[26]—the term "overspreading" suggests an *aerial* or *flying* character to his arrival at the time he invades Jerusalem to terminate the temple sacrifices. Whether by conventional aircraft, or something otherworldly, the word *kanáph* hints at an *over*-spreading that, it seems, must surely involve an aerial invasion. Though *kanáph* can refer to a military wing (another anticipated facet of his take-over, incidentally), in the overwhelming majority of cases it is used to refer to wings (for flying) and flying fowl. Thus, it is a very small stretch indeed to imagine the abomination coming on the wings of the "Mother

Ship" (to use the words of the Rev. Louis Farrakhan).

Whatever the case, I find it awfully intriguing that so much of Hollywood's movie magic (and lavish budgets) is devoted these days to elaborating images of aliens and extraterrestrials. We are fed a steady diet of these alien-oriented sci-fi productions both in the box office theaters as well as in our home theaters via television. We can't seem to get enough of the theme. My contention is that a key and timely principle is at work in these last days which is as ancient as the practice it has roots in—that of heralding, such as by forerunner or harbinger. Though even unwittingly to the scriptwriters and production chiefs, Hollywood is playing a key role in preparing the way of the Beast, very much like John the Baptist was commissioned to "prepare the way of the Messiah."

Our psyches and sensibilities are being conditioned by the *"prince of the power of the air, the spirit that now worketh in the children of disobedience,"* as Apostle Paul put it, to accept and welcome the Abomination. The task of a herald is that of making ready an appropriate public response in advance of the arrival of a dignitary or other official, etc. I too, by means of this "Voice of the 7th Angel" narration have undertaken to help prepare an appropriate response to the conditions of the days in which we live, and to the associated occurrences prophesied for our time (of the end). Monumental events are about to overwhelm us with stunning haste; and evidently, the Transdimensional Alien Intellect senses the same urgency, because his inspired minions are certainly working overtime to prepare our mentalities and environment for his epiphany.[27]

Hi-tech Synthetic God

To complete the synopsis of the final "week's" bizarre sequence of events, *the abomination of desolation* comes now under closer examination. (Stipulating that great tribulation—such as has never been since the beginning of the world, nor ever again shall be—would follow the sight of this detestable and sacrilegious displacement of holiness from the holy place when it stands *"where it ought not,"* Christ Yeshua referred us back to Daniel for clues about this last-hour phenomenon.) In the eyes of the world, naturally, there will be nothing particularly abominable, unholy, or despicable about this high-tech marvel of "human" achievement. In fact, the people of the world will be persuaded to worship this fabulous fabrication of their own fingers and work of their own hands. They themselves will be induced to provide materials, engineering and technology for its construction.[28]

This phenomenal product of high science and technology (no longer sci-fi fantasy), in large part, may likely be attributable to *technology transfer* from contact with extraterrestrials (as already hinted) who then also empower the man-god after whom it is fashioned.[29] Remember that, by some uncanny power, the very potent usher, prime advocate and power-broker (a.k.a. the false prophet) of the Antichrist will "give *life* unto the image of the beast!" In any event, the associated prophetic scriptures of Daniel, John the Revelator, and Christ concerning *the abomination of desolation* depict an image or some fabricated facsimile erected to a blasphemous and powerful political figure which is *"made" (Rev.13:14), "set up" (Dan.12:11), "placed" (Dan.11:31), "stands" (Mrk.13:14), "lives" and "speaks" (Rev.13:15).*

Unlike the graven images—carved or hand-fashioned idols—of all previous ages and types which were inanimate and silent, this hi-tech image will not only speak and display animation, but will have powers of cognition and awareness of the whereabouts of the human subjects who will be coerced to worship it. In essence, it will be able to "see," recognize, identify, and track every individual on planet Earth (esp. those who possess *the Mark*). And, those who refuse the Mark, refuse to worship the image (of the new supreme world ruler), and decline to pledge allegiance to or to participate in the new world order will be identified and tracked for reprogramming or termination. (Thus begins the great tribulation.)

Lest we doubt the feasibility of such an imminent technological wonder, let us consider the recent announcement by Bill Gates of Microsoft Corporation (computer software) fame, that within ten years computers will see, hear, learn, and speak—presumably at levels beyond present capabilities, which already include moderate-capacity voice recognition and voice synthesis. As reported by CBS Telenoticias (September 1996), Gates, now the wealthiest man in America, according to Forbes magazine, is already committing $2 billion a year in research toward the development and refining of these computer technologies.

This calls to remembrance the words of Daniel (c. 550 BCE) in chapter 11 of his book regarding the king who rules with unchecked will and whim, one who exalts himself above every god, honoring a *strange god* whom his ancestors knew not *"with gold and silver, and with precious stones, and pleasant things."* (Please note, no suggestion is even hinted that Gates should be associated with the beast or the prince of the covenant; rather, that great sums of wealth are and will be further committed to fulfillment of these prophecies.)

In terms of images and very hi-tech idolatry, *precious stones* are already being utilized in the projection of ethereal, yet almost life-like, electronic 3-dimensional images that fascinate and enchant modern-day audiences. No longer are these simply futuristic fantasies featured in science fiction movies and film productions, such as Star Trek. This image generation technology is reportedly (though unconfirmed by this author) now used by high class department stores in New York City in place of mannequins to model clothing. These computer-controlled holographic images (in 3-D)—an already operational technology in the process of refinement to incorporate full animation—are generated by the use of lasers fabricated from *precious stones. Ruby rods* are utilized as the core material in the optically pumped, pulsed lasers used in holographic technology. The sophisticated system used to create the images is driven by computers that control the precise timing of the light pulses, which are measured in nanoseconds (millionths of a second).

The coupling of holographic technology with high-speed computer technology is the perfect hi-tech marriage capable of fulfilling the apocalyptic vision of Apostle John in Revelation 13. Whatever the technology used, the image is intimately linked to the mandated veneration of the Antichrist by every would-be citizen of the new world order (under penalty of death) and the receiving of his mark—either in the right hand or forehead. The tracking technology built into the image will undoubtedly link everyone who is marked (perhaps with a type of bionic implant) and possibly even receive "radioed" alert signals back at image central processor headquarters at the sighting of or contact with an unmarked dissident.

Unquestionably though, installation of the abomination of desolation ushers in the worldwide initiative to unify the economies (and political systems) of all the nations of Earth into one central cashless system which functions much like the credit card systems of VISA, Mastercard, and American Express, etcetera—on unique numerical account identifiers issued to individual account holders. According to Revelation 13, every individual on earth will be forced or seduced into taking a number and/or a mark in order to participate in business, in the marketplace, or in the simplest of trading transactions. No purchase or sale of any goods or services will be legally transacted without the identifier by anyone, regardless of status or station in life.

Every transaction involving "money" will soon be conducted without cash, much as it is already with credit and debit cards. The "currency" of the new global establishment will be *the mark, the number, or the name* of the Führer of the new Global Federation of Earth. Groceries, gasoline, or medical services; clothing, household items or electronic goods; much less autos, houses, or furnishings will not be purchased without it. Wages, salaries, or other compensations will not be paid or collected without it, not to mention taxes. Utility bills, bank loans, or mortgages will not be negotiated without it. Driver's licenses, passports, airplane tickets, or vehicle registrations will not be issued without it. It will be the ultimate centralization and international control mechanism ever devised, or heretofore even possible!

Until the present-day age of electronic computers (now everyday household items in 30% of American homes), and now the incredibly fast generation of *supercomputers* (the fastest known computers in the world), it would have been tactically impossible to track the world's 6 billion inhabitants and all of their individual transactions on a round-the-clock daily basis. The capacity and potential for this exceeding technological achievement is now a very clear and present danger. Today's supercomputers currently provide this never-before-conceivable technological capability.

First developed by Seymour R. Cray, an American electronics engineer, the Cray-1 model in 1976 could perform 240 million calculations in one second. Now, only 20 years later those speeds have not doubled, tripled, or quadrupled, but are more than 1000% faster (some, like the ETA-10, more than 40 times faster). According to the *Encyclopaedia Britannica*, the Cray Y-MP is capable of 3 billion calculations per second; and, at nearly 3 times that speed, the ETA-10 is capable of performing 10,000,000,000 per second.

Late-breaking, headline news reported on October 11, 1996, on the front page of the Los Alamos Monitor, the daily newspaper published in the birthplace of the Cray supercomputer, Los Alamos, New Mexico, announced major new federal funding for development of another generation of supercomputers with 300 times more computing power than the ETA-10. According to the article, the U.S. Department of Energy awarded $110.5 million to build a computer at Los Alamos National Laboratory capable of more than three trillion (3 to 5,000,000,000,000) calculations per second, to be in operation by December 1998.[30]

So, in only 22 years, the power of the world's fastest computers will have increased more than 12,500 times. And, in terms of data/information storage, even *home computers* are now available with more than 8 gigabytes (8 billion bytes, which will probably more than triple by the time this book is published) of internal storage capacity, enough to store as much information as would be contained in about 32 complete sets of the *Encyclopaedia Britannica*; that's 44 million words contained in *each set* of thirty-two printed volumes! To give you some idea of the speed and processing power of "Blue Mountain," the new Los Alamos computing marvel discussed in the previous paragraph, as compared to a typical home or office computer, it will operate about 100 million times faster, which is far beyond my capacity to even conceive or imagine! President Clinton, in his recent February, 1997 visit to Los Alamos, put it another way: according to his calculations, "That's as many calculations *per second* as you or I with a hand-held calculator could perform in 32 million years."

In even later late-breaking news from Los Alamos, the lab's top nuclear weapons official, Stephen Younger in an interview with Keith Easthouse of the *Santa Fe New Mexican* (12/24/97 edition), spoke in some detail of the "generation-after-next system." Slated for installed in no more than 10 years, this super supercomputer will be capable of 100 trillion calculations per second. According to Younger as per the article, "The supercomputer may allow for other achievements that have previously only existed in the realm of science fiction—such as the projection of three-dimensional 'holographic' images and computers that can carry on conversations with humans."

On another front very strategic to the function of the hi-tech speaking image of the Antichrist, which will also seek out dissidents for termination, is the advent of worldwide satellite and other advanced electronic telecommunications technologies. These have made possible the instantaneous linkage of almost every part of Earth with any other part of the globe. Intelsat, the international telecommunications satellite network, was launched in 1964 as a joint venture of 11 countries; it now includes over 125 with 500 earth stations receiving and transmitting communications signals. In addition, there are numerous domestic satellite systems operated by individual countries, such as Canada, Russia, Japan, the USA, etc., as well as military systems of various countries that fill the skies with electromagnetic signals that carry not only telephone conversations and television programs, but also computer-generated data. And the number and capabilities of these systems grow each year.

It is easy to see that what was never before possible in the history of humankind, especially in terms of centralized global tracking and manipulation of the masses, has become a fearful and awe-inspiring reality in just the last 2 decades.

At the time of the Apostle John (c. 90 CE), the possibility for fulfillment of the prophetic vision of Revelation 13 was of a scale far beyond even the conception of the most imaginative of visionaries. How could such a sweeping planetary system as the Apocalypse describes ever be achieved?

Well, these days, the actual fabrication of the dream is only down the hallway from imagination. Successful tissue generation technologies now hold promise even for human organ synthesis, which could be used to regenerate damaged tissue, thereby curing and healing fatal injuries and wounds. The world is prepared to welcome the regeneration from death of an assassinated hero as a matter of high "science," especially if he promises to share the healing and life-saving technology with all his worshipping fans.

Even mind-blowing, miraculous wonders from the heavens are now man-made possibilities. For example, the Galileo planetary exploration spacecraft recently arrived and now in orbit around Jupiter is said to be carrying 49 pounds of plutonium (as power source for its mechanisms, controls, and electrical equipment). Speculation (by William Clark in his book *Behold a Pale Horse*) has it that it could be used as a nuclear trigger device which, when plunged into the enormous hydrogen/helium mass of Jupiter and then detonated, would ignite a nuclear fusion reaction of that hydrogen mass (almost 90% hydrogen, like the sun) which could be self-sustaining and result in another small sun in our sky. Astonishing! But then it's been 30 years ago that men walked *on the moon!* These days, we find that fabrication of the dream is now only a door or two down the hall from imagination; but, quite often those doors are bolted shut with the word "Classified" plaqued across them.

Moreover, beyond mere man-made wonders, the horizon is looming with promise of new technological discoveries and bizarre, unearthly innovations to be garnered or transferred, as suggested earlier, from beings of origins beyond earth. In fact, that same horizon rumbles with loud rumor of that very thing already going on in top-secret environments and under classified conditions. But, who knows? Since knowledge is power, it would violate the oligarchical agenda of the government to release its secrets and relinquish its ability to maintain control of the masses dependent upon it.

But, regardless of top secret classifications, or not, *"the eyes of the LORD are in every place, beholding the evil and the good,"* and nothing escapes the scrutiny of the Spirit of Truth. Christ promised that that Spirit would show us things to come, if we qualified as disciples of Truth. And we have seen from our study that the Truth Disciples of 2,000 years ago had phenomenally far-reaching insights into the very days in which we live. I wonder how they knew?

Hi-tech, modern-day prognosticators of a mere week in advance of weather forecasts require multimillion-dollar satellite, radar, and computer systems to guess at a few days worth of weather. The God of the Hebrews knew what the weather and every other detail of our endtime lives would be like before we were even born (in fact since the foundation of the world). [31]

Produce your cause, saith the LORD; bring forth your strong reasons, saith the King of Jacob. Let them bring them forth, and shew us what shall happen: let them shew the former things, what they be, that we may consider them, and know the latter end of them; or declare us things for to come. Shew the things that are to come hereafter, that we may know that ye are gods: yea, do good, or do evil, that we may be dismayed, and behold it together. Behold, ye are of nothing, and your work of nought: an abomination is he that chooseth you. . . . Who hath declared from the beginning, that we may know? and beforetime, that we may say, He is righteous? yea, there is none that sheweth, yea, there is none that declareth, yea, there is none that heareth your words. . . . For I beheld, and there was no man; even among them, and there was no counsellor, that, when I asked of them, could answer a word. Behold, they are all vanity; their works are nothing: their molten images [computers of molten glass, plastic, and metal] are wind and confusion.—Isaiah 41:21-29

Remember the former things of old: for I am God, and there is none else; I am God, and there is none like me, declaring the end from the beginning, and from ancient times the things that are not yet done, saying, My counsel shall stand, and I will do all my pleasure:—Isaiah 46:9-10

7

THE FUNDAMENTAL DREAD

Then shall be great tribulation, such as was not since the beginning of the
world to this time, no, nor ever shall be. And except those days should be
shortened, there should no flesh be saved: but for the elect's sake those
days shall be shortened.—Matthew 24:21-22
For in those days shall be affliction, such as was not from the beginning of
the creation which God created unto this time, neither shall be.
—Mark 13:19
And at that time shall Michael stand up, the great prince which standeth for
the children of thy people: and there shall be a time of trouble,
such as never was since there was a nation even to that same time:
and at that time thy people shall be delivered,
every one that shall be found written in the book.—Daniel 12:1
Because thou hast kept the word of my patience, I also will keep thee from
the hour of temptation, which shall come upon all the world, to try them
that dwell upon the earth.—Revelation 3:10

Past is Prologue

Appearance on the world scene of the notorious Abomination of Desolation will herald a period of persecution, oppression, affliction, trouble, and distress such as has never before been experienced upon earth. Although widespread international adversities will erupt during this calamitous period, this afflictive event falls particularly hard upon certain targeted groups of people (as identified in earlier chapters). The prophecies given by Messiah and others in the Bible, which we'll now proceed to examine further make reference to a HOLOCAUST of all holocausts yet to come, one surpassing, if imaginable, what we have already witnessed in this severely troubled century of ours.

Some folks may relate the concept of holocaust to the nuclear ravages of both Nagasaki and Hiroshima, and with good reason, for the rational mind can consider them nothing less. We have yet to see whether other similar desolations of this nature shall yet occur again on earth. Though the Scriptures are not clear on the issue, they hint very strongly at the possibility. The book of the prophet Zechariah describes a destructive plague of such unimaginable ferocity and power that the flesh of a victim is consumed off the bones in a flash of such intensity that it all occurs before the victim even hits the ground; while still standing upon the feet, eyes and tongues vaporize in their sockets and mouths, and flesh off the bones. Prior to the mid-1940's, such a horror may have been very hard to imagine, but not anymore.

This very generation, more than any other, can now relate to such horrific power; hardly more than 50 years ago, men actually witnessed the unleashing of such forces. Temperatures in the tens of millions of degrees, generated in only a millionth of a second in the nuclear blast of a modern atomic weapon, are known to even fuse bones together. However, the plague that Zechariah describes is not attributed to the handiwork of man, but to a proprietary power of YHWH Himself (the architect, after all, of all atomic, as well as non-nuclear, forces).[1]

For many others, the term "holocaust" with a capital H calls to remembrance the atrocities of Hitler and the Nazis. Yet, the implication in the oracles of Scripture is overwhelming that even *that* ghastly historical monument to human brutality shall be soon overshadowed. On the basis of the prophecies, I will even venture to say (without intending offense or any insensitivity) that much of the Holocaust of the Nazi and Stalinist eras can be reckoned "tame" and "humane" compared to what is yet to come.

Moreover, it is clearly indicated in the passages referenced above that the brunt of the tribulation will most immediately strike those who reside in the region of *Judea*—overlaid today by the southern portion of what is politically called the West Bank—over which Jerusalem was capital in ancient times. And, the onslaught of this great storm of calamity will be with such sweeping fury that fleeing to the hills for your life will be of utmost urgency. So critical will it be that attempting to gather up personal effects out of one's house for the flight into the wilderness will fatally compromise or sabotage any escape whatsoever—probably resulting in death or, even worse, capture.[2]

That particular region is already extremely tense in terms of a continuous hostile threat to the safety and well-being of the minority Jewish population inhabiting such cities as Hebron in the heart of the region. As of the date of this writing, outbreaks of ethnic violence have occurred in Israel said to be the worst in 30 years. Rock-throwing, firebomb-hurling Palestinians, joined by police of the Palestinian Authority with automatic weapons, have engaged in numerous assaults on Israeli soldiers and army field outposts, such as the one stationed in the city of Hebron to protect the 450 Israeli settlers there.

These recent attacks were triggered by the opening of an archaeological tunnel site near the Al Aqsa mosque in Jerusalem and were ostensibly motivated by Palestinian frustration over supposed Israeli "stalling" and "non-compliance" with peace accord agreements. So you see, extreme bitterness and vengeful, jealous hatred is already lethally seething there. And when the desolation and treading down of Jerusalem and the holy place occurs, the anti-Jew pathology will rage with such an angry vengeance that even pregnant women and mothers with nursing infants will see no mercy.[3]

Marked by an initial onslaught of severe hostility particularly upon the residents of Jerusalem and Judea, the *great tribulation* is spoken of as a period of holocaust in which all "flesh" would perish were it not for divine intervention to shorten those days. Again however, Sabbath observers in particular—who would be especially unprepared for such an event on such a day—are admonished by the Master to pray that it not break out at such a time. The obvious indication is that Jerusalem and the Jews of Israel will be the frontline targets.

Following this invasion of Jerusalem, for the next three-and-one-half years (1260 days), the desperate struggle for control and global domination by the Despot of All Ages takes on a grisly tyrannical twist, which even involves *beheading* as a form of punishment and dissident deterrence.[4] During this notorious period of prophetic history, the Christians shall not this time escape the appointed holocaust of all holocausts, unless they fall to kiss the "neo-Hitlerian" feet of the coming Son of Perdition and take his nefarious name or his mark of cowardly conformity. No longer will they find cover in the shadows of their churches, temples, and cathedrals. For those will either become their mass graves and funeral pyres *or* their centers of registration and reprogramming in the reverence and worship of the great new "messiah" of prosperity, power and glory (mistake him not!—see Chapter 10).

Great Tribulation Politics and Power Struggles

During those three-and-a-half years, two high-profile opponents of the new, politically-adjusted Hitlerian-style regime will arise onto the worldwide public square (the "iconoclasts" introduced in Chapter 4). They shall boldly confront and vehemently oppose the policies and practices of the recently-emerged, wonder-working, and very captivating Emperor of Earth 2000. Clothed in sackcloth garments they will lead the denunciation and repudiation of the New Humanist Empire of Earth and its evil new champion.

These two potent prophets of YHWH will be supernaturally empowered to countervail the diabolical program and schemes of the Antichrist by means of their catastrophic curses upon the blasphemers, God-haters, and persecutors of the righteous believers.[5] They in turn will be hated and dreaded for withholding rain, turning the waters of earth to blood, perhaps calling meteoroid bombardments out of space, as well as for various other curses proclaimed at their discretion as often as necessary to turn the nations of earth from their wickedness. As witnesses to the sovereignty and might of the Creator, they will likely command the power of God at the hand of the angels of the Seven Trumpets[6] to urge the endtime societies to repentance.[7]

Beside the wars waged by the new anti-God global power broker to dominate the international political scene—such as in the crushing conquest of 3 members of a newly-merged, ten-state super confederacy of an East-West bloc of nations—he must further contend with these two sackclothed prophets. Not only so, but these two shall be joined by their own dissident following, an innumerable number of spiritual comrades all of whom totally renounce participation in the new diabolical order of man-worship and hi-tech secularism. This powerful, warmongering "little horn" will subsequently conduct a murderous war of repression upon them all, Jew and Christian alike, reviving the practice of decapitation as a form of execution of these "infidels" (which, as you may already know, is their official Koranic classification, in the nations of Islam).

The pertinent passages of Scripture that support these conclusions come from the prophecies of Daniel and Revelation. They are provided below with the symbolism explained in the bracketed insertions; brackets are mine.

First, let us look at the prophecies about the East-West super-bloc of endtime nations:

There is a God in heaven that revealeth secrets, and maketh known to the king Nebuchadnezzar [c. 600 BCE] *what shall be in the latter days. Thy dream, and the visions of thy head upon thy bed, are these. . . .*

Thou, O king, sawest, and behold a great image. This great image, whose brightness was excellent, stood before thee; and the form thereof was terrible. This image's head was of fine gold, his breast and his arms of silver, his belly and his thighs of brass, his legs of iron, his feet part of iron and part of clay. Thou sawest till that a stone was cut out without hands, which smote the image upon his feet that were of iron and clay, and brake them to pieces. Then was the iron, the clay, the brass, the silver, and the gold, broken to pieces together, and became like the chaff of the summer threshingfloors; and the wind carried them away, that no place was found for them: and the stone that smote the image became a great mountain, and filled the whole earth. This is the dream; and we will tell the interpretation thereof before the king. . . .

Thou [king Nebuchadnezzar] *art this head of gold* [emperor of Babylon]. *And after thee shall arise another kingdom inferior to thee* [silver; with two arms = allied Medes & Persians], *and another third kingdom of brass* [Greece], *which shall bear rule over all the earth. And the fourth kingdom shall be strong as iron* [Rome; Holy Roman Empire of **west**, and Byzantine Empire of **east** = its 2 legs]: *forasmuch as iron breaketh in pieces and subdueth all things: and as iron that breaketh all these, shall it break in pieces and bruise* [typical Rome; ravaging, sweeping, devastating and brutal]. *And whereas thou sawest the feet and toes* [the latter-day extremities; with ten toes], *part of potters' clay, and part of iron, the kingdom shall be divided* [unlikely & incompatible confederacy]; *but there shall be in it of the strength of the iron* [militaristic authoritarianism], *forasmuch as thou sawest the iron mixed with miry clay. And as the toes of the feet were part of iron, and part of clay, so the kingdom shall be partly strong, and partly broken* [containing powerful elements, yet somewhat fragmented].

And whereas thou sawest iron [militant, law-based, authoritarian republics] *mixed with miry clay* [wishy-washy, carnal, convenience-driven, majority-whim democracies], *they shall mingle themselves with the seed of men* [note that even many despotic, authoritarian "republics" of the East & Middle East hold populace-pleasing "elections"]: *but they shall not cleave one to another, even as iron is not mixed with clay* [the bonds of confederacy will be politically incompatible, non-cohesive, and problematic].

And in the days of these kings [the endtime extremity of history] *shall the God of heaven set up a kingdom* [the New World Order of Zion], *which shall never be destroyed: and the kingdom shall not be left to other people* [never supplanted or overthrown; permanent], *but it shall break in pieces and consume all these kingdoms* [entirely vanquish all], *and it shall stand for ever.—Daniel 2:28-44*

We see from this passage out of Daniel chapter 2 that a ten-state confederacy of highly dissimilar political composition is predicted to emerge in the latter days. At the historical extremities of the two-legged Roman Empire; after centuries of Caesars, kaisers, tsars, and czars (until 1917), and Byzantines and Ottomans (also 'til 1917), and after first, second, and "third" Reichs ('til 1945), at last we are to see the end of man's iniquitous history. But this will not be without the ultimate in atrocities and the holocaust of the "Fourth Reich," which, after their utter abolishment, will be followed in the end, thank God, by the Ultimate Kingdom of Messiah! Finally, the *"desire of all nations"* spoken of by Haggai the prophet shall at last be established upon earth.[8]

The prophet Daniel goes on in chapter 7 of his book, this time to tell his own dream and "psychic" glimpse into the future, rather than that of the king of Babylon. In his personal revelation, greater and more intimate detail of the latter days is given, *especially including the fate of God's people* at the hands of the Antichrist. Again, the brackets indicate my own insertions.

In the first year of Belshazzar king of Babylon [c. 540 BCE] *Daniel had a dream and visions of his head upon his bed: then he wrote the dream, and told the sum of the matters. Daniel spake and said, I saw in my vision by night, and, and, behold, the four winds of the heaven* [spiritual forces, which are the invisible powers behind worldly political hegemonies] *strove upon the great sea* [repository of evil spirits].

And four great beasts [worldly political powers] *came up from the sea, diverse one from another. The first was like a lion, and had eagle's wings* [regal and exalted Babylon, contemporary to Daniel]: *I beheld till the wings thereof were plucked, and it was lifted up from the earth, and made stand upon the feet as a man, and a man's heart was given to it* [speaking of the dramatic conversion of Nebuchadnezzar]. *And behold another beast, a second, like to a bear* [Medo-Persia, specifically named in Daniel chapter 8], *and it raised up itself on one side* [dominant Persians], *and it had three ribs in the mouth of it between the teeth of it* [having devoured predecessors Babylon, Assyria, and Egypt]: *and they said thus unto it, Arise, devour much flesh. After this I beheld, and lo another, like a leopard, which had upon the back of it four wings of a fowl* [Greece, also named in Dan.8; powerfully fierce and swift under Alexander the Great]; *the beast had also four heads* [four provincial divisions—Macedonia/Greece, Egypt, Syria, and Anatolia/Turkey]; *and dominion was given to it* [with significant legacy of influence even today].

After this I saw in the night visions, and behold a fourth beast, dreadful and terrible, and strong exceedingly; and it had great iron teeth [Rome; exceeded in military, engineering, and political prowess]: *it devoured and brake in pieces, and stamped the residue with the feet of it* [brutally crushed all opposition and uprising, as with the Jews and Jerusalem in both 69-70 AD & 132, but particularly the **endtime remnant** of the saints]: *and it was diverse from all the beasts that were before it* [certainly in vastness and might; a professional standing army; but mostly for its unique *res publica*, its institution of public government, constitutional republicanism]; *and it had ten horns* [endtime legacy of political progeny, 10 latter day nations].

I considered the horns, and, behold, there came up among them another little horn [an eleventh spontaneous political figure to head up the ten], *before whom there were three of the first horns plucked up by the roots* [three utterly vanquished]: *and, behold, in this horn were eyes like the eyes of man, and a mouth speaking great things* [personified political entity].

I beheld till the thrones [worldly political dominions] *were cast down* [thoroughly abolished], *and the Ancient of days did sit* [Messiah & His New World Order], *whose garment was white as snow, and the hair of his head like the pure wool: his throne was like the fiery flame, and his wheels as burning fire. A fiery stream issued and came forth from before him: thousand thousands ministered unto him, and ten thousand times ten thousand stood before him: the judgment was set, and the books were opened.*

I beheld then because of the voice of the great words which the horn spake [outrageous boastings of the bombastic demagogue]: *I beheld even till the beast was slain, and his body destroyed, and given to the burning flame* [see Rev. 19:19-20]. *As concerning the rest of the beasts, they had their dominion taken away* [temporal regimes collapsed]: *yet their lives were prolonged for a season and time* [cultural and political legacies endured].—*Daniel 7:1-12*

Interpretation:

I Daniel was grieved in my spirit in the midst of my body, and the visions of my head troubled me. I came near unto one of [the angels] that stood by, and asked him the truth of all this. So he told me, and made me know the interpretation of the things.

These great beasts, which are four, are four kings [empires, political do-
minions], *which shall arise out of the earth. But the saints of the most High
shall take the kingdom, and possess the kingdom for ever, even for ever and
ever* [to ultimately be the indisputable, inalienable, invincible governors of Earth].

Then I would know the truth of the fourth beast [being particularly in-
trigued by Rome to be, several hundred years later], *which was diverse from
all the others, exceeding dreadful, whose teeth were of iron, and his nails of
brass; which devoured, brake in pieces, and stamped the residue with his
feet; and of the ten horns that were in his head, and of the other* [little horn]
*which came up, and before whom three fell; even of that horn that had eyes,
and a mouth that spake very great things, whose look was more stout than his
fellows* [more outstanding]. *I beheld, and the same horn made war with the
saints, and prevailed against them; until the Ancient of days came, and judgment was given to the saints of the most High; and the time came that the
saints possessed the kingdom.*

Thus he said, The fourth beast shall be the fourth kingdom upon earth [in
chronological order of conquest from the time of Daniel in Babylon], *which
shall be diverse from all kingdoms, and shall devour the whole earth, and
shall tread it down, and break it in pieces* [as Rome certainly did].

And the ten horns out of this kingdom are ten kings that shall arise [fu-
ture states at the extremities of history; part of iron and part of clay, according
to Daniel chapter 2]: *and another shall rise after them; and he shall be diverse from the first* [the little-horn Antichrist, distinctly unique and apart],
*and he shall subdue three kings. And he shall speak great words against the
most High* [the boastful, high-minded blasphemies to which I have so often
referred in characterizing this Antichrist], *and shall wear out* [afflict, lay waste,
consume] *the saints of the most High, and think to change times and laws*
[new calendar and legal codes—perhaps in part as restructuring and recovery
from the coming dreaded Y2K computer calamity in the year 2000]: *and they*
[the worshippers of YHWH] *shall be given into his hand* [to be persecuted]
until a time [1 year] *and times* [plus 2 years] *and the dividing of time* [plus
half a year].

But the judgment shall sit, and they [the persecuted adherents of the Law
and Faith of YHWH] *shall take away his dominion, to consume and to destroy
it unto the end* [totally annihilate and abolish the Secular Order of the Beast].
*And the kingdom and dominion, and the greatness of the kingdom under the
whole heaven, shall be given to the people of the saints of the most High,*

whose kingdom is an everlasting kingdom, and all dominions shall serve and obey him [the Most High].—*Daniel 7:15-27*

Six times the book of Revelation (c. 600 years later) mentions the *same ten horns* as Daniel. The first appearance in the Apocalypse of these horns is in the chapter 12 vision of the adversarial conflict between the cherished nation of YHWH and her "nemesis," the great red Dragon: *"And there appeared another wonder in heaven; and behold a great red dragon, having seven heads and ten horns, and seven crowns upon his heads (Revelation 12:3)."* The second instance was in John's vision of the dual-beast regime of the Antichrist and his powerful prophet, detailed in Revelation 13: *"And I stood upon the sand of the sea, and saw a beast rise up out of the sea, having seven heads and ten horns, and upon his horns ten crowns, and upon his heads the name of blasphemy (Revelation 13:1)."*

In the remaining four instances, John sees these same ten horns upon the same spiritual, seven-headed, anti-God Dragon, but with additional key particulars. This famous revelation details the symbiotic relationship of this blasphemous titanic nemesis of the chosen people with their other more worldly rival-counterpart, the Great Whore of Revelation 17; and it stipulates that these ten final-hour political entities exert global authority and power when they confederate under the Beast: *"So he carried me away in the spirit into the wilderness: and I saw a woman sit upon a scarlet coloured beast, full of names of blasphemy, having seven heads and ten horns. . . . And the angel said unto me, Wherefore didst thou marvel? I will tell thee the mystery of the woman, and of the beast that carrieth her, which hath the seven heads and ten horns. . . . And the ten horns which thou sawest are ten kings, which have received no kingdom as yet; but receive power as kings one hour with the beast. . . . And the ten horns which thou sawest upon the beast, these shall hate the whore, and shall make her desolate and naked, and shall eat her flesh, and burn her with fire (Revelation 17:3-16)."*

By way of these six references in the context of their related passages, John establishes that: (1) the little-horn-dominated alliance of Daniel's prophecy is the seventh and final pagan world empire of planet Earth (relative to Israel-Palestine centrism); (2) the blasphemous "little horn" of Daniel's vision is the same entity identified as "the beast" of chapter 13 of Revelation who tyrannizes the planet *for 42 months* (3½ years), during which he "makes war with the saints, and overcomes them"; and (3) the little horn/beast of blasphemy is of the *same essence as the Devil* and is actually Satan incarnate, intent upon subjugating every human soul under his dominion and destroying every soul who opposes his agenda—all the People of the Book, Jew and Christian alike.[9]

The Apocalypse thus expands more fully upon the vision of this endtime ten-nation confederacy than Daniel. In it, John reveals that all ten of these nations (three of them having been utterly overthrown) turn over their military might and political authority to the Beast. The new superstate formed by this alliance merges with the "indomitable" and death-defying Caliph of Marvels in a campaign to overthrow and destroy the Whore (of Revelation 17-18) which has so long dominated (and oppressed) them and all the other inhabitants of Earth. And finally, this God-hating coalition of nations also joins the Beast for the climactic stellar war of all ages—the final-hour war of insurgency and resistance against the return of the intergalactic Founder of Earth coming to repossess and govern His creation.

Very commonly known as the Battle of Armageddon, this massive conflict, probably involving an army of at least 200 million troops—most likely led and consisting primarily of red and Islamic hordes, previously amassed to purge the planet of all vestiges of whorish First-world (Western) civilization[10]—will represent the climax and consummation of 3½ years of persecution and genocide against the cultures of saints who worship the Creator.

The Politics of Persecution

Tragically, the mammonized Judeo-Christian cultures of the hedonistic First World—in the end, having forsaken loyal love for the Provider and Source of their prosperity—will have at length succeeded in provoking their namesake God to irreconcilable jealousy by their unmitigated worship of their material prosperity and providence.[11] This waxing adultery of spirit and soul has (already) rendered those reprobate societies corrupt, egotistical, degenerate, perverse and subject to judgment and destruction.[12]

Even *more tragic*, is that the world associates the idolatrous materialism of the West with the names of Christ, Adonai (YHWH), and GOD; and no less, those too who genuinely take these names in *faithful espousal* to the Creator have been reckoned alike with those religiously reprobate cultures; such that no aspect of the holy remains unprofaned or unbesmirched. All of this further serving to constitute cause for spite, provide rationale for persecution, and *"give occasion to the enemies of the LORD to blaspheme (2 Sam., chap. 2)."*

Thus, the genocidal aspect of this Period of Purging will not only represent a malicious campaign of hateful, self-righteous persecution of those who truly honor God, *but also* a vengeful, retributive assailing of institutionalized hypocrisy (daughter of the materialist religions of the established order).[13] The Whore will be hated as well as the saints. Not only will the corruption of the rapturist epicurean religious institutions be eradicated in its furnace of Great Tribulation, but individual integrity too will emerge refined from hedonist impurities and Establishment dross. In just such manner shall we see the Great Tribulation take on its furious, fierce and fiery aspect; and in the fullest sense, it shall constitute the thorough purging of all spurious belief, resulting in the ultimate refinement of the true-gold saints.

Great but Short, yet All-inclusive Tribulation

As previously iterated in earlier chapters, the dreaded Great Tribulation is clearly intended to afflict the entire world, most definitely including all believers (saints) who inhabit the earth when it erupts. Some will endure differing degrees of affliction than others; some will escape to wilderness refuge and escape the severest aspects; others will indeed suffer capture, confiscation of all worldly goods and assets, imprisonment, torture, and yes, capital execution. But without a quibble or doubt whatsoever, it is not meant merely as a period of punishment or affliction upon the pagan societies of earth. In fact, an honest and courageous study of the prophecies related to this abbreviated three-and-a-half-year period of future history reveals that one of the most significant features of that tribulation is a war of horrible persecution perpetrated by the Beast *specifically upon the saints.*[14]

The verses we cited earlier in this chapter from chapter 7 of Daniel's prophecy clearly show that the boastful blaspheming little horn *"makes war with the saints . . . wears them out"* and *"prevails against them"* for a period of *"a time (1 year), times (2 years), and the dividing of time (half year)."* In perfect parallel to Daniel, Revelation illuminates the scenario even more vividly in this respect by specifying that this same blaspheming beast is empowered for a limited period of *42 months,* during which he subsequently proceeds to *"make war with the saints, and to overcome them."*[15] And, lest any uncertainty or confusion might persist about the period of war, persecution and great tribulation to be suffered by the saints, Revelation chapter 12 clarifies the issue with even greater specificity:

And there appeared a great wonder in heaven; a woman clothed with the sun [bride of the Creator] *and the moon* [symbol of the ruler of darkness] *under her feet,*[16] *and upon her head a crown of twelve stars* [probably the preeminent Apostles of the Lamb]:[17] *And she being with child* [bearing the promised Seed] *cried, travailing in birth, and pained to be delivered.*

And there appeared another wonder in heaven; and behold a great red dragon, having seven heads [trans-historical governments (relative to the Holy Land) through which Satan exerts his power and influence] *and ten horns* [ten last political dominions], *and seven crowns* [imperial powers] *upon his heads. And his tail drew the third part of the stars of heaven* [seduced & corrupted spirit sons of God], *and did cast them to the earth: and the dragon stood before the woman which was ready to be delivered, for to devour her child as soon as it was born* [vicariously through Herod].[18] *And she brought forth a man child* [begotten through Mary, the virgin mother of Yeshua; she also part and parcel of *the woman,* the larger corporate body of the ekklesía], *who was to rule all nations with a rod of iron:*[19] *and her child was caught up unto God, and to his throne* [ascension after resurrection].[20] *And the woman fled into the wilderness* [fleeing persecution], *where she hath a place prepared of God, that they should feed her there a thousand two hundred and threescore days* [equaling 42 months, or 3½ years].

And there was war in heaven: Michael and his angels fought against the dragon; and the dragon fought and his angels, and prevailed not; neither was their place found any more in heaven.[21] *And the great dragon was cast out, that old serpent, called the Devil, and Satan, which deceiveth the whole world: he was cast out into the earth, and his angels were cast out with him.*

And I heard a loud voice saying in heaven, Now is come salvation, and strength, and the kingdom of our God, and the power of his Christ [**after** the Luciferian mother ship delivers her extraterrestrial surprise]: *for the accuser of our brethren is cast down, which accused them before our God day and night* [brethren still on earth must now face maximum adversity of Great Tribulation]. *And they overcame him* [foil Satan, holding fast to their devotion] *by the blood of the Lamb* [the ultimate love], *and by the word of their testimony* [the spirit of prophecy, foreknowledge of the Satanic agenda and eventual conquest by Christ]; *and they loved not their lives unto the death* [having washed their robes in the blood of the Lamb].[22] *Therefore rejoice, ye heavens, and ye that dwell in them. Woe to the inhabiters of the earth and of the sea! for the devil is come down unto you, having great wrath, because he knoweth that he hath but a short time.*

And when the dragon saw that he was cast unto the earth, he persecuted the woman [same strategy as in Job chapters 1 & 2] *which brought forth the man child. And to the woman were given two wings of a great eagle, that she might fly into the wilderness, into her place, where she is nourished for a time, and times, and half a time, from the face of the serpent* [see Daniel 7:25 & 12:7].[23]

And the serpent cast out of his mouth water as a flood [the hordes of the ungodly] *after the woman, that he might cause her to be carried away of the flood.[24] And the earth helped the woman, and the earth opened her mouth, and swallowed up the flood which the dragon cast out of his mouth* [probably massive rifting by earthquake, as in the case of Korah, Num. 16]. *And the dragon was wroth with the woman, and went to make war with the remnant of her seed, which keep the commandments of God, and have the testimony of Jesus Christ.—Revelation 12.*

Because of the very nature of the (hyperphysical) Spirit and the scriptures inspired by it, understanding the symbolism utilized in this passage (like many others) can be tricky. But though somewhat tricky, it is still not really difficult, *if* one can free the mind from the constrictions of customary material-physical perspectives. Just as your own shadow cannot possibly convey the full dimension of your own lovely, three-dimensional form, so can physical images hardly describe spiritual realities; nonetheless, they are very helpful in outlining the real thing. So, as we proceed in our attempt to decode the ciphers of the symbolism, don't get stuck in two-dimensional "shadowland"; try instead to see what is casting the shadows.

Interpretation of the symbolism in this passage is not difficult when it is properly fitted together with the complimentary pieces of the whole biblical jigsaw puzzle, which we will try to frame shortly. The graphic symbols and metaphors used in this chapter, very befitting of the transcendent nature of John's vision, effectively create a vivid picture of the culmination of *a long-running historical conflict*, and of the hyperphysical (supernatural) forces engaged in it. The metaphorical depictions used to represent the entities illustrated in this conflict are not new, but appear repeatedly in early Scriptures of the Old Testament era.

First of these, clothed with a garment of resplendent light, is the *Bride of The Creator*. The entity pictured here is not an individual person but a corporate assembly of persons typified as an individual woman. In keeping with the standard imagery used throughout the Bible in both Old and New Testaments, this is none other than the *"daughter of Jerusalem,"* or the City of God, the *city of peace* (not in reference to physical location or geography, but to **people** as *spiritual citizens*). Again from a Spirit viewpoint, she is not only the *progeny of peace*, but at the same time, as a bride with her espoused Husband, is *also the co-progenitor of peace* and literally gives birth to the Prince of Peace (in the flesh)—daughter, mother, bride and wife in one.

You may be saying, how could this be possible? How can she (the City of Peace) be pregnant with her own husband (the Prince of Peace)? Well, even notable and respected scholars indeed stumble over this strange concept embodied in the mysterious imagery of the woman in Revelation 12. They, in fact—thoroughly fixated on their flat "shadowland" perspective—insist that such an interpretation does not make sense. And they argue therefore, that this image is not the picture of the bride of Christ, but actually the "wife of God." (This artificially imposed distinction is quite important to them, as we shall see.) After all, they argue, this couldn't be a vision of the bride of Christ, because she doesn't even marry until some time later (as per Revelation chapter 19), yet this woman is *"great with child!"* (The pregnancy seems to present them with an irreconcilable moral dilemma.)

And so, completely daunted by the challenge of accepting the strange facts as they stand and trying to simply grasp their meaningfulness, they instead go about to actively provide themselves with "untempered mortar" (to use the words of the prophet Ezekiel, chapter 13 & 22) with which to restructure the revelation into something more agreeable and self-serving. The end result is a doctrinal fallacy which conveniently supports their skewed preconceptions—all of which consistently slant away from the Christian obligation (mandated by the Master) to take up our crosses after His own personal example and admonition.

You see, the argument that this woman "just cannot be" the bride of the Creator, on the basis that it is totally "unacceptable" that she could be found pregnant before her marriage, is really based ulteriorly in pride, fear, and unbelief. For, to concede that this pregnant woman *does* represent the bride of Christ would be to admit that Christians too must indeed suffer and endure the Great Tribulation as the final phase of the ancient conflict with the Dragon.

The terrible dread of *that* thought, however, completely quenches any such admission; beside which, they somehow also feel themselves to be *above* such suffering and any need to prove their devotion.

Thus, *their fearful view* is that this can only mean that this pregnant woman is the Old Testament "wife of GOD," as distinct from the virgin Bride of Christ. Their "married wife" theory identifies her as the Jewish people (a collective wife) who, they assent, did give birth to The Child *"who is to rule all nations with a rod of iron,"* but then generally rejected her own Messiah—rendering the Jewish "wife" subject to holocaust and Great Tribulation, which *they*, the "undefiled virgins," couldn't possibly merit.

As surely as sweet is favored over bitter, *that* much more *palatable* interpretation definitely suits them quite a bit better, because it obviously excludes them (as a "virgin Gentile Church") from common sharing in the ultimate trial. It allays their fears and dread of sacrifice, defers for them the demands of loyal devotion, and effectively suspends the standards of faith and love which would otherwise need to be demonstrated by a much more humble, yielding and courageous obedience to the doctrine of Christ.

Essentially then, this fundamentalist exercise in moralizing and theologizing on this pregnant woman—which by their reckoning requires a second (undefiled) spiritual spouse for Messiah—is nothing more than a *disguised form of unbelief* based in fear of sacrifice and suffering.

In this artificial dichotomy of interpretation, which they have contrived, the fundamentalists proudly regard themselves as devout believers in Christ— the Bride of Christ supposedly—a separate and distinct woman (as yet only espoused and not married). Quite apart, they characterize the Jews (as a "generally unbelieving" people supposedly of the "Old Testament" era) as the *married wife of God* the Father (and legitimately able to bear a child); and not only so, but also as an often wandering adulteress gone a whoring from her Husband. Thus, by their logic, the wandering wife merits the afflictions of the Tribulation to purge and cleanse away the filthiness of her estrangements; while they, of course, view themselves as separate, *undefiled virgins* who need no such purification.

To believe there could only be one woman, one wife, one bride, one calling (out), and one destiny is just not congruent with the obsessive fundamentalist desire to escape tribulation. But, if this woman of our interpretive controversy *is verily* the unified, singular symbol of the one and only Bride of the Creator, irrespective of era and certainly *irrespective of persons* (or, ethnicities, as the Christians themselves ostensibly teach), then their worst fear will have befallen them. They then, together with the ethnic Jews, will also have to tread the terrifying trail of trial that they have so exclusively sought to skip. So you see, the symbolism embodied in John's vision of the woman clothed with the sun is actually not quite so difficult to understand; at least not as hard as it is to *accept!*[25]

I said a few paragraphs earlier that the symbolism can be more *tricky* than difficult. Well, isn't it strange that Christians (again, chiefly the fundamentalists) strain with so much difficulty at the notion of a pregnant woman giving birth (before getting married) to the same person that she later is to marry; while, at the same instance, they manage to gulp down other equally "tricky" concepts with no difficulty at all? Consider the following passage, which seems to present absolutely no problem to them, and which they apparently have no trouble interpreting.

For unto us a child is born, unto us a son is given: and the government shall be upon his shoulder: and his name shall be called Wonderful, Counsellor, The mighty God, The everlasting Father, The Prince of Peace.—Isaiah 9:6

Is this not *another* of those apparent "contradictions" that impugns logic and common sense, as well as biblical doctrine? How can this *child*, this flesh-born *son*, this *Prince* at the same time be *The mighty God* and *The everlasting Father* in the same person? How can this be? To whom does this "shadow" belong; what figure does it reveal? (Gen.1:26-27 & Deut.6:4)

Evenhandedly now, if the fundamentalists were to remain true and consistent to the two-dimensional, flatland perspective which they apply to the woman clothed with the sun in the Book of Revelation, then they must of necessity concoct another dichotomous interpretation to explain how this multi-aspect individual spoken of by Isaiah "simply cannot be" *both persons* in one. Yet, if you check with them about it, you will find that they have no trouble swallowing and digesting this camel; but the vision of the Bride of the Creator, by the same token, brings them to choking and gagging.[26]

Well, as inveterate masters of double standards, they simply always swallow what is palatable and spit out what does not appeal. Their biblical interpretations, from all appearances, evidence that their doctrines are as "situational" as the ethics in today's modern societies. But, let us leave this straining at gnats and swallowing camels lesson, to get down to some serious deciphering.

Holy Incest? Holy Whoredom?—or Wholly Arrogance and Fear?

As if to always keep the focus on the spirit and on the intimate relation YHWH maintains with His children, rather than on mere material place or geography (though that link is *also maintained*) carefully chosen language is used to refer to His people in the Scriptures. Certain idiomatic language came into usage by the Prophets that (with only some variation probably for variety's sake) consistently expressed His special view of His chosen people.

Time and again, throughout the Prophets and Writings, we hear them referred to as the *daughter of Jerusalem*, the *daughter of Zion*, the *virgin daughter of Zion*, and the *daughter of Judah*. Jerusalem (where *Mt. Zion* is located) and Zion are synonymous in terms of geography, one and the same place, known as the city of David and the *city of the great King* (2 Samuel 5:7, Psalm 48:2, Matthew 5:35). But the *daughter* of Jerusalem is a specific reference to a beloved *people* whom YHWH regards with tenderness.

From its Hebrew roots, *Jerusalem* means *"teaching of peace"* or *"aimed at peace as an objective."* "Jerusalem" is often used interchangeably and synonymously with these other monikers of tenderness, or expressive nicknames of God's people, His nation, and His City.[27] She is the epitome as well as the heart and soul of Israel and Zion. In the TaNaKh (Old Testament) the prophets Isaiah, Jeremiah, Micah, Hosea, Zephaniah and Zechariah all expounded extensively on the relationship of YHWH's people (His City) to Himself as one of a maid to her betrothed/husband.[28]

As is evident from the scriptures cited in the preceding footnote, a majority of these prophets were also compelled by the Spirit of Truth to reprove their nation and fellowcitizens for their adulterous unfaithfulnesses to YHWH, and to characterize their backslidings and idolatrous apostasies as the wandering wantonness of a whorish woman. Such that, not only were His darling people regarded as a delight, but often as a major grief of heart. (Not much has changed; not even with the New Jews of Christianity.)

Despite the fact, however, that the history of the *chosen ekklesia*—Old and New Testament eras alike—has been so severely marred and mostly characterized by apostasy, rebellion and backsliding, yet the Lord has always preserved unto Himself a *remnant*.[29] The New Testament era represents a virtually spontaneous blossoming and sudden boom of renewal for the ekklesia, which is only attributable to the hyperphysical action of the Holy Spirit. Prior to the coming of Messiah, the power of the Spirit had been manifested and dispensed in only limited measure (primarily to prophets). The post-messianic era, on the other hand, introduced what John the Baptist first called the *"baptism of the Holy Spirit,"* with which John proclaimed that his imminent successor, Messiah, would *immerse* the devout. The devout, of course, being those remnant daughters of Jerusalem devoted to *"the teaching of peace"*—i.e., the gospel of the Kingdom of God.

The radiantly gleaming clothing in the picture symbolizes the ultimate glory that eventually adorns the daughter of Jerusalem. Being clothed with the sun is symbolic of being clad with a heavenly righteousness beyond human.[30] This imagery exemplifies the brilliance of Messiah's Gospel—the wonder of grace and truth, and the marvel of Divine love and mercy. It has long been understood by the community of faith in the Lamb that, despite all our human shortcomings, the gracious favor, forgiveness and righteousness of the crucified Mashiach is imputed unto those who sincerely accept Him (via His teachings and mandates) in humble repentance from sin. Our garments (spiritual adornment) are washed by the Word of Jesus, when we pursue Him in full faith as His friends.[31] And, it's in this fervent, obedient pursuit of Him that we consequently clash with the Satan-mentored world systems of mankind and the Force of Evil which dominates them; it is thereby that we evoke the virulent wrath of both, just as Christ also did;[32] and it is in that very process that the robes of the Bride are washed to match her Husband's.[33]

And so, working our way through to the end of Revelation chapter 12, it becomes unmistakably plain that this pregnant woman is beleaguered by persecution. Most intense is the final period of 1,260 days during which the Dragon is cast down to the earth (verses 9-13) and proceeds to take out his vengeful wrath upon the woman. During this short time of all-out war upon the woman and her seed, she must be provided a wilderness refuge where she can be fed, sheltered from persecution, and elude annihilation.

Verses 6 and 14 establish that the duration of this repressive warfare by the Serpent will be 3½ years. This is further corroborated and reinforced as we move on to chapter 13 of Revelation where we are given notice that the same Beast—now personified in the role of a flesh and blood demigod who is empowered by the Dragon—takes global authority for *"forty and two months"*; and, as part of that three-and-a-half-year totalitarian regime, conducts a concerted war upon the saints and palpably overcomes them (yet not entirely, as the Scriptures promise and as we see in our next chapter).

And there was given unto him a mouth speaking great things and blasphe-
mies; and power was given unto him to continue forty and two months. And
he opened his mouth in blasphemy against God, to blaspheme his name, and
his tabernacle, and them that dwell in heaven. And it was given unto him to
make war with the saints, and to overcome them: and power was given him
over all kindreds, and tongues, and nations. And all that dwell upon the earth
shall worship him, whose names are not written in the book of life of the
Lamb slain from the foundation of the world.—Revelation 13:5-8

All discriminatory and dichotomous theologizings aside, any good student of the Bible can demonstrate that the term "saints" here does not just
refer to the Jews, anymore than only to believing Gentiles. A saint, by biblical
definition, is a believer who *truly heeds the teachings of the Holy Scriptures*
(and thus, worships YHWH), regardless of his nationality or ethnicity. (Some
even do it without ever having read the Scriptures or even hearing of them;
see Romans 2:11-29.) **All believers** of this variety *are Jews* (the elect, the
chosen ones), whether Old or New Testament era.[34] In fact, every Christian *is
a Jew (adopted)* by virtue of their faith in the Judaism of their ultra Jewish
Master, Christ Yeshua, who came not to destroy Judaism (the teachings of
Torah and the Prophets), but to fully live it, and to teach others the same
(Matthew 5:17-20). So, "Jacob's trouble" is for *all his seed*, natural *and*
adopted. You cannot be a saint only in the Rapture, but not in the Tribulation;
except in your imagination!

To what end, you may ask, is all this exposition on the subject of the
mysterious sun-clothed woman? Largely, it's to debunk the rapture fantasies
and set the record straight. Because so many other ill-informed and self-de-
luded sources are continually leading millions astray with arrogant, fearful,
and unbelieving doctrines of escapist exclusivism. And most importantly because, if you don't believe the woman is you and you are a part of the woman,
then you won't be prepared to meet her fate with courage, or wear her glory
with honor. You won't be prepared or able to *overcome*, if you go to *sleep*
dreaming about the *rapture!*

As "saints" we are supposed to separate ourselves from Babylon the
Whore, *not* from the Daughter of Zion—the one and only Bride of the Creator! It is the height of arrogance and presumptuousness to rank oneself as an
undefiled virgin while self-righteously discriminating against the Mother of

virginity. Beware the exclusivist doctrinaires!

Don't be fooled by the dread-stricken fundamentalists! Shed their dread and get back to the fundamentals, which they deny! Wash your robes in the Blood of the Lamb and join the joyful crowd of the courageous in the Holy City New Jerusalem.

*He that overcometh shall inherit all things; and I will be his God, and he shall be my son. But the **fearful**, and **unbelieving**, and the abominable, and murderers, and whoremongers, and sorcerers, and idolaters, and all liars, shall have their part in the lake which burneth with fire and brimstone: which is the second death. . . .*

And I saw no temple [in New Jerusalem]: for the Lord God Almighty and the Lamb are the temple of it. And the city had no need of the sun, neither of the moon, to shine in it: for the glory of God did lighten it, and the Lamb is the light thereof. And the nations of them which are saved shall walk in the light of it: and the kings of the earth do bring their glory and honour into it. And the gates of it shall not be shut at all by day: for there shall be no night there. And they shall bring the glory and honour of the nations into it. And there shall in no wise enter into it any thing that defileth, neither whatsoever worketh abomination, or maketh a lie: but they which are written in the Lamb's book of life.—Revelation 21

8

THE GATES OF HELL PREVAIL

Fear not them which kill the body,
but are not able to kill the soul . . .
Matthew 10:28

Contradictions, contradictions . . . and more contradictions! The Bible is loaded with contradictions; at least it often seems that way.

How can Christ promise to His disciples that *"there shall not an hair of your head perish,"* and yet later declare to John in the Apocalypse that many would be *beheaded* for their testimony of Messiah?[1] Well, how can a person lose their entire head and none of the hair thereof perish? And, how can Messiah promise his disciples on the one hand that *"nothing shall by any means hurt you,"* and on the other hand pronounce that they would be delivered up to be *afflicted* and *killed*, and that some would be crucified, scourged, and persecuted from city to city?[2]

And then again, on the subject to which this chapter is dedicated, how can the people of God prevail, and yet be prevailed against? Is it not an obvious inconsistency to be told in one place that the Beast *will overcome* the ekklesía, and yet elsewhere that, *"the gates of hell shall not prevail"* against them?[3] Just what are we to believe? Are these really contradictions, as it might appear? Are they overcome, or do they prevail?

Well, what indeed does appear to prevail, sadly, is a cloud of theological gainsaying and contrary debate over these issues. Yet it is my hope that, as in the previous chapter, we shall see that it is really not so hard to understand these teachings, though their concepts may seem to be contrary one to another. With the Scriptures, the difficulty in comprehension almost always arises from an unyielded, contrary attitude toward their lessons, which I hope may itself be overcome in our study by an honest, open approach.

Prevailing Over That Which Prevails

It has been declared and broadcast by somewhat muddled, and often self-contradictory Bible scholars who promote and subscribe to tribulation escapism that one of the scriptural evidences that the Christian Church will supposedly not be subject to the Great Tribulation (presumably being raptured before) is a certain special promise made to them by Christ. In this particular pronouncement of Jesus to the Apostle Peter, He is quoted (in Matt.16:18) as supposedly declaring that *"the gates of hell shall not prevail against [my ekklesía]."* Whereas, this interpretation is really nothing more than a popular misconstruing of the topical subject which Jesus had raised.

They claim that this singular proclamation, misunderstood as it is, secures them against the numerous other prophetic declarations—repeated and blatant as they are—that the anti-Christ Beast *will indeed prevail* against the saints and overcome them. In fact, no less than seven separate Bible references, as we shall see shortly, clearly state the latter case. Yet these folks are summarily quick to blend this gates-of-hell teaching into their soothing repertoire of misunderstood references which dutifully scratch their itching ears and feignedly support their rickety rapture theories; as usual, they do so regardless of the preponderance of other teachings which patently contradict these mainstream fundamentalist misgivings.

Let us, at this point in our endtimes prophecy tour, veer only slightly into an intriguing side-street exploration of biblical contradictions. It will be brief and not terribly impertinent to the thrust of this section. The contents of this chapter are primarily intended to show that the apparent contradictions which we have highlighted in the opening paragraphs are really not irreconcilable; it also addresses the issue particularly of who does prevail and how, and what that might mean exactly.

The great majority of perceived contradictions in the Scriptures are almost exclusively a matter of misinterpretation and misapplication arising out of misunderstanding and unseasoned judgment or discernment. Allow me one quick, off-course excursion to illustrate this truism.

This little detour is into the proverbs of Solomon to briefly examine only two of them, side-by-side, and very conspicuously contradictory in their counsel. Consider these two completely opposite teachings set one against another in the very same passage; perhaps you may have stumbled across this biblical oddity already:

Answer not a fool according to his folly, lest thou also be like unto him.
—*Proverbs 26:4*
Answer a fool according to his folly, lest he be wise in his own conceit.
—*Proverbs 26: 5*

Could this pair of proverbs represent a lapse in the famed *wisdom of Solomon,* that he should be found to contradict himself so blatantly and overtly? Shouldn't one of these lines of advice have been deleted from the script, or at least inserted in some other random location so as not to contraposition them so patently?

Doesn't this example of contradictoriness make very foolishness out of the Bible itself and decertify it as a valid literary guide to the divine and as the preeminent practical guide to life? Maybe the secular gainsayers are right when they assert that the Bible couldn't be the word of God because it's full of contradictions. Well, that you will have to decide for yourself. But before you hang up your holy hopes, or try to deposit this two-sided coin in the bank of unbelief, contemplate one other of Solomon's precepts: *"A wise man's heart discerneth both time and judgment. Because to every purpose there is time and judgment . . ." (Ecclesiates 8:5-6)*

In other words, there are occasions when it is unprofitable, nonsensical and vain to be caught up in the foolish debate of that which is unprofitable and nonsensical; stooping to such vanity renders one as much a fool as the one who spawned the debate. There are other instances, though, when a fool's conceit needs to be quenched by the demonstration of how obviously idiotic his position and attitude is manifest to be. According to Solomon, a wise man will understand what is called for in each instance and be able to discern what is appropriate to the circumstance at the time.

In the case of endtimes Bible prophecy, foolishness and a foolhardy attitude is a very high-risk mentality with potentially dire consequences. The chapter entitled "Ten Virgins" at the conclusion of this book focuses on just this issue. But to return now to the issue at hand—who, or what, prevails—I hold that it is absolutely critical to one's survival to sort out these issues by a sober quest to understand the facts free of any hasty and foolhardy presumptions which ostensibly negate them.

Will the Messiah fulfill the will of the "blessed hope" escapists and rapture them prior to any of the Great Tribulation afflictions, thereby also satisfying their comfy interpretation of the promise that the gates of hell shall not prevail against them? Or do they instead need to forsake their (extremely) foolhardy interpretive attempts to revise God's will to suit their own, in order to gain a healthier understanding?

Well, as most of us realize, *understanding* (of the Scriptures and God's will) is just like *faith* (and essentially based in it too): **people believe what they** *want* **to believe**; and in terms of *understanding*, they likewise tend to understand things as it suits them best. Now, to answer the questions I've just posed, let's see what understanding we can gain from the words of the prophet Daniel.

According to Daniel, those who do understand shall *not* escape! Contrariwise, he proclaimed that *"many shall be purified, and made white, and tried; but the wicked shall do wickedly: and none of the wicked shall understand; but the wise shall understand"*; and that *"they that understand among the people . . . shall fall by the sword, and by flame, by captivity, and by spoil . . . to try them, and to purge, and to make them white, even to the time of the end: because it is yet for a time appointed."*[4]

Isn't it highly suspicious that the blessed hope cult wishes to assign this *"appointment"* to the Jews while setting their own *earlier* appointment for an exclusive pre-tribulation rapture special to themselves? To *their* best understanding, evidently, it's okay and even necessary that the gates of hell should prevail against the Jews, since they supposedly missed the "Church" boat, and so, require cleansing. Thus, according to that "understanding," only the Jews must remain to be tried and made white, while they, on the favored hand presumably, escape *already* "white and pure."

This all takes us back again to the staggeringly presumptuous false doctrine that the Gentile Christians hold some *exclusive and elevated rank* above the Jewish Ekklesía (who in the end, as in the beginning, are really the most Christian of all).[5] Such an attitude is *the* most void of wisdom and understanding that anyone could possibly take; it flies in the face of scores and scores of admonitions that stud the Holy Scriptures with censures against divisive self-exaltation. That presumptuous dogma, in our present context of the wise versus the foolish, is truly the height of folly (and in the light of the above references from Daniel, also nigh unto very wickedness)!

Somehow, they just don't seem to attain the most critical of all understandings: that they too are appointed to be "purified, made white, and tried"— for their own sakes and for the very purpose of their own overcoming! So desperately desirous are they to find a way of escape from this joint holy fate, that the meanings of all these scriptures seem to commonly and continually escape these escapists. And very tragically, it is by becoming ensnared in their fool's paradise of *ill-interpreted precepts* that they shall find themselves also *ill-prepared* to prevail and overcome, especially when it comes time to stick it out with the Jews for 42 months while *"it is given unto [the Beast] to make war with the saints, and to overcome them."* Nor much less shall they, as Lot's wife was not, be found prepared to escape into the wilderness.

Who Overcomes Whom?

As with so many other popular misinterpretations, a very manifest haste to skip the suffering and sacrifice inherent to the Faith of Christ is revealed in the anemic and spiritless teaching which we hear so often spouted: namely, that to be subject to the Great Tribulation is contrary to the promise that the gates of hell shall not prevail against Messiah's called-out ones. This feeble sort of teaching renders its disciples feeble, and spiritless, expecting not to have to strive to overcome or struggle to prevail, or to even prepare for the appointed engagement.

A little earlier in the previous section I promised you a set of at least seven scriptures that clearly make the case for the gates of hell "prevailing" indeed against the saints and "overcoming" many of them. Any doubt surrounding the issue cannot survive the litany of the numerous prophetic instances in the Bible that plainly state the case to be so. And in terms of contradiction, I believe our study of them will reveal that it's all a matter of how one views and interprets the concepts of victory and defeat that affects the ability to understand and resolve the apparent inconsistency in prophetic prospects, as well as the disagreement between opposing perspectives on the future.

These seven quotations come from key endtime passages out of the books of Daniel and the Apocalypse, and begin with chapter 7 of Daniel in which the prophet retells a vision he receives in the night (c. 550 BCE) about the empires of the future. In the portion of the vision which foretold of the final kingdom of mankind upon earth, just before the coming of "the Ancient of days" and the establishment of His domain, Daniel foresees a *"war with the saints"* at that future time in which the Little Horn *"prevailed against them."* *(Dan.7:21)* Four verses later, he further expands on the vision by saying that the little horn *"shall wear out the saints of the most High."* *(Dan.7:25)*

Then in the following chapter describing a follow-up vision he had two years later, he again sees the Little Horn, arising this time to exceeding greatness and magnificent prominence. Upon this rise to greatness, Daniel sees the horn *"cast down some of the host and of the stars to the ground [referring to the hosts of the heavenly Prince and to angels also overcome in the conflict],"* and notes that the horn *"stamped upon them."* In the same place, Daniel is told that *"both the sanctuary and the host"* are to *" be trodden under foot."* (Dan.8:9-13) A little later in chapter 8, the Little Horn is further elaborated on as a *"king of fierce countenance"* who *"shall destroy the mighty and the holy people."* (Dan.8: 23-24)

Three chapters later, and several years later, in another detailed vision concerning *"what shall befall [Daniel's] people in the latter days,"* the oracle provides not only more detail on the "king of fierce countenance" but elaborates more specifically on the plight of the "mighty and holy people" in his hand at that time. Daniel is told by a preeminent angelic spirit that *"the people that do know their God, shall be strong, and do exploits . . . yet they shall fall by the sword, and by flame, by captivity, and by spoil . . . to try them, and to purge, and to make them white, even to the time of the end"* (Dan.11:32-35); and finally, in the concluding prophesies of his last chapter, that *"when [this king] shall have accomplished to scatter the power of the holy people, all these things shall be finished."* (Dan.12:7) In other words, they shall not simply fall, but the power and might of these holy people shall be overcome and dashed to pieces, and then the end will come.

(It is precisely this "bleak" prospect that drives the mainstream Christian fundamentalists to craftily invent another separate class of "holy people" which will be raptured out of this rather dismal finale, which they contend only Daniel's people will have to endure. Thus do they not only disown Daniel's people, but Daniel himself! And of course, since Christ Yeshua also insisted that his own disciples—all Jews, except perhaps Simon the Canaanite—would have to endure unto the end, likewise do He and His disciples suffer disowning by such cowardly doctrinaires.)

The seventh biblical citation on the ultimate "demise" of these saints is found in the last book of the Bible. In this instance from the book of Revelation, John writes of his own vision of this same future time saying, *"And it was given unto [the beast] to make war with the saints, and to overcome them."* (Rev.13:7) The entire 13th chapter of the Apocalypse is dedicated to the same blaspheming, big-mouthed character whom Daniel saw typified as a "little horn" (actually an 11th horn) dominating and presiding over ten others and *"speaking great things . . . against the most High" (Dan. 7:8, 20 & 25)*—the very same beastly assassin and crusher of the holy people in the Apocalypse.

As a bonus now, we must also consider an *eighth* instance, one which does not even exempt the most exemplary or the mightiest of the "holy people." For, again according to John's apocalyptic vision, the two most prominent and powerful saints of the day will also be dashed by the Beast: *"And when they shall have finished their testimony, the beast that ascendeth out of the bottomless pit shall make war against them, and shall overcome them, and kill them." (Rev. 11:7)* Alas, as Daniel also foresaw, the king of fierce countenance *"shall have accomplished to scatter the power of the holy people"*; and now, *"all these things shall be finished." (Dan. 12:7)*

Well, in the face of all this overwhelming evidence from their own revered Scriptures, the mother of invention has been hastily summoned to the rescue of the desperate rapture doctrinaires who erroneously insist on separate destinies for Jews and "Christians." Superlative creative genius has inventively risen on this issue to meet the daunting challenge of *suffering for Christ*—by the concocting of sophisticated and heretical fables which presumptuously exempt a certain class of believers from having to do so, but meanwhile obligate the other.

Instead of keeping their spiritual wits about them, the panic and fear of suffering, and the dread of material, physical, fleshly insecurity has driven them to devise elaborate theologies to comfort feeble fellow Christians who just wouldn't know what to do at the thought of the prophecies of Great Tribulation applying to them. It is therefore that we hear and read of clever theories that split up God's people into dichotomous groups of different dispensations, different destinies, different testaments and different classifications, expectations and standards.

All this, of course, completely contradictory to the basic, simple truth taught by Messiah, and His prophets and apostles.[6] The simple matter of fact is that the consistent message of the Hebrew Bible, from Genesis to Revelation is that Yahweh God seeks to be known and worshipped as one, constant, unchanging, uncompromising, unmistakable, undeniable, unwavering Lord of all the universe—*unified and undivided.*[7] Discriminatory and divisive doctrines that separate between sheep and sheep (certain ones from other ones) spring from the desperate wickedness and deceitful pride of men's hearts, not from the teachings of the Bible. Speaking strictly factually, the issues of who overcomes and what "prevailing" actually consists of is totally irrelevant to ethnicity, just as it is irrelevant to any other fleshly measure.

Beyond Flesh

For the unseasoned student of Scripture who does not yet recognize the distinction between the multiple dimensions of the creation, confusion *could* conceivably arise about the notion of just who overcomes or prevails. I am referring to the basic biblical teaching of "dimensional pluralism" and what pertains to these plural dimensions, particularly those commonly acknowledged as the physical and the spiritual (i.e., hyperphysical, or supernatural). The confusion and apparent contradiction on this question of overcoming is easily dispelled and laid to rest by persevering in one's study of the holy teachings. For, any serious student quickly comes to understand that the Bible provides an account of dual, overlapping, coexistent realms and the continual meshing of the two, as well as the preeminence and predominance of the one which will ultimately prevail.[8]

The supposed contradiction on this issue is readily apparent within a passage of Scripture only eighteen verses long (which we have already examined in parts), found between Revelation 12:7 and 13:7.

We read (in 12:7-8) that the Great Red Dragon engaged against Michael the archangel—along with their respective extraterrestrial hosts—in actual combat on an astral level and that the Dragon was unable to prevail in that theater. He is subsequently cast out of the celestial domain into the earth, along with his angels (12:9). This demise of the Dragon on that plane and his banishment from it into Earth subsequently prompts the heralding of the imminent coming of the kingdom of God and the redemption of the earth (12:10). However, Satan definitely prevails in the theater of earth prior to the ensuing appearance of Messiah.

In the same breath, the heavenly herald announces that the "brethren" *have overcome* this expelled extraterrestrial foe *"by the blood of the Lamb, and by the word of their testimony."* However, this triumph is said to have been accomplished even at the expense of their lives, which *"they loved not . . . unto the death." (Rev.12:11)*

A few verses later, in chapter 13, verse 7, we learn that in the earthly arena the Dragon does indeed manage to conduct a successful cultural cleansing campaign against the saints. This cultural genocide in which the dragonish alien "prevails" is accomplished through a human beast he empowers of strikingly similar characteristics to his own (spiritually speaking; see 13:1), who institutes an obligatory planetary citizenship mark and capital execution for any refusing to take it. Not only does he overcome the saints through this "human" agent, but moreover exercises global totalitarian power over all the populations of Earth imposing the new worldwide culture of alien worship (13:7-18).

At this point, we must ask whether this would-be eradication of the saints is any more a victory for the Dragon and his protégé (the incarnate son of perdition) than was his crucifixion of the Lamb of God in 32 AD. Indeed, physically speaking, from the material point of view, the Messiah and His gospel appeared to have suffered a lethal blow at the time, which seemingly signaled their demise. In fact, even His own disciples and most trusted friends—thoroughly versed in His spiritual teaching and well acquainted with his hyperphysical powers (to even raise the dead)—sunk into deep depression at the event of His death thinking the revolution had been quashed. To them, it seemed more than apparent that the gates of Hades had prevailed against the Rock.

The historical record, however, testifies to the contrary. The revolution was not dead! Rather, the spark of the Lamb's blood ignited a fire that victoriously overcame the fierce opposition and persecution of the prevailing mighty Roman empire; until, within three hundred years, Christianity had become the prevailing religion of the empire. That being good or bad, the fact is that billions of souls since have bowed the knee to Christ over that last 1900 years in honor to His Revolution of Love and Truth.

The evil Dragon who unsuccessfully attempted to "devour the man child as soon as it was born" (Rev.12:4-5) did finally succeed in killing the Son of man at Golgotha; he thought! He thought he had prevailed; but his victory was ever so temporary and overwhelmingly hollow. The Messiah could not be overcome by death. On the contrary, He Himself *prevailed* by the resurrection and overcame by a Love, Life, Truth and Spirit that cannot be quenched.

To this very day, martyrs still lose their lives for that Love, Life, Truth and Spirit that *cannot* be quenched in the hearts of those who devotedly *overcome* for the sake of His Gospel. Faithful twentieth century believers are regularly imprisoned, tortured and killed in various parts of the world, even as we speak, for the love of this "dead" Savior who is known worldwide by a simple emblem or icon that symbolizes the way He gave His life for all. As the consummate symbol of overcoming, that cross by which the Dragon imagined to prevail against Him *itself prevails* in millions of homes, overshadowing cities, on mountaintops, in grave yards, in the finest of works of art, and is worn by countless millions as jewelry motifs; and more especially, it prevails in the hearts and on the shoulders of those who still bear it daily for the sake of the One Who died upon it.

And notwithstanding the plethora of odd sects, denominations and cultic variations on Christ's Gospel, which have sprung up throughout the world over the last 1900 years, yet there is no denying among any but the most nominal of them that *the Lamb and His Love are worthy* of worship, emulation and propagation; and that the promise of His Kingdom and His life eternal is a hope to be greatly anticipated. He has indeed prevailed and shall continue to prevail in the hearts of men, until He shall at last *utterly prevail* on earth as KING OF KINGS AND LORD OF LORDS (in the company of those who have also victoriously overcome by their own self-denying faith)!

Almost the entire world reckons time by the date of His first coming to the planet, and only a few isolated regions have yet to hear His name—which the sacrifice and passion of some of today's most dedicated believers may soon reduce to none, God helping them! All this despite the brutal effort by the Dragon to prevail against Christ's Gospel by a torturous and murderous persecution campaign against the Lamb and His devotees. Obviously, the Savior was not vanquished, instead, through His remnant saints has constantly overcome the force of pride, hate, envy, and rebellious blasphemy, and shall prove to be the ultimate victor! And in spite of every wicked prevailing effort to murderously quash and slaughter the witnesses of truth, His Gospel of the ultimate kingdom *"shall be preached in all the world for a witness unto all nations, and then shall the end come." (Matt.24:14)*

And then shall appear the sign of the Son of man in heaven: and then shall all the tribes of the earth mourn, and they shall see the Son of man coming in the clouds of heaven with power and great glory.—Matthew 24:30

The concept of overcoming, it seems plain to me, needs to be understood in terms beyond the mundane.[9]

Those who seek to spare themselves from tribulation have taken on a worldly, flesh-obsessed perspective on the principle of overcoming. They perceive Bible prophecy and teachings of Scripture from a point of view that caters to the flesh and facilitates an easy way out of suffering and sacrifice. And, it is upon that foundation of sand that strange, untenable doctrines and complicated theological interpretations are synthesized to artificially discriminate between the supposedly different destinies of Israel and the so-called Christian Church, which some very naively or misguidedly characterize as gentile. According to those spiritless doctrines, to suffer affliction and die for the faith of Christ in the Great Tribulation amounts to being prevailed against; and they're *right*, but only in terms of the *flesh*—their primary preoccupation, apparently!

Again, in their would-be scenario, the (flesh) seed of Israel are seen as the ones having to endure the Great Tribulation; and therefore, to suffer being overcome, trampled under foot, scattered, destroyed, worn out, and otherwise prevailed against. Meanwhile, the mistitled "Gentile" Church is raptured into heaven and spared all the trials and purging of this event; this includes, of course, not having to hazard their lives, nor their well-being and wealth by standing against the New World Order, its dragonish demagogue, and his bio-implanted passport to the new global Order. They want to leave that up to the *other* saints, the *other* class of holy people, while they watch from the "mezzanine."

Well, if there is any distinction as purported, just who are the "holy people," and who are the "saints?" Am I interpreting Scripture correctly in this study of mine? Might it be possible that my contentions are completely wrong? Perhaps Israel and the Church really are two different entities with separate destinies. What is a Jew? Who are the Gentiles? What is the seed of Abraham? Just who and what is the Church? And, who and what is Israel? Maybe the following section will help clear up these questions.

The Goyim, or the Goyim?

A careful study of the Scriptures reveals plainly that there is no difference between a Jew or a Gentile, except in the covenant relationship that God initiated with a certain line of people descended from Abraham who were to bear the mark (circumcision) of Yahweh's promise to him.[10] Note that Abraham himself was a Gentile (uncircumcised till the age of 99); not only so, but God's covenant with him was that Abraham would be the father of many gentiles/nations, and that in him would all the families of the earth be blessed.[11]

The original Hebrew word—gowy, or plural gowyim (as transliterated)—from which our English translations give us the word "gentile" is exactly the same word which is frequently translated as "nation(s)." The promise is that Yahweh would multiply Abraham exceedingly, make him exceeding fruitful and the father of many *gowyim* (modern, goyim).

Why would Yahweh specifically choose to multiply Abraham? Because, He had found in him a man whom He could regard as a *friend*—someone who had *unconditional faith* in Him.[12] Someone who would believe in Him, appreciate Him, love Him above everything, and do whatever He asked.[13] Someone who would even sacrifice the son Yahweh had promised him—a twenty-five year-old promise and the son of his old age (100 years)—the only son of his heretofore barren wife Sarah, miraculously born of her past ninety years of age. (Genesis chapters 17, 21 & 22) It was Abraham's qualities of faith, obedience and love of God that the Lord was interested in replicating and multiplying in "like father, like son" fashion; which speaks to another trait Yahweh recognized in him, faithfulness to pass on the teaching of Yahweh.[14]

So it is that through Abraham's lineage a people were called out as a chosen people *of promise* unto whom Abraham's God would forever also be their God, and unto whom the possession of the land of Canaan would be granted (Gen.17:7-8). In the process of time, through the son of Abraham's faith, Isaac, the covenant promise began to descend from generation to generation. It was in the third generation that a uniquely interesting phenomenon occurred to forever redefine the name and nature of things divine or of God, including the name of the chosen people, not to mention the understanding of very character of God. The third generation produced two very famous twins and a fork in the road of promise and destiny.

The promise to Abraham, however, was not split or in any way shared between this pair of his grandsons. Instead, it was literally captured by the younger twin son of second-generation Isaac and his wife Rebekah. It was this singularly uncommon son whose legacy of name the offspring and the land promised to Abraham still bear to this very day. It was this younger fraternal twin, later called the "Prevailer with God"—because he actually did prevail in contest with God by his unrelenting pursuit and struggle to seize the promise and blessing of God—who ultimately won the favored affection of the Almighty and was renamed by Yahweh Himself to a more "dignified" title.[15]

This particular son was not due the right of the firstborn (by primogeniture), because he was not the elder twin. This twin, in contrast however, embraced a particularly overriding and preeminent sense of worth as regards the Promise of God given to his grandfather for transference to his heirs; a value that drove him to even abandon all ethics to clinch by subtlety and outright deception that which he treasured, though it belonged by right of birth to his older brother. His original name means "supplanter;" or also "to restrain, circumvent, seize." These meanings derive from a remarkable peculiarity that accented the birth of these twin brothers—the seizing of the heel of the elder babe by the clenching baby hand of the younger at the time of their very emergence from the womb of Rebekah.

We know these twins as Esau and Jacob, who was later called "Israel." The people we know as the twelve tribes of Israel were fathered by the twelve sons of Jacob, and were of course the direct descendants of Abraham and now primary heirs according to the promise that Jacob seized.

According to the Genesis story, Jacob's brother Esau—and *his* descendants—might have been that primary line of inheritance had Esau not despised his birthright and esteemed a bowl of escape from fleshly privation (actually lentil soup) to have had more worth. (See this fascinating story in Genesis 25.) As the Scriptural account reveals, and indeed particularly points out, the competition from Jacob for the birthright was too dogged and fierce for Esau to have presumed any guarantees whatsoever about his destiny, or to have taken anything promised *for granted*—a particularly poignant lesson in this context of exactly who the chosen people of God are.

Moreover, Esau's cavalier attitude toward the promised blessing of God was clearly not the tradition of their grandfather Abraham who had sacrificed (in virtue) his most precious earthly treasure to please his God and insure acquisition of that promise. And so, it was in that tradition that Jacob—who in like fashion greatly *prized* the promise—supplanted the rightful heir to then seize upon his primary right of inheritance (see follow-up on story in Gen.27), which was subsequently passed on to his own twelve sons.

Yet, the contest was apparently not sealed. For not until twenty years later, in a mystical nighttime encounter with a man-angel whom Jacob called "God" (the same Elohiym of Creation, evidently) did the blessing get confirmed. It was as a result of an actual grappling match with the man-angel in which Jacob prevailed, getting permanently crippled in the process, that he clinched the promise he had so fervently sought.

Many scholars believe this man-angel with whom Jacob wrestled to have been the Mashiach. The prophet Hosea testified that the angel was indeed *"the LORD God of hosts."*[16] One thing is clear: The name Jacob gave to the place of this contest (Peniy'el) testifies to Jacob's personal conviction that he had seen the face of God. We can assume, however that the view was probably somewhat fleeting and vague, and that this shadowy figure himself was not desirous of being fully revealed, since He hastened to terminate the match before daybreak, while the shadows of night still obscured the view.

Shadow of the Chosen Faith

In terms of figurative literature and language, "shadows" and "types" indeed abound throughout the Bible, as the New Testament Apostle Paul pointed out so often.[17] The figurative portraits in these Genesis accounts we've been examining reveal the distinct shadow of an *ekklesia* being specially elected and set apart.[18] We see this dynamic occurring by a divine promise of a uniquely special blessing and by a uniquely appropriate response to it.

The very distinct shadow that is cast in Genesis also very clearly implies that acquisition of the promise is not by sheer right, nor by mere grace, as the free-salvation-by-grace doctrinaires propound. Instead, the clear outline of this shadow reveals that a relentless, Jacob-type pursuit of the blessing—driven by bona fide respect for the promises of God—is what procures and literally clinches the favor of God.

Laying hold of the promises made to YHWH's chosen seed is not accomplished by an indolent attitude of lackadaisical, easy-come-easy-go devotion. Taking *nothing* for granted, resolute Jacob-style faith is marked by devotion often exercised at considerable cost to one's person, life and well-being. Equally implicit in this Jacob-Esau history is that those who cavalierly repose upon their claims to privilege (or grace), presumptuously taking their election for granted, merely earn Yahweh's disdain.[19]

The bottom line of the history lesson we have been reviewing here in somewhat cursory fashion was more than adequately summed up by the famous grace-advocating Apostle Paul in one verse from the book of Hebrews: *"Without faith it is impossible to please Him: for he that cometh to God must believe that He is, and that He is a rewarder of them that diligently seek Him." (Hebrews 11:6)*

It is *this* key element that eliminates any and all difference between so-called Israel and the so-called Church. Those who prevail—by their ardent,

tenacious faith, thereby having power with God to become the sons of God—
are spiritually grafted into the Abrahamic Promise and *become one* with Israel, even taking on the full significance of the name.[20] This in no way takes
anything away from the biological seed of Israel. But it definitely identifies
one with the other and strips away the erroneous notion that they do not share
a common destiny, particularly including the Great Tribulation.[21] If any difference exists, it is simply the difference that arises from two disparate types
of faith: one that diligently seeks to be spared the cost of faith (i.e., tribulation
and testing), and another that heartily seeks *"the fellowship of His sufferings."*[22]

The name *Israel*, meaning *to prevail, to have power with God*, casts a
defining shadow of character that identifies both a unique person of special
qualities and a nation whom God loved and chose as His namesake people.
Contrary to Esau's gratify-me-now character, it was because of the resolute,
passionate, no-holds-barred faith of Jacob that his descendants, the Israelites,
became the inheritors of the promise to Abraham and the people of Abraham's
God. The shadow of Israel is the shadow of the ekklesía.

According to the martyr, Stephen—stoned to death for his outline of the
Old Testament shadow—the Messiah was with *"the church in the wilderness"* during the Exodus at the time of Moses.[23] Not only, then, was Christ
actively engaged with Israel at that pre-Christian era, but also so was the
"church" in existence at that time!

That same Christ *"whose goings forth have been from of old, from everlasting"* (according to Micah 5:2) promised that he would be with his disciples *"even unto the end of the world"* as they faithfully set about to pass on
to all nations the teachings of their Master.[24] He also declared that the end
would *not* come *until this* was accomplished; and in the same instance taught
that *those who endured* unto that end would be saved; and never, ever, that
only certain ones would have to go to that extent.[25]

But of course, we are about to stir up the same polemics; because the
minds that stedfastly resist the truth will then begin to argue that certain of the
words of Christ (as some which we have been referencing) were spoken to
and intended specifically for the *Jews*, since the disciples were Jews. They of
course, in their blind insistence on the would-be escape from tribulation of an
alleged gentile church (to which they pertain, of course), thoroughly overlook
the undeniable fact that the Christian Mother Church of the first century was
primarily a Jewish Church, one with Jewish leaders and Jewish disciples fol-

lowing a Jewish Messiah, and observing Jewish law and custom, especially in the earlier years when the church was almost exclusively Jewish. Not until after the sweeping missionary efforts of the Apostle Paul in Asia and Europe did non-Jews begin to outnumber the Hebrews in Church membership.

So, contrary to the doctrines of the dispensation cultists, there is absolutely no partition or distinguishing line of division between Israel (the true seed) and the Church (Messianic Israel, the same true seed, which increasingly incorporated gentiles as time passed).[26] They are one and the Same Ekklesía; and what is sauce for the goose is sauce for the gander, as they say.

Typically, it is those who do not believe that they will have to experience the Great Tribulation who also do not believe in the common destiny and oneness of the Church and Israel (the original and enduring Church). As with so many other straightforward teachings, concepts, precepts and principles which they do not embrace with *simple faith*, elaborately contrived fables which originate from an unwillingness to accept *simple facts* are deviously invented to supplant the *simple truth*.

And so, rather than diligently seeking The Truth and His message of the *cross*, they diligently apply themselves instead to find routes of escape. It is thereby that heaps of fallacious theories of convenience, promulgated by hosts of therapeutic doctors of divinity (and sundry other evangelistic charlatans) who specialize in scratching itching ears, become the Christian prescription pain-relievers of the day, as per the prophecy of the apostle Paul:

For the time will come when they will not endure sound doctrine; but after their own lusts shall they heap to themselves teachers, having itching ears; and they shall turn away their ears from the truth, and shall be turned unto fables.—2 Timothy 4:3-4

So, to begin wrapping up this chapter, the overwhelming scriptural evidence presented herein does not teach that one group of chosen people must suffer great tribulation and be overcome, while the "other ones" are especially chosen to be exempted from tribulation (and thus be non-prevailed against). Rather, the Scriptures testify to a single city constructed on a single foundation with a single chief cornerstone, built according to a single blueprint by a single architect, and destined to be a singular temple for the habitation of its Builder and Maker. And though the components and building blocks of this New Jerusalem be many and varied, yet they are brought together in **one**.[27]

This singular ekklesía also holds an undivided understanding that to lose ones life in the struggle for the advancement of the love and truth of the Kingdom of God is only a very temporary and hollow victory for their arch-enemy. And, in reality it is they who ultimately overcome at the resurrection by their hyperphysical regeneration into new bodies in which they will rule in the New World jointly with the Savior, Conqueror of Death and Hades. Remember, *"whosoever shall lose his life shall preserve it!" (Luke 17:33)*

That ultimate regeneration at the last day will be a full and complete (and immortal) reconstitution down to the last cell and follicle; for indeed *"there shall not an hair of your head perish."* This declaration of Christ Yeshua cited in the opening paragraph of this chapter continues with the statement of the critical element to this ultimate "possession" of your own soul: *"In your patience possess ye your souls." (Luke 21:18-19)*

And what does such patience require? Resolute faith of the type Abraham, Jacob and the other patriarchs demonstrated; formidable faith that prevails to seize promises and fears nothing (except "Esau-ism"); faith which can withstand being prevailed against and can endure tribulation, including that of the Great variety to come; the type of faith which can endure the Wicked One's temporal destruction of the body.

For those who embrace such faith, at the very hub of John the Revelator's chapter on the overpowering domination of the Antichrist during the last 42 months is found a rather grisly reassurance toward reinforcing their resolve. John is given the following divine assurance for those who face the grim persecutory wrath of the Dragon: *"He that leadeth into captivity shall go into captivity: he that killeth with the sword must be killed with the sword. Here is the patience and the faith of the saints." (Rev.13:10)* In other words, the saints understand as an integral part of their *faith*, as I have said, that being wickedly abused in this world and even killed for that faith is something to be expected; and that they will most definitely be avenged when it's all over. Their faith is in the promise of eternal life *and* the transcendent justice of God. Thus, patience is the key, not tribulation anxiety!

" And not only so, but we glory in tribulations also: knowing that tribulation worketh patience," admonishes Paul to the gentile Romans *(Rom.5:3).* James adds this in his address to the 12 tribes of Israel, *"Knowing this, that the trying of your faith worketh patience." (James 1:3)* (We should note that without respect of persons and without variance either to the non-Jews or to the Hebrews, the biblical message is always unified and consistent—faith in

the absence of tribulation is mere illusion, of no substance, and casts no shadow.) James continues, *"But let patience have her perfect work, that ye may be perfect and entire, wanting nothing* [i.e., not lacking substance]. *" (James 1:4)*

In essence then, overcoming is not a matter of any sort of overpowering deadly force, or worldly might, or power of the Evil One to bruise; nor is it *escape* from any of this. Neither is it a matter of mere untested or unproven belief among alleged believers.[28] Rather, it is a matter of sustained faith even in the shadow adversity, and especially in the face of mortal sacrifice.[29] This key spiritual theme of *overcoming* was well comprehended by St. John who wrote about it extensively in his epistles, in his gospel, and especially in the book of Revelation.

In his epistles, his multiple exhortations on overcoming are summed up in his teaching that deeply actualized *faith* (and manifest love of God) is the prevailing victory that overcomes both the world and "the wicked one."[30] And earlier, in the Gospel according to John (and contrary to the gospel of the anti-tribulation rapturists), he affirms that Christ promised his followers tribulation in this world, without hope of escape, urging them even to "be of good cheer" at this prospect—cheer, because He has "overcome the world," its devices, and the Wicked One. A few verses later in this same gospel, John testifies that Yeshua's express intent for His ekklesía was not that it should be precipitously removed from the adverse evil world. Rather, the Savior's prayer for his followers was simply that they should be kept from the evil of temptation while in the world.[31]

And finally, in the profound prophetic conclusion of the awesome spectacle of the Book of Revelation, John repeatedly echoes numerous specific rousings and urgings on the highly-rewarded call to overcome. This is particularly so when the faithful find themselves in the throes of the intensely adverse future circumstances predicted to come in this famous endtime vision (as per the accompanying footnote). Obviously, these repeated admonitions and exhortations, mostly regarding the time of the end, are highlighted in the Apocalypse because overcoming is *not* a wholesale unconditional guarantee or something to be presumptuously taken for granted.[32]

The summary of it all is that *faith* and her sister, *patience, shall ultimately prevail* with eternally enduring prizes at the finale; while the cowardly, feeble twins of *fear and unbelief* are classed together in the ranks of the "wicked, abominable, and murderers, etc."[33]

Key to the Contradiction

The key to resolving the conflict of apparently contradictory teachings on the subject of overcoming, or prevailing, is the same key needed to understand the Bible as a whole. An understanding must be gained that Scripture and its Author are beyond flesh and transcend the mere physical dimension in which we are temporarily constituted. As Paul put it, *"the natural man receiveth not the things of the Spirit of God: for they are foolishness unto him: neither can he know them, because they are spiritually discerned." (1 Corinthians 2:14)*

Attempts to decipher the Spirit-based scriptures of the Bible by employing a mere natural mentality will prove fruitless and frustrating. An understanding (by the "sixth sense" of faith) that all things physical and material were created of things invisible and emanating from a higher dimension is the key to beginning to understand the Holy Writings. For they issued from the same point of origin as the created universe—the powerful utterance of the Almighty God, the Word that proceeded from His Spirit Being. Things of that dimension are more real, solid and enduring than this "lower" form of materialization of spirit in which we live. It is with that more realistic perspective of the Universe that we can begin to understand that *"he that loveth his life shall lose it; and he that hateth his life in this world shall keep it unto life eternal." (John 12:25)*

That kind of worldview cannot be achieved without faith; and it is completely contrary to everything we are taught and conditioned with in the modern world of "empirical" skepticism and obsessive dialectical materialism. (Yet, even dialectics and true empiricism demand that there must be a mighty Creator God—otherwise known as the Big Bang in today's world of so-called "science.") Faith is really more natural than we moderns care to contemplate, but because we care not for it, it has become harder than ever to have it. What we have come to obsess over as a global community is mere materialism—to the denial of the essence and origin of the material world—with a myopic craving for the things of this life.

Overwhelmingly so, it is this pervasive obsession with the carnal being and its baser lusts which actually quenches faith and breeds fear and unbelief. Fear of deprivation of the flesh and loss of our all-important carnal "satisfactions" is inextricably tied together with *unbelief* that there is anything beyond this lust-based carnal existence: "Gotta make the most of this world, you know, 'cuz there ain't no guarantees of the next." Unfortunately, not only atheists and hedonists are stricken with this universal malady, but even those who have a basic belief in God are all too often infected with this fear. Though Christianity was founded to enlighten the human heart and mind to the ultimate and enduring essence of the Spirit, yet so many of its nominal subscribers still cherish what Christ censured and decried as thorns and weeds which choke out the truth. They still fear the loss of life in this world, unbelieving that He could make that loss so very worth their while.

Thus, they too have become infected with fear and unbelief in their interpretation of His teachings and sayings. Rather than the good cheer and peace Jesus urged, they anxiously fear and shun being prevailed against and overcome in the coming Great Tribulation, because they believe (in their excessively fleshly orientation) that *that* is what is actually happening. When quite to the contrary, Messiah assured that *"whosoever shall lose his life for my sake and the gospel's, the same shall save it." (Mark 8:35)*

What is meant by *overcoming* (for a convinced Christian) is prevailing over the prevailing materialist-fleshly mentality that enslaves and imprisons worldly unbelievers in the carnal chains of fear; fear of loss and suffering; fear of pain and death to the flesh; fear of tribulation and affliction.[34] In real terms, the realest of all terms, those who are physically overcome and prevailed against during the Great Tribulation—having their "heels bruised" for their enduring convictions of faith—are those who in all reality shall ultimately overcome to obtain their crowns of life and rods of iron (prevailing authority). It is *they* who actually prevail to eventually avenge their shed blood and finally "bruise" the head of their Persecutor. On the other hand, those who believe they will be raptured before the Great Tribulation so as not to be prevailed against have already been overcome—by a lying spirit dutifully scratching the itching ear of fear!

Gates of Hades Endnote

When Jesus came into the coasts of Caesarea Philippi, he asked his disciples, saying, Whom do men say that I the Son of man am? And they said, Some say that thou art John the Baptist: some, Elias; and others, Jeremias, or one of the prophets. He saith unto them, But whom say ye that I am? And Simon Peter answered and said, Thou art the Christ, the Son of the living God. And Jesus answered and said unto him, Blessed art thou, Simon Barjona: for flesh and blood hath not revealed it unto thee, but my Father which is in heaven. And I say also unto thee, That thou art Peter, and upon this rock I will build my church; and the gates of hell shall not prevail against it.—Matthew 16:13-18

As an endnote on the Mashiach's famed proclamation that *"the gates of hell shall not prevail,"* I urge you, please, to personally repeal centuries of conditioning in papal authoritarianism and ecclesiastical self-glorying to consider that He was not referring to the church/ekklesía in that profound passage. The ekklesía was not the subject of that conversation, nor was Simon Pétros; the topic was who and what *Yeshua Himself* was rumored to be. It is far more likely that He was here referring to the ancient *seed prophecy* of the Torah from the Book of Beginnings (Genesis). This "seed prophecy" actually took the form of a series of ancient prophecies iterated in various pronouncements beginning with one to the Serpent, then to Abraham, and later to Jacob, as follows:

Not long after the very inception of earth's history, while uttering the curses upon all three of the original Eden transgressors (Adam and Eve included), the Lord addressed the Serpent individually with a prophetic curse declaring his ultimate demise. This profound proclamation doomed the gleeful Serpent to a very hollow victory on earth in which he would ultimately prevail no more than to merely bruise the heel of the promised Seed:

And the LORD God said unto the serpent, Because thou hast done this [deceived the man and woman and destroyed His paradise], thou art cursed above all cattle, and above every beast of the field; upon thy belly shalt thou go, and dust shalt thou eat all the days of thy life: And I will put enmity between thee and the woman, and between thy seed and her seed; it shall bruise thy head, and thou shalt bruise his heel. (Genesis 3:14-15)

There is no question here about which is the prevailing bruise, or the prevailing seed.

Note that this was a prophecy of double entendre, or dual meaning, having a general as well as a more particular application. It applied to "the seed" in general, the human children of the Mother of All Living (i.e., Eve, whose name means *life, living, life-giver*),[35] all of whom would henceforth be universally beset by evil and destruction at the hands of the children of death and evil. (This wicked breed was the spiritually begotten seed of their murderous father the Devil, the author of destruction and death.) But more specifically, it was a reference to a *singular* and special Seed who would ultimately crush the head of the Serpent, although His "heel" (symbolically speaking) would sustain a "bruising" by him.

Overall, enmity and an ongoing adversarial contest was prophesied to be the earthly order of affairs. But in the final analysis, the contest was to result in the seed of the woman sustaining what was considered only minor injury, as compared to the skull crushing which is to be suffered by the enemy of Life.

It is also noteworthy to establish here that the woman bears no seed of her own, since, physiologically speaking, that is the exclusive function of the male gender that actually produces seed. The woman only bears seed that has been *implanted*. In the case of the Christian account of the virgin birth of Christ, and in accordance with promise of the Hebrew prophet Isaiah (Is. 7:14-9:7), a virgin was implanted and bore a seed called Immanuel (i.e., "with us is God," per the literal Heb.).[36] This divinely implanted Seed is the Life and the Light of men, which cannot be prevailed against; and moreover, *His* seed (spiritual offspring), though it "die" and fall into the ground, shall remain only temporarily buried before it once again springs to back to life (that can never be quenched). Death is only a very temporal bruising of minor consequence for the children of Life and Light.

Later, but still quite early in history, another pearl in this string of intriguing seed promises shows that the Lord introduced long ago to Abraham in no uncertain terms this theme of *"the gates of hell versus the Seed."* According to this Genesis pronouncement upon Abraham's Seed, ultimately *"the gate of his enemies"* shall certainly succumb to conquest.

In this prophecy He solemnly proclaims, *"By myself have I sworn, saith the LORD, for because thou hast done this thing, and hast not withheld thy son, thine only son: That in blessing I will bless thee, and in multiplying I will multiply thy seed as the stars of the heaven, and as the sand which is upon the sea shore; and thy seed shall possess the gate of his enemies; and in thy seed shall all the nations of the earth be blessed; because thou hast obeyed my voice." (Genesis 22:16-18)* We find here a reference to a Seed of Abraham—beside the multiplied seed of his innumerable descendants—who prevails to seize and "possess" the gate of *His* enemies.

That, of course, was the prophesied role of the Mashiach, the Anointed One who was to *"proclaim liberty to the captives and the opening of the prison to them that are bound"* and *"set at liberty them that are bruised."* *(Isaiah 61:1 & Luke 4:18)*

Finally now, to tie these Genesis pronouncements together in parallel with Christ's own classic proclamation on the gates of Hades, we shall reference a prophecy given by Jacob over his twelve sons just before he died. A beautiful and telling "parenthetical insertion" finds its way into the serial foretelling and blessing of the fortunes of his heirs, the patriarchs-to-be of all the progeny of Israel. This "incidental" inclusion speaks of the coming of a *distinctive shepherd.*

Appearing in verse 24 of Genesis chapter 49 in the fortune forecast over Joseph, is the mention of "the shepherd, the *stone* of Israel" proceeding from the divine strength of Jacob: *"Joseph is a fruitful bough, even a fruitful bough by a well; whose branches run over the wall: The archers have sorely grieved him, and shot at him, and hated him: But his bow abode in strength, and the arms of his hands were made strong by the hands of the mighty God of Jacob; (from thence is the shepherd, the stone of Israel . . .)"* *(Gen.49:22-26)*

Christ Yeshua—of the loins of Jacob descended through Mary from the tribe of Judah—was the fulfillment of that shepherd-stone prophecy. And when expounding in Matthew chapter 16 on Simon's revelation (from The Father) that *He was the rock*, Jesus even further fleshed out the prophetic picture of *"the stone of Israel"* forecast by the Torah. He did so by adding the declaration, from Genesis 22, that the gates of His enemies, Death and Hades—the tandem mortal duo on the back of the pale horse of Revelation 6:8—would not prevail against *The Rock*, the Stone of Israel. And indeed, Death and Hades—and the presiding power over them, the Devil—are all ultimately subdued in the final analysis and cast into the perpetual liquid fire incinerator spoken of in chapter 20 of the Apocalypse (Rev.20:10-14).

The word *hell* in the phrase *gates of hell* is actually referring to the Greek name of the holding place of the dead, Hades. According to Apostle Peter, it is into this prison that Messiah passed after his crucifixion during His time "in the tomb" when actually *"he went and preached unto the spirits in prison."* *(1 Pe.3:19)*[37] Apostles Paul and Luke also confirm this hyperphysical activity in passages out of the Epistle to the Ephesians and in the Book of Acts, respectively.[38] The gates of Hades indeed have not, cannot, and shall not prevail against either the Rock *or* the Ekklesía founded upon it. For death is only a temporary phenomenon that has already been conquered—a central conviction of Christian faith.

So when this corruptible shall have put on incorruption, and this mortal shall have put on immortality, then shall be brought to pass the saying that is written, Death is swallowed up in victory. O death, where is thy sting? O grave, where is thy victory? (1 Corinthians 15:54-55)

And fear not them which kill the body, but are not able to kill the soul: but rather fear him which is able to destroy both soul and body in hell.[39] (Matthew 10:28)

So you see, the only contradiction in this concept and theme of overcoming is the prevailing cowardly contrariness stubbornly maintained *against* the biblically-insured *promise* of Tribulation by the pre-Tribulation rapture gainsayers. Sadly, their prevailing fear of having to die to themselves in this world has essentially overcome their faith in the supremely rewarding promise it brings. Beware their itchy-ear contagion, lest you turn your ears to their contradictory fables for relief, and thereby shun the fellowship of Christ's suffering for the fellowship and comfort of their congregations of cowardice.

9

MARVEL, OR REVOLT?

Then if any man shall say unto you, Lo, here is Christ, or there;
believe it not.
For there shall arise false Christs, and false prophets,
and shall shew great signs and wonders; insomuch that,
if it were possible, they shall deceive the very elect.
Behold, I have told you before.
Wherefore if they shall say unto you, Behold, he is in the desert; go not
forth: behold, he is in the secret chambers; believe it not. For as the
lightning cometh out of the east, and shineth even unto the west;
so shall also the coming of the Son of man be.
Matthew 24:23-27

Dire Straits

The days under consideration in this manifesto—including times of tribulation such as have never before occurred in all of history—are indeed days
from which we should all hope to be able to escape. The unimaginable horrors of these approaching days are spoken of in bleak (yet hopeful) terms;
days which even the holy "Green Berets" (i.e., the spiritual elite) of the Ekklesia
would hardly be able to endure had they not been deliberately abbreviated to
a very limited period. Various Scriptures, as follows, conclude that these times
we are contemplating as soon to transpire on earth have no comparison in the
history of the world:

For in those days shall be affliction, such as was not from the beginning of the
creation which God created unto this time, neither shall be. And except that the
Lord had shortened those days, no flesh should be saved: but for the elect's
sake, whom he hath chosen, he hath shortened the days.—Mark 13:19-20

For then shall be great tribulation, such as was not since the beginning of the world to this time, no, nor ever shall be. And except those days should be shortened, there should no flesh be saved: but for the elect's sake those days shall be shortened.—Matthew 24:21-22

Woe to the inhabiters of the earth and of the sea! for the devil is come down unto you, having great wrath, because he knoweth that he hath but a short time. . . . And the dragon was wroth with the woman, and went to make war with the remnant of her seed, which keep the commandments of God, and have the testimony of Jesus Christ.—Revelation 12:12-17

And at that time shall Michael stand up, the great prince which standeth for the children of thy people: and there shall be a time of trouble, such as never was since there was a nation even to that same time: and at that time thy people shall be delivered, every one that shall be found written in the book.— Daniel 12:1

But, it's not just widespread holocaust that is prophesied to prevail during this brief, but frightful and impending epoch. Indeed, practically unimaginable and inconceivable wonders will, during this same time, enrapture the populace of earth with a flood of "miracles" and marvels that shall sweep them off their feet (and into perpetual perdition).

As certainly must have been gathered by this time, it is especially not the intent of this book to in any way lull its readers, nor, if it can helped, to even stand for them to be by any other means lulled into any sense of false security or hollow hope as regards this notoriously unparalleled and imminent period of history. Quite to the contrary, the voice being resounded here is one that desperately cries the opposite. Indeed, this quite unflattering and uncompromising voice is often much like a sharp and heavy ax laid to the root of the trees, so to speak. It has flaunted convention and mild manners to "talk straight" and confront prophetic issues and related traditional mainstream views head-on, the chips falling where they may!

Without any "pussy-footing" around, this unabashedly brazen voice has shouted loudly that it is high time to prepare the way of the Lord and *"make His paths straight!"* The dire character of our times demands it!

What do I mean "prepare" and "make His paths straight?" I mean, if the overall spirit of this book is heeded, people will radically revolutionize their way of thinking as regards the times in which we live. And as a consequence, they will also thoroughly revise their lifestyles to match the colossal difference between what Messiah and the Prophets teach about the value of the things of this world and our life in it, as opposed to what the overwhelming established order's carnal program dictates.

Elijah and the Revolution

As first proclaimed by Isaiah, and later by the prophet Malachi, the era just prior to the coming of Yahweh is established in their prophecies as a preparatory period meant to involve the heralding of a *divine manifesto which sets things straight*. Affairs, conditions, understandings, etcetera, are all meant to be suitably realigned. A reversal, remission and correction of error is called for and *urged* by the "manifesto" to be heralded. This crucial priming of the way of the LORD constitutes a laying of essential groundwork, which basically consists of the appropriate preparing of *hearts and minds* for the advent of the coming of the Great (and dreadful) Day of the LORD.[1]

The obvious implication in the prophetic proclamations of Isaiah and Malachi is that preexisting conditions and the prevailing ways of earth's contemporary societies are definitely not in good enough order to be considered fitting for the arrival of the holy and all-good Supreme Being, Creator of Heaven and Earth. In fact, the unacceptable conditions on our planet are described as crooked, broken and uneven, as well as obstructed and virtually impassable.

A close study of the passage to which we are referring from Isaiah chapter 40 (cited in the preceding footnote) tells of a voice that comes not from a theological institute, a seminary, or the campuses of Christian universities, rabbinical schools, churches or synagogues. Its origins are *not* in the heavily trafficked thoroughfares of metropolitan centers; nor does it issue from the mass media fountainheads which are cradled there; nor is it heard in the floods of voices that stream from them. Instead, Isaiah describes the preparatory proclamation as being heralded by a voice *"that crieth in the wilderness."*

These two prophecies saw a primary fulfillment already in the illustrious 1st century life of John the Baptizer, the famous herald of Yeshua Ha'Mashiach. His lone, nonconformist, and sometimes even confrontational voice, attracted the seekers of truth out into the wilderness to his purification rites in the

Jordan River. His message, in anticipation of Messiah's coming, was straight-forward and radical: Clean up your act, abandon your routine error, return from deviance to a right way, *and* definitely take *not* your supposed *chosen* status for granted.[2] He resounded the proclamation of the prophet Isaiah, de-creeing that global revolutionary reversals should be the preparatory order of the day. (Our times, so very obviously, scream out the indisputable urgency for nothing short of radical revolutionary change, which contrasts sharply with the feeble "revivals" some so mildly call for.)

Along these corrective lines, the preparatory manifesto calls for that which has not been esteemed to be exalted (e.g., the stranger-and-pilgrim mentality of the Patriarchs, which once renounced Egyptian-ism—that is, affection for the established order) and what has been highly esteemed and exalted (esp. institutionalized prosperity worship) to get set to be toppled.[3] The twisted, deviant, fraudulent crookedness of the establishment's beaten path must be straightened, according to the herald prophecy.[4]

That same radical spirit of reversal (or *repentance*) is the essence of the message being proclaimed in this book. Accordingly, no aspect of the status quo (socio-political, religious, or otherwise) is in any way regarded herein as sacrosanct, as was exactly the case in the days of the baptizing herald of Christ Yeshua. John unrelentingly assailed both the corrupt political estab-lishment of his day (esp. Herod) as well as the viperish venom of the toxic religious institutions of the time.[5] There is certainly no interest here in "reviv-ing" or returning to any institutionalized system or established order—par-ticularly to erring, convoluted, traditional religious systems, though they be highly esteemed—other than a program of straight compliance with the un-adulterated Law of God as given by Messiah and the Prophets.

Indeed, the Kingdom of God is at hand! But the end is definitely not yet. Thorough purging of the threshing floors of final harvest by a preceding bap-tism of Truth and fire must be accomplished first. That is, the hollow hulls of chaff which only mimic the shape and form of the real wheat must be sepa-rated for discarding and eradication. This is accomplished at the harvest by a threshing or "assailing" of the genuine grain to purge it of that which is un-desirable, unavailing, and worthless. This to me, is another clear indication that great tribulation is a preparatory process that is not impertinent even to the "cream of the crop."

According to Malachi's "Elijah prophecy," which calls for spiritual revo-lution, doom and annihilation shall be the fate of Earth, if not for the turning *"of the heart of the fathers to the children, and the heart of the children to their fathers."* This *turning of hearts* is precisely the nature of the redemptive mission of the herald that Malachi promised—*"to make ready a people prepared for the Lord."*[6] That group of hearts is still being qualified, incorporated, and readied; but, sad to say, the contrary heart of the great masses of earth will, in the final threshing, revolt against the good God of Creation.

Preparing people for *the ultimate reality* of one world under Yahweh begins with reconnecting them to their Roots. Namely, restoring their relation to their Creator and Father and reinstating His Ways as *the* blueprint for life. This was Elijah's task, John's task, and always that of any serious disciple of the I AM (YHWH, the ever-existing and omnipotent one): to strive to turn hearts from the Establishment Lie to the truth and righteousness of God.

Malachi's turning of the heart of the children to the fathers and the heart of the fathers to the children signifies that very reconnection, reversal, and repentance, or *revolution* against the paradigm of self-serving secularism and hedonistic idolatry. If this were not to be accomplished, according to the prophecy, the annihilation of humanity would be sweeping and global. As it is, only few are chosen, though many be called.[7] But it is those relatively few seekers of The Transcendent Truth that must be sought out for reconnection. The reconnection, as implied in the prophecy, consists in essence of a revolution—accomplished first and above all in the heart.

Almost going without saying, it is practically a given that the revolution should begin with turning the hearts of the *fathers*. To turn the heart of the "fathers" to the children involves a revolt from self-centered "adult" preoccupations and passions to the primary welfare of the children. It means sparking concern and compassion among caring leaders for the generations of posterity, so as to redeem them from error, waywardness, and faithlessness (all of which are now thoroughly institutionalized in our modern pagan, highly hedonistic societies structured primarily for adult ambitions and appetites).[8]

Contrary to the heretical experimental philosophies of contemporary secular social "scientists" and their dismally manifest (yet unacknowledged) failure—who have fulfilled the *"evil men and seducers"* prophecy of Apostle Paul by their politically correct *"form of godliness, which denies the power thereof,"* namely, *GOD* (see II Timothy 3)—this redemption and revolt from humanist error is **the only** compassionate formula for sparing the children, or anyone else, from destruction and perdition! Turning *"the disobedient to the wisdom of the just"* (Luke 1:17) is the quintessential objective of the Elijah

Revolution. And, this duty is incumbent upon the fathers, not a matter of the initiative of the children! What the fathers sow, they shall reap.[9]

Turning the heart of the fathers to the children is only accomplished by an abandoning of their adultist selfishness and a forsaking of their egoistic adult preoccupations with anti-God materialism. It is only then that they shall be able to rightly live for the children. And it is only then that they may truly bless their lives and maximize their future happiness by teaching them the Truth.

Moreover, unless we all jettison our spiritual adultism and accept the unadulterated faith of Christ in childlike fashion—rather than in analytically adultist, skepticist, escapist, and revisionist fashion—there shall be no entrance for us into the New World Order of the Prince of Peace.[10] (Let's face it, it takes the sophistication of an analytical adult to figure out how to evade biblical facts that require a non-evasive response, like "no man can serve two masters" and "he that shall endure unto the end shall be saved.")

The Revolution of Love and Truth completes is full cycle when the heart of the children is turned to *"the wisdom of the just."* To turn the heart of the "children" to *the fathers* is to reach out to those posterior generations (esp. vulnerable youth, though not necessarily only youth) to sway them back from apostasy and paganism to the faith of the just and faithful *patriarchs.*[11]

Again, the prime objective is to turn all who do not honor God—particularly those who have descended from a heritage of worshipping God—back *"to the wisdom of the just."* What would the overall goal and "big picture" then be? To restore Truth the world over, that it might be a solid foundation for building Faith in YHWH in the hearts of *all* people.[12]

(An interesting note to interject here is that more than one of every three persons in today's world of almost 5.8 billion people, or about 2,000,000,000 are under age 25; staggering numbers to work with toward restoring to the justness and wisdom of the ancient believing fathers!)

"Fathers" in the spiritual sense are those who beget and lead children of faith.[13] Leaders are essentially fathers. And it is *they who are responsible* for their flocks of spiritual (or political) children.[14] Good leaders who truly care about those who follow them, as Christ taught, are those who *give their lives* for the sheep.[15] On the other hand, "hirelings" are mere self-interested profiteers working for money or some other form of self-aggrandizement. Messiah cautioned us that they could be discerned just as good or bad trees are—by their fruit. Obviously, a good leader will not lead someone into a pit or any other type of harmful situation (unless he himself can't even see where he's going).

But followers, too, bear responsibility for seeking out good leadership and sound doctrine; and they do make their own choices (for which they shall be held individually accountable) as they are presented with the assortment of selections. Here too is where the wheat is separated from the chaff. The spiritual children of Faith are distinguished from the flesh-oriented children of the world, the lovers of the here-and-now, by what they choose to pursue and devote their lives to. Either the hearts of the children will prefer to turn to the wisdom of the just fathers of The Faith, or *"they shall turn away their ears from hearing the truth, and shall be turned unto fables."* (2 Timothy 4:4)

As for revolution, the turning of one's allegiance and devotion from the hallowed halls of the prosperity-worshipping establishment to the love-not-the-world, Kingdom of God doctrine of Messiah is the only authentic or meaningful revolution of any consequence. If the hailed and much-promoted Christian "revival" can accomplish *this*, rather than a mere revival of moralistic materialism and "holy mammonism," then perhaps they shall escape the threshingfloors of the Great Tribulation. Meanwhile, their false prophets and false-Christ establishments, which sport a form of godliness but only deny the Truth, should be turned away from and revolted against.

And now also the axe is laid unto the root of the trees: therefore every tree which bringeth not forth good fruit is hewn down, and cast into the fire . . . He that cometh . . . shall baptize you with the Holy Ghost, and with fire: Whose fan is in his hand, and he will throughly purge his floor, and gather his wheat into the garner; but he will burn up the chaff with unquenchable fire.—Matthew 3:10-12

Mind-Benders and Marvels

The largest reason why false Christs and false prophets are so plentiful in today's world is simply because the plain Truth is so unpopular. Teachings and doctrines of high regard that gain broad acceptance and popularity are almost always the products of false prophets.[16]

Zealous materialism and committed devotion to a mundane lifestyle, as popular wisdom promotes, may indeed gain a person all the world has to offer, this is true. The finest universities in the world and most other institutions of higher learning now generally and unashamedly promote this very style of life as the major brand of success. And our publicly funded schools (now thoroughly secular in the USA and elsewhere) are fully committed to an academic objective with precisely that emphasis—preparation for unmitigated participation in the world of mammon (while denying the power and priority of God). It's the standard conditioning.

So then, when Truth teaches that such purely materialistic goals are absolute vanity and a revolt against God, the great majority of people automatically react against it. Almost as an involuntary reflex, they impulsively reject such "unacceptable" precepts as untenable and fanatical.[17] They almost always opt for more pleasing (i.e., self-satisfying) ideas and readily tune in to those who promote them.[18]

The biblical idea of putting spiritual values above carnal ones, with the promise of reaping unseen benefits in a future beyond the door of death, requires more faith than most folks can muster. And as we have noted, it most certainly is not the standard programming advanced by the political, economic, and educational establishments of the world. Sadly, an ungodly number even of religious cultures regularly go to bed with the standard establishment program, prosperity worship (mammonism). And, as has already been extensively examined in earlier chapters, many have commonly made serving two masters an adulterous art as well as a religious science. Even supposed pious Bible believers regularly and commonly fall prey to the popular "standard program."

Isn't the interest in some form of personal benefit or reward what generally drive most all of us? Well, what exactly is our itch, and who will scratch it? And, around whom does the generally covetous, prosperity-seeking populous seem to gather and pay most tribute? Isn't that which is popular, pleasing, or broadly promoted by the powers-that-be—especially *prosperity*—generally the standard platform of the prophets-for-profit which dominate our social landscape, be they political or evangelical?

The allure of material prosperity (i.e., fulfillment of fleshly lusts, translating ultimately to self-aggrandizement) holds an overwhelming power over most people. In fact, the great majority see it not as a snare, but quite popularly as the indisputable standard purpose in life. And they almost instantly follow those who openly promote it, including those who more subtly offer it—with ulterior motive—as one of the perks or incidental benefits of being a contributing program "partner" (take the common brand of pious prosperity prophets of television notoriety as a prime example).

The captivating power of these assorted scratchers of the popular itch—be they pagan or pious—can sometimes be rather fleeting however. So, clinching the devotion of the itchy public often requires a certain boost in order to maintain subscribership, control, power and profit. What other allure, then, might be added to that of sheer material satisfactions to seize and capture the unwitting populace more effectively?

Miracles and marvels, of course! Scientific miracles, paranormal miracles, spiritual miracles, metaphysical manifestations, any kind of miracle most often serves the purpose! When the occasional demonstration of great signs and wonders is blended into the allurement, the capacity for captivation is greatly enhanced.

Today's world is one where marvels are so commonplace that we fail to take adequate stock of them. And in our day and age, the great majority of marvels and wonders are of the scientific and technological variety, demonstrated in the arenas of medicine, electronics, mechanization, weaponry, manufacturing, chemistry, and other fields where high technology now flourishes. Our modern era, especially within the last 100 years, but more especially within the last few decades—and more so with each passing year, or week as the case may be—is replete with *marvels!* Each new wonder exhibited or publicly announced is quickly surpassed these days by another that rapidly follows on its heels. Wonders have become so commonplace that they are routinely *expected* now as part of everyday life.

Whether it be a new wonder drug, or landing a man on the moon or a space probe on Mars, operating a space station, exploding a nuclear weapon, building a skyscraper or a supercomputer, projecting moving images and sounds out of thin air on glass "windows" in our living rooms, compacting concerts, movies or entire encyclopedias on shiny plastic discs, deploying a space-based laser weapon or a Hubble telescope, divining the future or the past (e.g., next week's weather, or the origins of the universe), transplanting a heart (and now whole bodies!),[19] growing body parts in a laboratory (such as the famed human-shaped ear on the mouse's back),[20] or bringing an assassinated political figure back to life (as we shall soon see), it all serves to add to the power of the persuasion, to rally the devotees, to boost the passion of the patriots, and to solidify the controlling influence of the miracle workers.

Wonders and signs always woo and bedazzle the multitudes and effectively sway them into assorted fan clubs, whether they be nations or denominations, or any other popular fad or fashion.

Spiritual miracles or paranormal wonders, such as faith-healings of cripples or cancer patients are no less effective in galvanizing the public. Which is not to say that miracles and wonders of any and all sorts are intrinsically evil or deleterious. Messiah Himself certified His own authenticity by performing innumerable assorted miracles; as did various other prophets of the Bible. Miracles and great wonders can and do serve as convincing signs that establish authenticity. But therein also lies a power that can be utilized in very pernicious ways.

Moreover, the power of miracles and wonders to captivate people throughout history has never yet reached its zenith, at least not on a global scale, such as it will within the next few years. According to the Hebrew prophets, wonders of unbelievable magnitude and power are yet to be exhibited on planet Earth. The following chapter discusses more about this future phenomenon, which we have yet to witness and experience, to be demonstrated for more than just sheer entertainment, you can be sure. The magnitude of these upcoming mega-marvels will be such that no one will be untouched by their awesome power.

Mind-blowing signs and wonders of both good and evil intent will occur before the eyes of the whole 21st century world, galvanizing us all into one of two possible camps. The camp of the revolutionary new order of Elijah will rally behind the two sackclothed prophets of YHWH who will manifest supernatural powers aimed at countering the evil agenda of the Antichrist. The other camp will be the camp of the "new" world order of the *Old Serpent*. They will be enticed headlong into selling their souls to this tyrannical lizard when this unholy Dragon parades his mighty miracles and potent power before earth's peoples to seduce us into submission to his highminded, diabolical hegemony of our planet.

The Serpent's grandiose, miracle-reinforced agenda will of course have the *same popular appeal* of every other age before—lust-based, human ego-serving prosperity.

Appealing to *"the lust of the flesh, the lust of the eyes, and the pride of life,"* he will successfully seduce the entire world (including you and me, if we love not the truth) into serving his real purpose. What this evil-minded epitome of narcissism seeks above all is the global validation of himself as the supreme being of the cosmos. In order to fully attain this outrageously haughty ambition, you and I and all of earth's people must be persuaded to acknowledge, adore and submit to him without reservation. And indeed the great majority will be sweepingly seduced by the allure of his ostensible human prosperity agenda, including many so-called Christians and other "holy peoples."

Let's never forget Messiah's somber admonition for the "chosen ones" noted earlier: Even the elite among them might be seduced and deceived, He said, by the absolutely astounding phenomena which the lying lizard—cloaked in savior guise—will produce in order to certify himself as "God" and to validate his global prosperity plan as viable and attainable.

The promise of prosperity and peace beyond all previously imagined limits will be the platform of the subtil serpent's appeal to the human race. The fabulously outrageous claims and grandiose worldly promises made by the supreme egotist of all ages will require the persuasive power of incredible "lying wonders" to successfully induce the people of the world into selling their souls for his brand of "salvation and immortality." The brand is already being advertised and promoted to Earth's anxious consumers, *coming soon* under his "divine and immortal" leadership and supremacy. You guessed it, the preserving and indefinite prolonging of the pursuit of our insatiable carnal cravings and passions will be the appeal.

The Evil One's world prosperity plot will be heavily studded with fantastic marvels of mega-magnitude to pump up his claims that humanity will achieve carnal immortality with him under his program. This time, just before the closing of the curtains on the final act of the serpent-human drama, all the stops will be pulled. Even those of us who already anticipate the challenge of being tempted by the fabulously incredible marvels we are all about to see— and consider ourselves spiritually and mentally armed to withstand—ought not to presume ourselves so completely immune to the power of the universal allure.

The "Universal" Allure and The Race Against Time

I had hoped originally to appeal in this book to a general audience outside of just religious or Christian folk, but I congratulate any reader who has managed to wade with me through this much of this unadulterated diatribe, especially Christians. My off-road tour through the prophetic scriptures of the Bible (& the related detours) has admittedly been rough, rocky, and unpaved with smooth lecture. Much of it has likely been even unintelligible to the uninitiated in Holy Writ, those unfamiliar, that is, with the Sacred Scriptures of the Bible. I offer my apologies for my style, and can only hope and pray that you are still with me to finish off the rest of this "classic" thesis.

If you are not Christian, perhaps it is because you know what you are "missing"; that is, you've elected against the idea for your own good reasons. If you are a Christian and still reading this book, you are stronger, hungrier, or more courageous than most about having your beliefs questioned and challenged (which is why I congratulate you). It could, however, be that you are simply seeking to try my spirit for evidence of false prophethood; which I'm glad of, and I again applaud you. For those who are not Christians in the mainstream sense, forgive me for tiring you with my repeated hacks to the roots of the trees of traditional and modern mainstreet religious cults. But, a great many are either fruitless or bearers of toxic fruit, and I purpose to steer you away from involvement with them, for obvious reasons.

At this point, I wholeheartedly encourage you to keep reading and stick with me to the end, whether you are "religious," or not. I am committed, in terms of seeking the Truth and its furtherance in the best way I know how, to both you who are and you who are not. If my fruit seems tough, hard and uninviting on the outside, perhaps its merits are at its core. If it's just too strong, or bitter, or acrid, or pungent, or simply too foul to swallow, I'm sure you will have already spit it out. Strong medicine can be very unpleasant to take. Beware of what is easy and appealing. The choices of fruits I am outlining in this book are not easy, I know, but they are critical to survival.

Trees are known by their fruits, and the evil ones are not always so easy to discern, until after you've ingested them. Consider them carefully; for what you swallow can kill you; and a deadly fruit is being cultivated even now on the tree of 20th century life which will be fully ripe and ready for worldwide consumption in just a few years. As I said, it's already being advertised. It will have universal appeal to the human race, and many are even now partaking of its green, unripened firstfruits. Some can hardly wait. Mouths are watering in anticipation. The fruit is one that no one could possibly turn down. Imagine, the promise of "life," enduring life on the edge of immortality!

Does this hold any allure for you? Does an extended life on earth appeal to you? What might be so "universally" appealing about living 100 or 150 years, or 200, or 250, or practically forever? Well, I suppose that longevity without prosperity and health would not have much appeal; but suppose it did. Naturally, I cannot personally begin to answer these questions on your behalf, or anyone else's.

Let me, instead, ask you personally: Would *you* take advantage of a new treatment or medical advance which could double your life span (healthfully, of course)? And, what would be so "deadly" or dreadful about that, as I am seeming to suggest?

Well, I cannot be sure, of course, what your individual answer might be. But I do know what the broad consensus seems to be on the part of the general public, and I imagine you might probably agree with my assessment. Though I have never done an official survey on the subject, there are many, many evidences that make it very apparent what the society at large feels in this regard—most Christians and non-Christians alike.

From my nearly half-century's experience on earth, much of it heavily involved with folk and studies of a religious/spiritual kind, little of it convinces me that Western Christians embrace or embody the original, fundamental character and elements of their mother Faith, which serve to set a person apart from the "heathenism" of the world. The very great majority of them that I have encountered along the way, and hereby testify to, seem to be just as covetous, materialistic, and sold out to the secular establishment program ("the cares of this life and the deceitfulness of riches" Christ taught against) as practically any non-believer. Only, they espouse a "moralism" (quite superficially usually) which they fancifully imagine to be of some sanctifying or redeeming value and to set them apart from the "sinners."

Worldliness is a malady that Christians, by Christ's own definition, should technically be untainted of; yet it permeates their congregations and denominations as pervasively as the Black Death of the 14th century that swept through Europe. Uninfected survivors are rare and hardy individuals indeed. I see precious little that comforts me about the modern Christian resolve here in the West to resist the plague of the Establishment Agenda (or its Tyrannosaurean New World Order program—thanks for allowing me to coin a word now and then). They will be as apt to swallow The Lizard's luciferian agenda as anyone, perhaps for reasons that need at little more exposé and may yet be a little less than obvious. (Again, please stick with me.)

Simply put, there is just no detectable solid quality to their religious philosophies, or any unshakable feature of their lifestyles, which I can detect, that would render them anywhere near able to withstand the pressures of the Great Trial into which we shall all soon be thrust. (Of course they largely don't believe they even need to be, and take it totally for granted they won't even be here!) They broadly profess belief in the Bible and Heaven, and in being "born again" to a new life and new love. But, their true first love is unquestionably manifest in what they *live for and invest in* today and everyday, and yesterday, and in all the days before yesterday. Really, the only ones fooled regarding their fundamental beliefs are, well, you know.

From all I can see, their diet of "fruit" comes primarily from the same Establishment tree that everyone else eats from. And it is without qualm that they liberally partake. There is absolutely no visible reason to believe that when the present Established Order flowers into the coming worldwide regime of the satanic Secular Savior the presently pious church folk will not readily turn to pay him worshipful homage. Which, of course, means they will (perhaps only haltingly) *take his Mark too*, in exchange for their continued material security and sustained carnal well-being, being unable to bear the curtailment of their steady supply of establishment fruit. Once the Lizard looses his genie of marvels from its bottle, the wishes to be granted will be "impossible" to resist. Aren't they already?

What makes me voice such critical and harsh surmisings, you may wonder? Well, again, from all of the evidences, they are already hooked, along with the rest of society, on the popular produce of the present secular tree that caters so attentively to the satisfactions of the flesh. This is quite apparently so, even to the point of having acquired quite a taste for the *sorcery* which pervades it.

Sorcery!? . . . in today's world? You mean, magic, as in Merlin, or David Copperfield? Well, not exactly. The word can be misleading, and even the dictionary is not particularly helpful in this case. As in the case of the word "church," which we covered in a previous chapter, we find ourselves somewhat shortchanged by the English translators of the Holy Scriptures. Let us, nonetheless, consider the daily sorceries we all partake of, and that even Christians succumb to quite commonly.

Preserving our lives for the mere worldly satisfaction of living is a primary health maintenance objective of practically every one of us, whether we denominate ourselves as Christian or not. Any of us would be hard pressed to dispute that. Were this not the actual case, the medical and pharmaceutical industries in the Western World would not be the outrageously lucrative commercial enterprises they indeed are, outstripping nearly every other industry in terms of sales, expenditures and profit, except perhaps weapons manufacture and trade (I lack the actual statistics).

The people of the (Judeo-Christian) West spare themselves *no cost what-

soever to preserve their lives and health so as to be able to continue to prolong their material-carnal enjoyment and prosperity.[21] They are fanatical in
the extreme about preserving their lives on earth, and literally cannot face
death as an acceptable option (much less any other discomfort). Absolutely
all efforts must be made, as per the Western worldview, to sustain the life of
the flesh for as long as our technologies can make possible, whether by me-
chanical, surgical, pharmaceutical, or any other means. Westerners' fear of
death is only surpassed by their inordinate love of the pleasures of life in this
cursed world of mammon, whether, as I said, they call themselves Christian
or not.

So-called Bible believers and the majority of fundamentalist Christians
are equally as hooked on the sorceries of Western medicine as any other run-
of-the-mill person. They are just as addicted to the modern pain-relieved
lifestyles of the Tylenol and Advil generation as the next person. Their medicine chests are just as crammed with the pharmaceutical potions and com-
pounds of the 20th century sorcerers as any non-Bible believer. Valium, Prozac,
Ritalin, and probably Viagra are not categorically off-limits for them, if it's
"doctors orders." And they get in line as fast as any other "Joe" or "Jane" for
life-saving treatments or organ transplants. "Sorceries?" you may still be asking. . . . "How can any of this be called *sorcery!?* Medicine is not sorcery!"

Let it suffice to be said that of the little more than a dozen mentions of the
practice of "sorcery" in the Bible (actually about 14), a significant number (nearly
30%) refer *not* to what most Christians classify as some sort of occult magic,
which they quickly and categorically condemn, but rather to, yes, "medicine."

A particular set of references (found in the Book of Revelation)[22] use the
word "sorcery" as a translation for the following Greek terms found in the
ancient manuscripts from which our popular English translations are derived:
pharmakeía (φαρμακεία) meaning *medication*, or *"pharmacy"* (also translated as *"witchcraft"* in Galatians 5:20); *pharmakeús or pharmakós* (variously found in the Gk. manuscripts in plural forms as φαρμάκοις, φαρμακοι,
and also φαρμακων) having the same meaning of *druggist or pharmacist*; all
are rooted in the word *phármakon* (φαρμακον) meaning *a drug, or potion.*

Now are you ready to toss that "backward" piece of literature called the
Bible into the trash? Or is it me and my extremist reading of it that ought to be
run through the garbage disposal? Or perhaps I'm just being a bit too literal
and fanatical, and maybe pharmacology is really okay in God's eyes. Well
again, you are at liberty to decide that for yourself.[23]

What most Christians do when they cannot reconcile their hallowed personal views with what the Scriptures actually say is excuse and justify, or try to reason and explain away what is just not acceptable to them (while priding themselves at how loyally they honor God's Word how literally they take it). Most self-denominated Christians who are aware that pharmacology is what the Scriptures refer to by the term "sorcery" justify their own indulgence in it by claiming that it is only a reference to *illegal* drugs and narcotics. "After all," they are ever so quick to rationalize, "God gave man the wisdom and knowledge to develop these modern marvels of chemistry and science for our benefit." Apparently, nobody knows where to draw the line these days about what is ethical or not, what is right or wrong, what is good or bad, or what is of God or not—not even the holy "Christians."

What I am driving at here is the universal allurement, the universal "lust," the universal snare. People in general, regardless of any religious devotion or affiliation, will accept **anything**—even Satan as Messiah!—if it promises or provides the most elementary desire of all.

Speaking for myself, that core human desire would be *"life to the full,"* or at least to the fullest possible, down the last drop, as much as I can possibly get of it! I think most honest folks would agree with me on this. All people, of course, don't view "Life" in the same light. What makes it meaningful does vary somewhat from person to person and sometimes from culture to culture. For some it is defined differently than for others. Very fundamentally though, and absolutely beyond debate, "life" is always connected with the *body*, the human flesh.

And anything that threatens, or curtails, or diminishes the satisfaction of that which is connected with the body becomes a dreaded enemy. Which is the reason why people go to such great lengths to counter and attempt to defeat all that which, in turn, threatens to defeat their bodies and their daily fleshly fulfillments. Thus, multibillions of dollars in the USA alone are spent each year on synthesized chemical formulations to kill pain, to combat microbes which threaten to kill us, treating or researching cures for cancer and other diseases, or to artificially sustain and prolong the life of the flesh. Everybody's on drugs here, including the Christians, because of the universal love of the flesh!

Now, don't get me wrong! Human life is a sacred and precious divine gift to be protected and treasured. But, obsessive efforts of an inordinate degree to preserve the flesh and its enjoyments are the fearful desperations of unbelieving pagans and hedonists who have no knowledge, faith, hope or trust in an ever-living God, the Almighty Creator and God of the Hebrews who has vowed to abolish death and restore His children to life (in the body). The trouble is even the nominal Christians, who swear by the God of Abraham, Isaac, Jacob and Christ, doubt and disbelieve this fundamental, core element of their Faith! My assessment is factually supported by the very way they live!

Their fervent devotion to the pursuit of materialism and carnal, worldly satisfactions, and the highly artificial means employed for preserving that style of life belies their dubious profession of faith in Christ.[24] Covetousness and carnality, no matter how moralistically practiced, is still covetousness and carnality. And by carnality, I mean catering to the desires of the flesh; sexual appetite being only one of the many lusts included in that package and definitely not the worst of them (as the sanctimonious moralists might have you believe). The "rat race" of the Babylonish West, in which the Christians run side by side with all the other blind mice, is a race against time.[25]

Time in the West (speaking for my own culture) is not viewed as an opportunity to learn to *live* (eternally, immortally); it's a sickle-wielding skeleton in a hooded cloak from which we run or hide for most of our "lives." For most, it is gauged, valued, and perceived according to the old capitalist adage: "Time is money." And what is money? Well, in the succinct summation of John the Apostle, it buys *"the lust of the flesh, the lust of the eyes, and the pride of life."* (Can you think of anything else?) Time in this culture is not a matter of living to seek and attain the secret of life. In the West, it's merely the "one and only" chance we get to eat, drink, see, hear, touch, feel, and experience merriment, pleasure, and pride (which includes self-expression). That is the Western "quintessence of life" which we strive so madly to capture and preserve. And, the longer we can put off death, the greater the illusion that we have lived!

And so, "the race is on," to savor the nectar of life, to suck all that we can from all the blossoms of this world that we can possibly drink from, and to gather all the sweetness possible; only to die in short order and leave all that honey behind.

Meanwhile, tenuously obscured behind the mad pursuits of the materialist masses, all chasing the same self-serving passions and lusts, lies the haunting, unavoidable truth: No one has ever perpetuated for themselves even the most satisfying earthly experience. That is to say, no one has ever conquered that terminal condition which guarantees an inevitable and inescapable **end** to everything that people so feverishly strive for. As King David noted, *"None can keep alive his own soul." (Ps.22:29)* Yet the venerated modern-day sorcerers ceaselessly seek to beat that end by their surgical techniques and transplants, cryogenics, new drug concoctions and ever-advancing pharmaceutical research, genetic engineering, life-support devices, tissue regeneration technologies, and various other desperate attempts to defy or defer the universal inevitability. Everything but look to the Creator and His blueprint for relief (and short-circuit their profit goals?—never!).

Every single person's opportunity to define (or discover) the meaning of life for her or himself is abruptly terminated within about 70 years (and for the great majority of the world's people residing in non-western and underdeveloped countries, considerably sooner). Rare indeed are the cases of those centenarians who have had an extended opportunity to give life meaning and to enjoy its favors. Defining life for ourselves, or having others define it for us, and then savoring it as defined is a very short-lived endeavor with an unrelenting conclusion—death for us all. What pointlessness![26]

And whatever the particular definition applied, the fact remains that unless Truth is found in the process of living, death will be the only enduring reality of which we can all be assured. Because, so-called "life" for the average person is merely the few passing pleasures between the first breath and the last, an extremely fleeting experience, which, in the final analysis, is only as real and enduring as last night's dream. *"For what is your life? It is even a vapour, that appeareth for a little time, and then vanisheth away." (James 4:14)*

For the sun is no sooner risen with a burning heat, but it withereth the grass, and the flower thereof falleth, and the grace of the fashion of it perisheth: so also shall the rich man fade away in his ways.—James 1:11

Prepare the Way of the "Maestro of Marvels"

As much as we all try not to think about death, ignoring it as long and as best we can, yet we are stalked by it. It constantly lurks to enslave people with a looming fear that unless they unreservedly indulge in the cares and pleasures of this life *while they can*, there will be no other time to do so. But a mighty one cometh who shall free us from this fear by his power to perform great signs and wonders to convince the world of some very alluring claims.

One of those magnificent marvels will be his own "resurrection" from the dead. This incredible feat of modern magic will be capitalized upon to convince the world that he holds the key to life and death, and therefore should be worshipped as God. And he *will be* universally embraced, almost! His incredible feats of power and staggering signs will certify his authenticity and convince nearly all the world that he is, alas, the god mankind has long awaited. A god who will flatteringly cater to the age-old thirst for the fountain of youth, promising relief from and conquest of the *primeval dread*—the feared and hated curse of death.

Tribute must be made at this point to one of the greatest signs humanity has ever witnessed—for which there is abundant testimony, as well as historical record, and which has had globally sweeping repercussions—the life of Christ. For over 1900 years, billions of lives have been impacted and radically changed by the words and deeds of this man who only passed through the public square of life for three-and-a-half years. In less than the single term of an American President—and without the mass media—this one man revolutionized the entire course of history.

His life is characterized not by powerful armies which He commanded, nor by empires that He ruled, but by poverty, simplicity, and the single-minded advancement of a transcendent, timeless realm not of this world, which He called "the Kingdom of Heaven." Not only did He suffer torture and death for His uncompromising furtherance of this otherworldly loyalty, but He also subsequently *returned from His grave* to unequivocally substantiate His authenticity (as having origins in Heaven) and firmly establish the veracity of His claim to the existence of this Kingdom of God. His resurrection was intended to prove He was the offspring of a timeless and immortal God, and that earthly death and the expiration of the temporal world would only reveal the indestructible domain of an all-powerful, eternal God.

How ironic it is that extraordinary and exceedingly great signs and wonders have already been performed to authenticate the biblical premise that life is a hyperphysical event connected to a divine metaphysical dimension beyond time and space. Yet, those signs and wonders are regularly and commonly discounted, diminished, denied, and often disparaged as unsubstantiated nonsense. And their author is often repudiated as the mythological figurehead of a superstitious legend promoted by overzealous devotees of a fanatical fantasy—who, it must be noted, have continually suffered cruel persecution, torture and death (for that "fantasy") at the hateful hands of their ever so "sane and rational" critics and assailants.

And in terms of sanity and rationality, contemporary Establishment schools featuring the finest products of 20th century thought and "scientific" hypothesis refuse to even consider the most logical and likely of all probabilities—that the universe is (obviously) a product of (super) intelligent design. Contrariwise (and deliberately so), they insanely prefer to irrationally relegate its formation to a totally illogical, random, unintelligent, undirected, chance-driven, unauthored process (so sophisticated and complex that they still cannot fathom the depths of it). Although they arrogantly and presumptuously profess themselves to have eyes (the mighty Hubble telescope) which can now nearly see to the very edges of the universe, back to the beginnings of time, yet, even the basic building block of life, the so-called "simple" cell, leaves them reeling from its unfathomable complexity.

For all their wisdom, understanding, "intelligence," skill and technological know-how, all they can manage to do is tinker with those microscopic cells. They cannot *make* one; for that—according to the insidious fools that pump our children's minds with their foul poison of idiocy—requires an unintelligent, unguided, random (and highly superstitious) process, to which they have even given a name, which is above every other name. It's called Big Bang Evolution, the mighty, mindless, mythological creator of heaven and earth. (And they laugh and mock at the mythologies of the ancient Greeks, Egyptians, and Canaanites etc., while they feed us this crackpot fairy tale! What a total farce!)

According to the Holy Scriptures of the Hebrews, the origin of life is with an Almighty Creator who exists outside time and space. Those ancient Scriptures give record of the very creation of time and space—and the universe contained by them—as the product and design of an eternal, all-powerful Being known to the Hebrews as the I AM. The indisputable fact that every single human being born into the world lives to witness I AM's incredible and incomparable creation constitutes the premiere and most undeniable "great sign and wonder!" The Creation and Life itself are a "magic" of extraordinarily supernatural proportions, plainly evident as such to any sentient person, whether simple child or sophisticated scientist.

Yet, like fools, our most "brilliant" thinkers and "scientific" minds conclude that the universe had its beginning in a "Big Bang" of no explainable origin. Magnificent magic—but *no magician!* Ha!

The incredibly complex and perfectly seamless design of everything from the "simplest" living cell to the precision-balanced solar system all plainly testify against the completely impossible notion that some spontaneous and unguided random process can be assigned the credit for such magnificence. Much more so does the infinite variety, beauty, intricacy and vitality of an earth exploding with life to the countless galaxies of the vast reaches of space that appear as only tiny stars in the limitless expanse of the heavens decry and negate such nonsense. It takes years of brainwashing in the "educational" institutions of the Established Order to strip people's minds of the common sense that even children possess, which tells them there is no such magic without a magician.

What is really going on is clever slight-of-hand trickery by the promulgators of such random, spontaneous magic-without-a-magician (a.k.a. scientists, professors, and educators) who have deftly swapped a ludicrously fallacious fairy tale for the simple Truth: The fable that the universe formed *by itself!* Mysterious Big Bang magic, without any cause. And of course, since there is no cause, there is also no purpose, except as either they or we, or some other cunning schemer whims to define it. There is no Creator God in their insidious evolutionary scheme. So there is therefore no purposed reason for our existence, but to become our own god and do our own will as we see fit. This is the conclusion of the heretical fable of evolutionary folly.

Secular humanist evolution teaches that God is the final product of the evolutionary chain. For God would not exist, were it not for the evolution of the human mind which has itself created God as a product of human imagination, along with all the other "mythologies." So, if we have imagined God by evolution's gift of the mind, then simple logic has it that God would not exist, if it weren't for evolution. Accordingly then, we humans (and God, in the process) are a product of "nothing" but some supposed titanic puff of magic smoke out of "nowhere" some 10-15 billion years ago. (Talk about myths, this to me is the most farcical of all fairy tales; in fact, Aladdin or Santa Claus is more credible; but they say a sucker is born every minute, and some even become scientists—with a fixation for fiction.)

You see then that *we* are really God, since *we created Him* as a figment of our collective imaginations. Poof! (or Bang!, rather) and 15 billion years later, there is God! Pretty good magic, wouldn't you say? (The slight-of-hand is just all too obvious, though, when you'd rather not be tricked.)

Evolutionary theory teaches (by logical deduction, following the hypothetical process to its ultimate end) that the eventual final product of the self-driven, autogenous, "natural" selection process will be nothing less than gods of superlative intelligence, power, might and dominion—the most advanced end result of the evolutionary chain. (Intelligence from non-intelligence, pretty smart, huh?) According to the scheme, natural selection supposedly gives rise to those creatures which will be the most fit to survive, those which most successfully adapt to their (changing) environment and, ideally, master the forces of nature. The survivors, then, are the most likely to thrive and dominate the environment and are the ultimate object of evolution.

In the broader cosmological arena dealing with the universe and its make-up and origins, few cosmogonists or cosmologists endure who do not subscribe to the universal application of evolutionary theory throughout the Cosmos. Which is to say that popular belief among the "scientific elite" of Cosmos worshippers has it that we simply cannot be alone in the apparently limitless expanse of the Big Bang universe. There *must be* life evolved on other planets elsewhere, if evolution holds true. (Which of course it must; otherwise, we should then have to acknowledge a Creator.—How unthinkable!) And without contradiction or question, untold billions of dollars are spent on SETI programs (radio astronomical Search for Extra-Terrestrial Intelligence), space telescopes (such as Hubble), and planetary exploration spacecraft and missions. All this in hope of validating the theory that we (the proud theorists) are right—evolution must be our progenitor, not God.

Sporting a noble but absolutely false humility, the Cosmos-worshipping cosmologists and cosmogonists—which includes most astrophysicists and astronomers, joined by most paleontologists, anthropologists, biologists and geneticists, and professional "educators," etc.—"humbly" concede that there must be equally advanced, if not more advanced beings of superior mastery and power somewhere out there in the universe.[27] In fact, this theory often forms the basis for modern-day rationalizations given for the past manifestations of various unexplainable, great, miraculous wonders known to have occurred throughout earth's history (other than that they are mere "myth or legend"). And, it is not such a far-fetched theory, actually.

According to the theory, beings of more advanced evolutionary progression, possessing prowess and technology ahead of our own, occasionally appeared on earth exercising powers to execute supernatural feats which were far beyond the understanding, ability and technology of the societies of the time, which were, naturally, awed by them. Those miracle workers of ages past, then, according to the ET theory, were either visitors from other worlds of more advanced civilizations, or they somehow developed powers ahead of their time. As these hypothetical explanations would have it, the witnessing of these signs and wonders in times past prompted underdeveloped cultures to deify, idolize and worship the miracle workers as gods, and also to weave the various myths surrounding them. (The fact is, as per the Bible, we're *not alone* and there *are aliens* of greater power, ability and knowledge than our own, and they have visited earth; only they are *not* products of evolution.)

Notwithstanding any of this, the fact remains that miracles and wonders do indeed capture the veneration and worship of the general public. People grasp at and latch on to power that holds out promise for greatness in which they too might share, or a power that gives them some assurance of security, which usually comes with domination.

Whether they be terrestrial or extraterrestrial in origin, the wonders and the wonder workers are dramatically on the increase, *and we ain't seen nuthin' yet!* We are right in the middle of the age of great signs and wonders. They are evident everywhere for the uninoculated observer.

Ours is the flowering age of flying machines. A mere 100 years ago men only dreamed of flying like birds. Now our scientists actually, actively formulate plans for setting our nests among the stars, terraforming and colonizing other planets.[28]

The overwhelming rash of UFO sightings in the last 50 years has sparked extensive speculation that we are not alone in the universe and may soon make open contact with more advanced civilizations from other worlds (where phantom Evolution has spawned advances beyond any we have yet seen on Earth). Scoff as we may, otherwise serious and credible experts claim that we already have made contact. And for the most part, the general public—especially its youth—is now practically prepared and open to a UFO/ET arrival and encounter.

So, what sweet and juicy evil fruit could the flowering of this humanist age soon dangle temptingly from its godless limbs—an ET-human alliance, perhaps? Will you partake because of promise of earthly "security," or a longer more prosperous life on earth?

Master Yeshua (Jesus) long ago foretold the coming of pseudo divine ones (counterfeit Messiahs and powerful spurious saviors), and of fallacious prophets (preparing the way for the pseudo saviors), who He said would precede and preempt His own coming. He warned that they would arise showing great signs and wonders to captivate the world. So fantastic would these mighty future wonders be that He even predicted His own elite disciples might possibly be seduced by them.

This same passage of endtime prophecy also cautioned against being taken in by rumors and reports that underground bunkers in top secret facilities in the desert—such as the now famed "Area 51" in the Nevada desert of the USA, or any other like it—were quarters or refuge of a "select" or advanced being come to lead humanity to divinity. And as for unidentified flying objects (UFOs), of which we have only begun to see but a fleeting few, the identity and description of the most spectacular one yet to appear in our skies is also given by Jesus in our anchor passage of prophecy from Matthew, chapter 24.[29]

Be mindful too that, as the UFO and ET phenomenon blossoms into 21st century prevalence—attaining politically correct status—you dare not denounce or blaspheme these *close encounters.* Jeopardy of ridicule or persecution as a reactionary religious mythologist awaits you. "Everybody knows" that Evolution has not left us alone in the universe; and only the superstitious, narrow-minded "God freaks" believe in antiquated notions of spirits and demons, and Jesus. Even the Pope (John Paul II) has now compromised with Evolution, according to front page headlines in local and national newspapers across the USA on Friday, October 25, 1996.[30]

Before we can even spell the word "extraterrestrials," they and the UFO phenomenon (along with their evil father, a.k.a. Evolution) will completely displace God and the Holy Scriptures as the belief system of the younger generation now being bred by the Novus Ordo Seclorum. In fact, unless I am mistaken, I believe we have already spelled "extraterrestrials!"

And great earthquakes shall be in divers places, and famines, and pestilences; and fearful sights and great signs shall there be from heaven. But before all these, they shall lay their hands on you, and persecute you, delivering you up to the [assemblies, translated as "synagogues" in the KJV Bible], and into prisons, being brought before kings and rulers for my name's sake. And it shall turn to you for a testimony. Settle it therefore in your hearts, not to meditate before what ye shall answer: For I will give you a mouth and wisdom, which all your adversaries shall not be able to gainsay nor resist.

And ye shall be betrayed both by parents, and brethren, and kinsfolks, and friends; and some of you shall they cause to be put to death. And ye shall be hated of all men for my name's sake. But there shall not an hair of your head perish. In your patience possess ye your souls.

And when ye shall see Jerusalem compassed with armies, then know that the desolation thereof is nigh. Then let them which are in Judaea flee to the mountains; and let them which are in the midst of it depart out; and let not them that are in the countries enter thereinto. For these be the days of vengeance, that all things which are written may be fulfilled. But woe unto them that are with child, and to them that give suck, in those days! for there shall be great distress in the land, and wrath upon this people. And they shall fall by the edge of the sword, and shall be led away captive into all nations: and Jerusalem shall be trodden down of the Gentiles, until the times of the Gentiles be fulfilled.

And there shall be signs in the sun, and in the moon, and in the stars; and upon the earth distress of nations, with perplexity; the sea and the waves roaring; men's hearts failing them for fear, and for looking after those things which are coming on the earth: for the powers of heaven shall be shaken. And then shall they see the Son of man coming in a cloud with power and great glory.—Luke 21:11-27

Are you prepared for the coming of Antichrist? Will you sucker for his grandiose, worldly promises and mystifying marvels and fabulous wonders? Or, will you be made a sap by the Christian escapist prophets who dupe believers into false hopes of security and safety by foolish fables of rapture theory?[31] If not prepared to marvel, the Elijah Revolution urges your own personal revolt from the web of lies that make up the secular fabric of the Established Order. Disentangle yourself today![32]

10

MESSIAH MISTAKE

Now we beseech you, brethren,
by the coming of our Lord Jesus Christ,
and by our gathering together unto him,
that ye be not soon shaken in mind, or be troubled,
neither by spirit, nor by word, nor by letter as from us,
as that the day of Christ is at hand.
Let no man deceive you by any means: for that day shall not come, except
there come a falling away first, and that man of sin be revealed, the son of
perdition; who opposeth and exalteth himself above all that is called God,
or that is worshipped; so that he as God sitteth in the temple of God,
shewing himself that he is God. . . . And now ye know what withholdeth that
he might be revealed in his time.
II Thessalonians 2:1-6

In this chapter, we shall be visiting a couple of prophetic markers which were left to us by a famous Hebrew who is so revered by the Christian peoples that he is practically reckoned as a sort of new testament Moses. He is, in fact, more read, "revered" and quoted as a premier spiritual authority by the Christians than Moses himself. (This is apparently connected with their quasi-shelving of the "Old" Testament, especially the Torah, the 5 books of Moses, as a virtual religious "relic.") All that aside, a highly noteworthy prophecy was left to us by this extraordinarily inspired figure who articulated some very key clues to help in piecing together the "big picture" of the last days.

Before his conversion to the transcendent Judaism of Christ Yeshua (later dubbed Christianity by the Greeks of Antioch) this famed Jew was called by the Hebrew name of Saul. Later, however, he took on a name of Latin origin meaning "small" or "little" and became popularly known as Paul (the Apostle).

The opening quotation cited above is from Paul's second epistle to the converted Greeks of Thessalonica in which he endeavors to calm a rumor: namely, that Messiah could appear at any moment! In this passage, he categorically states to these gentile disciples that such cannot by any means occur until two other crucial occurrences come to pass **first**.

Still to this day, however—as is also exactly the case with the teachings of Christ—a tragic irony obscuringly shadows this inspired legacy of Holy Scripture. Namely, that for the great volume of ecclesiastical lip service given to the reverencing of Paul's teachings as holy writ, yet his unambiguous divine declarations are regularly contradicted by that very same ecclesiastical cult. These folks have taken Paul's divine foreknowledge of the future and turned to negate that it means precisely what it says; the same as they have with Jesus' words!

As hinted by the subtitle of this book, the prime objective intended by it is to help effectively prepare the sober members of this last generation to prepare for the coming of Messiah while opportunity yet remains to do so. Central to that objective is driving home the realization that the Great Prince of Peace will *unequivocally not* come tomorrow or the day after, much less at any other randomly unexpected moment, as is proclaimed by the cult of the mezzanine Christians.

This particular cult is the same strain of ear-scratchers discussed earlier in chapter 2 (section entitled *Thief in the Night?*) who teach that only the Jews will have to endure the Great Tribulation, while the supposed Church escapes into the sky to merely view the event from the "mezzanine." The mezzanine, of course, being some point in the sky halfway between Earth and Heaven attained by these escapists as they rise in rapture to purportedly meet their savior in the clouds upon his return.

Integral to this particular half-way perspective is the teaching that Christian believers will not be present during the unveiling, debut and inauguration of the "son of perdition," often referred to as the Antichrist. Thus, they will also not have to be concerned about taking the mark of this beast (or resisting it), nor in any other way with having to experience the tribulation ordeal, as per the mezzanine doctrine.

"Son of Man" First, or "Man of Sin?"

Notwithstanding the half-baked prophesyings of the mezzanine cult, according to the esteemed Apostle Paul quoted at the head of this chapter from this famous epistle to the Thessalonians, the coming of Messiah must, by divine decree, be *preceded* by the revelation of the "man of sin." In addition, a preliminary period of *apostasy* (falling away, which we will discuss more shortly) must also occur before Christ's return to earth.

Note too that in addressing this prophecy to the Greek believers in Thessalonica, Paul made it eminently clear that the *"gathering together unto Him"* of *"all them that believe in that day"* is simultaneous with the coming of the LORD.[1] I iterate this (again) to emphasize that the oracle of Scripture speaks of *only one* gathering together of all the saints *at one time*; not a preliminary gathering for the Gentiles followed later by a second for the Jews—nonsense!

Paul was not addressing Hebrews or ethnic Jews in this passage. Clearly, these were primarily gentile Greek compatriots and brethren in the heart of the Grecian homeland, whom he was endeavoring to enlighten and comfort. Here, he was schooling these gentile saints concerning the aerial gathering together of all the saints unto Messiah at His second coming out of the heavens. This is important to note, because it disproves what the mezzanine cult teaches about the Jews being left behind while the gentile saints are taken out. These were *not Jews* being advised that they must witness the advent of the Antichrist prior to the coming of Christ.

Contrary to the separatist, spectator perspective of the mezzanine doctrinaires, the Gentiles as well as the Jews will see the "man of sin" be revealed before any appearance whatsoever of the rescuing Messiah. He *will not* appear spontaneously to gather the "gentile" church and leave the Jews (or any other believer) behind to suffer the Great Tribulation under the reign of the Man of Sin.

"Okay, okay, so what does it matter?" you may be thinking. "Why are you harping on this issue?" Well, in some small way, I am not just trying to set the record straight, but I'm apologizing for all of the crackpot falsehoods being promulgated by those that have the unashamed gall to associate themselves with the great name of Christ and with His (blood-sealed) gospel only to then profane them both with lies, deception, and half-hearted devotion. Believe me, there would be less than half as many folks out there calling themselves Christians, if the understanding that they must all endure the Great Tribulation before any so-called rapture were the prevailing mainstream teaching. Additionally, in apologizing for this travesty, I am also imploring you to guard against their perilous and pernicious preachings which do not prepare anyone at all for the realities of life as shall befall us all in the next few years!

If you seek truth in the least, it is better that you shut yourself up alone in a closet with the Bible and the Holy Spirit to teach you (and He will!) than to give any ear to their half-truths. The half-baked cake being served up by the half-hearted spectator-Christians who make up the half-way mezzanine cult of escapism is not merely sweet fantasy; even worse, it's pure candy-coated poison.

Not only is such insidious teaching pure cowardly fancy, it is also diametrically in conflict with the desperate need for facing the prophetic facts—in order to appropriately make ready a people prepared for the coming of the Great Prince and His Great Day. To sell such weak and watered-down formula to already anemic Christians is to prepare them for nothing but to fall headlong into perdition. For, since they expect the Messiah at any moment, for them He shall indeed arrive at a time when they least expect Him—much later, *after* the *Great Test* of faith, love and loyalty, *which they also least expect.*[2]

Consider, if their love and devotion is already strained at simply believing the clearly articulated spirit of prophecy embodied in the holy Scriptures as they stand, with what faith shall the soul of the mezzanine believer endure unto the end?[3] It is imperative, therefore, to re-examine what kind of preparation one would be compelled to make in the face of the inevitable scenario of confronting *first* the arrival and global regime of the Man of Sin.

But, proper preparation is difficult to achieve when following the counsel and direction of cowardly leaders who themselves are not prepared to set an example of faith themselves. Contrary to the tradition of the Apostle Paul, whose writings and prophetic legacies are being highlighted in this chapter, most of our modern-day apostles specialize in compromise and mezzanine-ism. Paul's example—on the other, non-escapist extreme—was of unceasing toil, travail, sacrifice and relentless striving against evil so as to spread the gospel of God.[4]

In fact, both his epistles to the Thessalonians were written to comfort and encourage them in their own related afflictions and persecutions suffered after having turned from serving idols to serving God.[5] It was Paul's expressed hope that those Greek saints would not, as a consequence of tribulation, lose patience, quit following his Spartan example, fall into temptation, and go back into serving idols and the lusts of the flesh.[6]

It was while endeavoring to foster hopeful encouragement to these persecuted Gentile brethren that Paul articulated his quite famous narration of the *first resurrection and gathering together* of all the saints (living and dead, Jew and Gentile). Referring to this in combination with several other matching passages of prophecy, it can be easily shown that this event occurs at the sounding of 7th Trumpet, which announces the Second Coming of Messiah:

But I would not have you to be ignorant, brethren, concerning them which are asleep [i.e., dead], that ye sorrow not, even as others which have no hope. For if we believe that Jesus died and rose again, even so them also which sleep in Jesus will God bring with him. For this we say unto you by the word of the Lord, that we which are alive and remain unto the coming of the Lord shall not prevent [precede or preempt] them which are asleep. For the Lord himself shall descend from heaven with a shout, with the voice of the archangel, and with the trump of God: and the dead in Christ shall rise first: Then we which are alive and remain shall be caught up together with them in the clouds, to meet the Lord in the air: and so shall we ever be with the Lord. Wherefore comfort one another with these words.—1 Thessalonians 4:13-18

Consistent with the truth, to which I am a witness, the very next point made in this same hope-and-patience epistle is just as incongruent with the Jesus-could-come-at-any-moment doctrines as all the rest of it. Paul next declares that the day of the Lord should **not** overtake these *children of light* as a thief in the night.[7]

Then, following up later with this same theme, in his second epistle to the Thessalonians (see quote at the head of this chapter), he in no uncertain terms placed the day of Christ *"after the working of Satan with all power and signs and lying wonders." (2 Thessalonians 2:9)*

This explicitly unambiguous declaration is introduced by Paul with an explanation that the mysterious dynamics of Evil were already quite active, though not fully unbridled; for, at the same time, another overarching force exercises a restraining power over evil. This greater Dynamic exerts a restraining rein upon the evil force of iniquity, effectively bridling it until it's fully unleashed; at which time it shall ultimately give birth to the son of perdition (who appears **before** the coming of Christ). In verses 6-8 of this second epistle to the Thessalonians, we read of the Force that hinders iniquity:

And now ye know what withholdeth that [the man of sin] might be revealed in his time. For the mystery of iniquity doth already work: only he who now letteth will let, until he be taken out of the way. And then shall that Wicked be revealed, whom the Lord shall consume with the spirit of his mouth, and shall destroy with the brightness of his coming.—2 Thessalonians 2:6-8

Now, in gathering the meaning of this passage, let us remember that for most modern English speakers the word "let" comes from an Old English term meaning "hinder," "impede," or "prevent." In fact, our contemporary Webster's dictionaries remain true to the Old English and give the primary meaning of let exactly as such. Even the connotation of let as "permitting" or "allowing" has its roots in the archaic meaning of let. Essentially stated here, some restraining power is withholding and preventing iniquity from fully flourishing, for the time being.

These verses speak plainly of that withholding force as *"he"* which restrains—until *"he"* be taken out of the way. The English translation here is consistent with the Greek manuscripts, where *"ho katéchoon"* is literally "he that holds down." This "he" is nothing other than the Almighty Sovereign Himself. The same power we read about in the first two chapters of the Old Testament book of Job (believed to be the oldest book in the Bible). In verses 6-12 of its first chapter, an interesting account is given of the typical activity of Satan, which reveals that YHWH God is the restraining power over him.

Again, in the first seven verses of chapter 2, we see reiterated that Satan's power is bridled by the authority and will of YHWH.[8] Yeshua also restated the supreme sovereignty and power of the Almighty in chapter 19 of John's Gospel when challenged by Pontius Pilate, who proudly asserted he had the power to either crucify or spare and release the imprisoned Christ. Yeshua responded, *"Thou couldest have no power at all against me, except it were given thee from above." (John 19:11)* Scores of other references throughout the Bible echo this very principle.

Yet, defying the obvious, here the mezzanine cult of escapists remains consistently true to themselves in twisting the straightforward and simple truth into treacherous winding paths of crooked reasonings, all to justify their theory of rapture before the final test.

Without attempting to provide a comprehensive exegesis of their elaborate rationalizings, let us at least summarize the gist of their illogical theory. Basically, they suppose the restraining "he" to be the Holy Spirit of God *as contained within the community of believers*—which they also must label as the Gentile Christian Church (see *Who Overcomes Who?* in chapter 8) in order for their theory to work. They, conveniently enough, see the Holy Spirit as **confined** to dwelling in the bodies of the believers in Christ; such that when the entire corporate body of believers they call "the Church" is raptured into the sky, then, according to their very self-centered views, the Holy Spirit too is removed from the Earth.

Supposedly, removal of the Spirit from Earth by this presumed theoretical process thus fulfills the prerequisite condition delineated by Paul in his second epistle to the Thessalonians: *"Only he who now letteth will let, until he be taken out of the way. And then shall that Wicked be revealed . . ."* *(2Th.2:7-8)* So, according to the escapists, the Man of Sin ("that Wicked") will not be revealed until they (embodying the Holy Spirit) are removed from Earth taking with them the Holy Spirit which supposedly "in-dwells" them, as they put it. This then presumably clears the way for *"the working of Satan with all power and signs and lying wonders," (verse 9)* which they say they will not (of course) be present to have to brave, but will, instead, enjoy only a bird's-eye view of from the "mezzanine!" (The ensuing state of affairs on Earth is left for the Jews and other heathen to endure and hopefully overcome.)

Even if this view were correct, yet there remains irreconcilable inconsistency in this arrogant interpretation. The love of the truth—and, consequently, the Holy Spirit of truth too—has evidently escaped the escapists.[9] For the actual truth, as it is clearly stated in verses 8 and 9 (see footnote), remains completely consistent with the rest of Paul's revelations on this subject and perfectly consistent too with the testimony of Christ Himself, according to Matthew, Mark, and John (in the Apocalypse). That testimony states definitively that *immediately after* the Abomination of Desolation (the unveiling of the Man of Sin and his Image) and *after* the ensuing Great Tribulation, which he ushers in, shall the sign of Messiah's own coming appear in the heavens. This is coupled inseparably with the first resurrection, namely the gathering together of the saints at the Second Coming (when the mystery of God is finished).

Again, sad to say, clear thinking on this issue has been conspicuously clouded by fear and pride. And it is precisely *this* woeful blend of ingredients that has produced the deceptively sweet, yet irrational conclusion, which they so fanatically savor and embrace, of escapist pre-tribulation rapture.[10]

To further dispute the discrepant and deluded view of these exclusivist "vessels of the Holy Spirit," consider (for hypothesis' sake): Once they have vanished from the Earth and presumably taken the "in-dwelling" Spirit with them, with what spirit will the two mighty sackcloth witnesses of Revelation chapter 11 be empowered to testify, who prophesy (before the last trumpet) during the entire term of the Great Tribulation? What about the all the Jews—including the 144,000 from each of the 12 tribes of Israel which are sealed and "left behind" to endure the Great Tribulation? And where does that leave the innumerable multitudes of all other nations, kindreds, peoples and tongues who go through and come out of that Tribulation victoriously?[11]

Will there be no Comforter, no Spirit of Truth, no Holy Spirit to empower, or teach, or lead, or keep them, much less to testify of Christ in those perilous days?[12] Will this "left behind" pariah of unfortunates be deprived of the gift of the Holy Spirit? Does the Holy Spirit now discriminate between classes of believers? Or, is this just more of the same convenience-oriented, self-glorifying exceptionism by which this mezzanine cult sets themselves above the genuine believers (tried and proven) and the martyrs of Mashiach?[13]

Only a presumptuous and unseemly brand of belief could contrive and advance such irrational interpretations of Scripture, which are so completely out of character with the classical teachings of Christ. It is, however, in perfect character with the endtime fulfillment of Paul's prediction to the Thessalonians under review in this section: *That day shall not come, except there come a falling away first. . . . with all deceivableness of unrighteousness in them that perish; because they received not the love of the truth, that they might be saved. And for this cause God shall send them strong delusion, that they should believe a lie . . ." (2Th.2:3-10)*

"Falling Away?" Apostasy?"—A Premier Sign of the Times

This future-tense prerequisite to the arrival of Christ—the "falling away" feature—is already upon us. And, although the escapist heresy we have studied is a major facet of it, other more widespread aspects also reflect the rapidly advancing climate of apostasy that is engulfing today's world with thick clouds of darkness. A darkness which the hypocritical religious establishments have indeed aided and abetted—and have now likewise become engulfed by it—having opted to wallow and steep in a lifestyle of prosperous self-satisfaction and indulgent intoxication on the materialism of the "Great City." This has been their adulterous preference, rather than to loyally preserve the pursuit of the City of God.[14] Yet, the pandemic apostasy we are about to examine more fully is actually of global proportions.

In today's highly materialist world, the climate is shifting dramatically away from any acknowledgment of God whatsoever (except in denunciatory terms), especially at the official and institutional levels of public life, which most affect the general public. A code name for this state-sponsored atheism in the USA is "separation of church and state." As even the most casual observer must agree, the governmental, educational, scientific, and informational (mass media) institutions regularly and routinely discard and delete Divine Origins and Purpose (God) from their programs, curricula, and agendas (when not outrightly denigrating or blaspheming them). The growing trend is obvious, and relentless.

And, rather than stemming the tide of waxing apostasy, the hypocritical religious establishments have married into and virtually condoned it by their straining to offer low-cost lip service to a God they conveniently construe to suit their own materialist passions.[15] Rather than extricating themselves, refusing participation, renouncing the materialist agenda, and observing the mandate not to become "unequally yoked together" with a reprobate society, they have equally (though more insidiously) denied the Truth (God) and substituted fraud for God.[16] The fraud is in their representation of the Gospel of God as a set of values which is compatible and harmonious with the harlotrous agenda of the Great Materialist Megalopolis of spiritual Babylon's idolatrous world order. (Revelation 17 & 18)

Descending ominously over us all, whether in secular or religious sectors, the prevailing climate is one in which honor for the God of Abraham, Moses, David, and Christ is either generally forsaken, feeble, or fickle; one in which faith and fear of God is commonly scoffed as a backward "relic of primitive history"; and, one in which love for God is only a frosty second-rate affection compared to the steaming passion for materialism and doctrines of pious prosperity. Pervasive apostasy is the prevalent mood and trend of modern societies, as well as the degenerate substance of their institutional pillars.

Whereas once a large majority of nations, empires, governments and states upheld the authority of the Judeo-Christian concept of law—as supernaturally sourced in the God of Abraham, Isaac, Jacob, Moses, David and Christ Yeshua—now the tide has swept away all but nominal remnants of adherence to those traditional precepts and principles. In only about 150 years, since the middle-to-late 19th century—or only about the last 7% of the Common Era (since Christ)—has the majority world undergone the sweeping secularization of its social and political systems. The God of the Bible is either already dead or rapidly passing away in today's world.

Even Muslim theism, which in only very recent days has seen dramatic and sweeping revival, experienced a similar divorcement from a tradition of religious devotion in nation-states and empires that historically once honored its theology. Numerous states formerly subscribing to Islam fell prey to the modern era of either soviet totalitarian atheism or the emulation of western democratic secularism (promoting the ousting of God from public life and institutions by devious separation-of-church-and-state politics).

The anti-God climate shift can be traced to the mid-nineteenth-century and the uncannily synchronous rise of Marxism and Darwinism. Spawned practically at the same moment in history, these two philosophical cancers formed a malignant tag team that has metastasized throughout the body politic of 20th century global humanity.

Charles Darwin we all know was the "inspired mind" who fathered the theory of evolution by natural selection. His fanciful theory on the origin of the species, though later modified by discoveries in genetics and molecular biology—both of which, in recent advanced studies, constantly challenge and discredit the very rationality of the theory—still remains stubbornly central to the modern evolutionary theory so commonly (and blindly) accepted in today's world.

Politically speaking, our modern world has also suffered massively calamitous impacts from Karl Marx's materialistic theories of social evolution driven by class struggle and mere economics.

Marx's conclusions were heavily colored by the influences of the German philosopher and moralist, Ludwig Feuerbach, remembered in history for his humanistic theologizing. Regarded by some as one of the most important 19th century atheists, Feuerbach contended that the God of Christianity is an illusion and mere outward projection of man's inward nature and ideals. That is, man assigns characteristics to and expresses an invented God in a manner that fits his own human needs—for morality, law, justice, mercy, love, understanding, etc. In his book *Das Wesen des Christentums (The Essence of Christianity)* Feuerbach argued that humanity itself was the "new religion" embodying the projection of man's own divinity, such that "man is God to man." Under Feuerbach's influence Marx came to view religion as "the opium of the people" and ideally sought the abolishing of religion, which he came to view as an obstacle to man's full self-realization in the struggle for economic justice—a thoroughly materialistic objective!

During the middle 1800s, other virulent seeds of apostasy were cultivated by the anti-Christian publicists David Friedrich Strauss, author of *Das Leben Jesu Kritisch Bearbeitet (The Life of Jesus Critically Examined)*, and Bruno Bauer a radical theologian and historian under whom Marx studied at the University of Berlin. Bauer, a biblical critic and skeptic, had begun to advance the argument that Christ had not even been a historical person and that the Christian Gospels were merely a fabrication of human fantasy rather than a valid historical record. According to the *Encyclopaedia Britannica* in the article "Karl Marx and Marxism: Life and Works of Marx," Bauer predicted the advent of a "new social catastrophe" of greater magnitude than Christianity. Perhaps he foresaw the flowering of our present age of sweeping denial of the Creator and Supreme Sovereign of the Universe.

It is inconclusive whether Marx may have also been influenced by Strauss, who was only ten years older and also studied at the University of Berlin. But Strauss definitely sowed a seed of skepticism that has flourished into full-blown atheism well into the 20th century. His legacy was the "novel" advancement of the mythological view of Christ, which denied the historical accuracy as well as the supernatural accounts of the Gospels (miracles, etc.), calling them "historical myth." His argument was that the memory of the historical Jesus was idealized by his early believers and ultimately transfigured into the Messianic grandeur of a miracle-working Christ, around which a religion was created that was based on ideas, rather than facts—as are all religions, according to Strauss.

While Marx and his philosophical contemporaries rocked the political, social and religious institutions, Darwin similarly undermined them from a "scientific" angle with his removal of the involvement of a supernatural God out of the arena of biology and nature, so that Nature alone was now the creative force.[17] Further, according to Darwin, man was also *not separate from the animals* by the divine decree of the Creator, but essentially *one of them* and only just part of the continuum of nature. And, though England (where Darwin was published) was intensely evangelical at the time and many there regarded his theory as blasphemous, heretical, and seditious, yet, by the time of his death, in less than 25 years from publication of his first abstract on the origin of the species, evolution by natural selection was *generally accepted*, especially in British scientific circles.

Then of course, the turn of the 20th century saw the atheistic psychoanalytical theories of Sigmund Freud also being sown and beginning to take root in the garden of apostasy. Freud analyzed belief in God to be a regression to a childlike state in which helpless humans psychologically project a comforting father figure upon nature. (Thank you, Sigmund, for enlightening us!)

Also leading up to the 20th century era of pandemic atheism was the existentialist strain of the likes of the infamous Friedrich Nietzsche (d. 1900) who proclaimed the "death of God." Nietzsche's philosophical tradition—of humankind being liberated by the "death of God" so as to fulfill itself and find its own essence—was carried on in this century by Jean-Paul Sartre, Albert Camus, and others who continued to promote the theme that man is (at last) freed from the "myth" of God and thus unfettered to determine his own values. These, and many others almost too numerous to name, exalt freedom, choice, happiness and materialism as the new hedonistic idols of humanity—which naturally entails the denial of God, who would otherwise ostensibly threaten man's "freedom" and unrepressed choice.

Also alive and well today is the essentially anti-God, seeing-is-believing philosophical movement known as "logical positivism" or logical empiricism, also called scientific empiricism. *Encyclopaedia Britannica* defines this movement as a "a philosophical doctrine formulated in Vienna in the 1920s, according to which scientific knowledge is the only kind of factual knowledge and all traditional metaphysical doctrines are to be rejected as meaningless." By "scientific" it is meant that only that which is capable of being verified or falsified by human experience (in some measurable degree) can be considered to fall into the realm of factual meaningfulness. So that, if a statement, claim or belief cannot be scientifically confirmed (or disconfirmed), it is discardable as meaningless.

The group to formulate and formally advance this empiricist worldview came to be known as the Vienna Circle. Forefathers of this atheistic school of thought are the likes of David Hume (1711-76), recognized founder of positivism Auguste Comte (1798-1857), John Stuart Mill (1806-1873), Thomas Huxley (1825-95, defender of Darwin and promoter of his *Origin* theory), and Ernst Mach (1838-1916). Some of the members of the Vienna Circle itself were Gustav Bergmann, Rudolf Carnap, Herbert Feigl, Philipp Frank, Kurt Gödel, Otto Neurath, and Friedrich Waismann, Wiener Kreis, and founder and leader Moritz Schlick. A sister group in Berlin, "Society for Empirical Philosophy," included Carl Hempel and Hans Reichenbach. In 1929 the Circle published a manifesto entitled "Scientific Conception of the World: The Vienna Circle." Almost ten years later they evidently disbanded when World War II broke out and largely fled to the USA and Britain (new fields in which to sow their insidious seed). This movement is attested also by *Encyclopaedia Britannica* to have been a major proponent of modern atheism.

As a matter of prophetic course into our modern era—so accurately fore-told—the seeds of *skepticist apostasy* have already flowered to paint our con-temporary world with the pallid shades of atheism. In very short order, we shall see them bring forth their supremely bitter fruit in the closing season of man's history. It is the presently blossoming season of God-hating which shall soon bring to fruition the complete removal, or "taking out of the way" of "He who now letteth" (i.e., restrains) the Ultimate Wickedness.

It is only the power of the Good Force of Almighty God that prevents rampant iniquity from overrunning the Earth. (Only in the fantasies of rap-ture-struck Christian escapists could it be *they* that restrain the flood of iniq-uity now sweeping the planet. GOD help us!)

The institutional rejection of the Good Force throughout the global estab-lishment—now an irreversible trend and malignant social cancer in our present world—will result in the impending demonic reign of the Seed of Satan over the entire face of the earth. That rejection is already reflected and clearly manifested in the abandonment and casting away of His Law, moral codes, precepts of behavior, and principles of wholesome living, as delivered to man-kind principally by the Hebrew Prophets and recorded in their Scriptures. It is those supernaturally inspired writings, referenced throughout the pages of this book as the Word of God, which also detailed the future (in which we now live) thousands of years in advance. Those ancient Scriptures tell us we are about to come face to face in this generation with the Wicked One, and worship him as God!

The "taking out of the way of He who now letteth" is not some meta-physical or fabled spiritual event that occurs by the rapture of wishful Chris-tians who, upon their presumed departure, strip the planet of the Spirit of Truth as they fly away into the sky. Rather, it is the actual casting away by endtime societies of the Truth itself, which the preceding paragraphs have been attempting to trace and sketch the latter day pattern of. The process and the logical sequence of this trend are easy to follow.

Essentially, by undermining the foundation of *acknowledging the existence of God*, as a matter of course the words and law traditionally attributed to

Him then get downgraded to the mere man-made formulations of "primitive" people ("backward" being the implication). Following the path of logical convenience, God's words and law get reclassified by the "enlightened empiricists" as purely part of the larger "myth" of a Creator God, who now exists solely in the imagination of ("unenlightened") man. As a result of this "progressive" empiricism, truth becomes whatever anyone wants it to be— any arbitrary and relative construct of contemporary societies, political bodies, or powerful, persuasive individuals inventing their own customized rule of convenience by which to act out whatever seems most expedient, or pleasing, or satisfying in any given situation. You see, if God is dead, then so is His standard.

When God is removed from man's increasingly secularized world, there is no longer any universal absolute truth. The reference point for truth then shifts to relative, personal and individual (or group) *preferences*, which then become adopted as the generally accepted *rule*. Such as: "A human fetus is not a true person, much less a creation of God, but merely a blob of fleshy tissue" (viewed by millions of modern-day pagans essentially as a *malignant tumor!*); or, "Sodomy is not aberrant sexual perversion, it's a perfectly correct lifestyle choice (politically correct, that is) and a civil right not to be discriminated against"; or, "Jews and Blacks aren't human, but really sub-human vermin" (according to the neo-Nazi supremacists). The point is easily deduced: Dispose of Truth, and you dispose of the reference point for discriminating clearly between good and evil![18]

When God is removed, anyone who commands enough power can be "God" and establish whatever indiscriminate standard or law happens to be commodious. Then, what is right is established by might, whether it be political might, financial or economic might, or military might—or a fusion of all these—such as that of the present Powers That Be (though not for long). The politics of self-serving convenience then emerges as the new law.

That is precisely what the prophets foretold about the consummate Man of Sin to come:

And the king shall do according to his will; and he shall exalt himself, and magnify himself above every god, and shall speak marvellous things against the God of gods, and shall prosper till the indignation be accomplished: for that that is determined shall be done. Neither shall he regard the God of his fathers, nor the desire of women, nor regard any god: for he shall magnify himself above all.—Daniel 11:36-37.

Who opposeth and exalteth himself above all that is called God, or that is worshipped; so that he as God sitteth in the temple of God, shewing himself that he is God.—(Paul) 2 Thessalonians 2:4.

And he opened his mouth in blasphemy against God, to blaspheme his name, and his tabernacle, and them that dwell in heaven. . . . And all that dwell upon the earth shall worship him, whose names are not written in the book of life of the Lamb slain from the foundation of the world.—(John) Revelation 13:6 & 8.

And he shall speak great words against the most High, and shall wear out the saints of the most High, and think to change times and laws: and they [the believers/saints/martyrs] shall be given into his hand [to be robbed and plundered, tortured, imprisoned, enslaved, executed, and otherwise oppressed and persecuted] until a time and times and the dividing of time [3½ years].— Daniel 7:25.

Antichrist, the swiftly overrunning new power to be, will *"think to change times and laws (Dan.7:25),"* thereby reordering the global establishment to suit his new social purpose. Perhaps the pending crash of the international stock markets and the accompanying worldwide economic collapse will effectively plow under the current system and leave the ground broken for a fresh, new "seed." The much dreaded Y2K, or Millennium, Computer Bug may very likely be the catalyst to precipitate the calamitous ground-breaking crisis which will invite a powerful "new order" to reseed the earth. And, as the signs of the times so clearly spell out, other natural and unnatural disasters will likely contribute to the harrowing of the present establishment, clearing the way for a new world order.

In any event, we know that the Antichrist Beast *"shall have power over the treasures of gold and silver" (Dan.11:43);* and that, with all that newly appropriated wealth, *"in his estate [the new establishment] shall he honour the God of forces [strength and military might]: and a god whom his fathers knew not shall he honour with gold, and silver, and with precious stones, and pleasant things. Thus shall he do in the most strong holds with a strange [hi-tech] god, whom he shall acknowledge and increase with glory: and he shall cause them to rule over many, and shall divide the land for gain [a "flattery" tactic; see Dan.11:21, 32 & 34]."* (Dan.11:38-39) We also know that *"he shall enter peaceably upon the fattest [oil-rich] places of the province"* and redistribute much wealth; and that *"he shall forecast his devices against the strong holds [of the "Great Satan?"], even for a time."* (Dan.11:24)

What is most at issue here, however, is **the only thing** that restrains evil—and the willful discarding of it, which then disposes of the restraint. Remove Truth, remove God's law and moral code, and you remove God; and vice versa. Impeach God (as undesirable, or an evil lie), and not only will the empty office not be occupied by the "lesser of two evils," but the crowning glory of all evil will then be unrestrained from seizing the power! And the most frightening thing about it is that Evil will be hailed as good, and Good will be renounced as evil.

We should all be familiar with that twisted syndrome: The same phenomenon happened at the Crucifixion, when Pontius Pilate opted for what he thought was the lesser of two evils, as he wrestled with the question, "What is **truth?**" Barabbas became the hero, and Christ the villain! (And a good many doubting folks are still stubbornly confused about that issue!)

An incredible marvel is about to hatch from the displacing of God out of the public square of 20th century life by secular humanism. A man with demonic alliances and possessing powers and technologies very likely derived from a nexus with extraterrestrials is soon to capture the imagination of the whole world (except for the martyrs). In this age of burgeoning paganism, where even the religious majorities of the Christian West hardly believe their own traditional Scriptures and Founding Principles in totality, we are experiencing a world where "anything goes." The environment is almost perfectly primed for the rise of the Son of Satan to the top of the opinion polls as the preferred candidate for Savior of the World.

The worldwide quest—for answers and solutions, peace and safety, order and security, wealth and prosperity, social and economic equity and justice; for relief from disease, poverty and famine, as well as from protests, terrorism, war, crime, black marketeers, gangs, narcotics cartels, guerrilla insurgencies, revolts, not to mention from governments riddled with corruption, lies, conspiracies, exploitation and oppression; and let alone the unabashed individual quest for **self**-fulfillment and **self**-satisfaction—has all become a wildly chaotic, virtually anarchist "free-for-all." Just switch on the television set to see and hear all about it. World over, chaos and lawlessness rule almost unchecked in the international striving for self-gratification. There is no order or law in any segment of society that provides a secure and dependable source of security for anyone anywhere. And no wonder![19]

Families, homes and children are not secure from invasions and abuse by governments, humanistic educators/schools (with liberal, atheistic, perverted, yet politically-correct agendas); nor from gangs, drugs, rapists, molesters, burglary, random violent crime, including home-centered television violence and moral undermining.

Marriages are not secure from seduction, entertainment industry assaults, liberal legal incompatibility divorce clauses, or radical homosexual redefinement of the institution, or other creeping cultural corruptions providing catalysts to undermine their integrity.

Communities are not secure from industrial, commercial, and governmental abuses, exploitation, or toxic waste despoiling.

Individual's properties are not secure from avaricious (tax-crazed, regulation-mad and land-grabbing) tyrannical governments, profiteering lawyers and developers, or exploitive industrialists (often government sponsored).

Nations and states are not secure from overthrow, extraterritorial coup conspiracies, covert subversion or invasion by power-hungry imperialist regimes or other political rivals.

The general public is not safe from heinous manipulation and exploitive deceit by the mass media moguls and entertainment industry giants, nor from rampant street crime and white-collar crime undeterred by liberal, molly-coddling judicial systems and legislative bodies.

Babies in the womb are not safe from murderous butchery and despicable fetal infanticide in the name of "medicine."

Peace and safety are nowhere to be found, because the God who offered it has been rejected. In fact the only thing that we seem to be "safe" from is the interference of the Creator in our everyday affairs. All that remains now is for the "author of confusion" himself to be elected to remedy the chaos (Ha!).[20] A couple of big-time power plays, spiked with miraculous signs and wonders, will be all it will take to crown him "savior of the world."

Occupy? as in Occupant, or as in Occupation?

So, what do we do when ("that Wicked") Mr. Marvel appears with his masterful agenda to resolve all the world's ills? Shall we all breathe a sigh of relief at the rise of someone who will at last bring peace and order to the earth—someone with the power and authority to reorder the collapsing colossus of Babylon on the back of the Dragon? Do we simply conform to the New Order and pledge allegiance to it, or do we dissent and refuse cooperation? Are we in fact already conformed and cooperating? And if so, when will we divorce ourselves from that affair—now, never, or at the very last minute?

If we rank ourselves among the Cult of the Christian Escapists, then we have nothing to worry about. According to the tenets of that cult, our "faith" in Christ grants us eternal salvation and promises us escape from the hour of trial. What more can you ask for? What greater assurance could anyone enjoy? Everything is fine and dandy.

And such being the case, nothing compels us to divorce ourselves from Babylon. All we have to do is just "hang in there" and keep reading our Bibles until the rapture happens (haplessly citing *"occupy till I come"* as the justification for such lackadaisical beliefs). Accordingly, we need simply continue to eat and drink, build and plant, buy and sell, mate and marry, and prepare our kids for their "promising" future in Babylon (or better yet, in the new world order of the Great Red Dragon)—all the while of course keeping ourselves "pure" as a bride "prepared" for the Rapture.[21] Well, what preparation is really in progress among these rapturists?

To go along with the rapture revelers is to believe that rescue could come out of the sky at any moment, as was discussed and analyzed in the opening chapters of this book. The most serious flaw in that bogus readiness dogma is that their preparedness is a feigned readiness that is disconnected from practical reality. It amounts to both a spiritual and practical fraud.

Noah (of the Great Flood) is the single most classic example of active preparation. He was faced with a practical reality that demanded more than simply being spiritually *"just"* and *"perfect in his generations,"* and far more than his having continually *"walked with God."* (Genesis 6:9) His preparation did not consist of merely keeping himself pure and preaching about the coming of the flood in hopes of converting sinners, while in the meantime actively participating in the established order (or "occupying till I come," as some construe it). Noah showed his faith by a practical response to the implications of impending catastrophe and actively occupied himself with appropriate preparations. The rapturists, on the other hand, have excused themselves from a practical response by vagueness and ambiguity hypocritically framed and couched in imminency doctrines.

That is to say, their rhetoric does not jive with their actions, which betray what they truly consider to be the most appropriate response: namely, eating and drinking with the drunken; or in other words, practicing routine, common, every-day materialism just like every other occupant of Great Babylon. So that with their words they profess the Lord could come at any moment, while by their actions they say, "Not to worry, my lord delayeth his coming; it *could be* tomorrow, *but* it might not be for another 20 years; so let us occupy the same old materialistic routine till then."

Their preparation is not for the advent of leaving behind the worthless wealth of this world to obtain treasures in Heaven, which according to Messiah is *the* most practical and sensible thing a person could do. Instead, their energies and preoccupations are routinely invested in money, possessions and worldly values, which they continue to heap up as though these things were indeed of some enduring and realistic value. It shows you where their hearts are at and how they interpret the "occupy" mandate.[22]

If they truly believed the Messiah could return at any moment to rescue them by rapture, they would sell all that they have to advance the Kingdom of God and do nothing else with their time and resources but seek first the true values of that eternal domain. But of course, how *practical* would *that* be? Let's be *"realistic,"* Messiah might not return for many years yet. How could He expect us to forsake our pursuit of mammon? How will we live? Sure, when he takes us away in the Rapture, we will have to leave it all behind; but that might not be for a long time. We need to be *prepared* to "occupy till he comes." We must remain prepared to maintain viable and effective participation in the world of mammon.

What nearly every single one of the rapturists is clearly and undeniably most well prepared for is to *carry on the materialistic routine* of the anti-God established world order while the Messiah tarries (delays His coming). What they are *not prepared for* is to be forced to choose between taking the Mark of the Beast or refusing it. For *that* they see *no need* to be prepared, because their blind leaders have played upon their covetousness and love of this life and the things of this world to convince their double hearts that they will not have to face that day.

They have no concept of preparing for the day when they will no longer be able to conduct any type of business, buy or sell, receive a pay check, pay a bill, own a car, own a house or a business, travel wherever they please, cross borders, or even get medical treatment without the number or name of the Beast. Those who do not pledge allegiance as law-abiding citizens of the coming Global Fascist Federation of Earth will lose their "freedom" by imprisonment, lose their properties and fortunes by confiscation, and lose their lives by execution, starvation, or unprepared exposure to the elements of nature (if they even manage to flee to escape apprehension and arrest).

Come now, let us talk *seriously* of preparation!

The loss of all these Establishment amenities is really no big deal for a true believer; nor is even the loss of his or her life. It is the call of every disciple of Christ Yeshua, in fact, to renounce and forsake the affection for and attachment to of all these values—so as to seek first the ultimate and highest value, the eternal order and domain of YHWH. *That* is a true disciple's abiding *occupation.*

But, if *that precept* is *not* the guiding light of all our endeavors, *what is?* Really now, is the recitation of a hollow set of imminency and rapture platitudes the best preparation we can muster for the most crucial, dramatic, cosmos-and-consciousness-altering event in the history of mankind!? Let's face it, we're talking about the resurrection to the Kingdom of God on Earth preceded by the greatest tribulation the world has *ever seen* and the full-blown rule of *Satan* among men!

Do you suppose that a sincere recitation of a prayer such as, "Lord Jesus, forgive me of my sins; come into my heart; help me to live for you everyday and tell others about You; and make me ready for Your coming, I pray" is adequate preparation for the evil days to come (as I've heard on TV). Well, let's hope so. Because that's about the most guidance and preparation the great majority of "converts" get from the rapturists. The escapist cult of these heretical rapturists ignores and denies the necessity of any more substantial preparation, because they also ignore and, in essence, deny the teachings of the Messiah and His prophets. This is evident by their blatant refusal to acknowledge and accept the plain facts of Scripture.

Among the many salient facts to which I refer (and have already presented) is one particularly significant one, especially for consideration by the mezzanine rapture cult who presume they shall not be among those "left behind," as they put it, to endure Great Tribulation. That fact: There are only two (mass) resurrections mentioned and specified in the Holy Scriptures; one for the just (unto life eternal), and one for the wicked (unto eternal damnation), according to Messiah Himself.[23] There is **not** more than one resurrection for the just believers (one before the tribulation and one after—one for the "escaping gentile Church" and one later for the Jews and Tribulation converts).

Further, Christ Yeshua specifically repeated four different times within one passage (in the space of only 16 verses) that the resurrection of the just believers would be a singular event on *the last day*.[24]

His friend Martha must have paid attention to the words of Messiah, because she certainly knew the resurrection was to be on the last day. (John 11:24) Yet somehow the rapturists formulate a special resurrection for themselves sometime **before** the last day...before the 7th angel sounds the last trump...before the Man of Sin is revealed...before the Abomination of Desolation is set up...before the working of Satan with all power, signs, and lying wonders...before the Mark of the Beast...before his reign of terror...before the Great Tribulation...before their sincerity can be put to the test...before they can no longer "get away with" serving two masters...before they are *forced* to forsake all their worldlinesses to love God with *all* their heart, *all* their soul, *all* their mind, and *all* their strength...

Again we must ask:

How can the escapists possibly believe they will be gathered together in rapture to meet the Lord in the sky *before* the Antichrist is revealed, when Paul makes it so completely clear that the day of Christ, and the gathering together of the all the saints, happens *after* the working of Satan with unbridled power, signs and wonders? Will there be a *special* resurrection and rapture for the mezzanine cultists *before* the son of perdition sits in the temple of God declaring that he is God? They are evidently counting on it (called the "secret rapture" by some).

Only a very few of them demonstrate any serious preparation of the sort that testifies to their reputed faith in the Kingdom of God; a kingdom so great that nothing in this world matters to them.[25] One of which they are so convinced that even their personal lives and fortunes are daily sacrificed upon the altar of consummate offering to God, in order to singularly seek the advancement of that kingdom.[26]

Instead, we see lives lived as though serving mammon and God simultaneously were a perfectly blessed thing to do. Prosperity doctrines are propounded with passion, in which gathering and heaping up money and material goods is hailed as the "abundant life" of the blessed children of the King. Christian narcissism consumes us here in the Babylonish West, a culture in which Christian financial strategies are the popular subject of extensive seminars for preserving (and thus wallowing in) Christian wealth. While the Messiah's own financial strategy—of selling and giving away—is routinely discounted and discarded (see footnote 25, *"treasure in Heaven"*), along with so much else He taught, as we have already observed and will continue to see.

In terms of Christian narcissistic wallowing—as opposed to genuinely and faithfully "preparing the way of the Messiah" in this last generation—let me cite some figures presented by George Otis, Jr. in his book *The Last of the Giants*.[27] Otis is president of the Sentinel Group, an organization dedicated to facilitating Christian ministry in the world's most severely underserviced mission frontiers. Quoting other statistical data-gathering sources, he testifies in his book to the travesty that is become Western Christianity (which we see tragically transfigured into an egotistical piety obsessively doting upon itself).

Introducing his statistical information, he says (p. 237), "The only way to discover believers' *real* intentions is to follow their wallets." He goes on to cite authors Barrett and Reapsome from page 116 of their publication, *Seven Hundred Plans to Evangelize the World,* wherein they state the 1988 annual combined personal income of church members worldwide (both Catholic and Protestant) to be in the range of "a staggering 8.2 trillion dollars." Where does it all go? Again citing Barrett and Reapsome, from page 25, Otis notes that they report that less than 2% went "to operate organized global Christianity." Well, to momentarily pat Christians on the back, the actual sum amounts to $145 billion spent on (non-personal) church expenses and all their attendant agency endeavors (such as outreach and missions). But as Otis points out, "While $145 billion is unquestionably a lot of money, the fact that it represents such a pitifully small percentage of the Church's overall resources offers an important clue as to Christian priorities."

Even greater perspective on this issue of priorities is provided by Otis (p. 238) citing another Barrett report (this time Barrett and Johnson in *Our Globe and How to Reach It)*. According to Otis, Barrett reports that "the average Christian family income in 1990 was $19,280," while "the weekly foreign missions giving per church member was a paltry ten cents." Worst of it all, as Otis then says (using information gleaned from a separate source, unnamed but quite believable), "most of what is given in the name of 'missions' today, at least in America, is used to propagate the Gospel among people who have the opportunity to hear the Good News *up to one hundred times a day."* In other words, it's virtually a case of repeatedly preaching to the choir! How much more unavailing and vainglorious can such evangelization be!?

"Only 0.1 percent of all Christian income is spent on direct ministry outside of the Christianized world—and a microscopic 0.01 percent on the hard-core unevangelized world," says Otis (again using data from Barrett and Johnson).

I ask, is *"occupy till I come"* a mandate for Christian occupation of a narcissistic part in the drunken drama of the Great Whore; or, is it a mandate to a *vocational occupation* that should faithfully obey the "come-out-of-her" proclamation and pattern of the Master who issued it? (Rev.18:4) There is a huge world to prepare for the Day of the LORD. And, it is already quite well acquainted with self-serving egotism, secular as well as religious. Will it ever see Christians wholly lay down our lives (much less our wallets) for the loving cause of Christ? What we are steadily and regularly occupied with defines conclusively what we *really* cherish.

Don't Be Mistaken

"Take heed lest any man deceive you," were Messiah's key watchwords for the end of the age. Being mistaken begins at the fork in the road. Getting drawn away of one's own selfish lusts onto a path that promises to provide self-serving ends which appeal to the satisfying of the cravings of the flesh is the most fundamental mistake that can ever be made.

A Savior is coming who will restore the paradise that was originally intended for mankind, the children of God. It is a paradise that can only function under the rule of *selflessness*. But, another "savior" shall precede the Self-sacrificial One and attempt to preempt Him altogether; this one hoisting the banner and allure of self-ism, proposing to quench that egotistical thirst with his own techno-utopia—a synthetic utopia geared to instant gratification of the human lust to "be as gods."

Almost all of earth's inhabitants will succumb to the appeal of the thirst-quenching egomania of the self-magnifying, self-serving one who exalts SELF. All self-centered humans will hitch their wagons to this rising star hoping to achieve self-glory with him (unrestrained by YHWH's order and law of self-deferring love). The choice will be between the here-and-now, self-serving techno-utopia that he will promise or the "organic" paradise of patience, faith and self-postponing, self-sacrificing love for others in the world to come. According to Christ, that world to come ought to be our first priority of life, and it is supposed to be a present living reality in the heart of every believer:

Seek ye first the kingdom of God, and his righteousness.—Matthew 6:33

Neither shall they say, Lo here! or, lo there! for, behold, the kingdom of God is within you.—Luke 17:21

"Take heed lest any man deceive you," were Messiah's watchwords for the end of the age, the days of His return to lay hold on His inheritance. Well, this book is not accompanied by signs and wonders by which it might seek to persuade its readers of its veracity. It is, however, accompanied by extensive references to the ancient Holy Scriptures of the Hebrew prophets. The greatest wonder, and the most incredible sign of all, is the ability of those prophets to foresee the future in which we now live. They knew (by supernatural revelation) that the world of man would dramatically degenerate in its final days into a global hedonistic culture of blasphemy against the Designer and Maker of the Cosmos; that it would be filled with self-worship, materialism, deceit, theft, fraud, lasciviousness, violence, anarchy, murder, worship of devils and hate for worshippers of God; and that we would worship an ultra-demonic man presenting himself as God and commanding beams of high-energy heat rays ("fire") out of the sky.[28] The greatest sign of all is the fulfillment of their prophecies.

Signs or no, the burden of critical analysis of what is being presented herein is left up to you, the reader. Considerable footnoting—consisting almost entirely of references from the Holy Scriptures—are provided for your convenience. But beware of convenience. Your soul hangs in the balance. Hesitate not to check it all out and make sure the testimony given herein is true and faithful.

Flattery and candy-coating are not the style employed in this book; nor is its intent to lure half-hearted believers into a discount religion of easy-street devotion. That type of approach is for the smooth-talking deceivers who neither know God nor love Him. You will know them by their fruits.

The *Jesus testimony* is the true spirit of prophecy, according to the fellowservant who delivered Messiah's revelation to John.[29] If what you read or hear isn't the testimony that Jesus bore, it's the prophecy of a lying spirit. Beware. Fall down at no man's feet. Don't buy their tapes, books or propaganda, or send them a single dime, if you don't hear them preach the cross.[30] And I don't mean Christ's cross, but yours![31] (See also footnote 26, *"a sacrifice, or an honor?"*) Worship God; not **convenience**—for that indeed is the nature of the Mark of the Beast!

And remember the testimony of the true Messiah:

"I pray not that thou [Father] shouldest take them out of the world, but that thou shouldest keep them [disciples] from the evil."—John 17:15

"These things I have spoken unto you [disciples], that in me ye might have peace. In the world ye shall have tribulation: but be of good cheer; I have overcome the world."—John 16:33

11

THE SIEVE OF VANITY

Behold, the name of the LORD cometh from far, burning with his anger, and the burden thereof is heavy: his lips are full of indignation, and his tongue as a devouring fire: And his breath, as an overflowing stream, shall reach to the midst of the neck, to sift the nations with the sieve of vanity: and there shall be a bridle in the jaws of the people, causing them to err.
Isaiah 30:27-28

Tracing the endtime outline provided for us by Christ Jesus in the New Testament as our basic itinerary for this exploration of last generation prophecies, we return again to the famous Gospel of Matthew. Messiah's testimony, as recorded by this apostle in his own testimony of witness to the life and teachings of Christ, is especially free of any fog of ambiguity, or cloud of disputation. It leaves no room for argument. Only outright denial of the LORD's testimony can dismiss its substance and meaning, denoted here in very plain language and recorded in perfect clarity by Matthew (in the following citation from chapter 24).

Immediately after the tribulation of those days shall the sun be darkened, and the moon shall not give her light, and the stars shall fall from heaven, and the powers of the heavens shall be shaken:
And then shall appear the sign of the Son of man in heaven: and then shall all the tribes of the earth mourn, and they shall see the Son of man coming in the clouds of heaven with power and great glory. And he shall send his angels with a great sound of a trumpet, and they shall gather together his elect from the four winds, from one end of heaven to the other.—Matthew 24:29-31

The second coming of Messiah—this time not on a donkey's colt nor cradled in its manger—when He returns to resurrect and gather up His loved and loyal ones, dead and alive, will not be until **after** the *"time of trouble such as never was since there was a nation even to that same time (as the prophet Daniel also foretold in chapter 12, verse 1)."*

Providing perfectly parallel corroboration to Matthew's account, the Apostle Mark likewise testified, almost identically, to the very same forewarning and promise of the Master, leaving even less room for dispute. According to the Gospel of Mark in chapter 13, Yeshua put his disciples on notice that it would be *"after that [unparalleled] tribulation"* that the Son of man (Messiah, human-born) would be seen *"coming in the clouds with great power and glory."* *"And then,"* he goes on, *"shall he send his angels, and shall gather together his elect from the four winds, from the uttermost part of the earth to the uttermost part of heaven." (verses 24-27)* Both these witnesses agree perfectly that Jesus declared He would send for the gathering up of His elect after the Great Tribulation. Did they both get it wrong?

This sum total *gathering together of the elect* (of all ages), leaving no grave unturned nor any corner of the earth unsearched, happens *after* the unrivaled Tribulation (unmatched in all earth's history) specified and described by both Mark and Matthew (& Daniel). How is it that any literate, clear-headed reader of these prophetic passages can come to any other conclusion about the chronology of this event, especially with the particular emphasis added by the word *"immediately"* in Matthew 24?

Immediately When?

Where does the confusion of terms arise? "Before" and "after" are opposite terms, like "black" and "white," "light" and "dark," "good" and "evil."

If the *gathering together*—alternately referred to in fonder terms by the escapist Christians as *the Rapture*—were before the tribulation, why doesn't the above passage from Matthew read, "Immediately *before* the tribulation of those days . . ?" Perhaps it is not only the pain-banishing connotation of the term "rapture" which endears the escapists to its common adoption into regular usage, but also that it disconnects the event it signifies from the Scripture references which place it squarely in the context of a (dreaded) *post*-tribulation time frame. Could it be that the confusion arises as a result of a condition spelled out in the proverbial words of the sage who taught, "There are none so blind as those who will not see?"

Those **who do not refuse to see** understand that, according to the key passage of prophecy from Matthew quoted above, at least three things occur *immediately after* the Great Tribulation. Major cataclysm occurs in the skies (atmosphere & outer space); the sign of the celestial Messiah appears in the heavens (no Hollywood special effects needed); all nations upon earth grieve, mourn and even wail at His appearing (when the "Myth" materializes!);[1] and, the Messiah sends His angels to gather together His elect (signaled by a mega-blast of the final trumpet).

In terms of a time table, the second appearance of Christ Yeshua (this time in His original splendor and magnificence) is practically simultaneous with the gathering together of the believing elect. It is, in fact, the primary reason for His majestic preliminary appearance in the heavens. I say "pre-liminary," because only about a month or so later, His *re*appearance (techni-cally a third coming) will culminate in the quashing of a global rebellion at Armageddon and the seizure and occupation of planet Earth as His eternal inheritance. The initial phase of the 2nd Coming—for retrieval of His king-dom constituents—is solely an aerial event not involving an actual "touch down" upon Earth. It follows right on the heels of the Tribulation, preceding Armageddon, and, please note, comes with the heralding blare of the Last Trumpet.

With it, the spirit agents (angels) of Earth's Founder not only announce the return of Christos to separate the wicked from the just (by the *gathering together*), but also the completion of the "mystery of God" and the expiration of man's wicked dominion of Earth as well. What then ensues upon earth, once the wicked have been isolated, is their sweeping annihilation and the cleansing of the earth. This all precedes establishment of Messiah's domin-ion. All this, at very last, occurs only after the saints of all ages, living and dead, Jew and Gentile alike, are indeed raptured and removed for a short season from the earth while judgment is executed upon the wicked. (Isaiah 26:19-20, quoted later in this chapter, is one of the proof-texts which substan-tiates this.)

It is largely for this reason that the just are removed from Earth—to spare them *not* from the purgings of the Great Tribulation, but to isolate them from the devastating retribution of Earth's Maker upon the vile destroyers of His Earth, who have grievously defiled His superbly-crafted and laboriously-fash-ioned planet.[2] This pent-up, patiently withheld wrath has been accumulating now for about 4,000 years, since its previous release at the time of the Great

Flood of Noah (c. 2345 BCE).[3] Once the just people are temporarily transported away from earth, the raging righteous indignation of the Almighty will be poured out, without dilution, upon the reprobate perverters of Creation's purpose.[4]

This vengeful retribution is detailed in many passages of the Bible, both in the TaNaKh (Old Testament) and the New Testament. In chapters 14-16, the New Testament book of Revelation provides a classic synopsis of this horrific climax of mankind's history. Further detail is contained in chapters 17-19, where the primary focus is on the utter demise of the "Great Megalopolis," but which close with the devastating decimation of the "Beast" and his antichrist hordes

The ultimate destruction of both (metaphorical) Babylon, as well as the Beast, is the climax of an intense, though brief, period of wrathful vengeance, fiery indignation, fierce anger and ravaging recompenses for the controversy of Zion, for fornication with Babylon, and for the worship of the Beast. It is *this* period—not that of the Great Tribulation—which Apostle Paul speaks of to the Grecian congregation of Thessalonica (in chapter 5 of his first epistle to them) when he gives those saints assurance that the *"children of light . . . are not appointed unto wrath"* in the day when the Lord comes *"as a thief in the night."* Numerous scriptures indicate that the saints (i.e., all just and faithful believers) will actually participate as the conquering hosts in the final battle to vanquish the League of Antichrist Nations and strip earth out of their wicked grip.

To give you some idea of the extensive coverage by the Hebrew prophets of this catastrophic and colossal event of cosmic proportions, let us at least excerpt a few accounts of it from among the numerous scriptures they left us on the subject of YHWH's wrath.

Galactic Blackout—Power, Gloom, and Fright

The coming Great and Notable Day of the LORD is tagged by the prophets with characteristic celestial phenomena very similarly described by several of them. Describing a mammoth cataclysm in the heavens, Matthew, Mark, Luke, John, Joel, and Isaiah (almost identically all) foretell of signs in the galaxy which include the sun and moon being darkened, as well as the stars failing (and falling), and the heavens and the powers of the heavens being shaken.

As we have already noted, Matthew attests that Jesus foretold that *"immediately after the tribulation of those days shall the sun be darkened, and the moon shall not give her light, and the stars shall fall from heaven, and the powers of the heavens shall be shaken."*

Well, Matthew's New Testament contemporary, the apostle Mark, likewise affirms the prophetic testimony of Christ in chapter 13 of his Gospel (verses 24-26): *"But in those days, after that tribulation, the sun shall be darkened, and the moon shall not give her light, and the stars of heaven shall fall, and the powers that are in heaven shall be shaken. And then shall they see the Son of man coming in the clouds with great power and glory."*

Luke, another New Testament compatriot of both Matthew and Mark, gives the following account of Messiah's prophecy: *"And there shall be signs in the sun, and in the moon, and in the stars; and upon the earth distress of nations, with perplexity; the sea and the waves roaring; men's hearts failing them for fear, and for looking after those things which are coming on the earth: for the powers of heaven shall be shaken. And then shall they see the Son of man coming in a cloud with power and great glory. And when these things begin to come to pass, then look up, and lift up your heads; for your redemption draweth nigh."*

(At this point, let us note again that all three of the preceding citations conclusively place the gathering together and redemption—i.e., the physical transformation and reconstitution of "the elect" into their immortal hyperphysical bodies at the resurrection—*after* the Tribulation at the time when the powers of the heavens shall be roused to rock our planet with their signs of final doom.)

The most up-to-date biblical account of the events pertaining to the time of the end were received by the apostle John, and recorded in the New Testament Book of Revelation (c. 90 CE). In a previous chapter it was noted that the Revelation contains *new information granted to Messiah* following His self-sacrifice as the Lamb of God. Subsequent to His death at the crucifixion, His resurrection, and His ascension to the celestial dimension of the Father God, previously unrevealed and tightly sealed secrets were released to Him. In perfect corroboration of earlier passages of prophecy (and even enhancing them with key detail and specified time frames), none of the new Revelation negates earlier revealed understandings.

Such is the case with the opening of the conclusive "sixth seal" in Revelation chapter six. Seal number six reveals the same signs provided earlier by Matthew, Mark and Luke, as well as by even more ancient Old Testament prophets.

About the Great Day of God, John says, *"And I beheld when [the Lamb] had opened the sixth seal, and, lo, there was a great earthquake; and the sun became black as sackcloth of hair, and the moon became as blood; and the stars of heaven fell unto the earth, even as a fig tree casteth her untimely figs, when she is shaken of a mighty wind. And the heaven departed as a scroll when it is rolled together; and every mountain and island were moved out of their places. And the kings of the earth, and the great men, and the rich men, and the chief captains, and the mighty men, and every bondman, and every free man, hid themselves in the dens and in the rocks of the mountains; and said to the mountains and rocks, Fall on us, and hide us from the face of him that sitteth on the throne, and from the wrath of the Lamb: For the great day of his wrath is come; and who shall be able to stand?"* (Revelation 6:12-17)

Even before this horrifying "great day of wrath," however, John is shown a preceding series of catastrophic chastisements that are unleashed upon earth during the Tribulation period, against which the servants of God have largely been protectively sealed in advance. These disastrous calamities are actually precursors to the Seven Last Plagues of Wrath and serve as selective punishments meant to urge the peoples of earth to repentance before the final grain of sand in the hourglass drops. Let us quickly detour into an exploration of the ultimatum sounded by the Trumpets of Tribulation.

The blast of the Fourth Trumpet by the fourth angel (*during the period of Great Tribulation*, which is punctuated by a series of 7 trumpets) initiates a precursory *darkness* that appears may, in part, be a result of the plagues brought on by the sounding of the first three trumpets.

The first three trumpets of tribulation invoke judgments that entail a great deal of fire and objects falling to fiery impacts on the Earth and in the oceans.[5] All of these catastrophic flaming cataclysms coming down upon Earth could produce tremendous volumes of smoke, ash, and airborne debris easily capable of blocking out the light of the sun, moon and stars even to pitch-blackness in the daytime. Recent awesome examples of this phenomenon have been witnessed by victims of local volcanic eruptions such as those in Monserrat a few months ago (1997) and in Mt. Pinatubo in the Philippines only a few years ago (1991-92).

The Tribulation judgment connected with the *First Trumpet* brings *"hail and fire mingled with blood"* to be cast upon the earth. The result is one third of earth's vegetation burning up, as well as a considerable death toll ("blood"). Hail, *"chálaza"* (χάλαζα) in the original Greek manuscripts, does not necessarily signify stones of precipitated ice, but any hail of stones (or projectiles) falling out of the sky. This, therefore, likely signifies some other type of hail, such as that of a shower of meteoroids of sufficient diameter to achieve a flaming impact with earth, capable of igniting an incendiary disaster of enormous proportions.

For that matter, an unexpected shower of icy comets, or "dirty snowballs" as they are otherwise dubbed by astronomers and astrophysicists, could produce similar results. Even *one* strategic comet strike in a densely populated area could not only cause raging fires, but cast up great quantities of bleeding human remains and water vapor to stratospheric altitudes. Launched into the freezing temperatures of those extreme altitudes, and beyond, they would then condense and return to earth in the form of hail mingled with blood, as part of the "ejecta" of the impact. Blazes over vast regions, blackening the atmosphere with soot, would result from the clumps of impact debris launched in all directions by the tremendous force of the impact (the ejecta) descending back to earth as showers of fireballs.

Most of us, thanks to 20th century technology, have probably seen close-up photos of our moon, which testify to the potential for a massive bombardment of roving cosmic rocks out of the dark reaches of space. The hundreds of huge craters visible on the surface of the moon provide a silent yet thunderous record of a violent past. A past that could very similarly repeat itself at any time, according to astronomers that have already called a worldwide alert to the estimated 2,000 asteroids in rogue, eccentric solar orbits which pose an unpredictable and potentially imminent threat to Earth. Due to the relatively small astronomical size of these asteroids and the limited resources available to scan and monitor the skies, they say a potential collision could occur with *zero forewarning* at any time. Presently, a mere handful of about 25 astronomers worldwide is dedicated to this monitoring, scanning only about 2% of the nighttime sphere of the heavens per month. So far these small teams of astronomers have reported identifying at least 200 of these dangerous "rogues." Near misses have already occurred that were not noticed until the asteroid was spotted speeding away from Earth after whizzing by undetected at incredible velocities.[6]

The *Second Trumpet* of (pre-wrath) Tribulation signals *"a great mountain burning with fire . . . cast into the sea."* Catastrophic destruction results, with a third of the ships and ocean-going vessels destroyed, as well as a third of the sea life, and probably a third of the sea coast populations.

One of the most active volcanoes in the world is Kilauea in the Hawaiian Islands (soon likely to be first place in the world to legalize homosexual marriages, incidentally). The potential of nearby Mauna Loa and Mauna Kea, both towering nearly 14,000 feet above sea level in the middle of the Pacific Ocean, is staggering. A Krakatoa-type eruptive explosion at the center of the Pacific basin could lay waste and ravage countless population centers up and down the west coasts of both North and South America, as well as cities in Japan, Taiwan, the eastern coasts of China, possibly even Hong Kong, the Philippines, Australia, New Zealand and innumerable South Pacific islands.[7] Thousands of tankers, trading, fishing and military vessels of every type would be destroyed, not to mention the abundant sea life.

The fact is, any number of the massive volcanic peaks along the almost continuous chain of Circum-Pacific volcanoes, known as the Ring of Fire, could fill the devastating bill of the second angel in Revelation chapter eight. According to the U.S. Geological Survey, more than 500 active volcanoes posing a danger to mankind are presently being monitored around the world.

At the sounding of the trumpet of the *third angel*, a *"great star"* falls to Earth *"burning as it were a lamp."* It falls upon *"the third part of the rivers, and upon the fountains of waters; and the name of the star is called Wormwood: and the third part of the waters became wormwood; and many men died of the waters, because they were made bitter."*

Whatever this "star" may be, it brings a plague of toxic contamination affecting the water supplies of the region where it collides. The poisonous residues it deposits and spews about are fatal to a wide population of people dependent on these sources of water that it contaminates. Some have speculated that this astral object may be radioactive, because of the supposed connection between the name of the star, Wormwood, and the name of the site in the Ukraine of the worst nuclear accident in history in 1986. Chernobyl, translated into English, reportedly means "wormwood." The coincidence certainly is striking, as is the fact that the bitter wormwood plant, Artemisia absinthium, is native to Eastern Europe.[8]

Taking these three Tribulation plagues in to account, is it any wonder now that at the sounding of the *fourth trumpet* a plague of *darkness* engulfs a third of the planet?

Scientists commonly agree that the aftermath of even a limited nuclear conflict, an impact by an asteroid or comet, or a massive volcanic disaster, would likely result in severe ecological damage, particularly from contamination of earth's atmosphere. This would include atmospheric repercussions of the same kind predicted by nuclear scientists who warn of a "nuclear winter" catastrophe which would result from the enormous quantities of smoke that would fill the air from the burning of cities and industrial complexes. The smoke would block out the sunlight, causing temperatures to plummet, destroying crops and producing famine, as well as causing extreme, freak weather and severe storms of incalculable magnitudes. These are scenarios posed not by doomsday religious prophets, but by 20th century scientific schools.

Admittedly, the understanding of many of these prophecies is inconclusive. But it is extremely intriguing and provocative that prominent secular sources—such as planetary scientists, nuclear and astro-physicists largely disconnected from religious tradition—are incidentally corroborating and even illuminating more vividly the prophetic landscapes painted by ancient prophets. Some of the best hypothetical computer modeling done with up-to-date scientifically-based information seems to remarkably support the visions of the ancients. Even special-effects Hollywood and the most credible science-fiction writers and producers are now regularly and prolifically pumping out films and books to flood the airwaves, theaters, video and book stores with doomsday scenes which uncannily resemble the visions of the Prophets of the Bible. Frighteningly enough, it does seem that the signs of the times are upon us.

Before leaving the troublous precursory period of Great Tribulation to return to our discussion of the even more dreadful period of indignation and wrath which ensues, there is a fifth scourge signaled in the series of seven trumpets:

At the sounding of the *Fifth Trumpet*, a "bottomless pit" is opened releasing a weird calamity that defies the imagination. Eerie insect-type creatures are released upon the earth to torment mankind for a period of five months. These extremely weird "mutant" creatures are described as armored locusts resembling war-horses having wings, with humanoid-like faces, teeth like lions, and hair like women. Apparently sentient creatures with a guided agenda, these hellish mutants resemble something out of either the annals of ancient mythology, or the science fiction visions of 21st century aliens portrayed by the special effects wizards of Hollywood (as in the recent blockbuster *Independence Day*). Their most striking characteristic is the scorpion-like tail they wield, with which they strike and torment only the God hating population.

The appearance of these mutant aliens on the scene marks a period of horror during which the terror of living practically outstrips the fear of death.[9]

But, to overlook these bizarre "locusts" for the moment, let us note particularly that the initial element of this fifth calamity does relate directly to our current theme of blackened skies and the sun, moon and stars being blocked out over huge regions of the globe. Whatever this bottomless pit may be to which John refers, he says that in his vision the pit was opened and *"there arose a smoke out of the pit, as the smoke of a great furnace: and the sun and the air were darkened by reason of the smoke of the pit." (Rev.9:2)* Dark days do indeed await us.

Jumping back now to a time considerably more ancient than John's, two prophets from the Old Testament spoke of similar conditions of gloomy obscurity connected with the Great Day of God.

First, ponder the words of Zephaniah (c. 630 BCE): *"The great day of the LORD is near, it is near, and hasteth greatly, even the voice of the day of the LORD: the mighty man shall cry there bitterly. That day is a day of wrath, a day of trouble and distress, a day of wasteness and desolation, a day of darkness and gloominess, a day of clouds and thick darkness, a day of the trumpet and alarm against the fenced cities, and against the high towers. And I will bring distress upon men, that they shall walk like blind men, because they have sinned against the LORD: and their blood shall be poured out as dust, and their flesh as the dung. Neither their silver nor their gold shall be able to deliver them in the day of the LORD's wrath; but the whole land shall be devoured by the fire of his jealousy: for he shall make even a speedy riddance of all them that dwell in the land (Zph.1:14-18)."*

Now consider chapter 2 of the prophecy of Joel (c. 800 BCE) announcing the same day: *"Blow ye the trumpet in Zion, and sound an alarm in my holy mountain: let all the inhabitants of the land tremble: for the day of the LORD cometh, for it is nigh at hand; a day of darkness and of gloominess, a day of clouds and of thick darkness . . ." (Joel 2:1-2)*

In this same passage, Joel goes on to describe the ultimate military force of all time, the invincible army of YHWH accompanying Him in the final conquest of the evil usurpers of Earth and of His Holy Land:

As the morning spread upon the mountains: a great people and a strong; there hath not been ever the like, neither shall be any more after it, even to the years of many generations. A fire devoureth before them; and behind them a flame burneth: the land is as the garden of Eden before them, and behind them a desolate wilderness; yea, and nothing shall escape them [a vast, omnipotent, sweeping, relentless force with flaming weaponry]. The appearance of them is as the appearance of horses; and as horsemen, so shall they run. Like the noise of chariots on the tops of mountains shall they leap [able to master gravitational limitations], like the noise of a flame of fire that devoureth the stubble, as a strong people set in battle array. Before their face the people shall be much pained [being thoroughly overpowered and dismayed]: all faces shall gather blackness [be it hopelessness of soul or environmental blackness].

They shall run like mighty men [swift and omnipotent]; they shall climb the wall [ascend and surmount fortifications] like men of war; and they shall march every one on his ways [independently targeted, and yet . . .], they shall not break their ranks [fully unified as if by telepathic communications]: Neither shall one thrust another [no confusion or casualties by "friendly fire"]; they shall walk every one in his path: and when they fall upon the sword [when fired upon and struck by any weapon], they shall not be wounded [remain unscathed and invincible].—Joel 2:2-8

Evidently, the relentless, indefensible onslaught of these supernatural warriors includes the ability to defy gravity and easily scale elevated positions to engage in direct combat: *"They shall run to and fro in the city; they shall run upon the wall, they shall climb up upon the houses; they shall enter in at the windows like a thief. The earth shall quake before them; the heavens shall tremble: the sun and the moon shall be dark, and the stars shall withdraw their shining: And the LORD shall utter his voice before his army: for his camp is very great: for he is strong that executeth his word: for the day of the LORD is great and very terrible; and who can abide it?"* (Joel 2:9-11) There will be no place to hide or escape the vengeance of this invading force from the skies, though shelter will be desperately sought underground.[10]

The great prophet Isaiah complements Joel's prophecy regarding this invasion from space when he describes "the battle mustered by the Lord," saying:

I have commanded my sanctified ones, I have also called my mighty ones for mine anger, even them that rejoice in my highness. . . . They come from a far country, from the end of heaven, even the LORD, and the weapons of his indignation, to destroy the whole land.

Howl ye; for the day of the LORD is at hand; it shall come as a destruction from the Almighty. Therefore shall all hands be faint, and every man's heart shall melt: And they shall be afraid: pangs and sorrows shall take hold of them; they shall be in pain as a woman that travaileth: they shall be amazed one at another; their faces shall be as flames [reflecting the only available light]. Behold, the day of the LORD cometh, cruel both with wrath and fierce anger, to lay the land desolate: and he shall destroy the sinners thereof out of it. For the stars of heaven and the constellations thereof shall not give their light: the sun shall be darkened in his going forth, and the moon shall not cause her light to shine. And I will punish the world for their evil, and the wicked for their iniquity; and I will cause the arrogancy of the proud to cease, and will lay low the haughtiness of the terrible. (Isa.13:3-11)

To resume and conclude chapter 2 of the prophecy of Joel (in summary), verses 12-17 tell of a call to mass repentance in Zion and a solemn rallying back to the LORD. The call to general fasting, weeping and mourning is followed by a promise (in verses 18-29) of ultimate restoration to righteousness, peace, prosperity, plenty and prestige—after the driving off of the "northern army" toward what evidently appears to be the barren regions of the Jordan valley.[11] This vision is perfectly consistent with the very detailed prophecy of Ezekiel (chapters 38 & 39) where the northern armies of Gog and his league of allies (discussed in detailed shortly) are ultimately slaughtered and allocated a place for the burial of their flesh-scavenged bones to the "east of the sea."[12]

The voice of prophecy in Joel closes chapter 2 saying, *"And I will shew wonders in the heavens and in the earth, blood, and fire, and pillars of smoke. The sun shall be turned into darkness, and the moon into blood, before the great and the terrible day of the LORD come. And it shall come to pass, that whosoever shall call on the name of the LORD shall be delivered: for in mount Zion and in Jerusalem shall be deliverance, as the LORD hath said, and in the remnant whom the LORD shall call." (vss.30-32)*

Chapter 3 of the book of Joel adds even more to the particulars of the endtime scenario, characteristically marked by the awesome and fateful signs in the sky that we have been studying. In verses 14-15, he associates the darkened heavens with the gathering of all nations into the "valley of decision" at the time when "the day of the LORD is near."

Setting the stage in verses 1-2, Yahweh pledges, *"For, behold, in those days, and in that time, when I shall bring again the captivity of Judah and*

*Jerusalem [regather Jews and restore their capital city, as it is today], I will
also gather all nations, and will bring them down into the valley of Jehoshaphat
[also known as the Kidron Valley running between Jerusalem and the Mt. of
Olives], and will plead with them there for my people and for my heritage
Israel, whom they have scattered among the nations, and parted my land [to
occur (once again) at the reneging and double-crossing of the covenant when
Antichrist seizes Jerusalem as his capital]."*[13]

Lebanon (Tyre and Zidon) and the Palestinians are mentioned specifically in this passage of chapter 3. We are led to believe that it will not go well
for these Israel-haters in the valley of decision. Undoubtedly, that shall be as
a result of their spiteful intent to push Israel into the sea, as per the still un-
amended Palestinian Charter.

The ruthless rip-off and hateful dispossession of the Jews is not over yet,
according to Joel. As is obvious to the wakeful eye, the constant ganging up
of the nations of the world against the so-called "occupationist" Israelis is
preparing the world community for the next, upcoming holocaust of the Great
Tribulation period. With the support of the one-sided, pro-Arab (actually pro-
petroleum) propaganda machine operated by the hypocritical, establishment
news media moguls (feigning objectivity), the next holocaust rationale
continues to be trumped up on a daily basis.

What they all fail to recognize, in their staggering pagan pride and covetousness, is that The Almighty has declared Jerusalem and Israel (the people
and the land) as *"my people . . . my heritage . . . my land!"* Well, their big, fat
heads will soon be plump, ripe grapes in the winepress of the wrath of Almighty God!

Blood Flood—The Vintage of Earth Matures

An example of the successful "management" of public opinion to manipulate mass public bias is evident in the recent United Nations vote—130
to 2, with 2 abstentions—to ratify Yasser Arafat's resolution to condemn the
Har Homa housing development in Jerusalem. (Nobody even thinks of telling
Germany, France, or even Serbia or Iraq whether they can or cannot create
housing in their own capitals!) But, any close observer of United Nations
proceedings knows this is strictly typical of the UN voting pattern regarding
nearly *every issue related to Israel!* Is it any wonder that "all the heathen"
and "all nations" should be summoned to Jehoshaphat for an encounter with

He who holds the title to Jerusalem and Israel? The controversy of Jerusalem will be settled—but not by the United Nations or by the mass media moguls:[14]

Proclaim ye this among the Gentiles; Prepare war, wake up the mighty men, let all the men of war draw near; let them come up: Beat your plowshares into swords, and your pruninghooks into spears: let the weak say, I am strong. Assemble yourselves, and come, all ye heathen, and gather yourselves together round about: thither cause thy mighty ones to come down, O LORD. Let the heathen be wakened, and come up to the valley of Jehoshaphat: for there will I sit to judge all the heathen round about.—Joel 3:9-12

Rather, settlement of the Israeli Issue shall come by the very decision of the Allied Global Federation (of rebellion against God's Will) to defy YHWH the Almighty and deny Him his right.[15] When the anti-Christ nations of the world assemble their armies and armaments, and surround Jerusalem in the mountains and valleys of Israel for the ultimate battle of all ages, The Issue will be settled. The fully ripe cluster of the wicked vine of the earth will be reaped, gathered and *crushed* in the "winepress" outside Jerusalem:

Put ye in the sickle, for the harvest is ripe: come, get you down; for the press is full, the fats [vats] overflow; for their wickedness is great. Multitudes, multitudes in the valley of decision: for the day of the LORD is near in the valley of decision. The sun and the moon shall be darkened, and the stars shall withdraw their shining. The LORD also shall roar out of Zion, and utter his voice from Jerusalem; and the heavens and the earth shall shake: but the LORD will be the hope of his people, and the strength of the children of Israel. So shall ye know that I am the LORD your God dwelling in Zion, my holy mountain: then shall Jerusalem be holy, and there shall no strangers pass through her any more.—Joel 3:13-17

Then Messiah will rule; and Israel (despite their own waywardnesses and rebellions) will be redeemed; and all the blood-spilling, terrorism-loving, illegitimate aliens (translated "strangers") laying fraudulent claims to God's possession—driven by covetousness, envy and ancient hatred—will be banished for a thousand years.

In the Apocalypse, John the Revelator described *the same* final harvest and reaping of the earth spoken of by Joel. He conclusively wrapped up Earth's

Dragon-Whore-dominated history (i.e., the Satan-inspired, power-pleasure-driven history of materialist man) in the famous "grapes-of-wrath" passage. Reading chapter 14 of Revelation, we learn of two back-to-back reapings.

The first one is by someone resembling *"the Son of man"* upon a white cloud but *"having on his head a golden crown, and in his hand a sharp sickle,"* who *"thrust in his sickle on the earth; and the earth was reaped." (Rev.14:14-16)* This harvest is followed by a second, nearly trailer-hitched reaping by an angel with a similarly sharp sickle who was subsequently commanded, *"Thrust in thy sharp sickle, and gather the clusters of the vine of the earth; for her grapes are fully ripe." (Rev.14:17-20)*

When this angel of the subsequent harvest thrusts in his sickle, the wicked produce of the evil vine of the earth is finally gathered and cast into *"the great winepress of the wrath of God"* and trodden. This wrathful crushing is such that *"blood came out the winepress"* enough to fill the gullies and river valleys in the regions around Jerusalem *"even unto the horse bridles, by the space of a thousand and six hundred furlongs [furlong = approx. 185 meters]."* That's nearly two hundred miles! Sounds outrageously incredible, doesn't it?[16]

John was not the lone apocalyptic "lunatic" who foretold a horrendous, bloody slaughter. Jeremiah, Ezekiel, David and Isaiah also described the massive carnage that befalls the blasphemers in the Day of YHWH's vengeance:

In chapter 46, verse 10, Jeremiah describes *"the day of the Lord GOD of hosts"* as *"a day of vengeance, that he may avenge him of his adversaries: and the sword shall devour, and it shall be satiate and made drunk with their blood: for the Lord GOD of hosts hath a sacrifice in the north country by the river Euphrates [region common to Syria, Iraq & Turkey]."* And though this fierce anger is focused primarily on the Middle East—for the controversy of Zion[7]—the prophet is even more global and comprehensive in chapter 25.

Here, Jeremiah foretold of the *"wine cup of [YHWH's] fury"* which the LORD God would *"cause all the nations . . . to drink,"* moving them to madness *"because of the sword that [He] will send among them."* The prophecy specifically listed 21 nations and peoples by name who would drink of this cup of fury (Jerusalem and the cities of Judah included); but it also made anonymous mentions of various *"mingled peoples,"* as well as kingdoms in countries abroad (noncontiguous with the Middle East)—namely, *"kings of the isles which are beyond the sea . . . and all that are in the utmost corners."* This practically universal enmity includes *"all the kings of the north, far and near"* in league *"one with another,"* and *"all the kingdoms of the world, which are upon the face of the earth."* This passage from Jeremiah 25 (verses 13-33) reemphasizes the global scale of *YHWH's controversy* with all the nations of Earth:

For, lo, I begin to bring evil on the city which is called by my name, and should ye be utterly unpunished? Ye shall not be unpunished: for I will call for a sword upon all the inhabitants of the earth, saith the LORD of hosts.

Therefore prophesy thou against them all these words, and say unto them, The LORD shall roar from on high, and utter his voice from his holy habitation; he shall mightily roar upon his habitation; he shall give a shout, as they that tread the grapes, against all the inhabitants of the earth.

A noise shall come even to the ends of the earth; for the LORD hath a controversy with the nations, he will plead with all flesh; he will give them that are wicked to the sword, saith the LORD. Thus saith the LORD of hosts, Behold, evil shall go forth from nation to nation, and a great whirlwind shall be raised up from the coasts of the earth. And the slain of the LORD shall be at that day from one end of the earth even unto the other end of the earth: they shall not be lamented, neither gathered, nor buried; they shall be dung upon the ground.—Jeremiah 25:29-33

David, in the Psalms, also foresaw the *"striking through"* of multitudes of kings *"in the day of [God's] wrath."* It is then that *"He shall judge among the heathen, he shall fill the places with the dead bodies; he shall wound the heads over many countries." (Ps.110:5-6)*

Isaiah, in chapter 34, describes the call to assembly of the nations and their armies to the battle of the Great Day of God Almighty: *"Come near, ye nations, to hear; and hearken, ye people: let the earth hear, and all that is therein; the world, and all things that come forth of it. For the indignation of the LORD is upon all nations, and his fury upon all their armies: he hath utterly destroyed them, he hath delivered them to the slaughter. Their slain also shall be cast out, and their stink shall come up out of their carcasses, and the mountains shall be melted with their blood." (Isa.34:1-3)* And in verses 6-8, Isaiah elaborates further on the locale and cause of YHWH's anger: *"The sword of the LORD is filled with blood . . . for the LORD hath a sacrifice in Bozrah, and a great slaughter in the land of Idumea. . . . And their land shall be soaked with blood . . . For it is the day of the LORD's vengeance, and the year of recompenses for the controversy of Zion."*

(Bozrah-Idumea is the region surrounding the southern end of the Dead Sea where Jordan, Saudi Arabia and Egypt converge with Israel in the area of the Negev. It also encompasses the trouble spots of Gaza and the southern end of the West Bank that includes Hebron, which are all presently seething with controversy over Jerusalem. This is also the homeland of Herod the Great, the jealous Idumean perpetrator of the heinous Slaughter of the Innocents—the viscous mass murder of infants two years of age and under—at the time of Messiah's birth. At last, blood for blood, terror for terror.)

Again in chapter 63, Isaiah provides another reference to the slaughter that will take place in this region (of the Negev, S. Jordan being the modern-day location of Bozrah). This passage speaks of the righteous Savior returning with his garments dyed garishly red in blood from the furious treading down of the wicked at a time when the entire world has exalted themselves in defiance of YHWH:

Who is this that cometh from Edom, with dyed garments from Bozrah? this that is glorious in his apparel, travelling in the greatness of his strength? I that speak in righteousness, mighty to save. Wherefore art thou red in thine apparel, and thy garments like him that treadeth in the winefat? I have trodden the winepress alone; and of the people there was none with me: for I will tread them in mine anger, and trample them in my fury; and their blood shall be sprinkled upon my garments, and I will stain all my raiment. For the day of vengeance is in mine heart, and the year of my redeemed is come. . . . And I will tread down the people in mine anger, and make them drunk in my fury, and I will bring down their strength to the earth.—Isaiah 63:1-6

No power or might on earth, no high-tech military or even advanced "extraterrestrial" weaponry, nor any other force summoned from any other realm will be able to stand when the fury of YHWH is finally wreaked upon the pompous "gods" of Earth and the mountains melt with their mortal blood.

Isaiah identifies the timing of this massive exhibition of blood upon the earth and the worldwide littering of it with unburied carcasses. He places it at the time of God's wrath, once the resurrection of YHWH's people has occurred and they are ushered into protective isolation from the "vials" of wrath to be poured out upon the wicked. Isaiah writes, *"Thy dead men shall live, together with my dead body shall they arise. Awake and sing, ye that dwell in dust: for thy dew is as the dew of herbs, and the earth shall cast out the dead.*

Come, my people, enter thou into thy chambers, and shut thy doors about thee: hide thyself as it were for a little moment, until the indignation be overpast. For, behold, the LORD cometh out of his place to punish the inhabitants of the earth for their iniquity: the earth also shall disclose her blood, and shall no more cover her slain." (Isa.26:19-21)

Armageddon Hosts "Gog" Convention and Vulture Banquet

Now let us examine the prophecies of Ezekiel regarding this same massive slaughter. This scenario also involves the northern peoples of the regions of the Black and Caspian Seas, including the various other allied nations joining with them to invade Israel *"in the latter years."* Chapters 38 and 39 of the book of Ezekiel merit detailed studies in themselves, and provide enough subject matter to fill the pages of a whole book focused on their topic alone. Fine and thoroughly researched studies on these two chapters, which this author highly recommends, are available in bookstores.[18]

For our purposes here, we simply wish to reference these prophecies of Ezekiel by way of excerpts that match the corresponding features of the prophecies of the other ancient Hebrews we have been studying. In this case, we shall pursue one of the most notable features of the Great and Notable Day of the LORD—the Battle of Armageddon. Ezekiel's inspiration reveals considerable and intriguing details of this concluding event.

This prophet's writings (c. 587 BCE) detail an endtime invasion of the land of Israel by a coalition of nations led by a legendary entity called Gog—practically synonymous with the associated *"land of Magog."* The land of Magog is traceable as the ancestral home of the descendants of the grandson of Noah by the same name.

This grandson of Noah by Japheth (the eldest son of Noah), according to Greek and Jewish historians, evidently fathered the nomadic tribes of the famed Scythians. These descendants of Magog in Greek history dominated the vast steppe regions of southern Russia and central Asia from as far back as the 8th century BC until about the 1st century AD, when their empire appears to have dissolved. Since the Greeks (particularly Herodotus, "The Father of History") clearly identified the Scythians with Magog, many scholars feel there is fairly solid ground on which to base the identity of the land of Magog with Russia and the now independent, former Soviet republics of central Asia—Kazakhstan, Turkmenistan, Uzbekistan, Tadzhikistan, and Kyrgyzstan.

Gog and Magog, then, evidently refer to a spiritual-political entity that has roots in this region of the world, north of Israel. Gog is characterized with a definite degree of supremacy in a region that also includes modern day Turkey, Armenia, Azerbaijan, Georgia, Chechnya, and other Transcaucasus districts. Author J. D. Pentecost in *Things to Come* (p. 327) tells us that "the very word 'Caucasus' means Gog's fort." Gog is spoken of as the chief prince, or head leader of Meshech and Tubal—names of the brothers of Magog, also sons of Japheth. The ancient homelands of these two other grandsons of Noah include Armenia and northern Anatolia (modern-day Turkey) from whence their descendants migrated northward.

It may be of interest to note that this ancient region of the Earth is recorded as being the new point of origin of humankind after the Great Flood. Turkey and bordering Armenia and Iran are home to the mountains of Urartu and Mount Ararat, Turkey's highest peak, which lies just inside its eastern border with Armenia. These mountains are recorded by the Hebrews as being the landing site of Noah's Ark.[19] They have been the site of numerous exploratory expeditions, at least one of which has resulted in the discovery of the actual remains of a huge ship perfectly fitting the description of Noah's Ark eleven miles south of Mt. Ararat itself.[20]

Other allies in league with Gog and Magog include more close relatives. Descendants of another of the sons of Japheth, *Gomer* and his son *Togarmah*, form part of this coalition as well. (Armenians to this day regard themselves as the "house of Togarmah".) *Gomer* refers to the Cimmerian peoples of the shore regions of the Black Sea, who ultimately migrated, or were driven, north and westward to become the peoples of the land now known as *Germany*. Gomer is rendered "Germania" in the Babylonian Talmud (the authoritative body of Jewish instructive tradition, consisting of the oral law and its respective commentary).

The ancient name Askenaz, that of another son of Gomer, is to this day borrowed and applied by Jews themselves to the division of Diaspora Jewry (Ashkenazim) established in Eastern Europe, particularly Germany. It is interesting to note that despite the core cultural differences between Turkey and Germany, Germany is one of Turkey's most significant trading partners and their principal source of machinery and equipment.

Germany is, in fact, one of the major Western trading partners of several Middle Eastern countries, including Iran and Iraq. Besides machinery, transportation equipment, and electrical and electronic equipment—for which it is world renowned—as a world leader in chemicals production, it also supplies Iran and Iraq with these materials. As has been reported recently by the weekly television edition of *The International Intelligence Briefing*, Germany sells equipment to Middle Eastern countries to build bacteriological weapons and persists in selling restricted chemicals to Iraq.[21] For some years now, the endtime alliances have been taking shape right before our eyes in this latter-day generation, amazingly in accord with these prophecies.

It is not surprising at all to students of Bible prophecy to see the mention of Gomer's troops included in the Gog-Magog military confederation of Ezekiel's prophecy, since their ties to the controversy of Zion are weighed heavily on the side of Israel's enemies. All public political posturing aside, Germany is not neutral on the issue of Jerusalem, as is conspicuously mani-fest in their joining Yasser Arafat's effort to condemn Israel for attempting to build on their own land (as well as in all similar UN votes against Israel).

Alongside Gomer, we see Iran, North Africa, and Black Africa also listed as part of the Gog-Magog alliance in chapter 38 of Ezekiel (verse 6). Again, however, their identities are provided by way of their ancestors and their cor-responding homelands after the Great Flood. Iran is listed, under the name *Persia*, as the *primary ally* in this Gog-led campaign to invade Israel. The name Persia, in fact, remained with us until the 1930s, before being changed to Iran. The significance of Iran (Persia) being listed first is not to be over-looked, as it has definitely developed major ties with the land of Magog. Moreover, as most everyone knows, Iran is among the chief and most ardent of Israel's avowed enemies.

Despite the culture clash between the atheistic establishment of formerly soviet Russia (also considered part of the "Great Satan" by radical Muslims) and the intensely theistic nation of Iran, yet major exchanges and cooperative dealings have been going on between them since the break up of the USSR. They seem to have found mutually beneficial grounds for an unlikely partner-ship.

Iran needs the now readily available military hardware and nuclear tech-nology that post-Cold War Russia has to offer—in order to muscle-up for achieving its *Grand Design*. This term refers to Iran's declared objective of leading the nations of Islam in conquering the world for Allah and uniting the Muslim world into the *Superpower of the 21st century.*

Severely depressed Russia, hard-up for hard currency even to pay its army, much less its scientists and engineers, is quite pleased to be able to do business with one of its biggest weapons customers—oil-rich, militaristic Iran. Iran has been engaged in a massive armaments build-up in recent years, spending billions upon billions of dollars from its oil revenues to purchase military hardware from Russia, as well as from China and North Korea. In addition, Iran's petro-dollars are also ready sources of cash to fund the high technology transfers that now keep many of Russia's engineers and nuclear scientists employed developing nuclear power facilities in a country that has absolutely no need for an alternative energy source (to "generate electricity," they say).

As part of the Russo-Iranian deal, Iran—the chief dynamo of the sweeping, international Islamic Revolution—promises not to overtly foment Islamic insurgencies in the troubled Central Asian republics of the former Soviet Union. This includes the various other Muslim republics seeking to break away from Russia, such as we have seen happen within the last year in Chechnya (and now Dagestan, 1999). The successful revolt in Chechnya has resulted in the imposition by the new government of *Shari'ah*, or Islamic religious law as the civil code. A similar, though stricter form, has been imposed in Afghanistan, which we all witnessed via television last year (1996) when the Taliban rebels overthrew the government there. The Taliban rebel leaders were reportedly trained in Iran.

As a matter of delicate strategy then, Russia is keenly interested in preserving Kazakhstan, Turkmenistan, Uzbekistan, Tadzhikistan, and Kyrgyzstan in a stable Russian orbit, along with Dagestan and the other republics of the Caucasus region (near Chechnya) which might be inclined to follow in the footsteps of Chechnya. And Iran, pursuing its own ambitions, is even willing to deal strategically with "the devil" (the Great Satan) if it might strengthen their own position.

In the final analysis, the ancient hatred for the Jews will unite these diverse forces for a final assault on the Holy Land. This time, according to the prophecies, they will have to reckon with the forces of Almighty God in order to attempt to try to rip off what is not theirs. Now, let us complete the review of the list of the doomed Gog conglomeration.

It was mentioned that north, and more southerly Black Africa, will also join the Armageddon forces of Gog. Indeed, they are the very next names following Persia in the list, and even precede Gomer (probably in significance as well). The King James Version of the Bible gives their names as *Libya* and *Ethiopia*. And lest we mistakenly limit our perspective only to the modern-day countries going by these same names, we need to return to the original names of these peoples out of the Hebrew manuscripts of Ezekiel. The King James translators applied the name Libya to the region of Africa settled by the descendants of Phut, or also translated Put (Heb. פוט, *Puwt*). Phut was another of the grandsons of Noah, this time by his son Ham. His descendants migrated to inhabit North Africa—which includes the countries we know today as Libya, Tunisia, Algeria, Morocco, and probably Mali and Mauritania as well.

In like manner, "Ethiopia" was applied to the ancestral lands of the descendants of Cush (Heb. כוש, *Kuwsh*), a brother of Phut. It refers to a much greater expanse of territory than is now defined by the current boundaries of "Ethiopia," including Sudan and beyond. Note that the name Cush means "black" in the original language, and hence we can logically extend the application of the name Ethiopia even as far as the nation of South Africa in our consideration of the implications of this prophecy. Again we find few friends of Israel among the majority of these African nations. Many are either officially Muslim (some radical), or harbor radical Muslim nationalist movements, or are experiencing a significant growth of Islam.

Even those who do not yet figure with large populations of Muslims demonstrate anti-Israeli sympathies in their choice of partners. As is the case with South Africa, whose president recently rebuked the United States for attempting to pressure his country against a policy decision to sell hi-tech weapons systems to Syria, another of Israel's rabid archenemies. Defending his position against what he called American attempts to dictate South Africa's foreign policy, President Nelson Mandela justified his policy stance with the following declaration in January of 1997:

"All countries sell arms to other countries. The only condition we make is that our arms should not be used to disturb the peace in any region of the world. But, every country is entitled to have its own defense force, to equip itself, to defend its borders and its country. And it is in that spirit that we will conclude agreements with any country whether that country is popular in the West or not. And that is what we are likely to do in this case."[22]

This deal involves $8 billion in sales of tank parts and equipment, such as night vision scopes, fire control systems, and other combat capabilities to allow Syria to upgrade their 1,500 T-72 tanks to a par with Israel.

African unity seems to have recently found a new theme around which to rally. And though Egypt is not specifically listed by name among the allies of Gog and Magog, it seems, nonetheless, to be serving as a catalyst at this point for coalescing an anti-Israeli sympathy among the black African states. This is probably a ploy to deflect the heat of the internal turmoil that the Mubarak administration is feeling from Islamic radicals within his own borders—as well as pressures from without—who have regularly engaged in terrorism aimed at undermining the secular government of Egypt. The radicals also resent Egypt's official status of peaceful relations with Israel under the 1977 peace treaty signed by the late Anwar Sadat. Probably hoping to placate the radicals and sustain a semblance of leadership and prestige among Arab countries, Egypt has rallied 11 African states into a tentative anti-Israeli agreement.

Among them are countries not formerly hostile toward Israel, such as South Africa, Kenya, and the Ivory Coast. Egypt even convinced Ethiopia, Niger, and the Ivory Coast to abandon existing joint military agreements that they entered into only last year with Israel. The eleven-nation draft agreement will ban Israel from establishing military bases on the African continent, and also prohibits member states from engaging in joint military exercises with Israeli troops.[23]

The visions of the prophets are materializing more solidly as each week passes. The tension over the controversy of Zion will continue to build and very soon reach critical mass, until the situation becomes so explosive that only a miracle worker can de-fuse the bomb. An artificial political peace will be miraculously synthesized in the region by a cunning crafter of deceit and conniving betrayal. This amazing diplomatic triumph will mark the debut of the consummate warlord of all ages ("guised" in sheep's clothing) who is subsequently elevated to the status of a god by the masses of his worshipful constituents. Soon to arise, this man of marvels will be the infamous "Beast," of whom we have already spoken in detail, who will ultimately manage to rally the nations of the world to defy Almighty God at the battle of Armageddon.

Gog, however, should not be confused with the Beast. The Beast is an individual man empowered by Satan and embodying the ambitions of his insolent mentor. Gog, on the other hand, is a collective spirit of rebellion and defiance to the Order of YHWH (the rule of Truth and Righteousness and the authority of the Author of Creation). Gog is the corporate driving spirit of political pride, particularly that which is headquartered in the land of Magog that possesses mankind to exalt himself against the Creator. In this instance,

Gog is an aggressive, anti-Israel collective with strongholds in the land of Magog to the north of Israel resentful of its prosperity. Ostensibly, Gog seeks to dominate the strategic land of Israel and the wealth of the entire region, the oil-rich Middle East—including its other riches: stashes of precious metal oil revenues; high technology centers; and modern weapons caches.[24]

In spiritual terms, the controversy of Zion (Jerusalem) is the envious struggle for the "throne of God" as the seat of government over all Earth, which Lucifer covets in his jealous ambition.[25] The Battle of Armageddon is a preemptive "coup" rallied by the luciferian-empowered Beast against YHWH's coming to establish His New World Order (the Kingdom of God on earth with Jerusalem as capital).

In more practical terms, the battle will take form as a multi-pronged, allied invasion of the land of Israel "in the latter days," of which Gog apparently leads the primary contingent, almost surely for the reasons given above. And of course, among the many other nations which will also join the multinational fray, will be the kings of the rapidly rising powers of the far eastern nations also seeking a piece of the middle-eastern pie.

Gog's colossal defeat by the forces of the Almighty Mashiach at the time of the Battle of Armageddon constitutes the day of the Great Slaughter that we have studied in this chapter as the climax of the wrath of God. Though this battle is concentrated in and about the valley Meggido (also known as the Plain of Esdraelon in northern Israel, "the valley of the passengers" from ancient times), it also includes battlefronts and invasions from the south.[26] The central focal point is the land of Israel which will soon become the final battleground of the titanic struggle for the possession of Earth as well as the location of the mass burial grounds of the Hamongog International Cemetery (please refer back to footnotes 11, "demise of the northern army," and 12, "the international cemetery").

Gog is crushed at the battle of Armageddon. His coalition hordes are decimated, leaving only a fraction of his people as survivors in his land. A massive mop-up campaign then follows the carnage and slaughter of the great battle—beginning with the birds and beasts of prey summoned to the "supper of the great God":

Therefore, thou son of man, prophesy against Gog, and say, Thus saith the Lord GOD; Behold, I am against thee, O Gog, the chief prince of Meshech and Tubal: And I will turn thee back, and leave but the sixth part of thee, and will cause thee to come up from the north parts, and will bring thee upon the mountains of Israel: And I will smite thy bow out of thy left hand, and will cause thine arrows to fall out of thy right hand. Thou shalt fall upon the mountains of Israel, thou, and all thy bands, and the people that is with thee: I will give thee unto the ravenous birds of every sort, and to the beasts of the field to be devoured. Thou shalt fall upon the open field: for I have spoken it, saith the Lord GOD.

And I will send a fire on Magog, and among them that dwell carelessly in the isles: and they shall know that I am the LORD. So will I make my holy name known in the midst of my people Israel; and I will not let them pollute my holy name any more: and the heathen shall know that I am the LORD, the Holy One in Israel. Behold, it is come, and it is done, saith the Lord GOD; this is the day whereof I have spoken.

And they that dwell in the cities of Israel shall go forth, and shall set on fire and burn the weapons, both the shields and the bucklers, the bows and the arrows, and the handstaves, and the spears, and they shall burn them with fire seven years: So that they shall take no wood out of the field, neither cut down any out of the forests; for they shall burn the weapons with fire: and they shall spoil those that spoiled them, and rob those that robbed them, saith the Lord GOD.

And it shall come to pass in that day, that I will give unto Gog a place there of graves in Israel, the valley of the passengers on the east of the sea: and it shall stop the noses of the passengers: and there shall they bury Gog and all his multitude: and they shall call it The valley of Hamongog. And seven months shall the house of Israel be burying of them, that they may cleanse the land. Yea, all the people of the land shall bury them; and it shall be to them a renown the day that I shall be glorified, saith the Lord GOD. And they shall sever out men of continual employment, passing through the land to bury with the passengers those that remain upon the face of the earth, to cleanse it: after the end of seven months shall they search [full-time grave-diggers continue the interment after the initial collective burial campaign]. And the passengers that pass through the land, when any seeth a man's bone, then shall he set up a sign by it, till the buriers have buried it in the valley of Hamongog [Jezreel valley, site of Armageddon]. And also the name of the city shall be Hamonah [i.e., "the multitude of Gog"]. Thus shall they cleanse the land.

And, thou son of man, thus saith the Lord GOD; Speak unto every feathered fowl, and to every beast of the field, Assemble yourselves, and come; gather yourselves on every side to my sacrifice that I do sacrifice for you, even a great sacrifice upon the mountains of Israel, that ye may eat flesh, and drink blood. Ye shall eat the flesh of the mighty, and drink the blood of the princes of the earth, of rams, of lambs, and of goats, of bullocks, all of them fatlings of Bashan. And ye shall eat fat till ye be full, and drink blood till ye be drunken, of my sacrifice which I have sacrificed for you. Thus ye shall be filled at my table with horses and chariots, with mighty men, and with all men of war, saith the Lord GOD. And I will set my glory among the heathen, and all the heathen shall see my judgment that I have executed, and my hand that I have laid upon them. So the house of Israel shall know that I am the LORD their God from that day and forward.—Ezekiel 39:1-22

Thus, the cleanup process inaugurates the millennial reign of Messiah and marks the establishment of His Kingdom of peace in which no weapon of war will be tolerated. At last, all wrongs will be righted, all transgressions terminated, all unholinesses halted, all corruptions cleansed, all abominations abolished, all pride purged, and all controversies concluded. All mysteries will be resolved, all uncertainties dispelled, all misunderstandings clarified, and absolutely no doubt will remain about who YHWH God is and what His Will is; nor will any debate remain as to what The Truth is.[27] (Least of all, there will be no more controversy over Zion.)

Finally, Truth Distilled From Muddy (or perhaps Bloody) Waters

The "mystery of God" will then be finished. The Jews will grasp the essence of what it is to be a "Jew"; and so will the Gentiles.[28] They will comprehend who the King of Israel is; and so will the Gentiles. The house of Israel will come to understand that the Creator does not equivocate and keeps His word; and so will the heathen. All people will understand that God only is truly good and righteous; not any man or race, Gentile or Jew. Everyone will see that God keeps His promises (of blessing and curse), irrespective of persons, both to the Gentile as well as the Jew. And, when He sits on His throne in Jerusalem and returns the genuine remnant of the house of Israel to possess the land promised to Abraham, Isaac, and Jacob for ever (exactly as promised), no one will challenge that YHWH is Sovereign to chose as He pleases.—At least not for 1000 years!

So the house of Israel shall know that I am the LORD their God from that day and forward. And the heathen shall know that the house of Israel went into captivity for their iniquity: because they trespassed against me, therefore hid I my face from them, and gave them into the hand of their enemies: so fell they all by the sword. According to their uncleanness and according to their transgressions have I done unto them, and hid my face from them.

Therefore thus saith the Lord GOD; Now will I bring again the captivity of Jacob, and have mercy upon the whole house of Israel, and will be jealous for my holy name; after that they have borne their shame, and all their trespasses whereby they have trespassed against me, when they dwelt safely in their land, and none made them afraid.

When I have brought them again from the people, and gathered them out of their enemies' lands, and am sanctified in them in the sight of many nations; then shall they know that I am the LORD their God, which caused them to be led into captivity among the heathen: but I have gathered them unto their own land, and have left none of them any more there. Neither will I hide my face any more from them: for I have poured out my spirit upon the house of Israel, saith the Lord GOD.—Ezekiel 39:22-29

Zephaniah, too, prophesied very eloquently of YHWH's diligent sifting process and the final outcome:

The just LORD is in the midst thereof [having definitely manifested Himself & illuminated the world with the knowledge of good, as opposed to evil]; he will not do iniquity: every morning doth he bring his judgment to light, he faileth not [to illuminate good vs. evil]; but the unjust knoweth no shame [unrestrainedly favoring evil]. I have cut off the nations: their towers are desolate; I made their streets waste, that none passeth by: their cities are destroyed, so that there is no man, that there is none inhabitant. I said [greatly hoping], Surely thou wilt fear me, thou wilt receive instruction; so their dwelling should not be cut off, howsoever I punished them: but they rose early, and corrupted all their doings [refused correction, anxious for reprobate pursuits].

Therefore wait ye upon me, saith the LORD, until the day that I rise up to the prey: for my determination is to gather the nations, that I may assemble the kingdoms, to pour upon them mine indignation, even all my fierce anger: for all the earth shall be devoured with the fire of my jealousy.

For then will I turn to the people a pure language, that they may all call upon the name of the LORD, to serve him with one consent. . . . In that day shalt thou not be ashamed for all thy doings, wherein thou hast transgressed against me: for then I will take away out of the midst of thee them that rejoice in thy pride, and thou shalt no more be haughty because of my holy mountain. I will also leave in the midst of thee an afflicted and poor people, and they shall trust in the name of the LORD. The remnant of Israel shall not do iniquity, nor speak lies; neither shall a deceitful tongue be found in their mouth: for they shall feed and lie down, and none shall make them afraid. Sing, O daughter of Zion; shout, O Israel; be glad and rejoice with all the heart, O daughter of Jerusalem. The LORD hath taken away thy judgments, he hath cast out thine enemy: the king of Israel, even the LORD, is in the midst of thee: thou shalt not see evil any more.

In that day it shall be said to Jerusalem, Fear thou not: and to Zion, Let not thine hands be slack. The LORD thy God in the midst of thee is mighty; he will save, he will rejoice over thee with joy; he will rest in his love, he will joy over thee with singing. I will gather them that are sorrowful for the solemn assembly, who are of thee, to whom the reproach of it was a burden. Behold, at that time I will undo all that afflict thee: and I will save her that halteth, and gather her that was driven out; and I will get them praise and fame in every land where they have been put to shame. At that time will I bring you again, even in the time that I gather you: for I will make you a name and a praise among all people of the earth, when I turn back your captivity before your eyes, saith the LORD.—Zephaniah 3:5-20

Zechariah contributes the following to the final analysis of the Zion Controversy:

Thus saith the LORD of hosts; It shall yet come to pass, that there shall come people, and the inhabitants of many cities: And the inhabitants of one city shall go to another, saying, Let us go speedily to pray before the LORD, and to seek the LORD of hosts: I will go also. Yea, many people and strong nations shall come to seek the LORD of hosts in Jerusalem, and to pray before the LORD. Thus saith the LORD of hosts; In those days it shall come to pass, that ten men shall take hold out of all languages of the nations, even shall take hold of the skirt of him that is a Jew, saying, We will go with you: for we have heard that God is with you.—Zechariah 8:20-23

The Armageddon scenario that precedes the New World Order of YHWH is also described in the New Testament by the writer of the Apocalypse. In the apocalyptic visions of chapter 19 of the Book of Revelation, John's prophecy heavily supplements the prophecies of Ezekiel (nearly 700 years more ancient). John contributes additional particulars and adds fresh perspective, while also reinforcing the corresponding features of Ezekiel's vision to establish the event as identical to the one foretold in such vivid detail by Ezekiel (and others).

In his vision, John sees the "KING OF KINGS" come out of the heavens upon a white horse, leading His own armies to a battle at which are gathered together *"the beast, and the kings of the earth, and their armies . . . to make war against him that sat on the horse, and against his army."* This KING is called "Faithful and True," and His name is called "The Word of God":

And out of his mouth goeth a sharp sword, that with it he should smite the nations: and he shall rule them with a rod of iron: and he treadeth the winepress of the fierceness and wrath of Almighty God. And he hath on his vesture and on his thigh a name written, KING OF KINGS, AND LORD OF LORDS.

And I saw an angel standing in the sun; and he cried with a loud voice, saying to all the fowls that fly in the midst of heaven, Come and gather yourselves together unto the supper of the great God; that ye may eat the flesh of kings, and the flesh of captains, and the flesh of mighty men, and the flesh of horses, and of them that sit on them, and the flesh of all men, both free and bond, both small and great.

And I saw the beast, and the kings of the earth, and their armies, gathered together to make war against him that sat on the horse, and against his army. And the beast was taken, and with him the false prophet that wrought miracles before him, with which he deceived them that had received the mark of the beast, and them that worshipped his image. These both were cast alive into a lake of fire burning with brimstone. And the remnant were slain with the sword of him that sat upon the horse, which sword proceeded out of his mouth: and all the fowls were filled with their flesh.—Revelation 19:15-21

What the weapon wielded by this Supreme Ruler might actually consist of is a matter of pure conjecture. Essentially though, it is deployed as a mere matter of the command of His mouth—just as the power of His word also created the heavens and the earth.[29] No defense whatsoever will be found by the warmongering, weapons-mad nations of Earth, not even in the lofty high technologies of the 21st century. Their weaponry will become scrap and junk fit only to be recycled into farming implements, or as fuel for the fire; and their slain carcasses will be a flesh banquet for the fowls and beasts of prey.

We know this future battle to be the one mustered in the valley of Megiddo (also known as the Valley of Jezreel, or the Plain of Esdraelon), because John specifically identifies this *"battle of that great day of God Almighty"* as an event that occurs in *"a place called in the Hebrew tongue Armageddon."*[30] Armageddon in the Hebrew is *Har-Megiddown*, a compound of two words signifying *"the mount or hill country of Megiddown."* The town of Megiddo still exists today under the modern name Tel Megiddo. It lies about 18 miles (29km) southeast of Haifa in northern Israel overlooking the Plain of Esdraelon. This valley of Meggido runs northwest from the northern boundary of the so-called West Bank toward the Mediterranean coastland just to the north of Haifa. Nazareth also lies at close proximity to this geography. Armageddon is "ground zero" for the "showdown" we have discussed at length in this chapter.

An interesting report by the Associated Press in February 1997 related the vision for a project by Israel's National Parks Authority to use advanced computer graphics to bring the Battle of Armageddon to life for modern day tourists visiting the site. Park director Zeev Margalit expanded on the vision explaining that transparent screens were planned for installation at 14 different sites among Megiddo's excavated archaeological ruins, which would serve as hi-tech display stations. Holographic images would be projected on the screens, which would thereby create lifelike depictions superimposed over the backdrop of the actual site. Some of the images would simply depict ancient buildings as they originally existed, while at least one station is intended to dramatize the scenario of the Armageddon showdown, presumably with 3-D realism. The project deadline, according to Margalit, is by the year 2000.

In terms of the real thing, our deadline for choosing sides is when the Mark of the Beast is issued. (But then, your deadline could be this very day, unless you have some guarantee of tomorrow that the rest of us don't.) The nations of earth are soon to be sifted in the sieve of vanity. Will you fall through to the bloodstained ground, or will you be redeemed? I guess it's a matter of whether you hunger for the Truth or foolishly embrace the vanity of Godless iniquity. Be careful what you love, lest it become the bridle by which you are led.

Behold, the eyes of the Lord GOD are upon the sinful kingdom, and I will destroy it from off the face of the earth; saving that I will not utterly destroy the house of Jacob, saith the LORD.

For, lo, I will command, and I will sift the house of Israel [and those who have joined themselves to his house] among all nations, like as corn is sifted in a sieve, yet shall not the least grain fall upon the earth. All the sinners of my people shall die by the sword, which say, The evil shall not overtake nor prevent us [no one exempt from the sifting, despite their escapist rapture theories].

In that day will I raise up the tabernacle of David that is fallen, and close up the breaches thereof; and I will raise up his ruins, and I will build it as in the days of old [Jerusalem and Israel completely restored]: That they may possess the remnant of Edom [their jealous rival brethren], and of all the heathen, which are called by my name [converted Gentiles, including the so-called Church], saith the LORD that doeth this.—Amos 9:8-12

12

TIME NO LONGER
OR
THE SEVEN LAST PLAGUES

Agents everywhere! The FBI has agents, the CIA, and the KGB. Governments, auto rental companies, insurance companies, and many others employ agents. All of us are accustomed to dealing with agents and agencies of various sorts, and we understand the concept and principle. Well, the Author of the "Big Bang" also employs agents. They are commonly called angels, a word that originally signified a messenger, an envoy, or a representative dispatched as a deputy on behalf of the head authority. The Hebrews and their prophets spoke often of encounters with YHWH's envoys and of their messages. The Book of the Revelation is no exception and, in fact, highlights the activities and duties of numerous special agents. Angels are mentioned 76 times in the Apocalypse alone.

Among them, there were seven angels assigned to the seven 1st century churches detailed in the first three chapters. Another group of seven notable angels were charged with initiating, punctuating and concluding the Great Tribulation by the sounding of seven separate trumpets which are blown in sequence, detailed in chapters 8-11. The angels of the *final group of seven* were given charge of seven bowls ("vials" as per the KJV) and the pouring out of their terrible contents upon the earth and its Beast-marked survivors. The seven final downpours of God's Wrath are borne and poured out upon the lovers of iniquity by these seven angels of wrath in the final end.

For purposes of our prophecy tour, the activities of the last two groups of seven angels have been, and continue to be our focus. The distinction between these two groups is of utmost significance to the understanding of the development of endtime events. The seven angels of the Seven Trumpets are quite apart from the seven which have the "golden vials" full of the Seven

Last Plagues. Just as implied, the Seven Last Plagues are the *final* retributive acts of The Creator upon earth to avenge the wicked transgressions of mankind in violation of His holy design. Thus, the commissioned task of the *last seven* spirit agents of God should not be confused with the prior seven agents who signal the previously-occurring plagues of the Tribulation period (studied in earlier chapters).

John the Revelator detailed each of *"the seven last plagues"* (in the which are *"filled up the wrath of God"*) in chapters 15 and 16 of the prophecies of the Apocalypse. In his stunning vision, seven angels are given seven broad, shallow gold containers *"full of the wrath of God." (Rev.15:1 & 7)* (The term "vials" was used by the KJV Bible translators; the terminology used in the early Greek manuscripts, however, actually describes them as more akin to bowl-type containers, denoting rapid emptying of volume.) The transfer of these "seven golden vials" into the hands of these seven angels occurs at a key transitional point in the drama of the last hours of human horror—the transition from Tribulation to intense Indignation, namely, the Day of Vengeance upon YHWH's enemies.[1]

The passage from Tribulation into Wrath is signaled by the sounding of the Seventh Trumpet, the last in the foregoing series of Tribulation Trumpets, which occurs just prior to the swift and thoroughly devastating period of the "wrath of God" to follow.[2] The great sifting "with the sieve of vanity" will have essentially been completed by the time of the 7th Trumpet. That, indeed, is the whole purpose of the Great Tribulation, as we studied in earlier chapters, to sort the wicked from the just. What shall follow next is reserved specifically for God's enemies.

That last apocalyptic trumpet in the series of seven is the famed *"last trump"* spoken of by Apostle Paul as the signal of the renowned and much-celebrated Rapture.[3] It is also the trumpet mentioned by Messiah in the prophecy from Matthew chapter 24, which provides the thematic title for this book. The seventh trumpet **marks the end** of the Great Tribulation. It is outlined and described by John from the first verse of Revelation chapter 7 through chapter 14 (ending at verse 16). It's at that point that Messiah finally gathers and reaps His harvest of friends who have not compromised with the Beast and his new world order program.

It is after the gathering of the saints into a celestial (probably hyperspace) dimension that the seven last plagues proceed to be poured out in rapid succession upon the wickedly intransigent God-haters, who rally in anger to defy

YHWH's repossession of planet Earth. This in particular is the period (with its series of associated plagues) that constitutes the event spoken of so frequently by the Hebrews as the *Great Day of the Wrath of God.*

Completely distinct from the Great Tribulation, the ensuing period of the Wrath of God is not intended to be any type of trial or event aimed at proving the devotion of the just, nor at sorting or separating them from the wicked. It is the period in which God takes vengeance on them that have hated His followers and chosen ones, and thus also hated Him as an enemy, having thereby ultimately sealed their own condemnation of themselves.[4] Such spite for YHWH by the wicked usurpers of Earth shall be thoroughly manifest in the brutal campaign of the coming World Order of the Beast to viciously assail, repress, and crush the endtime saints during the Tribulation period.[5]

Again, the principal aim of the Great Tribulation is to sort the wheat from the chaff, the sheep from the goats, and the good seed from the tares, so to speak.[6] Every soul alive will be compelled, without convenient resort to escape, to chose an allegiance: the evil Dragon, or the righteous Christ whom he and the wicked world blaspheme.

Another of the Tribulation's directly connected purposes is to purge "the gold" of all its dross in the fires of persecution. That is to say, to remove all the impurities of the world system and its influences from the lives and hearts of multitudes of corrupted believers who are torn in their devotion between "two masters."[7] In the very process, the perpetrators of persecution, who inflict tribulation upon the saints who refuse to compromise and conform, simultaneously fulfill yet another critical goal—filling up the measure of their own wickedness by their hateful assaults upon the righteous. Thus, having filled their cup of iniquity to overflowing wickedness, they then plainly and patently merit the vengeance and wrath of the Almighty God. Conversely, the uncompromising saints will then merit laundered white robes, and also avert the shame of "nakedness," empty-handedness, and being forever stripped of any personal recompense or reward.[8] These are the key functions of the immediately preceding stage of Tribulation.

Once the crucial sifting functions of the Great Tribulation are accomplished, the seventh angel of the Seven Trumpets blows the final horn, signaling the end of the line for the blaspheming, pagan societies of Earth:

And the angel which I saw stand upon the sea and upon the earth lifted up his hand to heaven, and sware by him that liveth for ever and ever, who created heaven, and the things that therein are, and the earth, and the things that therein are, and the sea, and the things which are therein, that there should be time no longer: But in the days of the voice of the seventh angel, when he shall begin to sound, the mystery of God should be finished, as he hath declared to his servants the prophets.—Revelation 10:5-7

(Behold, I shew you a mystery; We shall not all sleep [die], but we shall all be changed, in a moment, in the twinkling of an eye, at the last trump: for the trumpet shall sound, and the dead shall be raised incorruptible, and we shall be changed.—1 Corinthians 15:51-52)

And the seventh angel sounded; and there were great voices in heaven, saying, The kingdoms of this world are become the kingdoms of our Lord, and of his Christ; and he shall reign for ever and ever. . . . And the nations were angry, and thy wrath is come, and the time of the dead, that they should be judged, and that thou shouldest give reward unto thy servants the prophets, and to the saints, and them that fear thy name, small and great; and shouldest destroy them which destroy the earth.—Revelation 11:15-18

The Wrath of God

The Wrath does not come until the voice of the last trump of the seventh angel is sounded. This is unambiguously articulated in the Apocalypse. And, as has already been demonstrated in a previous section (chapter 10), the judgment and the resurrection do not come until this *last day*, when it is declared *"that there should be time no longer."*[9] We can therefore conclude that the seventh trumpet draws the line that separates the Tribulation phase from the stage of Wrath that immediately follows, heralding the end of the former and the start of the latter. (I don't deny that the Great Tribulation will incorporate acts of anger and ire on the part of The Almighty, from which believers will be largely protected; but none quite as harsh as those reserved for the following weeks of Wrath, from which the faithful will be removed altogether.)

It is at this point that the real horror of horrors begins, in terms of cataclysm and catastrophe upon Earth; some of which we have examined in the previous chapter, with a particular focus on the Battle of that Great Day (Armageddon, etc.). Here is where the promise conveyed to the believers by Apostle Paul regarding the *wrath* of God is to be applied and claimed: *"For*

God hath not appointed us to wrath, but to obtain salvation by our Lord Jesus Christ." (1Thes.5:9) "And to wait for his Son from heaven, whom he raised from the dead, even Jesus, which delivered us from the wrath to come." (1Thessalonians 1:10)

In an earlier chapter, it was pointed out that the word "tribulation" in the ancient Greek manuscripts of the New Testament is *thlipsis* [θλι□ψις], meaning *pressure* as a pressing or squeezing through straits. Whereas, the "wrath" referred to by Paul in the above quotes (as well as in other pertinent cross-references) comes from the Greek *orgé* [ὀργὴ], signifying *anger* or *indignation* as a violent passion. Two clearly dissimilar concepts are denoted by these words, which need to be kept distinct from one another so as to understand the Tribulation-versus-Wrath difference. Otherwise, great confusion results, clouding not only the purpose but also the timing of these two disparate events.

Beyond question, the plagues of the Tribulation period are certainly nothing less than catastrophic. Still, they are not to be compared in magnitude with those of the period of Wrath, when YHWH no longer purposes merely to *"try them that dwell upon the earth" (Rev. 3:10)*, but now to tread the wicked in *"the winepress of the fierceness and wrath of Almighty God." (Rev. 19:15)*

The *"seven last plagues"* of Wrath are swift, devastating punishments accomplished within the period of about a month. As regards the order of unfolding of the terminal events forecast in the Apocalypse, these very last plagues are to be fulfilled at a time when the triumphant disciples of the Lamb are now safely sanctuaried in heaven, having overcome the beast and his image, his mark and number.[10]

These seven plagues constitute the full volume of God's wrath to be unleashed upon the wicked blasphemers remaining on planet Earth (Rev. 15:1). A wrath so awesome and horrible that *"the kings of the earth, and the great men, and the rich men, and the chief captains, and the mighty men, and every bondman, and every free man, hid themselves in the dens and in the rocks of the mountains; and said to the mountains and rocks, Fall on us, and hide us from the face of him that sitteth on the throne, and from the wrath of the Lamb: For the great day of his wrath is come; and who shall be able to stand?" (Rev.6:16-17)*

To kick off this dreadful period of scourging and annihilation, men are afflicted with an especially baneful and grievous sore. At the unleashing of the *first plague*, the Greek manuscripts suggest a horrible ulcerous wound or disease will break out upon the remaining populations of Earth having the mark of the Antichrist.[11]

The *second and third plagues* to follow are alike. Together, they affect all the waters of Earth, turning them to "blood."[12] Although I do not doubt in the least that the meaning here is quite literal, blood, in this passage, may very well be symbolic of death by polluted water rendered lethally toxic; I don't know. In any event, I find it needless to seek to offer a scientific explanation for what is easily within the capabilities of the Almighty God to perform; for indeed, it won't be the first time in history that waters have been turned to blood. In any event, even in scientifically understood terms, the vision of the prophet, in which he evidently saw the waters of Earth turn blood red, is not an outlandish nor unknown phenomenon by any account.

Red tides of toxic waters, lethal to fish and other marine life, as well as to birds, have periodically been reported in various parts of the world, especially in warm waters. *Earth* magazine reported in its August 1997 edition on a red tide that occurred on April 11 of that same year, which forced thousands of rock lobsters onto the beaches of Elands Bay in South Africa. These red tides are caused by "blooms" (exploding populations) of teeming millions (per liter of water) of microorganisms causing discoloration of sea water (often bright red or yellow). These microscopic one-celled creatures—protozoa/algae dinoflagellates ("half plant, half animal") of a couple of different species—also release toxins into the water. Besides killing fish and birds, the toxins are also poisonous to humans. They sometimes force the closings of seaside resort areas, due to the quite irritating toxic substances released even into the air by breaking waves.

Various encyclopedias give account of two major infestations in recent history caused by *Gymnodinium brevis* dinoflagellates. One occurred off the Gulf coast of Florida in 1947, which reportedly killed thousands of fish; the second along the Northumberland coast of England in 1968, which even killed local bird populations. Among the other species of these strange, toxic micro-creatures, *Gonyaulax polyedra* is another, responsible for recorded red tides off Portuguese and California coasts. Chile, Japan, eastern Australia, Peru and Texas are other listed locations of this strange phenomenon.

In light of these, it is not at all hard to imagine that a worldwide toxic scourge of just this nature could be brought to bear upon the death-dealing, genocidal barbarians that have contrived to murder millions with demonic chemical and biological weapons of mass destruction! But again, literal blood is not out of the question: *"For they have shed the blood of saints and proph-*

*ets, and thou [O LORD] hast given them blood to drink; for they are worthy."
(Rev.16:6)*

Plague four is a curse of intense heat and incendiary disaster triggered by a solar event—perhaps nearly nova or supernova in nature—which generates searing fires, such that men are *"scorched with [mega] heat."* The prophets Isaiah (particularly) and Malachi both confirm a last-day event of this nature.[13]

Next, *"the fifth angel poured out his vial upon the seat [throne, capital, headquarters] of the beast; and his kingdom was full of darkness; and they gnawed their tongues for pain, and blasphemed the God of heaven because of their pains and their sores, and repented not of their deeds." (Rev 16:10-11)* Whether this darkness, which prevails particularly over the headquarters of the Antichrist (soon to be) in Israel,[14] is due to smoke and atmospheric contaminants, or to blindness caused by the hyperactivity of the sun, it is hard to say. But the tormenting conditions and agonizing sores experienced by these hardened "humans" does not move them to desist in their defiance of the (returning) Founder of Earth. Rather, they unrelentingly persist in their rebellious blasphemy against the Almighty.

The spilling out of the *sixth bowl* results in the drying up of *"the great river Euphrates . . . that the way of the kings of the east might be prepared." (Rev 16:12-16)* Now occurs the great gathering together of the nations for the final Armageddon showdown, as we have fairly broadly examined already in the preceding chapter. In particular, the stage is set here for the massing of troops to the Great Battle from the Asian countries to the east. The Dragon manages to recoup his partially crippled forces and rally the Eastern contingent—China, India, Pakistan, etc.[15]—to engage with his other coalition forces in the preemptive *coup de resistance* against the Prince of Peace.

Viewing a globe of Earth and following a line directly east of Israel just above the 30th parallel takes us through a striking geopolitical zone. We cross the Euphrates through Iraq, Iran, Afghanistan, Pakistan, India, and on to China, *none of which* (we should note) are friends of Israel or the West. Into that basket category of anti-Western sympathies are tossed not only Israel, but America, England, and other Western allies too, whether they be Judeo-Christian in heritage or essentially neo-pagan in orientation.

Cast in together by association with these decadent societies is, of course, the profaned GOD (of Abraham, Isaac, Jacob, Moses, David, and Jesus) whose name has been taken in vain by them. This worst of tragedies can be attributed in large part to the degeneration and corruption of these Western societies and cultural groups—thanks to their miserable misrepresentation of the religion of those faithful patriarchs of GOD (just listed in parenthesis). Not that the countries of the Orient are to be justified for their virulent, self-righteous antipathies for the societies and peoples of The Book, or its Author; but the perversion and hypocritical piety of those peoples lends significant impetus to the Eastern disdain for, and their eventual mass revolt against, the namesake GOD "of the West."[16]

The writer of the Apocalypse was able, by some phenomenal means, to penetrate 2,000 years into the future to foresee the formidable foe that the countries of the orient would become to the establishment of the New World Order of Messiah.

The People's Republic of China, in particular, is now viewed by numerous political, economic and military analysts as *"the rising superpower of the 21st century."* This, in combination with its official government stance on religion (particularly Christianity),[17] its stance on human rights, its technology piracy practices and violations of international copyrights, its implication in the illegal smuggling of assault weapons into California, never mind its "blindfold bribery" of the American political machine to purchase the winking of the eyes of the incumbent White House administration at China's atrocious official state policies and practices—with illegal contributions to the 1996 presidential campaign—all taken together manifest China's character as an unscrupulous, insidious, and treacherous menace to any world order or culture of a Judeo-Christian ethic. China, however, is not alone. It's just the most notable and powerful of the numerous looming oriental threats—a devious, dastardly "dragon" reawakening to fulfill its defiant destiny!

And the sixth angel poured out his vial upon the great river Euphrates; and the water thereof was dried up, that the way of the kings of the east might be prepared. And I saw three unclean spirits like frogs come out of the mouth of the dragon, and out of the mouth of the beast, and out of the mouth of the false prophet. For they are the spirits of devils, working miracles [extraordinary phenomena], which go forth unto the kings of the earth and of the whole world, to gather them to the battle of that great day of God Almighty. Behold, I come as a thief. Blessed is he that watcheth, and keepeth his garments, lest he walk naked, and they see his shame. And he gathered them together into a place called in the Hebrew tongue Armageddon. And the seventh angel poured out his vial into the air; and there came a great voice out of the temple of heaven, from the throne, saying, It is done.—Revelation 16:12-17

By whatever means it is accomplished, in this vision of the imminent future, the militaries of the endtime antichrist world are consolidated and assembled; and the very significant eastern element is mobilized to *join* the coup. The supreme sultan of this satanic earthwide regime, together with his miracle-working prophet/prime minister, mobilizes all their armies and armaments for the ultimate engagement, the final contest..

The communications logistics employed in this achievement are apparently not of the conventional sort. In fact, it is quite likely that the conventional telecommunications facilities will have been largely destroyed or disabled by the earlier geologic, cosmic, and solar cataclysms that plague the earth during this period of wrath. Some quite anomalous and extraordinary phenomenon is commanded to rally the different armies together, very possibly being of an alien type, perhaps involving UFO "leaps" to remote locations to call the various international contingents to the Holy Land vicinity. A telepathic communications technique (of supernatural and spirit nature) may be used to coordinate the urgent deployment and mobilization of disparate forces (of different languages).

Evidently too, these forces are not entirely mechanized, but include colossal numbers of infantry and, particularly, *mounted troops*. This is the clear inference made by both John and Ezekiel in their respective prophecies of the *"great sacrifice"* and the *"supper of the great God,"* which immediately follow the great battle of Armageddon.

And I saw an angel standing in the sun; and he cried with a loud voice, saying to all the fowls that fly in the midst of heaven, Come and gather yourselves together unto the supper of the great God; that ye may eat the flesh of kings, and the flesh of captains, and the flesh of mighty men, and the flesh of horses, and of them that sit on them, and the flesh of all men, both free and bond, both small and great. And I saw the beast, and the kings of the earth, and their armies, gathered together to make war against him that sat on the horse, and against his army. And the beast was taken, and with him the false prophet that wrought miracles before him, with which he deceived them that had received the mark of the beast, and them that worshipped his image. These both were cast alive into a lake of fire burning with brimstone. And the remnant were slain with the sword of him that sat upon the horse, which sword proceeded out of his mouth: and all the fowls were filled with their flesh.—Revelation 19:17-21

Son of man, set thy face against Gog, the land of Magog, the chief prince of Meshech and Tubal, and prophesy against him, and say, Thus saith the Lord GOD; Behold, I am against thee, O Gog, the chief prince of Meshech and Tubal: And I will turn thee back, and put hooks into thy jaws, and I will bring thee forth, and all thine army, horses and horsemen, all of them clothed with all sorts of armour, even a great company with bucklers and shields, all of them handling swords: Persia, Ethiopia, and Libya with them; all of them with shield and helmet: Gomer, and all his bands; the house of Togarmah of the north quarters, and all his bands: and many people with thee.

After many days thou shalt be visited: in the latter years thou shalt come into the land that is brought back from the sword, and is gathered out of many people, against the mountains of Israel, which have been always waste: but it is brought forth out of the nations, and they shall dwell safely all of them. Thou shalt ascend and come like a storm, thou shalt be like a cloud to cover the land, thou, and all thy bands, and many people with thee. . . . And thou shalt come from thy place out of the north parts, thou, and many people with thee, all of them riding upon horses, a great company, and a mighty army.—Ezekiel 38:2-15

And I will turn thee back, and leave but the sixth part of thee, and will cause thee to come up from the north parts, and will bring thee upon the mountains of Israel: And I will smite thy bow out of thy left hand, and will cause thine arrows to fall out of thy right hand. Thou shalt fall upon the mountains of Israel, thou, and all thy bands, and the people that is with thee: I will give thee unto the ravenous birds of every sort, and to the beasts of the field to be devoured.—Ezekiel 39:2-4

And, thou son of man, thus saith the Lord GOD; Speak unto every feathered fowl, and to every beast of the field, Assemble yourselves, and come; gather yourselves on every side to my sacrifice that I do sacrifice for you, even a great sacrifice upon the mountains of Israel, that ye may eat flesh, and drink blood. Ye shall eat the flesh of the mighty, and drink the blood of the princes of the earth, of rams, of lambs, and of goats, of bullocks, all of them fatlings *of Bashan [speaking of the anti-Israel Syrians and their financed guerrillas to be sacrificed in recompense]. And ye shall eat fat till ye be full, and drink blood till ye be drunken, of my sacrifice which I have sacrificed for you. Thus ye shall be filled at my table with horses and chariots, with mighty men, and with all men of war, saith the Lord GOD.—Ezekiel 39:17-20*

(*"Horses, swords, bows and arrows?"* you may be asking. The term "swords" is, of course, nothing more than ancient terminology for hand-held weapons; and modern "bows and arrows" simply take the form of hi-tech weapons that launch projectiles. Horses, on the other hand, though they too could have a modern mechanized counterpart, probably will actually be the military transport of choice in the final analysis. We have already seen how failures of state-of-the-art computerized technologies can paralyze critical operations of modern equipment so utterly dependent upon them.

For example, let us call to mind the recent massive failures of paging and communications devices when the Galaxy 4 telecommunications satellite suddenly blinked out in May of 1998 due to failure of the onboard automated stabilizing system. Not only were 4 million customers of the paging system affected, but relayed radio broadcasts and television signal transmissions were also interrupted, as well as certain credit card and ATM transactions. The cause is evidently still undetermined.

In another case, the reported cause of a massive electric power outage lasting 6 hours across 15 states and even parts of Canada and Mexico in July of 1996 was a simple short circuit. A tree growing too close to a transmission line in Idaho provided the short circuit that blew out the system. State employees in the state capitol of Idaho were sent home when state agencies and offices were unable to operate functionally with their "plug pulled." Vital water supplies delivered from remote locations to Los Angeles by huge pumps eked to a drip. Businesses were paralyzed without lights, computers, cash registers, etc., forcing closure of stores, banks, and others. People on amusement park rides in Los Angeles and in rail cars on San Francisco's Bay Area Rapid Transit System were stranded when they all lost power and ground to a halt.

Yet another similar demonstration of the fragility of our modern systems occurred in the spring of 1998 at what some believe to have been a century date-change test by AT&T (which was reported as a software problem). Probably exploring the potential for Y2K problems with their automated (computerized) systems at the turn of the century, one of AT&T's switching hubs went haywire. Communications services all around the USA were affected, including basic phone services, fax, Internet and e-mail services. Manufacturers were unable to place or receive orders; banking transfers could not be made; and many other industries and businesses were crippled over wide areas because over 40 other telephone "hubs" linked in the network were jolted out of whack by the original malfunction.

With all its advancements in high technology and all the accompanying advantages, our modern 20th century society has become more fragile than ever. Our modern, highly mechanized military machines are easier to paralyze or severely cripple than ever before. The Year 2000 (Y2K) Computer Bug (a.k.a. the Millennium Bug) has already sent shivers of dread throughout the Pentagon, the US Department of Defense and Capitol Hill. Every facet of the military machine is computerized, from the common infantry battalion to the most powerful nuclear weapons delivery systems in the world, and not least of all, the monitoring, tracking and defensive systems continually on alert for foreign attack. One tiny software oversight—Y2K—now threatens to unravel it all!

A meteor shower in November of 1988 is predicted to have the potential to wreak havoc on any number of the thousands of satellites we have placed in orbit around the earth for various reasons, some of them utterly critical to the GPS guidance systems of naval, airborne, and ground-based military equipment.[18] This is only a small sample of the natural disasters that are due to befall the earth in the last days. One of the Seven Last Plagues before the amassing of the multinational armies to the final Battle of Armageddon is a searing solar cataclysm which will scorch Earth, its people, its machines, its cities, its satellites (unprotected by atmosphere, clouds, or even shrouds of smoke), etcetera, as its burns seven times hotter than usual.

Conditions such as these will render our machines and hi-tech devices useless. Those machines which are petrol-powered (gasoline, diesel, kerosene, etc.) are sure to suffer crippling lacks of fuel. Imagine the likelihood of refineries and stores of fuel surviving the heat, quakes, meteor and asteroid assaults. And even in the case of a scant survival rate, how will the fuel be transported to refueling points when so many automated systems critical to piloting and navigation of tankers are likewise crippled? In addition, normally impassable terrain or nonexistent or demolished roadway infrastructures are not nearly the obstacle to horses as they would be to land-based vehicles. Even four-wheel-drive vehicles are easily surpassed by horses in rugged ground conditions. The days to come will see the old-fashioned horse, unmatched for dependability, once again prove indispensable to military operations.

Now, of course, the scorching heat of a hyperactive solar phenomenon would certainly kill horses as well as people. But remember, huge areas of the earth will be shrouded in smoke and airborne ash during this period, so that we can expect that not all regions will be directly exposed to the extreme heat at that time. According to the prophecies, vast numbers of troops will be amassed at that time to battle at Armageddon, so that enormous armies will still survive and be maintained (always a #1 priority with the world's nations) until the time of the final conflict. The issue is: How will they effectively cover the distances they must travel in order to descend upon Israel without the aid of mechanized vehicles?

The foreknowledge of God conveyed to us through the Hebrew Prophets has already provided the answers and laid out the whole future scenario with uncanny precision. Doubt all that we might, the fact that China and Russia are two of the leading producers of horses in the world ought to strike any rational, thinking person with awe and the fear of God.[19] The hordes of Gog and Magog and the Kings of the East shall descend upon the Holy Land on horses— but only to be overwhelmingly squashed like grapes by the Lion of Judah in the valleys of Megiddo, Jezreel, Jordan, Jehoshaphat and the land of Edom. THE WORD OF YHWH WILL NOT FAIL IN THE LEAST!

Hailstones, Skyscrapers, and Bombshelters

The grand conclusion of the *seven last plagues* of the Great Day of God's Wrath is at last announced at the pouring out of the very *last bowl into the air*—with the words *"It is done." (Rev 16:17)* (These are the same words, we should note, declared in the related prophesy of Ezekiel, chapters 38 & 39, reviewed in this and the previous chapter.)[20]

And the seventh angel poured out his vial into the air; and there came a great voice out of the temple of heaven, from the throne, saying, It is done. And there were voices, and thunders, and lightnings; and there was a great earthquake, such as was not since men were upon the earth, so mighty an earthquake, and so great. And the great city was divided into three parts, and the

*cities of the nations fell: and great Babylon came in remembrance before
God, to give unto her the cup of the wine of the fierceness of his wrath. And
every island fled away, and the mountains were not found. And there fell upon
men a great hail out of heaven, every stone about the weight of a talent [about
114 pounds, according to Vine's Expository Dictionary]: and men blasphemed
God because of the plague of the hail; for the plague thereof was exceeding
great.—Revelation 16:17-21*

The declaration of the "great voice" out of the temple of heaven, from the
throne of God, saying, *"It is done,"* is the final word of destiny for the expired dominion of wicked men upon earth.

Modern man has ungratefully chosen to give God credit for nothing but
destruction, and "evolution" for Creation. YHWH has been stripped by the
arrogant contemporary blasphemers in today's world of any credit for creation of life, or the earth, or the heavens, or the powers contained therein. The
only place He is acknowledged is in legal disclaimers for those "natural disasters" beyond the control of man: storms, tornadoes, hurricanes, floods,
earthquakes, volcanic eruptions, the sky falling, etcetera—termed as "acts of
God." Well, ironically enough, destruction and blasphemy will be the overflowing cups of destiny which wicked humanity will drink and (once again)
drown in. They will be the violent end and final undoing of the proud and
highminded, evolution-bent human spawn.

Enough superlatives cannot be used to describe the fierceness of the wrath
of Almighty God. Yet the Hebrew prophets were prompted to endeavor to
communicate the extent of the unimaginable devastation that lies at the end
of the last leg of the road that mankind now carelessly treks to his impending
doom. John the Revelator, as we have just read, described a gargantuan earthquake greater than man has ever known. *"So mighty an earthquake, and so
great"* that the cities of the nations are left ruinous heaps. Islands vanish and
mountains are leveled. *(Rev.16:18-20)*

The epicenter of this titanic quake is likely the land of Israel itself, if the
prophecies of John, Ezekiel, Joel, and Zechariah can be validly pieced together:

*For in my jealousy and in the fire of my wrath have I spoken, Surely in that
day there shall be a great shaking in the land of Israel; so that the fishes of
the sea, and the fowls of the heaven, and the beasts of the field, and all creep-*

ing things that creep upon the earth, and all the men that are upon the face of the earth, shall shake at my presence, and the mountains shall be thrown down, and the steep places shall fall, and every wall shall fall to the ground.— Ezekiel 38:19-20

The LORD also shall roar out of Zion, and utter his voice from Jerusalem; and the heavens and the earth shall shake: but the LORD will be the hope of his people, and the strength of the children of Israel.—Joel 3:16

For I will gather all nations against Jerusalem to battle; and the city shall be taken, and the houses rifled, and the women ravished; and half of the city shall go forth into captivity, and the residue of the people shall not be cut off from the city. Then shall the LORD go forth, and fight against those nations, as when he fought in the day of battle. And his feet shall stand in that day upon the mount of Olives, which is before Jerusalem on the east, and the mount of Olives shall cleave in the midst thereof toward the east and toward the west, and there shall be a very great valley; and half of the mountain shall remove toward the north, and half of it toward the south.—Zechariah 14:2-4

And of course, the Apocalypse confirms and corroborates these related prophecies by linking Jerusalem with the initial impacts of the quake. John says, *"And the great city was divided into three parts, and the cities of the nations fell: and great Babylon came in remembrance before God, to give unto her the cup of the wine of the fierceness of his wrath. And every island fled away, and the mountains were not found." (Rev. 16:19-20)* We can conclude that "the great city" is Jerusalem from an preceding reference to this same location as the city *"where also our Lord was crucified." (Rev. 11:8)*

Identifying the epicenter of the quake is perhaps not of great consequence, and perhaps rather, only an interesting footnote. What is interesting to note is that a least four different prophets from four different eras, separated by hundreds of years over a span of nearly nine centuries, forecast the same event with specificity, implicating Jerusalem and the land of Israel as the focus of this major endtime cataclysm.

Beyond all of that, the colossal degree of devastation from this quake is what is most striking. To imagine it is nothing short of nightmarish, particularly when we contemplate the skylines and contemporary architectural character of so many of the modern cities in today's world. From Hong Kong to

Johannesburg to Toronto, the globe is dotted with city after city not just sprawling outward, but scaling upward, after the American pattern of scraping the skies with the towering high-rise glories of the 20th century. The prophetic outlook for these proud, gleaming structures and the cities they adorn is dismally bleak.

As may have been noted in the passages cited above from both Ezekiel and Joel, this one last earthquake will be so massive that the Earth's atmospheric shroud also will be rocked with gigantic shock waves affecting even the birds in the sky. At least three other prophets confirm this phenomenon, Isaiah describing the horror most vividly:

Howl ye; for the day of the LORD is at hand; it shall come as a destruction from the Almighty. Therefore shall all hands be faint, and every man's heart shall melt: And they shall be afraid: pangs and sorrows shall take hold of them; they shall be in pain as a woman that travaileth: they shall be amazed one at another; their faces shall be as flames.

Behold, the day of the LORD cometh, cruel both with wrath and fierce anger, to lay the land desolate: and he shall destroy the sinners thereof out of it. For the stars of heaven and the constellations thereof shall not give their light: the sun shall be darkened in his going forth, and the moon shall not cause her light to shine. And I will punish the world for their evil, and the wicked for their iniquity; and I will cause the arrogancy of the proud to cease, and will lay low the haughtiness of the terrible. I will make a man more precious than fine gold; even a man than the golden wedge of Ophir.

Therefore I will shake the heavens, and the earth shall remove out of her place, in the wrath of the LORD of hosts, and in the day of his fierce anger.—Isaiah 13:6-13

Whose voice then shook the earth: but now he hath promised, saying, Yet once more I shake not the earth only, but also heaven.—Paul's epistle to the Hebrews (12:26)

Mankind has been put on notice with ample advance warning (thousands of years) by the abundant testimony of a plethora of holy prophets: His defiant efforts to create a civilization that denies the Creator of heaven and earth His own sovereignty and right to establish the laws by which earth's societies may viably operate will be quashed and his civilizations annihilated.

The power of Earth's people to exercise freedom of choice does not translate into the right to defy the will and might of Him who created life and the universe that sustains it. That transitory human power of self-will misused to choose to deny and defy Truth is merely a demonstration of the power men and women have to delude themselves. Their creative genius and free will has been opportunistically exercised to exalt themselves against God in an attempt to redefine life and the universe to suit their own lusts for self-aggrandizement and unbridled egotism; thus, in pretense, they act as their own "gods," rewriting their own self-serving laws of convenience. While YHWH refrains from any tyrannical imposition of forced restraint upon men, they exploitatively take up their own tyranny against His revealed will, His poor people, His Savior, His planet and all that abides therein.[21]

This evil aggrandizement of self is thoroughly manifest in the vainglorious city systems of mankind, which he has haughtily founded upon this earth that he did not—and could never—create. "Grand" cities are they, where greed and self-aggrandizement are the dreams, goals and societally defined purposes of the urbanized populations of our planet.[22] Cities where unfettered avarice and worship of self is the cultural core of their state educational systems, and where protecting those egotistical pursuits is the bedrock of their political, legislative, judicial, and religious systems. Cities where rape of the earth and oppression of its poor for profit is unscrupulously plotted with subtle genius and carried out by evil acumen and ruthless chicanery and tyranny. Cities that embody and represent a thorough perversion of the purpose for which the Creator formed the earth and engendered its human inhabitants.[23]

The cities of men are generally the building blocks and central hubs of empires.[24] And imperialism, almost without exception, either fosters or is founded upon *tyranny*. Make no mistake, though, tyranny is not an exclusive trait of autocratic dictatorships. It is an equally villainous (and more insidious) aspect of all mercenary "democracies" (fueled by money for the buying and selling of votes and politicians to do the bidding of occult, treasury-monopolizing oligarchies). Tyranny is no less constituted in the contemptuous aggression inherent in political systems that impose one group's will upon others by the mob mentality of ganged democratic "majorities." These "majority" power groups regularly trample under foot the less powerful minorities *along with* the constitutional laws intended to protect all citizens equitably (not just to serve the advantageous, constitution-flaunting mob). Interestingly, the biblical record accounts that the author of tyranny was also the author of the first city, which he named after his son, Enoch.[25]

The tyrannical tools and control mechanisms of today's city-based states and warmongering nations are not much of an esoteric secret anymore. Yet, though they're fairly common knowledge to many, they have become widely accepted, approved of, and even subscribed to. This is largely due to the carefully engineered narrowing of options by the entrenched powers-that-be. These establishment powers, rather than promote real choices (true freedom) for the common citizen, engineer dependency-based populations addicted to Big Brotherism.

Those pervasive, powerful establishment mechanisms of control include the military-industrial machine, the political-legislative complex, the information-education (i.e., mind-control-and-conditioning) mediums of mass manipulation, and, not the least of all, the economic-financial resource extortion apparatuses (treasuries, banks, and stock markets)—all of them cleverly managed and coordinated from behind the scenes by the intelligentsia and elite oligarchies, "the great men of the earth," as the Bible names them (Revelation 17 & 18, etc.).

All of these systems are rife with corruption, as the most casual of observers (even the average couch-potato television addict) will often acknowledge; unless, that is, they have thoroughly savored the pro-establishment propaganda and bought wholesale into the delusion. The glorious high-rise cities that embody and house these corrupt systems are also irredeemably contaminated by them. Therefore, the decadent civilization they incarnate is slated for obliteration by the fierce indignation of the just and holy God they have pridefully snubbed, scorned, mocked, and censured. The exalted towers that rise to dominate the skyline of men's sinful cities will be rocked to the ground, according to the prophets. These lofty monuments to mankind's pride will scarcely remain even as heaps of twisted steel mingled with shards of shattered glass and fragments of crumbled concrete.[26]

For the day of the LORD of hosts shall be upon every one that is proud and lofty, and upon every one that is lifted up; and he shall be brought low. . . . And upon all the high mountains, and upon all the hills that are lifted up, and upon every high tower, and upon every fenced wall. . . . And upon all the ships of Tarshish [myriad fleets of merchant marine vessels}, and upon all pleasant pictures. And the loftiness of man shall be bowed down, and the haughtiness of men shall be made low: and the LORD alone shall be exalted in that day.

And the idols [of mammon and materialism] he shall utterly abolish. And they shall go into the holes of the rocks, and into the caves of the earth, for fear of the LORD, and for the glory of his majesty, when he ariseth to shake terribly the earth. In that day a man shall cast his idols of silver, and his idols of gold, which they made each one for himself to worship, to the moles and to the bats; to go into the clefts of the rocks, and into the tops of the ragged rocks [such as Cheyenne Mountain - home of NORAD center - and other mountain fortresses], for fear of the LORD, and for the glory of his majesty, when he ariseth to shake terribly the earth.—Isaiah 2:12-21

The great day of the LORD is near, it is near, and hasteth greatly, even the voice of the day of the LORD: the mighty man shall cry there bitterly. That day is a day of wrath, a day of trouble and distress, a day of wasteness and desolation, a day of darkness and gloominess, a day of clouds and thick darkness, a day of the trumpet and alarm against the fenced cities [defended by mighty militaries], and against the high towers. And I will bring distress upon men, that they shall walk like blind men, because they have sinned against the LORD: and their blood shall be poured out as dust, and their flesh as the dung. Neither their silver nor their gold shall be able to deliver them [the madness of the vain pursuit for wealth and power will prove to be sheer folly] in the day of the LORD's wrath; but the whole land shall be devoured by the fire of his jealousy: for he shall make even a speedy riddance of all them that dwell in the land.—Zephaniah 1:14-18

I have cut off the nations: their towers are desolate; I made their streets waste, that none passeth by: their cities are destroyed, so that there is no man, that there is none inhabitant.—Zephaniah 3:6

And there shall be upon every high mountain, and upon every high hill, rivers and streams of waters [massive tidal floods, tsunamis, and torrential storms] in the day of the great slaughter, when the towers fall. Moreover the light of the moon shall be as the light of the sun, and the light of the sun shall be sevenfold, as the light of seven days, in the day that the LORD bindeth up the breach of his people, and healeth the stroke of their wound [makes restoration for the violations of His chosen people, His holy land, and His original plan for Earth]. Behold, the name of the LORD cometh from far, burning with his anger, and the burden thereof is heavy: his lips are full of indignation, and his tongue as a devouring fire: And his breath, as an overflowing stream, shall reach to the midst of the neck, to sift the nations with the sieve of vanity: and there shall be a bridle in the jaws of the people [possessed by their own insane obsessions], causing them to err.—Isaiah 30:25-28

And it shall come to pass, that he who fleeth from the noise of the fear shall fall into the pit; and he that cometh up out of the midst of the pit shall be taken in the snare: for the windows from on high are open [to the rocketing meteoric rogues of space], and the foundations of the earth do shake. The earth is utterly broken down, the earth is clean dissolved, the earth is moved exceedingly. The earth shall reel to and fro like a drunkard, and shall be removed like a cottage [torn down as a shack]; and the transgression thereof shall be heavy upon it; and it shall fall, and not rise again. And it shall come to pass in that day, that the LORD shall punish the host of the high ones that are on high, and [both the extraterrestrial alien allies and] the kings of the earth upon the earth.—Isaiah 24:18-21

Generous amounts of space and time are being dedicated herein to this topic of *"the day of the great slaughter, when the towers fall"* for various reasons. Beside the fact that so many of the ancient Hebrew prophets had so much to say about it, it provides highly relevant commentary on the current state of affairs in our endtimes era. This is particularly so with respect to the developments and trends that characterize our "civilization" at the turn of the 21st century—namely, a return to the pre-diluvian paganism of the days of Noah. More than that, the intention is to highlight not only the very fitting applications of the prophecies to our present-day modern world, but to impress upon the reader the dramatic difference between the (post-Rapture) day of great wrath and the (pre-Rapture) days of great tribulation.

The Great Day of God Almighty, when He comes as a thief with destructive vengeance to strip the earth away from corrupt mankind, is day of annihilation and obliteration—not to be confused as a day of trial, testing, or mere tribulation. So frighteningly horrendous will be the magnitude of this destruction that terror will drive people like foolish ostriches to seek uncertain shelter in any hole, cave, rocky crag or crevice (as indicated in the prophecies above). Preferring to be buried alive by heaps of rubble, than to face the horror of standing nakedly defenseless upon the surface of the earth in the tempestuous fury of a Richter-ravaging global earthquake, continent-threatening tidal waves, savagely violent atmospheric convulsions, and flaming 100-pound meteors pummeling the planet like torrential downpours of fiery hail, now the crazed populations that persistently dared to defy the Creator madly scramble like frightened cockroaches to hide from the face of GOD!

Frustrated in their own deluded vanity, they could only hope to trade, for hapless refuge, their entire stockpile of material idols—stocks, bonds, treasury holdings, gold, silver, and "almighty dollars"—to purchase the subterranean real estate of the moles and the bats (their deep burrows and dim cavern refuges) as hiding places. (See quote from Isaiah, chapter 2, above.)

In recap, we again quote the writer of the Apocalypse, this time from his classic, panoramic overview of history in chapter 6 of the Book of Revelation in which he distills the quintessential elements of earth's history. It concludes with the calamitous event we have just been highlighting:

And I beheld when he had opened the sixth seal, and, lo, there was a great earthquake; and the sun became black as sackcloth of hair, and the moon became as blood; and the stars of heaven fell unto the earth, even as a fig tree casteth her untimely figs, when she is shaken of a mighty wind. And the heaven departed as a scroll when it is rolled together; and every mountain and island were moved out of their places. And the kings of the earth, and the great men, and the rich men, and the chief captains, and the mighty men, and every bondman, and every free man, hid themselves in the dens and in the rocks of the mountains; and said to the mountains and rocks, Fall on us, and hide us from the face of him that sitteth on the throne, and from the wrath of the Lamb: For the great day of his wrath is come; and who shall be able to stand? (Revelation 6:12-17)

Unable to endure the horrifying ferocity of this wrathful event, these remaining rebel populations flee in hopeless futility for any cover they can find. For what the earthquake and all its associated catastrophes do not completely devastate, evidently the "hail" will demolish. Whether widespread, global, or only isolated bombardments, is not absolutely certain. What is certain is that the plague of the hail will be *"exceeding great!"* And, in combination with the quake, the demolished city systems of the world will leave only a fraction of the human population to emerge from the ashes and rubble to which man's proud civilization will be reduced.[27]

Behold, the Lord hath a mighty and strong one, which as a tempest of hail and a destroying storm, as a flood of mighty waters overflowing, shall cast down to the earth with the hand [direct active power exceeding oral commands]. . . . Judgment also will I lay to the line, and righteousness to the plummet [to set things straight]: and the hail shall sweep away the refuge of lies [earth's corrupt earthly civilization], and the waters shall overflow the hiding place. . . . From the time that it goeth forth it shall take you: for morning by morning shall it pass over, by day and by night: and it shall be a vexation only to understand the report [much less to endure the tempest]. For the bed is shorter than that a man can stretch himself on it: and the covering narrower than that he can wrap himself in it [finding no adequate relief or refuge]. For the LORD shall rise up as in mount Perazim [when the Rephaim giants were vanquished by His personal intervention], he shall be wroth as in the valley of Gibeon [where He decimated the imperial armies of the Amorite empire (c. 1450 BCE) with "great stones from heaven"], that he may do his work, his strange work; and bring to pass his act, his strange act. Now therefore be ye not mockers, lest your bands be made strong [and you become inescapably subject]: for I have heard from the Lord GOD of hosts a consumption, even determined upon the whole earth.—Isaiah 28:2-22

In all of this, the greatest tragedy is that the outcome is totally alien to what the Almighty had originally intended in his plan for Earth. Isaiah points this up by his choice of words to express that this destructive fury is foreign to God's nature. His wrath has been reluctantly provoked, forcing him to unwillingly engage in *"strange work"* and to bring to pass *"his strange act,"* against a grievously revolting generation of wayward earth creatures.

This is indeed a wicked generation of hypocritical accusers, who blaspheme the Creator with maligning slanders, like, "If God is so good, why does He allow starvation in the world? or war? or suffering of innocents?" and so on. All these, while they themselves fully participate in multitrillion-dollar warmongering industries and economies (either on the job and production line, in the stock market, or in the ballot box); or, spend trillions on space programs, searching for the origins, purpose, and keys to "life" (Ha!); or cast away billions of pounds of food annually as waste (96 billion pounds in the USA alone in 1996); or, spend $4.6 trillion per year on sightseeing and tourism; or worse yet, $586 billion (in the USA in 1997) on gambling and casino gaming.

The human problems of the world are of our own doing, and the solutions are within our own hands. But, the will of the average person is devoted to greedy covetousness and pursuing our own petty lusts. Yet the world's people have the insolent audacity to find fault with the Great God and Creator of the infinitely wonderous universe which He made for all our benefit. In a world where World Health Organization studies show that the availability, on a worldwide per capita basis, of caloric nutrients (food) far surpasses that of any other time in history, it's not overpopulation that's killing us. It's a combination of greed, hatred, indifference, and a plain old obsession with self-importance.

This indeed is an evil and adulterous generation, who have estranged themselves from their Creator now to even go to bed with the extraterrestrial, demon-alien phenomenon they are coming to adore with worshipful fascination. Billions of dollars annually flow to the "burning of incense" and worship of these new evolutionary gods, exalting and making idols of them. Take, as only one example, the billion-dollar science-fiction entertainment industry—especially movies, television, and video—now capitalizing on this perverse adoration of ETs.[28]

Moreover, our generation has spent multibillions on gigantic radio telescope arrays,[29] space telescopes (Hubble, and the latest space-based X-ray telescope), and extensive efforts at venturing toward deep space exploration (NASA programs, etc.) to probe for evidences—signals, sights, sounds, and signs from outer space—that will tell us exactly what we want to hear:

"The Bible is wrong!...There is no Creator such as it bespeaks...There will be no day of reckoning...We shall not have to give account to anyone but ourselves...The Universe itself is god...Its power is god...The key to that power is nearly within our grasp...Our fellow space beings, by their advanced technologies, have already unlocked many of those powers of the formerly impossible...We too shall have the power...They can show us the way...Let them be our gods, that we might share in their powers to become gods as they..."

Meanwhile, back on Earth, teeming millions starve and drink putrid water, perishing from ravaging diseases as a consequence. Their lands get expropriated by special-interest power mongers, and they get driven by racist, genocidal maniacs from refugee camp to refugee camp (or is that mass grave to mass grave?). Or they slave in third world sweatshops for $2 a day to support the addictive consumerism of the First World Babylonians. Or else, they are forced to sacrifice their blood on the altars of the oligarchs (let alone the petty despots) to be cannon fodder in the armed conflicts instigated by those perverse ogres in competition for domination of territories and resources. The statistics and casualties for this century alone surpass those of the previous 1900 years combined. They are staggering, atrocious, and abominable!

And man wants to be his own evolved god! (To borrow the poignant lyrics of famed song artist Tina Turner, "We don't need another hero!") GOD spare us his insane arrogance; and may He tarry not to avenge the peacemakers, the righteous and the poor of evil man's heinous, death-dealing egomania. GOD help us when the wicked worldlings make their proud alliance and pact with the bestial, satanic Alien!

Even now, the righteous languish longingly for the words *"It is done!"*

13

FIGS AND GENERATION FINÁLE

Now learn a parable of the fig tree; When his branch is yet tender,
and putteth forth leaves, ye know that summer is nigh:
So likewise ye, when ye shall see all these things, know that it is near,
even at the doors. Verily I say unto you,
This generation shall not pass, till all these things be fulfilled.
Heaven and earth shall pass away, but my words shall not pass away.
But of that day and hour knoweth no man, no, not the angels of heaven,
but my Father only.—Matthew 24:32-36

Let us return now to the "Olivet Discourse," as certain scholars have termed it, since this endtime dissertation was delivered upon the Mount of Olives. It was spoken by Yeshua to a private group of His disciples as they conferred about the end of the world, the sign of His return and the coming of His kingdom...

"I can't tell you exactly how many miles it is from here; but, when you come to a very steep hill in the road, you're almost there; in fact, the highway comes to an end right over the hill," is an alternate (paraphrased) version that Messiah might have used, had the metaphor been more fitting. However, the figurative language He selected to illuminate the last stretch of this road is perhaps less than just a random choice of word pictures. Although saying essentially the same thing, the parable of the fig tree uses language that would have conjured pictures already very familiar to the Jewish people, from the writings of their ancient prophets. Familiar depictions that made reference to their very own nation—especially by Joel and the great seer Jeremiah—which now would also link that nation to the signs of the end of the world.

Fig-uratively Speaking

In chapter 24 of Jeremiah, we find two distinct groups of Judah-ites and Jerusalem-ites figuratively represented by two different types of *figs*. Those Israelites that would submissively yield to the yoke of chastisement, which the Lord would impose upon the Jews for their rebellions against Him, were classed as the basket of "good figs," tasty as the first ripe figs of the season. The other basket of "very evil figs," which were deemed absolutely inedible, were those Israelites who refused to submit, but resolved rather to resist the instrument of punishment (the imperial occupation of the Babylonian empire), and rebelled more persistently still.

The account and scope of this chastisement and servitude, to which the Jews were obliged to yield by the prophecy of Jeremiah, stretches on into chapter 30, eventually spanning centuries, and even millennia beyond the seventy years of the original judgment obligation. It finally culminates in the unparalleled "time of Jacob's trouble." This exquisite passage (Jeremiah 30:3-24), also foretelling the eventual (and final) return of the Jews to their homeland, ends with the words, *"in the latter days ye shall consider it (v.24)."*

This homeland is also popularly known as the Promise (or, Promised) Land. And indeed, the promise rehearsed by Moses to the children of Israel, after their deliverance and departure from the bondage of Egypt, described this land as a land of fig trees (among other amenities): *"For the LORD thy God bringeth thee into a good land, a land of brooks of water, of fountains and depths that spring out of valleys and hills; a land of wheat, and barley, and vines, and fig trees, and pomegranates; a land of oil olive, and honey." (Deuteronomy 8:7-8)* Again, in another place, upon encountering hardship on their trek for that promised land, the Israelites took up a murmur against Moses, complaining that their harsh wilderness surroundings did not smack at all of such a lush, promised "place of figs": *"Wherefore have ye made us to come up out of Egypt, to bring us in unto this evil place? it is no place of seed, or of figs, or of vines, or of pomegranates; neither is there any water to drink." (Numbers 20:5)*

Besides Jeremiah, and reckoned about 200 years more ancient, the prophet Joel (c. 800 BCE), also using "fig" symbols, predicted successive desolations and afflictions of Judah and Jerusalem (even before the *first* siege and captivity of 586 BCE by the Babylonians, during the time of Jeremiah). In his prophecies about "the great and the terrible day of the LORD,"[1] he foretold of the ultimate return in that day from these captivities, confiscations, extortions, and other abuses and oppressions by their captors and enemies. However, prior to the ultimate, permanent restoration of Israel to prosperous dominion in the land of promise—under the reign of Messiah in Jerusalem—Joel also prophesied of the ravaging of Israel, in the following symbolic terms: *"For a nation is come up upon my land, strong, and without number, whose teeth are the teeth of a lion, and he hath the cheek teeth of a great lion. He hath laid my vine waste, and barked my fig tree: he hath made it clean bare, and cast it away; the branches thereof are made white." (Joel 1:6-7)*

Thus, we see that Christ's choice of symbols in the parable of the fig tree would have had great meaning to the Jews who were well versed in the writings of their prophets of old. The summer He referred to would, of course, be the time of fruition for this tree, the time in which Israel would dwell safely in Zion, "every man under his vine and under his fig tree," and under the rulership of Mashiach. Such a time of peaceful prosperity has not been a part of Jewish history since the glorious days of King Solomon (c. 1000 BCE).[2]

But in the last days it shall come to pass, that the mountain of the house of the LORD shall be established in the top of the mountains [superseding all other dominions], and it shall be exalted above the hills; and people shall flow unto it. And many nations shall come, and say, Come, and let us go up to the mountain of the LORD, and to the house of the God of Jacob; and he will teach us of his ways, and we will walk in his paths: for the law shall go forth of Zion, and the word of the LORD from Jerusalem. And he shall judge among many people, and rebuke strong nations afar off; and they shall beat their swords into plowshares, and their spears into pruninghooks: nation shall not lift up a sword against nation, neither shall they learn war any more. But they shall sit every man under his vine and under his fig tree [individual proprietary liberty and pursuit of happiness]; and none shall make them afraid [no more voracious imperialists]: for the mouth of the LORD of hosts hath spoken it. For all people will walk every one in the name of his god, and we will walk in the name of the LORD our God for ever and ever. In that day, saith the LORD, will I assemble her [children of Israel] that halteth [crippled from assaults and victimization], and I will gather her that is driven out [scattered and exiled], and her that I have afflicted [by numerous chastisements]; and I will make her that halted a remnant [preserved portion], and her that was cast far off a strong nation: and the LORD shall reign over them in mount

Zion from henceforth, even for ever. And thou, O tower of the flock, the strong hold of the daughter of Zion, unto thee shall it come, even the first [primary or chief] dominion; the kingdom shall come to the daughter of Jerusalem.— Micah 4:1-8

"Summer," we know, alludes to the coming of the Messianic Kingdom with the return of Christ Yeshua to Earth. This is understood by referring back to the wording of the original question Christ was responding to at the outset of the Olivet Discourse: *"When shall these things be? and what shall be the sign of thy coming, and of the end of the world?" (Matthew 24:3)* The apostle Luke makes this even more obvious in the parallel passage from his Gospel: *"And he spake to them a parable; Behold the fig tree, and all the trees; when they now shoot forth, ye see and know of your own selves that summer is now nigh at hand. So likewise ye, when ye see these things come to pass, know ye that the kingdom of God is nigh at hand. Verily I say unto you, This generation shall not pass away, till all be fulfilled." (Luke 21:29-32)*

This prophetic summer seems inexorably linked to the restoration of Israel and the return of the Jews to their promised land, according to Psalm 102, verse 16: *"When the LORD shall build up Zion, he shall appear in his glory."* Quite remarkably, this is a phenomenon that has seen formal political fulfillment on the world stage only within the last 50 years, with the establishment of Israel as a nation-state on May 14, 1948. Those familiar with Middle Eastern and Jewish history understand the profound significance of this occurrence, since it marks the rebirth of a nation that was scattered and went completely out of existence nearly 19 centuries ago.

In the year 135 CE, the Romans effectively extinguished the state of Israel in the hard fought Bar Kochba revolt of 132 CE, in which nearly 1,000 villages were destroyed and almost 600,000 Jewish insurgents lost their lives, not counting those who died of hunger and disease in the Roman siege. Thereafter, the Romans renamed the provincial region Syria Palaestina. Hadrian, the Roman emperor at that time, established a Roman colony on the site of former Jerusalem, which he converted into a Greco-Roman city under the name Aelia Capitolina, where he erected temples to himself and Jupiter on the very site of the former Jewish temple to Jehovah. Jews were officially barred from entry to Jerusalem and the surrounding district from that time on. For more than 1,800 years since, only minority populations of ethnic Jews inhabited the land known as Palestine, while millions lived in exile scattered across the globe.

In 1947, after the close of the Second World War, Palestine was partitioned by the UN into respective Jewish and Palestinian states, providing an official homeland for the Zionist Jews who longed to emigrate there from Europe, Russia, America and many other lands of the Diaspora. The Zionists, by armed struggle to secure their own sovereignty and after several successful military offensives, captured key territories in early 1948, and on May 14 of that year proclaimed the sovereign State of Israel. In accordance with a decision of the United Nations General Assembly, with the support of the United States and the Soviet Union, the State of Israel was established. By the summer of the following year, they joined the United Nations and were recognized by more than 50 governments.

This Generation Shall Not Pass

This remarkable history of the fig tree, coupled with the amazing fulfillments of numerous other prophecies given by Christ in His Olivet Discourse of Matthew 24, Mark 13, and Luke 21, make for extraordinary evidence that the last generation of secular history is, at this moment, winding down to its expiration deadline. The implication by Messiah in those passages is that the complete realization of the specific set of prophesies He gave related to the advent of the Messianic summer would occur within a single, last generation of mankind. In fact, that particular generation, according to the Mount-of-Olives prophecy, *"shall not pass, till all these things be fulfilled."* (Matthew 24:34) That is, before that particular generation dies out, it shall witness the fulfillment of all those signs, including the coming to Earth of the Son of man in the heavens with power and great glory. Again, it seems important to note that this limited time frame is couched within a passage that appears to link the revival of the "fig tree"—as a major endtime element—to the last-generation scenario.

Other last-generation phenomena (more extensively detailed in previous sections) surrounding the comeback of the proverbial fig tree, include the savage and devastating conflicts of this century of *multitudinous wars*—civil, international, and world scale—as well as the *numerous famines, diseases, and earthquakes around the globe*. We have noted that together these have caused immeasurable destitution, staggering casualties, and horrendous loss of life for countless millions in this century alone, with much more yet to come. Hardly overshadowed by these international calamities, the more micro scale of local life in this century is travailing painfully under the modern plagues of domestic forms of rage, hatreds, betrayals, abuses, and conflicts. These have multiplied out of the disastrous *disintegration of natural affection* between parents and children, wives and husbands, employers and employees, neighbors and friends, community members, and even among strangers.[3] Road rage, employee (union/syndicate) rage, gang rage, ethnic and race rage, guerrilla and terrorist rage, political rage, religious rage, and every other form of rage has consumed our societies, and is regularly ravaging all courtesy, respect, decency, and peaceful resolution with *pervasive, ever-rising levels of violence*, evil, and insanity. Meanwhile, mirroring the insanity, the assortments of "enlightened" prophets, gurus, sects, cults, denominations, and political, scientific, economic, as well as religious *saviors and "Christs" proliferate* like commercial ads on prime-time television.

In the midst of all this, and despite the very troublous times of our 20th century, Israel has been miraculously restored and built up—against towering odds and amidst overwhelming populations of hostile neighbors—to very prosperous and powerful status among the nations of the world. By comparison on world scale, the average household income in Israel exceeds that of the British, the gross national product per capita is almost 80% that of Great Britain, and Israel is rated by the London-based *Jane's Intelligence Review* as the world's third most powerful military. According to Yeshua's parable, a sure indication that *summer is indeed near* is that the fig tree has already begun to manifest obvious signs of its return to vitality, and, naturally, of its preparation for bearing its fruit/sweetness. The prophetic "shoe" of verse 16 from Psalm 102 seems quite a good fit on the "foot" of the last 50 years of Zionism.

The metaphor of the fig tree must be carefully considered when applied to the proverbial, and highly anticipated, final restoration of the Israel spoken of by the prophets. Isaiah (chapter 62) spoke of it in prophecies about the "acceptable year of the Lord."

A bountiful array of prophesies from the ancient Hebrew texts deal with the restoration and redemption of the Jewish people, even from before the time of their first national desolation, captivity, exile and dispersion from the land of their original statehood in ancient Canaan, now often called Palestine. The first desolation was actually a fairly lengthy process of collapse. For 235 years, between 721 and 586 BCE, Israel actually experienced a sort of gradual dissolution, by stages. This included only a few periods of reformation and recovery, confined solely to the southern portion of the kingdom, known by the name of the dominant tribe Judah, which was also last to fall. A look back at history also reveals the occurrence of a second sweeping desolation of Judah by the Romans (beginning in 70 CE, completed in 135) that brought to an end the *first recognized restoration* of the Jewish nation.

Since the 10th century BCE, after the deaths of its greatest kings, David and son Solomon, the history of the nation of Israel developed into a tragic and tumultuous period of division, rebellions, power struggles, internal conflict, as well as assaults and invasions from external enemies, and eventually complete demise. The once united kingdom of Israel under David and Solomon subsequently split into two: the northern kingdom under the name Israel, and the kingdom of Judah (with Jerusalem as its capital) to the south. By 721 BCE the northern breakaway fragment (of Israel) collapsed under the assault of the Assyrian Empire, which deported in captivity the great majority of the northern ten tribes of Israelites, and subsequently transplanted them far and wide throughout their empire, importing other foreign nationals to take their place.[4] About 235 years later, the remaining southerly kingdom of Judah also fell, on this occasion to the succeeding empire of Babylon.

This event, in which the people of Judah were now carried away in captivity, enslaved, and slaughtered by the thousands in the siege of Jerusalem, is well established and commonly known, even by secular historians, as the Babylonian Exile of 586 BCE. Occasioned by the conquests of the famous Babylonian king Nebuchadnezzar, it, more than any other in a series of several blows to Israel's hegemony and political independence in the region, represented the final nail in the coffin of the original state of Israel, particularly for predominant Judah (from whence the name "Jew" is derived).

The siege and Exile of 586 BCE actually occurred twenty years after the initial conquest of the region by Babylon. It came as a last resort option for king Nebuchanezzar, who had been provoked by Judah's repeated rebellions against their vassalage to Babylonian domination. It was under defiant Zedekiah, the last of Judah's kings (whose eyes were put out after his capture), that Nebuchadnezzar finally besieged and destroyed the city of Jerusalem. He burned the magnificent temple erected there over 400 years earlier by King Solomon, took the great majority of the population of the kingdom of Judah captive, and deported them to Babylon as slaves (including king Zedekiah in chains).

Seventy years of servitude to Babylon ended in 536 BCE, under the subsequent hegemony of the Medo-Persians (conquerors of the Babylonians), when Cyrus the Great issued a decree permitting the Jews to return to their homeland to rebuild. All this transpired according to the very word of Jeremiah given in prophecy 11 or 12 years earlier during the reign of Josiah (one of the last kings of Judah): *"And this whole land shall be a desolation, and an astonishment; and these nations shall serve the king of Babylon seventy years. . . . For thus saith the LORD, That after seventy years be accomplished at Babylon I will visit you, and perform my good word toward you, in causing you to return to this place."* (*Jer. 25:11 & 29:10)* The emancipation decree of Cyrus marked the beginning of the *first return* of the Jews to their homeland.

For the next 600 years, Israel existed for the most part as the restored *Province of Judah* under tribute to the supremacy of foreign powers. First as a satrapy of Persia, then under the Hellenistic dominance of the Grecian Empire, including the later Egyptian (Ptolemaic) and Syrian (Seleucid) rival fragments of Alexander's domain, and finally as a province of the Roman Empire when Palestine was conquered by Pompey in 63 BCE. Though Judah enjoyed some semblance of autonomy in their own land under various of their own governors during this extended period of renewed vitality, in which they also restored their temple from ruin, only about 80 years of that period can be accounted as an era of actual political independence. The Jewish Wars of Independence, beginning in about 167 BCE with the successful Maccabean Revolt, led to a period of sovereignty during which the reigning Hasmonean dynasty (also known as the Maccabees) even struck their own coinage. This, of course, all ended with the Roman conquest of 63 BCE. After that time, the rulers of Judah were procuratorial vassals appointed by ultimate authority of the Roman emperors, as in the case of the infamous King Herod (the "Great").

It was during the reign of Herod's son Antipas, whom John the Baptist censured, that Christ was condemned and crucified. And, the Zealot revolt of 66 CE occurred during the reign of his great-grandson Agrippa II, who supported the Roman invasion under Titus, which finally resulted in the destruction of Jerusalem and the reduction of the Temple (that Herod had so grandly remodeled and enlarged) to ashes in the fateful year 70 CE.

Thus, in summary form, is comprised the abbreviated history of Israel's first destruction and desolation, their first restoration, and then their *second devastation* that effectively extinguished their place among the nations of the world. Until only within the recent "days" of this very generation has Israel been rebirthed after nearly 2,000 years of dormancy! An absolutely amazing and highly improbable outcome that could only be the result of divine intervention. Perhaps other students of history can name a similar case of a nation who was reborn after 19 centuries of extinction. I cannot.

This very generation has witnessed, on an ongoing basis, the fulfillment of the ancient and far-reaching Messianic prophecy of Isaiah written more than 700 years before Christ (implying *a second* desolation *and* restoration 100 years even before Israel's *first* desolation):

And it shall come to pass in that day, that the Lord shall set his hand again the second time to recover the remnant of his people, which shall be left, from Assyria, and from Egypt, and from Pathros, and from Cush, and from Elam, and from Shinar, and from Hamath, and from the islands of the sea [the numerous lands of scatteration of the "Wandering Jew," including the distant, New World "isles of the sea," such as South and North America]. And he shall set up an ensign for the nations [as the (often-desecrated) blue and white flag of Israel], and shall assemble the outcasts of Israel, and gather together the dispersed of Judah from the four corners of the earth." (Isa.11:11-12)

Even as we speak, immigrants of Israeli ancestry and Jews from all over the world continue to arrive on the shores of their ancient national homeland in the newly restored State of Israel under the banner of the Star of David on a daily basis.

Since the founding of the State of Israel in 1948, 2,762,328 Jewish immigrants from around the world have been absorbed into this little country about the size of New Jersey, and half the size of Holland. Just for reference, prior to 1995, the breakdown of the origins of the "olim" by country is roughly as follows: about 33% of the olim had come from the FSU (Former Soviet Union); 14% from Morocco, Algeria and Tunisia; 11% from Romania; almost 8.5% from Iraq and Iran combined; 7% from Poland; 3% from the USA; 2.5% from Turkey; 2% from Yemen; nearly another 2% from Ethiopia, followed closely by Argentina with 1.8%; the remaining 15% of the total, about 374,000 originated in a wide variety of other countries—namely, Bulgaria, Egypt and Sudan, Libya, France, Hungary, India, the UK, Czechoslovakia, Germany, South Africa, Yugoslavia and Syria (in descending order of percentages). Since 1995 to the present and following the trend of post-USSR immigration, the ratio of olim coming from the FSU, as opposed to other countries, is more than 8 out of 10.[5]

This year alone, through September 1999, a total of 48,809 immigrants (or, "olim" as they're known in Israel) have made their "aliyah" to Israel (meaning their "going up"). That's an average of 184 olim a day, with roughly 85% of them coming from the Former Soviet Union. In the last 10 years, since the doors to the massive aliyah from the one-time Soviet Republics of the FSU were flung open at the collapse of the USSR in 1989, nearly a million Jews have emigrated from the FSU to the land of the "fig tree."[6]

This "putting forth of leaves" by the fig tree is nothing less than an obvious sign that summer is near. And though the summer has not yet come, yet the days of that grand event are surely upon us, according to the prophets. Jeremiah (2,600 years ago) spoke of the same metaphorical putting forth of leaves in anticipation of the Righteous Age of the Summer of Messiah. He first clearly identified the age to which he made future reference: *"Behold, the days come, saith the LORD, that I will raise unto David a righteous Branch [son of David], and a King shall reign and prosper, and shall execute judgment and justice in the earth [Millennial reign of MESSIAH, obviously unfulfilled as yet]. In his days Judah shall be saved, and Israel shall dwell safely [at last, the ultimate destiny of the chosen people]: and this is his name whereby he shall be called, THE LORD OUR RIGHTEOUSNESS." (Jer. 23:5-6)* And how do we know this summer is near?

Jeremiah goes on to say, *"Therefore, behold, the days come, saith the LORD, that they shall no more say, The LORD liveth, which brought up the children of Israel out of the land of Egypt [exodus in days of Moses]; but, The LORD liveth, which brought up and which led the seed of the house of Israel out of the north country, and from all countries whither I had driven them; and they shall dwell in their own land." (Jer. 23:7-8)*

This specific gathering and restoration is not a reference to the first restoration, outlined in preceding paragraphs, which occurred by return out of the easterly oriented kingdom of Babylon. Rather, this exodus speaks of a *second* regathering from a *global* scatteration, and particularly from the *north*—which is exactly what we have seen in our day. The great majority of Zionist resettlers of modern day Israel has come from Russia and Eastern/Central Europe to the north. In fact, the first prime minister of modern Israel, David Ben-Gurion (1948-53, 1955-63), was a native of Poland under the Russian Empire; and, the "father" of political Zionism, Theodor Herzl, founder and first president of the World Zionist Organization (1897), a native of Hungary. In view of all this then, it is evident that this second time the children of Jacob are being gathered constitutes the Springtime Days of the approaching, and long-awaited prophetic Summer.

The modern, endtime restoration of Israel which we have been witnessing in our lifetime is the precursor to the full and ultimate establishment of Israel as the ruling power of Earth, with Jerusalem as the capital and Yeshua Ha'Mashiach as King. But, as repeatedly stressed by this author, the end is not yet. As evidenced in earlier chapters of this book, the rising swell of anti-Israeli and anti-Semitic sympathies throughout the world parallels the prenatal conditions of travail that beset a pregnant woman before giving birth. For though the sudden, contemporary reemergence of Israel in our time signals the day of her magnificent salvation and incontestable authority over the nations of the world, yet in keeping with the parable of the pregnant woman in travail, there must come a severe—albeit brief—period of affliction *before* the Birth of the Kingdom of God on Earth.

Isaiah, speaking of the uncommon set of circumstances surrounding the sudden coming(s) of Messiah and the swift establishment of His Kingdom (of Israel), put it this way: *"Who hath heard such a thing? who hath seen such things? Shall the earth be made to bring forth in one day? or shall a nation be born at once? for as soon as Zion travailed, she brought forth her children. Shall I bring to the birth, and not cause to bring forth? saith the LORD: shall I cause to bring forth, and shut the womb? saith thy God."* (Isa. 66:8-9) Indeed, the whole regathering and birthing phenomenon is relatively sudden and, for all practical matters, an unexpected marvel (except by those who are familiar with the words of the Hebrew prophets). Yet the process is *not complete*, until the final fruit is born; and that will not come without *tribulation*. Unusual as the process may seem, Zion, both as a fig tree and as the beloved (pregnant) bride, shall inexorably bring forth her ultimate fruit—but not before the accompanying, inevitable travail.

[As a parenthetical note on this passage of prophecy quoted above from Isaiah chapter 66 regarding the coming kingdom of Zion under Messiah, a look at the immediately preceding verse in this passage reveals a strange concept of considerable interest: *"Before she travailed, she brought forth; before her pain came, she was delivered of a man child."* (Isa. 66:7) In verses 8 & 9 above, Isaiah infers an odd and bizarre aspect about Israel's birthing process...

The strangeness in the whole passage, highlighted in this verse (7), is that Zion was to bear a proverbial "man child" *before* all of the travail which leads up to the birth of His Kingdom on Earth. In this last chapter of the Book of

Isaiah, focusing on the coming of Messiah and the ultimate State of Israel, he also alludes to misguided *temple-building* and *offering of sacrifices*, implying a *seriously erring religion* catering to self-serving agendas. All of this subsequently results in the future *division* of the self-willed religionists from their submitted, believing brethren, whom they then self-righteously *hate and persecute*. If only (as this author surmises) the "Orthodox" could have unassumingly accepted that the humble King of the Jews had *already been born* in exemplary meekness, perhaps their centuries of travail since might have been averted, while they rather coveted *power and glory first*. Adopting a matching attitude of Messianic meekness and brokenheartedness would surely have led to a better grasp of Isaiah's earlier alert to the "acceptable year of the Lord (Isa. 61:1-3)." Many of us *are awakening* to this understanding.[7]

As Christ and so many of the prophets before Him (as well as following) taught, serious travail, affliction, persecution, and great tribulation shall befall the people of God before their deliverance is accomplished. Even now, those who are not drunk on the wine of the spiritual fornication of Babylon the Great see the telltale clouds of warning gathering on the horizon. Thanks to the modern mediums of communication and diligent journalistic and intelligence sources, information is publicly available revealing that Russia, China, and other anti-Western states are very actively engaged in arming the hostile neighbors of Israel to the eyeballs with the latest high-tech weaponry. Included are weapons of mass destruction, both nuclear as well as chemical and biological, and the long-range missile batteries necessary to deliver them (in formidable barrages). Even the USA, in trying to play both ends against the middle for the sake of its own selfish interests in the Middle East (primarily oil), has played a huge part in inadvertently arming Israel's enemies, not the least of which is peace-cloaked Egypt. At this very time, Israel is almost completely surround by heavily armed adversaries who are ardently antagonistic to its very existence. Travail, and much more yet to come, is, unfortunately, the order of the day—not peace.

It is with strained difficulty that anyone could deny that the "beginning of sorrows" foretold by Christ has commenced. Increased terrorism, for example, translates perfectly into figurative birth pangs, of increased intensity and frequency. Taking into account the most recent suicide bombings in Jerusalem of July 30 and September 4, 1997, more Israeli citizens have been killed since 1993 than died from such attacks in all the years prior, dating back to 1948.[8] The consequent breakdown of the Israeli-Palestinian "peace process" is no doubt the outcome of a deliberate strategy to systematically and thoroughly isolate and seek utter eradication of Israel by a forced confrontation, which, it is hoped, would lead to its defeat. The terror attacks figure, if not as unofficial declarations of war, then certainly as provocations of it.

Heavily bolstered now by the recent massive infusion of fresh tactical and hardware support from Russia and China, *International Intelligence Briefing* commentator Cliff Ford surmises that the Arab and Islamic foes in the region believe they have "effectively neutralized Israel's nuclear deterrent." That is to say, they now believe their combined military readiness to be sufficient to overwhelm the defensive capabilities of the Jewish State, even if Israel were to consider a nuclear option—which formerly kept full-scale aggression at bay. The new strategic layout promises, and almost guarantees the outbreak of war, which Ford predicts will occur as soon as 1998.[9] Thus we see that the noise of "wars and rumors of wars" continues to build more loudly than ever to a very alarming crescendo.[10]

Turkey, Israel's key and sole military ally in the region, is under pressure both from within and without to dump its alliance with Israel. A groundswell of ever more belligerent, popular fundamentalist Islamic forces—shown via video camera toting placards condemning western-style regimes in Turkey with the slogan "To HELL With Your Democratic Mentality"[1]—threaten the stability of this unlikely ally with a political upheaval that would leave Israel *completely cut off* from anything but remote (and steadily waning) allies, such as the USA. The pressure, of course, is for Turkey to realign itself with its Eastern and Muslim roots. A strong swing in that direction was displayed recently with the 1996 election of Islamic fundamentalist Necmitten Urbakhan to the presidency, advocating a public policy of Islamization of the nation. Urbakhan only lately resigned on June 18, 1997, after barely a year in office, under pressure from the Turkish military, which feared his fundamentalist push away from a modern secular state.

News analyst and commentator Cliff Ford notes also that the strength of the uprising has gathered such momentum that "the Turkish military has been making preparations to meet an Algerian style insurgency" (with uncertainty about whether it can be contained).[12] Some idea of the strength of the radical Algerian Muslim insurgency can be gleaned even from the past nine months of repeated bombings, raids and massacres by Islamic guerrillas. Daily television news broadcasts over that period have covered at least six bloody terror bombings and two vicious massacres of villagers, which combined have killed

600 people. The massacres have involved slashing, burning, stabbing, and shooting of victims, after which in one instance their homes were subsequently looted. According to a *CBS Evening News* report of August 29, 1997, more than 60,000 have been killed in Algeria since the Algerian government canceled the 1992 general elections in an effort to nullify what had already shaped up as certain victory for the Islamic Salvation Front, with radical Muslim candidates in the lead.

Again, *International Intelligence Briefing's* Cliff Ford proposes that, from the outside, Russia is simultaneously seeking to strategically squeeze Turkey through a knothole to compel it to shed its mutual defense pact with Israel by committing to arm its long-standing rival over Cyprus. This arms deal is in the form of a sale of "a number of Russian S-300 (anti-aircraft) missiles" to its traditional enemy Greece (as also recently reported in Turkish newspapers), under the guise of supposedly seeking to adjust the military imbalance that exists between the two countries. Ford also points out that the former prime minister of Turkey, Tansu Ciller, in a public announcement, threatened war with Russia, if it delivered the missiles to Greece.[13] As noted in an earlier chapter, the only thing louder and more frequently noised than the relentless drumbeats of war is the fanciful talk of peace.

Notably, the major focus of all this peace and war talk centers on Israel and Jerusalem and the "controversy of Zion."[14] Unfortunately, the overwhelming testimony of the Hebrew scriptures is that the Spring Season just before Zion's Summer is not to be without its tempestuous tribulations and stormy assaults. It is to be a season when *Jerusalem will once again be trodden down of the Gentiles (Luke 21:24 & Revelation 11:2)*, the land of Israel "parted" in extorted land-for-peace deals, and the Jews betrayed and sold out for gain as they are once again partially scattered for a very brief period (Joel 3:1-3).[15] The concise book of the prophet Joel, in its three-chapter preview (28 centuries ago) of the great "day of the Lord," raises the endtime trumpet of alarm and attests that the fig tree shall be stripped of its bark and languish near death before reaching the zenith of its restoration at the climax of world history.

The only salvation for Israel, and the conclusive halt to the ravaging and dividing of the spoils of Zion (to occur yet once again), will be direct intervention by the Almighty God Himself, as Zechariah foretells:

Behold, the day of the LORD cometh, and thy spoil shall be divided in the midst of thee. For I will gather all nations against Jerusalem to battle; and the city shall be taken, and the houses rifled, and the women ravished; and half of the city shall go forth into captivity, and the residue of the people shall not be cut off from the city. Then shall the LORD go forth, and fight against those nations, as when he fought in the day of battle. . . . And the LORD shall be king over all the earth: in that day shall there be one LORD, and his name one. All the land shall be turned as a plain from Geba to Rimmon south of Jerusalem: and it shall be lifted up, and inhabited in her place, from Benjamin's gate unto the place of the first gate, unto the corner gate, and from the tower of Hananeel unto the king's winepresses. And men shall dwell in it, and there shall be no more utter destruction; but Jerusalem shall be safely inhabited.— Zechariah 14:1-3 & 9-11

Not until the actual arrival and presiding of Messiah in Jerusalem will true peace and safety be absolutely established and permanently assured.

This time to which Zechariah refers is the very same time of the awesome appearing of the LORD that Joel writes of—the days when Messiah returns to cleanse Jerusalem of its vile usurpers (as well as its pretentious claimants invoking mere fleshly Judaic covenants, with no spiritual authenticity).[16] This is also the day when He will finally dwell there in the flesh:

The LORD also shall roar out of Zion, and utter his voice from Jerusalem; and the heavens and the earth shall shake: but the LORD will be the hope of his people, and the strength of the children of Israel. So shall ye know that I am the LORD your God dwelling in Zion, my holy mountain: then shall Jerusa-lem be holy, and there shall no strangers pass through her any more. . . . But Judah shall dwell for ever, and Jerusalem from generation to generation. For I will cleanse their blood that I have not cleansed: for the LORD dwelleth in Zion.—Joel 3:16-17 & 20-21

Isaiah too insists that a precursory purging must be accomplished, in-cluding a separation of the sheep from the goats:

In that day shall the branch of the LORD be beautiful and glorious, and the fruit of the earth shall be excellent and comely for them that are escaped of Israel [i.e., its anti-God rebellion and wickedness, detailed in the first three chapters of Isaiah's book]. And it shall come to pass, that he that is left in Zion, and he that remaineth in Jerusalem, shall be called holy, even every one that is written among the living in Jerusalem: When the Lord shall have washed away the filth of the daughters of Zion, and shall have purged the blood of Jerusalem from the midst thereof by the spirit of judgment, and by the spirit of burning.—Isaiah 4:2-4

Ezekiel likewise testifies to a prerequisite cleansing:

So the house of Israel shall know that I am the LORD their God from that day and forward. And the heathen shall know that the house of Israel went into captivity for their iniquity: because they trespassed against me, therefore hid I my face from them, and gave them into the hand of their enemies: so fell they all by the sword. According to their uncleanness and according to their transgressions have I done unto them, and hid my face from them. Therefore thus saith the Lord GOD; Now will I bring again the captivity of Jacob, and have mercy upon the whole house of Israel, and will be jealous for my holy name; after that they have borne their shame, and all their trespasses whereby they have trespassed against me, when they dwelt safely in their land, and none made them afraid. When I have brought them again from the people, and gathered them out of their enemies' lands, and am sanctified in them in the sight of many nations; then shall they know that I am the LORD their God, which caused them to be led into captivity among the heathen: but I have gathered them unto their own land, and have left none of them any more there. Neither will I hide my face any more from them: for I have poured out my spirit upon the house of Israel, saith the Lord GOD.—Ezekiel 39:22-29

God's Name in the Center of the World

Regardless of what you, or I, or anyone may opinion about God's choices, Israel is the center of the Earth, according to The Prophets. Everything revolves around Jerusalem and the land of Israel, were YHWH has chosen to place His Name.[17] This includes particularly the future historical developments on this planet, in accordance with the very sure words of prophecy, as they pertain to the New World Order of Zion. For it is not the New World Order of George Bush, Mikail Gorbachev, the United Nations, the Council on Foreign Relations, the Trilateral Commission, the Bilderbergers, the Rockefellers, the Lucis Trust, the Round Table Groups, or of the *coming Mahdi* (the Twelfth Imam) that shall inherit and rule the world. Instead, the Supreme

Order of Melchizidec, the King of Right, the King of Jerusalem, the King of Peace, the King of the Jews, the Lamb of God, the Faithful and True Witness shall surely rule. At least, whether you choose to believe them or not, the unfailing Hebrew prophets tell us so.

And the greatest prophet of all, the Martyred Son of God signed, sealed, and certified the testimony of those ancient prophets as His own. For as the Lamb declared to John in the Apocalypse, the spirit of prophecy—knowledge of truth, true knowledge, and revelation of the future—is *"the testimony of Yeshua Ha'Mashiach."*[18] As the Prophets preached the Kingdom of God on Earth, so did Mashiach; and He did so with specificity about the *"acceptable year"* of that Summer of the Fig Tree, as we shall study more in the next chapter.

One of the tiniest nations on Earth has, in less than 50 years of its existence in the modern world, come to be the biggest pebble in the shoe of the World that anyone might have ever imagined. Just we can hardly walk a city block without stopping to untie our shoe to clear out the annoyance of even the tiniest bit of gravel or sand, so not a day goes by that the concern over that minute piece of real estate in the Middle East does not rumble troublously across the airwaves of our daily news broadcasts. And we are on the other side of globe from it, not in Europe, Asia, or Africa where the pebble is a huge stumbling stone. Not surprisingly, this is just as the Zechariah, by the spirit of prophecy predicted so precisely almost 2,500 years ago:

And in that day will I make Jerusalem a burdensome stone for all people: all that burden themselves with it shall be cut in pieces, though all the people of the earth be gathered together against it. . . . In that day shall the LORD defend the inhabitants of Jerusalem; and he that is feeble among them at that day shall be as David; and the house of David shall be as God, as the angel of the LORD before them. And it shall come to pass in that day, that I will seek to destroy all the nations that come against Jerusalem. And I will pour upon the house of David, and upon the inhabitants of Jerusalem, the spirit of grace and of supplications: and they shall look upon me whom they have pierced, and they shall mourn for him, as one mourneth for his only son, and shall be in bitterness for him, as one that is in bitterness for his firstborn.—Zechariah 12:3-10

Even now, this envious preordained rally against the People and the Place of The Book is no longer an amorphous, scattered, or isolated phenomenon;

but it is more and more unified and coherent, just as we discussed in greater detail in an earlier chapter (11). As various other authors and scholars have so rightly pointed out, Israel is indeed God's timepiece in the chronology of eschatology (the study of the ultimate destiny of mankind). As we see the Fig Tree putting forth leaves, we know that "Summer" is presently imminent. And when the other nations of the world attack and batter that tree, leaving it barked and languishing near death, the Lamb will rise up as the Lion of the tribe of Judah to defend it.

Don't be distracted by the latest manic developments of the stock market, either on Wall Street, London, Tokyo, or Hong Kong, with all their bull market euphorias and Black Monday depressions. Babylon the Great will most definitely crash and burn, "to be found more at all!"[19] But Jerusalem will be forever—the city of the Great King over the World Order of Zion! This generation shall not pass, till all these things be fulfilled!

Thus saith the Lord GOD; When I shall have gathered the house of Israel from the people among whom they are scattered, and shall be sanctified in them in the sight of the heathen [highly honored, not regarded as anathema and a curse word], then shall they dwell in their land that I have given to my servant Jacob. And they shall dwell safely therein [not under threat of katyusha rockets, Scud missiles, the Hizbollah, Hamas, Syria, Iran, Sadam Hussein, or the PLO], and shall build houses, and plant vineyards; yea, they shall dwell with confidence [not with gas masks beside their beds as they do now], when I have executed judgments upon all those that despise them round about them; and they shall know that I am the LORD their God.—Ezekiel 28:25-26

For I will set mine eyes upon them for good, and I will bring them again to this land: and I will build them, and not pull them down; and I will plant them, and not pluck them up. And I will give them an heart to know me [at last!], that I [guess Who] am the LORD: and they shall be my people, and I will be their God: for they shall return unto me with their whole heart.— Jeremiah 24:6-7

And I will make an everlasting covenant with them, that I will not turn away from them, to do them good; but I will put my fear in their hearts, that they shall not depart from me. Yea, I will rejoice over them to do them good, and I will plant them in this land assuredly with my whole heart and with my whole soul [only atheists and agnostics can fail to grasp the inexorable power of that pledge!]. For thus saith the LORD; Like as I have brought all this great evil [desolations, holocausts, and unceasing persecutions] upon this people, so will I bring upon them all the good that I have promised them.—Jeremiah 32:40-42

In that day will I raise up the tabernacle of David that is fallen, and close up the breaches thereof; and I will raise up his ruins, and I will build it as in the days of old [total grand scale restoration]:—Amos 9:11

This most assuredly refers to "the city of David" and the house of LORD David intended to build and Solomon completed. One thing for certain is that David will literally resurrect to rule in Israel: See Ezekiel 34:23-24, 37:24-27; and Hosea 3:4-5.

And I will bring again the captivity of my people of Israel, and they shall build the waste cities [after Armageddon and the seven last plagues—see my chapter 12], and inhabit them; and they shall plant vineyards, and drink the wine thereof; they shall also make gardens, and eat the fruit of them. And I will plant them upon their land, and they shall no more be pulled up out of their land which I have given them, saith the LORD thy God.—Amos 9:14-15

And when this cometh to pass, (lo, it will come,)
then shall they know that a prophet hath been among them.—Ezekiel 33:33

14

TELL US WHEN!

But of that day and that hour knoweth no man, no, not the angels which are
in heaven, neither the Son, but the Father.—Mark 13:32

Take ye heed, watch and pray: for ye know not when the time is.
For the Son of man is as a man taking a far journey, who left his house,
and gave authority to his servants, and to every man his work,
and commanded the porter to watch. Watch ye therefore: for ye know not
when the master of the house cometh, at even, or at midnight, or at the
cockcrowing, or in the morning: Lest coming suddenly he find you sleeping.
And what I say unto you I say unto all, Watch.—Mark 13:33-37

Kingdom-Come Ideology

As we finally approach the last leg of our tour through the prophetic
records of the Hebrews, we arrive at a major point of interest—one that has
been a source of considerable consternation and frustration for a great many
hopefuls throughout the last two millennia, and probably well before.

At least as far back as 700 years before the time of Christ and His apostles,
great anticipation had been sparked over the fabulous attributes assigned by the
prophets to the promised Kingdom of God to come on Earth. Time and space
fail me here to recount all the biblical accounts of those spectacular promises
and visions; but the prophet Isaiah is certainly the most eloquent and expansive
in his written record of revelations of the glorious future promised to the people
of Earth, and especially to Israel. It is only natural that Isaiah's prophetic visions
should feature Israel so prominently, since of all peoples, the Hebrews were
bestowed with particularly unique favor in the plan of YHWH. In Isaiah's
revelations, Israel was one day to be lavished with incredible wealth, majesty,
and global dominion under an Anointed King of supreme power and authority.

The Apostles in Christ's day, owing to their particular cultural heritage as Jews, were most certainly well aware of the general, if not the specific, features of this highly anticipated Kingdom awaited by the Jews. Practically every Jew in their day would have been, due to the strict customs of their culture, which included regular attendance at weekly Sabbath convocations in the local synagogues. Besides prayer, these weekly gatherings convened in large part for reading of the Torah (the books of Moses) and the Prophets.[1]

Week after week, and often more, counting the various other sabbaths of the feast days, the customary reading of the Scriptures in the synagogues promoted periodic revisiting of the same passages of scripture. Which, taken on an annual cycle, means the congregations would have had occasion to hear the same readings repeated many times over during their lifetime. Though not all were able to read and quite often only listened, this regular exposure would, of course, have fostered broad familiarity with the words of their prophets, and would have resulted in the congregations being fairly well versed throughout. Such was surely the case with Christ's disciples, certain of which were expressly acknowledged in one place to be illiterate—by a certain crowd (see Acts 4:13) that was otherwise amazed at their remarkable abilities, which were subsequently attributed to their having been in the company of The Master.[2] The point being that even the illiterate enjoyed by custom a substantial familiarity with the writings of the Prophets.

This familiarity with the Kingdom prophecies related to Israel and Zion was frequently demonstrated by the Disciples in the attitudes and ambitions they manifested, and in their repeated queries of the Messiah about *when* it would come. In fact, the very outline pursued in the organization of this book came from the oral dissertation on the end of the world (the Olivet Discourse) that Yeshua was prompted to give when being interrogated by a certain four of His followers, who happened to be illiterate fishermen, trying to pin down the day.[3] Two of them (Peter & John) were specifically named as illiterate in the account of their activities in the Book of Acts (as referenced above). However, after that whole lengthy briefing He gave them, which included the long list of signs He provided, still that was not the last time they would press Him with questions about *when* exactly the Kingdom would come. And, it was really no wonder.

Their anxious absorption with when the Kingdom would be established is quite easy to understand, when the incredible miracles and events they witnessed firsthand are taken into account. Witnessing the power of their

Master to command the forces of nature, to multiply food by the ton, to heal hopeless lepers, cure the blind, lame, deaf, dumb, and palsied, and even to raise the dead (from four days in the grave in one instance), convinced them that this man who could walk on water could also easily conquer the world. They recognized He was the Chosen and Anointed Prince of Peace heralded to come by so many of their prophets. Which to them meant that, "obviously," the Kingdom of God *was indeed "at hand!"*

After all, even Christ Himself had proclaimed that very thing from the beginning of His vocational circuit.[4] And not only so, but right before His debut, His radical desert forerunner, the camel-skin-clad, grasshopper-and-wild-honey-munching Baptist, had also distinguished his own renowned precursory calling with his vociferous announcements of exactly the same proclamation—saying, *"Repent ye: for the kingdom of heaven is at hand." (Matthew 3:2)*

And not only did John the Baptist and Yeshua too proclaim the imminency of the Kingdom, but then the Disciples themselves were also commissioned out on "internship" forays and practice missions, during their discipleship training years, to *"preach the Kingdom of God and heal the sick."*[5] Their every waking moment, as well as probably their slumbering ones too, must have been saturated with excitement, anticipation and even anxious disbelief sometimes at the thought that the New World Order of Zion was at hand.

By all of this, these twelve, hand-picked hopefuls of Yeshua were so overtaken with excitement about the advent of the New World Order—and especially their own status and position in it—that in their private moments among themselves, they often argued about who would be the "top drawer," or "biggest cheese." One of these top-dog disputes even occurred on the occasion of The Last Supper. Apostles Mark and Luke (in two separate accounts) recorded the occurrence of these status squabbles.[6] And Matthew recorded the occasion when the aspiring mother (of two ambitious fisherman) worshipfully petitioned The Master on behalf her sons James and John, *"Grant that these my two sons may sit, the one on thy right hand, and the other on the left, in thy kingdom." (Matt. 20:21)*

It's uncertain exactly whether they all engaged in the vying for vice presidency, the seat of prime minister, or chief of staff, or whether only certain of the more ambitious were most guilty. However, we see by the reported general attitude, there is no question but what an anxious expectation of the great event definitely pervaded their thinking as a whole, especially when they all had been promised "thrones" in the new government.[7] We do know that the entire group was resentful (probably jealous) of the personal ambitions of Mother Zebedee's sons.[8]

Toward the end, the momentous events of the very last week—preceding the tragic temporal crushing of all these dreams and ambitions—signified for them an imminency so proximate that they could now no longer contain their curiosity over the enigmatic behavior, disclosures, and assertions of their Master. The senior Disciples just had to take Messiah aside to pin things down and get some definite answers—*"Tell us, When shall these things be? and what shall be the sign of thy coming, and of the end of the world?" (Matt. 24:3)* Certain strange, and also wonderful, occurrences and declarations of the final few days of their company with Yeshua obviously must have forced the issue among them: *This had to be the time; but if not, then when?!*

The last few weeks, and particularly the last few days before the crucifixion of the Master, I surmise, must have given rise to what was an almost overwhelming sense of expectancy and excitement among these yearning colleagues. They must have been thoroughly stricken with the impression that the tangible establishment of the Kingdom was set to occur *any day!*

Consider that in only the last four days or so, they had beheld the spectacular "Triumphal Entry" of Messiah into Jerusalem. It was on that famous improvised-red-carpet day, that the crowds—gathered in Jerusalem for the annual feast of the Passover—stripped themselves of their coats and cloaks, and tore branches from palm trees to spread on the street before Yeshua, welcoming Him into the "city of the Great King" with resounding hails of, *"Hosanna: Blessed is the King of Israel that cometh in the name of the Lord." (John 12:13)* "Hosanna," from its Hebrew derivation, is literally a victory plea or prayer of *"save, rescue, deliver, avenge us presently."* Apostles Matthew and Mark both record that the hail of "Hosanna!" by the cheering multitudes was appended by many of them with a phrase actually making it more lavish and maximal in character—*"Hosanna . . . in the highest!"*[9]

This crowning event, in which Yeshua—for the first time—allowed Himself to be revered and proclaimed as King,[10] was followed by another, almost equally stunning episode that must have exhilarated the disciples. All four of the Gospels (Matthew, Mark, Luke, and John) all give an account of this incident, which probably pretty well shocked them.

According to Mark, on the day after the Hosanna episode, *"they come to Jerusalem: and Jesus went into the temple, and began to cast out them that sold and bought in the temple, and overthrew the tables of the moneychangers, and the seats of them that sold doves."* (Mark 11:15) Matthew's parallel account goes on to say, *"And [he] said unto them, It is written, My house shall be called the house of prayer; but ye have made it a den of thieves. And the blind and the lame came to him in the temple; and he healed them."* (Matt 21:13-14) The physical force Yeshua used to rededicate the Temple as a house of prayer, rather than a religious shopping mall, probably added a keen new dimension to the tension His disciples felt about the likelihood of a very imminent take-over by the King with His freshly fired-up revolutionists.

Some interesting detail is added to the episode of this angry eviction of the merchants and shoppers from the Temple by Apostle John, which definitely adds to the stun factor which thundered through all Jerusalem that day. The rather notorious feature of the expulsion in John's account is that the force exercised in the eviction process also included the use of *"a scourge [whip] of small cords"* which *"he had made"* (i.e., personally fashioned) and with which He thereby literally *"drove them all out of the temple."* (John 2:15) From then on, for the next few days, according to Luke, *"he taught daily in the temple. But the chief priests and the scribes and the chief of the people sought to destroy him, and could not find what they might do: for all the people were very attentive to hear him."* (Luke 19:47-48)

To top all this off, over the next couple days, the now rabid scribes and Pharisees (who functioned as rabbis and community leaders)—feeling severely threatened by this powerful and popular revolutionist—stepped up their campaign to discredit the whip-wielding king. Their vehement challenges to Yeshua's authority were met by Him at one point with scathing denunciations of these otherwise "reverend" leaders. Matthew (in chapter 23) provides the fullest account of Christ's stinging indictment of these "exemplary" officials, whom He labeled as oppressive and presumptuous "hypocrites" obsessed as they were with exalted titles and political image, cloaking their religious extortion and thievery of the poor behind "long prayers." He railed on them as "fools and blind guides" with twisted materialist values and priorities. Cursing them with woe after woe, He exposed them as murders and blood-guilty persecutors of the righteous, and essentially condemned them to hell as a *"generation of serpents and vipers!"* (Matt.23, whole chapter)

It takes but a very little imagination to picture the wild-eyed astonishment of His nervous and, by this time, trigger-happy disciples, now ready to risk their lives for the Revolution.[11] As far as they could tell, the time could never be riper. *"This must be it! The Master must be ready to make His move!"*

(This author believes that even Judas Iscariot was acting on this conviction, and that his act of betrayal was intended to force a confrontation with the establishment, knowing full well that Yeshua could prevail—especially "now" with so much popular support by the masses. His support was enough to even provoke intense alarm among the leaders of that establishment.[12] This, I think, is manifest in the fact that Judas deeply regretted the outcome.[13] He certainly had every reason to believe that Christ was prepared to engage even in armed uprising, having advised the purchase of a weapon for the first time.[14])

The fact is though, that the Disciples were summarily confused and uncertain *what* to think. The Scriptures indicate plainly that Yeshua had been preparing them (repeatedly) for His betrayal, arrest, and execution; and that, as prophesied 700 years earlier by Isaiah, he would be *"reckoned among the transgressors."* (See Isaiah 53:12 & Luke 22:37.) A few months before this was to take place, when He had fixed His intent on making His final Passover appearance in Jerusalem—where a capital warrant was already out for His arrest[5]—Luke, Matthew, and Mark record that He had begun to forewarn His intimate followers of an inglorious "end" to His career. We see from Luke's record that the advance notice didn't quite register in their minds:

Then he took unto him the twelve, and said unto them, Behold, we go up to Jerusalem, and all things that are written by the prophets concerning the Son of man shall be accomplished. For he shall be delivered unto the Gentiles, and shall be mocked, and spitefully entreated, and spitted on: and they shall scourge him, and put him to death: and the third day he shall rise again. And they understood none of these things: and this saying was hid from them, neither knew they the things which were spoken."—Luke 18:31-34

Evidently though, at the first such declaration that He would be apprehended by the officials and killed, Peter did react particularly to the announcement:

From that time forth began Jesus to shew unto his disciples, how that he must go unto Jerusalem, and suffer many things of the elders and chief priests and scribes, and be killed, and be raised again the third day. Then Peter took him, and began to rebuke him, saying, Be it far from thee, Lord: this shall not be unto thee. But he turned, and said unto Peter, Get thee behind me, Satan:

thou art an offence unto me: for thou savourest not the things that be of God, but those that be of men.—Matthew 16:21-23

The whole notion was obviously unthinkable to Peter. It spoiled his entire conception of what he had thought was *the plan*, and the imminent outcome—*"that the kingdom of God should immediately appear."*[16] Blinded by ambition, misplaced priorities, and, therefore, misplaced hope (as the whole group evidently was) none of the words of the Prophets with regard to Messiah being cut off,[17] nor the various pronouncements and caveats of the Master made any proper sense to him.

What Peter "savoured" was the power and glory of a palpable and tangible Kingdom of God, where the earthly, material dreams of his people could be immediately and presently realized. *"The Kingdom of Zion"* was the dream, the object of all their desire—The Ultimate Hope. Prophet after prophet of theirs had proclaimed the coming of this bejeweled hope, and even detailed its glamorous facets.

How could this not be the time of its coming? The King Himself was on the scene! The taste of it was in their mouths. They could smell it, hear it, feel its warmth. It seemed they were on the very threshold of sitting on those thrones they had been promised! Not even the powerful pagan empire of Rome, nor the pervasive, hypocritical religious establishment of the scribes and Pharisee, nor their own personal poverty, lack of resources—nothing—nothing could prevent the power of this Miracle Man from fulfilling His destiny, *and theirs!*

Well, we see from the passage cited above that Peter's misplaced values earned him quite a vile epithet. The great Apostle Peter, here tagged as "Satan," had not yet gotten the picture, nor had his fellows either. His obsession with the material aspect of the Kingdom promises—minus the associated tribulation and cost involved—warranted, in the Master's estimation, the severe characterization Peter received as an asinine sap for the wares of Satan, actually making him a collaborator and associate! (Remember, this was the very same commodity the Devil tried to sell Yeshua Himself at the start, during the Wilderness Temptation.)[18]

Wasn't Christ's reaction to Peter's "concern" for Him a bit extreme and overblown? Or was it, on the other hand, more precisely, a simple, easy-to-read gauge of Jesus' tolerance (or intolerance, in this case) for petty affections for the mundane "things of men/Satan?"

Hosanna Hearts and the Barabbas Factor

Poor Peter! Hadn't he and his fellows really been led astray by the Master, right into this eager fixation with the Kingdom-Come Ideology? Let's get real—what impression would you gather, if you had been in the presence of the Master when He said, *"Verily I say unto you, That there be some of them that stand here, which shall not taste of death, till they have seen the kingdom of God come with power?" (Mark 9:1)*[19] Had you witnessed the raising of the dead on several occasions, and been taught that, *"If a man keep my saying, he shall (verily, verily) never see death" (John 8:51)* and, moreover, had you been commissioned by the Master to go out yourself and exercise the same power to defeat death, I doubt your mindset would have been any different. Speaking for myself, I believe I would have thought, felt, and reacted just like Peter and the others. Fortunately, we have the advantage of all this retrospect and history.

But unless you had been keenly in tune with the Spirit, and been astute enough to catch on when Yeshua also taught that *"the kingdom of God cometh not with observation,"* you would quite likely have fallen into the same typical frame of reference as Peter and company. Luke records that, *"when [Yeshua] was demanded of the Pharisees, when the kingdom of God should come,"* He only elaborated by saying, *"Neither shall they say, Lo here! or, lo there! for, behold, the kingdom of God is within you." (Luke 17:20-21)* In this *signal* admonition, Messiah was clueing his audience in to the issue of "primary-ness" and principal essence, as touching the plan and intention of the Creator. That is, He was literally stressing the essential nature of the Kingdom of God as a matter not so much of where and when and what it would look like, but what it is *really all about*—a matter of the heart!

In this we see reflected the essence of Yeshua's core concept of conversion to *"childhood"* and being "born again." It involves the forsaking of ego and prideful adultist mind-sets fraught with covetous lusts for grandiosity and ego-centered self-fulfillment. It's a return in heart to "the garden" and to simple devotion to loving, self-sacrificial interrelations, as taught by Yeshua to His disciples whom He preferred to call "brethren," rather than "servants."[20] The selfless innocence, optimistic trust, sensitivity, tenderness, and unpretentious humility of a little child were revered by Messiah as the prime qualities of His Kingdom constituents.[21] The Kingdom of God is primarily a kingdom of the heart.

Unless the heart is converted, the environment too will eventually be corrupted, not matter how perfect it may be. In fact, the coming Messianic Order of Zion (Mashiach's Millennium) will itself also finally be corrupted by the unconverted ones, even after an entire child-oriented millennium of peace, plenty, liberty, justice, and the pursuit of happiness. [22]

The "Millennium of the Child" in the New World Order of Messiah will be a one-thousand-year experience of virtual harmlessness. "Virtual," because a remnant of unconverted carnal humans will survive the decimation of the evil endtime civilization of man, and require governing by rigid enforcement of the Law of Love and Peace—which will necessitate occasional severe sentences of retribution for rebellion and violation. Yet, the broad general Order will be maintained as an environment of absolute security fitting for children. According to the Apocalypse, one of the major factors contributing to the peace of this idyllic period will be that the dynamic force of evil (Satan the Adversary) will be imprisoned for the duration:

And I saw an angel come down from heaven, having the key of the bottomless pit and a great chain in his hand. And he laid hold on the dragon, that old serpent, which is the Devil, and Satan, and bound him a thousand years, and cast him into the bottomless pit, and shut him up, and set a seal upon him, that he should deceive the nations no more, till the thousand years should be fulfilled: and after that he must be loosed a little season.—Revelation 20:1-3

In very short order, upon Satan's brief release from his 1,000-year sentence, we find that he has not rehabilitated. And not only has he personally not experienced a change of heart, but millions of humans meanwhile, even under the global reign of love and peace for that entire millennium, have not either. The remnant of the unconverted, having multiplied during that period (by usual human reproductive means) into masses of "obliged" and not entirely willing hearts, organize a massive *coup d'état* against the beloved, theocratic Kingdom of Zion.

And when the thousand years are expired, Satan shall be loosed out of his prison, and shall go out to deceive the nations which are in the four quarters of the earth, Gog and Magog [again, second & final round], to gather them together to battle: the number of whom is as the sand of the sea. And they went up on the breadth of the earth, and compassed the camp of the saints about, and the beloved city: and fire came down from God out of heaven, and devoured them.—Revelation 20:7-9

Under the leadership of the proud, unreformed, discontented, envious, never-satisfied Tempter—still coveting to ascend to divine supremacy—the unwilling "subjects" of the Messianic order, who have had no change of heart, rally in a fateful democratic insurgency against the Prince of Peace. Until the very end, we see that people reserve the right to make their own choices; and some refuse the way of God, no matter how beautiful and ideal it is even manifest to be.

The lesson we can reap from this peace of future history: Even the perfect conditions of the Millennium of Children will not result in complete change of heart for a huge majority of those who are married to their covetous, adultist love of self.

Precisely the same principle of "unrepentant heart" was at work among the rapturous Hosanna crowds in Jerusalem 2,000 years ago. Despite all the hoopla of that cheering populous, no profound change of heart had taken place in Jerusalem that week. Within that same week of the fateful Last Passover Supper, no sooner had the echoing cheer of hope and optimism fallen in the streets of Jerusalem, but the vindictive outcry of soured adultist expectation quickly rose up to replace it, with spiteful demands for blood and cruel vengeance. The Kingdom of God was indeed "at hand," but the unconverted hearts of the avaricious and self-seeking failed to recognize the essence of it.

According to Luke, the day Christ entered into the city of Jerusalem—riding on that asses' colt over the "red carpet" of fickle devotion offered by that *"very great multitude [which] spread their garments in the way [and] cut down branches from the trees, and strawed them in the way". (Matt 21:8)*—He wept over it. (See Luke 19:41-42.) Rather than being elated at the worshipful welcome and the tumultuous hails of "Hosanna in the highest," He instead mourned *to tears* over what He knew was in that crowd's heart. For within *the same week*—this time as He stood in the mock garb of the "gorgeous purple robe" with which had Herod ridiculed Him, a crown of thorns jammed upon His head, face slimed with spit, bruised, bloody and lacerated after harsh beatings while blindfolded by a group of hardened soldiers—the chant now of the nearly rioting crowd had changed. Now it was, *"Crucify him, crucify him!"*

From glorified king to capital convict only within a matter of days!

Because the masses viewed Messiah's unpreparedness to presently promote the Kingdom of Zion by armed revolt and violent overthrow as a manifest sign of weakness, and an unwillingness to support their materialist agenda, they quickly turned against Him. They opted instead for the violent modus operandi of Barabbas and his militant brand of force-premised liberation politics, of whom Mark testified in the following words:

And there was one named Barabbas, which lay bound with them that had made insurrection with him, who had committed murder in the insurrection. And the multitude crying aloud began to desire him to do as he had ever done unto them.—Mark 15:7-8

Wishing to free the arrested King of the Jews, whom even Pontius Pilate recognized as a just and peace-loving man of good will, he saw the rabid masses would have none of it, but would instead riot over it. When this consummate politician compromised his integrity for personal advantage (in the scurry for escape from potential career damage) by offering to release Jesus—after ordering a vicious, flesh-ripping scourging, which he thought would appease the blood-thirsty crowds—they threateningly taunted, *"If thou let this man go, thou art not Caesar's friend!"* And they cried out all the more loudly in chorus, *"Away with this man, and release unto us Barabbas! We have no king but Caesar!"*[23]

Now, under the sway of the latest negative campaign ads blared by the party bosses and the incumbent administration, the capricious democratic mob had reversed their opinion and suddenly changed their vote:

And Pilate, when he had called together the chief priests and the rulers and the people, said unto them, Ye have brought this man unto me, as one that perverteth the people: and, behold, I, having examined him before you, have found no fault in this man touching those things whereof ye accuse him: No, nor yet Herod: for I sent you to him; and, lo, nothing worthy of death is done unto him. I will therefore chastise him, and release him. (For of necessity he must release one unto them at the feast.) And they cried out all at once, saying, Away with this man, and release unto us Barabbas: (Who for a certain sedition made in the city, and for murder, was cast into prison.) Pilate therefore, willing to release Jesus, spake again to them. But they cried, saying, Crucify him, crucify him. And he said unto them the third time, Why, what evil hath he done? I have found no cause of death in him: I will therefore chastise him, and let him go. And they were instant with loud voices, requiring that he might be crucified. And the voices of them and of the chief priests prevailed.—Luke 23:13-23

The Apostle Matthew confirms the leading role of the corrupt administration in stirring up the tumult:

But the chief priests and elders persuaded the multitude that they should ask Barabbas, and destroy Jesus. The governor answered and said unto them, Whether of the twain will ye that I release unto you? They said, Barabbas. Pilate saith unto them, What shall I do then with Jesus which is called Christ? They all say unto him, Let him be crucified. And the governor said, Why, what evil hath he done? But they cried out the more, saying, Let him be crucified. When Pilate saw that he could prevail nothing, but that rather a tumult [riot, or violent uprising] was made, he took water, and washed his hands before the multitude, saying, I am innocent of the blood of this just person: see ye to it. Then answered all the people, and said, His blood be on us, and on our children.—Matthew 27:20-25

So, in less than a week the hearts of those wildly cheering fans *had switched* to that of monstrous murdering mobs. One day, praise and blessing, the next, violent spite and cursing. Because the hallelujah crowds didn't get their kingdom of rapturous glory when and how they wanted it, *they turned* to viciously betray the now despised "no-show messiah" for deferring to oblige them with their "blessed hope"; *and, they joined the pagans* in allegiance to "The Emperor" and the world establishment of the day. Thus goes the politics (and religion) of convenience. (Any connection to real persons and actual contemporary settings is lamentably unmistakable, and strictly intended.)

What will your personal course of action be on the deadline date of the final governmental order to appear at the registrar's office to receive your assigned number and/or mark of the Evil Emperor? This time it will be your arrest, imprisonment, and "crucifixion" (i.e., *beheading*)[24] in the sentencing mandate. Will the cock crow twice for you, before you recall the words of Christ? Is your devotion as staunch as Peter's, who vowed he would go to prison and to death for the Master? Well, one thing Peter was certainly never mistaken about—which contrasts sharply with the fickle "Peters" of contemporary Christianity—was *the cost* of being a Christ-following *mathetés (disciple,* Gk. μαθητής, *one applied to learning, a pupil, and hence, a follower of the teaching).*[25]

The disciples originally came by the name "Christians," not because they simply acknowledged a belief in Christ, but because they followed His teachings, walked in His footsteps, and took His cross upon themselves. We have seen that the original Christians were under their own set of illusions initially (concerning the coming of Messiah and His Kingdom), but hardly under any misconceptions about the nature of their calling, vocation, and the associated commitment.

Today's "Christians," however, desperately need serious reevaluation of their faith and intensive self-examination of their belief systems. A very large majority of them are under very grave illusions of rapture and escape from tribulation, which are the telltale evidences of heresy based in delusive doctrines of "low-cost kingdom and no-cross convenience." It seems to me that "preparing the way of the Lord" in this last generation, calls for much more than birdbath baptisms of repentance, in order to aggressively flush away apostate 20th century Christian illusions.

The prophet Jeremiah provided an astute psychological profile of humanity from which Christians are not exempt. His caveat: *"The heart is deceitful above all things, and desperately wicked: who can know it?" (Jer.17:9)* In other words, we are all quite susceptible and prone to self-deceit, illusion, and error. There is, however, a key to this quandary. It was later spelled out to the Hebrews by Apostle Paul: *"The word of God is quick, and powerful, and sharper than any two-edged sword, piercing even to the dividing asunder of soul and spirit, and of the joints and marrow, and is a discerner of the thoughts and intents of the heart." (Heb.4:12)* Simple faith in the sacred texts on which this book is based provide a gauge to help determine where our hearts are at, and to guide us in making appropriate adjustments.

Sophistication is not the key; it is rather, in pure, child-like obedience and faith in the ways and wisdom of God. Elaborate, complicated, desperately stretched and twisted interpretations of Scripture, which are not straightforward and consistent, should always be highly suspect. For therein lies the soul of deception. And herein, too, is the rule and not the exception.

The foregoing retrospective tour of the apostolic era of Yeshua and His Disciples is not only to examine their own perspectives, errors in judgment, understandings, and misunderstandings, so as to gain a better grasp of the "big picture" for ourselves. It is also to contribute to accurately framing that true picture of when the Kingdom of God will actually come.

Yet, though a major thrust of this section and this book as a whole is about what is acceptable as well as not, in terms of timing, it's definitely not the sole purpose. For although timing is important, the constituency of that Kingdom is far more so. Kingdom "constituents" with only pre-tribulation rapture and glory on their mind will find themselves unfit for the New World Order of The Lamb and seriously deceived about the type and quality of soul to be welcomed there. Those in that case would do well to plan a trip to the Laundromat of Great Tribulation to wash their robes in the blood of the Lamb, and cancel all plans to be airlifted to their fanciful Destination Glory. They, like the naked king in the fable of "The King Who Wore No Clothes," are victims of their own dissatisfaction with the truth.

Dispelling illusions is absolutely *key* to getting a true picture—and thus being also able to truly prepare. Understanding that deceit is almost always sweet, and truth more akin to reproof, every effort made has been in this thesis to err in favor of the wise ear.[26] Being prepared for the coming of the Great Day of God Almighty is not something to be even mildly mistaken about, in my opinion.

The Acceptable-Year-Acceptable-Witness Link

One of the stipulated purposes of the coming of the LORD's Anointed One, according to Isaiah (61:1-3) was that He should "proclaim the accept-able year of the LORD." Messiah did indeed proclaim what was acceptable in that regard during His first visit with us. But even His most intimate followers at that time failed to fully recognize the appointed season intended for it. This wasn't due to any inherent complexity in the proclamation, but instead to other problems (i.e., errors of the mind, which clouded understanding). We have examined the probable whys and wherefores fairly extensively, in hopes that we in our day might learn not only when the acceptable year is to be expected, but also, more importantly, to come to simply *accept the time as it is proclaimed*—clear of any misconceptions spawned by deceitful hearts.

Critical to understanding the *acceptable year of the Lord* is grasping the meaning of the renowned proclamation introduced in the previous section—"the Kingdom of Heaven is at hand!" We saw that even among the most de-voted and intimate of Christ's followers there was considerable perplexity surrounding that idea, and a general belief at one point that the Kingdom of God would "immediately appear."

The concept of The Kingdom is absolutely central to the teachings of Christ, as well as those of all the Hebrew prophets. It is, without a doubt, the *heart and soul* of the biblical message, and the hope for which millions have waited throughout the ages—the much-acclaimed "blessed hope." With respect to the coming of that hope, Messiah conclusively stipulated a prerequisite condition: That mankind's wicked world order would not be finally replaced with God's righteous order until *"this gospel of the kingdom shall be preached in all the world for a witness unto all nations." (Matt.24:14)* "Gospel" (originally *euangélion* in the Greek, and more literally the root of the English word *evangelism*) means *good tidings/message/news*. In terms of message content, Christ's objective was that the good tidings of His *specially defined Kingdom*—as He personally taught and demonstrated—should first be published and proclaimed to all nations.

The intent is evidently that all peoples should be given full advance notice of the will and purpose of the Creator for His Creation. Thus, they should be able to make an informed selection, when faced with the choice of allegiance to either the global regime of the Beast, or the Messianic New World Order. Ignorance of the Messianic Kingdom, nor unsuspected surprise at its advent, cannot and will not be a factor in the public acceptance or rejection of it, nor in the judgment of the selection made. The Kingdom is being heralded at this very moment, and will be proclaimed even more ardently and fully as the days progress, until the sheep have all been divided from the goats. And as the end draws near, there shall be no misgivings about its nature either.

Faithful witnesses shall give testimony to that Kingdom, even at the expense of their lives—which is really the only believable testimony that could effectively impact the decisions of millions of already perplexed earthlings, who don't know what to believe. The twelfth-hour age of astonishment into which we are even now beginning to transition will yet give rise to a final pair of extraordinary prophets. Two powerful terminal-era prophets, previously studied in Chapters 4 and 7, are destined to spearhead the final witness campaign, providing straightforward, unmuddled testimony of the coming Theocratic Order, versus the luciferian option.[27] They will be heeded and supported by multitudes of other witnesses, equally committed to the testimony of Christ during the last hour of supreme contest and trial in the war of the worlds.

And I will give power unto my two witnesses, and they shall prophesy a thousand two hundred and threescore days, clothed in sackcloth. These are the two olive trees, and the two candlesticks standing before the God of the earth. And if any man will hurt them, fire proceedeth out of their mouth, and devoureth their enemies: and if any man will hurt them, he must in this manner be killed. These have power to shut heaven, that it rain not in the days of their prophecy: and have power over waters to turn them to blood, and to smite the earth with all plagues, as often as they will. And when they shall have finished their testimony, the beast that ascendeth out of the bottomless pit shall make war against them, and shall overcome them, and kill them.—Revelation 11:3-7

And the great dragon was cast out, that old serpent, called the Devil, and Satan, which deceiveth the whole world: he was cast out into the earth, and his angels were cast out with him. And I heard a loud voice saying in heaven, Now is come salvation, and strength, and the kingdom of our God, and the power of his Christ: for the accuser of our brethren is cast down, which accused them before our God day and night. And they overcame him by the blood of the Lamb, and by the word of their testimony; and they [the believing brethren on earth] loved not their lives unto the death. . . . And the dragon was wroth with the woman [corporate body of believers], and went to make war with the remnant of her seed [remaining saints & witnesses], which keep the commandments of God, and have the testimony of Jesus Christ.—Revelation 12:9-11 & 17

The description of the casualties in this endtime conflict reflect the degree of commitment to that testimony:

And when he had opened the fifth seal, I saw under the altar the souls of them that were slain for the word of God, and for the testimony which they held: And they cried with a loud voice, saying, How long, O Lord, holy and true, dost thou not judge and avenge our blood on them that dwell on the earth? And white robes were given unto every one of them; and it was said unto them, that they should rest yet for a little season, until their fellowservants also and their brethren, that should be killed as they were, should be fulfilled.—Revelation 6:9-11

After this I beheld, and, lo, a great multitude, which no man could number, of all nations, and kindreds, and people, and tongues, stood before the throne, and before the Lamb, clothed with white robes, and palms in their hands. . . . And one of the elders answered, saying unto me, What are these which are arrayed in white robes? and whence came they? And I said unto him, Sir, thou knowest. And he said to me, These are they which came out of great tribulation, and have washed their robes, and made them white in the blood of the Lamb.—Revelation 7:9

And I saw thrones, and they sat upon them, and judgment was given unto them: and I saw the souls of them that were beheaded for the witness of Jesus, and for the word of God, and which had not worshipped the beast, neither his image, neither had received his mark upon their foreheads, or in their hands; and they lived and reigned with Christ a thousand years.—Revelation 20:4

As Christ gave His life to conclusively validate His credentials and as authentication of His testimony of the Theocratic Order, so shall the multitudes of martyrs of these last days also do. Miracles were one of the certifying trademarks of Messiah, and will also certify the two sackcloth prophets soon to appear. But, power to do miracles is not the exclusive domain of the Good Force; for, the Dark Force will unleash its full ability in these last days to also manifest miracles. Hence, the most conclusive measure of veracity and authentic belief in this age of "strong delusion" will be the *"washing of robes in the Lamb's Blood."*

The lives of the witnesses are already supposed to be sacrificed upon their crosses of daily death to self and to material world ambitions, as validation of the "testimony of Jesus Christ." Quite tragically however, as has been harped on so repeatedly by this author, rapture and escape doctrines most commonly prevail among the mainstream of would-be "witnesses," which only serve to belittle and denigrate that sacred testimony. On the other hand, a witness that actually forsakes the opportunity to achieve material comfort, success, and prosperity for the sake of the "world to come," is a witness to be believed. The duplicity of all those witnesses that, contrariwise, manifest Babylonish affections renders their witness dubious and fully unworthy of serious credibility. *"For where your treasure is, there will your heart be also."* (Matthew 6:21)

Those who truly believe in the promise of the Kingdom and in the testimony of Jesus do not make committed investments in the fleeting substance of the mammonistic order of "Great Babylon." Rather, they join the great patriarchs of Apostle Paul's "hall of fame" in his epic chapter to the Hebrews (chapter 11) on the crucial theme of *faith*. According to Paul, it is "impossible to please God without faith" (Heb.11:6)—faith that is manifest by action. His definitive statement on faith highlighted the lifestyles and conduct of Abraham, Isaac, Jacob, Moses and many others who clung to their faith in the Promises *unto the death*. The distinguishing factor in their tenacious embrace of God's promises was that they were so persuaded of them that they declared and maintained their status as that of *"strangers and pilgrims on the earth." (Heb.11:13)*

Paul goes on in Hebrews 11, verses 14-16, to point out that such lifestyles of faith *" declare plainly"* a conviction in *"a better country, that is, an heavenly [one]."* The unmistakable conviction of those patriarchs, which they faithfully lived out in a lifelong, dedicated quest for that promised country, is what earned them the distinction, as Paul puts it, that *"God is not ashamed to be called their God."* The clear lesson is, of course, that those who doubt that God has *"prepared for them a city"* will instead earn shame and disgust unto themselves in the sight of God. And, what is it that "declares plainly" whether one doubts, or has faith? Plainly understood from Hebrews 11—either a lifestyle of affection for materialism, or one that opts to renounce it all for a *"better country."*

Beyond that (in verses 24-27), Paul further expands on this principle by adding *affliction* to the ingredients of faith, when he notes that Moses chose *"rather to suffer affliction with the people of God, than to enjoy the pleasures of sin for season."* By forsaking his potential inheritance to the throne of Egypt (being regarded the son of Pharaoh's daughter), Paul indicated that Moses esteemed the expatriation and vagabond character of Messiah's calling as *"greater riches than the treasures in Egypt,"* because he had *"respect unto the recompense of the reward."* That is, he had faith in the greatness of the Messianic Kingdom to come, and demonstrated it, gladly accepting the associated suffering. Paul finally concludes, in chapter 13 of Hebrews, *"Let us go forth therefore unto [Christ] without the camp [join Him outside the acceptable establish order], bearing his reproach [banishment for non-conformity]. For here [in this world] have we no continuing city, but we seek one to come."* (Heb.13:13-14)

We touch on this aspect of genuine faith in the Promise of the Kingdom to draw attention to an understanding which the ancient Hebrew patriarchs had of the fabulous substance and essence of the "city, country, and kingdom" to come. Centuries later, the Disciples of Yeshua Ha'Mashiach got a living taste of that essence, in the flavor of the very King Himself. For it is the king that defines the nature and character of his kingdom by the laws he establishes for the conduct of its affairs and governance of its citizens. It is in that light that we, more than even the great Hebrew forefathers, have much greater insight into the flavor of the Kingdom of God, by our own taste of the very quintessence of that kingdom in the person of Messiah Himself. And, it is for that simple reason that John the Baptist, Christ, and His Disciples all proclaimed—at the time of Messiah's physical presence on Earth in the land of Israel 2000 years ago—that *"the Kingdom of God is at hand."*

At the very hub of this central Kingdom theme is the Perfect Model of the sum and substance of Kingdom life. Yeshua's life and teachings while on Earth were the quintessential example of that sum and substance. His otherworldly Kingdom is not made up of mere material superstructure, or comprised primarily of a physical construct of cities, buildings, and other material elements (with a bunch of humans tossed in to adorn it). In fact, when His Disciples approached Him with worldly grandiosity in their eyes— as they ogled the magnificent superstructures they thought they would shortly be lords over in the New Order—Yeshua found it necessary to employ some shock therapy in an attempt to readjust their misplaced sense of values:

And as he went out of the temple, one of his disciples saith unto him, Master, see what manner of stones and what buildings are here! And Jesus answering said unto him, Seest thou these great buildings? there shall not be left one stone upon another, that shall not be thrown down.—Mark 13:1-2

His thorough devaluation of their material significance is conspicuous in the severe curse He pronounced upon those "great buildings," such a sweeping destruction that not a single stone would remain standing upon another! (So much for the glory of man.) Physical buildings and cities are not the essence of the Kingdom of God.[28]

For all practical matters, that is the least of it and the easiest, simplest portion of it to produce (if even all that desirable!). Consider that God created the perfect physical environment and setting for the establishment of this Kingdom, with all its abundance of resources, in only six days. But in terms of properly suited inhabitants, it has taken thousands of years to recondition and prepare the participants and citizens of that heavenly world order for entry and functional participation in that order. (Thanks go to Adam's and Eve's unleashing of the Pandora's Box of Corruption when they chose the Serpent as their mentor and ally to their ambition). The viability of that divinely designed realm is dependent on the nature and character of the beings that are to inhabit it as its citizens, not on buildings and superstructures.[29] In fact, in terms of temples and buildings and cities, the biblical concept is one of *living stones and a living temple.*[30]

Priorities in Order

Evidently, it was part of a Divine strategy—to neutralize any preoccupation with the physical or material features of the New World Order of YHWH— that even Messiah Himself was initially uninformed exactly of the "the day and the hour" when the world would end, giving birth to the full-scale Kingdom of God. Thus, the primary endeavor toward establishment of the Kingdom, and the key element stressed, was preparation of the way of the Lord by first preparing the *hearts* of men to enter into that Kingdom—in spirit. Herein lies the key to comprehending why Messiah insisted that the Kingdom of God *"cometh not with observation,"* but rather that *"the kingdom of God is within you." (Luke 17:20-21)*

The strategy was first of all to gather the *"lost sheep of the house of Israel" (Matt.10:5-7),* and then to go *"into all the world and preach the gospel to every creature." (Mark 16:15)* As stated in the previous section, Messiah made it clear that, before the end, *"the gospel must first be published among all nations." (Mark 13:10)* This was the established priority, of far greater concern than *when* the full-blown physical manifestation of the gospel promise should occur. According to Christ, the whole world needed to hear about it and have an opportunity to make their selection and exercise their faith preference, one way or the other.[31] As Apostle Paul urged, *"For whosoever shall call upon the name of the Lord shall be saved. How then shall they call on him in whom they have not believed? and how shall they believe in him of whom they have not heard? and how shall they hear without a preacher?" (Romans 10:13-14)*

This was Christ's preoccupation, which He wisely hitched to the excited energy of His very anxious team of workhorse Disciples. In a sense, Yeshua made full advantage of their "chomping on the bit" to provide the impetus and momentum for delivering His payload (the gospel of the Kingdom) to all the ends of the earth. And, to insure that the momentum would be sustained for the duration, He kept them guessing as to the exact day and hour of His return, admonishing them in these words:

But of that day and that hour knoweth no man, no, not the angels which are in heaven, neither the Son, but the Father. Take ye heed, watch and pray: for ye know not when the time is. For the Son of man is as a man taking a far journey, who left his house, and gave authority to his servants, and to every man his work, and commanded the porter to watch. Watch ye therefore: for ye know not when the master of the house cometh, at even, or at midnight, or at the cockcrowing, or in the morning: Lest coming suddenly he find you sleeping. And what I say unto you I say unto all, Watch.—Mark 13:32-37

The strategy, we see, was to keep them fully alert and working steadily on their assignment. We should also note that this strategy originated with The Father. For as Yeshua confessed in His own words, *not even He knew the exact time*. Had he known the day and hour at that time, He probably would not have withheld it from them; because, He considered His Disciples such intimate friends that He committed to full disclosure with them.[32]

Earlier in this chapter it was stated that the intense interest of the Disciples in knowing exactly when the Messiah's world government would come prompted them to repeated probing of the Master for the date. One of the most notable of those instances occurred again only about a month-and-a-half after the Olivet interrogation. This time (again upon the Mount of Olives), it was after His crucifixion and resurrection. As Luke points out in the Book of the Acts of the Apostles, Yeshua *"showed himself alive after his passion by many infallible proofs"* and was *"seen of them forty days . . . speaking of the things pertaining to the kingdom of God." (Acts 1:3)* Well, at the conclusion of that additional forty-day period spent with His Disciples, elaborating further on the New World Order of YHWH, the time for His departure from Earth arrived and again gave rise to another round of questioning.

What must have triggered the inquiry was Yeshua's instruction (in verse 4) *"that they should not depart from Jerusalem, but wait for the promise of the Father, which,"* He reminded them, *"ye have heard of me"* (from earlier teachings prior to His death).[33] Then, after revisiting the symbolism of John the Baptist's priming call to radical repentance and complete renewal, He pledged (in verse 5), as He had before, that they would be immersed in His very own Spirit after a mere wait of *"not many days hence."* This Spirit, the Power by which Messiah Himself had been operating, was now to be theirs as well in a matter of days!

Well, as you can imagine, this announcement drew them into a tight huddle around Him with nothing but the big question in the forefront of their minds— *"Lord, wilt thou at this time restore again the kingdom to Israel?"* (Acts 1:6) His reply was point-blank: *"It is not for you to know the times or the seasons, which the Father hath put in his own power."* (Acts 1:7)

And with that, He immediately turned their attention back to the Number-one Priority: *"But ye shall receive power, after that the Holy Ghost is come upon you: and ye shall be witnesses unto me both in Jerusalem, and in all Judaea, and in Samaria, and unto the uttermost part of the earth."* (Acts 1:8) They had their marching orders. On top of that, as if to underscore the mandate and reemphasize its priority, while they stood staring up into the sky as they beheld Yeshua ascend up into the clouds, *"two men stood by them in white apparel; which also said, Ye men of Galilee, why stand ye gazing up into heaven? This same Jesus, which is taken up from you into heaven, shall so come in like manner as ye have seen him go into heaven."* (Acts 1:10-11) In other words, *"You all know the score, now let's get back to the game and play some serious ball!"* (Please pardon the sporting metaphor.)

It's Different Now

Messiah, at the time of this "post-crucifixion questioning" which we just examined from the Book of Acts, did not state as He had before crucifixion, that He didn't know the day and the hour. Rather, He pointedly replied this time that it just wasn't for them to have that precise information, which The Father had reserved unto Himself.

But especially for the sake of the stubborn nobody-knows-the-day-or-the-hour buffs, it must be made perfectly clear that things are not quite the same now as they were prior to the crucifixion at the time of the Olivet Discourse. Dear brother John the Apostle, also often referred to as John the Revelator, author of the "Apocalypse," made us to understand by the Book of the Revelation, that the Lamb—having been slain—was since found worthy to open the Holy Scroll of the Future, sealed with seven seals, which no one else in heaven or in earth, nor under the earth was found worthy to open, or to even look upon (Revelation 5, whole chapter).

After John tells us that he *"wept much, because no man was found worthy to open and to read the book, neither to look upon" (v. 4)*, he speaks of an heavenly-based elder who comforted him with these words: *"Weep not: behold, the Lion of the tribe of Juda, the Root of David, hath prevailed to open the book, and to loose the seven seals thereof." (v.5)* Probably approaching the age of 90, John still had not been able to let go of his ardent desire to know when the great Restoration would come and put an end to iniquity. I imagine he would have died broken-hearted had this great secret not been revealed.

In chapter 7, we studied what was revealed to John about the veiled day and hour *"when there should be time no longer,"* and when the Voice of the Seventh Angel finally trumpets that *"the mystery of God should be finished, as he hath declared to his servants the prophets." (Rev.10:5-7)* What John learned was especially intended to be passed on to us. And in fact, the whole book of the Apocalypse was given as a fulfillment of the Lamb's promise to guide His friends "into all truth" and to show them "things to come." (See footnote 33, "The Promise.") Specifically included was the very day of the end of the world, though still in partially inconclusive terms. That is to say, the Apocalypse does indeed specify the day when time will be no longer, but only in terms of placing it 1,260 days after another signal point in time, which is only described and not dated.[34] So that, once the sign appears as described, there will be no quibble about exactly how much time is left. John's patient wait for this information took him up almost to the end of his life at the turn of the 1st century. But he got it!

It's important to ask, how did John come about this prized top-secret file detailing the last few years of history? The answer: From someone who confessed he did not previously have access to it, before he died. That same someone who had before declared to John and his compatriots that *no one*—not he, nor the angels in heaven—had the clearance to view that file, except God Himself. Now, however, things had changed. This same Someone, spoken of in the Apocalypse as The Lamb, had offered His life in supreme sacrifice to the Love of The Father and His children, The Lamb's brethren. Consequently, this Lamb now merited the exclusive right to crack the seals and view the secrets of the Scroll, and to pass them on to the brethren.

A good many prophecy "experts" fail to note that the first five words of the very first verse of the Apocalypse attest to the fact that Jesus Christ learned something after His death that He did not know before; and also, that the whole purpose for *"The Revelation . . . which God gave unto him"* was *"to shew unto his servants things which must shortly come to pass . . ."* So, as I have said, though there is still some temporary uncertainty, for deliberate reasons, about the date and time of the Zero Hour, there is a conclusive, well-defined point at which it is time to begin the countdown to the Trumpet of the Seventh Angel.

That seventh voice will herald the "acceptable year of the LORD," which the Lord did proclaim when He walked the earth with Peter and John and the others. He, in fact, proclaimed it by stipulating that the acceptable year was *not yet*, but must follow some dramatic developments upon earth, including some major witness accomplishments. Not least of all, He also expressly specified that the Great Tribulation and the Abomination of Desolation would precede it.

Not until the ultimate Beast Order of Luciferian Man hatches upon earth, when the people of the world have filled the cup of their iniquity to the brim, will the acceptable year of the LORD come. When mankind has fully realized himself as the despicably proud and ungrateful rebel that he is, when his materialist achievements reach their pinnacle as he enters into blasphemous alliance with Lucifer himself, jointly partnering with him in his own ambition to *be God* and fully defy the intent and purpose of GOD, then will the end come. When mankind's insane, covetous obsession with his own power and glory becomes so pervasive that it compels him to set himself up as God, via the global rally to adore the man-god person of their techno-miracle-manifesting Antichrist hero, then YHWH will be compelled to destroy the destroyers.[35]

Until then, the marching cadence of the authentic corps of cross-bearers must be stepped up dramatically to advance against the anti-God forces of the specious New World Order, which exalt war and the technology of destruction to defend and advance covetous greed, dominance, and vainglory under the beguiling banner of "peace, prosperity and world unity." For even now, two would-be world orders actually vie for supremacy, East pitted against West. One ensnares and enslaves by advancing the hedonistic religion of mammon and humanistic democracy as supreme. The other, by self-righteous advocacy of the supposed superiority of its holier-than-thou religion over all others, per which the Resurrected Jew is only but a mere "prophet." Which world order has captured your allegiance?

In the end, the Order of the Great Whore will be severely scourged by the Beast and his cohorts, for her idolatrous wandering harlotry. But then too, the momentarily triumphant Order of the Beast of Blasphemy will ultimately be crushed with blood-wringing fury in the Great Day of the Vengeance and Wrath of Almighty God.

Neither of these two orders holds anything but hollow, temporary promise. Their deceitful allure is terminal, and their fruit is certain death with no remedy. The only escape to freedom and true life (the everlasting pursuit of happiness) is in the New World Order of Messiah, the Kingdom of God. But the only entrance there is by death to self and worldly ambitions,[36] which requires *faith* to renounce any allegiance to the world orders of the Whore or the Beast. Faith for such death unto life lies in the testimony of Jesus Christ, who sacrificed his blood to seal and certify a solemn, binding pledge that we can be born again into everlasting life.[37] There are only two promises to consider: glory now, or glory later.

The admonitions are also two—one for those who stumble in the intoxicating shadow of the Whore, and the other for those who have been allured by the rising star and new moon of the specious "salvation" of the "omnipotent" Beast to come. First, for those who have been rendered senseless by stupefaction on the consummate materialism of the "great city," BABYLON THE GREAT, THE MOTHER OF HARLOTS AND ABOMINATIONS OF THE EARTH (Rev.17:5 & 18):

Come out of her, my people, that ye be not partakers of her sins, and that ye receive not of her plagues.—Revelation 18:4

For those who are possessed with envy and jealous hatred, and covet to overthrow the Great City superpower, so as to take her place as the ultimate power brokers and rulers of the world:

If any man worship the beast and his image, and receive his mark in his forehead, or in his hand, the same shall drink of the wine of the wrath of God, which is poured out without mixture into the cup of his indignation; and he shall be tormented with fire and brimstone in the presence of the holy angels, and in the presence of the Lamb: And the smoke of their torment ascendeth up for ever and ever: and they have no rest day nor night, who worship the beast and his image, and whosoever receiveth the mark of his name. Here is the patience of the saints: here are they that keep the commandments of God, and the faith of Jesus.—Revelation 14:9-12

Two hundred virgins do not await you in paradise for sacrificing your life to devils and their violent doctrines of covetousness. The commandments of YHWH and the faith of Yeshua Ha'Mashiach are the key to your salvation, peace, paradise, pleasure and most likely virgins too!

And he spake to them a parable; Behold the fig tree, and all the trees; when they now shoot forth [not just Israel, but numerous recently budding states from Taiwan to Sri Lanka to Chechnya, to Serbia, Bosnia, El Salvador and Cuba, Poland, Hungary, Czechoslovakia and Afghanistan, to the new Democratic Republic of the Congo (formerly Zaire) and the Republic of South Africa, et cetera, not to mention all the countries of Latin America only within the last couple decades emerging out of repressive dictatorships to American-style democracies], ye see and know of your own selves that summer is now nigh at hand. So likewise ye, when ye see these things come to pass, know ye that the kingdom of God is nigh at hand.—Luke 21:29-31

Providing the answer to the question of "When shall the end come?" has been the major endeavor of this book and its wandering tour through the ancient prophetic records of the Hebrews. Answering that question as straighforwardly as possible with sound, well-laid bases, is the driving motivation that has compelled its writing. Though the perspective contained herein is a very minority-held view these days, it is really nothing new or different than what the ancients have already declared.

All that remains, actually the hardest part of the equation, once we have been convinced of the divine inspiration of the Bible's prophets is to act upon their counsels. The fact that The End is **not quite yet** is not reason to be lulled into complacency, but **opportunity** to **PREPARE**. My deepest hope is that the magnitude of the import of all that I have endeavored to share with you will result in the most fabulous joy a human could ever know. Flee the foolish and LIVE!

15

TEN VIRGINS

Then shall the kingdom of heaven be likened unto ten virgins, which took their lamps, and went forth to meet the bridegroom. And five of them were wise, and five were foolish. They that were foolish took their lamps, and took no oil with them: But the wise took oil in their vessels with their lamps. While the bridegroom tarried, they all slumbered and slept. And at midnight there was a cry made, Behold, the bridegroom cometh; go ye out to meet him. Then all those virgins arose, and trimmed their lamps. And the foolish said unto the wise, Give us of your oil; for our lamps are gone out. But the wise answered, saying, Not so; lest there be not enough for us and you: but go ye rather to them that sell, and buy for yourselves. And while they went to buy, the bridegroom came; and they that were ready went in with him to the marriage: and the door was shut. Afterward came also the other virgins, saying, Lord, Lord, open to us. But he answered and said, Verily I say unto you, I know you not. Watch therefore, for ye know neither the day nor the hour wherein the Son of man cometh.—Matthew 25:1-13

This very intriguing parable of Christ's, using a reference to a polygamous marriage, is part and parcel of the mother text flowing from the preceding chapter (24) of Matthew's Gospel and continuing through to the end of chapter 25. (The original manuscripts provide no chapter breaks or verse numbering, which were added later by the translators.) Hence, the parable is intimately attached to the endtime theme of chapter 24 and concerned with the coming of Messiah. Making this obvious is the last verse in this striking passage, which reads, *"Watch therefore, for ye know neither the day nor the hour wherein the Son of man cometh."*

Couched among at least three other parables, all aimed from different angles at stressing the importance of the state and quality of true readiness, the parable of the ten virgins stands out in its penetrating uniqueness. It illus-

trates a *special angle* on preparation for the advent of the Second Coming—
that of taking nothing for granted.

Five Wise, Five Foolish

Both sets of virgins were well aware the bridegroom was about to arrive.
Both went expectantly forth to meet him. But only one group took the event
seriously enough to fully contemplate the preparations for readiness in holistic fashion. The other group took it for granted that possessing and fulfilling
only certain significant requisites was quite sufficient, thereby actually fool-
ing themselves that they were truly all set to go into the marriage. As virgins,
they too certainly met the eligibility qualifications, and they had taken some
important steps to get set for the event. They did at least take lamps and apparently had enough light to be able to find their way nearly to the threshold
of the marriage chamber.

Lamps in hand, and happy in the moment with the limited view their
shallow little lamps afforded, they shortsightedly assumed a giddy sense of
confidence that all was well. After all, in their typically myopic and negligent
manner, they must've concluded that the bridegroom would *surely* arrive *at
any moment*. What more could they possibly need to do but sit pretty and wait
to be carried away by the Groom in this rapturous event.

Well, the bridegroom tarried, and didn't come as *soon* as they had foolishly *expected*. Meanwhile, as they all waited and finally dozed, the oil in
their lamps was exhausted and their lamps burned out. Then, in the middle of
the night, the shout came announcing the arrival of the groom. At that critical
point, a significant crisis arose. While quickly refueling and trimming their
lamps for the momentous occasion they had so conscientiously prepared for,
the group of wise virgins—who hadn't carelessly abandoned their senses—
found themselves put upon at the last minute by the other witless virgins
who'd neglected to prepare. The foolish virgins, now desperate for oil, rashly
expected their wiser counterparts to furnish them with their own precious oil
that they'd *bought beforehand*. The irresponsible virgins, in keeping with their
typical pattern of taking things for granted and wanting something for nothing, now assumed the wise virgins would be willing to share their oil with
them at this crucial moment.

Well, no such luck. Oil was not only quite a precious commodity and
hard to come by too, but also very essential to the consummation of this joy-

ful event. Realizing this, the wise ones had gone *all out* to *make sure* they were *ready* for this occasion. And they had paid a goodly price to acquire the necessities that would assure them of making the best of one of the finest moments ever. These virgins had not in any way taken their betrothal nonchalantly; no way would they compromise now the joy of the marriage to make up for the inconsiderate laxness of their ill-prepared fellow brides. Rather, the wise prudently admonished the foolish that they had better go back out and buy their own! (A good lesson to beware of "coattails religion" that supposedly confers righteousness and/or holiness upon individuals by means of group membership—such as, ride-on-the-coattails-of-our-denomination churchianity or temple-ism.)

Quite unfortunately for the five hitherto just-a-little-too-cavalier maids, their desperate, last minute scramble to do what they should've already done did not serve them well. Upon return from their hustle to make up for their half-baked disposition and chronic myopia they found themselves *too late* to undo their folly.

The door was shut! They had missed the grand moment of moments, which they had presumed, as virtually guaranteed "shoo-ins," could not possibly happen to them. (You know, like the cocky fundamentalist notion of "eternal salvation—once saved, always saved"; the-Lord-owes-it-to-me kind of attitude.) In its tragic conclusion, the parable closes with these foolish virgins clamoring desperately for tardy admittance, but being refused and repudiated for their derelict and capricious attitude. Instead of being welcomed late at the door with open arms and "Oh, my darlings, I knew that if I waited long enough for you, you wouldn't disappoint me," they were met with doors bolted shut and words that essentially say, *"Miss Who is knocking? Tell them all to go away, they've got the wrong house. I have no idea who they are, or what they could possibly want!"*

Unique Circumstances Demand Unique Responses

The advent of the Great Prince and Messiah of Peace returning to finally reclaim His Earth is no everyday event of just any nondescript era at just "any old time" in history. That is the very point of the "Olivet Discourse" (our pilot passage from Matthew 24 traced throughout this book)—to provide a sure handle on the unique signs that mark the celebrated days of His appearance. Just so that we might have a positive understanding of what to anticipate *and prepare for.* It is a highly unparalleled and supremely special event that merits much more than being complacently satisfied with the mere knowledge that it is imminent and that we qualify as candidates for inclusion (even possibly having *some* "light" to our credit).

The voice of the *Seventh Angel* (the *Last Trumpet)* in this parable of the ten virgins is the voice which cries, *"Behold, the bridegroom cometh; go ye out to meet Him!"* This is the climax voice that crucially juxtaposes the greatest of all joys with the most woeful of all tragedies. Here is where the sheep are divided from the (nearly acceptable) goats, the authentic from the pretenders, those that excel from the merely "acceptable." At this point the pretentious wanna-bes are separated from the earnest devotees, and those who are smugly contented with merely possessing lamps from those who realize talk is cheap and cannot be traded for the real oil that keeps them burning.[1] Those who get out to push will soon be separated from those who are only along for the rapture, I mean, the ride. The Last Trumpet is not an announcement of general amnesty! Quite to the contrary, it is the concluding call to the gathering and "marriage" of the truly prepared *and invested* virgins.

Also evident in the parable of the ten virgins is that readiness was *more* than a matter of mere *awareness of the imminency* of this rapturous event, which they all jointly expected. It was a matter of having some insight into what exactly was to be anticipated, and what to do to be prepared for the most probable of all likelihoods—*a delay.* But, because the foolish virgins based their course of action on anxious presumptions (that they were satisfactorily prepared for the general event by sheer virtue of their qualifying eligibility, even betrothal no less—"Once betrothed, always betrothed," they thought), they committed a serious and tragic miscalculation. Rooted in their recklessly lax and flighty foolishness was a seriously unviable illusion surrounding the marriage—that all they had to do was show up and just let the good times roll, as they say.[2] On the other hand, what characterized the other five virgins as wise was their sensibility and alertness of mind, a more realistic and responsive grasp of what exactly to anticipate, and a mind and motivation to take appropriate measures to prepare.

The alertness of the prudent virgins was evident in their invested style and manner. Their well-contemplated conviction was that whether the groom returned promptly or tarried, they were to be prepared for all contingencies. As opposed to the foolish outlook, an early arrival was neither their bet nor their persuasion, nor were they deluded by any unfounded hopes of that capricious sort. Rather, they wisely invested in their promised hope, as eligible virgins, by thoroughly committing themselves to absolutely assuring the uncompromised consummation of their selection (by betrothal). Their supremely sensible strategy of single-mindedly preparing for the eventual fullness of their marital bliss set them worlds apart from their "airheaded" counterparts.

To spell out the meaning of the parable, so as to avert any equivocation of its practical application, the wise go well beyond reading their Bible and preaching its promised salvation (i.e., lighting and bearing their lamps); they *sell out* wholly to become fully invested in the Promise contained therein.[3]

Oil—Key to Readiness

Not knowing with exactness when the Kingdom of God might come is precisely the reason why *alertness* was so strongly stressed by Christ Yeshua in this parable to His disciples (as well as in numerous other instances) as a central key to preparation. The essence of the matter is not in the timing, nor in exactly when the return of The Bridegroom should be. Instead, it is in the vigilance of *ever-readiness* and in the devotion to the anticipation of that return. Watchfulness, as so repeatedly emphasized by Messiah, is always a matter of *undivided dedication to the commission* He mandated for His servants and followers.

Preparedness was enjoined from every angle: (a) Beware not to fall asleep on the job simply because delay stretches out the anticipation (Matthew 24:42-51 & Mark 13:32-37); (b) take caution not to redefine the commissioned task for sake of convenience (Matthew 25:14-30); (c) look out for getting lured into the cares of this life, eating and drinking with the drunken (Luke 21:34-35); and (d) definitely don't take anything for granted, particularly that you have done enough to be ready (Matthew 25:1-13, our current parable under review).

According to the following passage, alertness is substantially more than just watching the sky for signs of the Rapture while indulgently carrying on in "Babylon":

Fear not, little flock; for it is your Father's good pleasure to give you the kingdom [the "community property" inheritance of the virgins]. *Sell that ye have, and give alms* [the virgins' oil-acquisition strategy & investment "portfolio"]; *provide yourselves bags* [for stashing valuables] *which wax not old, a treasure in the heavens that faileth not* [like Wall Street will!], *where no thief approacheth, neither moth corrupteth* [totally secure financial strategy of Christ]. *For where your treasure is, there will your heart be also. Let your loins be girded about* [never abandoned to relaxation and leisure], *and your lights burning* [well supplied with "oil" for unfaltering illumination]; *and ye yourselves like unto men that wait for their lord, when he will return from the wedding; that when he cometh and knocketh, they may open unto him immediately* [expectantly & attentively on duty]. *Blessed are those servants* [and "virgins" alike], *whom the lord when he cometh shall find watching: verily I say unto you, that he shall gird himself, and make them to sit down to meat, and will come forth and serve them* [special honors to the diligently prepared]. *And if he shall come in the second watch, or come in the third watch* [suggesting that he will likely return later than earlier], *and find them so, blessed are those servants.—Luke 12:32-38*

We see in this passage from Luke, that readiness is not just a condition of ever-constant expectation and alertness, without regard for a particular day or time; instead, the general era of the wedding period entails a heightened sense of alertness.

The core message—the heart and soul of this book—is precisely in this: the end *is not yet!* Though the era is indeed upon us and the marriage set, the wedding is not concluded and the groom is not yet due. Moreover, let us not be fooled meanwhile into thinking that we are so completely ready for the "marriage" simply because we regard ourselves a betrothed virgin and carry a shallow little lamp around, believing the Messiah could show up for us at any minute. We need to complete our preparations, with no silly, simplistic assumptions that the groom will show up *early* in the *first watch*.

It is imperative that we ask ourselves, "What hinders us from going *all the way, all out,* if we *really believe* these are the last days and the royal Groom is truly coming in *this* generation?" There is, literally, no time to play "Christian" and put on an act. It behooves us, rather, to put presumptions aside and refresh ourselves from the dictionary on the meaning of the term "hypocrite." No longer can we risk being satisfied with *acting* like a Bible-believer, or appearing as a Christian (esp. in our own eyes); but now, more than ever, it is crucial that we *be the disciples defined in the Bible.* Being only complacently semi-prepared with shallow lamps, and no adequate substance to fuel them, is tantamount to not being prepared at all—according to Christ, that is.

Talking the talk (bearing shallow lamps, with only *limited commitments* of oil) is a far cry from walking the walk (forgive the cliché). It's time to strip our Bibles of their heirloom-edition, fine leather covers—imitation leatherette too—and bind them in good ole authentic, well-worn *shoe leather!* The time is far spent for us to have bound up those Bibles in leather *that walks*, so non-believers can **see** something to believe in! They don't need to hear more illusory rap about the Rapture and the call up to the "marriage," they need to learn about the Kingdom agenda, and what it takes to effectively participate in this marriage. The trumpet and alarm of this volume of mine is, "*Enough talk* about cheap grace, with no price to pay, and no serious preparations to make."

To borrow from the astute insights of Caribbean-based Myles Monroe, the liberal evangelical preachers of "born-again-ism" would do well to reread their New Testaments and take account of how many instances they can find of Christ broadcasting the notion of being "born again" during the three-and-one-half years He so purposefully carried out His mission. (Search it out for yourself.) On the other hand, a comparative count of how many times He is recorded as having proclaimed and taught about *the Kingdom of God* would reveal a gross and very conspicuous imbalance between what you hear from the "evangelicals" as opposed to what Christ's overwhelming emphasis was.

Those who know their Bibles well already have the answer: Only **once**, in the stealth of the night, to a Pharisee so infamous for his secret, under-cover visit with Yeshua that *every instance* of his mention in the Bible is qualified with "he which came to Jesus by night."

My point is not intended to deny the meaningfulness of a valid concept; not in any way. However, had the principle of being born again been so "high-level," why did *not* Messiah himself make it a point to popularize it and spread it abroad in *all* of His broad-daylight teachings to his multitudinous audiences, as He most certainly did with the voluminous declarations on the Kingdom? Nowhere either did He definitively teach that a person should "ask Jesus into their heart as their personal Lord and Savior." Again, there are no persnickety qualms on my part about this overly simplistic notion, which should—in all good faith—lead to a *repentance and conversion* from mentorship by the Prince of Evil to learning submission to Righteousness. But just as the five foolish virgins were sorely short on insight, so is this myopic brand of "gospel" woefully lacking in depth of perspective and substance!

But on the extreme opposite end of the spectrum indeed, Yeshua very graphically taught that *"except ye eat the flesh of the Son of man, and drink his blood, ye have no life in you" (John 6:53-56)*—a far cry from the unsavory staleness of today's miserably bland and banal Christian TV dinners. No wonder they are delusional about Pre-tribulation Rapture; malnutrition of spirit has induced hallucination and sapped their strength and will to live up to the radical Messianic pattern and tradition of martyrdom. Christian junk food (cheap-grace style) has infiltrated and permeated nearly the entire culture of modern Christendom. (God be thanked that a remnant of profound believers has been preserved.)

The discount-Christianity evangelicals stress how easy it is to get your hands on a "born-again-style" lamp that hardly costs you a thing ('cuz Jezuz aw'ready paid the pryce on Calv'ry); but as rare as Mother Teresas are is how often they are ever heard to teach what it really means to stock up on that expensive oil that makes those lamps burn!

Getting our hands on a lamp (even a lighted one) is just not sufficient. Those little Middle-Eastern clay lamps in the parable Christ told are cheap and easy to come by. Any serious disciple knows that simply laying hold of one of those rather common commodities, figuratively speaking, does not constitute the substance of the true Gospel, nor the Testimony of Jesus Christ. Instead, Messiah's unequivocal witness is that those who suffer the loss of all worldly things for His name's sake will be among those counted worthy of the marriage. It is they who will be honored with the ensuing co-inheritance in all the Bridegroom's grand, eternal Estate (having *"provided [themselves] bags which wax not old, a treasure in the heavens,"* as quoted above). True believers, who are genuinely convinced of the fabulous reality of this notion, do not hesitate to go and sell all that they have to buy the oil they will need to fully insure the undeterred celebration of their marriage. It is with unreserved totality and complete abandon of all other earthly concerns that they do so.

On the other hand, failing to insure well-prepared participation in that event is a categorical act of contempt for the Gospel and Testimony of the Groom. This we rightly gather from the "welcome" the foolish virgins got at the groom's door upon returning from vainly attempting to remedy their folly. It was just too late to revise their cocky foolishness.

Those of us who at least regard ourselves as eligible virgins surely should be prompted by this parable to examine ourselves for which of the two categories we fall into. Unfortunately, it is probably not an unreasonable stretch to state that at least half of all the perfectly eligible virgins will fail to qualify for final entry to the marriage supper of the Lamb;[4] and only afterward will they belatedly awaken to the hard realities—beyond the point of any remedy!

Christi-any-way-you-want-it

Lackadaisical, lukewarm and too late—summarily characterizes the lamentable attitude and style evident in the demeanor of the consummately foolish virgins of our parable. Their lukewarmness so disgusted the groom that they were resolutely denied entrance to the marriage chambers at the last. Not only so, but they were further denied even the slightest recognition of *ever* having been betrothed candidates for the marriage. Deemed unworthy of *any* acknowledgment whatsoever, their silly illusions were brutally dashed! They had presumed their betrothal to be practically a matter of warranty and had *neglected to exercise earnest intent* to fully guarantee that hopeful status.

Now, scrambling madly to catch Rapture Airlines flight 777 at the last minute, they discovered the boarding gate closed, the plane on the runway and their tickets void. Their names had been deleted from the reservation roster, and no way would the flight be delayed or the plane recalled to board this bunch of slouchy slackers. (Please pardon my mixing of metaphors again, but the Rapturists relate much more readily to flying away, than to being included in a multiple sex partner marriage.)

The shallow lamps of the five lagging ladies served to get them tentatively to the door of delight. But their careless failure to convert their assets—in timely fashion—into a provision of oil left these half-hearts holding flickering, useless lamps, which now only illuminated their tragedy as overconfident, unprepared castaways completely unwelcomed at their tardy attempt to make up for what they should have already done.

I suppose that many of us might be inclined to view such harsh fate as *excessively austere* in this case of what otherwise might seem to be nothing more than a simple mistake on the part of these hapless virgins. But, in all fairness, it seems *that* assessment would really depend on whose shoes we might choose to try on.—Those of the obviously unappreciative, half-hearted virgins?—or the shoes of the Groom they foolishly took for granted? Perhaps donning the shoes of the unpresumptuous and prudent virgins who shirked no sacrifice to thoroughly prepare for their "honeymoon" would yield a sufficiently judicious outlook.

Most unfortunately, it is the shoes and sentiments of the *Groom* that are so rarely ever tried on, or even considered. In fact, it is with callous and contemptuous insensitivity that His viewpoint is most often thoroughly disregarded. Without a doubt though, the most enlightened perspective is only achievable from that standpoint.

The Biblical portrait of the Groom is one of a loyal, long-suffering, and supremely loving person, compelled to sacrifice His own blood and very life to make full accommodations for the overflowing joy of the virgins to whom He is betrothed. No other priority carried more weight in the life of the Groom than to call together and prepare His betrothed. His undistracted, unwavering, all-consuming passion to that end left no room in His life for the pursuit of other personal pleasures or mundane self-gratification. Absolutely no glory, no grand importance, nor eminent value at all did He attach to the material life of this "divorced" world.[5] Unfalteringly, it was always the future enduring Estate of His Father that He raved about and sought to call and prepare His virgins for. It was that promise of joy and preparation for the bliss of that marriage that took precedence in every single facet of His singularly dedicated life.

Considering the supreme sacrifice(s) made by Messiah to demonstrate His devotion to this hope, both to His Father and His Bride, a half-hearted response on the part of His beloved virgins is, frankly, utterly unbecoming and thankless. The degree of care taken on the part of the virgins—or carelessness, as the case may be—to prepare for the marriage is a manifest token of their own level of appreciation for His loyal zeal and affection. It is obvious the foolish virgins could hardly have cared less about joining their Groom. As we noted before, they plainly took far too much for granted. Their meager preparations were as shallow as their lamps, which, in the end, were only sufficient to illuminate the shallow, superficial attitude of faith, love and appreciation that they personified in the parable.

As suggested a few paragraphs earlier, *not* to reciprocate in some mutual fashion—though perhaps not perfectly, since none of us can—is, in the light of a sensitive and factual perspective, nothing short of despite and disdain for the love, word, and wedding covenant of the Groom. The fact is, Messiah gave His life (and also sacrificed just and rightful recognition of His true person, His fully-entitled status as the King of Earth) to testify to another (future) life and a transcendent world of promise. A future realm that shrivels the glory of this present world to a decrepit, sin-ridden existence of disease, covetousness, egotism, lies, theft, murder, violence, war, avarice, inordinate affection, perversion, incontinence, fornication, adultery, injury, abuse, mercilessness, maliciousness, injustice, rank adultism, societal insanity, pervasive neuroses, rampant psychopathy, and every other manner of pandemic ungodly human pathology. To cling, even "inadvertently," to any of this, or to the worldly environment and spirit of Evil that nurtures it, is in itself pathological, *and* moreover redefines us as the *enemies* of God Himself!

Modern, apostate Christians *and* Jews have *revised* the religion of their devout forefathers, to accommodate a new and all-too-widely-accepted *double* standard. One, which in effect, serves nothing more than to *nullify the sacred standard* establish by Christ in His core doctrinal dissertation upon the Mount of Olives (the "Sermon on the Mount"), as well as that set out by Moses in the Torah, between which there is no difference.[7] This is precisely what uncommitted hearts and minds seek to arrive at—a means by which to eliminate the stringency of Biblical demands and the conflict of interests that arises while striving to have the best of both worlds. As a bonus, their revisionism helps to resolve the great difficulty they seem to have in deciding whether or not to *believe* the Bridegroom's extravagant promises about His future estate of inheritance, which they would then have to *act* on. Their double-duty revisions are apparently intended to create a more "pragmatic" approach to the prime Bible mandate of *"No other gods before YHWH.* According to the dictates of their earthly wisdom, the prudent religious approach seems to be, "A little idolatry here and there can't hurt; and we'd better get in *some* while we can, in case this Love-thy-God-with-all-thy-might notion doesn't pan out."

"For," in the words of Apostle Paul, *"here have we no continuing city* [no worthwhile patrimony or citizenship], *but we seek one to come." (Hebrews 13:14)* Those who, instead, love this present world, thereby express and demonstrate a loathing for the promised realm of Messiah and the privilege of citizenship therein (by marriage). This principle is so in the very same way that the unbelieving children of Israel in the wilderness with Moses *"despised the pleasant land"* and *"in their hearts turned back again into Egypt."*[8] In explicitly unflattering terms, the apostle James put it very succinctly: *"Ye adulterers and adulteresses, know ye not that the friendship of the world is enmity with God? whosoever therefore will be a friend of the world is the enemy of God. . . .Draw nigh to God, and he will draw nigh to you. Cleanse*

your hands, ye sinners; and purify your hearts, ye double minded." (James 4:4 & 8)

After all, what if that future world of the Kingdom is not as great as He claimed it to be (you know, so ecclesiastically "sterile" that it has no appeal)? Or, what if Christ's resurrection is only a myth, invented and perpetuated by wishful-thinking disciples who had nothing better to live for than to compulsively advance a certain selected noble cause they chose to embrace, much as the Chinese martyrs for democracy in Tienemen Square?

Their thinking seems to be, "Well, at least we will have made the most of the present material existence, and we won't have lost out on the gratification and cheap thrills this world has to offer, however short-lived they may be. And besides, how practical is it that we should *'take no thought for our lives'* and refrain from preoccupation about, *'What shall we eat? or, What shall we drink? or, What clothing and shelter shall be provided us?' (Matthew 6:25 & 31)* How can we literally be expected not to *'take thought for the morrow' (Matt.6:34),* and hence neglect to prepare for the future with good educations, secured jobs, investments, and retirement plans? Everybody knows it's practically impossible and simply not pragmatic in today's world to *'hate mammon, seek first the kingdom of God, and not serve two masters.' (Matt.6:24 & 33)* Anyway, wasn't that sermon really meant for the original disciples back in primitive times?"

All too commonly these days, modern "believers" affirm, "This the 20th century!—these are the '90s! Times have changed, we have to keep in step and adjust our faith, our gospel, and our interpretations to keep them viable within the trends and demands of modern society. It doesn't make us divided in our devotion, or double minded, or heretical, or apostate to pursue a decent standard of living in this world. We can't always be giving everything away, or working only for the kingdom of God. What would we do, and where would we go, if we sold all our goods to give to the poor? Everybody can't be a missionary. And anyway, didn't Jesus pray that we should not be taken out of the world, but only kept from the evil? Don't you think we do our part by going to church, reading our Bibles, and living morally clean lives? You have to be careful not to misapply all that out-dated, radical Gospel stuff to our days. Haven't you heard that we are under a different 'dispensation'?"[9]

Well, exaggerated as they all may sound, rationalizings and excuses of this very nature are as prolific in contemporary Christendom as poesies among laureates. Verses are snatched out of context and skillfully parroted to justify pitiful reasonings for not following in the footsteps of the biblical Christ, who is most often only superficially or professedly revered.

For, to return to the passage from John, chapter 17, a select portion of which was referenced (and misused) above, the Messiah was actually reiterating a recurrent and standard theme, spelled out often to His dedicated disciples. Namely, that those who follow wholly committed in His footsteps will most certainly not, just as He didn't, enjoy a gratifying relationship with the established order in their obliged sojourn through this cursed world. What factor, according to this often misused passage (quoted below), shatters any viability of effectively serving two masters, two different agendas, or more than one kingdom?—The uncompromising (and undispensationalized) truth, the Word of God, which Christ entrusted and commissioned to His faithful followers. In full context, John's more complete record of the Lord's prayer in this passage reads:

I have given [my disciples] THY word; and the world hath hated them, because they are not of the world, even as I am not of the world. I pray not that THOU shouldest take them out of the world, but that THOU shouldest keep them from the evil. They are not of the world, even as I am not of the world. Sanctify them through THY truth: THY word is truth. As THOU hast sent me into the world, even so have I also sent them into the world.—John 17:14-18

Again, we have touched upon the dread of so many nominal converts to this radical faith, and begin to understand *why* all the rationalizing and "dispensational" dispensing of the foundational fundamentals of Christ's teachings.

Popularly considered impractical, inconvenient, and clearly incompatible with the contemporary lifestyle agenda of modern-day, so-called fundamentalist Bible-believers, this "unthinkable" Faith of following in *those* one-track Footsteps has gotten conveniently shape-shifted by the dispensationalists. By very sophisticated, yet entirely lame reasoning it's been revised and reshaped into a compromised religion of *one foot in Babylon and the other in the kingdom of God.* Apparently, this comprises the "new and improved," and much less exacting, dispensationalist fundamentalism we hear so much about. Perhaps "Christi-any-way-you-want-it" best denominates this new dual-devotion religion of convenient compromise between the two *mutually exclusive opposites*!

Whereas, venturing back almost as far as you can go (Genesis chapter

12), we learn that the founding father of the original faith became the beloved friend of God by a single-minded zeal to marry himself unconditionally to the sole worship of YHWH; and in the process, *forsook Babylon* for the Promise of God in compliance with His wishes. Paul testifies to this in his exhortation to the New Testament Hebrew Christians of the 1st century:

By faith Abraham, when he was called to go out into a place which he should after receive for an inheritance, obeyed; and he went out, not knowing whither he went. By faith he sojourned in the land of promise, as in a strange country, dwelling in tabernacles [tents] with Isaac and Jacob, the heirs with him of the same promise: For he looked for a city which hath foundations, whose builder and maker is God.—Hebrews 11:8-10

By simply looking around at this century's religious landscape, it is readily obvious that Abraham's devout pattern of faith is now regarded much like a *committed marriage* in today's western world—as a practically abandoned vestige of the past. The overwhelming majority of so-called children of Abraham (Christians included of course) today completely defy the patriarchal pattern and deny the original faith, by their inimical love affair with "BABYLON." Their particular friendship, faith, and zeal—manifest in their routine daily pursuits—is rooted in the pagan materialism of that metaphorical city-system, after which they have gone a whoring. Yet, at the very same time, they double-speakingly espouse a pretense of devotion to that famous promise of a future city and kingdom of divine design and origin, as well as to its Maker and Builder. You won't find many "children of Abraham" with the real faith or courage to "dwell in tents," so to speak, and to forsake their Babylonian materialism. To be trite, the majority of them want to eat their cake, and have it still.

Messiah, on the other hand, declared that absolutely no friendship could be successfully established between Himself and the established order; nor could His true friends and followers even remotely expect any such friendship with it. Addressing His unbelieving family members (siblings), He defined the relationship between the world and Himself with these words: *"The world cannot hate you; but me it hateth, because I testify of it, that the works thereof are evil."* (John 7:7) Exhorting His disciples in this same regard, He said, *"If the world hate you, ye know that it hated me before it hated you. If ye were of the world, the world would love his own: but because ye are not of the world, but I have chosen you out of the world, therefore the world hateth you." (John 15:18-19)* This testimony strongly counters the modern popular notion that a symbiosis or a mutually inclusive compatibility can be struck between the interests and values of the Babylonish world order and the kingdom of GOD.

At the risk of being dismissed for nagging, or rebuffed for hammering at these centrally fundamental principles of biblical doctrine, I cannot but insist that it is expressly (and inherently) unacceptable to make any attempt *explain away* the teachings of the martyred Messiah and His devout following of martyrs, who all sacrificed their lives to uphold a clear-cut, uncompromised testimony. Messiah's word and testimony must either be accepted as it is recorded, or flatly discarded as flawed or unbelievable.

Canceling all double-mindedness, and betting ones life on the testimony of Christ, is the only practical way to prepare for the marriage (or contrariwise, even to get the most out of Babylon!). Rationalizing a devotion to mammon will be the tragedy of all eternity—for the foolish among virgins—when the celebrated but tenuous dream of earthly life is suddenly shattered by the wake-up call of the Groom.

And though this author vehemently insists that the days of the last generation are presently ticking down to their final hours, and that the return of the Groom is visibly on the horizon, still the admonition remains constant— *"the end is not yet."* None of us had better sleep until we have secured our store of "oil"; unless we intend to try to "bum" some from our wiser counterparts when the alarm goes off, or to try to bail out of our folly at the very last moment when the Rapture has obviously not spared us.

But maybe we're all wrong, you say. Maybe our interpretations and understandings are erroneous. Look at all the doomsday prophets who have been wrong in the past! What if there yet remain 20 years, or 50, or more. What course do we take in that case? How do we live and function in the world?

Well, suppose this author's hypothesis may be in error; or, that it were even possible that the imminency doctrinaires (discussed in Chapters 1 & 2) were not mistaken and Messiah could contravene His own testimony to come at any moment. *Regardless* of the case, the original call of Christ remains unadulterated still (as well as immutably unalterable)[10]—except, of course, in the shallow-lamp interpretation of the denying dispensationalists. They refuse to accept that Messiah's call to The Kingdom really means our life in this world is not to be savored or preserved, but rather hated and renounced.[11]

Those questions about the course true believers should take are clearly answered in the teachings of the One they name as their "personal" Savior and Lord. The call is unmistakable, the course clearly mapped, the footsteps traced unmistakably in martyr's blood, and the shoes—well, they've been dispensed with into the attic or the basement of the neo-fundamentalists and very rarely does anyone dare wear them or even try them on.[12]

The Marturéo Complex

So, as it stands, many, many "virgins" possess these metaphorical "lamps" from the parable we have just analyzed. Most of them expect to be raptured into the "marriage," and also realize the "bridegroom" is soon to come. But, though many might even know who He is, few truly know Him; for if they did, they would presently jettison BABYLON like so much trash, and trade all its wealth to acquire the oil they need for a befitting consummation of the union they expect to see.[13]

Millions know this groom by the name Jesus. The people of his own (flesh) ancestry know Him as Yeshua. Many altogether deny that He could even be the promised Messiah. All men, however, that do truly come to know Him know Him as Love, Truth, Justice, Mercy, Peace, Faith, Faithfulness and Freedom. His testimony was faithfully recorded by His own consummately devoted apostles and preserved in the pages of the Bible. Those who really believe His testimony do not hesitate (unlike the unwilling rich young ruler)[14] to trade in every scrap of worldly worth to then follow in the footsteps of the Son of God:

The One who knew no certain dwelling place, nor where He might next lay His head; born in an animal stall, laid in a feed trough, nurtured in humble simplicity, dependent as the birds on the Hand of God to feed and clothe Him; tirelessly healing, comforting, gathering, defending, teaching, preaching, redeeming, advocating the qualities of an unseen kingdom; and most of all, setting an example (to the death), of a *whole-hearted,* undivided devotion to the Holy, Loving, and Long-suffering Sovereign of this Kingdom of Love, as well as to the precious human subjects of His Love.

This book is not written to supplant the incomparable testimony of Yeshua Ha'Mashiach, or to pretend to have other, or better advice about what actions you, the reader, ought to take to prepare for the incontrovertible fact that He must shortly appear. It is written to shake your beliefs to their foundations, to shatter illusions and cast down any falsehoods or vain imaginations; and to spur and implore you to reread the Holy Bible with a passion to get it right, because it's a matter of *more* than simple life or death. No trivial risk or gamble whatsoever is implicated here. It's a fearsome matter of taking the Mark of the "New" World Order (already well under final stages of construction), and of unending damnation as a result! Consider carefully: By the time you get desperate enough to sell out and believe the Gospel, you may have already taken the mark of your true devotion—in your forehead! Be not a fool among eligible virgins, gambling on being able to bum off the virgins who did sell out to prepare themselves, or to ride on their coattails.

The Rapture is not our salvation! Obedient faith in the gospel of Christ is. Without any question whatsoever, that always means trial and tribulation first, consistent with the biblical principle of suffering, sacrifice, cost and price to pay, which is iterated time and time again throughout the Scriptures, beginning with Genesis 3:15-17, through Revelation 7:14-17. Christ's gospel is a gospel of tribulations, affliction, persecution, paying your way,[15] and patient enduring through it all, for the sake of the Promise. As they say, "no pain, no gain,"—no crown without a cross.

As documented in the pages of this book, it is readily apparent (and even more so in the very pages of the Bible itself) that tribulation is an expected, accepted, and predicted experience that almost every single recorded prophet and apostle of the Holy Scriptures acknowledged and spoke of, except perhaps Jude (for one). In light of all that testimony, let whosoever wishes foolishly indulge in playing the instant-win, double-your-odds gamble, if they must. As for me and my house, we neither trust nor bid blessings upon those treacherous tempters who teach compromise with Babylonish mammonism, or rapturous religions of preemptive escape from tribulation, demanding nothing but extended dependency on their easy-chair TV fan clubs. This they do while simultaneously blessing spiritual lasciviousness and delicious living with the Great Whore of Revelation 17 & 18 (extensively referenced in Chapter 4 of this book, and particularly characterized, incidentally, as staunchly affirming that *no suffering is due* her—Rev.18:7).

Jude did, however, provide this perfectly pertinent passage of scripture to add to this commentary:

Beloved, when I gave all diligence to write unto you of the common salvation [general and one-for-all], *it was needful for me to write unto you, and exhort you that ye should earnestly contend for the* [original] *faith which was once delivered unto the saints. For there are certain men crept in unawares* [in sheep's clothing], *who were before of old ordained to this condemnation, ungodly men, turning the grace of our God into lasciviousness* [license for whorish Babylonish indulgence], *and denying the only Lord God, and our Lord Jesus Christ. . . .*

Woe unto them! for they have gone in the way of Cain [egotistically-oriented sacrifices], *and ran greedily after the error of Balaam* [prophesying, or even evangelizing] *for reward, and perished in the gainsaying of Core* [Korah & company of Numbers 16—exalting themselves to anointed status, assembling separate congregations of their own in defiance of God's specific will]. . . .

These are murmurers, complainers [against God's way of tribulation, affliction, and crucifixion of self], *walking after their own lusts* [self-gratifying, self-aggrandizing pursuits]; *and their mouth speaketh great swelling words* [of anointing of the Spirit, or prophecy expertise, promise of prosperity, special election for rapture, etc.], *having men's persons in admiration* [billing great evangelist, pastor, & prophecy expert "So-and-so"] *because of advantage* [power, prestige, and money—"just send in your $200 dollar gift for the whole must-have set of prophecy tapes, and bless this ministry," etc.]...

But, beloved, remember ye the words which were spoken before of the apostles of our Lord Jesus Christ; how that they told you there should be mockers in the last time [making a scoffing mockery of the Gospel—evangelical television is replete with examples], *who should walk after their own ungodly lusts. These be they who* [ironically] *separate themselves* [as elite and chosen moral high-grounders], *sensual* [actually see-touch-feel materialists & prosperity prophets], *having not the Spirit* [though with great swelling words they claim to].—*Jude 1:3-4, 11, 16-19*

This voice (of mine) is raised to vehemently urge you to forget every shred of propaganda, or potential and likely propaganda, that may have reached your ears from the mouths of men who did not actually (and indeed do not now, despite what they claim) walk with Christ. *"For,"* in the words of the Apostle Paul, *"many walk* [endless assortment of impostors], *of whom I have told you often, and now tell you even weeping, that they are the enemies of the cross of Christ: Whose end is destruction, whose God is their belly* [self-centered core lusts that constitute their cloaked agendas and true objects of worship], *and whose glory* [grandiosity] *is in their shame* [hypocritical pretense], *who mind earthly things* [like more and more money and material gratification]. " *(Philippians 3:18-19)*

For serious-minded believers, so-called Christian financial strategies should be viewed with intense skepticism, in my opinion. Most often, you will note, they are attempts to sanction—on God's behalf, using cleverly crafted patchwork quilts of selected scriptures—the preservation of earthly wealth. They are attempts to validate a view that minding earthly things is such a perfectly Christian preoccupation, or even a sanctioned vocation as God's steward, and that those extremists who advocate forsaking all such values are obsessed with a *martyr complex.* Interesting, isn't it, that the word "martyr," from the Greek *martus,* or *martur,* denotes a *witness* giving testimony to his view particularly by his/her death. Equally of note—though perhaps not of "interest" (by many who cloak themselves in stewardship doctrines for the sake of interest)[16]—is the straight doctrine of Christ, as recorded by Luke, related to death:

And he said to them all, If any man will come after me, let him deny himself, and take up his cross daily, and follow me. For whosoever will save his life shall lose it: but whosoever will lose his life for my sake, the same shall save it. For what is a man advantaged, if he gain the whole world, and lose himself, or be cast away?—Luke 9:23-25

So much for preserving earthly wealth! Indeed, Messiah considered denying those very values that gratify the flesh a part of our obligatory death, on an everyday basis—that is, if we sincerely imagine to faithfully follow Him. In so doing, we become daily martyrs, obsessed with losing our lives for the sake of Christ's testimony; and thus, obtain a far more excellent life and wealth in the world to come.

For those wealthy believers, and good stewards of the gifts of God, Paul wrote a healthy word of admonition to the famed disciple Timothy: *"Charge them that are rich in this world, that they be not highminded, nor trust in uncertain riches, but in the living God, who giveth us richly all things to enjoy; that they do good, that they be rich in good works, ready to distribute, willing to communicate* [from Gk. *"koinonikos,"* more closely denotes "liberally share with fellows"]; *laying up in store for themselves a good foundation against the time to come, that they may lay hold on eternal life." (1 Timothy 6:17-19)* With respect to Christian financial strategies, none other is more well-articulated, or strictly based upon the teachings of Christ than this very one from the eminently devout Apostle Paul; nor is there, according that same disciple, any other more sound investment to be made toward readiness for the time to come. If there were, both he and Jesus, not to mention the other apostles, would have certainly declared it.

And for those who dispute the veracity of this teaching, Timothy was further exhorted by Paul, *"If any man teach otherwise, and consent not to wholesome words, even the words of our Lord Jesus Christ, and to the doctrine which is according to godliness; he is proud, knowing nothing, but doting about questions and strifes of words, whereof cometh envy, strife, railings, evil surmisings, perverse disputings of men of corrupt minds, and destitute of the truth, supposing that gain is godliness: from such withdraw thyself. But godliness with contentment is great gain. For we brought nothing into this world, and it is certain we can carry nothing out. And having food and raiment let us be therewith content. But they that will be rich fall into temptation and a snare, and into many foolish and hurtful lusts, which drown men in destruction and perdition. For the love of money is the root of all evil: which while some coveted after, they have erred from the faith, and pierced themselves through with many sorrows."*—*1 Timothy 6:3-10*

The parable of the ten virgins is clear to me. I know what I must do to prepare. Everyone else will have to draw their own conclusions based on the information that reaches them. I have liberally shared my view as truly and faithfully as I have been able in this book, trusting it might be of service to you. Three years of my life have I "sacrificed" to compile and publish this writing; and likewise many other years previous to live by the exhortation on personal contentment with mere food and clothing, in order to travel about proclaiming and "communicating" this testimony. I am sharing my oil with you now; but lest there be not enough for me and thee in the days to come, I urge you to go now and sell all that you have, and purchase for yourself a worthy supply.

After all, it didn't seem that the foolish virgins lacked the resources or the wherewithal to buy the oil they needed, but merely that they were reticent about giving it up—until it became absolutely unavoidable to do so. I supposed they felt that the wealthy Groom, so well known for His generosity and grace, would be so overtaken with their virgin purity and desirability that He would be falling all over Himself to mollycoddle them at every turn.

There was no need to relinquish the enjoyment of their assets or to go out of the way at all to make their own preparations for something that would just be "taken care of" like all the rest. That, they presumed, is what should be expected from this Groom who was reputed for a characteristic inclination to indulge his maids with liberal, incessant gifts of grace. It seems, in fact, that they had been hoarding their assets with this thought in mind, imposing upon the Groom to live up to their idealized, albeit lopsided, image of Him and just keep doling out the gifts and goodies at absolutely no cost or trouble to them. (Free grace, I believe they call it—something we just cannot merit or earn.) And so, of course, they clung to their personal possessions until the very last, when it finally became obvious their strategy was wrong—and until it was *too late* to remedy their false notions about the Groom or to correct their foolish egotistical course.

More inanely yet, they had the unadulterated audacity to further impose upon their fellow virgins this time for a free ride into the party. Now they expected that their wiser comrades should allow them to squeeze into their prepaid honeymoon limo chartered with their own outlay of hard-earned cash.

"No way, cheapskates!" was their response. "You want free grace, free forgiveness, free salvation, free rides, and to be free from suffering and sacrifice. Well, sorry, but now pay your own way, you bunch of freeloaders! Don't try to ride in on the coattails of the martyrs! Get out and carry your own crosses for a change!"

In conclusion let me offer the Bible's primary and perennial wisdom: Love the Groom with **all** your heart, **all** your soul, **all** your mind, and **all** your strength, no matter what it costs. If so, you'll never be left banging desperately on the closed door after the fact saying, "It's us, your brides, remember?" Then only to hear the dreaded reply, "I have no idea who you are—go away!" The End is not yet; there's still a chance to purchase your "oil." Jettison the foolish freeloader mentality of the Rapturist and Dispensationalist "virgins" and stash up on some oil with the Tribulationists (truly great company, I assure you). In my view you will be all the wiser for it.

I hope I've been a blessing to you. The rest of the road, until the 7th Trumpet, will be very difficult; so if I've helped to get you prepared, I could not be happier! May the Lamb be with you unto . . .

the End.

NOTES

Chapter 1—So Many Voices

[1]**cleanse the land of Earth's defilers**

Isaiah 24:1-6 Behold, the LORD maketh the earth empty, and maketh it waste, and **turneth** it upside down, and scattereth abroad the inhabitants thereof. . . . The land shall be utterly emptied, and utterly spoiled: for the LORD hath spoken this word. The earth mourneth and fadeth away, the world languisheth and fadeth away, the haughty people of the earth do languish. *The earth also is defiled under the inhabitants thereof; because they have transgressed the laws, changed the ordinance, broken the everlasting covenant.* Therefore hath the curse devoured the earth, and they that dwell therein are desolate: therefore the inhabitants of the earth are burned, and few men left.

Revelation 11:18 And the nations were angry, and thy wrath is come, and the time of the dead, that they should be judged, and that thou shouldest give reward unto thy servants the prophets, and to the saints, and them that fear thy name, small and great; and shouldest *destroy them which destroy the earth.*

[2]**learn war no more**

Isaiah 2:4 And he shall judge among the nations, and shall rebuke many people: and they shall beat their swords into plowshares, and their spears into pruninghooks: nation shall not lift up sword against nation, neither shall they learn war any more.

Ezekiel 39:9-12 And they that dwell in the cities of Israel shall go forth, and shall set on fire and burn the weapons, both the shields and the bucklers, the bows and the arrows, and the handstaves, and the spears, and they shall burn them with fire seven years. . . . And seven months shall the house of Israel be burying [armies], that they may cleanse the land.

[3]**New Order of Messiah**

Micah 4:1-2 But in the last days it shall come to pass, that the mountain [symbolic of kingdom] of the house of the LORD shall be established in the top of the mountains, and it shall be exalted above the hills; and people shall flow unto it. And many nations shall come, and say, Come, and let us go up to the mountain of the LORD, and to the house of the God of Jacob; and he will teach us of his ways, and we will walk in his paths: for the law shall go forth of Zion, and the word of the LORD from Jerusalem.

Daniel 2:44 And in the days of [the last 10] kings shall the God of heaven set up a kingdom, which shall never be destroyed: and the kingdom shall not be left to other people, but it shall break in pieces and consume all these kingdoms, and it shall stand for ever.

Psalm 96:10-13 Say among the heathen that *the LORD reigneth*: the world also shall be established that it shall not be moved: he shall judge the people righteously. Let the heavens rejoice, and let the earth be glad; let the sea roar, and the fullness thereof. Let the field be joyful, and all that is therein: then shall all the trees of the wood rejoice before the LORD: *for he cometh*, for he cometh to judge the earth: *he shall judge the world with righteousness*, and the people with his truth.

Revelation 12:5 And [Israel] brought forth a man child, who was to rule all nations with a rod of iron: and her child was caught up unto God, and to his throne.

Revelation 19:13-16 And he was clothed with a vesture dipped in blood: and his name is called The Word of God. And the armies which were in heaven followed him upon white horses, clothed in fine linen, white and clean. And out of his mouth goeth a sharp sword, that with it he should smite the nations: and he shall rule them with a rod of iron: and he treadeth the winepress of the fierceness and wrath of Almighty God. And he hath on his vesture and on his thigh a name written, KING OF KINGS, AND LORD OF LORDS.

Isaiah 9:6-7 For unto us a child is born, unto us a son is given: and the government shall be upon his shoulder: and his name shall be called Wonderful, Counsellor, The mighty God, The everlasting Father, The Prince of Peace. Of the increase of *his government and peace there shall be no end*, upon the throne of David, and upon his kingdom, to order it, and to establish it with judgment and with justice from henceforth even for ever. The zeal of the LORD of hosts will perform this.

[4]meek inherit the earth

Psalm 37:11 But the meek shall inherit the earth; and shall delight themselves in the abundance of peace.—King David

Matthew 5:5 Blessed are the meek: for they shall inherit the earth.—Christ Yeshua

Revelation 1:4-6 Grace and peace from . . . Jesus Christ, who is the faithful witness, and the first begotten of the dead, and the prince of the kings of the earth. Unto him that loved us, and washed us from our sins in his own blood, and *hath made us kings and priests* unto God and his Father; to him be glory and dominion for ever and ever. Amen.—Apostle John

Revelation 5:10 [He] made us unto our God kings and priests: and we shall reign on the earth.—John

1 Corinthians 6:2 Do ye not know that the saints shall judge the world? and if the world shall be judged by you, are ye unworthy to judge the smallest matters?—Apostle Paul

Revelation 2:26-27 And he that overcometh, and keepeth my works unto the end, to him will I give power over the nations: And he shall rule them with a rod of iron; as the vessels of a potter shall they be broken to shivers: even as I received of my Father.

[5]the law

Isaiah 11:1-10 And there shall come forth a rod out of the stem of Jesse, and a Branch shall grow out of his roots: and the spirit of the LORD shall rest upon him, the spirit of wisdom and understanding, the spirit of counsel and might, the spirit of knowledge and of the fear of the LORD; and shall make him of quick understanding in the fear of the LORD: and he shall not judge after the sight of his eyes, neither reprove after the hearing of his ears: but *with righteousness* shall he judge the poor, and reprove with *equity* for the meek of the earth: and he shall smite the earth with the rod of his mouth, and with the breath of his lips shall he slay the wicked. And *righteousness* shall be the girdle of his loins, and faithfulness the girdle of his reins. The wolf also shall dwell with the lamb, and the leopard shall lie down with the kid; and the calf and the young lion and the fatling together; and a little child shall lead them. And the cow and the bear shall feed; their young ones shall lie down together: and the lion shall eat straw like the ox. And the sucking child shall play on the hole of the asp, and the weaned child shall put his hand on the cockatrice' den. *They shall not hurt nor destroy in all my holy mountain:* for the earth shall be full of the knowledge of the LORD, as the waters cover the sea. And in that day there shall be a root of Jesse, which shall stand for an ensign of the people; to it shall the Gentiles seek: and his rest shall be glorious. (See also Isaiah 65:25.)

John 15:12 This is my commandment, That ye love one another, as I have loved you.—Prince Jesus

Matthew 22:37-40 Jesus said unto him, Thou shalt love the Lord thy God with all thy heart, and with all thy soul, and with all thy mind. This is the first and great commandment. And the second is like unto it, Thou shalt love thy neighbour as thyself. *On these two commandments hang all the law and the prophets.*

[6]**restoration**

Isaiah 58:12 And they that shall be of [the house of Jacob] shall build the old waste places: thou shalt raise up the foundations of many generations; and thou shalt be called, The repairer of the breach, The restorer of paths to dwell in.

[7]**that blessed hope & associated lifestyle**

Hebrews 9:28 So Christ was once offered to bear the sins of many; and unto them that look for him shall he *appear the second time* without sin *unto salvation.*—Apostle Paul

Titus 2:11-14 For the grace of God that bringeth *salvation* hath appeared to all men, teaching us that, *denying ungodliness and worldly lusts,* we should live soberly, righteously, and godly, in this present world; *looking for that blessed hope, and the glorious appearing* of the great God and our Saviour Jesus Christ; who gave himself for us, that he might redeem us from all iniquity, and purify unto himself a peculiar people, zealous of good works.—Paul

2 Timothy 3:12 Yea, and all that will live godly in Christ Jesus shall suffer persecution.—Paul

Revelation 2:10-11 Be thou *faithful unto death,* and I will give thee a *crown of life.* He that hath an ear, let him hear what the Spirit saith unto the churches; He that overcometh shall not be hurt of the *second death.*—Yeshua

John 16:33 These things I have spoken unto you, that in me ye might have peace. *In the world ye shall have tribulation:* but be of good cheer; I have overcome the world.—Yeshua Ha'Mashiach

Acts 14:22 We must through much tribulation enter into the kingdom of God.—Paul

1 Thessalonians 3:4 For verily, when we were with you, we told you before that we should suffer tribulation; even as it came to pass, *and ye know.*—Paul

[8]**average life expectancy**

Psalm 90:10 The days of our years are threescore years and ten; and if by reason of strength they be fourscore years, yet is their strength labour and sorrow; for it is soon cut off, and we fly away.

[9]**for our sake**

Matthew 24:21-22 For then shall be great tribulation, such as was not since the beginning of the world to this time, no, nor ever shall be. And except those days should be shortened, there should no flesh be saved: but for the elect's sake those days shall be shortened.

[10] common pitfalls
1 Corinthians 10:13 There hath no temptation taken you but such as is common to man . . . —Paul

[11] the pattern of history
Isaiah 24:5 The earth also is defiled under the inhabitants thereof; because they have transgressed the laws, changed the ordinance, broken the everlasting covenant.

Isaiah 30:9-10 This is a rebellious people, lying children, children that will not hear the law of the LORD: Which say to the seers, See not; and to the prophets, Prophesy not unto us right things, speak unto us smooth things, prophesy deceits:

[12] the source of light, and darkness
Matthew 6:19-24 Lay not up for yourselves treasures upon earth, where moth and rust doth corrupt, and where thieves break through and steal: But lay up for yourselves treasures in heaven, where neither moth nor rust doth corrupt, and where thieves do not break through nor steal: For where your treasure is, there will your heart be also. The light of the body is the eye: if therefore thine eye be single, thy whole body shall be full of light. But if thine eye be evil, thy whole body shall be full of darkness. If therefore the light that is in thee be darkness, how great is that darkness! No man can serve two masters: for either he will hate the one, and love the other; or else he will hold to the one, and despise the other. Ye cannot serve God and mammon.

Luke 11:34-36 The light of the body is the eye: therefore when thine eye is single, thy whole body also is full of light; but when thine eye is evil, thy body also is full of darkness. Take heed therefore that the light which is in thee be not darkness. If thy whole body therefore be full of light, having no part dark, the whole shall be full of light, as when the bright shining of a candle doth give thee light.

[13] morality zealots
Romans 10:2-3 For I bear them record that they have a zeal of God, but not according to knowledge. For they being ignorant of God's righteousness, and going about to establish their own righteousness, have not submitted themselves unto the righteousness of God.

[14] the quest for mammon
Matthew 6:32-33 (For after all these things do the Gentiles seek:) . . . your heavenly Father knoweth that ye have need of all these things. But seek ye first the kingdom of God, and His righteousness; and all these things shall be added unto you.

[15] beware the funky frequencies!
1 Corinthians 14:33 For God is not the author of confusion, but of peace, as in all churches of the saints.

[16] true love
Titus 1:16 They profess that they know God; but in works they deny him, being abominable, and disobedient, and unto every good work reprobate.

John 3:19 And this is the condemnation, that light is come into the world, and men loved darkness rather than light, because their deeds were evil.

[17] blind watchmen
Isaiah 56:10-11 His watchmen are blind: they are all ignorant, they are all dumb dogs, they cannot bark; sleeping, lying down, loving to slumber. Yea, they are greedy dogs which can never have enough, and they are shepherds that cannot understand: they

all look to their own way, every one for his gain, from his quarter.

[18]pure religion

James 1:27 Pure religion and undefiled before God and the Father is this, To visit the fatherless and widows in their affliction, and to keep himself unspotted from the world.

[19]a totally distorted concept—The concept of *the church* is a highly misunderstood phenomenon, particularly by "church people" themselves, who insist on *going* to church, rather than *being one.* It is discussed in detail in the chapter entitled "The Gates of Hell Prevail."

[20]either sell out or be spit out

Revelation 3:15-16 I know thy works, that thou art neither cold nor hot: I would thou wert cold or hot. So then because thou art lukewarm, and neither cold nor hot, I will spue thee out of my mouth.

[21]beware of Rev. Flatterie N. Compromeiss

Ephesians 4:14-15 That we henceforth be no more children, tossed to and fro, and carried about with every wind of doctrine, by the sleight of men, and cunning craftiness, whereby they lie in wait to deceive; but speaking the truth in love, may grow up into him in all things, which is the head, even Christ . . .

Isaiah 29:13-14 Wherefore the Lord said, Forasmuch as this people draw near me with their mouth, and with their lips do honour me, but have removed their heart far from me, and their fear toward me is taught by the precept of men: Therefore, behold, I will proceed to do a marvellous work among this people, even a marvellous work and a wonder: for the wisdom of their wise men shall perish, and the understanding of their prudent men shall be hid.

1 Corinthians 1:19 For it is written, I will destroy the wisdom of the wise, and will bring to nothing the understanding of the prudent.

Romans 1:21-22 Because that, when they knew God, they glorified him not as God, neither were thankful; but became vain in their imaginations, and their foolish heart was darkened. Professing themselves to be wise, they became fools . . .

Psalm 12:1-3 Help, LORD; for the godly man ceaseth; for the faithful fail from among the children of men. They speak vanity every one with his neighbour: with flattering lips and with a *double heart* do they speak. The LORD shall cut off all flattering lips, and the tongue that speaketh proud things [e.g., that they are the bride of Christ, and not Israel]:

Psalm 5:9 For there is *no faithfulness* in their mouth; their inward part is very wickedness; their throat is an open sepulchre; they flatter with their tongue . . .

Proverbs 29:5 A man that flattereth his neighbour spreadeth a net for his feet.

Proverbs 28:23 He that rebuketh a man afterwards shall find more favour than he that flattereth with the tongue.

1 Thessalonians 2:4-5 But as we were allowed of God to be put in trust with the gospel, even so we speak; not as pleasing men, but God, which trieth our hearts. For neither at any time used we flattering words, as ye know, nor a cloke of covetousness; God is witness . . .

[22]cunningly devised fables

2 Timothy 4:4 And they shall turn away their ears from the truth, and shall be turned unto fables.

2 Peter 1:16 For we have not followed cunningly devised fables, when we made known unto you the power and coming of our Lord Jesus Christ, but were eyewitnesses of his majesty.

2 Corinthians 4:2 But have renounced the hidden things of dishonesty, not walking in craftiness, nor handling the word of God deceitfully; but by manifestation of the truth commending ourselves to every man's conscience in the sight of God.

Ephesians 4:14 That we henceforth be no more children, tossed to and fro, and carried about with every wind of doctrine, by the sleight of men, and cunning craftiness, whereby they lie in wait to deceive;

[23]**special knowledge**—Their claim to an elevated status of exemption is apparently the "knowledge of Jesus Christ" through a supposed "personal relationship with Him as Lord and Savior." This knowledge/relationship presumably begins with inviting Him to enter one' s heart, which, according to popular teaching, produces a conversion/salvation. Well, leaving nothing unchallenged, the authenticity of this "experience" must also be questioned.

It must be noted for the record that Christ did teach the notion of a deep level of belief, in terms that He concisely defined as *receiving Him* and His *word*, with the emphasis always on His *word*. The reason for the emphasis is obviously that His word unequivocally defines Him for who He is and what He stands for. In fact, Apostle John, in no uncertain terms, defines Christ as The very Word of God made flesh. (John 1:1-14) To know Him, therefore, is a matter of having that "Word" communicated to one's understanding and accepting it, thereby producing a conversion of heart, soul, and mind by one's faith in that word. However, a would-be relationship with Christ, according to Christ himself, is an extreme unlikelihood, when the words of His teaching are patently disregarded: *"And why call ye me, Lord, Lord, and do not the things which I say?"* *(Luke 6:46)* In the same passage, the Lord went on to liken just such a belief system to a house founded upon sand, which will only collapse under adversity (such as the Great Tribulation!).

Belief systems that purport to bring one into a personal relationship with Christ by such easy methods as praying to invite Him into one's heart need to be scrutinized with a high degree of skepticism. The same John, referenced above, went on to admonish the following in a later epistle: *"He that saith, I know him, and keepeth not his commandments, is a liar, and the truth is not in him. But whoso keepeth his word, in him verily is the love of God perfected: hereby know we that we are in him. He that saith he abideth in him ought himself also so to walk, even as he walked."* *(I John 2:4-6)* While lips may beguile; only feet go the extra mile!

And, though Christ *never* definitively taught the concept of praying to receive Him into the heart, He did teach a much more radical, all-or-nothing concept of receiving Him, phrasing it very graphically in these words: *"Verily, verily, I say unto you, Except ye eat the flesh of the Son of man, and drink his blood, ye have no life in you."* *(John 6:53)* It is in another all-or-nothing passage (in Revelation chapter 3, condemning mediocrity of faith and lifestyle) that Christ presented Himself as a willing conversant and friend, standing at the door and knocking, prepared to enter into fellowship, *if* a zealous repentance from *"lukewarmness"* were accomplished. (See Rev.3:14-20) Again, popular applications of this out-of-context precept conveniently skirt the extreme demands of truth, in favor of a watered-down, mediocre approach to Christianity.

[24]**it was given, not taken**

John 10:17-18 Therefore doth my Father love me, because I lay down my life, that I might take it again. No man taketh it from me, but I lay it down of myself. I have power to lay it down, and I have power to take it again. This commandment have I received of my Father.

[25]slave to the flesh

Romans 8:6-8 For to be carnally minded is death; but to be spiritually minded is life and peace. Because the carnal mind is enmity against God: for it is not subject to the law of God, neither indeed can be. So then they that are in the flesh cannot please God.

[26]love not the darkness of worldly values

Colossians 3:2 Set your affection on things above, not on things on the earth.

I John 2:15 Love not the world, neither the things that are in the world. If any man love the world, the love of the Father is not in him.

John 18:36 Jesus answered, My kingdom is not of this world: if my kingdom were of this world, then would my servants fight, that I should not be delivered to the Jews: but now is my kingdom not from hence.

Hebrews 13:14 For here have we no continuing city, but we seek one to come.

Matthew 6:19-21 Lay not up for yourselves treasures upon earth, where moth and rust doth corrupt, and where thieves break through and steal: But lay up for yourselves treasures in heaven, where neither moth nor rust doth corrupt, and where thieves do not break through nor steal: For where your treasure is, there will your heart be also.

Mark 10:21-22 Then Jesus beholding him loved him, and said unto him, One thing thou lackest: go thy way, sell whatsoever thou hast, and give to the poor, and thou shalt have treasure in heaven: and come, take up the cross, and follow me. And he was sad at that saying, and went away grieved: for he had great possessions.

Luke 12:20-21 But God said unto him, Thou fool, this night thy soul shall be required of thee: then whose shall those things be, which thou hast provided? So is he that layeth up treasure for himself, and is not rich toward God.

James 5:1-3 Go to now, ye rich men, weep and howl for your miseries that shall come upon you. Your riches are corrupted, and your garments are motheaten. Your gold and silver is cankered; and the rust of them shall be a witness against you, and shall eat your flesh as it were fire. Ye have heaped treasure together for the last days.

Mark 8:36-37 For what shall it profit a man, if he shall gain the whole world, and lose his own soul? Or what shall a man give in exchange for his soul?

[27]the Great Spirit

John 4:24 God is a Spirit: and they that worship him must worship him in spirit and in truth.

Chapter 2—Sorting Out the Facts

[1]**the Jewish Bible**—The **TaNaKh**, a term familiar to Jews, is the Hebraic term for the Bible; but specifically what is distinguished as the "Old Testament" as apart from the New. It is actually an acronym derived from the names of its three divisions: Torah (hence, *Ta*), Nevi`im (*Na*), and Ketuvim (*Kh*). The *Torah* consists of the 5 books of Moses, which comprises the Instruction, or Law, and is also called the Pentateuch. The *Nevi`im* comprise eight books, which are generally known as the Prophets. These include Isaiah, Jeremiah, Ezekiel, and the Twelve Minor (i.e., briefer) Prophets (Hosea, Joel, Amos, Obadiah, Jonah, Micah, Nahum, Habakkuk, Zephaniah, Haggai, Zechariah, and Malachi, who were all formerly written on a single scroll and thus reckoned as one book). Also contained in *Nevi`im* are the four historical works, Joshua, Judges, Samuel, and Kings, called the Former Prophets. And finally, the religious poetry and wisdom literature is grouped into the *Ketuvim*, or Writings. These include Psalms, Proverbs, and Job, a collection known as the "Five Megillot" ("scrolls")—Song of Songs, Ruth, Lamentations, Ecclesiastes, and Esther, which have been grouped together according to the annual cycle of their public reading in the synagogue—and the books of Daniel, Ezra and Nehemiah, and Chronicles.

[2]**sinning saints**—Note that the concept of sainthood has been much exaggerated over the centuries, particularly by certain churches which have contrived a religious culture of cultic saint worship. In these ecclesiastical cultures, certain devout believers, because of their exemplary lifestyles, are unduly exalted to a status of "saintliness" of a type that confers upon them an inordinate quality of sinlessness or holiness that is beyond measure for any flesh. Such exaltation of persons—considering the clear prohibition of such practices by the Law of the God of the Hebrews—is really tantamount to idolizing of humans. *In actuality*, the Holy Scriptures plainly define a *saint* as a consecrated individual who has committed him- or herself to observance of the Law of God out of faith in the divine nature of that law, and who consequently defies or resists temptation and error by pursuing that law. In other words, a saint is a person who is committed to the pursuit of righteousness, despite human weakness, error, and the inescapable tendency to sin; and by virtue of that commitment to strive toward that end, is regarded as "sinless" in the understanding eyes and lovingkindness of the Creator, although absolute carnal sinlessness is patently unachievable in any present fleshly state of being. Perfection of a human soul (virtual sinlessness) is ultimately accomplished primarily through a dynamic process of the Creator's own cleansing activity. It is not a natural state of being, let alone a self-attainable one. Saints are those who have willingly submitted themselves to that hopeful process and do not feign to be sinless or perfect by any means. They are simply believers, and hence followers of the Holy Word, who are consequently cleansed by that very faith in the teaching. Christ declared: *"Now ye [disciples] are clean through the word which I have spoken unto you (John 15:2)."* Solomon in his keen understanding of such matters taught that *"a just man falleth seven times, and riseth up again: but the wicked shall fall into mischief." (Prov. 24:16)* Saints are stumblers, bumblers, and sinners as much as any; they just don't settle comfortably in the mire when they happen to slip into it.

[3]**all-inclusive guarantee**

John 16:33 These things I have spoken unto you, that in me ye might have peace. In

the world ye shall have tribulation: but be of good cheer; I have overcome the world. —
Yeshua Ha'Mashiach

2 Timothy 3:12 Yea, and all that will live godly in Christ Jesus shall suffer persecution. —Apostle Paul

⁴comfort for the committed

1 Corinthians 15:51-54 Behold, I shew you a mystery; We shall not all sleep, but we
shall all be changed, in a moment, in the twinkling of an eye, at the last trump: for the
trumpet shall sound, and the dead shall be raised incorruptible, and we shall be changed.
For this corruptible must put on incorruption, and this mortal must put on immortality.
So when this corruptible shall have put on incorruption, and this mortal shall have put
on immortality, then shall be brought to pass the saying that is written, Death is swallowed up in victory.

Mark 13:24-27 But in those days, *after that tribulation*, the sun shall be darkened,
and the moon shall not give her light, and the stars of heaven shall fall, and the powers
that are in heaven shall be shaken. And then shall they see the Son of man coming in the
clouds with great power and glory. And then shall he send his angels, and shall gather
together his elect from the four winds, from the uttermost part of the earth to the uttermost part of heaven.

1 Thessalonians 4:16-18 For the Lord himself shall descend from heaven with a
shout, with the voice of the archangel, and with the trump of God: and the dead in Christ
shall rise first: Then we which are alive and remain shall be caught up together with
them in the clouds, to meet the Lord in the air: and so shall we ever be with the Lord.
Wherefore comfort one another with these words.

⁵hosanna choirs and the hosanna syndrome—Please see the section *"Hosanna Hearts
and the Barabbas Factor"* in the chapter (14) entitled "Tell Us When" for an in-depth
look at this phenomenon. Essentially, it refers to the on-again-off-again affections of the
here-today-gone-tomorrow worshippers who presently hail the King in adoration, only
to later repudiate and deny Him when their personal expectations of Him are not met.

⁶vestigial organs?

Matthew 13:13-16 Therefore speak I to them in parables: because they seeing see
not; and hearing they hear not, neither do they understand. And in them is fulfilled the
prophecy of Esaias, which saith, By hearing ye shall hear, and shall not understand; and
seeing ye shall see, and shall not perceive: For this people's heart is waxed gross, and
their ears are dull of hearing, and their eyes they have closed; lest at any time they
should see with their eyes, and hear with their ears, and should understand with their
heart, and should be converted, and I should heal them. But blessed are your eyes, for
they see: and your ears, for they hear.

Isaiah 6:9-10 And he said, Go, and tell this people, Hear ye indeed, but understand
not; and see ye indeed, but perceive not. Make the heart of this people fat, and make
their ears heavy, and shut their eyes; lest they see with their eyes, and hear with their
ears, and understand with their heart, and convert, and be healed.

⁷the acceptable year — Please refer to the chapter (14) entitled "Tell Us When!" for more
detail on Kingdom-come Ideology, and the Acceptable Year.

⁸Common Era — The dating abbreviation CE (Common Era) is used throughout this
book as the equivalent of the more generally used AD And, BCE (Before the Common
Era) is used instead of BC as its equivalent.

⁹**stewards of earth**

Genesis 2:15-16 And the LORD God took the man, and put him into the garden of Eden to dress it and to keep it. And the LORD God commanded the man, saying, Of every tree of the garden thou mayest freely eat:

¹⁰**to the thief as a thief**

Psalm 18:26-27 With the pure thou wilt shew thyself pure; and with the froward *thou wilt shew thyself froward.* For thou wilt save the afflicted people; but wilt bring down high looks.

¹¹**the real thief vs. the "thief"**

John 10:10 The thief cometh not, but for to steal, and to kill, and to destroy: I am come that they might have life, and that they might have it more abundantly.

¹²**the warring Lamb**

Revelation 19:11-16 & 19 And I saw heaven opened, and behold a white horse; and he that sat upon him was called Faithful and True, and in righteousness he doth judge and make war. His eyes were as a flame of fire, and on his head were many crowns; and he had a name written, that no man knew, but he himself. And he was clothed with a vesture dipped in blood: and his name is called The Word of God. And the armies which were in heaven followed him upon white horses, clothed in fine linen, white and clean. And out of his mouth goeth a sharp sword, that with it he should smite the nations: and he shall rule them with a rod of iron: and he treadeth the winepress of the fierceness and wrath of Almighty God. And he hath on his vesture and on his thigh a name written, KING OF KINGS, AND LORD OF LORDS. . . . And I saw the beast, and the kings of the earth, and their armies, gathered together to make war against him that sat on the horse, and against his army.

Revelation 17:14 These shall make war with the Lamb, and the Lamb shall overcome them: for he is Lord of lords, and King of kings: and they that are with him are called, and chosen, and faithful.

¹³**son of perdition — the beast**

Revelation 17:11-14 And the beast that was, and is not, even he is the eighth, and is of the seven, and goeth into perdition. And the ten horns which thou sawest are ten kings, which have received no kingdom as yet; but receive power as kings one hour with the beast. These have one mind, and shall give their power and strength unto the beast. These shall make war with the Lamb, and the Lamb shall overcome them: for he is Lord of lords, and King of kings: and they that are with him are called, and chosen, and faithful.

II Thessalonians 2:3-12 Let no man deceive you by any means: for that day shall not come, except there come a falling away first, and that man of sin be revealed, the son of perdition; Who opposeth and exalteth himself above all that is called God, or that is worshipped; so that he as God sitteth in the temple of God, shewing himself that he is God. Remember ye not, that, when I was yet with you, I told you these things? And now ye know what withholdeth that he might be revealed in his time. For the mystery of iniquity doth already work: only he who now letteth will let, until he be taken out of the way. And then shall that Wicked be revealed, whom the Lord shall consume with the spirit of his mouth, and shall destroy with the brightness of his coming: Even him, whose coming is after the working of Satan with all power and signs and lying wonders, and with all deceivableness of unrighteousness in them that perish; because they received not the love of the truth, that they might be saved. And for this cause God shall send them strong delusion, that they should believe a lie: That they all might be damned who believed not the truth, but had pleasure in unrighteousness.

[14] what you want is what you get

II Thessalonians 2:10-12 They received not the love of the truth, that they might be saved. And for this cause God shall send them strong delusion, that they should believe a lie: That they all might be damned who believed not the truth, but had pleasure in unrighteousness.

Psalm 106:15 And he gave them their request [satisfied their lust]; but sent leanness into their soul. (an Exodus experience of the chosen people & lesson to all)

Isaiah 66:3-4 Yea, they have chosen their own ways, and their soul delighteth in their abominations. I also will choose their delusions, and will bring their fears upon them; because when I called, none did answer; when I spake, they did not hear: but they did evil before mine eyes, and chose that in which I delighted not.

[15] don't even touch it

Leviticus 18:3-4 After the doings of the land of Egypt, wherein ye dwelt, shall ye not do: and after the doings of the land of Canaan, whither I bring you, shall ye not do: neither shall ye walk in their ordinances. Ye shall do my judgments, and keep mine ordinances, to walk therein: I am the LORD your God.

2 Corinthians 6:14-18 Be ye not unequally yoked together with unbelievers: for what fellowship hath righteousness with unrighteousness? and what communion hath light with darkness? And what concord hath Christ with Belial? or what part hath he that believeth with an infidel? And what agreement hath the temple of God with idols? for ye are the temple of the living God; as God hath said, I will dwell in them, and walk in them; and I will be their God, and they shall be my people. Wherefore come out from among them, and be ye separate, saith the Lord, and touch not the unclean thing; and I will receive you, and will be a Father unto you, and ye shall be my sons and daughters, saith the Lord Almighty.

Ephesians 5:11 And have no fellowship with the unfruitful works of darkness, but rather reprove them.

Revelation 18:4 And I heard another voice from heaven, saying, Come out of [BABYLON THE GREAT, THE MOTHER OF HARLOTS AND ABOMINATIONS OF THE EARTH], my people, that ye be not partakers of her sins, and that ye receive not of her plagues.

Psalm 106:35-40 But [they] were mingled among the heathen, and learned their works. And they served their idols: which were a snare unto them. Yea, they sacrificed their sons and their daughters unto devils, and shed innocent blood, even the blood of their sons and of their daughters, whom they sacrificed unto the idols of Canaan: and the land was polluted with blood. Thus were they defiled with their own works, and went a whoring with their own inventions. Therefore was the wrath of the LORD kindled against his people, insomuch that he abhorred his own inheritance.

Ephesians 5:5-7 For this ye know, that no whoremonger, nor unclean person, nor covetous man, who is an idolater, hath any inheritance in the kingdom of Christ and of God. Let no man deceive you with vain words: for because of these things cometh the wrath of God upon the children of disobedience. Be not ye therefore partakers with them.

[16] blind leaders of the blind

Luke 6:39 And he spake a parable unto them, Can the blind lead the blind? shall they not both fall into the ditch?

[17]**choked by materialism**

Mark 4:19 And the cares of this world, and the deceitfulness of riches, and the lusts of other things entering in, choke the word, and it becometh unfruitful.

[18]**name only**

Revelation 3:1-3 I know thy works, that thou hast a name that thou livest, and art dead. Be watchful, and strengthen the things which remain, that are ready to die: for I have not found thy works perfect before God. Remember therefore how thou hast received and heard, and hold fast, and repent. If therefore thou shalt not watch, I will come on thee as a thief, and thou shalt not know what hour I will come upon thee.

[19]**material certainty**

Job 1:20-21 Then Job arose, and rent his mantle, and shaved his head, and fell down upon the ground, and worshipped, and said, Naked came I out of my mother's womb, and naked shall I return thither: the LORD gave, and the LORD hath taken away; blessed be the name of the LORD.

1 Timothy 6:7 For we brought nothing into this world, and it is certain we can carry nothing out. —Paul

[20]**treasures for thieves** (see Rev. 3:3 in footnote 18 also)

Matthew 6:19-20 Lay not up for yourselves treasures upon earth, where moth and rust doth corrupt, and where thieves break through and steal: But lay up for yourselves treasures in heaven, where neither moth nor rust doth corrupt, and where thieves do not break through nor steal.

[21]**seizure and confiscation of assets**

Daniel 11:24 He [Antichrist-prince of the holy covenant detailed later] shall enter peaceably even upon the fattest places of the province; and he shall do that which his fathers have not done, nor his fathers' fathers; he shall *scatter among them the prey, and spoil*, and riches: yea, and he shall forecast his devices against the strong holds, even for a time.

Daniel 11:28 Then shall he return into his land with great riches [seized spoils]; and his heart shall be against the holy covenant; and he shall do exploits, and return to his own land.

Daniel 11:31-39 And arms shall stand on his part, and they shall pollute the sanctuary of strength, and shall take away the daily sacrifice, and they shall place the abomination that maketh desolate. And such as do wickedly against the covenant [the underhanded underminers and betrayers of the "peace process"] shall he corrupt by flatteries (from the Hebrew *chalaq,* meaning dividing up, apportioning, distributing of gifts and spoil): but the people that do know their God shall be strong, and do exploits. And they that understand among the people shall instruct many: *yet they shall fall* by the sword, and by flame, *by captivity, and by spoil*, many days. Now when they shall fall, they shall be holpen with a little help: but many [erstwhile believers] shall cleave to [turn to and embrace] them with flatteries [the new socialist regime]. And some of them of understanding [God's people] shall fall, to try them, and to purge, and to make them white, even to the time of the end: because it is yet for a time appointed. And the king shall do according to his will; and he shall exalt himself, and magnify himself above every god, and shall speak marvellous things against the God of gods, and shall prosper till the indignation be accomplished: for that that is determined shall be done. Neither shall he regard the God of his fathers, nor the desire of women, nor regard any god: for he shall magnify himself above all. But in his estate shall he honour the God of forces [military might]: and a god whom his fathers knew not shall he honour with gold, and silver, and with precious stones, and pleasant things. Thus shall he do in the most strong holds with a *strange* god, whom he shall acknowledge and increase with glory: and he shall cause them to rule over many, *and shall divide the land for gain [money and/or other reward, e.g. political gain].* (Note that "divide" here is the same "chalaq" translated as "flattery" above.)

[22] **form of godliness**

2 Timothy 3:5 Having a form of godliness, but denying the power thereof: from such turn away.

[23] **the beast first**

II Thessalonians 2:3-4 Let no man deceive you by any means: for that day shall not come, except there come a falling away first, and that man of sin be revealed, the son of perdition; who opposeth and exalteth himself above all that is called God, or that is worshipped; so that he as God sitteth in the temple of God, shewing himself that he is God.

[24] **take your pick**

Revelation 13:15-17 And he had power to give life unto the image of the beast, that the image of the beast should both speak, and cause that as many as would not worship the image of the beast should be killed. And he causeth all, both small and great, rich and poor, free and bond, to receive a mark in their right hand, or in their foreheads: And that no man might buy or sell, save he that had the mark, or the name of the beast, or the number of his name.

Revelation 14:9-12 And the third angel followed them, saying with a loud voice, If any man worship the beast and his image, and receive his mark in his forehead, or in his hand, the same shall drink of the wine of the wrath of God, which is poured out without mixture into the cup of his indignation; and he shall be tormented with fire and brimstone in the presence of the holy angels, and in the presence of the Lamb: And the smoke of their torment ascendeth up for ever and ever: and they have no rest day nor night, who worship the beast and his image, and whosoever receiveth the mark of his name. Here is the patience of the saints: here are they that keep the commandments of God, and the faith of Jesus.

[25] **escape what?!**

Luke 21:34-36 And take heed to yourselves, lest at any time your hearts be overcharged with surfeiting, and drunkenness, and cares of this life, and so that day come upon you unawares. For as a snare shall it come on all them that dwell on the face of the whole earth. Watch ye therefore, and pray always, that ye may be accounted worthy to escape all these things that shall come to pass, and to stand before the Son of man.

[26] **reminder of "the appointment"**

1 Thessalonians 3:3-4 No man should be moved by these afflictions: for yourselves know that we are appointed thereunto. For verily, when we were with you, we told you before that we should suffer tribulation; even as it came to pass, and ye know.

Acts 14:22b We must through much tribulation enter into the kingdom of God.

Chapter 3—The Signposts

[1]irrevocable, immutable—the Word of YHWH God to the People of the Book

Numbers 23:19 God is not a man, that he should lie; neither the son of man, that he should repent: hath he said, and shall he not do it? or hath he spoken, and shall he not make it good?

Deuteronomy 7:9 Know therefore that the LORD thy God, he is God, the faithful God, which keepeth covenant and mercy with them that love him and keep his commandments *to a thousand generations* . . .

Genesis 17:7-8 And I will establish my covenant between me and thee [Abraham] and thy seed after thee in their generations for an *everlasting covenant*, to be a God unto thee, and to thy seed after thee. And I will give unto thee, and to thy seed after thee, the land wherein thou art a stranger, *all the land of Canaan* [millennia later called Palestine by the Romans], for an *everlasting possession*; and I will be their God.

Psalm 105:6-11 O ye seed of Abraham his servant, ye *children of Jacob his chosen*. He is the LORD our God: his judgments are in all the earth. He hath remembered his covenant for ever, the word which he commanded to a thousand generations. Which covenant he made with Abraham, and his oath unto Isaac; and confirmed the same unto Jacob for a law, and *to Israel for an everlasting covenant*: saying, Unto thee will I give the land of Canaan, the lot of your inheritance:

Isaiah 61:6-9 But *ye shall be named the Priests of the LORD*: men shall call you the Ministers of our God: ye shall eat the riches of the Gentiles, and in their glory shall ye boast yourselves. For your shame ye shall have double; and for confusion they shall rejoice in their portion: therefore in their land they shall possess the double: everlasting joy shall be unto them. For I the LORD love judgment, I hate robbery for burnt offering; and I will direct their work in truth, and I will make an *everlasting covenant with them*. And *their seed* shall be known among the Gentiles, and *their offspring* among the people: all that see them shall acknowledge them, that *they are the seed* which the LORD hath blessed.

Jeremiah 32:37-41 Behold, I will gather them out of all countries, whither I have driven them in mine anger, and in my fury, and in great wrath; and I will bring them again unto this place, and I will cause them to dwell safely: And *they shall be my people*, and I will be their God: And I will give them one heart, and one way, that they may fear me for ever, for the good of them, and of their children after them: And I will make an *everlasting covenant with them*, that I will not turn away from them, to do them good; but I will put my fear in their hearts, that they shall not depart from me. Yea, I will rejoice over them to do them good, and I will plant them in this land *assuredly with my whole heart and with my whole soul*.

Ezekiel 37:25-28 And they shall dwell in the land that I have given *unto Jacob my servant*, wherein your fathers have dwelt; and they shall dwell therein, even they, and their children, *and their children's children for ever*: and my servant David shall be their prince for ever. Moreover I will make a covenant of peace with them; it shall be an *everlasting covenant* with them: and I will place them, and multiply them, and will set my sanctuary in the midst of them for evermore. My tabernacle also shall be with them: yea, I will be their God, and they shall be my people. And *the heathen shall know that I the LORD do sanctify Israel*, when my sanctuary shall be in the midst of them for evermore.

[2]you can't beat 'em—join 'em!— By adopting the Jew's worship of Jah (also known as Yahweh, Jehovah, El Shaddai, Adonai—the God of Abraham, Isaac, and Jacob) you become a Jew, not a distinct or separate class of "church" people . . .

Esther 8:17 And in every province, and in every city, whithersoever the king's commandment and his decree came, the Jews had joy and gladness, a feast and a good day. And *many of the people of the land [Persian Gentiles] became Jews* [during the days of the Persian Empire in the reign of Ahasuerus & Esther]; for the fear of the Jews fell upon them.

1Thessalonians 2:14 (Jewish Apostle Paul writes to the Greek Gentile believers of Thessalonica:) For ye, brethren, *became followers* of the *churches of God* which *in Judaea* are [strictly "Ju-ish" believers] in Christ Jesus . . .

Ephesians 2:14 &18-22 (Paul to the Gentile Ephesians:) For [Christ] is our peace, who hath *made both one*, and hath broken down the middle wall of partition between us. . . . For through him we *both have access* by one Spirit unto the Father. Now therefore ye are *no more strangers and foreigners*, but *fellowcitizens* with the saints, and of the household of God; and are built upon the foundation of the apostles and prophets, Jesus Christ himself being the chief corner stone; in whom all the building fitly framed together groweth unto an holy temple in the Lord: In whom ye also are *builded together* for an habitation of God through the Spirit.

[3]the People of the Book

Romans 11:1-2 & 16-27 I say then, Hath God cast away his people? God forbid. For I also am an Israelite, of the seed of Abraham, of the tribe of Benjamin. God *hath not cast away his people* which he foreknew. . . . If the root be holy, so are the branches. And if some of the branches be broken off, and *thou [Gentile], being a wild olive* tree, wert graffed in among them, and with them partakest of the root and fatness of the olive tree; boast not against the branches. But if thou boast, thou bearest not the root, but the root thee. Thou wilt say then, The branches were broken off, that I might be graffed in. Well; because of unbelief they were broken off, and thou standest by faith. *Be not highminded, but fear.* For if God spared not the natural branches, take heed lest he also spare not thee. Behold therefore the goodness and severity of God: on them which fell, severity; but toward thee, goodness, if thou continue in his goodness: *otherwise thou also shalt be cut off.* And they also, if they abide not still in unbelief, shall be graffed in: for God is able to graff them in again. For if thou wert cut out of the olive tree which is wild by nature, and wert *graffed contrary to nature into a good olive tree*: how much more shall these, which be the natural branches, be graffed into their own olive tree? For I would not, brethren, that ye should be ignorant of this mystery, lest ye should be wise in your own conceits; that blindness in part is happened to Israel, until the fulness of the Gentiles be come in. And so all Israel shall be saved: as it is written, There shall come out of Sion the Deliverer, and shall turn away ungodliness from Jacob: For this is my covenant unto them, when I shall take away their sins.—Saul (Apostle Paul)

[4]Christian anti-Semitism— Various books and literary works can be obtained to document the presumptuous spiritual coup de'état perpetrated against the People of the Book in an effort to displace and supplant them from the immutable scheme of the Scriptures—in order, it appears, to usurp their position and promises, as provided in the Book. An excellent, comprehensive, and yet succinct treatise on the subject is available from EICB, P.O. Box 668, Dyer, Indiana 46311-0668, USA.

Please request a copy of *Does Jacob's Trouble Wear A Cross?* by Randall A. Weiss.

Dyer, Indiana, Excellence in Christian Books, 1995. (My copy was delivered for a very worthwhile gift of $15 US.)

⁵**deceitful, divisive, and distancing different-destiny doctrines**— A later chapter, entitled "Gates of Hell" details more of this heretical and divisive "different destiny" doctrine, teaching that Jews will go through Great Tribulation, while Gentile "Christians" rate themselves exempt.

⁶**church??**— The etymology of this word is traced in Webster's dictionary back to the Greek *kyriakos*, meaning *of the Lord*, from *kyrios*, lord or master. Then, from Greek to Old English, the word evidently became *cirice*, and subsequently evolved through Middle English into *chirche*, to become what it is today, meaning simply "of the Lord." Indeed, to be *called out* is to be "of the Lord"; but a huge loss in meaning came about by the substitution of a different word, which was very likely already long since used to apply to congregations that met in buildings (by the time the English-speaking world ventured at a translation of the Bible into the language of their common people). It is also quite likely that the conceited anti-Jew bias had already set in, reckoning the Jews and their synagogues as *not of the Lord*, while the now Gentile-dominated assemblies supplantingly considered themselves *as kyriakos*, or *cirice*, and later *chirche*.

⁷**establishment vanity vs. the call of Israel**

John 17:14-18 I have given them thy word; and the world hath hated them, because they are not of the world, even as I am not of the world. I pray not that thou shouldest take them out of the world, but that thou shouldest keep them from the evil. They are not of the world, even as I am not of the world. Sanctify them through thy truth: thy word is truth. As thou hast sent me into the world, even so have I also sent them into the world.

Matthew 6:31-33 Therefore take no thought, saying, What shall we eat? or, What shall we drink? or, Wherewithal shall we be clothed? (For after *all these things do the Gentiles seek:*) for your heavenly Father knoweth that ye have need of all these things. But seek ye first the kingdom of God, and his righteousness; and all these things shall be added unto you.

⁸**the original Hebrew calling out**

Genesis 12:1-5 Now the LORD had said unto Abram, *Get thee out* of thy country, *and from* thy kindred, and from thy father's house, unto a land that I will shew thee: And I will make of thee a great nation, and I will bless thee, and make thy name great; and thou shalt be a blessing: And I will bless them that bless thee, and curse him that curseth thee: and in thee shall all families of the earth be blessed. So Abram departed, as the LORD had spoken unto him; and Lot went with him: and Abram was seventy and five years old when he departed out of Haran. And Abram took Sarai his wife, and Lot his brother's son, and all their substance that they had gathered, and the souls that they had gotten in Haran; and they went forth to go into the land of Canaan; and into the land of Canaan they came.

⁹**the Exodus Church with Moses in the wilderness**—*called out* of Egypt

Acts 7:37-38 (Stephen the martyr, just before his stoning, testified of Moses' prophesy of a Hebrew Messiah to come, Who had actually already been in spiritual company with the children of Israel in their exodus wanderings—*the church* in the wilderness:) This is that Moses, which said unto the children of Israel, A prophet shall the Lord your God raise up unto you of your brethren, like unto me; him shall ye hear. This is he, that was in *the church in the wilderness* with the angel which spake to him in the mount Sina, and with our fathers . . . (Obviously, this did not refer to a group of Gentiles; and

---

404

it existed long prior to the heretical notion that the Church was born in 32 AD, as the fundamentalists teach.—Now watch 'em explain this away! with the on-this-rock-I-will-build-my-church doctrine, which they also misconstrue.)

10calling out of Jewish sheep by Jewish shepherd

Matthew 15:24 I am not sent but unto the lost sheep of the house of Israel.—Jesus

John 15:18-19 If the world hate you, ye know that it hated me before it hated you. If ye were of the world, the world would love his own: but because ye are not of the world, but I have *chosen you out of the world*, therefore the world hateth you.

11the LORD's portion

Deuteronomy 32:9 For the LORD's portion is *his people*; *Jacob* is the lot of his inheritance.

12Daniel's vision of the New World Order of the Ancient of Days and his saints

Daniel 2:44 And in the days of these [last 10] kings shall the God of heaven set up a kingdom, which shall never be destroyed: and the kingdom shall not be left to other people, but it shall break in pieces and consume all these kingdoms, and it shall stand for ever.

Daniel 7:18-22 But the saints of the most High shall take the kingdom, and possess the kingdom for ever, even for ever and ever. . . . I beheld, and the same horn [Antichrist] made war with the saints, and prevailed against them; *until* the Ancient of days came, and judgment was given to the saints of the most High; and the time came that the saints possessed the kingdom.

13back to Eden—the law of God

John 13:34-35 A new commandment I give unto you, That ye love one another; as I have loved you, that ye also love one another. By this shall all men know that ye are my disciples, if ye have love one to another.

I John 2:7-10 Brethren, I write no new commandment unto you, but an old commandment which ye had from the beginning. The old commandment is the word which ye have heard from the beginning. Again, a new commandment I write unto you, which thing is true in him and in you: because the darkness is past, and the true light now shineth. He that saith he is in the light, and hateth his brother, is in darkness even until now. He that loveth his brother abideth in the light, and there is none occasion of stumbling in him.

I John 3:23 And this is his commandment, That we should believe on the name of his Son Jesus Christ, and love one another, as he gave us commandment.

14another order

John 18:36 Jesus: *My kingdom is not of this world*: if my kingdom were of this world, then would my servants fight, that I should not be delivered to the Jews: but *now* is my kingdom not from hence.

Isaiah 9:6-7 Unto us a child is born, unto us a son is given: and the government shall be upon his shoulder: and his name shall be called Wonderful, Counsellor, The mighty God, The everlasting Father, The Prince of Peace. Of the increase of his government and peace there shall be no end, upon the throne of David, and upon his kingdom, to order it, and to establish it with judgment and with justice from henceforth even for ever.

15the wine of that Great City

Proverbs 23:31-33 Look not thou upon the wine when it is red, when it giveth his colour in the cup, when it moveth itself aright. At the last it biteth like a serpent, and stingeth like an adder. Thine eyes shall behold strange women, and thine heart shall utter perverse things.

Revelation 17:18 & 2 And the woman which thou sawest is that great city, which reigneth over the kings of the earth. . . . With whom the kings of the earth have committed fornication, and *the inhabitants of the earth have been made drunk with the wine of her fornication.*

Revelation 18:3-4 For all nations have drunk of the wine of the wrath of her fornication, and the kings of the earth have committed fornication with her, and the merchants of the earth are waxed rich through the abundance of her delicacies. And I heard another voice from heaven, saying, Come out of her, my people, that ye be not partakers of her sins, and that ye receive not of her plagues.

Revelation 14:8 And there followed another angel, saying, Babylon is fallen, is fallen, that great city, because she made all nations drink of the wine of the wrath of her fornication.

[16]Christian power struggles

Mark 9:33-35 And (Jesus) came to Capernaum: and being in the house he asked (his disciples), What was it that ye disputed among yourselves by the way? But they held their peace: for by the way they had disputed among themselves, who should be the greatest. And he sat down, and called the twelve, and saith unto them, If any man desire to be first, the same shall be last of all, and servant of all.

Mark 10:42-45 Ye know that they which are accounted to rule over the Gentiles exercise lordship over them; and their great ones exercise authority upon them. But so shall it not be among you: but whosoever will be great among you, shall be your minister: And whosoever of you will be the chiefest, shall be servant of all. For even the Son of man came not to be ministered unto, but to minister, and to *give his life* a ransom for many.

[17]mission aborted

Isaiah 26:17-18 Like as a woman with child, that draweth near the time of her delivery, is in pain, and crieth out in her pangs; so have we been in thy sight, O LORD. We have been with child, we have been in pain, we have as it were *brought forth wind; we have not wrought any deliverance in the earth;* neither have the inhabitants of the world fallen [their idolatrous vanity/covetousness has not been conquered for failure to bear out the saving power of truth and love].

[18]back-up plan

Revelation 14:6-11 And I saw another angel fly in the midst of heaven, *having the everlasting gospel to preach unto them that dwell on the earth,* and to every nation, and kindred, and tongue, and people, saying with a loud voice, Fear God, and give glory to him; for the hour of *his* judgment is come: and worship him that made heaven, and earth, and the sea, and the fountains of waters. And there followed another angel, saying, Babylon is fallen, is fallen, that great city, because she made all nations drink of the wine of the wrath of her fornication. And the third angel followed them, saying with a loud voice, If any man worship the beast and his image, and receive his mark in his forehead, or in his hand, the same shall drink of the wine of the wrath of God, which is poured out without mixture into the cup of his indignation; and he shall be tormented with fire and brimstone . . . And the smoke of their torment ascendeth up for ever and ever: and they have no rest day nor night, who worship the beast and his image, and whosoever receiveth the mark of his name.

[19]tree known by its fruits

Luke 6:43-46 A good tree bringeth not forth corrupt fruit; neither doth a corrupt tree bring forth good fruit. For every tree is known by his own fruit. For of thorns men do not gather figs, nor of a bramble bush gather they grapes. A good man out of the good treasure of his heart bringeth forth that which is good; and an evil man out of the evil treasure of his heart bringeth forth that which is evil: for of the abundance of the heart his mouth speaketh. And why call ye me, Lord, Lord, and do not the things which I say?

[20]dynamic patriarch of the established orders of men

Revelation 12:9 & 13:3-4 And the great dragon was cast out, that old serpent, called the Devil, and Satan, *which deceiveth the whole world*: he was cast out into the earth, and his angels were cast out with him. . . . And all the world wondered after the beast. And they *worshipped the dragon which gave power* unto the beast: and they worshipped the beast, saying, Who is like unto the beast?

Luke 4:5-8 And the devil, taking [Christ] up into an high mountain, shewed unto him *all the kingdoms of the world in a moment of time*. And the devil said unto him, *All this power will I give thee*, and the glory of them: *for that is delivered unto me*; and to whomsoever I will I give it. If thou therefore wilt worship me, all shall be thine. And Jesus answered and said unto him, Get thee behind me, Satan: for it is written, Thou shalt worship the Lord thy God, and him only shalt thou serve.

Chapter 4—New World Order Options

¹the ultimate great holy civilization of God upon Earth

Revelation 21:1-5 And I saw a new heaven and a new earth: for the first heaven and the first earth were passed away; and there was no more sea. And I John saw the holy city, new Jerusalem, coming down from God out of heaven, prepared as a bride adorned for her husband. And I heard a great voice out of heaven saying, Behold, the tabernacle of God is with men, and he will dwell with them, and they shall be his people, and God himself shall be with them, and be their God. And God shall wipe away all tears from their eyes; and there shall be no more death, neither sorrow, nor crying, neither shall there be any more pain: for the former things are passed away. And he that sat upon the throne said, Behold, I make all things new. And he said unto me, Write: for these words are true and faithful.

Revelation 21:9-27 And there came unto me one of the seven angels which had the seven vials full of the seven last plagues, and talked with me, saying, Come hither, I will shew thee the bride, the Lamb's wife. And he carried me away in the spirit to a great and high mountain, and shewed me that great city, the holy Jerusalem, descending out of heaven from God, having the glory of God: and her light was like unto a stone most precious, even like a jasper stone, clear as crystal; and had a wall great and high, and had twelve gates, and at the gates twelve angels, and names written thereon, which are the names of the twelve tribes of the children of Israel: On the east three gates; on the north three gates; on the south three gates; and on the west three gates. And the wall of the city had twelve foundations, and in them the names of the twelve apostles of the Lamb. And he that talked with me had a golden reed to measure the city, and the gates thereof, and the wall thereof. And the city lieth foursquare, and the length is as large as the breadth: and he measured the city with the reed, twelve thousand furlongs [approx. 1,400 miles, or 2,250 kilometers]. The length and the breadth and the height of it are equal. And he measured the wall thereof, an hundred and forty and four cubits, according to the measure of a man, that is, of the angel. And the building of the wall of it was of jasper: and the city was pure gold, like unto clear glass. And the foundations of the wall of the city were garnished with all manner of precious stones. The first foundation was jasper; the second, sapphire; the third, a chalcedony; the fourth, an emerald; the fifth, sardonyx; the sixth, sardius; the seventh, chrysolyte; the eighth, beryl; the ninth, a topaz; the tenth, a chrysoprasus; the eleventh, a jacinth; the twelfth, an amethyst. And the twelve gates were twelve pearls; every several gate was of one pearl: and the street of the city was pure gold, as it were transparent glass. *And I saw no temple therein: for the Lord God Almighty and the Lamb are the temple of it.* And the city had no need of the sun, neither of the moon, to shine in it: for the glory of God did lighten it, and the Lamb is the light thereof. And the nations of them which are saved shall walk in the light of it: and the kings of the earth do bring their glory and honour into it. And the gates of it shall not be shut at all by day: for there shall be no night there. And they shall bring the glory and honour of the nations into it. And there shall in no wise enter into it any thing that defileth, neither whatsoever worketh abomination, or maketh a lie: but they which are written in the Lamb's book of life.

²enter the heart of the Creator—*"For the Lord God Almighty and the Lamb are the temple of it."*

John 17:20-23 Neither pray I for these alone, but for them also which shall believe on me through their word; that they all may be one; as thou, Father, art in me, and I in thee, that they also may be one in us: that the world may believe that thou hast sent me. And the glory which thou gavest me I have given them; *that they may be one, even as we are one: I in them, and thou in me, that they may be made perfect in one*; and that the world may know that thou hast sent me, and hast loved them, as thou hast loved me.

⁴**war of annihilation of the building blocks of New Jerusalem, the Bride of Christ**— As follows, the *persecuted woman* is the Bride of Christ, also referred to as the Heavenly City, and New Jerusalem. The "woman" is a corporate concept better understood in terms of a living building made up of individual, living blocks. (First, consider the spiritual concept of the living structure specifically titled New Jerusalem in Revelation chapter 21, already provided in the 1st footnote of this chapter.)

Ephesians 2:19-22 (Apostle Paul to the Gentile Ephesians) Now therefore ye are no more strangers and foreigners, but fellowcitizens with the saints, and of the household of God; and are built upon the foundation of the apostles and prophets, Jesus Christ himself being the chief corner stone; in whom all the building fitly framed together [same spiritual building, the Bride of Christ of Revelation 21, made up of living stones, Gentiles included with Jews, with Christ as chief cornerstone] groweth unto an holy temple in the Lord: In whom ye also are builded together for an habitation of God through the Spirit.

1 Peter 2:5, 9-10 (Apostle Peter to the Gentiles:) Ye also, as lively stones, are built up a spiritual house, an holy priesthood, to offer up spiritual sacrifices. . . . Ye are a chosen generation, a royal priesthood, an holy nation, a peculiar people . . . which in time past were not a people, but *are now the people of God . . .*

Next, we see that the same woman is targeted for extermination by the Beast:

Revelation 12:13, 17 And when the dragon saw that he was cast unto the earth, he *persecuted the woman* which brought forth the man child *[the flesh-born offspring of the corporate body of devoted human lovers of God (the Jewish ekklesia, the "woman"), begotten by Yahweh's Holy Spirit through Miryam (the virgin Mary), also a building block and part of the whole "woman"]. . . .* And the dragon was wroth with the woman, and went to make *war with the remnant of her seed*, which keep the commandments of God, and have the testimony of Jesus Christ [Jew and Gentile alike who endure to the end].

Revelation 13:5-8 And there was given unto [the Dragon-empowered Beast, or Anti-Christ] a mouth speaking great things and blasphemies; and power was given unto him to continue forty and two months [1260 days, or 3½ years]. And he opened his mouth in blasphemy against God, to blaspheme his name, and his tabernacle, and them that dwell in heaven. And it was given unto him to make *war with the saints [Jew and Gentile alike]*, and to overcome them: and power was given him over all kindreds, and tongues, and nations. And all that dwell upon the earth shall worship him, whose names are not written in the book of life of the Lamb slain from the foundation of the world.

Revelation 20:4 And I saw the souls of them that *were beheaded* for the witness of Jesus, and for the word of God, and which had not worshipped the beast, neither his image, neither had received his mark upon their foreheads, or in their hands; and they lived and reigned with Christ a thousand years [Jew and Gentile alike].

⁵**human animals doing what comes naturally**

2 Peter 2:9-13 The Lord knoweth how to deliver the godly out of temptations, and to reserve *the unjust* unto the day of judgment to be punished: but chiefly *them that walk after the flesh* in the lust of uncleanness, and despise government [rule, law, authority of God]. Presumptuous are they, *selfwilled*, they are not afraid to speak evil of dignities [e.g., blaspheming or denouncing the Creator]. . . . These, as *natural brute beasts*, made to be taken and destroyed, speak evil of the things that they understand not; and shall utterly perish in their own corruption; and shall receive the reward of unrighteousness, as they that count it pleasure to riot [Gk. *truphé*, to revel in the luxuries and pleasures of the materialist world] in the day time [all their waking hours].

Jude 1:10 These speak evil of those things which they know not: but what they know *naturally*, as brute beasts, in those things they corrupt themselves.

⁶**cast your vote for president of the New Secular Order**

Daniel 11:36-39 And the king shall do according to his will; and he shall exalt himself, and *magnify himself above every god*, and shall speak marvellous things against the God of gods, and shall prosper till the indignation be accomplished: for that that is determined shall be done. *Neither shall he regard the God of his fathers*, nor the desire of women, *nor regard any god*: for he shall magnify himself above all. But in his estate *shall he honour the God of forces*: and *a god whom his fathers knew not* shall he honour with gold, and silver, and with precious stones, and pleasant things. Thus shall he do in the most strong holds with *a strange god*, whom he shall acknowledge and increase with glory: and he shall cause them to rule over many, and shall divide the land for gain.

Luke 4:5-8 (The ancient Luciferian ambition) And the devil, taking [Messiah] up into an high mountain, shewed unto him all the kingdoms of the world in a moment of time. And the devil said unto him, All this power will I give thee, and the glory of them: for that is delivered unto me; and to whomsoever I will I give it. If thou therefore wilt *worship me*, all shall be thine. And Jesus answered and said unto him, Get thee behind me, Satan: for it is written, Thou shalt worship the Lord thy God, and him only shalt thou serve. (This temptation was couched among two others in the same passage that both attempted to lure Yeshua into the prideful worship of self with the taunting words, "If thou be the Son of God . . .")

⁷**Jah** is the short form of the name of GOD by which He identified Himself to Moses in the voice which spoke to him out of the midst of the fiery burning bush in Horeb (land of Midian). In the following quotation from the book of Exodus, translated into English by the team of translators commissioned by King James of England in their 1611 version, the Hebrew word YHWH is rendered LORD. YHWH is the "ineffable" name of GOD which is deliberately not pronounced at all by many Jews. Other folks variously pronounce it as Yahweh and other times as Jehovah (Yehovah, or even Yehovih) It's often shortened to Jah as in Hallelu-Jah (Praise ye Jah!). Jews generally prefer to refer to Him as Adonai (meaning Lord), instead of using the YHWH form of GOD's name. The difficulty in pinning down the pronunciation seems to arise from the fact that the word YHWH (in Hebrew, and as we see transliterated here) contains no vowels, which is true of the entire Hebrew alphabet. Thus, the original sound of the name may have been lost in time. I, however, accept the conventional Yahweh pronunciation as close enough to the generally accepted modern verbalization of יְהוָה (Hebrew form of YHWH). After all, mispronunciation of His name is surely much more forgivable than twisting of His Word which He personally exalts "above all His name." (Ps.138:2)

Exodus 3:13-15 And Moses said unto God, Behold, when I come unto the children of Israel, and shall say unto them, The God of your fathers hath sent me unto you; and they shall say to me, What is his name? what shall I say unto them? And God said unto Moses, I AM THAT I AM: and he said, Thus shalt thou say unto the children of Israel, I AM hath sent me unto you. And God said moreover unto Moses, Thus shalt thou say unto the children of Israel, The LORD (יהוה) God of your fathers, the God of Abraham, the God of Isaac, and the God of Jacob, hath sent me unto you: *this is my name for ever,* and this is my memorial unto all generations.

[8]**love the Lord your God as He loves you—with a whole heart**

Exodus 34:14-16 For thou shalt worship no other god: for the LORD, whose name is Jealous, is a jealous God: Lest thou make a covenant with the inhabitants of the land, and they go a whoring after their gods, and do sacrifice unto their gods, and one call thee, and thou eat of his sacrifice; and thou take of their daughters unto thy sons, and their daughters go a whoring after their gods, and make thy sons go a whoring after their gods.

Deuteronomy 31:16 And the LORD said unto Moses, Behold, thou shalt sleep with thy fathers; and this people will rise up, and go a whoring after the gods of the strangers of the land, whither they go to be among them, and will forsake me, and break my covenant which I have made with them.

Judges 2:17 And yet they would not hearken unto their judges, but they went a whoring after other gods, and bowed themselves unto them: they turned quickly out of the way which their fathers walked in, obeying the commandments of the LORD; but they did not so.

Psalms 106:35-39 But were mingled among the heathen, and learned their works. And they served their idols: which were a snare unto them. Yea, they sacrificed their sons and their daughters unto devils, and shed innocent blood, even the blood of their sons and of their daughters, whom they sacrificed unto the idols of Canaan: and the land was polluted with blood. Thus were they defiled with their own works, and went a whoring with their own inventions.

Ezekiel 6:9 And they that escape of you shall remember me among the nations whither they shall be carried captives, because I am broken with their whorish heart, which hath departed from me, and with their eyes, which go a whoring after their idols: and they shall lothe themselves for the evils which they have committed in all their abominations.

Ezekiel 23:29-30 And they shall deal with thee hatefully, and shall take away all thy labour, and shall leave thee naked and bare: and the nakedness of thy whoredoms shall be discovered, both thy lewdness and thy whoredoms. I will do these things unto thee, because thou hast gone a whoring after the heathen, and because thou art polluted with their idols.

[9]**black light**

Luke 11:34-35 The light of the body is the eye: therefore when thine eye is single, thy whole body also is full of light; but when thine eye is evil, thy body also is full of darkness. Take heed therefore that the light which is in thee be not darkness.

[10]**PA CRIM keeping up with the Joneses**—The current Pacific Rim economic crisis dominating the daily news (Nov.-Dec. 1997), which has severely rocked financial systems worldwide and even threatens the mighty American stock market, underscores the magnitude of this religious obsession with materialist power and glory. The principal reason

for the virtual collapsing of the economies of the Philippines, Malaysia, Thailand, Indonesia, Hong Kong, South Korea, and now also seriously threatening Japan (2nd largest economy in the world) is the extravagant spending spree launched with borrowed money over the last couple decades or so, both by governments as well as private sector enterprises.

Additionally, rampant corruption in numerous PACRIM nations is responsible for the siphoning off of billions of dollars by lucre-crazed leaders. For example, Roh Tae-Woo, S. Korean president from 1987-1993 admitted last year (1996) to amassing $650 million in bribes while in office for favors to private sector interests. This is just one example.

Everything from outrageous, world class, high-rise office buildings (rivaling those in USA) to lucrative real estate purchases, to electronics and other manufacturing plants, were financed with borrowed money that was not adequately secured. Now the uncollectible bad debt ($1 trillion in Japan alone) has thrown the economies of these nations into a tail spin, bankrupted their financial institutions, and devastated their stock markets. All of this highlighting the age-old craze for material glory that rules over the societies of covetous men; and, that, in the case of S.E. Asia, spun completely out of control as those nations strove to compete with and outdo the MOTHER OF HARLOTS.

(Bible basics on covetousness)

Jeremiah 51:13 (Speaking of Babylon, the prophet characterizes her almost identically as John in the Apocalypse:) O thou that dwellest upon many waters, abundant in treasures, thine end is come, and the measure of thy *covetousness.*

Luke 12:15 Take heed, and beware of covetousness: for a man's life consisteth not in the abundance of the things which he possesseth.—Christ Yeshua

Mark 7:21-23 For from within, out of the heart of men, proceed evil thoughts, adulteries, fornications, murders, thefts, covetousness, wickedness, deceit, lasciviousness, an evil eye, blasphemy, pride, foolishness: All these evil things come from within, and defile the man.—Yeshua

Colossians 3:5 Mortify therefore your members which are upon the earth; fornication, uncleanness, inordinate affection, evil concupiscence, and *covetousness, which is idolatry.*—Apostle Paul

Exodus 18:21 (Wise counsel to Moses by his father-in-law for sound system of governance and leadership:) Moreover thou shalt provide out of all the people able men, such as fear God, *men of truth, hating covetousness*; and place such over them, to be rulers of thousands, and rulers of hundreds, rulers of fifties, and rulers of tens . . . .

Psalms 119:35-37 (Prayer of the Psalmist for corruption-free direction and godly guidance:) Make me to go in the path of thy commandments; for therein do I delight. Incline my heart unto thy testimonies, and not to covetousness. Turn away mine eyes from beholding vanity; and quicken thou me in thy way.

Proverbs 28:16 (Counsel of Solomon to wise leaders:) The prince that wanteth [lacks] understanding is also a great oppressor [tax-and-spend fiend]: but he that hateth covetousness shall prolong his days.

Jeremiah 6:13 (The true prophet reproving his own people for their corruption:) For from the least of them even unto the greatest of them every one is given to covetousness; and from the prophet even unto the priest every one dealeth falsely [for the "fast buck," or "violence, spoil, and oppression (vs.6-7)"].

[11]"and the (metropolitan) beat goes on"

Psalm 49:11-13 Their inward thought is, that their houses shall continue for ever, and their dwelling places to all generations; they call their lands after their own names. Nevertheless man being in honour abideth not: he is like the beasts that perish. This their way is their folly: yet their posterity approve their sayings.

[12]**Cain and the new alternative religion**

Genesis 4:17 And Cain knew his wife; and she conceived, and bare Enoch: and he builded *a city*, and called the name of the city, after the name of his son, Enoch.

[13]**hooked by lust**

1 Corinthians 6:16 What? know ye not that he which is joined to an harlot is one body? for two, saith he, shall be one flesh.—Paul

Matthew 5:28 I say unto you, That whosoever looketh on a woman to lust after her hath committed adultery with her already in his heart.—Christ Yeshua

[14]**financial "freedom"**

Proverb 22:7 The rich ruleth over the poor, and the *borrower is servant to the lender*.

[15]φαρμακεία (**translated** *"sorcery"*) = **Gk.** *pharmakeia* = **Eng.** *pharmaceuticals, medications, drugs*

Revelation 18:21-24 And a mighty angel took up a stone like a great millstone, and cast it into the sea, saying, Thus with violence shall that great city Babylon be thrown down, and shall be found no more at all. . . . for *by thy sorceries were all nations deceived.* And in her was found the blood of prophets, and of saints, and of all that were slain upon the earth.—Consider that, in 1997 alone, the major daily television news programs announced the development of no less than 28 new drugs (more than one every other week), to treat everything from baldness and failing memory to obesity and wrinkles . The latest, most promising pharmaceutical research and developments are in the realms of genetic manipulation techniques. November and December of 1997 saw the announcements of discoveries at UCLA and MIT that researchers expect will soon lead to the development of a pill or drug to dramatically slow the aging process. At last, by his advanced 20th century medical technologies, modern man touts himself to be on the scientific threshold of discovering the proverbial and much-sought-after "Fountain of Youth!" What is more, this research could advance dramatically with the announcement on December 26, 1997 on ABC's "Cutting Edge" segment of their daily news broadcast of a new microchip "laboratory" that incorporates micro-miniature scale "test tube" capability—actually manifold test chambers—promising virtual obsolescence of the conventional medical lab. Billed as a "scientific revolution—an entire medical lab on a chip," as many as 10,000 lab tests can be performed simultaneously within a single chip! One of the greatest promises of the new technology, according to the report, is in the development of new drugs to treat everything from aids to cancer. The expensive, labor-intensive tests of conventional laboratories can now be replicated in the microscopic environment of the multi-layered chip where fluids are pumped electronically through mazes of channels approximately the size of a human hair into thousands of tiny test chambers no larger than a speck of dust, all etched within the chip. (BABYLON now promises to be able to "cure it all" and heal whatever ails you, supposedly, including the inexorable process of aging—and perhaps even death, if we may stretch the logic!? Who needs God, anyway? The "Myth" will soon be abolished!)

(Unable to reconcile their love of mammon and their affection for the glory of BABYLON with the indisputable biblical sanctions against the characteristic materialism of it, hardly a single Bible prophecy "expert" dares to venture a truly objective analysis of the meaning of the above passage on the great whore quoted from the Apocalypse. To a man, almost every one turns a blind eye to the significance of this identifying feature of the Great City, merely assigning this highly prophetic item a pitifully shallow interpretation, by narrowly applying it to the (albeit) rampant abuse, traffic, and black market of *illicit drugs*. Whereas, there is absolutely no basis whatsoever for such a narrowly constricted application or interpretation. In fact, the repeated, severe condemnation of chemical manipulations for medical purposes—punishable by death, and called sorcery in the Scriptures—is based in the essence of that "art/science" as a form of robbing the Creator God of His own glory and sovereign right to regulate the lives and affairs of men through managing their ultimate health and well-being. Sickness and health are plainly evident in the Scriptures as divine instruments of either correction or reward for violation or cooperation with the purposes of God. Playing "God" is tantamount to blasphemy, according to the Hebrews. The strict prohibition of "sorcery" is a manifest token of the Creator's disdain for the iniquitous self-glorification of unrighteous men, who purpose to defy the course of nature, defeat the purposes of God, and to displace divine action in the lives of men with their own devices, as well as to diminish the value of all the natural remedies already made available in nature by the Hand of the Creator. It's not by narcotics and psychedelics that "all nations" are being deceived, but by the seriously erroneous notion that man, by his own sciences and technologies, can do without his dependence on the Creator, and thus impeach God from His throne to then assume that seat unto himself!)

¹⁶**the twilight preference**

John 3:19-21 And this is the condemnation, that light is come into the world, and men loved darkness rather than light, because their deeds were evil. For every one that doeth evil hateth the light, neither cometh to the light, lest his deeds should be reproved. But he that doeth truth cometh to the light, that his deeds may be made manifest, that they are wrought in God.

¹⁷**international dominion of BABYLON**

Revelation 17:15 And [the angel] saith unto me, The waters which thou sawest, where the whore sitteth, are peoples, and multitudes, and nations, and tongues.

¹⁸**nations and souls on the market**

Nahum 3:4-5 Because of the multitude of the whoredoms of the wellfavoured harlot, the mistress of witchcrafts [feminist power struggles], that *selleth nations* through her whoredoms [e.g., by mega-bucks loans, other forms of capitalizing, and finally "bailouts" of bankrupted countries and governments, as we see going on in the ASEAN region now], and families through her witchcrafts [feminist-advanced international family planning agenda, i.e., birth-rate control, meant to sew up the holes and prevent losses in the economic net of opulent Western prosperity which scorns "useless eaters" in favor of manageable slave populations able to participate in Babylonish consumerism]. Behold, I am against thee, saith the LORD of hosts; and I will discover thy skirts upon thy face, and I will shew the nations thy nakedness, and the kingdoms thy shame [all fully exposed in the end].

¹⁹**is, was, and yet to come—timelessness of spiritual dimensionalities**—The realities of the foundational dimension of pre-material "matter" (i.e., spirit) form the basis of the developments which take place in the physical world; that is, the physical is a manifestation of the spiritual. Concerning our study of the 3 competing world orders—Zion (or

New Jerusalem), the Beast, and the Whore—it is important to understand that these entities transcend time and are not confined to any single era in which they are manifested. However, each has a conclusive and ultimate manifestation in which it culminates with a definitive expression (or physical manifestation) on Earth. That is to say, the world orders of Zion, the Beast, and the Whore each have their ultimate fulfillments as defined, global-scale socio-political entities, or "states," on the planet. Verses of Scripture that attest to this timeless, transcendent character are provided below:

Revelation 1:8 I am Alpha and Omega, the beginning and the ending, saith the Lord, *which is, and which was, and which is to come,* the Almighty.

Revelation 17:8 The beast that thou sawest *was, and is not; and shall ascend* out of the bottomless pit, and go into perdition: and they that dwell on the earth shall wonder, whose names were not written in the book of life from the foundation of the world, when they behold the beast that *was, and is not, and yet is.* (And of course, by virtue of indisputable association, *"the woman . . . that great city which reigneth over the kings of the earth"* is also partaker of this transcendent quality, eventually also finding her ultimate megalopolis manifestation on earth in the endtime epitome of metropolism.)

[20]**the seventy week prophecy of Daniel**—Please contact Koinonia House, P.O. Box D, Coeur d'Alene, ID (USA) 83816-0347, or call 1-800-546-8731 to request a copy of Volume 6, No. 3, March 1996 issue of the Koinonia House newsletter, *Personal Update* and see "The Unexpected King," by Chuck Missler. (Please be thoughtful and consider a worthy donation to cover costs.)

Chapter 5—Not Yet

[1]the believer's mandate, mission, and motivation

Matthew 5:14-16 Ye are the light of the world. A city that is set on an hill cannot be hid. Neither do men light a candle, and put it under a bushel, but on a candlestick; and it giveth light unto all that are in the house. Let your light so shine before men, that they may see your good works, and glorify your Father which is in heaven.

Mark 16:15 And he said unto them, Go ye into all the world, and preach the gospel to every creature.

Matthew 24:14 And this gospel of the kingdom shall be preached in all the world for a witness unto all nations; and then shall the end come.

[2]subversive radicals

John 10:20 And many of them said, [Jesus of Nazareth] hath a devil, and is mad; why hear ye him?

Luke 23:2 And they began to accuse him, saying, We found this fellow *perverting the nation*, and forbidding to give tribute to Caesar, saying that he himself is Christ a King.

John 15:18-20 Jesus said: If the [established order] hate you, ye know that it hated me before it hated you. Remember the word that I said unto you, The servant is not greater than his lord. If they have persecuted me, they will also persecute you; if they have kept my saying, they will keep yours also. If ye were of the world, the world would love his own: but because ye are not of the world, but I have chosen you out of the world, therefore the world hateth you. (The following exemplifies the reactionary rage Jesus spoke of:)

Acts 17:5-7 But the Jews which believed not, moved with envy, took unto them certain lewd fellows of the baser sort, and gathered a company, and set all the city on an uproar, and assaulted the house of Jason, and sought to bring [Paul & Silas] out to the people. And when they found them not, they drew Jason and certain brethren unto the rulers of the city, crying, *These that have turned the world upside down* are come hither also; whom Jason hath received: and these all do contrary to the decrees of Caesar, saying that there is another king, one Jesus.

[3]Christ or conformity

Romans 12:1-2 I beseech you therefore, brethren, by the mercies of God, that ye present your bodies a living sacrifice, holy, acceptable unto God, which is your reasonable service. And be not conformed to this world: but be ye transformed by the renewing of your mind, that ye may prove what is that good, and acceptable, and perfect, will of God.

John 17:14-16 Father, I have given them thy word; and the world hath hated them, because they are not of the world, even as I am not of the world. I pray not that thou shouldest take them out of the world, but that thou shouldest keep them from the evil. They are not of the world, even as I am not of the world.—Yeshua

John 15:19 If ye were of the world, the world would love his own: but because ye are not of the world, but I have chosen you out of the world, therefore the world hateth you.

[4]she couldn't let go!

Luke 17:30-33 Even thus shall it be in the day when the Son of man is revealed. In that day, he which shall be upon the housetop, and his stuff in the house, let him not come down to take it away: and he that is in the field, let him likewise not return back. *Remember Lot's wife.* Whosoever shall seek to save his life shall lose it; and whosoever shall lose his life shall preserve it.

[5]the mark of conformity

Revelation 14:9-11 And the third angel followed them, saying with a loud voice, If any man worship the beast and his image, and receive his mark in his forehead, or in his hand, the same shall drink of the wine of the wrath of God, which is poured out without mixture into the cup of his indignation; and he shall be tormented with fire and brimstone in the presence of the holy angels, and in the presence of the Lamb: And the smoke of their torment ascendeth up for ever and ever: and they have no rest day nor night, who worship the beast and his image, and whosoever receiveth the mark of his name.

Matthew 7:21-23 Not every one that saith unto me, Lord, Lord, shall enter into the kingdom of heaven; but he that doeth the will of my Father which is in heaven. Many will say to me in that day, Lord, Lord, have we not prophesied in thy name? and in thy name have cast out devils? and in thy name done many wonderful works? And then will I profess unto them, I never knew you: depart from me, ye that work iniquity.

[6]extermination

Daniel 7:21 I beheld, and the same horn *made war with the saints*, and prevailed against them;

Daniel 7:25 And he shall speak great words against the most High, and shall *wear out the saints* of the most High, and think to change times and laws: and they shall be given into his hand until a time and times and the dividing of time.

Revelation 13:5-7 And there was given unto him a mouth speaking great things and blasphemies; and power was given unto him to continue forty and two months. And he opened his mouth in blasphemy against God, to blaspheme his name, and his tabernacle, and them that dwell in heaven. And it was given unto him to *make war with the saints, and to overcome them*: and power was given him over all kindreds, and tongues, and nations.

[7]**rivals compromise over common spite**—For the first half of the 7-year covenant period, the major religions of the new world order mainstream (and other assorted, compromising religious factions) in concert with the political powers-that-be will viciously target the so-called sects and "cults" of anti-institutional, establishment-censuring faiths— even with capital punishment (see footnote 9). However, once the "prince of the covenant" (the Beast) abolishes all religions, including that of his fathers (Dan.11:37), to replace them all with the exclusive monotheism of his own self-worship during the second half of the last 7 years, then the various swords of persecution become one brutal sword of his 3½ year totalitarian World Reich. The key to this foresight is: the apostasy is not some tame or passive fading of faith among the nominal people of God (as most interpreters seem to think), nor among the humanist pagans either. The real sign that apostasy has set in *with a vengeance*, so to speak, is the vengeance with which it sets in! In other words, neither the pagans nor the nominal religious are any friends of Truth, Christ, or YHWH (disciples included); their only friendly affections are for their own lusts. Their coats, we shall see, are of matching color, and their vile blood of the same type (as Cain's)—and yours, like Abel's, looks best to the lot of them when spilled on the ground, if you dare worship that baneful Christ who "deprives people" of their unbridled "freedom" to lust and "have it their way!"

⁸**in the name of God**

John 16:2 They shall put you out of the synagogues [Gr. *sunagogé* = assemblies or congregations, irrespective of denomination, Jewish, Christian or Muslim]: yea, the time cometh, that whosoever killeth you will think that he doeth God service.

Isaiah 66:5 Hear the word of the LORD, ye that tremble at his word; Your *brethren* that *hated you*, that *cast you out for my name's sake*, said, Let the LORD be glorified: but he shall appear to your joy, and they shall be ashamed.

⁹**dizzy spin-doctors of the Scriptures**

2 Peter 3:16-17 As also in all [Paul's] epistles, speaking in them of [the coming of the day of God]; in which are some things hard to be understood, which *they that are unlearned and unstable wrest [wrench, forcefully distort, pervert, twist as by violence], as they do also the other scriptures,* unto their own destruction. Ye therefore, beloved, seeing ye know these things before, beware lest ye also, being led away with the error of the wicked, fall from your own stedfastness.

¹⁰**"radical and bigoted"**—As reported by CBN's April 5th edition of the *700 Club*, 1996, the Media Research Center's 3rd annual study of the television industry, revealed that, of 44,000 news stories in 1995, only 1% highlighted religion or issues of faith. According to the report, the negative portrayals of devoutly religious characters in entertainment TV nearly doubled in 1995 over the previous year, rising from 35% to 65%. Terms commonly used by both the news and entertainment media to refer to the devout were "radical" and "bigoted." [Well, in terms of "bigotry," just as with racial discrimination, *reverse bigotry* is just as contemptible; and, after all, isn't it just as the case of the fool calling the moron an idiot? The popular neo-bigotry of the 90's is a politically-correct prejudice propagandized against Judeo-Christian orthodoxy, and anything Biblical, including GOD! And, with respect to democracy, self-determination, and pro-choice philosophies, like Love and Freedom, they are *all* classically *Biblical concepts, limited* in scope by the framework of the LAW established by GOD Almighty, Who, increasingly as the days go by, is Himself a victim of growing neo-bigotry intolerance. Modern humanists have succeeded in conveniently redefining "human rights" as self-originating and conforming to a pure interest in, gratification of, absorption with, and actualization of *self;* not as endowments from the Maker of heaven, earth and mankind, Who still holds *all rights* and constraints under His own sovereign authority—a principle which is detested by them. Yet, for the time being, GOD advocates total freedom and choice: *"He that is unjust, let him be unjust still: and he which is filthy, let him be filthy still: and he that is righteous, let him be righteous still: and he that is holy, let him be holy still."* But, without abdication of primal or ultimate authority, or any abrogation of the principles of personal responsibility, accountability and burden of consequence, He (THE Alpha and THE Omega, the Beginning and the End) adds, *"And, behold, I come quickly; and my reward is with me, to give every man according as his work shall be."* Needless to say, that judgment won't be up for referendum or the democratic vote of corrupt, egocentric humanists. *(Rev.22:11-13)*]

¹¹**Yahweh? or YHWH, the tetragrammaton (יהוה)**—*Vine's Expository Dictionary of Biblical Words* explains: "The Tetragrammaton YHWH appears without its own vowels [in the original manuscripts], and its exact pronunciation is debated (Jehovah, Yehovah, Jahweh, Yahweh). . .This use of the word occurs 6,828 times. The word appears in every period of biblical Hebrew. . .The divine name YHWH appears only in the Bible. Its precise meaning is much debated. God chose it as His personal name by which He

related specifically to His chosen or covenant people. Its first appearance in the Biblical record is Genesis 2:4: "These are the generations of the heavens and of the earth when they were created, in the day that the *LORD* God made the earth and the heavens . . ." (The KJV, King James Version—used throughout this book—translates each occurrence of יְהֹוָה as *"LORD,"* in all capitals.)

¹²the hooker

Genesis 3:1 Now the serpent was more subtil than any beast of the field which the LORD God had made. And he said unto the woman, Yea, hath God said, Ye shall not eat of *every tree* of the garden?

¹³think about it . . . you deserve better

Genesis 3:2-6 And the woman said unto the serpent, We may eat of the fruit of the trees of the garden: But of the fruit of the tree which is in the midst of the garden, God hath said, Ye shall not eat of it, neither shall ye touch it, lest ye die. And the serpent said unto the woman, Ye shall not surely die: For God doth know that in the day ye eat thereof, then your eyes shall be opened, and *ye shall be as gods*, knowing good and evil. And when the woman saw that the tree was good for food, and that it was pleasant to the eyes, and a tree to be desired to make one wise, she took of the fruit thereof, and did eat, and gave also unto her husband with her; and he did eat.

¹⁴beast as God

II Thessalonians 2:3-4 Let no man deceive you by any means: for that day shall not come, except there come a falling away first, and that man of sin be revealed, the son of perdition; who opposeth and exalteth himself above all that is called God, or that is worshipped; so that he as God sitteth in the temple of God, shewing himself that he is God.

Revelation 13:3-8 And I saw one of his heads as it were wounded to death; and his deadly wound was healed: and all the world wondered after the beast. And they worshipped the dragon which gave power unto the beast: and they worshipped the beast, saying, Who is like unto the beast? who is able to make war with him? And there was given unto him a mouth speaking great things and blasphemies; and power was given unto him to continue forty and two months. And he opened his mouth in blasphemy against God, to blaspheme his name, and his tabernacle, and them that dwell in heaven. And it was given unto him to make war with the saints, and to overcome them: and power was given him over all kindreds, and tongues, and nations. And all that dwell upon the earth shall worship him, whose names are not written in the book of life of the Lamb slain from the foundation of the world.

Daniel 8:23-25 And in the latter time of their kingdom, when the transgressors are come to the full, a king of fierce countenance, and understanding dark sentences, shall stand up. And his power shall be mighty, but not by his own power: and he shall destroy wonderfully, and shall prosper, and practise, and shall destroy the mighty and the holy people. And through his policy also he shall cause craft to prosper in his hand; and he shall magnify himself in his heart, and by peace shall destroy many: he shall also stand up against the Prince of princes; but he shall be broken without hand.

Daniel 11:36-37 And the king shall do according to his will; and he shall exalt himself, and magnify himself above every god, and shall speak marvellous things against the God of gods, and shall prosper till the indignation be accomplished: for that that is determined shall be done. Neither shall he regard the God of his fathers, nor the desire of women, nor regard any god: for he shall magnify himself above all.

[15]**short period**

Revelation 12:12-17 Woe to the inhabiters of the earth and of the sea! for the devil is come down unto you, having great wrath, because *he knoweth that he hath but a short time*. And when the dragon saw that he was cast unto the earth, he persecuted the woman which brought forth the man child. And to the woman were given two wings of a great eagle, that she might fly into the wilderness, into her place, where she is nourished for a *time, and times, and half a time [3½ yrs.]*, from the face of the serpent. . . . And the dragon was wroth with the woman, and went to make war with the remnant of her seed, which keep the commandments of God, and have the testimony of Jesus Christ.

Revelation 12:6 And the woman fled into the wilderness, where she hath a place prepared of God, that they should feed her there *a thousand two hundred and threescore days*.

Revelation 13:5, 7 And [the devil gave the beast] a mouth speaking great things and blasphemies; and power was given unto him to continue *forty and two months*. . . . And it was given unto him to make war with the saints, and to overcome them: and power was given him over all kindreds, and tongues, and nations.

Mark 13:20 And except that the Lord had shortened those days, no flesh should be saved: but for the elect's sake, whom he hath chosen, he hath shortened the days.

[16]**beheading**

Revelation 20:4 And I saw thrones, and they sat upon them, and judgment was given unto them: and I saw the souls of them that were beheaded for the witness of Jesus, and for the word of God, and which had not worshipped the beast, neither his image, neither had received his mark upon their foreheads, or in their hands; and they lived and reigned with Christ a thousand years.

[17]**bow or die**

Revelation 13:15 And [the false prophet] had power to give life unto the image of the beast, that the image of the beast should both speak, and cause that as many as would not worship the image of the beast should be killed.

[18]**that old serpent**

Revelation 12:9 And the great dragon was cast out, that old serpent, called the Devil, and Satan, which deceiveth the whole world: he was cast out into the earth, and his angels were cast out with him.

[19]**America's Godly Heritage**—Statistics courtesy of the Wallbuilder Press video production *America's Godly Heritage*, featuring noted historian David Barton. Available from Eden Communications, 1044 N. Gilbert Rd., Gilbert, AZ 85234 (USA), or toll free in USA at 1-800-332-2261 ($19.95)

[20]**sexual "objects" included**—Forceful and violent seizure of objects of desire includes *people* as sexual "objects." Rape, incest, child molestation, and sexual harassment are all heinous acts of violence and victimization for the satisfaction of purely covetous lusts. YHWH made that plain in the Laws of Moses. And in fact, simple analysis of the *Ten Commandments, reveals that virtually all ten are intended to counter impulses of *covetousness*—i.e., excessive lust and inordinate desire. In their conclusion, they are certainly wrapped up with that specific prohibition being clearly spelled out: "Neither shalt thou desire thy neighbour's wife, neither shalt thou covet thy neighbour's house, his field, or his manservant, or his maidservant, his ox, or his ass, *or any thing* that is thy neighbour's." (Deuteronomy 5:21)

*The Commandments: #I) To love God with all your heart immediately bars covetousness of any sort right from the very first. (As it is, He *is everything*, the All In All.) #2) Have no other gods—for obvious purposes of obtaining their favor toward your lusts which YHWH will not grant. #3) Take not YHWH's name in vain—by selfishly betraying Him in pursuit of other gods once He has favored you. #4) Remember the sabbath day to keep it holy—and take a break from your own self-profiting endeavors, lest you be consumed 365 days a year with your lust for profit. #5) Honor thy father and mother—lest you ultimately abandon them in pursuit of your own ungrateful interests. #6) Thou shalt not kill—to forcefully obtain another's possessions, or to cover up or defend your taking, or in jealousy over the blessings of others. #7) No adultery—one of the most hurtful and destructive of lusts, esp. to children and families. #8) Thou shalt not steal—for easy acquisition of your desires, or as a short-cut of legitimate endeavor. #9) Thou shall not bear false witness against thy neighbor—obviously, to wrongfully acquire a personal benefit (or else why lie about someone else?) #10) Thou shalt not covet thy neighbor's wife or any thing else you might lust after that belongs to your neighbor—or else you will end up committing adultery, stealing, killing (or provoking a killing), bearing false witness, taking YHWH's name in vain, and eventually worshipping another god who will condone these abominations.

[21]**universal covetousness**

Jeremiah 6:13 For from the least of them even unto the greatest of them every one is given to covetousness; and from the prophet even unto the priest every one dealeth falsely.

[22]**covetousness vs. YHWH**—YHWH teaches that we are meant to inherit and possess all things (Rom.8:32, 1 Pet.1:3-4, 2 Pet.1:3-4, Rev.21:7, 1 Cor.6:9-10) as long as we keep our priorities in order. In His domain and by His design, self-sacrificial love, not egotism, is the supreme law at the core of all existence. By YHWH's plan, naturally, the self-sacrifice comes before the reward. Preferring others to oneself is always the prime motivation in this design. That is love. That is God. To worship YHWH with all one's heart, soul, mind, and spirit is to do things His way, to obey His perfect directions (commands), according to the Perfect Design. That is the prime requisite of and for Life, the only life (perfection) that can be permitted to continue forever. All other alternatives and schemes are destructive of Earth's Perfect Design.

[23]**covetousness/idolatry**

Ephesians 5:5 For this ye know, that no whoremonger, nor unclean person, nor covetous man, who is an idolater, hath any inheritance in the kingdom of Christ and of God.

Colossians 3:5 Mortify therefore your members which are upon the earth; fornication, uncleanness, inordinate affection, evil concupiscence, and covetousness, which is idolatry:

[24]**the fruit of a Godless earth**

Revelation 14:19 And the angel thrust in his sickle into the earth, and gathered the vine of the earth, and cast it into the great winepress of the wrath of God.

[25]**the religious clique rife with envy**

Matthew 27:18 For he knew that for envy they had delivered him. *See also next two footnotes.*

[26]**lovers of the status quo**

John 12:19 The Pharisees therefore said among themselves, Perceive ye how ye prevail nothing? behold, the world is gone after him.

John 11:47-48 Then gathered the chief priests and the Pharisees a council, and said, What do we? for this man doeth many miracles. If we let him thus alone, all men will believe on him: and the Romans shall come and take away both our place and nation.

[27]**covetousness of religious leaders**

Luke 16:13-14 No servant can serve two masters: for either he will hate the one, and love the other; or else he will hold to the one, and despise the other. Ye cannot serve God and mammon. And the *Pharisees also, who were covetous,* heard all these things: and they derided him.

[28]**the loudest voices of hate**

Luke 23:13-23 And Pilate, when he had called together the chief priests and the rulers and the people, Said unto them, Ye have brought this man unto me, as one that perverteth the people: and, behold, I, having examined him before you, have found no fault in this man touching those things whereof ye accuse him: No, nor yet Herod: for I sent you to him; and, lo, nothing worthy of death is done unto him. I will therefore chastise him, and release him. (For of necessity he must release one unto them at the feast.) And they cried out all at once, saying, Away with this man, and release unto us Barabbas: (Who for a certain sedition made in the city, and for murder, was cast into prison.) Pilate therefore, willing to release Jesus, spake again to them. But they cried, saying, Crucify him, crucify him. And he said unto them the third time, Why, what evil hath he done? I have found no cause of death in him: I will therefore chastise him, and let him go. And they were instant with loud voices, requiring that he might be crucified. And *the voices of them and of the chief priests prevailed.*

Matthew 27:20 The *chief priests and elders persuaded the multitude* that they should ask Barabbas, and destroy Jesus.

[29]**established order destroyed**

Revelation 11:15, 18 And the seventh angel sounded; and there were great voices in heaven, saying, The kingdoms of this world are become the kingdoms of our Lord, and of his Christ; and he shall reign for ever and ever. And the nations were angry, and thy wrath is come, and the time of the dead, that they should be judged, and that thou shouldest give reward unto thy servants the prophets, and to the saints, and them that fear thy name, small and great; and shouldest destroy them which destroy the earth.

[30]**scarlet and purple vs. clothing of humility**—Inglorious sackcloth represents the antithesis of pomp and pride that comes with material prosperity and wealth. It has was worn often by prophets and others wishing to demonstrate their humility and repentance from sin. The king and every inhabitant (including the animals) of the capital of the mighty kingdom of Assyria once donned sackcloth to seek repentance and mercy, and to spare them the destruction prophesied against them for their pride. (See the book of Jonah.)

[31]**separation and sacrifice, or compromise and conformity?**

Romans 12:1-2 I beseech you therefore, brethren, by the mercies of God, that ye present your bodies a living sacrifice, holy, acceptable unto God, which is your reasonable service. And be not conformed to this world: but be ye transformed by the renewing of your mind, *that ye may prove* what is that good, and acceptable, and perfect, will of God.—Paul

John 15:19 If ye were of the world, the world would love his own: but because ye are not of the world, but I have chosen you out of the world, therefore the world hateth you.—Christ Yeshua

³²God's choice

James 2:5 Hearken, my beloved brethren, Hath not God chosen the poor of this world rich in faith, and heirs of the kingdom which he hath promised to them that love him?

³³Establishment hates light

John 17:14 I have given them thy word; and the world hath hated them, because they are not of the world, even as I am not of the world.—Christ Jesus

John 15:18 If the world hate you, ye know that it hated me before it hated you.— Christ

John 7:7 Me it hateth, because I testify of it, that the works thereof are evil.—Christ

John 3:19-21 And this is the condemnation, that light is come into the world, and men loved darkness rather than light, because their deeds were evil. *For every one that doeth evil hateth the light,* neither cometh to the light, lest his deeds should be reproved. But he that doeth truth cometh to the light, that his deeds may be made manifest, that they are wrought in God.—Christ

³⁴the costs & hazards of following The Non-conformist

Luke 9:23-24 And [Jesus] said to them all, If any man will come after me, let him deny himself, and take up his cross daily, and follow me. For whosoever will save his life shall lose it: but whosoever will lose his life for my sake, the same shall save it.

1 Corinthians 15:19 If in this life only we have hope in Christ, we are of all men most miserable.—Paul

John 15:20 Remember the word that I said unto you, The *servant is not greater* than his lord. If they have persecuted me, *they will also persecute you.*—Christ

2 Timothy 3:12 Yea, and all that will live godly in Christ Jesus shall suffer persecution.—Paul

³⁵last shall be first

Luke 6:20-25 And he lifted up his eyes on his disciples, and said, Blessed be ye poor: for yours is the kingdom of God. Blessed are ye that hunger now: for ye shall be filled. Blessed are ye that weep now: for ye shall laugh. Blessed are ye, when men shall hate you, and when they shall separate you from their company, and shall reproach you, and cast out your name as evil, for the Son of man's sake. Rejoice ye in that day, and leap for joy: for, behold, your reward is great in heaven: for in the like manner did their fathers unto the prophets. But woe unto you that are rich! for ye have received your consolation. Woe unto you that are full! for ye shall hunger. Woe unto you that laugh now! for ye shall mourn and weep.

³⁶the cause of conflict

James 4:1-3 From whence come wars and fightings among you? come they not hence, even of your lusts that war in your members? Ye lust, and have not: ye kill, and desire to have, and cannot obtain: ye fight and war, yet ye have not, because ye ask not. Ye ask, and receive not, because ye ask amiss, that ye may consume it upon your lusts.

³⁷gain, or godliness? (heads up, Christian prosperity buffs!)

1 Timothy 6:3-8 If any man teach otherwise, and consent not to wholesome words, even the words of our Lord Jesus Christ, and to the doctrine which is according to godliness; He is proud, knowing nothing, but doting about questions and strifes of words, whereof cometh envy, strife, railings, evil surmisings, perverse disputings of men of corrupt minds, and destitute of the truth, *supposing that gain is godliness:* from such withdraw thyself. *But godliness with contentment is great gain.* For we brought nothing into this world, and it is certain we can carry nothing out. And having food and raiment let us be therewith content.

[38]betrayal over materialism

Luke 21:16 And ye shall be betrayed both by parents, and brethren, and kinsfolks, and friends; and some of you shall they cause to be put to death.

Mark 13:12 Now the brother shall betray the brother to death, and the father the son; and children shall rise up against their parents, and shall cause them to be put to death.

Matthew 24:10 And then shall many be offended, and shall betray one another, and shall hate one another.

Isaiah 66:5 Your *brethren* that *hated you*, that *cast you out for my name's sake*, said, Let the LORD be glorified: but he shall appear to your joy, and they shall be ashamed.

John 16:2 Yea, the time cometh, that whosoever killeth you will think that he doeth God service.

[39]iconoclast Christianity

John 16:8 When [the Spirit of truth] is come, he will reprove the world of sin, and of righteousness, and of judgment:

Ephesians 5:11-13 And have no fellowship with the unfruitful works of darkness, but rather reprove them. For it is a shame even to speak of those things which are done of them in secret. But all things that are reproved are made manifest by the light: for whatsoever doth make manifest is light.

[40]the light of the world—YHWH's Values

—When challenged by the expert religious scholars about the greatest of the commandments in the Torah (Moses' books of the law), Christ summed up their entire collection of Hebraic teachings with this reply: *"Thou shalt love the Lord thy God with all thy heart, and with all thy soul, and with all thy mind. This is the first and great commandment. And the second is like unto it, Thou shalt love thy neighbour as thyself. On these two commandments hang all the law and the prophets." (Matthew 22:37-40)* These primordial values are the light of the world. He hoped the brilliance & intensity of them put into practice would be the convincing factor to draw all people to His gospel—one nation under God: *"Neither pray I for these [disciples] alone,"* he said, *"but for them also which shall believe on me through their word; that they all may be one; as thou, Father, art in me, and I in thee, that they also may be one in us: that the world may believe that thou hast sent me (John 17:20-21). . . . By this shall all men know that ye are my disciples, if ye have love one to another (John 13:35). . . . Greater love hath no man than this, that a man lay down his life for his friends (John 15:13)."* (O God, what a dark world these days.)

[41]Gentile lusts

Matthew 6:31-32 Therefore take no thought, saying, What shall we eat? or, What shall we drink? or, Wherewithal shall we be clothed? (For after all these things do the Gentiles seek:) for your heavenly Father knoweth that ye have need of all these things.

[42]the expectation

John 20:21 Then said Jesus to them again, Peace be unto you: *as my Father hath sent me, even so send I you.*

[43]profaning and taking of the Name in vain

Exodus 20:7 Thou shalt not take the name of the LORD thy God in vain; for the LORD will not hold him guiltless that taketh his name in vain.

Leviticus 19:12 And ye shall not swear by my name falsely, neither shalt thou profane the name of thy God: I am the LORD.

Ezekiel 22:26 They have put no difference between the holy and profane, neither have they shewed difference between the unclean and the clean . . . and I am profaned among them.

[44]pernicious "Christianity"

2 Peter 2:1-3 But there were false prophets also among the people, even as there shall be false teachers among you, who privily shall bring in damnable heresies, even denying the Lord that bought them, and bring upon themselves swift destruction. And many shall follow their pernicious [highly injurious] ways; *by reason of whom the way of truth shall be evil spoken of.* And *through covetousness* shall they with feigned words make merchandise of you: whose judgment now of a long time lingereth not, and their damnation slumbereth not.

[45]mark of the beast

Revelation 13:16-18 And he causeth *all*, both small and great, rich and poor, free and bond, to receive a mark in their right hand, or in their foreheads: And that *no man* might buy or sell, save he that had the mark, or the name of the beast, or the number of his name. Here is wisdom. Let him that hath understanding count the number of the beast: for it is the number of a man; and his number is Six hundred threescore and six.

[46]manifest by trial

1 Corinthians 3:13 Every man's work shall be made manifest: for the day shall declare it, because it shall be revealed by fire; and the fire shall try every man's work of what sort it is.

1 Peter 1:7 That the trial of your faith, being much more precious than of gold that perisheth, though it be tried with fire, might be found unto praise and honour and glory at the appearing of Jesus Christ:

James 1:3 Knowing this, that the trying of your faith worketh patience.

James 1:12 Blessed is the man that endureth temptation: for when he is tried, he shall receive the crown of life, which the Lord hath promised to them that love him.

Revelation 3:10 Because thou hast kept the word of my patience, I also will keep thee from the hour of temptation, which shall come upon all the world, to try them that dwell upon the earth.

[47]understanding the final fiery trial

Daniel 11:33, 35 And they that understand among the people shall instruct many: yet they shall fall by the sword, and by flame, by captivity, and by spoil, many days. . . . And some of them of understanding shall fall, to try them, and to purge, and *to make them white*, even to the time of the end: because it is yet for a time appointed.

Zechariah 13:9 And I will bring the third part through the fire, and will refine them as silver is refined, and will try them as gold is tried: they shall call on my name, and I will hear them: I will say, It is my people: and they shall say, The LORD is my God.

Revelation 7:14 These are they which came out of great tribulation, and have washed their robes, and *made them white* in the blood of the Lamb.

[48]woolen wanna-be's

Matthew 7:15 Beware of false prophets, which come to you in sheep's clothing, but inwardly they are ravening wolves.

Chapter 6—"Ye Shall Not Die. . . . Ye Shall Be As Gods"

[1]the Eve Syndrome

Genesis 2:15-17 And the LORD God took the man, and put him into the garden of Eden to dress it and to keep it. And the LORD God commanded the man, saying, Of every tree of the garden thou mayest freely eat: But of the tree of the *knowledge of good and *evil*, thou shalt not eat of it: for in the day that thou eatest thereof thou shalt surely die.

*evil, from Heb. רע, *rah*, is derived from the root *ra'á*, meaning *to spoil by breaking to pieces*; hence, *ruinous, destructive, hurtful, injurious*; and thus also signifying *power* (to destroy, ruin, hurt. etc.).

Genesis 3:1-7 Now the serpent was more subtil than any beast of the field which the LORD God had made. And he said unto the woman, Yea, hath God said, Ye shall not eat of every tree of the garden? And the woman said unto the serpent, We may eat of the fruit of the trees of the garden: But of the fruit of the tree which is in the midst of the garden, God hath said, Ye shall not eat of it, neither shall ye touch it, lest ye die. And the serpent said unto the woman, Ye shall not surely die: For God doth know that in the day ye eat thereof, then your eyes shall be opened, and *ye shall be as gods*, knowing good and evil. And when the woman saw that the tree was good for food, and that it was pleasant to the eyes, and *a tree to be desired to make one wise*, she took of the fruit thereof, and did eat, and gave also unto her husband with her; and he did eat.

[2]Please pardon the seemingly unending assortment of names and titles used in this book to refer to the Wicked human who will one day soon arise to rule the world in which we live. The intent is to broaden the imaginary perspectives by which we might form a mental picture of who and what this creature will appear to be; so that, when he appears we will all have contemplated the various possibilities and potentialities of his highly devious aspect, and *not mistake him by any means* as The Incomparable Messiah. This book is not written exclusively to and for Christians and/or Bible students. It is hoped it will be readable to a variety of audiences, including those of faiths competing with the Judeo-Christian worldview, not to exclude atheists and agnostics. The prophetic picture of the future is profound and heavily implicates the rise of the Eastern world into very prominent roles within that context. In fact, the so-called Antichrist will have more sweeping and influential sway "toward the East and toward the South" (& toward the Holy Land) than any other. The days of the age of Western hegemony are numbered. The Antichrist will not come out of Europe, contrary to Western Christian views. Hence, a deliberate attempt is made on my part to break the confining molds of those severely limited perspectives, and to introduce fresh and multi-aspect perspectives. Please bear with me, and consider all the other possibilities, which egocentrist religious mind-sets fail of. The "Beast" of the Hebrew Scriptures, will not readily appear as a beast to the untrained eye. In fact, so magnificent, sophisticated, persuasive, and crafty shall his appearing be that *many* of even the most prominent religious leaders (yes, even Christian) will fall into his grip. He will be the greatest man to walk the planet Earth since Christ Himself, and will quite convincingly make himself out to be even greater. Brace yourselves. Behold, he cometh, and you will marvel!

[3]white with blood!?

Revelation 7:13-14 And one of the elders answered, saying unto me, What are these which are arrayed in white robes? and whence came they? And I said unto him, Sir, thou knowest. And he said to me, These are *they which came out of great tribulation*, and have *washed their robes, and made them white in the blood of the Lamb.

"Mystic" Christians prefer to "spiritualize" the concept of washing one's robes in the Lamb's blood, by insisting on viewing this act as a *painless act of faith*—"faith" in the saving grace of Christ, by "belief" in the expiatory value of Christ shedding his blood to atone for our sins. They love to mysticize the concept, focusing on *the grace aspect* of the atoning bloodshed, for what I regard as pseudo-spiritual motives. After all, it is quite easy to plunge yourself in analgesic grace, by the simplistic, non-demanding, easy-come-easy-go belief that you will be painlessly cleansed of all your sins by merely confessing them and accepting the "free gift" of atonement and "salvation" (another excessively mysticized concept). On the other hand, it is quite another notion to plunge your "garments" (which we all know outwardly define who and what we are) in the reason, purpose, and cause for which that Precious Blood was shed. *It was shed for the keeping of the commandments of God.* For, indeed, it was the Father God who willed that His Son should shed His blood (i.e., sacrifice His life) to restore *that* very objective—*the keeping of the commandments of God* (as in, *"Thy will be done in earth as it is in Heaven"*). *That is* the putting away and remission of sins (i.e., disobedience to His will). To wash, or literally *plunge* (per the orig. Gk.) one's garments (symbolic of lifestyle) in the Lamb's blood, is to plunge yourself into His cause, His purpose, His passion, His tribulation, His sacrifice, and His obedience to the Father's will. Far from the painless grace of the spiritualist "Christians," this plunging will cost you *everything*, just as it did the Lamb of Obedience (Heb.5:8, 1Pe.2:21), whom the spiritualists love for His grace, but not for His commandment to go and do *the same (Jn.20:21)*. For the servant is not greater than his lord! Spiritual folks who simply swish around "grace-fully" in the delicate cycle of their spiritual "Maytag" washing machines, found in the local Christian Laundromats, called "churches," would do well to drain those machines (including all the fabric softener), fill them with blood, switch them to the "heavily soiled" cycle, and get down to the rough and tumble business of following in the Lamb's blood-stained footsteps. Enough mysticism, spiritualism, rapturism, escapism, God-and-mammonism, dispensationalism, denominationalism ("my-laundromat's-better-than-yours-ism"), and hokey tele-evangelism! Where have all the martyrs gone? What happened to the venerated *Tradition of Obedience* as per the martyred Apostles of the Lamb? (And for those who scoff cockily at the "martyr complex," my advice is, try some extra bleach on those dirty undergarments. Don't just white wash "the *outside* of the sepulcher," as the Lord said.)

James 1:27 Pure religion and undefiled before God and the Father is this, To visit the fatherless and widows in their affliction, and to keep himself *unspotted from the [established order]*.

⁴the abomination spoken of by Daniel the prophet

Daniel 9:27 And he shall confirm the covenant with many for one week: and in the midst of the week he shall cause the sacrifice and the oblation to cease, and for the *overspreading of abominations* he shall make it *desolate*, even until the consummation, and that determined shall be poured upon the desolate.

Daniel 11:31 And arms shall stand on his part, and they shall pollute the sanctuary of strength, and shall take away the daily sacrifice, and they shall place *the abomination that maketh desolate*.

Daniel 12:11 And from the time that the daily sacrifice shall be taken away, and *the abomination that maketh desolate* set up, there shall be a thousand two hundred and ninety days.

⁵the abomination standing where it ought not

Mark 13:14 But when ye shall see the abomination of desolation, spoken of by Daniel the prophet, *standing where it ought not*, (let him that readeth understand,) . . .

Daniel 11:31 They shall *pollute the sanctuary of strength*, and shall take away the daily sacrifice, and they shall place the abomination that maketh desolate.

Matthew 24:15 When ye therefore shall see the abomination of desolation, spoken of by Daniel the prophet, stand *in the holy place*, (whoso readeth, let him understand:)

⁶think in shabuwas—Similar to how we in the West refer to a group or period of 10 years as a *decade*, so the word *shabuwa* refers to a set of seven. Unfortunately, our English language has no specific term by which to translate the Hebrew *shabuwa* effectively. *Week* was the best choice available to the translators, for lack of a more appropriate alternative. Instead of *week*, the only other word that might have been used by the translators is *heptad*, which neither denotes nor connotes a period of time, but simply a group of seven; whereas, *week* clearly suggests a time element bundled in multiples of seven.

⁷the accord of 1993—In the wake of the Persian Gulf War, the USA sponsored regional (Middle East) peace talks in Norway during which secret negotiations occurred between Israel and the Palestine Liberation Organization. These culminated in the signing of an accord, called the Declaration of Principles, in Washington, DC by Yasser Arafat (chairman of the PLO) and Israeli Prime Minister Yitzhak Rabin on Sept. 13, 1993. This was the initiation of the notorious "peace process" we have heard so much about over the last couple of years, especially in terms of it *breaking down*. The breakdowns have occurred with each side citing the other for alleged violations of the terms of the agreements. In other words, the accord lacks firm and faithful adherence by each of the covenant parties. (Someone's cheating on the agreement, and the traditional scapegoats—guess who—are still getting the blame.) This is a perfect example of an existing covenant that apparently needs confirmation, reaffirmation, and committed implementation in order to produce the desired result, peace in the heart of the Middle East!

⁸determined upon Daniel's patrimony

Daniel 9:24 Seventy weeks are determined upon *thy people and upon thy holy city*, to finish the transgression, and to make an end of sins, and to make reconciliation for iniquity, and to bring in everlasting righteousness, and to seal up the vision and prophecy, and to anoint the most Holy.

⁹the burdensome controversy of Jerusalem

Zechariah 12:2-3 Behold, I will make Jerusalem a cup of trembling unto all the people round about, when they shall be in the siege both against Judah and against Jerusalem. And in that day will I make Jerusalem a burdensome stone for all people: all that burden themselves with it shall be cut in pieces, though all the people of the earth be gathered together against it.

Isaiah 34:8 For it is the day of the LORD's vengeance, and the year of recompences for the *controversy of Zion*.

¹⁰world headquarters of the beast

II Thessalonians 2:3-4 Let no man deceive you by any means: for that day shall not come, except there come a falling away first, and that man of sin be revealed, the son of perdition; who opposeth and exalteth himself above all that is called God, or that is worshipped; so that he as God sitteth *in the temple of God*, shewing himself that he is God.

Daniel 11:45 And he shall plant the tabernacles of his palace between the seas [Dead and Mediterranean] *in the glorious holy mountain* [at Jerusalem—see Isaiah 27:13] . . .

[11]planetary liberation front achieves hegemony under the "little horn" of galactic ambitions

Daniel 8:9-12 And out of one of [the provinces of the collapsed Grecian Empire] came forth *a little horn*, which waxed exceeding great, toward the south, and toward the east, and toward the pleasant land [Israel]. And it waxed great, even to the host of heaven [speaking perhaps of deep space or interplanetary ambitions, or his seduction and defeat of some of YHWH's astral cadres, as per Rev.12]; and it cast down some of the host and of the stars to the ground, and stamped upon them. Yea, he [the *"king of fierce countenance"* in verses 23-24] magnified himself even to the prince of the host [in reference to the celestial Monarch of the hyperdimensional corps, spuriously claiming himself to be the monarch of all intergalactic civilizations], and by him the daily sacrifice was taken away, and the place of his sanctuary [i.e., YHWH's] was cast down. And *an host* [masses of followers, esp. as organized for military campaign] was given him *against the daily sacrifice* by reason of transgression, and it cast down the truth to the ground; and it practised [successfully achieves establishment], and prospered [with sweeping, prolific expansion].

Daniel 11:21-24 And in his estate shall stand up *a vile person*, to whom they shall not give the honour of the kingdom: but *he shall come in peaceably, and obtain the kingdom by flatteries.* And with the *arms* of a flood shall they be overflown from before him, and shall be broken; yea, also [indeed him] *the prince of the covenant.* And after the league made with him he shall work deceitfully: for he shall come up, and shall become strong with a small people. He shall enter peaceably even upon the fattest places of the province; and he shall do that which his fathers have not done, nor his fathers' fathers; he shall scatter among them the prey, and spoil, and riches: yea, and he shall forecast his devices against the strong holds.

[12]prince of the covenant mortally wounded by deadly weapon

Revelation 13:3 And I saw one of his heads as it were *wounded to death; and his deadly wound was healed*: and all the world wondered after the beast.

Revelation 13:12, 14 And [another beast, the false prophet] exerciseth all the power of the first beast before him, and causeth the earth and them which dwell therein to worship the first beast, *whose deadly wound was healed.* . . . And deceiveth them that dwell on the earth by the means of those miracles which he had power to do in the sight of the beast; saying to them that dwell on the earth, that they should make an image to the beast, which *had the wound by a sword, and did live.*

[13]technological superiority—the gods of the New Secular Order

Daniel 11:38-39 But in his estate shall he honour the God *of forces* [military technologies & capabilities]: *and a god whom his fathers knew not* shall he honour with gold, and silver, and with precious stones, and pleasant things. Thus shall he do in the most strong holds with a *strange god* [doubtlessly hi-tech, New Age, Luciferian & probably alien], whom he shall acknowledge and increase with glory: and he shall cause them to rule over many, and shall divide the land for gain.

Daniel 11:37 Neither shall he regard the God of his fathers[Islamic, most likely], nor the desire of women [typically Muslim], nor regard any god: for he shall magnify himself above all [the new religion].

Revelation 13:4-5 And they worshipped the dragon *which gave power unto the beast*: and they worshipped the beast, saying, Who is like unto the beast? *who is able to make war with him?* And there was given unto him a mouth speaking great things and blasphemies; and power was given unto him to continue forty and two months.

[14]no other civilization shall be superior to ours

Daniel 8:10 And [the "little horn" antichrist] waxed great, *even to the host of heaven*; and it cast down some of the host and of the stars to the ground, and stamped upon them. (cf. footnote 11)

Revelation 13:6 And he opened his mouth in blasphemy against God, to blaspheme his name, and his tabernacle, and *them that dwell in heaven.*

[15]extraterrestrial "invasion" of Earth, or reclamation by owner?

Revelation 19:11-19 I saw heaven opened, and behold a white horse; and he that sat upon him was called Faithful and True, and in righteousness he doth judge and make war . . . And the armies which were in heaven followed him upon white horses, clothed in fine linen, white and clean. . . . And I saw the beast, and the kings of the earth, and their armies, gathered together to make war against him that sat on the horse, and against his army.

Jude 1:14-15 And Enoch also, the seventh from Adam, prophesied of these, saying, Behold, the Lord cometh with ten thousands of his saints, to execute judgment upon all, and to convince all that are ungodly among them of all their ungodly deeds which they have ungodly committed, and of all their hard speeches which ungodly sinners have spoken against him.

[16]electronic communications

Job 38:35 Canst thou send lightnings, that they may go, and say unto thee, Here we are? [Apparently, *yes!*]

[17]grandiose rhetoric of the alternate Messiah

Revelation 13:2-6 And all the world wondered after the beast . . . And they worshipped the dragon which gave power unto the beast: and they worshipped the beast, saying, Who is like unto the beast? who is able to make war with him? And there was given unto him *a mouth speaking great things and blasphemies*; and power was given unto him to continue forty and two months. And he *opened his mouth in blasphemy* against God, to blaspheme his name, and his tabernacle, and them that dwell in heaven.

Daniel 11:36-37 And the king shall do according to his will; and he shall exalt himself, and magnify himself above every god, and *shall speak marvellous things* against the God of gods, and shall prosper till the indignation be accomplished: for that that is determined shall be done. Neither shall he regard the God of his fathers, nor the desire of women, nor regard any god: for he shall magnify himself above all.

See also Daniel 7:7-8, 19-20 about "that horn that had eyes, and *a mouth that spake very great things.* . ."

[18]will flattery persuade you?

Daniel 11:21, 32 And in his estate shall stand up a vile person, to whom they shall not give the honour of the kingdom: but he shall come in peaceably, and obtain the kingdom by flatteries. . . . And such as do wickedly against the covenant shall he corrupt by flatteries . . .

[19]**inspiration is the key**

2 Peter 1:20-21 Knowing this first, that no prophecy of the scripture is of any private interpretation. For the prophecy came not in old time by the will of man: but holy men of God spake as they were moved by the Holy Ghost.

John 16:13 Howbeit when he, the Spirit of truth, is come, he will guide you into all truth: for he shall not speak of himself; but whatsoever he shall hear, that shall he speak: and he will shew you things to come.

Isaiah 45:11 Thus saith the LORD, the Holy One of Israel, and his Maker, Ask me of things to come concerning my sons, and concerning the work of my hands command ye me.

2 Timothy 2:15 Study to shew thyself approved unto God, a workman that needeth not to be ashamed, rightly dividing the word of truth.

[20]**"rapid-fire" knowledge growth**—"The rapid fire advance of cloning technology," reports CBS' Ed Bradley, "is now so fast the law can't keep up with it. . . . Just hours after the FDA said it would regulate key cloning research, scientists announced their latest breakthrough, cloned cows genetically altered to produce human medicine." (News report on "Pharming," *CBS Evening News*, Ed Bradley, CBS, 20 January 1998.)

[21]**the deaf hear**—"Cutting Edge," *World News Tonight*, rep. Gina Smith, ABC, 27 May 1998.

[22]**the blind see**—"Bionic Eyes," *World News Tonight*, rep. James Walker, ABC, 5 November 1998.

[23]**stem cells**—*Ibid.*, principal report by James Walker.

(Perhaps what Mr. Jennings was suggesting by the "frightening" implications of this stem cell technology has something to do with the potential commerce and profit to be made in the marketing of body parts and the fetal "raw material" from which they would stem. See Rev.18:12-13 in reference to the merchandising of *somáton*—translated "slaves"—actually meaning *bodies* from the Gk., dead or alive.)

[24]**the Genesis invasion of the Nephilym**

Genesis 6:1-7 And it came to pass, when men began to multiply on the face of the earth, and daughters were born unto them, that the **sons of God* saw the daughters of men that they were fair; and they took them wives of all which they chose [at will]. . . . There were ***giants* in the earth in those days; and also after that, when the sons of God came in unto the daughters of men, and *they bare children to them*, the same *became mighty men which were of old*, men of *renown* [such as the legendary, supposedly "mythological" characters of Hercules and others, reputed as half god, half man]. And GOD saw that the wickedness of man was great in the earth, and that every imagination of the thoughts of his heart was only evil continually. And it repented the LORD that he had made man on the earth, and it grieved him at his heart. And the LORD said, I will destroy man whom I have created from the face of the earth. . . .

*sons of God are the same *beney ha'Elohiym* spoken of in the book of Job: "Now there was a day when the *sons of God* came to present themselves before the LORD, and *Satan came also among them.* And the LORD said unto Satan, Whence comest thou? Then Satan answered the LORD, and said, From going to and fro in the earth, and from walking up and down in it (Job 1:6-7)."

**giants here refers to the *nephiliym*, or the *fallen sons of God*, who Jude says were *"the angels which kept not their first estate, but left their own habitation"* to evidently invade and subsequently corrupt the earth. So pervasive and profound was their influ-

ence that God grieved at the result and found it necessary to completely destroy (by the Flood) the evil generations of corrupted men who had mingled with these aliens. Jude went on in the same passage of his prophecy to indicate that these *nephiliym* have since been *"reserved in everlasting chains under darkness [wherever that may be] unto the judgment of the great day (Jude 1:6)."* It seems they shall reappear to fulfill their destiny at the final hour as per the prophecy of John the Revelator: *"And there appeared another wonder in heaven; and behold a great red dragon, having seven heads and ten horns, and seven crowns upon his heads. And his tail drew the third part of the stars of heaven, and did cast them to the earth. . . . And there was war in heaven: Michael and his angels fought against the dragon; and the dragon fought and his angels, and prevailed not; neither was their place found any more in heaven. And the great dragon was cast out, that old serpent, called the Devil, and Satan, which deceiveth the whole world: he was cast out into the earth, and his angels were cast out with him (Rev. 12:3-9)."*

[25]**1997 Phoenix sighting**—ABC's Brian Rooney on the June 18, 1997, edition of *World News Tonight* reported on the mass sighting of a UFO, which numerous witnesses claim to have seen in the evening of March 13, 1997. Sightings were reported for a period of 40 minutes along a two hundred mile path over Arizona, traversing from Paulden directly over Phoenix to Tucson, where it was last reported at 9:00 p.m. One of the first reports came from Paulden, where a former police officer reported seeing the object at about 8:20 p.m. According to Rooney, an air traffic controller at the Phoenix airport tower reports having seen the cluster of lights, though nothing supposedly appeared on radar. Many actually took photos and videotaped the apparently delta-shaped cluster of lights. The report included video footage submitted to ABC showing a string of evenly spaced lights "hovering" over the city of Phoenix.

[26]**the powerful aerial prince**

Ephesians 6:10-12 Finally, my brethren, be strong in the Lord, and in the power of his might. Put on the whole armour of God, that ye may be able to stand against the wiles of the devil. For we wrestle not against flesh and blood, but against principalities, against powers, against the rulers of the darkness of this world, against spiritual wickedness in *high places.*

Again, in Ephesians 2:2, Paul speaks of this *spirit* that works *"in the children of disobedience"* as *"the prince of the power of the air."* And Messiah declared that he *"beheld Satan as lightning fall from heaven (Luke 10:19)."* And of course, as pointed out elsewhere, this Alien does engage at some point in cosmic combat in space with the forces of Good, and is defeated and ousted from the celestial realm (Rev. 12).

[27]**time is short, obviously**

Revelation 12:9-12 And the great dragon was cast out, that old serpent, called the Devil, and Satan, which deceiveth the whole world: he was cast out into the earth, and his angels were cast out with him. And I heard a loud voice saying in heaven, Now is come salvation, and strength, and the kingdom of our God, and the power of his Christ: for the accuser of our brethren is cast down, which accused them before our God day and night. And they overcame him by the blood of the Lamb, and by the word of their testimony; and they loved not their lives unto the death. Therefore rejoice, ye heavens, and ye that dwell in them. Woe to the inhabiters of the earth and of the sea! for the devil is come down unto you, having great wrath, because he knoweth that he hath but a short time.

[28]**the ultimate creation of man**

Revelation 13:13-15 And [the false prophet] doeth great wonders, so that he maketh fire come down from heaven on the earth in the sight of men, and deceiveth them that dwell on the earth by the means of those miracles which he had power to do in the sight of the beast; saying to them that dwell on the earth, that *they should make an image* to the beast, which had the wound by a sword, and did live. And he had *power to give life unto the image* of the beast, that the image of the beast should both *speak, and cause that as many as would not worship the image of the beast should be killed* (able to identify, locate, monitor status, and order termination).

Isaiah 2:8-9 Their land also is full of idols; they worship the work of their own hands, that which their own fingers have made: And the mean man boweth down, and the great man humbleth himself: therefore forgive them not.

[29]**extraterrestrial technology transfer**

Revelation 12:7-9 And there was war in heaven: Michael and his angels fought against the dragon; and the dragon fought and his angels. . . . And the great dragon was cast out, that old serpent, called the Devil, and Satan, which deceiveth the whole world: *he* was *cast out into the earth*, and his angels . . . with him.

Revelation 13:3-4 And all the world wondered after the beast. And they worshipped the dragon which *gave power unto the beast:* and they worshipped the beast . . .

[30]**sure enough**—(Update:) Tuesday, October 27, 1998, it was reported on ABC's *World News Tonight* that IBM and the White House would be announcing (next day) development of the world's fastest supercomputer, able to perform nearly 4 trillion calculations per second (equivalent to what a person could do with a hand-held computer in 63k years). It is 20 times faster than IBM's Deep Blue, which last year defeated a human at chess for the first time ever, and equivalent to 15k desktop PC's, and will make possible computer modeling/simulation of nuclear explosion for the first time. In the report by Jack Smith, he also related expectations that weather can now be predicted "with real accuracy," and that "life-saving drugs that can take 10 years to find with hit-or-miss lab work [may now] be isolated in just 1½ years."

[31]**El Niño, El Diablo, Gran Temor, Gran Tribulación, Etc.**

Luke 21:25-26 And there shall be signs in the sun, and in the moon, and in the stars; and upon the earth distress of nations, with perplexity; *the sea and the waves roaring,* men's hearts failing them for fear, and for looking after those things which are coming on the earth: for the powers of heaven shall be shaken.

Chapter 7—The Fundamental Dread

[1]the "breath" of the Almighty

Zechariah 14:12 And this shall be the plague wherewith the LORD will smite all the people that have fought against Jerusalem; Their flesh shall consume away while they stand upon their feet, and their eyes shall consume away in their holes, and their tongue shall consume away in their mouth.

Revelation 19:15 And out of his mouth goeth a sharp sword, that with it he should smite the nations: and he shall rule them with a rod of iron: and he treadeth the winepress of the fierceness and wrath of Almighty God.

Isaiah 66:15-16 For, behold, the LORD will come with fire, and with his chariots like a whirlwind, to render his anger with fury, and his rebuke with flames of fire. For by fire and by his sword will the LORD plead with all flesh: and the slain of the LORD shall be many.

Psalm 50:3 Our God shall come, and shall not keep silence: a fire shall devour before him, and it shall be very tempestuous round about him.

2 Peter 3:10 But the day of the Lord will come as a thief in the night; in the which the heavens shall pass away with a great noise, and the elements shall melt with fervent heat, the earth also and the works that are therein shall be burned up.

[2]the primary targets—3 Apostles warn

Mark 13:14 But when ye shall see the abomination of desolation, spoken of by Daniel the prophet, standing where it ought not, (let him that readeth understand,) then let them that be in Judaea flee to the mountains:

Matthew 24:16-22 Then let them which be in Judaea flee into the mountains: Let him which is on the housetop not come down to take any thing out of his house: Neither let him which is in the field return back to take his clothes. And woe unto them that are with child, and to them that give suck in those days! But pray ye that your flight be not in the winter, neither on the sabbath day: For then shall be great tribulation, such as was not since the beginning of the world to this time, no, nor ever shall be. And except those days should be shortened, there should no flesh be saved: but for the elect's sake those days shall be shortened.

Luke 21:20-22 And when ye shall see Jerusalem compassed with armies, then know that the desolation thereof is nigh. Then let them which are in Judaea flee to the mountains; and let them which are in the midst of it depart out; and let not them that are in the countries enter thereinto. For these be the days of vengeance, that all things which are written may be fulfilled.

[3]the Gentile hoards and ultimate vengeance

Luke 21:22-24 For these be the days of vengeance, that all things which are written may be fulfilled. But woe unto them that are with child, and to them that give suck, in those days! for there shall be great distress in the land, and wrath upon this people. And they shall fall by the edge of the sword, and shall be led away captive into all nations: and Jerusalem shall be trodden down of the Gentiles, until the times of the Gentiles be fulfilled.

Revelation 11:2 And the holy city shall they tread under foot forty and two months [3½ years, at the end].

Revelation 12:13-17 And when the dragon saw that he was cast unto the earth, he persecuted the woman which brought forth the man child. And to the woman were given two wings of a great eagle, that she might fly into the wilderness, into her place, where she is nourished for a time, and times, and half a time [3½ years], from the face of the serpent. . . . And the dragon was wroth with the woman, and went to make war with the remnant of her seed, which keep the commandments of God, and have the testimony of Jesus Christ [Christians included in the coming holocaust].

Zechariah 14:1-3 Behold, the day of the LORD cometh, and thy spoil shall be divided in the midst of thee. For I will gather all nations against Jerusalem to battle; and the city shall be taken, and the houses rifled, and the women ravished; and half of the city shall go forth into captivity, and the residue of the people shall not be cut off from the city. Then shall the LORD go forth, and fight against those nations, as when he fought in the day of battle.

⁴don't be a "fanatic"—you might lose your head

Revelation 7:9 After this I beheld, and, lo, a great multitude, which no man could number, of all nations, and kindreds, and people, and tongues, stood before the throne, and before the Lamb, clothed with white robes, and palms in their hands;

Revelation 7:13-14 And one of the elders answered, saying unto me, What are these which are arrayed in white robes? and whence came they? And I said unto him, Sir, thou knowest. And he said to me, These are they which came out of great tribulation, and have washed their robes, and made them white in the blood [love] of the Lamb.

Revelation 20:4 And I saw thrones, and they sat upon them, and judgment was given unto them: and I saw the souls of them that were beheaded for the witness of Jesus, and for the word of God, and which had not worshipped the beast, neither his image, neither had received his mark upon their foreheads, or in their hands; and they lived and reigned with Christ a thousand years.

⁵two dissidents in sackcloth

Revelation 11:3-6 And I will give power unto my two witnesses, and they shall prophesy a thousand two hundred and threescore days, clothed in sackcloth. These are the two olive trees, and the two candlesticks standing before the God of the earth. And if any man will hurt them, fire proceedeth out of their mouth, and devoureth their enemies: and if any man will hurt them, he must in this manner be killed. These have power to shut heaven, that it rain not in the days of their prophecy: and have power over waters to turn them to blood, and to smite the earth with all plagues, as often as they will.

⁶seven angels, seven trumpets (of Tribulation)

Revelation 8:2-7 And I saw the seven angels which stood before God; and to them were given seven trumpets. . . . And the seven angels which had the seven trumpets prepared themselves to sound. The first angel sounded, and there followed hail and fire mingled with blood, and they were cast upon the earth: and the third part of trees was burnt up, and all green grass was burnt up. . . . (Please see continuation of passage through the end of Rev. chapter 11 for all seven angels and their respective plagues.)

⁷repent?!—of what?

Revelation 9:20-21 And the rest of the men which were not killed by these plagues [of the first 6 trumpet angels] yet repented not *of the works of their hands*, that they should not *worship devils* [channeled spirits; extraterrestrials; deceitful and diabolical inspirations in revered entertainment mediums which glorify violence, destruction and carnality; etc.], *and idols of gold* [symbolic of material wealth; also used extensively in modern microelectronics & satellite technologies], and *silver* [chief uses are in photography, mirrors, & electronics; all central to modern image technologies], and *brass* [really *copper*, primarily used in electrical products for powering the "indispensable" apparatuses and equipment of the 20th century], and *stone* [ores converted to all the metal products by which we are surrounded; also crystalline minerals such as diamonds and others essential to modern tooling & manufacturing industries of all sorts; let's not forget atomic fuels and weapons technologies uses, nor the silicone chip heart of our highest gods], and of *wood* [from which come *petroleum*-based plastics, which permeate our societies] *[all of these are heavily utilized in computers, television, entertainment devices, automobiles, airplanes, spacecraft, pharmaceuticals, chemistry, weapons and other hi-tech & not-so-hi-tech products of modern society—the works of our own hands!]*: which neither can see, nor hear, nor walk [although we're working on that too!]: *Neither repented they of their murders* [sundry assassinations and killings, either mass or otherwise, by war, terrorism, rivalries, etc.; ethnic cleansings; genocides; infanticides, *esp. prenatal*], nor of their *sorceries* [anti-God pharmaceutics; & other evil, toxic chemistries, esp. weapons of mass destruction], nor of their *fornication* [soul-cheapening, anti-child, anti-family, incontinent, irresponsible lusts of liberalism], nor of their *thefts* [countless scams & frauds; currency devaluations; unjust taxations; tax evasion; asset seizures & confiscations; & all sorts of *rampant* misc. rip-offs, from "petty" employee theft and embezzlement to managerial-level funds siphoning and misuse of corporate and public funds for personal benefit].

[8]**repossession of Earth, then Immanuel's House, peace, prosperity, & Eden-style utopia**

Haggai 2:6-7 For thus saith the LORD of hosts; Yet once, it is a little while, and I will shake the heavens, and the earth, and the sea, and the dry land; and I will shake all nations, and *the desire of all nations shall come:* and I will fill this house [Temple of YHWH in Jerusalem] with glory, saith the LORD of hosts.

[9]**For more on the People of the Book** to support this assertion, see chapters 3 & 8, "The Signposts" and "Gates of Hell Prevail."

[10]**WWIII holocaust army**

Revelation 9:13-18, 20-21 And the sixth angel sounded, and I heard a voice from the four horns of the golden altar which is before God, saying to the sixth angel which had the trumpet, Loose the four angels which are bound in the great river Euphrates. And the four angels were loosed, which were prepared for an hour, and a day, and a month, and a year, for to slay the third part of men. And *the number of the army of the horsemen were two hundred thousand thousand:* and I heard the number of them. And thus I saw the horses in the vision, and them that sat on them, having breastplates of fire, and of jacinth, and brimstone: and the heads of the horses were as the heads of lions; and out of their mouths issued fire and smoke and brimstone. By these three was the third part of men killed, by the fire, and by the smoke, and by the brimstone, which issued out of their mouths. . . . And the rest of the men which were not killed by these plagues yet repented not of the works of their hands, that they should not worship devils, and idols of gold, and silver, and brass, and stone, and of wood: which neither can see, nor hear, nor walk: Neither repented they of their murders, nor of their sorceries, nor of their fornication, nor of their thefts.

[11]**they that choose riches**

1 Timothy 6:9-11 But they that will be rich fall into temptation and a snare, and into many foolish and hurtful lusts, which drown men in destruction and perdition. For the love of money is the root of all evil: which while some coveted after, they have erred from the faith, and pierced themselves through with many sorrows. But thou, O man of God, flee these things; and follow after righteousness, godliness, faith, love, patience, meekness.

[12] spiritual philanderers

Psalm 50:22 Now consider this, ye that forget God, lest I tear you in pieces, and there be none to deliver.

Psalm 9:17 The wicked shall be turned into hell, and all the nations that forget God.

Romans 1:21-32 Because that, when they knew God, they glorified him not as God, neither were thankful; but became vain in their imaginations, and their foolish heart was darkened. Professing themselves to be wise, they became fools, and changed the glory of the uncorruptible God into an image made like to corruptible man, and to birds, and fourfooted beasts, and creeping things [Darwinian evolution?]. Wherefore God also gave them up to uncleanness through the lusts of their own hearts, to dishonour their own bodies between themselves: Who changed the truth of God into a lie, and worshipped and served the creature more than the Creator, who is blessed for ever. Amen. For this cause God gave them up unto vile affections: for even their women did change the natural use into that which is against nature: And likewise also the men, leaving the natural use of the woman, burned in their lust one toward another; men with men working that which is unseemly, and receiving in themselves that recompence of their error which was meet. And even as they did not like to retain God in their knowledge, God gave them over to a reprobate mind, to do those things which are not convenient; being filled with all unrighteousness, fornication, wickedness, covetousness, maliciousness; full of envy, murder, debate, deceit, malignity; whisperers, backbiters, haters of God, despiteful, proud, boasters, inventors of evil things, disobedient to parents, without understanding, covenantbreakers, without natural affection, implacable, unmerciful: Who knowing the judgment of God, that they which commit such things are worthy of death, not only do the same, but have pleasure in them that do them.

[13] hypocrisy purged

Isaiah 65:12 Therefore will I number you to the sword, and ye shall all bow down to the slaughter: because when I called, ye did not answer; when I spake, ye did not hear; but did evil before mine eyes, and did choose that wherein I delighted not.

Isaiah 66:4 I also will choose their delusions, and will bring their fears upon them; because when I called, none did answer; when I spake, they did not hear: but they did evil before mine eyes, and chose that in which I delighted not. Hear the word of the LORD, ye that tremble at his word; Your brethren that hated you, that cast you out for my name's sake, said, Let the LORD be glorified: but he shall appear to your joy, and they shall be ashamed.

Ezekiel 33:31 And they come unto thee as the people cometh, and they sit before thee as my people, and they hear thy words, but they will not do them: for with their mouth they shew much love, but their heart goeth after their covetousness.

Ezekiel 39:23-24 And the heathen shall know that the house of Israel [& her Christian daughter] went into captivity for their iniquity: because they trespassed against me, therefore hid I my face from them, and gave them into the hand of their enemies: so fell they all by the sword. According to their uncleanness and according to their transgressions have I done unto them, and hid my face from them.

14for whose sake?

Mark 13:19-20 For in those days shall be affliction, such as was not from the beginning of the creation which God created unto this time, neither shall be. And except that the Lord had shortened those days, no flesh should be saved: but *for the elect's sake, whom he hath chosen*, he hath shortened the days. (Isn't it funny how the Christians always regard themselves as "the chosen ones"—spiritual Israel—when it comes to the blessings of God, but never in terms of tribulation? Thank God that, for *all our sakes*, it shall last no more than 3½ years.)

15three-and-half-year war with the saints

Daniel 7:21-25 I beheld, and the same horn made war with the saints, and *prevailed against them.* . . . And he shall speak great words against the most High, *and shall wear out the saints* of the most High, and think to change times and laws: and *they shall be given into his hand* until a time and times and the dividing of time [*a time* equating to 1 year].

Revelation 13:5-7 And there was given unto him a mouth speaking great things and blasphemies; and power was given unto him to continue *forty and two months.* And he opened his mouth in blasphemy against God, to blaspheme his name, and his tabernacle, and them that dwell in heaven. And it was given unto him to *make war with* the saints, *and to overcome them:* and power was given him over all kindreds, and tongues, and nations.

16the ruler of the darkness under the foot of the ultimate victors

Genesis 1:16 And God made two great lights; the greater light to rule the day, and *the lesser light to rule the night* . . .

Ephesians 6:12 For we wrestle not against flesh and blood, but against principalities, against powers, *against the rulers of the darkness of this world*, against spiritual wickedness in high places.

Luke 10:19-20 Behold, I give unto you power to tread on serpents and scorpions, and over all the power of the enemy: and nothing shall by any means hurt you [in the enduring sense, of course]. . . . The spirits are subject unto you . . . —Christ Yeshua

Genesis 3:15 [Speaking prophetically to Satan, YHWH curses the devil] And I will put enmity between thee [the serpent] and the woman, and between thy seed and her seed [ongoing enmity between progenies]; [in the final analysis] *it shall bruise thy head, and thou shalt bruise his heel* [despite injury, Christ conquers, and His bride with him].

Isaiah 14:12 How art thou fallen from heaven, O Lucifer, son of the morning! how art thou cut down to the ground, which didst weaken the nations!

17seeds and stars and crowning saints

Exodus 32:13 [Moses praying to YHWH] Remember Abraham, Isaac, and Israel, thy servants, to whom thou swarest by thine own self, and saidst unto them, I will multiply *your seed as the stars* of heaven, and all this land that I have spoken of will I give unto your seed, and they shall inherit it for ever.

Daniel 12:3 And they that be wise shall shine as the brightness of the firmament; and *they that turn many to righteousness as the stars* for ever and ever.

Luke 22:29-30 And I [Yeshua] appoint unto you [twelve apostles] a kingdom, as my Father hath appointed unto me; that ye may eat and drink at my table in my kingdom, and sit on thrones judging the twelve tribes of Israel.

1 Corinthians 12:28 And God hath set some in the church, *first apostles*, secondarily prophets, thirdly teachers . . .

[18]**the baby killer**

Matthew 2:13-16 The angel of the Lord appeareth to Joseph in a dream, saying, Arise, and take the young child and his mother, and flee into Egypt, and be thou there until I bring thee word: for *Herod will seek the young child to destroy him*. When he arose, he took the young child and his mother by night, and departed into Egypt: and was there until the death of Herod: that it might be fulfilled which was spoken of the Lord by the prophet, saying, Out of Egypt have I called my son. Then Herod, when he saw that he was mocked of the wise men, was exceeding wroth, and sent forth, and *slew all the children* that were in Bethlehem, and in all the coasts thereof, from *two years old and under*, according to the time which he had diligently inquired of the wise men.

[19]**the Indisputable Ruler of Earth**

Psalm 2:7-12 The LORD hath said unto me, Thou art my Son; this day have I begotten thee. Ask of me, and I shall give thee the heathen for thine inheritance, and the uttermost parts of the earth for thy possession. Thou shalt break them with a rod of iron; thou shalt dash them in pieces like a potter's vessel. Be wise now therefore, O ye kings: be instructed, ye judges of the earth. Serve the LORD with fear, and rejoice with trembling. Kiss the Son, lest he be angry, and ye perish from the way, when his wrath is kindled but a little. Blessed are all they that put their trust in him.

Revelation 19:11-16 And I saw heaven opened, and behold a white horse; and he that sat upon him was called Faithful and True, and in righteousness he doth judge and make war. . . . And he was clothed with a vesture dipped in blood: and his name is called The Word of God. And the armies which were in heaven followed him upon white horses, clothed in fine linen, white and clean. And out of his mouth goeth a sharp sword, that with it he should smite the nations: and he shall rule them with a rod of iron: and he treadeth the winepress of the fierceness and wrath of Almighty God. And he hath on his vesture and on his thigh a name written, KING OF KINGS, AND LORD OF LORDS.

[20]**the ascension of resurrected Messiah**

Proverb 30:4 Who hath ascended up into heaven, or descended? who hath gathered the wind in his fists? who hath bound the waters in a garment? who hath established all the ends of the earth? what is his name, and what is his son's name, if thou canst tell?

Hebrews 9:24 For Christ is not entered into the holy places made with hands, which are the figures of the true; but into heaven itself, now to appear in the presence of God for us:

1 Peter 3:22 Who is gone into heaven, and is on the right hand of God; angels and authorities and powers being made subject unto him.

Mark 16:19 So then after the Lord had spoken unto them, he was received up into heaven, and sat on the right hand of God.

Acts 1:9-11 And when he had spoken these things, while they beheld, he was taken up; and a cloud received him out of their sight. And while they looked stedfastly toward heaven as he went up, behold, two men stood by them in white apparel; which also said, Ye men of Galilee, why stand ye gazing up into heaven? this same Jesus, which is taken up from you into heaven, shall so come in like manner as ye have seen him go into heaven.

[21]**astro-titans; star wars; astral intrigues, alliances, and conflicts**—The following verses are provided to provoke consideration that we are indeed "not alone in the universe," but actually at the heart of a cosmic conflict for domination of (essentially) the most beautiful planet in the cosmos, coveted by the most powerful beings throughout the

galaxies. These are only a small sampling of the Scriptural references to the extraterrestrial and interdimensional intrigues in which we are centrally embroiled. Christ Yeshua, who melded with our DNA and became flesh among us, to later suffer torturously in the flesh in order to demonstrate His love and commitment to humanity and its future on earth, confirmed that the ongoing cosmic conflict over Earth was linked to a diabolical alien who had invaded and overwhelmed the planet, temporarily dominating it. Now, it is only a matter of time before the demon will be defeated and incarcerated to await trial, sentencing, and final abolishment from all realms of life anywhere. He briefed His disciples in Luke 10:18, *"I beheld Satan as lightning fall from heaven"*; and in John 12:31, *"Now is the judgment of this world: now shall the prince of this world be cast out."*

The Apostle Paul also recognized the Alien's influence in world affairs in his briefing to the Ephesians when he advised them to resolutely detour from *"the course of this world"* which is, he said, *"according to the prince of the power of the air, the spirit that now worketh in the children of disobedience." (Eph.2:1-2)* Later in the same briefing, he made it explicitly clear what we are up against: *"Put on the whole armour of God, that ye may be able to stand against the wiles of the devil. For we wrestle not against flesh and blood, but against principalities, against powers, against the rulers of the darkness of this world, against spiritual wickedness in high places* [Gk., *epouranious* = above the sky]. *Wherefore take unto you the whole armour of God, that ye may be able to withstand in the evil day, and having done all, to stand.*

And, both Old and New Testament prophets, Daniel and his more modern counterpart, John, shed much light on the final assault of the alien Demon. They both testify that he shall actually establish himself openly on earth to subsequently defy and repudiate the authenticity of an Almighty Creator and Sovereign of all the universe, claiming instead to be the Almighty himself, to then also kill all who espouse YHWH or any other god then him. (See Daniel chapter 8 and Revelation 13.) Daniel also testifies that then *"there shall be a time of trouble, such as never was since there was a nation even to that same time"* and that *"at that time shall Michael stand up, the great [astral] prince which standeth for the children of thy people: and at that time thy people shall be delivered, every one that shall be found written in the book." (Dan.12:1)* (See Daniel 10 for more on the extraterrestrial alliance that includes this celestial prince, Michael, as well as the demonic arch-rival axis that he had to engage with before being able to penetrate their "stratospheric defensive shield" over the Middle East.)

[22]ultimate love, ultimate faith

Revelation 7:9-14 After this I beheld, and, lo, a great multitude, which no man could number, of all nations, and kindreds, and people, and tongues, stood before the throne, and before the Lamb, *clothed with white robes*, and palms in their hands. . . . And one of the elders answered, saying unto me, What are these which are arrayed in white robes? and whence came they? And I said unto him, Sir, thou knowest. And he said to me, *These are they which came out of great tribulation*, and have washed their robes, and made them white in the blood of the Lamb.

Galatians 5:6 For in Jesus Christ neither circumcision availeth any thing, nor uncircumcision; but *faith* which *worketh by love*. [That is, Jew or Gentile classifications are irrelevant to the real soul of the matter—*love* and the faith it breeds!]

[23]duration of Great Tribulation war of persecution

Daniel 7:25 And he shall speak great words against the most High, and shall wear out the saints of the most High, and think to change times and laws: and they shall be given into his hand *until a time and times and the dividing of time.*

Daniel 12:6-7 How long shall it be to the end of these wonders? And I heard the man clothed in linen, which was upon the waters of the river, when he held up his right hand and his left hand unto heaven, and sware by him that liveth for ever that *it shall be for a time, times, and an half,* and when he shall have accomplished to scatter the power of the holy people, all these things shall be finished.

24the flood

Isaiah 17:12-14 Woe to the multitude of many people, which make a noise like the noise of the seas; and to the rushing of nations, that make a rushing like the rushing of mighty waters! The nations shall rush like the rushing of many waters: but God shall rebuke them, and they shall flee far off, and shall be chased as the chaff of the mountains before the wind, and like a rolling thing before the whirlwind. And behold at eveningtide trouble; and before the morning he is not. This is the portion of them that spoil us, and the lot of them that rob us.

Psalm 18:4 The sorrows of death compassed me, and the floods of ungodly men made me afraid.

Psalm 144:7 Send thine hand from above; rid me, and deliver me out of great waters, from the hand of strange children;

Psalm 124:2-5 If it had not been the LORD who was on our side, when men rose up against us: Then they had swallowed us up quick, when their wrath was kindled against us: Then the waters had overwhelmed us, the stream had gone over our soul: Then the proud waters had gone over our soul.

25mystery of time as the womb of eternity—Useless and futile debate cannot alter the fact that the Bible is a unified whole, with no contradiction nor cancellation of the old as opposed to the new (no matter what Apostle Paul is understood to have said). *Christ Jesus said* not to even "think" that he had come "to destroy the law [Torah] or the prophets [the rest of the TaNaKh]," but rather that he had come *"to fulfill"* them. He moreover admonished, *"For verily I say unto you, Till heaven and earth pass, one jot or one tittle shall in no wise pass from the law, till all be fulfilled. Whosoever therefore shall break one of these least commandments, and shall teach men so, he shall be called the least in the kingdom of heaven: but whosoever shall do and teach them, the same shall be called great in the kingdom of heaven."* (Matt.5-17-20) Christ came to empower and enlarge Israel (The Church) and fulfill the promise to Abraham that he would be the father of many nations and his seed would bless all the families of earth. (Gen.17:2-6 & 12:3, Lk.2:32, Matt.12:18-21) Christ did not come to supposedly start a new ekklesía ("church"), but to build it henceforward on the unmistakable Rock of Truth—as revealed to each individual solely by the Father Himself—that He is (and always has been) the Messiah and the Son of the Living God, become flesh to dwell among us. (Matt.16:13-20, Jn.6:44, Jn.8:58, Jn.1:1-17) *There is only one Israel, one Jerusalem, one nation under God (Ep.4:4-6, etc.);* and she *does* marry the *same* person she gives birth to! Just because the concept is strange, mysterious and out of the ordinary does not invalidate it. (1Cor.2:7-14, Is.55:8-9) It is a dichotomous lie spoken by a dichotomous tongue out of a dichotomous heart that Israel and "the church" are two separate entities, as much as it is a lie that Christians will not have to endure Great Tribulation! Anyone who is not willing to lay down his or her life for Messiah and/or you is not credible. Beware! (In terms of mysteries, the only real mystery, to me, is that after centuries of Bible study, the fundamentals of the Scriptures still elude the fundamentalists!)

---

[26]the blindness & inconsistency of self-serving convenience

Matthew 23:24 Ye blind guides, which strain at a gnat, and swallow a camel.

[27]"New Jerusalem," the bride of the Creator

Revelation 21:2-23 And I John saw the holy city, new Jerusalem, coming down from God out of heaven, prepared as a bride adorned for her husband. . . . And there came unto me one of the seven angels which had the seven vials full of the seven last plagues, and talked with me, saying, Come hither, *I will shew thee the bride, the Lamb's wife.* And he carried me away in the spirit to a great and high mountain, and shewed me that great city, the holy Jerusalem, descending out of heaven from God, *having the glory of God.* . . . And the city had no need of the sun, neither of the moon, to shine in it: for the glory of God did lighten it, and the Lamb is the light thereof.

Revelation 22:5 And there shall be no night there; and they need no candle, neither light of the sun; for the Lord God giveth them light: and they shall reign for ever and ever.

Ephesians 5:23-32 The husband is the head of the wife, even as Christ is the head of the [ekklesía]: and he is the saviour of the body. Therefore as the [ekklesía] is subject unto Christ, so let the wives be to their own husbands in every thing. Husbands, love your wives, even as Christ also loved the [ekklesía], and gave himself for it; that he might sanctify and cleanse it with the washing of water by the word, that he might present it to himself a glorious [ekklesía], not having spot, or wrinkle, or any such thing; but that it should be holy and without blemish. So ought men to love their wives as their own bodies. He that loveth his wife loveth himself. For no man ever yet hated his own flesh; but nourisheth and cherisheth it, even as the Lord the [ekklesía]: For we are members of his body, of his flesh, and of his bones. For this cause shall a man leave his father and mother, and shall be joined unto his wife, and they two shall be one flesh. This is a great mystery: but I speak concerning Christ and the church [ekklesía].

Hebrews 12:22-23 Ye are come unto mount Sion [Zion], and unto *the city of the living God,* the *heavenly Jerusalem,* and to an innumerable company of angels, to *the general assembly and church [ekklesía]* of the firstborn, which are written in heaven, and to God the Judge of all, and to the spirits of just men made perfect . . .

[28]Old Testament references to the Bride (though frequently unfaithful one)

Jeremiah 6:2 I have likened the daughter of Zion to a comely and delicate woman.

Isaiah 1:1, 4, 21 The vision of Isaiah the son of Amoz, which he saw concerning Judah and Jerusalem in the days of Uzziah, Jotham, Ahaz, and Hezekiah, kings of Judah. . . Ah sinful nation, a people laden with iniquity, a seed of evildoers, children that are corrupters: they have forsaken the LORD, they have provoked the Holy One of Israel unto anger, they are gone away backward. . . How is the faithful city become an harlot! it was full of judgment; righteousness lodged in it; but now murderers.

Jeremiah 8:19 Behold the voice of the cry of the daughter of my people because of them that dwell in a far country: Is not the LORD in Zion? is not her king in her? Why have they provoked me to anger with their graven images, and with strange vanities?

Jeremiah 3:6-14 The LORD said also unto me in the days of Josiah the king, Hast thou seen that which backsliding Israel hath done? she is gone up upon every high mountain and under every green tree, and there hath played the harlot. And I said after she had done all these things, Turn thou unto me. But she returned not. . . . Turn, O backsliding children, saith the LORD; for *I am married unto you:* and I will take you one of a city, and two of a family, and I will bring you to Zion:

Hosea 4:12 My people ask counsel at their stocks, and their staff declareth unto them: for the spirit of whoredoms hath caused them to err, and they have gone a whoring from under their God.

Zechariah 2:10-12 Sing and rejoice, O daughter of Zion: for, lo, I come, and I will dwell in the midst of thee, saith the LORD. And many nations shall be joined to the LORD in that day, and shall be my people: and I will dwell in the midst of thee, and thou shalt know that the LORD of hosts hath sent me unto thee. And the LORD shall inherit Judah his portion in the holy land, and shall choose Jerusalem again.

Micah 4:8 And thou, O tower of the flock, the strong hold of the daughter of Zion, unto thee shall it come, even the first dominion; the kingdom shall come to the daughter of Jerusalem.

Zechariah 9:9 Rejoice greatly, O daughter of Zion; shout, O daughter of Jerusalem: behold, thy King cometh unto thee: he is just, and having salvation; lowly, and riding upon an ass, and upon a colt the foal of an ass.

Zephaniah 3:14-17 Sing, O daughter of Zion; shout, O Israel; be glad and rejoice with all the heart, O daughter of Jerusalem. The LORD hath taken away thy judgments, he hath cast out thine enemy: the king of Israel, even the LORD, is in the midst of thee: thou shalt not see evil any more. In that day it shall be said to Jerusalem, Fear thou not: and to Zion, Let not thine hands be slack. The LORD thy God in the midst of thee is mighty; he will save, he will rejoice over thee with joy; he will rest in his love, he will joy over thee with singing.

[29] uncancelled reservations

Amos 9:8 Behold, the eyes of the Lord GOD are upon the sinful kingdom, and I will destroy it from off the face of the earth; saving that *I will not utterly destroy the house of Jacob,* saith the LORD.

Isaiah 1:9 Except the Lord of hosts had *left unto us a very small remnant,* we should have been as Sodom, and we should have been like unto Gomorrah.

Jeremiah 46:28 Fear thou not, O Jacob my servant, saith the LORD: for I am with thee; for I will make a full end of all the nations whither I have driven thee: but I will *not make a full end of thee,* but correct thee in measure; yet will I not leave thee wholly unpunished.

Leviticus 26:44 And yet for all that, when they be in the land of their enemies, *I will not cast them away, neither will I abhor them, to destroy them utterly,* and to break my covenant with them: for I am the LORD their God.

Zephaniah 3:12-14 I will also leave in the midst of thee an afflicted and poor people, and they shall trust in the name of the LORD.

Micah 4:6-8 In that day, saith the LORD, will I assemble her that halteth, and I will gather her that is driven out, and her that I have afflicted; and I will make her that halted a remnant, and her that was cast far off a strong nation: and the LORD shall reign over them in mount Zion from henceforth, even for ever. And thou, O tower of the flock, the strong hold of the daughter of Zion, unto thee shall it come, even the first dominion; *the kingdom shall come to the daughter of Jerusalem.*

[30] glorious grace—the clothing of the daughter of Jerusalem

Psalm 50:2 Out of Zion, the perfection of beauty, God hath shined.

Matthew 13:41-43 The Son of man shall send forth his angels, and they shall gather out of his kingdom all things that offend, and them which do iniquity. . . . Then shall *the righteous shine forth as the sun* in the kingdom of their Father. Who hath ears to hear, let him hear.

Philippians 3:8-9 Yea doubtless, and I count all things but loss for the excellency of the knowledge of Christ Jesus my Lord: for whom I have suffered the loss of all things, and do count them but dung, that I may win Christ, and be found in him, *not having mine own righteousness,* which is of the law, but that which is through the faith of Christ, the *righteousness which is of God by faith* . . .

Revelation 19:7-8 Let us be glad and rejoice, and give honour to him: for the marriage of the Lamb is come, and his wife hath made herself ready. And to her was granted that *she should be arrayed in fine linen, clean and white:* for the fine linen is *the righteousness of saints.*

Revelation 21:10-11 & 23 And he carried me away in the spirit to a great and high mountain, and shewed me that great city, the holy Jerusalem, descending out of heaven from God, *having the glory of God.* . . . And the city had no need of the sun, neither of the moon, to shine in it: for *the glory of God did lighten it, and the Lamb is the light thereof.*

[31]laundered garments of the friends of Yeshua Ha'Mashiach

Revelation 1:5 Jesus Christ, who is the faithful witness, and the first begotten of the dead, and the prince of the kings of the earth. Unto him that loved us, and washed us from our sins in his own blood . . .

John 15:3-20 Now ye are *clean through the word* which I have spoken unto you. . . . If ye keep my commandments, ye shall abide in my love; even as I have kept my Father's commandments, and abide in his love. . . . This is my commandment, That ye love one another, as I have loved you. *Greater love hath no man than this, that a man lay down his life for his friends.* Ye are my friends, if ye do whatsoever I command you. . . . Remember the word that I said unto you, The servant is not greater than his lord. If they have persecuted me, they will also persecute you...

1 Peter 2:21 For even hereunto were ye called: because Christ also suffered for us, leaving us an example, that ye should follow his steps:

Revelation 7:13-14 And one of the elders answered, saying unto me, What are these which are arrayed in white robes? and whence came they? And I said unto him, Sir, thou knowest. And he said to me, These are they which came out of great tribulation, and have washed their robes, and made them white in the blood of the Lamb.

[32]hate—the common destiny of servant and Lord

John 15:18-20 If the world [Gk. *kosmos,* the ordered system, or "establishment"] hate you, ye know that it hated me before it hated you. If ye were of the world, the world would love his own: but because ye are not of the world, but I have chosen you out of the world, therefore the world hateth you... The servant is not greater than his lord. If they have persecuted me, they will also persecute you; if they have kept my saying, they will keep yours also.—Messiah

[33]we shall be like Him ("clothed with the sun")

I John 3:2 Beloved, now are we the sons of God, and it doth not yet appear what we shall be: but we know that, *when he shall appear, we shall be like him;* for we shall see him as he is.

Mark 9:2-3 Jesus taketh with him Peter, and James, and John, and leadeth them up into an high mountain apart by themselves: and he was transfigured before them. And his raiment became shining, exceeding white as snow; so as no fuller [cloth bleacher] on earth can white them.

Exodus 12:48-49 And when a stranger [Gentile] shall sojourn with thee, and will keep the passover to the LORD, let all his males be circumcised, and then let him come near and keep it; and he shall be as one that is born in the land: for no uncircumcised person shall eat thereof. One law shall be to him that is homeborn, and unto the stranger that sojourneth among you.

Leviticus 19:34 But the stranger that dwelleth with you shall be unto you as one born among you, and thou shalt love him as thyself; for ye were strangers in the land of Egypt: I am the LORD your God.

Numbers 9:14-16 And if a stranger shall sojourn among you, and will keep the passover unto the LORD; according to the ordinance of the passover, and according to the manner thereof, so shall he do: ye shall have one ordinance, both for the stranger, and for him that was born in the land. One ordinance shall be both for you of the congregation, and also for the stranger that sojourneth with you, an ordinance for ever in your generations: as ye are, so shall the stranger be before the LORD. One law and one manner shall be for you, and for the stranger that sojourneth with you.

Isaiah 14:1 For the LORD will have mercy on Jacob, and will yet choose Israel, and set them in their own land: *and the strangers shall be joined with them*, and *they shall cleave to the house of Jacob* [a.k.a. Israel].

Chapter 8—The Gates of Hell Prevail

[1]**Luke 21:18 & Revelation 20:4**
[2]**Luke 10:19, Matthew 24:9 & 23:34**
[3]**Revelation 13:7 & Matthew 16:18**
[4]**understanding separates the wise from the wicked**—Daniel 12:10 & 11:32-35
[5]**Jews—the first, the last, the finest**

   Revelation 14:1-4 And I looked, and, lo, a Lamb stood on the mount Sion, and with him an hundred forty and four thousand [of the 12 tribes of the children of Israel—Rev.7:3-8], having his Father's name written in their foreheads. . . . *These are they which follow the Lamb whithersoever he goeth.* These were redeemed from among men, being the firstfruits unto God and to the Lamb.

[6]**only one**

   John 10:15-16 As the Father knoweth me, even so know I the Father: and I lay down my life for the sheep. And other sheep I have, which are not of this fold: them also I must bring, and they shall hear my voice; and *there shall be one fold, and one shepherd.*—Yeshua

   Ephesians 4:4-6 There is *one body,* and one Spirit, even as ye are called in *one hope* of your calling; One Lord, one faith, one baptism, One God and Father of all, who is above all, and through all, and in you all.

   Romans 3:29-31 Is he the God of the Jews only? is he not also of the Gentiles? Yes, of the Gentiles also. . . . Seeing it is one God, which shall justify the circumcision by faith, and uncircumcision through faith. Do we then make void the law through faith? God forbid: yea, we establish the law.

   Numbers 15:15-16 One ordinance shall be both for you of the congregation, and also for the stranger [gentile] that sojourneth with you, an ordinance for ever in your generations: as ye are, so shall the stranger be before the LORD. *One law and one manner* shall be for you, and for the stranger that sojourneth with you.

   Malachi 2:9-10 Therefore have I also made you contemptible and base before all the people, according as ye have not kept my ways, but have been *partial in the law.* Have we not all one father? hath not one God created us? why do we deal treacherously every man against his brother, by profaning the covenant of our fathers?

   1 Timothy 2:5 & 4 For there is one God, and one mediator between God and men, the man Christ Jesus. . . . Who will have all men to be saved, and to come unto the knowledge of the truth.

[7]**undivided**

   Luke 11:17 Every kingdom divided against itself is brought to desolation; and a house divided against a house falleth.—Christ Yeshua

   Mark 12:29-30 Jesus answered [from De.6:4-5], The first of all the commandments is, Hear, O Israel; *The Lord our God is one Lord:* and thou shalt love the Lord thy God with all thy heart, and with all thy soul, and with all thy mind, and with all thy strength: this is the first commandment.

   John 17:20-23 Neither pray I for these alone, but for them also which shall believe on me through their word; *that they all may be one;* as thou, Father, art in me, and I in thee, *that they also may be one in us:* that the world may believe that thou hast sent me. And the glory which thou gavest me I have given them; that they may be one, *even as we are one:* I in them, and thou in me, that they may be *made perfect in one;* and that the world may know that thou hast sent me, and hast loved them, as thou hast loved me.— Yeshua's prayer for his followers and theirs

Zechariah 14:9 And the LORD shall be king over *all the earth: in that day shall there be one LORD, and his name one.*

[8]the ultimate dimension

John 4:23-24 The hour cometh, and now is, when the true worshippers shall worship the Father in spirit and in truth: for the Father seeketh such to worship him. God is a Spirit: and they that worship him must worship him *in spirit and in truth.*

1 Corinthians 2:14 But the natural man receiveth not the things of the Spirit of God: for they are foolishness unto him: neither can he know them, because they are spiritually discerned.

John 8:23 And [Jesus] said unto [the unbelieving Jews], Ye are from beneath; I am from above: ye are of this world; I am not of this world.

John 18:36 Jesus answered [Pilate], My kingdom is not of this world: if my kingdom were of this world, then would my servants fight, that I should not be delivered to the Jews: but now is my kingdom not from hence.

John 17:14 I have given [my disciples] thy word; and the world hath hated them, because they are not of the world, even as I am not of the world.—Yeshua, confirming the effective translation of His followers out of this dimension by the hyperphysical quality and transforming power of God's word

[9]the "prevailing" paradox

Romans 8:36-37 As it is written, For thy sake we are killed all the day long; we are accounted as sheep for the slaughter. Nay, in all these things we are *more than conquerors* through him that loved us.

Mark 8:35-36 For whosoever will save his life shall lose it; but whosoever shall lose his life for my sake and the gospel's, *the same shall save it.* For what shall it profit a man, if he shall gain the whole world, and lose his own soul?

Philippians 3:8 Yea doubtless, and I count all things but loss for the excellency of the knowledge of Christ Jesus my Lord: for whom I have suffered the loss of all things, and do count them but dung, that I may win Christ . . .—Apostle Paul

[10]no difference

Romans 4:11 And [Abraham] received the sign of circumcision, a seal of the righteousness of the faith which he had yet being uncircumcised: that he might be the *father of all them that believe, though they be not circumcised;* that righteousness might be imputed unto them also:

Romans 3:22 Even the righteousness of God which is by faith of Jesus Christ unto all and upon all them that believe: for there is *no difference* . . .

Ephesians 3:6 That the Gentiles should be *fellowheirs, and of the same body, and partakers of his promise* in Christ by the gospel:

Romans 10:12-13 For there is *no difference* between the Jew and the Greek: for the same Lord over all is rich unto all that call upon him. For whosoever shall call upon the name of the Lord shall be saved.

Romans 2:28-29 For he is not a Jew, which is one outwardly; neither is that circumcision, which is outward in the flesh: But he is a Jew, which is one inwardly; and circumcision is that of the heart, in the spirit, and not in the letter; whose praise is not of men, but of God.

John 8:39 [The Jews] answered and said unto him, Abraham is our father. Jesus saith unto them, If ye were Abraham's children, ye would do the works of Abraham.

Romans 9:8 That is, They which are the children of the flesh, these are not the children of God: but the children of the promise are counted for the seed.

Galatians 3:7-9 Know ye therefore that *they which are of faith, the same are the children of Abraham*. And the scripture, foreseeing that God would justify the heathen through faith, preached before the gospel unto Abraham, saying, In thee shall all nations be blessed. So then they which be of faith are blessed *with* faithful Abraham.

11 Abram, father of the Gentiles

Genesis 12:2-3 I will make of thee a great nation, and I will bless thee, and make thy name great; and thou shalt be a blessing: And I will bless them that bless thee, and curse him that curseth thee: and in thee shall all families of the earth be blessed.

Genesis 17:2-7 And I will make my covenant between me and thee, and will multiply thee exceedingly. And Abram fell on his face: and God talked with him, saying, As for me, behold, my covenant is with thee, and thou shalt be a father of many nations. Neither shall thy name any more be called Abram, but thy name shall be Abraham; for a father of many nations have I made thee. And I will make thee exceeding fruitful, and I will make nations of thee, and kings shall come out of thee. And I will establish my covenant between me and thee and thy seed after thee in their generations for an everlasting covenant, to be a God unto thee, and to thy seed after thee.

Genesis 17:8-11 And I will give unto thee, and to thy seed after thee, the land wherein thou art a stranger, all the land of Canaan, for an everlasting possession; and I will be their God. And God said unto Abraham, Thou shalt keep my covenant therefore, thou, and thy seed after thee in their generations. This is my covenant, which ye shall keep, between me and you and thy seed after thee; Every man child among you shall be circumcised. And ye shall circumcise the flesh of your foreskin; and it shall be a token of the covenant betwixt me and you.

12 the friend of God

Isaiah 41:8 But thou, Israel, art my servant, Jacob whom I have chosen, the seed of Abraham my friend.

2 Chronicles 20:7 Art not thou our God, who didst drive out the inhabitants of this land before thy people Israel, and gavest it to the seed of Abraham thy friend for ever?

James 2:20-24 But wilt thou know, O vain man, that faith without works is dead? Was not Abraham our father justified by works, when he had offered Isaac his son upon the altar? Seest thou how faith wrought with his works, and by works was faith made perfect? And the scripture was fulfilled which saith, Abraham believed God, and it was imputed unto him for righteousness: and he was called the *Friend of God*. Ye see then how that by works a man is justified, and not by faith only.

13 faith is obedience

Genesis 22:10-12 And Abraham stretched forth his hand, and took the knife to slay his son. And the angel of the LORD called unto him out of heaven, and said, Abraham, Abraham: and he said, Here am I. And he said, Lay not thine hand upon the lad, neither do thou any thing unto him: for now I know that thou fearest God, seeing thou hast not withheld thy son, thine only son from me.

Genesis 22:15-18 And the angel of the LORD called unto Abraham out of heaven the second time, And said, By myself have I sworn, saith the LORD, for because thou hast done this thing, and hast not withheld thy son, thine only son: That in blessing I will bless thee, and in multiplying I will multiply thy seed as the stars of the heaven, and as the sand which is upon the sea shore; and thy seed shall possess the gate of his enemies; And in thy seed shall all the nations of the earth be blessed; because thou hast obeyed my voice.

[14]Abraham & Sons, Inc.

Genesis 18:19 For I know him, that he will command his children and his household after him, and they shall keep the way of the LORD, to do justice and judgment; that the LORD may bring upon Abraham that which he hath spoken of him.

[15]love it or lose it

Genesis 32:24-31 And Jacob was left alone; and there wrestled a man with him until the breaking of the day. And when he saw that he prevailed not against him, he touched the hollow of his thigh; and the hollow of Jacob's thigh was out of joint, as he wrestled with him. And he said, Let me go, for the day breaketh. And he said, *I will not let thee go, except thou bless me.* And he said unto him, What is thy name? And he said, Jacob. And he said, Thy name shall be called no more Jacob, but *Israel:* for as a prince *hast thou power with God and with men,* and hast *prevailed.* And Jacob asked him, and said, Tell me, I pray thee, thy name. And he said, Wherefore is it that thou dost ask after my name? And he blessed him there. And Jacob called the name of the place Peniel: for I have seen God face to face, and my life is preserved. And as he passed over Penuel the sun rose upon him, and he halted upon his thigh.

Genesis 35:10-12 And God said unto him, Thy name is Jacob: thy name shall not be called any more Jacob, but Israel shall be thy name: and he called his name Israel. And God said unto him, I am God Almighty: be fruitful and multiply; a nation and a company of nations shall be of thee, and kings shall come out of thy loins; and the land which I gave Abraham and Isaac, to thee I will give it, *and to thy seed* after thee will I give the land.

(Note that although God had given Jacob this more "dignified" title, nonetheless, when He later first revealed Himself to Moses in Sinai, He chose rather to identify Himself as the God of Abraham, Isaac, and *Jacob*, thus distinguishing Jacob as His primary character preference. This also reveals a hint of God's own character; one that highly regards and honors those who cherish the *promise* of God with relentless determination and tenacity, regardless of "right." Look out Israel and/or "Spiritual Israel," lest your crown be stolen!)

[16]Jacob's challenger

Hosea 12:3-5 He took his brother by the heel in the womb, and by his strength he had power with God: Yea, he had power over the angel, and prevailed: he wept, and made supplication unto him: he found him in Bethel, and there he spake with us [Jacob's descendants, through Jacob]; *even the LORD God of hosts;* the LORD is his memorial.

[17]figures of foreshadowing

Hebrews 10:1 The law having *a shadow of* good things to come, and not the very image of the things . . .

Hebrews 11:17-19 By faith Abraham, when he was tried, offered up Isaac: and he that had received the promises offered up his only begotten son, of whom it was said, That in Isaac shall thy seed be called: Accounting that God was able to raise him up, even from the dead; from whence also he received him *in a figure.* [The shadow here was that of God the Father offering up His only-begotten Son—also miraculously born— to later receive him back restored from death.]

See also Hebrews 9:8-9 & 24.

[18]**shadow of the ekklesía**—For the benefit of readers who may only read certain selections from this book, *ekklesia* has been introduced in earlier chapters (esp. Chap. 3) and defined as the more accurate and appropriate term for which the word *church* has been substituted in the English versions of the New Testament to refer to the *called-out ones*. It is the word used in the early Greek manuscripts to refer to the believing corps of YHWH's followers, friends, and faithful devotees whom He has called out and separated from the secular luciferian world of pagan hedonism. The word *church,* in contrast, is really an extremely poor and inaccurate denotation of the called-out-ones concept and today connotes more of a religious clubhouse of weekly congregationalists whose members are mostly mired in the established order the majority of the week.

[19]**the Chosen Tree is known by its fruits**

Malachi 1:2-3 Was not Esau Jacob's brother? saith the LORD: yet I loved Jacob, and I hated Esau . . .

Romans 9:13 As it is written, Jacob have I loved, but Esau have I hated.

Luke 3:8-9 Bring forth therefore fruits worthy of repentance, and begin not to say within yourselves, We have Abraham to our father: for I say unto you, That God is able of these stones to raise up children unto Abraham. And now also the axe is laid unto the root of the trees: *every tree* therefore which bringeth not forth good fruit is hewn down, and cast into the fire.

1 Samuel 2:30 For them that honour me I will honour, and they that despise me shall be lightly esteemed.

[20]**becoming one by the power of faith**

John 1:11-13 [Christ Yeshua] came unto his own, and his own received him not. But *as many as received him,* to them *gave he power to become* the sons of God, even to them that *believe* on his name: *Which were born,* not of blood, nor of the will of the flesh, nor of the will of man, but *of God.*

Galatians 3:29 And if ye be Christ's, *then are ye Abraham's seed, and heirs* according to the promise.

Ephesians 3:6 That the Gentiles should be *fellowheirs,* and of the *same body,* and *partakers of his promise* in Christ by the gospel:

Romans 11:19-22 Thou [the gentile Romans] wilt say then [of the Jews], The branches were broken off, that I might be *graffed in.* Well; because of unbelief they were broken off, and thou standest by faith. *Be not highminded, but fear:* For if God spared not the natural branches, take heed lest he also spare not thee. Behold therefore the goodness and severity of God: on them which fell, severity; but toward thee, goodness, *if thou continue in his goodness: otherwise thou also shalt be cut off.*

Romans 9:6-8 Not as though the word of God hath taken none effect. For they are not all Israel, which are of Israel: Neither, because they are the seed of Abraham, are they all children: but, In Isaac shall thy seed be called. That is, They which are the children of the *flesh,* these are *not* the children of God: but the *children of the promise are counted* for the seed.

Galatians 4:28 Now *we,* brethren [gentile Galatian believers], as Isaac was, *are the children of promise.*

Romans 8:17 And if children, then heirs; heirs of God, and joint-heirs with Christ; *if so be that we suffer with him,* that we may be also glorified together.

[21]true Israel is the Church, and vice versa

Ephesians 4:4-6 There is one body, and one Spirit, even as ye are called in one hope of your calling; one Lord, one faith, one baptism, one God and Father of all, who is above all, and through all, and in you all.

John 10:16 And other sheep I have, which are not of this fold: them also I must bring, and they shall hear my voice; and there shall be one fold, and one shepherd.

Galatians 4:26 Jerusalem which is above . . . is the mother of us all.

[22]the faith of Christ

Philippians 3:8-10 Yea doubtless, and I count all things but loss for the excellency of the knowledge of Christ Jesus my Lord: for whom I have suffered the loss of all things, and do count them but dung, that I may win Christ, and be found in him, not having mine own righteousness, which is of the law, but that which is through the faith of Christ, the righteousness which is of God by faith: That I may know him, and the power of his resurrection, and the *fellowship of his sufferings,* being made *conformable unto his death. . . .* I press toward the mark for the prize of the high calling of God in Christ Jesus. Let us therefore, as many as be perfect, be thus minded . . .

Luke 9:24-25 For whosoever will save his life shall lose it: but whosoever will lose his life for my sake, the same shall save it. For what is a man advantaged, if he gain the whole world, and lose himself, or be cast away?

[23]the Church existed in the Old Testament!

Acts 7:38 This is he, that was in the church in the wilderness with the angel which spake to him in the mount Sina, and with our fathers [the children of Israel]: who received the lively oracles to give unto us:

[24]from the wilderness even to the end of the world

Matthew 28:19-20 Go ye therefore, and *teach all nations,* baptizing them in the name of the Father, and of the Son, and of the Holy Ghost: Teaching them to observe all things whatsoever I have commanded you: and, lo, I am with you alway, even unto the end of the world. Amen.

[25]the end is post-global-witness and post-endurance of the witnesses

Matthew 24:13-14 But he that shall endure *unto the end,* the same shall be saved. And this gospel of the kingdom shall be preached in all the world for a witness unto all nations; and *then shall the end come.*

[26]no respect of persons

Romans 2:10-11, 28-29 Glory, honour, and peace, to every man that worketh good, to the Jew first [only chronologically], and also to the Gentile: For there is *no respect of persons with God. . . .* For he is not a Jew, which is one outwardly; neither is that circumcision, which is outward in the flesh: But he [is] a Jew, which is one inwardly; and circumcision is that of the heart, in the spirit, and not in the letter; whose praise is not of men, but of God.

Ephesians 2:13-14 But now in Christ Jesus ye who sometimes were far off are made nigh by the blood of Christ. For he is our peace, who hath made both one, and hath broken down the middle wall of partition between us

See also Romans 9:6-8 & 8:17 already presented in footnote 20.

[27]fitly joined together

Ephesians 2:17-22 And [Christ] came and preached peace to you which were afar off, and to them that were nigh. For through him *we both* have access *by one Spirit* unto the Father. Now therefore ye are no more strangers and foreigners, but fellowcitizens with the saints, and of the household of God; and are built upon the foundation of the apostles and prophets, Jesus Christ himself being the chief corner stone; in whom all the building *fitly framed together* groweth unto an holy temple in the Lord: In whom ye also are *builded together* for an habitation of God through the Spirit.

1 Peter 2:6-10 (To the Gentiles:) Wherefore also it is contained in the scripture, Behold, I lay in Sion a chief corner stone, elect, precious: and *he that believeth on him shall not be confounded*. Unto you therefore which believe he is precious: but unto them which be disobedient, the stone which the builders disallowed, the same is made the head of the corner, and a stone of stumbling, and a rock of offence, even to them which stumble at the word, being disobedient: whereunto also they were appointed. But ye are a *chosen generation*, a *royal priesthood*, an *holy nation*, a peculiar people; that ye should shew forth the praises of him who hath called you out of darkness into his marvellous light: Which in time past were not a people, but *are now the people of God*: which had not obtained mercy, but now have obtained mercy.

28alleged faith demands more than mere belief

James 2:17-20 Even so faith, if it hath not works, is dead, being alone. Yea, a man may say, Thou hast faith, and I have works: shew me thy faith without thy works, and I will shew thee my faith by my works. Thou believest that there is one God; thou doest well: the devils also believe, and tremble. But wilt thou know, O vain man, that faith without works is dead?

29here is patience and faith (in justice, the second death, and the second life)

Revelation 13:10 He that leadeth into captivity shall go into captivity: he that killeth with the sword must be killed with the sword. Here is the patience and the faith of the saints.

Matthew 10:28 And fear not them which kill the body, but are not able to kill the soul: but rather fear him which is able to destroy both soul and body in hell.

Revelation 2:11 He that hath an ear, let him hear what the Spirit saith unto the churches; He that overcometh shall not be hurt of the second death [the real concern of any truly sentient person].

Revelation 20:6 Blessed and holy is he that hath part in the first resurrection: on such the second death hath no power, but they shall be priests of God and of Christ, and shall reign with him a thousand years.

Revelation 20:10-15 And the devil that deceived [the nations] was cast into the lake of fire and brimstone, where the beast and the false prophet are, and shall be tormented day and night for ever and ever. . . . And I saw the dead, small and great, stand before God; and the books were opened: and another book was opened, which is the book of life: and the dead were judged out of those things which were written in the books, according to their works. And the sea gave up the dead which were in it; and death and hell delivered up the dead which were in them: and they were judged every man according to their works. And death and hell were cast into the lake of fire. *This is the second death*. And whosoever was not found written in the book of life was cast into the lake of fire.

30the triumph: overcoming the flesh affinity

I John 2:14b-15 I have written unto you, young men, because ye are strong, and the word of God abideth in you, and *ye have overcome the wicked one. Love not the world, neither the things* that are in the world. If any man love the world, the love of the Father is not in him.—[Neither does he overcome!]

I John 5:4-5 For whatsoever is born of God overcometh the world: and *this is the victory* that overcometh the world, *even our faith.* Who is he that overcometh the world, but he that believeth that Jesus is the Son of God [who, strictly advocating the world to come, taught to recognize the fleshly lusts of this world as a self-destructive vanity].

(John's compatriot Paul offers this perfect complement on the theme: Romans 8:36-37 As it is written, For thy sake we are killed all the day long; we are accounted as sheep for the slaughter. Nay, in all these things we are *more than conquerors* through him that loved us.)

[31] keep them, not take them out

John 16:33 & 17:14-15 These things I have spoken unto you, that in me ye might have peace. *In the world ye shall have tribulation:* but be of good cheer; *I have overcome the world....* [Yeshua to the Father:] I have given them thy word; and the world hath hated them, because they are not of the world, even as I am not of the world. I pray *not that thou shouldest take them out* of the world, but that thou shouldest keep them from the evil.

[32] the prizes for ears that hear

Revelation 2:7 He that hath an ear, let him hear what the Spirit saith unto the churches; To him that overcometh will I give to eat of the tree of life, which is in the midst of the paradise of God.

Revelation 2:11 He that hath an ear, let him hear what the Spirit saith unto the churches; He that overcometh shall not be hurt of the second death.

Revelation 2:17 He that hath an ear, let him hear what the Spirit saith unto the churches; To him that overcometh will I give to eat of the hidden manna, and will give him a white stone, and in the stone a new name written, which no man knoweth saving he that receiveth it.

Revelation 2:26-28 And he that overcometh, *and keepeth my works unto the end*, to him will I give power over the nations: And he shall rule them with a rod of iron; as the vessels of a potter shall they be broken to shivers: even as I received of my Father. And I will give him the morning star.

Revelation 3:5 He that overcometh, the same shall be clothed in white raiment; and I will not blot out his name out of the book of life, but I will confess his name before my Father, and before his angels.

Revelation 3:12 Him that overcometh will I make a pillar in the temple of my God, and he shall go no more out: and I will write upon him the name of my God, and the name of the city of my God, which is new Jerusalem, which cometh down out of heaven from my God: and I will write upon him my new name.

Revelation 3:21 To him that overcometh will I grant to sit with me in my throne, even as I also overcame, and am set down with my Father in his throne.

Revelation 21:7 He that overcometh shall inherit all things; and I will be his God, and he shall be my son.

[33] fate of the faithless escapists and fearful rapturists

Revelation 21:8 But the fearful, and unbelieving, and the abominable, and murderers, and whoremongers, and sorcerers, and idolaters, *and all liars*, shall have their part in the lake which burneth with fire and brimstone: which is the second death.

[34] slaves of carnality in the prison of materialist mentality

Hebrews 2:14-15 Forasmuch then as the children are partakers of flesh and blood, [Messiah] also himself likewise took part of the same; that through death he might destroy him that had the power of death, that is, the devil; and deliver them who *through fear of death were all their lifetime subject to bondage.*

[35]the mother of Life

Genesis 3:20 And Adam called his wife's name Eve; because she was the mother of all living.

[36]God with us

Isaiah 7:14 & 9:6-7 Therefore the Lord himself shall give you a sign; Behold, a virgin shall conceive, and bear a son, and shall call his name Immanuel. . . . For unto us a child is born, unto us a son is given: and the government shall be upon his shoulder: and his name shall be called Wonderful, Counsellor, The mighty God, The everlasting Father, The Prince of Peace. Of the increase of his government and peace there shall be no end, upon the throne of David, and upon his kingdom, to order it, and to establish it with judgment and with justice from henceforth even for ever. The zeal of the LORD of hosts will perform this.

[37]body entombed, spirit on tour

Matthew 12:40 For as Jonas was three days and three nights in the whale's belly; so shall the Son of man be three days and three nights in the heart of the earth.

[38]the jailbreak jail break

Ephesians 4:8-9 When he ascended up on high, he led captivity captive, and gave gifts unto men. (Now that he ascended, what is it but that he also descended first into the lower parts of the earth?) [His descent resulted in the re-capture of the captives for release from Hades; then upon His ascent into hyperspacial heaven He administered special spirit gifts to His followers on earth, as were detailed by Paul in the remainder of the passage in this epistle to the Ephesians, vs. 10-16.]

Acts 2:24-32 Whom God hath raised up, having loosed the pains of death: because it was not possible that he should be holden of it. For David speaketh concerning him [in Psalm 16:8-10], I foresaw the Lord always before my face, for he is on my right hand, that I should not be moved: Therefore did my heart rejoice, and my tongue was glad; moreover *also my flesh shall rest in hope: Because thou wilt not leave my soul in hell,* neither wilt thou suffer thine Holy One to see corruption. Thou hast made known to me the ways of life; thou shalt make me full of joy with thy countenance. Men and brethren, let me freely speak unto you of the patriarch David, that he is both dead and buried, and his sepulchre is with us unto this day. Therefore being a prophet, and knowing that God had sworn with an oath to him, that of the fruit of his loins, according to the flesh, he would raise up Christ to sit on his throne; he seeing this before spake of the resurrection of Christ, that his soul was not left in hell, neither his flesh did see corruption. This Jesus hath God raised up, whereof we all are witnesses.

1 Peter 3:18-20 For Christ also hath once suffered for sins, the just for the unjust, that he might bring us to God, being put to death in the flesh, but quickened by the Spirit: By which also he went and preached unto the spirits in prison; which sometime were disobedient, when once the longsuffering of God waited in the days of Noah, while the ark was a preparing . . . [This obviously represented their opportunity for repentance and redemption; or else, why preach to them?]

Revelation 1:17-18 Fear not; I am the first and the last: I am he that liveth, and was dead; and, behold, I am alive for evermore, Amen; and have the keys of hell and of death.

[39]the ambiguously universal English word *Hell*—In this particular case, *"hell"* is not

translated from the Gk. *Hades*, but from *"geéna,"* which was a term used of Heb. origin, *Gehenna*, referring to a place of destruction by burning. By Hebrew analogy, the future place of eternal punishment of the soul was likened figuratively to the valley of Hinnom south of Jerusalem, Ge-Hinnom (or *Gehenna*), where refuse from the city was cast out and burned. Whereas the Devil is charged with authority over Hades and the power of Death, in this verse from Matthew chapter 10 God Himself, not Satan, has the power and authority over that ultimate place of fiery annihilation.

Chapter 9—Marvel, or Revolt?

[1]**make appropriate arrangements (the fire's hot and the lye is strong)**

Malachi 3:1-2 Behold, I will send my messenger, and he shall prepare the way before me: and the Lord, whom ye seek, shall suddenly come to his temple, even the messenger of the covenant, whom ye delight in: behold, he shall come, saith the LORD of hosts. But who may abide the day of his coming? and who shall stand when he appeareth? for he is like a refiner's fire, and like fullers' soap:

Malachi 4:1-6 For, behold, the day cometh, that shall burn as an oven; and all the proud, yea, and all that do wickedly, shall be stubble: and the day that cometh shall burn them up, saith the LORD of hosts, that it shall leave them neither root nor branch. But unto you that fear my name shall the Sun of righteousness arise with healing in his wings; and ye shall go forth, and grow up as calves of the stall. And ye shall tread down the wicked; for they shall be ashes under the soles of your feet in the day that I shall do this, saith the LORD of hosts. *Remember ye the law of Moses* my servant, which I commanded unto him in Horeb for all Israel, with the statutes and judgments. Behold, I will send you Elijah the prophet before the coming of the great and dreadful day of the LORD: And he shall *turn the heart* of the fathers to the children, and the heart of the children to their fathers, lest I come and smite the earth with a curse.

Isaiah 40:3 The voice of him that crieth in the wilderness, Prepare ye the way of the LORD, *make straight in the desert a highway* for our God.

[2]**the baptism of revolt from the status quo**

Luke 3:3-9 And he came into all the country about Jordan, preaching the *baptism of repentance* [*Gk. metanoia* = reversal] for the remission [*Gk., aphesis* = release, freedom] of sins; as it is written in the book of the words of Esaias the prophet, saying, The voice of one crying in the wilderness, Prepare ye the way of the Lord, make his paths straight. Every valley shall be filled, and every mountain and hill shall be brought low; and the crooked shall be made straight, and the rough ways shall be made smooth; and *all flesh shall see* the salvation of God. . . . And now also the axe is laid unto the root of the trees: *every tree therefore which bringeth not forth good fruit is hewn down*, and cast into the fire.

[3]**every valley exalted and every high thing humbled**

Luke 1:51-53 He hath shewed strength with his arm; he hath scattered the proud in the imagination of their hearts. He hath put down the mighty from their seats, and exalted them of low degree. He hath filled the hungry with good things; and the rich he hath sent empty away.

James 1:9 Let the brother of low degree rejoice in that he is exalted:

Isaiah 5:20-21 Woe unto them that call evil good, and good evil; that put darkness for light, and light for darkness; that put bitter for sweet, and sweet for bitter! Woe unto them that are wise in their own eyes, and prudent in their own sight!

Isaiah 29:14 Therefore, behold, I will proceed to do a marvellous work among this people, even a marvellous work and a wonder: for the wisdom of their wise men shall perish, and the understanding of their prudent men shall be hid.

Luke 10:21 In that hour Jesus rejoiced in spirit, and said, I thank thee, O Father, Lord of heaven and earth, that thou hast hid these things from the wise and prudent, and hast **revealed them unto babes**: even so, Father; for so it seemed good in thy sight.

1 Corinthians 1:19 For it is written, I will destroy the wisdom of the wise, and will bring to nothing the understanding of the prudent.

⁴make the crooked straight

In Isaiah 40:4, decreeing that the *crooked* shall be made straight and the *rough places* plain, *crooked* is translated from the Hebrew word *'aqob* (עָקֹב), meaning in the denominative sense *fraudulent*; various dictionaries give its meaning also as "deceitful, sly, insidious, polluted." Whereas, *rough places* comes from the Hebrew *rekec* (pronounced reh'-kes), meaning a mountain ridge (as of linked summits tied together), or *impeded* as in the impassability of a forbidding chain of mountains, suggesting (in my opinion) that many honest and good hearts will be welcomed by Messiah, though stringent traditional religious formulas and contrived salvation criteria which have been prohibitive and exclusionary are often self-righteously imposed by holier-than-thou pretenders to set themselves apart from "unworthy" others. The tragedy is, when the way to God is not fraudulently misrepresented one way, then it's blocked in another! The good news is, Ha'Mashiach will soon straighten it all out as it should be.

⁵beware the sting of establishment poison or the taste of its toxic fruit

Matthew 3:7-9 But when [John] saw many of the Pharisees and Sadducees [religious leaders] come to his baptism, he said unto them, O generation of vipers, who hath warned you to flee from the wrath to come? Bring forth therefore fruits meet for repentance: And think not to say within yourselves [or dare to presume that], We have Abraham to our father [or for that matter, "Christ is our savior"]: for I say unto you, that God is able of these stones to raise up children unto Abraham [and Jesus too]. [As was true in the case of the scribes, Pharisees and Sadducees, the way of traditional or establishment-oriented religious cults is often as crooked as it is prohibitive to passage into the Kingdom of Truth; see Matthew 23:13-14 et seq.]

⁶the battle for hearts and minds

Luke 1:17 (Prophecy about the destiny of John the Baptist given to his father Zacharias before his illustrious son's birth): And he shall go before [Messias] *in the spirit and power of Elias [Elijah]*, to turn the hearts of the fathers to the children, and the disobedient to the wisdom of the just; to make ready a people prepared for the Lord.

⁷popular myth, or painful fact

Matthew 7:13-14 Enter ye in at the strait gate: for wide is the gate, and broad is the way, that leadeth to destruction, and many there be which go in thereat: Because strait is the gate, and narrow is the way, which leadeth unto life, and few there be that find it.

⁸the battle for faith and the children

Hosea 4:1 Hear the word of the LORD, ye children of Israel: for the LORD hath a controversy with the inhabitants of the land, because there is no truth, nor mercy, nor knowledge of God in the land.

Isaiah 38:19 The living, the living, he shall praise thee, as I do this day: *the father to the children shall make known thy truth.*

3 John 1:4 I have no greater joy than to hear that my children walk in truth. (See continuation of 3rd epistle of John.)

Luke 1:17 And he [the herald] shall go before him [Messiah] in the spirit and power of Elias, to turn the hearts of the fathers to the children, *and the disobedient to the wisdom of the just*; to make ready a people prepared for the Lord.

Luke 18:8 Nevertheless when the Son of man cometh, shall he find faith on the earth?

[9]**Our damnable, despicable fathers**—the intellectual elites, political leaders, corrupt judges, social engineers and entertainment moguls, etc.—have turned our poor children into the children of hell, using them as guinea pigs to try out the anti-God social experiments of the last 3 decades. Since the early 60's, they have stripped them naked of spiritual and moral godliness in the public square and left them destitute of godly support to guide them into healthy, peaceful, and godly lives. Now children ironically sport "No Fear" T-shirts and caps while they walk the streets in fear, go the local parks in fear, go to work in fear, and even go to school in fear, with threats of violence and evil constantly looming over their innocent heads! The rash of school shootings and violent student massacres in just the 1997-98 school year—which we have all watched reports of in horror on our daily evening news broadcasts or read about in our newspapers—testify against the anti-Christ fathers of our country who will be held accountable before the Almighty GOD for their damnable rebellion against Him and their ravaging of the innocence of His children. Those fiendish fathers have condoned, sanctioned, sponsored, supported, and promoted infanticide, violence, licentious immorality, perversity, drugs, egotism, hedonism, and *humanist theophobia* in our society and among our children. And then they have the unmitigated gall to blame guns for the violence and murders; have the children tried as adults; and offer their pathetic counseling, mediation and anger-management therapies to our kids. They are the real smoking guns, riddling our society and children with rapid-fire projectiles of perversity, death, violence and terror launched from their wicked adult minds out of the canons of their malevolent mouths and public manipulation machines—from mass media to public schools—which teach *no fear of God!* They will be tried and punished as demons for promoting murder, massacre, money and lust, rather than Moses and prayer! (Matt.25:41)

[10]**only children, not the adultist wise and prudent ones**

Mark 10:15 Verily I say unto you, Whosoever shall not receive the kingdom of God as a little child, he shall not enter therein. (See continuation of Mark 10.)

Matthew 18:3-4 And [Jesus] said, Verily I say unto you, Except ye be converted, and become as little children, ye shall not enter into the kingdom of heaven. Whosoever therefore shall humble himself as this little child, the same is greatest in the kingdom of heaven.

Luke 10:21 In that hour Jesus rejoiced in spirit, and said, I thank thee, O Father, Lord of heaven and earth, that thou hast hid these things from the wise and prudent, and hast revealed them unto babes: even so, Father; for so it seemed good in thy sight.

[11]**get back to roots**

Micah 5:3 Therefore will he give them up, until the time that she which travaileth hath brought forth: then *the remnant of his brethren shall return* unto the children of Israel.

[12]**red and yellow, black and white . . . all are precious in His sight**

Isaiah 56:6-8 Also the sons of the stranger, that join themselves to the LORD, to serve him, and to love the name of the LORD, to be his servants, every one that keepeth the sabbath from polluting it, and taketh hold of my covenant; even them will I bring to my holy mountain, and make them joyful in my house of prayer: their burnt offerings and their sacrifices shall be accepted upon mine altar; for mine house shall be called an house of prayer *for all people.* The Lord GOD which gathereth the outcasts of Israel saith, Yet will I gather others to him, beside those that are gathered unto him.

[13]**spiritually speaking**

1 Corinthians 4:15-16 For though ye have ten thousand instructors in Christ, yet have ye not many fathers: for in Christ Jesus I have *begotten you through the gospel.* Wherefore I beseech you, be ye followers of me.—Apostle Paul

1 Timothy 1:2 [Paul] Unto Timothy, my own *son in the faith:* Grace, mercy, and peace, from God our Father and Jesus Christ our Lord.

2 Timothy 2:1-2 Thou therefore, *my son,* be strong in the grace that is in Christ Jesus.—Apostle Paul

[14]**leaders must give account**

Hebrews 13:17 Obey them that have the rule over you, and submit yourselves: for *they watch for your souls, as they that must give account,* that they may do it with joy, and not with grief: for that is unprofitable for you.

[15]**what does it taste like to you?**

John 10:11-13 I am the good shepherd: the good shepherd giveth his life for the sheep. But he that is an *hireling [mercenary pastor, politician, or leader],* and not the shepherd, whose own the sheep are not, seeth the wolf coming, and leaveth the sheep, and fleeth: and the wolf catcheth them, and scattereth the sheep. The hireling fleeth, because he is an hireling, and careth not for the sheep.

Matthew 7:15-20 Beware of false prophets, which come to you *in sheep's clothing, but inwardly* they are ravening wolves. Ye shall know them by their fruits. . . . Every good tree bringeth forth good fruit; but a corrupt tree bringeth forth evil fruit. . . . Wherefore by their fruits ye shall know them.

[16]**perspective on popularity**

Luke 16:15 And [Jesus] said unto [the covetous religious leaders], Ye are they which justify yourselves before men; but God knoweth your hearts: for *that which is highly esteemed among men is abomination in the sight of God.*

Luke 6:26 Woe unto you, *when all men shall speak well of you!* for so did their fathers to the false prophets.

[17]**the vanity & revolt* of the establishment program**

Isaiah 40:6-8, 17 The voice said, Cry. And he said, What shall I cry? All flesh is *grass,* and all the goodliness thereof is as the *flower* of the field: *The grass withereth, the flower fadeth:* because the spirit of the LORD bloweth upon it: surely the people is grass. The grass withereth, the flower fadeth: but the word of our God shall stand for ever. . . . All nations before him are as nothing; and they are counted to him less than nothing, and vanity.

James 1:9-11 Let the brother of low degree rejoice in that he is exalted: But the rich, in that he is made low: because as the flower of the grass he shall pass away. For the sun is no sooner risen with a burning heat, but it withereth the grass, and the flower thereof falleth, and the grace of the fashion of it perisheth: so also shall the rich man fade away in his ways.

Matthew 16:26 For what is a man profited, if he shall gain the whole world, and lose his own soul? or what shall a man give in exchange for his soul?

*James 4:4 Ye adulterers and adulteresses, know ye not that the friendship of the world is enmity with God? whosoever therefore will be a friend of the world is the enemy of God.

[18]**ear candy**

Isaiah 30:8-10 Now go, write it before them in a table, and note it in a book, that it may be for the time to come for ever and ever: That this a rebellious people, lying children, children that will not hear the law of the LORD: Which say to the seers, See not; and to the prophets, Prophesy not unto us right things, speak unto us smooth things, prophesy deceits:

[19]**how about a new body for that head?** The April 27, 1998 edition of ABC's *World News Tonight* featured a report by Peter Jennings on a stunning medical miracle which will, according to Dr. Robert White of Case Western Reserve University, "certainly within the year" see the possibility of total body transplants successfully achieved on humans. According to the report, the procedure—reconnection of a head to a different body—has already been performed successfully on monkeys at CWRU.

[20]**laboratory body part replicas**—First reported in late 1996 by the popular television program, *Discovery*, the same awe-inspiring achievement was covered again as recently as May 7, 1998 on that day's edition of the *CBS Evening News* in a report on biomedical "Tissue Engineering" by John Roberts. In his interview, the developer of the artificial living ear replication procedure, Dr. Charles Bicotti of the University of Massachusetts Medical Center, expressed his conviction that "probably in less than two years, maybe even one" the procedure is expected to be successfully performed on a human. Other bio-artificial body parts are also being successfully replicated, and other scientists are working on growing human organs, according to the report. Dr. Bicotti spoke of the future of tissue engineering as "a medical advance" which he suspects "will be as significant as antibiotics." To add to the intrigue, and to highlight the speed of technological advancement, consider the following news update of November 5, 1998: ABC's anchor man of *World News Tonight* led off the daily broadcast on what he said many people are likening to finding the "holy grail of biology," saying, "There is remarkable scientific news to report this evening, and some people are going to find it frightening—scientists have succeeded in growing stem cells in the laboratory." The report (by James Walker) was on embryo stem cells, the very unique human cells found only in embryonic stages, our most basic cells, which have the extraordinary capability of becoming any kind of cell—brain, bone, blood, heart, eye, etc. As per Dr. John Gearheart of Johns Hopkins Medical School, *they are now being grown in a laboratory culture dish!* "Beyond that, scientists at universities in Wisconsin and Maryland are learning how to turn the cells on to grow into just the type of human tissue they want," Walker reported. He went on to state the real potential of this technology, besides producing tissue for grafting and repairs of damaged tissue (e.g., heart attack cases), namely "to be able to grow any kind of human organ."

[21]**one trillion dollars, and growing**—The January 12, 1998 edition of the *CBS Evening News* reported that health care costs for 1997 in the USA hit a record high, over $1 trillion, surpassing the average $3,759 per person spent in 1996. (This staggering amount is equivalent to $31,710 spent *every second* year round.) Peter Jennings of ABC's *World News Tonight* reported on October 13, 1998 that by the year 2007 the annual health care bill is expected to double, reaching $2 trillion.

[22]**the occult, or the okay?—magic, or "medicine"**

Revelation 9:21 Neither repented they of their murders, nor of their sorceries, nor of their fornication, nor of their thefts.

Revelation 18:23 And the light of a candle shall shine no more at all in [Babylon the Great]; and the voice of the bridegroom and of the bride shall be heard no more at all in thee: for thy merchants were the great men of the earth; for *by thy sorceries were all nations deceived.*

Revelation 21:8 But the fearful, and unbelieving, and the abominable, and murderers, and whoremongers, and *sorcerers*, and idolaters, and all liars, shall have their part in the lake which burneth with fire and brimstone: which is the second death. (The continuation of Rev.21 is also pertinent.)

Revelation 22:15 For without [excluded from New Jerusalem] are dogs, and *sorcerers*, and whoremongers, and murderers, and idolaters, and whosoever loveth and maketh a lie.

Galatians 5:19-21 Now the works of the flesh are manifest, which are these; Adultery, fornication, uncleanness, lasciviousness, idolatry, witchcraft [Gk. *pharmakeia*], hatred, variance, emulations, wrath, strife, seditions, heresies, envyings, murders, drunkenness, revellings, and such like: of the which I tell you before, as I have also told you in time past, that they which do such things shall not inherit the kingdom of God.

[23]**The fact of the matter** is that drugs are used to defy the sovereignty of the Creator, Supreme God of heaven and earth. His sovereign good will was clearly stated in some of the earliest chapters of biblical history. Namely, that those who love Him and obey His Voice are promised every blessedness on earth, not the least of which is great health and length of days. As early as the giving of the Ten Commandments (in Exodus chapter 20) we find the promise of length of days attached to the 4th commandment to honor father and mother, which of course immediately established the "assurance" of a descendant chain of continuity of honoring and obeying God throughout future generations. Then in Deuteronomy (esp. chap. 7 & 28), the covenant of blessedness establishes upon God's people a sworn promise that illness shall only be inflicted in the case of neglect to heed the voice of the LORD and failure to observe His commandments and sovereign will. The insidious power of pharmacology is the sorcerer's black art of providing a means of defying the will of God and defeating His means of recourse and remedy for human rebellion (i.e., illness and physical affliction).

Deuteronomy 7:12-15 Wherefore it shall come to pass, if ye hearken to these judgments, and keep, and do them, that the LORD thy God shall keep unto thee the covenant and the mercy which he sware unto thy fathers: And he will love thee, and bless thee, and multiply thee: he will also bless the fruit of thy womb, and the fruit of thy land, thy corn, and thy wine, and thine oil, the increase of thy kine, and the flocks of thy sheep, in the land which he sware unto thy fathers to give thee. Thou shalt be blessed above all people: there shall not be male or female barren among you, or among your cattle. And *the LORD will take away from thee all sickness, and will put none of the evil diseases of Egypt*, which thou knowest, upon thee; but will lay them upon all them that hate thee.

[24]**does this dying body dictate the meaning of life for us?**

Matthew 6:25 Therefore I say unto you, Take no thought for your life, what ye shall eat, or what ye shall drink; nor yet for your body, what ye shall put on. Is not the life more than meat [food: eating, consuming, nourishing of lusts], and the body than raiment [clothing and accessories]?

John 6:27 Labour not for the meat which perisheth, but for that meat which endureth unto everlasting life, which the Son of man shall give unto you: for him hath God the Father sealed.

[25]**mice, or men?—the rat race, or Messiah's marathon?**

2 Corinthians 6:14-18 Be ye not unequally yoked together with unbelievers: for what fellowship hath righteousness with unrighteousness? and what communion hath light with darkness? And what concord hath Christ with Belial? or what part hath he that believeth with an infidel? And what agreement hath the temple of God with idols? for ye are the temple of the living God; as God hath said, I will dwell in them, and walk in them; and I will be their God, and they shall be my people. Wherefore come out from among them, and be ye separate, saith the Lord, and touch not the unclean thing; and I will receive you, and will be a Father unto you, and ye shall be my sons and daughters, saith the Lord Almighty.

Hebrews 12:1-4 Let us lay aside every weight, and the sin which doth so easily beset us, and let us run with patience the race that is set before us, looking unto Jesus the author and finisher of *our faith;* who for the joy that was set before him *endured the cross*, despising the shame. . . . For consider him that endured such contradiction of sinners against himself, lest ye be wearied and faint in your minds. Ye have not yet resisted unto blood, *striving against sin.*

[26]**vanity and vexation of spirit**

Ecclesiastes 2:22 What hath man of all his labour, and of the vexation of his heart, wherein he hath laboured under the sun?

Ecclesiastes 8:8-15 There is no man that hath power over the spirit to retain the spirit; neither hath he power in the day of death: and there is no discharge in that war; neither shall wickedness deliver those that are given to it. . . . But it shall not be well with the wicked, neither shall he prolong his days, which are as a shadow; because he feareth not before God. . . . Then I commended mirth, because a man hath no better thing under the sun, than to eat, and to drink, and to be merry: for that shall abide with him of his labour the days of his life, which God giveth him under the sun.

Ecclesiastes 9:3-6 This is an evil among all things that are done under the sun, that there is one event unto all: yea, also the heart of the sons of men is full of evil, and madness is in their heart while they live, and after that they go to the dead. . . . Also their love, and their hatred, and their envy, is now perished; neither have they any more a portion for ever in any thing that is done under the sun.

Ecclesiastes 1:14 I have seen all the works that are done under the sun; and, behold, all is vanity and vexation of spirit.—King Solomon

[27]**The Green Bank equation**, according to *Encyclopaedia Britannica,* postulates that, based on various factors—including the number of stars and possible planetary systems in our Milky Way Galaxy in which intelligent life may have evolved—that the nearest advanced civilization might be in the range of only 100 light years away from earth. This would put it clearly within range of radio communications (though the signal would be delayed 100 years). This equation was first discussed in 1961 at a SETI conference convened at the National Radio Astronomy Observatory in Green Bank, West Virginia. U.S. astrophysicist Frank Drake is in large part credited with having formulated the equation. *Encyclopaedia Britannica* also reports that, according to the equation, as many as 1,000,000 advanced civilizations at least on a par with our own could exist scattered around our galaxy, if even only one percent of the many more possible have learned to live with the technology of mass destruction, and with themselves. (So you see these are serious discussions by serious science-oriented minds.)

[28]**colonies in space**

Obadiah 1:4 Though thou exalt thyself as the eagle, and though thou set thy nest among the stars, thence will I bring thee down, saith the LORD.

("Terraforming," incidentally, is a new word coined by extraplanetary theorists who envision the possibility of men landing on other worlds in outer space to then artificially create earth-like environments in which they are able to survive, even if only on a limited or contained basis—such as the recent Arizona Biosphere project.)

[29]not in secret chambers in the desert

Matthew 24:23-27 Then if any man shall say unto you, Lo, here is Christ, or there; believe it not. . . . If they shall say unto you, Behold, he is *in the desert;* go not forth: behold, he is *in the secret chambers; believe it not. For as the lightning cometh out of the east, and shineth even unto the west; so shall also the coming of the Son of man be.*

Isaiah 66:15 For, behold, the LORD will come with fire, *and with his chariots like a whirlwind [flying craft],* to render his anger with fury, and his rebuke with flames of fire.

Psalm 68:17 The chariots [the only adequate term to describe these vehicles in ancient times] of God are twenty thousand, even thousands of angels: the Lord is among them . . .

[30]the great compromise, or *apostasia (falling away; defection from the Faith)*

Front page headline of *The Santa Fe New Mexican*, October 25, 1996: **"Pope sanctions theory of evolution."** In the lead article by columnist Greg Toppo, he quotes Pope John Paul II as having said that since 1950 "new knowledge" has led to the recognition that theory of evolution is "more than a hypothesis." (What "new knowledge" could that be?) This declaration was made the day before to the Pontifical Academy of Sciences where he reportedly affirmed Darwin's theory to be "compatible with the Christian faith." In the same article, a pastoral assistant for the local St. John the Baptist Catholic Church agreeing with the Pope is quoted as having said she attended a catholic university 20 years ago, where she learned about Darwin's theory, and that "it made perfect sense to [her]." Also quoted is a New Mexico state school board member describing himself as a "Catholic evolutionist," who said about the Pope's statement, "I think it's late but welcome on the part of the church to recognize the larger picture, which is both sacred and secular." (Interesting that the sacred is now secular, and the secular sacred! Sounds like mixing up apples with oranges, or perhaps, monkeys with men.)

[31]"don't worry, the Lord will save us"

2 Peter 2:19-22 While they promise them liberty, they themselves are the servants of corruption: for of whom a man is overcome, of the same is he brought in bondage. For if after they have escaped the pollutions of the world through the knowledge of the Lord and Saviour Jesus Christ, they are again entangled therein, and overcome, the latter end is worse with them than the beginning. For it had been better for them not to have known the way of righteousness, than, after they have known it, to turn from the holy commandment delivered unto them. But it is happened unto them according to the true proverb, The dog is turned to his own vomit again; and the sow that was washed to her wallowing in the mire.

[32]revolt

2 Timothy 2:3-4 Thou therefore endure hardness, as a good soldier of Jesus Christ. No man that warreth entangleth himself with the affairs of this life; that he may please him who hath chosen him to be a soldier.

Chapter 10—Messiah Mistake

[1]**that day & all them that believe—(same theme continued . . .)**

II Thessalonians 1:7-11 & continued in 2:1-3 And to you who are troubled *rest with us*, when the Lord Jesus shall be revealed from heaven with his mighty angels...*when he shall come* to be glorified in his saints, and to be admired in *all them that believe* . . . in *that day*. Wherefore also we pray always for you, that our God would count you worthy of this calling. . . . Now we beseech you, brethren, by the coming of our Lord Jesus Christ, *and by our gathering together unto him*, that ye be not soon shaken in mind, or be troubled, neither by spirit, nor by word, nor by letter as from us, as that *the day of Christ* is at hand. Let no man deceive you by any means: for *that day* shall not come, except there come a *falling away first, and that man of sin be revealed.*

[2]**when do you think He's coming?**

Matthew 24:44 Therefore be ye also ready: for in such an hour as ye think not the Son of man cometh.

Luke 18:8 Nevertheless when the Son of man cometh, shall he find faith on the earth?

[3]**weak hearts, weak theologies, weak perspectives do not make strong spirits**

Jeremiah 12:5 If thou hast run with the footmen, and they have wearied thee, then how canst thou contend with horses? and if in the land of peace, wherein thou trustedst, they wearied thee, then how wilt thou do in the swelling of Jordan?

Proverbs 24:10 If thou faint in the day of adversity, thy strength is small.

Hebrews 12:3-4 For consider him that endured such contradiction of sinners against himself, lest ye be wearied and faint in your minds. Ye have not yet resisted unto blood, striving against sin.

[4]**by their fruits ye shall know them?**

2 Corinthians 11:23-27 Are they ministers of Christ? (I speak as a fool) I am more; in labours more abundant, in stripes [floggings] above measure, in prisons more frequent, in deaths oft. Of the Jews five times received I forty stripes save one. Thrice was I beaten with rods, once was I stoned, thrice I suffered shipwreck, a night and a day I have been in the deep; in journeyings often, in perils of waters, in perils of robbers, in perils by mine own countrymen, in perils by the heathen, in perils in the city, in perils in the wilderness, in perils in the sea, in perils among false brethren; in weariness and painfulness, in watchings often, in hunger and thirst, in fastings often, in cold and nakedness.—Apostle Paul

1Thessalonians 2:9 For ye remember, brethren, our labour and travail: for labouring night and day, because we would not be chargeable unto any of you, we preached unto you the gospel of God.—Paul

[5]**the original pattern & example**

1Thessalonians 1:5-9 For our gospel came not unto you in word only, but also in power, and in the Holy Ghost, and in much assurance; as ye know what manner of men we were among you for your sake. And ye became followers of us, and of the Lord, having *received the word in much affliction*, with joy of the Holy Ghost: so that ye were ensamples to all that believe...also in every place your faith is spread abroad. . . . how ye turned to God from idols to serve the living and true God...

[6]**hang in there, despite the tribulation**

1Thessalonians 3:2-5 [I] sent Timotheus, our brother, and minister of God, and our fellowlabourer in the gospel of Christ, to establish you, and to comfort you concerning your faith: *That no man should be moved by these afflictions:* for yourselves know that *we are appointed thereunto.* For verily, when we were with you, *we told you before that we should suffer tribulation;* even as it came to pass, *and ye know.* For this cause, when I could no longer forbear, I sent to know your faith, lest by some means the tempter have tempted you, and our labour be in vain.—Paul

[7]**children of light, not victims of surprise**

1Thessalonians 5:4-5 But ye, brethren, are not in darkness, that that day should overtake you as a thief. Ye are all the children of light, and the children of the day: we are not of the night, nor of darkness.

[8]**He who holds down**

Job 1:6-12 Now there was a day when the sons of God came to present themselves before the LORD, and Satan came also among them. And the LORD said unto Satan, Whence comest thou? Then Satan answered the LORD, and said, From going to and fro in the earth, and from walking up and down in it. And the LORD said unto Satan, Hast thou considered my servant Job, that there is none like him in the earth, a perfect and an upright man, one that feareth God, and escheweth evil? Then Satan answered the LORD, and said, Doth Job fear God for nought? Hast not thou made an hedge about him, and about his house, and about all that he hath on every side? Thou hast blessed the work of his hands, and his substance is increased in the land. But put forth thine hand now, and touch all that he hath, and he will curse thee to thy face. And the LORD said unto Satan, Behold, all that he hath is in thy power; only upon himself put not forth thine hand. So Satan went forth from the presence of the LORD.

Job 2:1-7 Again there was a day when the sons of God came to present themselves before the LORD, and Satan came also among them to present himself before the LORD. And the LORD said unto Satan, From whence comest thou? And Satan answered the LORD, and said, From going to and fro in the earth, and from walking up and down in it. And the LORD said unto Satan, Hast thou considered my servant Job, that there is none like him in the earth, a perfect and an upright man, one that feareth God, and escheweth evil? and still he holdeth fast his integrity, although thou movedst me against him, to destroy him without cause. And Satan answered the LORD, and said, Skin for skin, yea, all that a man hath will he give for his life. But put forth thine hand now, and touch his bone and his flesh, and he will curse thee to thy face. And the LORD said unto Satan, Behold, he is in thine hand; but save his life. So went Satan forth from the presence of the LORD, and smote Job with sore boils from the sole of his foot unto his crown.

[9]**truth eludes the escapists**

II Thessalonians 2:8-12 And then shall that Wicked be revealed, whom the Lord shall consume with the spirit of his mouth, and shall destroy with the brightness of his coming: Even him [the LORD], *whose coming is after the working of Satan with all power and signs and lying wonders, and with all deceivableness* of unrighteousness in them that perish; *because they received not the love of the truth,* that they might be saved. And for this cause God shall send them strong delusion, that they should believe a lie: That they all might be damned who believed not the truth, but had pleasure in unrighteousness.

[10]sweet bread recipe

Proverbs 20:17 Bread of deceit is sweet to a man; but afterwards his mouth shall be filled with gravel.

[11]supposedly "left behind"

Revelation 7:2-4, 9, 13-15 And I saw another angel ascending from the east, having the seal of the living God: and he cried with a loud voice to the four angels, to whom it was given to hurt the earth and the sea, saying, Hurt not the earth, neither the sea, nor the trees, till we have sealed the servants of our God in their foreheads. And I heard the number of them which were sealed: and there were sealed an hundred and forty and four thousand of all the tribes of the children of Israel. . . . After this I beheld, and, lo, a great multitude, which no man could number, of all nations, and kindreds, and people, and tongues, stood before the throne, and before the Lamb, clothed with white robes, and palms in their hands. . . . And one of the elders answered, saying unto me, What are these which are arrayed in white robes? and whence came they? And I said unto him, Sir, thou knowest. And he said to me, These are they which came out of great tribulation, and have washed their robes, and made them white in the blood of the Lamb. Therefore are they before the throne of God, and serve him day and night in his temple: and he that sitteth on the throne shall dwell among them.

[12]the Comforter

John 14:16-17 & 26 And I will pray the Father, and he shall give you another Comforter, that he may abide with you for ever; even the Spirit of truth...for he dwelleth with you, and shall be in you. . . . But the Comforter, which is the Holy Ghost, whom the Father will send in my name, he shall teach you all things.

John 16:13 Howbeit when he, the Spirit of truth, is come, he will guide you into all truth: for he shall not speak of himself; but whatsoever he shall hear, that shall he speak: and he will shew you things to come.

John 15:26 But when the Comforter is come, whom I will send unto you from the Father, even the Spirit of truth, which proceedeth from the Father, *he shall testify of me* . . .—Christ Yeshua

Acts 1:8 But ye shall receive power, after that the Holy Ghost is come upon you: and ye shall be witnesses unto me both in Jerusalem, and in all Judaea, and in Samaria, and unto the uttermost part of the earth.

[13]above the rest—the cult of the exempt

Isaiah 65:2 & 5 I have spread out my hands all the day unto a rebellious people, which walketh in a way that was not good, after *their own thoughts*. . . . Which say, Stand by thyself, come not near to me; for *I am holier than thou*. These are a smoke in my nose, a fire that burneth all the day.

2 Timothy 3:4-5 Traitors, heady, highminded, lovers of pleasures more than lovers of God; having a form of godliness, but denying the power thereof: from such turn away.

Romans 12:3 For I say, through the grace given unto me, to every man that is among you, not to think of himself more highly than he ought to think; but to think soberly.

Philippians 2:5-8 Let this mind be in you, which was also in Christ Jesus: Who...made himself of no reputation, and took upon him the form of a servant...He humbled himself, and became obedient unto death, even the death of the cross.

Luke 6:40 The disciple is not above his master: but every one that is perfect shall be as his master.

[14]stumbling in the shadow of materialism, or sojourning in the light of the promise?

Revelation 17:1-2, 5, 15 & 18 And there came one of the seven angels which had the seven vials, and talked with me, saying unto me, Come hither; I will shew unto thee the judgment of the great whore that sitteth upon many waters: With whom the kings of the earth have committed fornication, and *the inhabitants of the earth have been made drunk* with the wine of her fornication. . . . And upon her forehead was a name written, MYSTERY, BABYLON THE GREAT, THE MOTHER OF HARLOTS AND ABOMI-NATIONS OF THE EARTH. . . . And he saith unto me, The waters which thou sawest, where the whore sitteth, are peoples, and multitudes, and nations, and tongues. . . . And the woman which thou sawest is that *great city*, which reigneth [superpower] over the kings of the earth.

Hebrews 11:10, 13-14 & 16 For [Abraham] looked for a city which hath founda-tions, whose builder and maker is God. . . . These [patriarchs] all died in faith, not having received the promises, but having seen them afar off, and were persuaded of them, and embraced them, and confessed that they were *strangers and pilgrims* on the earth. For they that say such things declare plainly that they seek a country. . . . But now *they desire a better country*, that is, an heavenly: wherefore God is not ashamed to be called their God: for he hath prepared for them a city.

[15]adultery of spirit and the love of Babylon

2 Corinthians 6:14-18 Be ye not unequally yoked together with unbelievers: for what fellowship hath righteousness with unrighteousness? and what communion hath light with darkness? And what concord hath Christ with Belial? or what part hath he that believeth with an infidel? And what agreement hath the temple of God with idols? for ye are the temple of the living God; as God hath said, I will dwell in them, and walk in them; and I will be their God, and they shall be my people. Wherefore come out from among them, and be ye separate, saith the Lord, and touch not the unclean thing; and I will receive you, and will be a Father unto you, and ye shall be my sons and daughters, saith the Lord Almighty.

1 Corinthians 6:15-17 Know ye not that your bodies are the members of Christ? shall I then take the members of Christ, and make them the members of an harlot? God forbid. What? know ye not that he which is joined to an harlot is one body? for two, saith he, shall be one flesh. But he that is joined unto the Lord is one spirit.

[16]God, or fraud?

Titus 1:16 They profess that they know God; but in works they deny him, being abominable, and disobedient, and unto every good work reprobate.

[17]the chicken or the egg?

Romans 1:21, 25 Because that, when they knew God, they glorified him not as God, neither were thankful; but became vain in their imaginations, and their foolish heart was darkened. . . . Who changed the truth of God into a lie, and worshipped and served the creature more than the Creator, who is blessed for ever. Amen.

Romans 1:23 And changed the glory of the uncorruptible God into an image made like to corruptible man, and to birds, and fourfooted beasts, and creeping things.

[18]impeach God on grounds of discrimination

Isaiah 5:20-24 Woe unto them that call evil good, and good evil; that put darkness for light, and light for darkness; that put bitter for sweet, and sweet for bitter! Woe unto them that are wise in their own eyes, and prudent in their own sight! Woe unto them that are mighty to drink wine [until they cannot discriminate], and men of strength to mingle strong drink [concoct everpowerful new brew]: Which justify the wicked for reward, and take away the righteousness of the righteous from him! Therefore as the fire devoureth the stubble, and the flame consumeth the chaff, so their root shall be as rottenness, and their blossom shall go up as dust: because they have cast away the law of the LORD of hosts, and despised the word of the Holy One of Israel.

[19] apostasy = rejecting the Rock of Truth for foundations of sand

Deuteronomy 32:4 He is the Rock, his work is perfect: for all his ways are judgment: a God of truth and without iniquity, just and right is he.

Psalm 33:4 For the word of the LORD is right; and all his works are done in truth.

Psalm 119:142 Thy righteousness is an everlasting righteousness, and thy law is the truth.

Matthew 7:24, 26-27 Therefore whosoever heareth these sayings of mine, and doeth them, I will liken him unto a wise man, which built his house upon a rock: . . And every one that heareth these sayings of mine, and doeth them not, shall be likened unto a foolish man, which built his house upon the sand: And the rain descended, and the floods came, and the winds blew, and beat upon that house; and it fell: and great was the fall of it.

Hosea 4:1 Hear the word of the LORD, ye children of Israel: for the LORD hath a controversy with the inhabitants of the land, because there is no truth, nor mercy, nor knowledge of God in the land.

Deuteronomy 8:11 Beware that thou forget not the LORD thy God, in not keeping his commandments, and his judgments, and his statutes, which I command thee this day:

Jeremiah 6:19 Hear, O earth: behold, I will bring evil upon this people, even the fruit of their thoughts, because they have not hearkened unto my words, nor to my law, but rejected it.

Psalm 78:10 They kept not the covenant of God, and refused to walk in his law;

Isaiah 5:24 Therefore as the fire devoureth the stubble, and the flame consumeth the chaff, so their root shall be as rottenness, and their blossom shall go up as dust: because they have cast away the law of the LORD of hosts, and despised the word of the Holy One of Israel.

Jeremiah 8:9 The wise men are ashamed, they are dismayed and taken: lo, they have rejected the word of the LORD; and what wisdom is in them?

Psalm 14:1-3 The fool hath said in his heart, There is no God. They are corrupt, they have done abominable works, there is none that doeth good. The LORD looked down from heaven upon the children of men, to see if there were any that did understand, and seek God. They are all gone aside, they are all together become filthy: there is none that doeth good, no, not one.

Proverbs 1:7 The fear of the LORD is the beginning of knowledge: but fools despise wisdom and instruction.

Jeremiah 9:3 And they bend their tongues like their bow for lies: but they are not valiant for the truth upon the earth; for they proceed from evil to evil, and they know not me, saith the LORD.

Psalm 9:17 The wicked shall be turned into hell, and all the nations that forget God.

Zechariah 7:11-12 But they refused to hearken, and pulled away the shoulder, and stopped their ears, that they should not hear. Yea, they made their hearts as an adamant stone, lest they should hear the law, and the words which the LORD of hosts hath sent in his spirit by the former prophets: therefore came a great wrath from the LORD of hosts.

Jeremiah 6:10 To whom shall I speak, and give warning, that they may hear? behold, their ear is uncircumcised, and they cannot hearken: behold, the word of the LORD is unto them a reproach; they have no delight in it.

[20]appointing the fox to guard the chicken coop?

1 Corinthians 14:33 For God is not the author of confusion, but of peace, as in all churches of the saints.

[21]the cult of the "prepared"

Luke 17:26-30 And as it was in the days of Noe, so shall it be also in the days of the Son of man. They did eat, they drank, they married wives, they were given in marriage, until the day that Noe entered into the ark, and the flood came, and destroyed them all. Likewise also as it was in the days of Lot; they did eat, they drank, they bought, they sold, they planted, they builded; but the same day that Lot went out of Sodom it rained fire and brimstone from heaven, and destroyed them all. Even thus shall it be in the day when the Son of man is revealed.

2 Corinthians 6:14-18 Be ye not unequally yoked together with unbelievers: for what fellowship hath righteousness with unrighteousness? and what communion hath light with darkness? And what concord hath Christ with Belial? or what part hath he that believeth with an infidel? And what agreement hath the temple of God with idols? for ye are the temple of the living God; as God hath said, I will dwell in them, and walk in them; and I will be their God, and they shall be my people. Wherefore come out from among them, and be ye separate, saith the Lord, and touch not the unclean thing; and I will receive you, and will be a Father unto you, and ye shall be my sons and daughters, saith the Lord Almighty.

James 1:27 Pure religion and undefiled before God and the Father is this, To visit the fatherless and widows in their affliction, and to keep himself unspotted from the world.

[22]values unveiled

Colossians 3:1-3 If ye then be risen with Christ, seek those things which are above, where Christ sitteth on the right hand of God. Set your affection on things above, not on things on the earth. For ye are dead, and your life is hid with Christ in God.

Luke 12:34 For where your treasure is, there will your heart be also.

Ezekiel 33:31 And they come unto thee as the people cometh, and they sit before thee as my people, and they hear thy words, but they will not do them: for with their mouth they shew much love, but their heart goeth after their covetousness.

[23]only one for each

John 5:28-29 Marvel not at this: for the hour is coming, in the which all that are in the graves shall hear his voice, and shall come forth; they that have done good, unto the resurrection of life; and they that have done evil, unto the resurrection of damnation.

[24]the last day

John 6:39-40, 44 & 54 And this is the Father's will which hath sent me, that of all which he hath given me I should lose nothing, but should raise it up again *at the last day*. And this is the will of him that sent me, that every one which seeth the Son, and believeth on him, may have everlasting life: and I will raise him up *at the last day*. . . . No man can come to me, except the Father which hath sent me draw him: and I will raise him up *at the last day*. . . . Whoso eateth my flesh, and drinketh my blood, hath eternal life; and I will raise him up *at the last day*.

[25]**treasure in Heaven**

Matthew 19:21-22 & 29 Jesus said unto him, If thou wilt be perfect, go and sell that thou hast, and give to the poor, and thou shalt have treasure in heaven: and come and follow me. But when the young man heard that saying, he went away sorrowful: for he had great possessions. . . . And every one that hath forsaken houses, or brethren, or sisters, or father, or mother, or wife, or children, or lands, for my name's sake, shall receive an hundredfold, and shall inherit everlasting life.

[26]**a sacrifice, or an honor?**

Luke 9:23-25 And [Yeshua] said to them all, If any man will come after me, let him deny himself, and take up his cross daily, and follow me. For whosoever will save his life shall lose it: but whosoever will lose his life for my sake, the same shall save it. For what is a man advantaged, if he gain the whole world, and lose himself, or be cast away?

Luke 14:26-27 & 33 If any man come to me, and hate not his father, and mother, and wife, and children, and brethren, and sisters, yea, and his own life also, he cannot be my disciple. And whosoever doth not bear his cross, and come after me, cannot be my disciple. . . . So likewise, whosoever he be of you that forsaketh not all that he hath, he cannot be my disciple.—Yeshua

Philippians 3:7-8 But what things were gain to me [Paul], those I counted loss for Christ. Yea doubtless, and I count all things but loss for the excellency of the knowledge of Christ Jesus my Lord: for whom I have suffered the loss of all things, and do count them but dung, that I may win Christ.

Matthew 10:38 He that taketh not his cross, and followeth after me, is not worthy of me.—Yeshua

Romans 12:1 I beseech you therefore, brethren, by the mercies of God, that ye present your bodies a living sacrifice, holy, acceptable unto God, which is your reasonable service.—Apostle Paul

John 15:13 Greater love hath no man than this, that a man lay down his life for his friends.—Yeshua

[27]Otis, George Jr. (1993) *The Last of the Giants: Lifting the Veil on Islam and the End Times.* Chosen Books, division of Baker Book House Co. Grand Rapids, Michigan 49516

[28]**high-tech miracles**

Revelation 13:13 And he doeth great wonders, so that he maketh fire come down from heaven on the earth in the sight of men...

[29]**the true spirit**

Revelation 19:10 And I fell at his feet to worship him. And he said unto me, See thou do it not: I am thy fellowservant, and of thy brethren that have the testimony of Jesus: worship God: for the testimony of Jesus is the spirit of prophecy.

[30]**whose tradition will you buy?**

II Thessalonians 3:5-6 & 14-15 And the Lord direct your hearts into the love of God, and into the *patient waiting for Christ.* Now we command you, brethren, in the name of our Lord Jesus Christ, that ye withdraw yourselves from every brother that walketh disorderly, and not after the tradition which he received of us. . .And if any man obey not our word by this epistle, note that man, and have no company with him, that he may be ashamed. Yet count him not as an enemy, but admonish him as a brother.—Apostle Paul

[31]**cross, or candy**

Mark 10:21 Then Jesus beholding him loved him, and said unto him, One thing thou lackest: go thy way, sell whatsoever thou hast, and give to the poor, and thou shalt have treasure in heaven: and come, take up the cross, and follow me.

Matthew 10:38 He that taketh not his cross, and followeth after me, is not worthy of me.—Yeshua

1 Peter 2:21 For even hereunto were ye called: because Christ also suffered for us, leaving us an example, that ye should follow his steps:

Chapter 11—The Sieve of Vanity

[1]**Welcome home, Yeshua Ha'Mashiach!**

Revelation 1:7 Behold, he cometh with clouds; and every eye shall see him, and they also which pierced him: and all kindreds of the earth shall wail because of him. Even so, Amen.

[2]**who should be angry?**

Revelation 11:18 And the nations were angry, and thy wrath is come, and the time of the dead, that they should be judged, and that thou shouldest give reward unto thy servants the prophets, and to the saints, and them that fear thy name, small and great; and shouldest destroy them which destroy the earth.

[3]**The year of the Noachian Flood**—has been "determined" to have occurred on May 14, 2345 BCE (Before the Common Era—marked by the birth of Christ and essentially equivalent to BC designation). This date is per the computer-aided astronomical dating methodologies used by Chronology History Research Institute in Iowa (USA). It is reported on page 111 of *The Incredible Discovery of Noah's Ark* by Charles E. Sellier and David W. Balsiger. New York: Dell, 1995.

[4]**pure, unmitigated indignation**

Revelation 14:9-10 And the third angel followed them, saying with a loud voice, If any man worship the beast and his image, and receive his mark in his forehead, or in his hand, the same shall drink of the wine of the wrath of God, which is poured out without mixture [Gk. *akrátou* (ἀκράτου) undiluted] into the cup of his indignation; and he shall be tormented with fire and brimstone in the presence of the holy angels, and in the presence of the Lamb:

[5]**target earth and sea—the first three trumpets of Tribulation**

Revelation 8:6-11 And the seven angels which had the seven trumpets prepared themselves to sound. The first angel sounded, and there followed hail and fire mingled with blood, and they were cast upon the earth: and the third part of trees was burnt up, and all green grass was burnt up. And the second angel sounded, and as it were a great mountain burning with fire was cast into the sea: and the third part of the sea became blood [probably the extent of deadly devastation in an oceanic region, like the Pacific bordered by the notoriously volcanic "Ring of Fire"]; and the third part of the creatures which were in the sea, and had life, died; and the third part of the ships were destroyed. And the third angel sounded, and there fell a great star from heaven, burning as it were a lamp, and it fell upon the third part of the rivers, and upon the fountains of waters; and the name of the star is called Wormwood*: and the third part of the waters became wormwood; and many men died of the waters, because they were made bitter.

[6]**near misses and the ever-present danger**—Articles reprinted from *The Washington Post* in local newspapers around the country on or around February 27, 1997 told of an object at least 1,000 ft. in diameter (305 m) that crossed our skies not much farther away than the moon in May of 1996. The same article relayed reports by planetary and astronomical scientists that a ton of micrometeorite dust hits the Earth every hour, and that a lump the size of a baseball survives the searing temperatures of atmospheric friction to reach the surface intact every few hours. Also, data (now declassified) from military satellites indicates that nearly once a month some speeding extraterrestrial object explodes in the upper atmosphere with the force of one kiloton of TNT or more. Same

article reports that an object a mile or more in diameter would cause "global ecological damage and disrupt civilization." Estimates are that 2,000 asteroids and comets approaching 1 mile or more in diameter currently move in orbits that could intersect with Earth's. Much of the information provided in the article was evidently provided by the NEAT (Near Earth Asteroid Tracking) science team, which is one of only 2 such search teams in the world. NEAT utilizes observatory equipment operated by the U.S. Air Force Space Command atop Haleakala volcano in Hawaii.

The FOX Television Special, *DOOMSDAY—What Can We Do?*, which aired in March 1997, showed daytime video footage of what was ostensibly the same 1000-foot object reported by the *Washington Post* (cited above) visibly skimming the Earth's atmosphere and leaving a distinct trail of smoke or vapor before escaping gravity to continue on its journey past Earth. According to this documentary-style FOX special, including its brief glancing of the atmosphere the asteroid was visible for 5 days traversing our skies before disappearing into space.

[7]**Krakatoa**—Krakatau, a volcano on Rakata Island in the Sunda Strait between Java and Sumatra, Indonesia, erupted violently on August 27, 1883. Its eruption was one of the most catastrophic in history and triggered tsunamis (tidal waves) estimated at 100-120 feet in height along the shores of Java and Sumatra. 36,000 people were killed in nearby coastal towns and the tsunamis were recorded as far away as South America and Hawaii. In addition, the surrounding region was plunged into darkness for two and a half days because of ash in the air. Dust and ash from the explosion caused spectacular red sunsets around the globe throughout the following year as it drifted several times around the Earth.

[8]**Wormwood**—Note that the significance of the term "wormwood" is difficult to pinpoint, except that it evidently refers to the bitterness of a plant, Artemisia absinthium, native to Eastern Europe. The wormwood plant, which though used as the primary ingredient in the liqueur *absinthe* and as an aromatic flavoring in vermouth (German *vermut*, hence *wormwood*), produces a bitter and toxic substance that is poisonous in high enough concentrations. Shortly after the turn of the century, Switzerland, France and many other countries prohibited the manufacture of absinthe as a health hazard that appeared to cause convulsions, etc. Though lacking confirmation, this author has learned that the name of the site of the world's worst nuclear disaster of April 1986, in the Ukraine—"Chernobyl," translated into English—means "wormwood." Perhaps the modern-day association of the nuclear disaster which spread radioactive fall-out over vast areas of Eastern Europe and Scandinavia with "Chernobyl" gives some clue as to the possible significance of the use of the term "wormwood." It is highly conceivable that the intent is to describe a highly toxic substance deposited by the collision of either an asteroid or large meteor consisting of a radioactive element or some chemical composite that spews a poisonous element or compound over vast areas of the planet upon impact. A man-made object such as a missile, warhead, or spacecraft should not be ruled out.

[9]**demonic invaders resembling locusts**

Revelation 9:1-12 And the fifth angel sounded, and I saw a star fall from heaven unto the earth: and to him was given the key of the bottomless pit. And he opened the bottomless pit; and there arose a smoke out of the pit, as the smoke of a great furnace; and the sun and the air were darkened by reason of the smoke of the pit. And there came out of the smoke locusts upon the earth: and unto them was given power, as the scorpions of the earth have power. And it was commanded them that they should not hurt the grass of the earth, neither any green thing, neither any tree; but only those men which have not the seal of God in their foreheads. And to them it was given that they should not kill them, but that they should be tormented five months: and their torment was as the torment of a scorpion, when he striketh a man. And *in those days shall men seek death*, and shall not find it; and shall desire to die, and death shall flee from them. And the shapes of the locusts were like unto horses prepared unto battle; and on their heads were as it were crowns like gold, and their faces were as the faces of men. And they had hair as the hair of women, and their teeth were as the teeth of lions. And they had breastplates, as it were breastplates of iron; and the sound of their wings was as the sound of chariots of many horses running to battle. And they had tails like unto scorpions, and there were stings in their tails: and their power was to hurt men five months. And they had a king over them, which is the angel of the bottomless pit, whose name in the Hebrew tongue is Abaddon, but in the Greek tongue hath his name Apollyon [the Destroyer]. One woe is past; and, behold, there come two woes more hereafter.

[10]**dens and caves of the earth**—It is quite common knowledge that nearly every government on Earth has constructed subterranean shelters for its presidents, prime ministers, and high ranking officials (such as cabinet ministers) in which to seek refuge in the case of a massive bomb attack or other devastating enemy invasion, as well as in cases of popular revolution or coups d'état. Even the poverty-stricken nations of Africa with their starving millions have, in tragic irony, joined this subterranean refuge club: e.g., Zambia, where a CBN news crew was guided on an exclusive tour of a two-mile-long, seven-story-deep, multi-million-dollar facility in secret tunnels beneath the statehouse of this central African nation. The report, providing video of portions of the facility, was broadcast by CBN on Nov. 9, 1995 as a feature of its daily *Newswatch Today* program.

Extensive underground excavations, tunnels and chambers have been and increasingly continue to be constructed (esp. with the vastly improved technologies of the last 3 or 4 decades) for a multitude of purposes. These range from "bomb-proof" military command centers, such a NORAD (North American Air Defense and Command Center in the rock of Cheyenne Mountain in Colorado) to subterranean shopping malls in Montreal, Canada. Dens and caves (esp. man-made) are used for warehouses and storage depots, hundreds of hydro-electric plant facilities in numerous countries, top secret laboratories and research and development facilities (such as those at Sandia and Los Alamos labs in New Mexico), as well as for weapons manufacture (Libyan chemical weapons plant, and Syrian missile factories by no means isolated cases), underground military bunkers and aircraft hangars (as in the Saudi Arabian deserts and elsewhere), extensive mining operations worldwide, not to overlook "simple" tunnels for transportation uses (railways, highways, and subways) common to millions around the world from the English Channel to Washington, DC, and Columbia to Japan. They are everywhere in our modern world and many are accessible to the soon-to-be terrified millions seeking to hide from those horrors of the wrath to come foreseen by the prophets. The tens of thousands of bomb shelters constructed especially during the Cold War need also be included in this listing.

Revelation 6:15-17 And the kings of the earth, and the great men, and the rich men, and the chief captains, and the mighty men, and every bondman, and every free man, hid themselves in the dens and in the rocks of the mountains; and said to the mountains and rocks, Fall on us, and hide us from the face of him that sitteth on the throne, and from the wrath of the Lamb: For the great day of his wrath is come; and who shall be able to stand?

Isaiah 2:19 And they shall go into the holes of the rocks, and into the caves of the earth, for fear of the LORD, and for the glory of his majesty, when he ariseth to shake terribly the earth.

[11]**demise of the northern army**

Joel 2:20 But I will remove far off from you the northern army, and will drive him into a land barren and desolate, with his face toward the east sea [a.k.a. Dead, or Salt Sea], and his hinder part toward the utmost sea [Great, or Mediterranean Sea], and his stink shall come up, and his ill savour shall come up, because he hath done great [magnific, pompous] things. (Note: The direction in which this northern army flees is toward the Jordan valley; see next footnote for the topographical link between the valley of Megiddo and Jordan valley.)

Ezekiel 38:14-16 Therefore, son of man, prophesy and say unto Gog, Thus saith the Lord GOD; In that day when my people of Israel dwelleth safely, shalt thou not know it? And thou shalt come from thy place out of the north parts, thou, and many people with thee, all of them riding upon horses, a great company, and a mighty army: And thou shalt come up against my people of Israel, as a cloud to cover the land; it shall be in the latter days, and I will bring thee against my land, that the heathen may know me, when I shall be sanctified in thee, O Gog, before their eyes.

Ezekiel 39:1-5, 11-13 Therefore, thou son of man, prophesy against Gog, and say, Thus saith the Lord GOD; Behold, I am against thee, O Gog, the chief prince of Meshech and Tubal: And I will turn thee back, and leave but the sixth part of thee, and will cause thee to come up from the north parts, and will bring thee upon the mountains of Israel: And I will smite thy bow out of thy left hand, and will cause thine arrows to fall out of thy right hand. Thou shalt fall upon the mountains of Israel, thou, and all thy bands, and the people that is with thee: I will give thee unto the ravenous birds of every sort, and to the beasts of the field to be devoured. Thou shalt fall upon the open field: for I have spoken it, saith the Lord GOD. . . . (11-13) And it shall come to pass in that day, that I will give unto Gog a place there of graves in Israel, *the valley of the passengers on the east of the sea:* and it shall stop the noses of the passengers: and there shall they bury Gog and all his multitude: and they shall call it The valley of Hamongog. And seven months shall the house of Israel be burying of them, that they may cleanse the land. Yea, all the people of the land shall bury them; and it shall be to them a renown the day that I shall be glorified, saith the Lord GOD.

[12]**the international cemetery**—Though Ezekiel 39:11 (cited in previous footnote) does not specify which "sea" it will be east of, it is most likely referring to the Great Sea (Mediterranean). The "valley of the passengers on the east of the sea" may refer to the much-visited Jordan valley, which drops to more than 1,300 feet below sea level and is extremely hot and barren (as per Joel 2:20), with the exception of river bank areas, rare oases, and limited areas of irrigated cultivation. The Jordan is both east of the (Great) sea, as well as east of Armageddon and east of Jerusalem. But also east of the Great Sea lie the connecting valleys of Meggido and Jezreel (linking both to the Jordan valley) which together represent the central siting of the Battle of Armageddon. These valleys and areas are not only modern touring sites, but were ancient (passenger) crossroads where major north-south, east-west trade routes coursed and intersected. They qualify highly as the possible site of "The valley of Hamongog (the multitude of Gog)," the

burial grounds for the staggeringly massive armies of the Armageddon invasion (who shall not flee all *that* far from the onslaught of YHWH).

[13] capital of the beast for last 3 and 1/2 years

Daniel 9:27 And he shall confirm the covenant with many for one week [7 yrs.]: and in the midst of the week [3.5 yrs.] he shall cause the sacrifice and the oblation to cease [break the covenant], and for the overspreading of abominations [great array of blasphemies] he shall make it desolate, even until the consummation [final end], and that determined [wrath & indignation] shall be poured upon the desolate [him and his devotees].

Daniel 11:45 And he shall plant the tabernacles of his palace [establish regime capital] between the seas [Mediterranean & Dead] in the glorious holy mountain [in Jerusalem]; yet he shall come to his end, and none shall help him.

[14] united nations general assembly—against Israel!

Zechariah 12:2-3 Behold, I will make Jerusalem a cup of trembling unto all the people round about, when they shall be in the siege both against Judah and against Jerusalem. And in that day will I make Jerusalem a burdensome stone for all people: all that burden themselves with it shall be cut in pieces, though all the people of the earth be gathered together against it.

[15] YHWH, the tetragrammaton (יְהֹוָה)—*Vine's Expository Dictionary of Biblical Words*

explains: "The Tetragrammaton YHWH appears without its own vowels, and its exact pronunciation is debated (Jehovah, Yehovah, Jahweh, Yahweh). . .This use of the word occurs 6,828 times. The word appears in every period of biblical Hebrew. . .The divine name YHWH appears only in the Bible. Its precise meaning is much debated. God chose it as His personal name by which He related specifically to His chosen or covenant people. Its first appearance in the biblical record is Genesis 2:4: "These are the generations of the heavens and of the earth when they were created, in the day that the LORD God made the earth and the heavens . . ." (The KJV—King James Version—used throughout this book translates each occurrence of יְהֹוָה as "LORD," in all capitals.)

[16] that much blood?—impossible!—Depending on the standard furlong measurement applied to this calculation, 1,200 furlongs ranges from 160-200 miles, or approx. 260-320 kilometers of blood flow.—Sounds incredible, huh? Yet a 200 million man army as mentioned in Revelation 9:16 spilling all its blood could fill a rectangular channel 2.5 meters wide and 1 meter deep with blood for a distance of 320 kilometers, or over 3 meters wide for 260 kilometers, if each soldier weighs an average of 68 kilos (150 pounds), yielding a typical 4 liters of blood each. In U.S. measurements that translates as a channel over 8 feet wide and 3 feet 4 inches deep over a distance of 200 miles; or, over the more conservative distance of 160 miles, a channel 9.25 feet wide and 3 feet 4 inches deep. Do you suppose John the Revelator had his handy Tozai calculator with him to facilitate making such an outrageous prophecy? Please note also that the army of Rev. 9:16 could be even larger by the time of the amassing of the anti-Christ hordes of Armageddon.

Should John have been speaking *figuratively* of blood, which is possible, the scenario he described simply illustrates the magnitude of the slaughter that takes place at the Battle of Armageddon where wounded, bleeding carcasses of millions of men will be strewn one atop another for hundreds of miles (especially) in the valleys, as well as on the mountains surrounding Jerusalem.

[17]**controversy of Jerusalem**

  Isaiah 34:8 For it is the day of the LORD's vengeance, and the year of recompences for the controversy of Zion.

[18]**Gog and Magog**—Additional reading on the subject matter of Ezekiel 38 & 39: *The Magog Factor*, by Chuck Missler and Hal Lindsay; also, *The Magog Invasion*, by Chuck Missler.

[19]**Ararat**

  Genesis 8:4 And the ark rested in the seventh month, on the seventeenth day of the month, upon the mountains of Ararat.

[20]**Noah's Ark—Fact or fiction?**—Fascinating further reading: Charles E. Sellier & David W. Balsiger, *The Incredible Discovery of Noah's Ark*. New York: Dell Publishing, 1995. Even more well documented and *conclusive evidence* is available (on video, etc.) from Wyatt Archaeological Research, 713 Lambert Dr., Nashville, TN 37220 (USA).

[21]**Gomer's endtime antics**—Between February 1997 and May 1997, *The International Intelligence Briefing*, a weekly television program offering world news and commentary, aired by Trinity Broadcasting Network (TBN), has reported on German involvement in the hotspots of the Middle East with a particular focus on strategic military developments. The February 20 edition reported that Germany continues to sell restricted chemicals to Iraq. These are no doubt used to revitalize the stockpiles of chemical weapons, much of which were destroyed by the Allies following Persian Gulf War of 1991. An April 1997 edition reported that both Germany and France have been involved for years in both nuclear and chemical projects in neighboring Iran, which could easily be converted to military use. And, the May 1, 1997 edition, discussing the trading status of Germany with Iran as its largest Western partner, reported on German sales of equipment to various Middle Eastern countries which is subsequently diverted for building bacteriological weapons.

[22]**Nelson Mandela—gone the way of all flesh**—Quote taken from statement aired on January 23, 1997 edition of *The International Intelligence Briefing*: Trinity Broadcasting Network.

[23]**Egypt and the controversy of Zion**—Reported by *The International Intelligence Briefing*, February 13, 1997 edition, aired by TBN.

[24]**is it for the spoil and the prey?**

  Ezekiel 38:11-13 And thou [Gog] shalt say, I will go up to the land of unwalled villages; I will go to them that are at rest, that dwell safely, all of them dwelling without walls, and having neither bars nor gates, to take a spoil, and to take a prey; to turn thine hand upon the desolate places that are now inhabited, and upon the people that are gathered out of the nations, which have gotten cattle and goods, that dwell [strategically] *in the midst of the land*. Sheba, and Dedan [Arabians of Saudi peninsula], and the merchants of Tarshish [unknown location, thought to be a European port headquartering international merchant marine trade and to have probably even shifted locations, even to London], with all the young lions thereof [perhaps signifying the "offspring" of British colonialism, lions being commonly used in English heraldry], shall say unto thee, Art thou come to take a spoil? hast thou gathered thy company to take a prey? to carry away silver and gold, to take away cattle and goods, to take a great spoil?

[25]**the capital city of Messiah**

  Isaiah 2:3-4 And many people shall go and say, Come ye, and let us go up to the mountain of the LORD, to the house of the God of Jacob; and he will teach us of his ways, and we will walk in his paths: for *out of Zion shall go forth the law, and the word of the LORD from Jerusalem*. And he shall judge among the nations, and shall rebuke many people: and they shall beat their swords into plowshares, and their spears into pruninghooks: nation shall not lift up sword against nation, neither shall they learn war any more.

Psalm 48:1-2 Great is the LORD, and greatly to be praised in the city of our God, in the mountain of his holiness. Beautiful for situation, the joy of the whole earth, is *mount Zion, on the sides of the north*, the city of the great King.

Isaiah 14:12-14 How art thou fallen from heaven, O Lucifer, son of the morning! how art thou cut down to the ground, which didst weaken the nations! For thou hast said in thine heart, I will ascend into heaven, I will exalt my throne above the stars of God: *I will sit also upon the mount of the congregation, in the sides of the north:* I will ascend above the heights of the clouds; I will be like the most High. (Vicariously, the Fallen One accomplishes this usurpation during the 42 months of Antichrist's reign, according to the prophecy of Daniel, chapter 11, verse 45: "And he shall plant the tabernacles of his palace between the seas *in the glorious holy mountain;* yet he shall come to his end, and none shall help him.")

[26] the day of the Great Slaughter

Isaiah 30:25 And there shall be upon every high mountain, and upon every high hill, rivers and streams of waters in the day of the great slaughter, when the towers fall.

Isaiah 34:6 The sword of the LORD is filled with blood, it is made fat with fatness, and with the blood of lambs and goats, with the fat of the kidneys of rams: for the LORD hath a sacrifice in Bozrah, and a great slaughter in the land of Idumea [south of Israel as previously identified].

[27] the end of controversy

Zechariah 14:9 And the LORD shall be king over all the earth: in that day shall there be *one* LORD, and his name *one*.

[28] true Judaism

Romans 9:6-8 Not as though the word of God hath taken none effect. For they are not all Israel, which are of Israel: Neither, because they are the seed of Abraham, are they all children: but, In Isaac shall thy seed be called. That is, They which are the children of the flesh, these are not the children of God: but the children of the promise are counted for the seed.

Romans 2:28-29 For he is not a Jew, which is one outwardly; neither is that circumcision, which is outward in the flesh: But he is a Jew, which is one inwardly; and circumcision is that of the heart, in the spirit, and not in the letter; whose praise is not of men, but of God.

[29] the Ultimate Power

Genesis 1:1 In the beginning God created the heaven and the earth.

John 1:1-3 In the beginning was the Word, and the Word was with God, and the Word was God. The same was in the beginning with God. All things were made by him; and without him was not any thing made that was made.

Colossians 1:16-17 For by him were all things created, that are in heaven, and that are in earth, visible and invisible, whether they be thrones, or dominions, or principalities, or powers: all things were created by him, and for him: And he is before all things, and by him all things consist.

Psalm 33:6 By the word of the LORD were the heavens made; and all the host of them *by the breath of his mouth.*

³⁰har-Megiddown, site of the great battle with God Almighty

Revelation 16:12-16 And the sixth angel poured out his vial upon the great river Euphrates; and the water thereof was dried up, that the way of the kings of the east might be prepared. And I saw three unclean spirits like frogs come out of the mouth of the dragon, and out of the mouth of the beast, and out of the mouth of the false prophet. For they are the spirits of devils, working miracles, which go forth unto the kings of the earth and of the whole world, to gather them to the battle of that great day of God Almighty. Blessed is he that watcheth, and keepeth his garments, lest he walk naked, and they see his shame. Behold, I come as a thief. And he gathered them together into a place called in the Hebrew tongue Armageddon.

Chapter 12—Time No Longer, or The Seven Last Plagues

[1]the Day of Vengeance

Isaiah 34:8 For it is the day of the LORD's vengeance, and the year of recompences for the controversy of Zion.

Isaiah 63:4 For the day of vengeance is in mine heart, and the year of my redeemed is come.

Isaiah 61:1-2 The Spirit of the Lord GOD is upon me; because the LORD hath anointed me . . . to proclaim the acceptable year of the LORD, and the day of vengeance of our God . . .

[2]the end of The Trial, end of The Mystery, end of mankind's sinful tenure—now wrath

Revelation 10:5-7 And the angel which I saw stand upon the sea and upon the earth lifted up his hand to heaven, and sware by him that liveth for ever and ever, who created heaven, and the things that therein are, and the earth, and the things that therein are, and the sea, and the things which are therein, that there should be *time no longer:* But in the days of the voice of the seventh angel, when he shall begin to sound, *the mystery of God should be finished,* as he hath declared to his servants the prophets. (See following footnote for "mystery.")

Revelation 11:15 & 18 And the seventh angel sounded; and there were great voices in heaven, saying, The kingdoms of this world are become the kingdoms of our Lord, and of his Christ; and he shall reign for ever and ever. . .(18) And the nations were angry, and *thy wrath is come*, and the time of the dead, that they should be judged, and that thou shouldest give reward unto thy servants the prophets, and to the saints, and them that fear thy name, small and great; and shouldest destroy them which destroy the earth.

[3]the last trumpet

1 Corinthians 15:51-54 Behold, I shew you a mystery; We shall not all sleep [die], but we shall all be changed, in a moment, in the twinkling of an eye, *at the last trump:* for the trumpet shall sound, and the dead shall be raised incorruptible, and we shall be changed. For this corruptible must put on incorruption, and this mortal must put on immortality. So when this corruptible shall have put on incorruption, and this mortal shall have put on immortality, then shall be brought to pass the saying that is written, Death is swallowed up in victory.

1 Thessalonians 4:16-17 For the Lord himself shall descend from heaven with a shout, with the voice of the archangel, and with the trump of God: and the dead in Christ shall rise first: Then we which are alive and remain shall be caught up together with them in the clouds, to meet the Lord in the air: and so shall we ever be with the Lord.

Matthew 24:31 And he shall send his angels with a great sound of a trumpet, and they shall gather together his elect from the four winds, from one end of heaven to the other.

[4]self-determination and self-condemnation

Luke 10:16 He that heareth you [disciples] heareth me; and he that despiseth you despiseth me; and he that despiseth me despiseth him that sent me.

John 12:47-48 And if any man hear my words, and believe not, I judge him not: for I came not to judge the world, but to save the world. He that rejecteth me, and receiveth not my words, hath one that judgeth him: the word that I have spoken, the same shall judge him in the last day.

John 3:17-21 For God sent not his Son into the world to condemn the world; but that the world through him might be saved. He that believeth on him is not condemned: but he that believeth not is condemned already, because he hath not believed in the name of the only begotten Son of God. And this is the condemnation, that light is come into the world, and men loved darkness rather than light, because their deeds were evil. For every one that doeth evil hateth the light, neither cometh to the light, lest his deeds should be reproved. But he that doeth truth cometh to the light, that his deeds may be made manifest, that they are wrought in God.

Titus 3:10-11 A man that is an heretick after the first and second admonition reject; knowing that he that is such is subverted, and sinneth, *being condemned of himself.*

[5] convicted by the evidence—hatred

Matthew 25:40 And the King shall answer and say unto them, Verily I say unto you, Inasmuch as ye have done it unto one of the least of these my brethren, ye have done it unto me.

Mark 9:41-42 For whosoever shall give you a cup of water to drink in my name, because ye belong to Christ, verily I say unto you, he shall not lose his reward. And whosoever shall offend one of these little ones that believe in me, it is better for him that a millstone were hanged about his neck, and he were cast into the sea.

[6] the sorting out

Matthew 3:11-12 He that cometh after me is mightier than I [John], whose shoes I am not worthy to bear: he shall baptize you with the Holy Ghost, *and with fire:* Whose fan is in his hand, and he will throughly purge his floor, and gather his wheat into the garner; but he will burn up the chaff with unquenchable fire.

Matthew 25:31-32 When the Son of man shall come in his glory, and all the holy angels with him, then shall he sit upon the throne of this glory: And before him shall be gathered all nations: and he shall separate them one from another, as a shepherd divideth his sheep from the goats . . .

Matthew 13:24-30 Another parable put he forth unto them, saying, The kingdom of heaven is likened unto a man which sowed good seed in his field: But while men slept, his enemy came and sowed tares among the wheat, and went his way. But when the blade was sprung up, and brought forth fruit, then appeared the tares also. So the servants of the householder came and said unto him, Sir, didst not thou sow good seed in thy field? from whence then hath it tares? He said unto them, An enemy hath done this. The servants said unto him, Wilt thou then that we go and gather them up? But he said, Nay; lest while ye gather up the tares, ye root up also the wheat with them. Let both grow together *until the harvest:* and in the time of harvest I will say to the reapers, Gather ye together *first the tares,* and bind them in bundles to burn them: but gather the wheat into my barn.

[7] the fires of purification

Isaiah 48:10 Behold, I have refined thee, but not with silver; I have chosen thee in the furnace of affliction.

Zechariah 13:9 And I will bring the third part through the fire, and will refine them as silver is refined, and will try them as gold is tried: they shall call on my name, and I will hear them: I will say, It is my people: and they shall say, The LORD is my God.

Malachi 3:3 And he shall sit as a refiner and purifier of silver: and he shall purify the sons of Levi, and purge them as gold and silver, that they may offer unto the LORD an offering in righteousness.

Daniel 11:35 And some of them of understanding shall fall, to try them, and to purge, and to make them white, even to the time of the end: because it is yet for a time appointed.

Revelation 7:9-14 After this I beheld, and, lo, a great multitude, which no man could number, of all nations, and kindreds, and people, and tongues, stood before the throne, and before the Lamb, clothed with white robes, and palms in their hands . . . These are they which came out of great tribulation, and have washed their robes, and made them white in the blood of the Lamb.

Revelation 6:9-11 And when he had opened the fifth seal, I saw under the altar the souls of them that were slain for the word of God, and for the testimony which they held: And they cried with a loud voice, saying, How long, O Lord, holy and true, dost thou not judge and avenge our blood on them that dwell on the earth? And white robes were given unto every one of them; and it was said unto them, that they should rest yet for a little season, until their fellowservants also and their brethren, that should be killed as they were, should be fulfilled.

⁸loincloth or fine wardrobe; mansion or palm frond shack—all have their reward

Revelation 3:18 I counsel thee to buy of me gold tried in the fire, that thou mayest be rich; and white raiment, that thou mayest be clothed, and that the shame of thy nakedness do not appear . . .

1 Corinthians 3:13-15 Every man's work shall be made manifest: for the day shall declare it, because it shall be revealed by fire; and the fire shall try every man's work of what sort it is. If any man's work abide which he hath built thereupon, he shall receive a reward. If any man's work shall be burned, he shall suffer loss: but he himself shall be saved; yet so as by fire.

Revelation 16:15 Behold, I come as a thief. Blessed is he that watcheth, and keepeth his garments, lest he walk naked, and they see his shame.

⁹the last day

John 11:24 Martha saith unto him, I know that he [deceased brother Lazarus] shall rise again in the resurrection *at the last day.*

John 6:39-40, 44 & 54 And this is the Father's will which hath sent me, that of all which he hath given me I should lose nothing, but should raise it up again *at the last day.* And this is the will of him that sent me, that every one which seeth the Son, and believeth on him, may have everlasting life: and I will raise him up *at the last day.* . . . No man can come to me, except the Father which hath sent me draw him: and I will raise him up *at the last day.* . . . Whoso eateth my flesh, and drinketh my blood, hath eternal life; and I will raise him up *at the last day.*

John 12:47-48 And if any man hear my words, and believe not, I judge him not: for I came not to judge the world, but to save the world. He that rejecteth me, and receiveth not my words, hath one that judgeth him: the word that I have spoken, the same shall judge him *in the last day.*

¹⁰the victors

Revelation 15:1-2 And I saw another sign in heaven, great and marvellous, seven angels having the seven last plagues; for in them is filled up the wrath of God. And I saw as it were a sea of glass mingled with fire: and them that had gotten the victory over the beast, and over his image, and over his mark, and over the number of his name, stand on the sea of glass [*before the throne* of God; see Rev. 4:6], having the harps of God.

Revelation 7:9, 14 I beheld, and, lo, a great multitude, which no man could number, of all nations, and kindreds, and people, and tongues, stood *before the throne*, and before the Lamb, clothed with white robes, and palms in their hands. . . . And he said to me, These are they which came out of great tribulation, and have washed their robes, and made them white in the blood of the Lamb.

Isaiah 26:20-21 Come, my people, enter thou into thy chambers, and shut thy doors about thee: hide thyself as it were for a little moment, until the indignation be overpast. For, behold, the LORD cometh out of his place to punish the inhabitants of the earth for their iniquity: the earth also shall disclose her blood, and shall no more cover her slain.

[11]*helkos* [ἕλκος], **ulcerous, pussy plague of the first bowl of wrath**

Revelation 16:2 And the first went, and poured out his vial upon the earth; and there fell a noisome [particularly baneful] and grievous sore *[helkos]* upon the men which had the mark of the beast, and upon them which worshipped his image.

[12]**death to drink**

Revelation 16:3-6 And the second angel poured out his vial upon the sea; and it became as the blood of a dead man: and every living soul [creature with breath] died in the sea. And the third angel poured out his vial upon the rivers and fountains of waters; and they became blood. And I heard the angel of the waters say, Thou art righteous, O Lord, which art, and wast, and shalt be, because thou hast judged thus. For they have shed the blood of saints and prophets, and thou hast given them blood to drink; for they are worthy.

[13]**ozone depletion?—or supernova furnace?**

Revelation 16:8-9 And the fourth angel poured out his vial upon the sun; and power was given unto him to scorch men with fire. And men were scorched with great heat, and blasphemed the name of God, which hath power over these plagues: and they repented not to give him glory.

Malachi 4:1 For, behold, the day cometh, that shall burn as an oven; and all the proud, yea, and all that do wickedly, shall be stubble: and the day that cometh shall burn them up, saith the LORD of hosts, that it shall leave them neither root nor branch.

Isaiah 30:26-30 Moreover the light of the moon shall be as the light of the sun, and the *light of the sun shall be sevenfold*, as the light of seven days, in the day that the LORD bindeth up the breach of his people, and healeth the stroke of their wound. Behold, the name of the LORD cometh from far, *burning with his anger*, and the burden thereof is heavy: his lips are full of indignation, and his tongue as *a devouring fire:* And his breath, as an overflowing stream, shall reach to the midst of the neck, to sift the nations with the sieve of vanity: and there shall be a bridle in the jaws of the people, causing them to err. . .And the LORD shall cause his glorious voice to be heard, and shall shew the lighting down of his arm, with *the indignation of his anger*, and *with the flame of a devouring fire*, with scattering, and tempest, and hailstones.

[14]**Antichrist headquarters; usurped land**

Daniel 11:45 And he [king of north] shall plant the tabernacles of his palace [establish regime capital] between the seas [Mediterranean & Dead] in the glorious holy mountain [Zion/Jerusalem]; yet he shall come to his end, and none shall help him.

Daniel 9:16 O Lord, according to all thy righteousness, I beseech thee, let thine anger and thy fury be turned away from *thy city Jerusalem, thy holy mountain:* because for our sins, and for the iniquities of our fathers, Jerusalem and thy people are become a reproach to all that are about us.

Ezekiel 20:40 For in mine holy mountain, in the mountain of the height of Israel, saith the Lord GOD, there shall all the house of Israel, all of them in the land, serve me: there will I accept them, and there will I require your offerings, and the firstfruits of your oblations, with all your holy things.

Isaiah 66:20 And they shall bring all your brethren for an offering unto the LORD out of all nations upon horses, and in chariots, and in litters, and upon mules, and upon swift beasts, to my holy mountain Jerusalem, saith the LORD, as the children of Israel bring an offering in a clean vessel into the house of the LORD.

[15]**East vs. West**—Common to nearly every Asian country is either a long-standing anti-Western sympathy, or a more recent, but ever-swelling one. There is hardly any need to mention the commonly known antipathy for the West among the Islamic countries of Asia, such as Iraq, Iran, Afghanistan, and Pakistan; not to mention India with its enormous Muslim population (over 100 million) and its rapid distancing from Western ties, as was evidenced by the recent popular uprising against the hosting of the "culturally seductive" 1997 Miss Universe beauty pageant. But more insidious is the snake in the grass with whom the USA does more business and commerce than hardly any other nation on earth, and to whom it has granted Most Favored Nation trading status since 1980, despite its consistently hideous record on human rights—Red China. This is a nation that threatened to "nuke" Los Angeles during the recent (1996) Taiwan crisis in the event of American intervention on behalf of Taiwan.

With respect to the Chinese military threat to the West, although the major (liberal, irresponsible, and commercialized) news media organizations here in the USA have deliberately blinked and grossly neglected to report on the issue, other alternative news sources have faithfully reported on China's anti-West belligerency. This includes reports on their massive arms race and eager dealings with other belligerent Asian and Middle Eastern states to supply armaments and weapons technologies & components. Radio broadcasts by Koinonia House, heard locally on KNKT FM 107.1, Albuquerque, have reported on the mammoth arms race in progress in the hostile Middle and Far East, SE Asian countries alone committing to $50 billion in military spending just over the last couple years.

On a January 1997 broadcast on this same station, author and lecturer Chuck Missler cited intelligence information from such respected intelligence sources as the *Intelligence Digest* and *Jane's Monthly Intelligence Review*. Missler reported that China's military budget has exceeded that of NATO and western Europe. Its nuclear arsenal, reportedly, contains at least 17 solid-fuel ICBMs (Intercontinental Ballistic Missiles). It, at that time, was negotiating a purchase of a major aircraft carrier from the Ukraine, as well as 20 Russian KILO class diesel submarines, which originally carried 12 single stage ICBMs and wake-homing torpedoes (against which American surface ships presently have no installed defense). Other purchases also being negotiated are for advanced air combat capability, such as additional MiG-29s, MiG-231s, AWACs (Airborne Warning and Control Systems aircraft), in-flight refueling aircraft, S-300 anti-aircraft systems, anti-sub helicopters, and cruise missals. In addition, not only are direct purchases being dealt, but China is also scheduled to produce (under license) 150 Russian SU-27 aircraft equipped with advanced Russian avionics. All this, of course, financed by an economy which, according to Missler, nearly equals that of the USA and is 10 times that of faltering Russia. Hard up for the welcomed cash flow, Russia has evidently been transferring huge amounts of arms and related technology to this historical communist arch rival. In terms of guidance systems to support their submarine operations, China has launched 9 of its own communications satellites, and fills the gaps by using down-link data readily available from Japanese (GMS) and American (LANDSAT & NOAA) satellites.—Chuck Missler, "The Sleeping Dragon Awakes," *The Grand Adventure*, KNKT, Albuquerque, 27 Jan. 1997.

In terms of China's role as a supplier of arms, weapons technologies, and components to its Asian and Middle Eastern clients, Missler reported, in the same program, that $4.5 billion in arms deals were recently announced between China and Iran. Some of this apparently includes advanced radar components and missile technologies, such as the 10 FAC-Ms (Fast Attack Craft Missiles) armed with C-802 anti-ship cruise missiles supposedly being delivered to Iran by Beijing (obviously for use in the strategic Persian Gulf). On top of those, according to Missler, the CIA has released reports that China has provided both Iran and Pakistan with key missile system components "believed to be used to improve the accuracy" of their current (North Korean supplied) Scud missile arsenals. (SS-1 limited-range Scuds are originally Russian-made, and may be fitted for various, including nuclear, warhead deliveries. New N. Korean missiles with strike ranges exceeding 500 miles, capable of targeting US bases in Japan, are reported to be under development.) Pakistan, by the same reports, was also to have taken delivery within the prior 3 months of medium-range M-11 missiles and parts from China. Much of this, Missler reminds, is in violation of China's signed agreements with international accords. Beside conventional weapons marketing, China also actively supports the build-up of weapons of mass destruction in these countries, also substantiated in Missler's report by an account of a recent sale of 400 tons of chemicals to Iran for manufacture of nerve agents.—Ibid.

The May 8, 1997 broadcast of the *International Intelligence Briefing*, on TBN, Atlanta, confirmed China's nefarious status as a leader in the Eastern marketplace of unconventional weapons of mass destruction, as well as the more conventional. That week's edition covered a *Jane's Defense Weekly* report that China had just sold 2 tons of chemicals used for weapons to Iran. Commentary in that edition reiterated reports by other major news sources, such as CBN, that China is leading supplier of *nuclear* hardware and technology to Iran, as well as selling other advanced weapons to Syria, Saudi Arabia, and Pakistan.

Ironic twists of 20th century political circumstances are yielding (esp. of late) unlikely strategic linkages and unexpected international bonds, as well as enmities, that only God could have predicted (and did). The March 3, 1997, edition of TBN's *International Intelligence Briefing* reported on the meeting that week of (former arch-rivals) Chinese Foreign Minister Kien Chen with Boris Yeltsin, apparently in a counterbalancing move to strengthen Sino-Russian relations in the face of NATO's threatening commitment to expand eastward. Continuation of the coverage of that week's news events, included the visit to Russia the same week by India's prime minister, Deve Gowda, who also met with Yeltsin, and discussed issues of technical and military cooperation. IIB reported that India and Russia have "agreed to finalize details of a new [Indo-Russian] military cooperation program, due for launch in the year 2000," and that 40 Russian jet fighters worth $1.8 billion were bought by India last year. They affirmed that of the 51 countries for which Russia is the official arms dealer, 60% of Russia's total arms sales now end up either in New Delhi or Beijing.

¹⁶**the Eastern disdain**

Revelation 17:16-18 & 19:19 And the ten horns which thou sawest upon the beast, *these shall hate the whore*, and shall make her desolate and naked, and shall eat her flesh, and burn her with fire. For God hath put in their hearts to fulfill his will, and to agree, and give their kingdom unto the beast, until the words of God shall be fulfilled. And *the woman* which thou sawest *is that great city [superpower metropolis]*, which reigneth over the kings of the earth. . . . And I saw the beast, and the kings of the earth, and their armies, gathered together to make war against him that sat on the horse [KING OF KINGS], and against his army [from heaven].

¹⁷**Red China's official sympathies**—On a June 6, 1997 television broadcast by CBN, correspondent Dale Hurd covered the Chinese human rights issue with a special report on their chief state mechanism for controlling dissidence: the **Laogai**—Chinese equivalent of the Soviet Gulag system—meaning *reform through labor*. More than a thousand (1,100) forced labor camps make up the system, which has reportedly swallowed up millions of political dissidents since 1949. According to the report, when not being brainwashed or tortured, prisoners are forced to work, often handling toxic or raw hazardous materials, as in asbestos mines. Many Laogai products are then exported to the USA, where they sell at very low prices, of course. Other exports include human organs, such as livers, kidneys, and corneas harvested from freshly executed prisoners [usually by firing squad], and then sold to wealthy Asians who can rely on China to maintain a steady supply. The CBN report declared China the leading persecutor of Christians in the world. The standard sentence for members of an unregistered [underground] church is 3 years in the Laogai, which in some known cases has stretched to 21 years.

In another CBN report aired May 8, 1996, China was again implicated, along with Sudan and Burma (now Myanmar), for severe persecution of Catholics and Evangelicals. Interviewed in the report, Christian demographer, David Barette, stated estimates of *over 150,000 martyrdoms* having occurred in the these countries during 1994 alone.

¹⁸**1998 meteor shower**— *CBS Evening News* reporter Diana Olick, when reporting (May 20, 1998 edition) on the Galaxy 4 satellite failure, alluded to the grave potential for widespread systemic failure in global communication later in the year. Referring to the more than 200 other communications satellites like the G-4 in high orbit above Earth, in a tone of alert and circumspection, she cautioned , "But wait till November—that's when a massive meteor shower may storm the atmosphere where all those satellites are spinning around." Her alert did not mention the various and sundry other spy, weather and guidance orbiters (**G**lobal **P**ositioning **S**ystem satellites) which will also be in dire jeopardy of being disabled, this time by tiny remnant particles crossing Earth's path at tens of thousands of miles per hour—"dust" supposedly left over from the tail of a bygone passing comet. A particle the size of a grain of sand traveling at such astronomical speeds could devastate the sensitive electronic systems on board any one of the 500 or more working satellites now in orbit in our skies. According to aerospace engineer Edward Tagliaferri, interviewed on the May 7, 1998 edition of ABC's *World News Tonight* about this November's meteor shower, "Every satellite's going to get hit; the question is how often and by what sized particles." (Note: The muzzle velocity of a speeding bullet from a high powered hunting rifle is a mere 2,000 mph.) (Also note that the meteor shower prediction did not pan out as expected. All this to simply state the fragile quality of our high technologies.)

¹⁹**the banquet of Armageddon**—According to *Encyclopaedia Britannica*, China is the

world's leading horse producing country at more than 10,000,000 head per annum. *Grolier Encyclopedia* confirms that the mountainous province of Qinghai is the primary source of China's horse breeding, constituting a major element if the economy of that province (next to the cultivation of wheat, barley, potatoes, and sheep raising). Other leading producers include Russia (2.4 million), Mongolia (2.4 million), and Kazakhstan (1.4 million). Together, these Asian states produce in excess of an estimated 16 million horses per year.

[20]"it is done"

Ezekiel 39:8 Behold, it is come, and *it is done*, saith the Lord GOD; this is the day whereof I have spoken.

[21]the title holder

Psalm 24:1-2 The earth is the LORD's, and the fulness thereof; the world, and they that dwell therein. For he hath founded it . . .

[22]urbanization of Earth—sucking in the covetous

Isaiah 14:12 & 21 How art thou fallen from heaven, O Lucifer, son of the morning! how art thou cut down to the ground, which didst weaken [by prideful delusion] the nations! . . .Prepare slaughter for his children for the iniquity of their fathers; that they do not rise, nor possess the land, *nor fill the face of the world with cities.*

By 1995, about 2,600,000,000 people, or 45% of the world's population, were living in urban areas. About 200 million now live in cities with populations exceeding 10 million; the total is expected to be 450 million in the next 20 years, almost all of the increase taking place in the developing world.—World Health Organization (WHO) 1995 Report

[23]the original plan

Genesis 1:27-28 God created man in his own image, in the image of God created he him; male and female created he them. And God blessed them, and God said unto them, Be fruitful, and multiply, and replenish the earth, and subdue it: and have dominion over the fish of the sea, and over the fowl of the air, and over every living thing that moveth upon the earth.

Genesis 2:7-8, & 15 And the LORD God formed man of the dust of the ground, and breathed into his nostrils the breath of life; and man became a living soul. And the LORD God planted a garden eastward in Eden; and there he put the man whom he had formed. . . .And the LORD God took the man, and put him into the garden of Eden to dress it and to keep it.

[24]New York—As an incidental point of interest, this author has often wondered which empire and which state is signified in the name of the erstwhile tallest building in the world: The Empire State Building.

[25]tyranny and the founder of the first city

Genesis 4:8-9 & 16-17 And Cain talked with Abel his brother: and it came to pass, when they were in the field, that Cain rose up against Abel his brother, and slew him. And the LORD said unto Cain, Where is Abel thy brother? And he said, I know not: Am I my brother's keeper? . . .And Cain went out from the presence of the LORD, and dwelt in the land of Nod, on the east of Eden. And Cain knew his wife; and she conceived, and bare Enoch: and he builded a city, and called the name of the city, after the name of his son, Enoch.

[26]high towers of the world—Kuala Lumpur, Malaysia is home soil to the world's tallest buildings, the Petronas Twin Towers, completed in 1996. At 1,483 feet (452m) high,

they surpass the Sears Tower in Chicago (1,454 ft.), the twin towers of the World Trade Center (1,350 ft.), and the Peking-based central Bank of China Building in Hong Kong (1,209 ft.), formerly the tallest building in the world outside the USA.

[27]back to the earth

Micah 7:17 They shall lick the dust like a serpent, they shall move out of their holes like worms of the earth: they shall be afraid of the LORD our God, and shall fear because of thee [the new governing administration of Messiah and His co-conquerors of Earth].

[28]another sign of the times

Revelation 18:2 Babylon the great is fallen, is fallen, and is become the habitation of devils [picture Hollywood's lovely ETs], and the hold of every foul spirit, and a cage of every unclean and hateful bird [flying thing].

[29]Chinese tower of Babel—Interestingly, it was reported by author/lecturer Chuck Missler on Koinonia House's *Grand Adventure* radio series, that even China has revealed serious intent to seek to make contact with extraterrestrial intelligence. In a country plagued with vast poverty-stricken populations, the $1,000,000,000 plan is, according Missler, to construct a 30-antenna complex of mammoth radio telescopes, superior in the world to any existing ones. This 20th century effort by the Chinese to "reach unto heaven," as the ancients of Babel intended to do with their famous space-oriented tower, is to be comprised of a sophisticated array of receivers supposedly designed to specifications that will render them 100 times more sensitive than any presently in operation today.—*The Grand Adventure*, KNKT, Albuquerque, 27 Jan. 1997.

Chapter 13—Figs and Generation Finále

[1]**the great and the terrible day of the LORD, according to Joel**

Joel 1:15 Alas for the day! for the day of the LORD is at hand, and as a destruction from the Almighty shall it come.

Joel 2:1-2 & 10-11 Blow ye the trumpet in Zion, and sound an alarm in my holy mountain: let all the inhabitants of the land tremble: for the day of the LORD cometh, for it is nigh at hand; a day of darkness and of gloominess, a day of clouds and of thick darkness, as the morning spread upon the mountains: a great people and a strong; there hath not been ever the like, neither shall be any more after it, even to the years of many generations. . . .The earth shall quake before them; the heavens shall tremble: the sun and the moon shall be dark, and the stars shall withdraw their shining: And the LORD shall utter his voice before his army: for his camp is very great: for he is strong that executeth his word: for the day of the LORD is great and very terrible; and who can abide it?

Joel 2:31 The sun shall be turned into darkness, and the moon into blood, before the great and the terrible day of the LORD come.

Joel 3:14-17 Multitudes, multitudes in the valley of decision: for the day of the LORD is near in the valley of decision. The sun and the moon shall be darkened, and the stars shall withdraw their shining. The LORD also shall roar out of Zion, and utter his voice from Jerusalem; and the heavens and the earth shall shake: but the LORD will be the hope of his people, and the strength of the children of Israel. So shall ye know that I am the LORD your God dwelling in Zion, my holy mountain: then shall Jerusalem be holy, and there shall no strangers [heathen] pass through her any more.

[2]**...life, liberty, and the pursuit of happiness**

I Kings 4:25 And Judah and Israel dwelt safely, every man under his vine and under his fig tree, from Dan even to Beersheba, all the days of Solomon.

[3]**"Because iniquity shall abound, the love of many shall wax cold."—Christ in Matthew 24:12**

2 Timothy 3:1-5 This know also, that in the last days perilous times shall come. For men shall be lovers of their own selves, covetous, boasters, proud, blasphemers, disobedient to parents, unthankful, unholy, **without natural affection**, trucebreakers, false accusers, incontinent, fierce, despisers of those that are good, traitors, heady, highminded, lovers of pleasures more than lovers of God; having a form of godliness, but denying the power thereof: from such turn away.

[4]**customs of Assyrian conquests**—As affirmed by Henry H. Halley, it is commonly understood among historians that "Assyrian policy was to deport conquered peoples to other lands, to destroy their sense of nationalism and make them more easily subject." (*Halley's Bible Handbook* [Grand Rapids, MI: Zondervan Publishing House, 1965], p. 209)

[5]**statistics**—Percentages calculated from statistics provided courtesy of the AICE (American-Israeli Cooperative Enterprise) website, www.us-israel.org (Source of figures: the *Jerusalem Report*)

[6]**thanks again**—Statistics courtesy of the Jewish Agency for Israel website, www.jazo.org.il (Source of figures: The Central Bureau of Statistics and The Ministry of Immigrant Absorption)

[7]**a high horse?**

Zechariah 9:9 Rejoice greatly, O daughter of Zion; shout, O daughter of Jerusalem: behold, thy King cometh unto thee: he is just, and having salvation; lowly, and riding upon an ass, and upon a colt the foal of an ass.

[8]**recent news reports on Israel's travail**—Cliff Ford & Hal Lindsay, "Special Report—Prelude to Apocalypse," *International Intelligence Briefing*, September 25, 1997, broadcast by TBN, Atlanta

[9]Ibid.

[10]**just the beginning**

Mark 13:7-8 And when ye shall hear of wars and rumours of wars, be ye not troubled: for such things must needs be; but the end shall not be yet. For nation shall rise against nation, and kingdom against kingdom: and there shall be earthquakes in divers places, and there shall be famines and troubles: these are the beginnings of sorrows.

[11]**"these shall hate the Whore"** (Revelation 17:16-17)—Video newsclip shown on *International Intelligence Briefing*, "Special Report—Prelude to Apocalypse," September 25, 1997, broadcast by TBN, Atlanta

[12]Ibid.

[13]Ibid.

[14]**tiny nation, huge controversy**

Isaiah 34:8 For it is the day of the LORD's vengeance, and the year of recompences for the controversy of Zion.

[15]**one last time!**

Joel 3:1-3 For, behold, in those days, and in that time, when I shall bring again the captivity of Judah and Jerusalem, I will also gather all nations, and will bring them down into the valley of Jehoshaphat, and will plead with them there for my people and for my heritage Israel, whom they have scattered among the nations, and parted my land. And they have cast lots for my people; and have given a boy for an harlot, and sold a girl for wine, that they might drink.

[16]**your genetics cannot save you**

John 8:31-47 Then said Jesus to those Jews which believed on him, If ye continue in my word, then are ye my disciples indeed; and ye shall know the truth, and the truth shall make you free. They answered him, We be Abraham's seed, and were never in bondage to any man: how sayest thou, Ye shall be made free? Jesus answered them, Verily, verily, I say unto you, Whosoever committeth sin is the servant of sin. And the servant abideth not in the house for ever: but the Son abideth ever. If the Son therefore shall make you free, ye shall be free indeed. I know that ye are Abraham's seed; but ye seek to kill me, because my word hath no place in you. I speak that which I have seen with my Father: and ye do that which ye have seen with your father. They answered and said unto him, Abraham is our father. Jesus saith unto them, If ye were Abraham's children, ye would do the works of Abraham. But now ye seek to kill me, a man that hath told you the truth, which I have heard of God: this did not Abraham. Ye do the deeds of your father. Then said they to him, We be not born of fornication; we have one Father, even God. Jesus said unto them, If God were your Father, ye would love me: for I proceeded forth and came from God; neither came I of myself, but he sent me. Why do ye not understand my speech? even because ye cannot hear my word. Ye are of your father the devil, and the lusts of your father ye will do. He was a murderer from the beginning, and abode not in the truth, because there is no truth in him. When he speaketh a lie, he speaketh of his own: for he is a liar, and the father of it. And because I tell you the truth, ye believe me not. Which of you convinceth me of sin? And if I say the truth, why do ye not believe me? He that is of God heareth God's words: ye therefore hear them not, because ye are not of God.

John 6:63 It is **the spirit** that quickeneth; the **flesh [gene pool] profiteth nothing**: the words that I speak unto you, they are spirit, and they are life.

[17]YHWH's choice by right

Numbers 6:27 And [the priests] shall put my name upon the children of Israel; and I will bless them.

Deuteronomy 12:5 But unto the place which the LORD your God shall choose out of all your tribes to put his name there, even unto his habitation shall ye seek, and thither thou shalt come:

I Kings 11:36 And unto his son [Solomon] will I give one tribe, that David my servant may have a light alway before me in **Jerusalem**, the city which I have chosen me to put my name there.

[18]the spirit of prophecy

Revelation 1:2 [John] bare record of the **word of God**, and of the **testimony of Jesus Christ**, and of all things that he saw.

Revelation 1:9 I John, who also am your brother, and companion in tribulation, and in the kingdom and patience of Jesus Christ, was in the isle that is called Patmos [exiled into isolation, after attempt to execute him by boiling in oil was unsuccessful], for the word of God, and **for the testimony** of Jesus Christ.

Revelation 12:17 And the dragon was wroth with the woman, and went to make war with the remnant of her seed, which keep the commandments of God, and **have the testimony** of Jesus Christ.

Revelation 19:10 And I fell at [the angel's] feet to worship him. And he said unto me, See thou do it not: I am thy fellowservant, and of thy brethren that have the testimony of Jesus: worship God: for **the testimony of Jesus is the spirit** of prophecy.

[19]no more mammonism!

Revelation 18:14, 21-24 And the fruits that thy soul lusted after are departed from thee, and all things which were dainty and goodly are departed from thee, and thou shalt find them **no more at all**. . . . And a mighty angel took up a stone like a great millstone, and cast it into the sea, saying, Thus with violence shall that great city Babylon be thrown down, and **shall be found no more at all**. And the voice of harpers, and musicians, and of pipers, and trumpeters, shall be heard **no more at all** in thee; and no craftsman, of whatsoever craft he be, shall be found **any more** in thee; and the sound of a millstone shall be heard **no more at all** in thee; and the light of a candle shall shine **no more at all** in thee; and the voice of the bridegroom and of the bride shall be heard **no more at all** in thee: for **thy merchants were** the great men of the earth; for by thy sorceries were all nations deceived. And in her was found the blood of prophets, and of saints, and of all that were slain upon the earth.

Chapter 14—Tell Us When!

¹Sabbath custom

Acts 15:21 For Moses of old time hath in every city them that preach him, being read in the synagogues every sabbath day.

Acts 13:27 the voices of the prophets . . . are read every sabbath day . . .

Luke 4:16 And [Yeshua] came to Nazareth, where he had been brought up: and, as his custom was, he went into the synagogue on the sabbath day, and stood up for to read.

²higher education

Acts 4:13 Now when they saw the boldness of Peter and John, and perceived that they were unlearned [Gk. *aggrámmatoi*, illiterate] and ignorant [Gk. *idiótai*, uneducated] men, they marvelled; and they took knowledge of them, that they had been with Jesus.

³inquiring fishermen want to know

Mark 13:3-4. And as he sat upon the mount of Olives over against the temple, Peter and James and John and Andrew asked him privately, Tell us, when shall these things be? and what shall be the sign when all these things shall be fulfilled?

Mark 1:16-19 Now as he walked by the sea of Galilee, he saw Simon and Andrew his brother casting a net into the sea: for they were fishers. And Jesus said unto them, Come ye after me, and I will make you to become fishers of men. And straightway they forsook their nets, and followed him. And when he had gone a little further thence, he saw James the son of Zebedee, and John his brother, who also were in the ship mending their nets.

⁴don't let it slip away

Mark 1:14-15 Now after that John was put in prison, Jesus came into Galilee, preaching the gospel of the kingdom of God, and saying, The time is fulfilled, and the kingdom of God is at hand: repent ye, and believe the gospel.

Matthew 4:17 From that time Jesus began to preach, and to say, Repent: for the kingdom of heaven is at hand.

⁵rehearsal

Matthew 10:5-8 These twelve Jesus sent forth, and commanded them, saying, Go not into the way of the Gentiles, and into any city of the Samaritans enter ye not: But go rather to the lost sheep of the house of Israel. And as ye go, preach, saying, The **kingdom of heaven is at hand**. Heal the sick, cleanse the lepers, raise the dead, cast out devils: freely ye have received, freely give.

Luke 9:1-3 & 10:1-9 Then he called his twelve disciples together, and gave them power and authority over all devils, and to cure diseases. And he **sent them to preach the kingdom** of God, and to heal the sick. And he said unto them, Take nothing for your journey, neither staves, nor scrip, neither bread, neither money; neither have two coats apiece. (10:1-9) After these things the Lord appointed other seventy also, and sent them two and two before his face into every city and place, whither he himself would come. . . . Go your ways: behold, I send you forth as lambs among wolves. . . . heal the sick that are therein, and say unto them, **The kingdom of God is come nigh unto you**.

⁶big cheese stinks

Mark 9:33-35 And he came to Capernaum: and being in the house he asked them, What was it that ye disputed among yourselves by the way? But they held their peace:

for by the way they had disputed among themselves, who should be the greatest. And he sat down, and called the twelve, and saith unto them, If any man desire to be first, the same shall be last of all, and servant of all.

Luke 9:46-48 Then there arose a reasoning among them, which of them should be greatest. And Jesus, perceiving the thought of their heart, took a child, and set him by him, and said unto them, Whosoever shall receive this child in my name receiveth me: and whosoever shall receive me receiveth him that sent me: for he that is least among you all, the same shall be great.

Luke 22:24-26 And [at their "last" Passover observance on the eve of the Crucifixion] there was also a strife among them, which of them should be accounted the greatest. And he said unto them, The kings of the Gentiles exercise lordship over them; and they that exercise authority upon them are called benefactors. But ye shall not be so: but he that is greatest among you, let him be as the younger; and he that is chief, as he that doth serve.

[7]**twelve stars**

Matthew 19:28-29 And Jesus said unto them, Verily I say unto you, That ye which have followed me, in the regeneration when the Son of man shall sit in the throne of his glory, ye also shall sit upon twelve thrones, judging the twelve tribes of Israel. And every one that hath forsaken houses, or brethren, or sisters, or father, or mother, or wife, or children, or lands, for my name's sake, shall receive an hundredfold, and shall inherit everlasting life.

[8]**the Zebedee affair**

Matthew 20:20-28 Then came to him the mother of Zebedee's children with her sons, worshipping him, and desiring a certain thing of him. And he said unto her, What wilt thou? She saith unto him, Grant that these my two sons may sit, the one on thy right hand, and the other on the left, in thy kingdom. But Jesus answered and said, Ye know not what ye ask. Are ye able to drink of the cup that I shall drink of, and to be baptized with the baptism that I am baptized with? They say unto him, We are able. And he saith unto them, Ye shall drink indeed of my cup, and be baptized with the baptism that I am baptized with: but to sit on my right hand, and on my left, is not mine to give, but it shall be given to them for whom it is prepared of my Father. And when the ten heard it, they were moved with indignation against the two brethren. But Jesus called them unto him, and said, Ye know that the princes of the Gentiles exercise dominion over them, and they that are great exercise authority upon them. But it shall not be so among you: but whosoever will be great among you, let him be your minister; and whosoever will be chief among you, let him be your servant: Even as the Son of man came not to be ministered unto, but to minister, and to give his life a ransom for many.

[9]**to the "max"**—The implication, by Hebrew idiom, of *"in the highest"* seems to be that they called for the ultimate deliverance foreseen and promised by the Prophets. Other equally acceptable translations might read, *by the Highest* (referring to the Most High God), or *at the highest*, or perhaps, *to the utmost*—all virtually synonymous in significance.

[10]**glory avoidance**—Only a few short months (apparently) prior to the commencement of Yeshua's pilgrimage to Jerusalem for the "final" Passover with His twelve disciples (probably just the summer before?)—during the tour of the region Galilee, in which he twice fed huge crowds of thousands with a few loaves and fishes—there was evidently a concerted effort made by those amazed, fish-feasted multitudes to rally a movement to

establish Yeshua as a king. According to John, *"Then those men, when they had seen the miracle that Jesus did, said, This is of a truth that prophet that should come into the world. When Jesus therefore perceived that they would come and take him by force, to make him a king, he departed again into a mountain himself alone." (John 6:14-15)*

[11] the guerrilla's vow

Luke 22:33 And [Peter] said unto him, Lord, I am ready to go with thee, both into prison, and to death. [Indeed this revolutionary did take up arms to defend the cause on the night of the betrayal and arrest of the Commander in Chief:]

Matthew 26:51-53 And, behold, one of them which were with Jesus stretched out his hand, and drew his sword, and struck a servant of the high priest's, and smote off his ear. Then said Jesus unto him, Put up again thy sword into his place: for all they that take the sword shall perish with the sword. Thinkest thou that I cannot now pray to my Father, and he shall presently give me more than twelve legions of angels? [John identifies the assailant:]

John 18:10-11 Then Simon Peter having a sword drew it, and smote the high priest's servant, and cut off his right ear. . . . Then said Jesus unto Peter, Put up thy sword into the sheath: the cup which my Father hath given me, shall I not drink it?

[12] it's not assassination—it's preserving the order, I mean, "keeping the peace"

John 12:19 The Pharisees therefore said among themselves, Perceive ye how ye prevail nothing? behold, the world is gone after him.

John 11:47-51 Then gathered the chief priests and the Pharisees a council, and said, What do we? for this man doeth many miracles. If we let him thus alone, all men will believe on him: and the Romans shall come and take away both our place and nation. And one of them, named Caiaphas, being the high priest that same year, said unto them, Ye know nothing at all, nor consider that it is expedient for us, that one man should die for the people, and that the whole nation perish not. And this spake he not of himself: but being high priest that year, he prophesied that Jesus should die for that nation . . .

[13] to hell with 30 pieces of silver . . . I wanted to rule the world!

Matthew 27:3-5 Then Judas, which had betrayed him, when he saw that [Christ] was condemned, repented himself, and brought again the thirty pieces of silver to the chief priests and elders, saying, I have sinned in that I have betrayed the innocent blood. And they said, What is that to us? see thou to that. And he cast down the pieces of silver in the temple, and departed, and went and hanged himself.

[14] things will be different now

Luke 22:35-38 And he said unto them, When I sent you without purse, and scrip, and shoes, lacked ye any thing? And they said, Nothing. Then said he unto them, But now, he that hath a purse, let him take it, and likewise his scrip: and he that hath no sword, let him sell his garment, and buy one. For I say unto you, that this that is written must yet be accomplished in me, And he was reckoned among the transgressors: for the things concerning me have an end. And they said, Lord, behold, here are two swords. And he said unto them, It is enough.

[15] wanted—dead or alive

John 7:1 After these things Jesus walked in Galilee: for he would not walk in Jewry, because the Jews sought to kill him.

Luke 9:51 And it came to pass, when the time was come that he should be received up, he stedfastly set his face to go to Jerusalem . . .

John 11:8 His disciples say unto him, Master, the Jews of late sought to stone thee;

and goest thou thither again?

John 11:57 Now both the chief priests and the Pharisees had given a commandment, that, if any man knew where he were, he should shew it, that they might take him.

¹⁶their impression

Luke 19:11 And as they heard these things, he added and spake a parable, because he was nigh to Jerusalem, and because they thought that the kingdom of God should immediately appear.

¹⁷Messiah to be "cut off"

Isaiah 53:7-10 He was oppressed, and he was afflicted, yet he opened not his mouth: he is brought as a lamb to the slaughter, and as a sheep before her shearers is dumb, so he openeth not his mouth. He was taken from prison and from judgment: and who shall declare his generation? for he was cut off out of the land of the living: for the transgression of my people was he stricken.

Daniel 9:26 And after threescore and two weeks shall Messiah be cut off, but not for himself: and the people of the prince that shall come shall destroy the city and the sanctuary; and the end thereof shall be with a flood, and unto the end of the war desolations are determined.

Psalm 22:15-18 My strength is dried up like a potsherd; and my tongue cleaveth to my jaws; and thou hast brought me into the dust of death. For dogs have compassed me: the assembly of the wicked have inclosed me: they pierced my hands and my feet. I may tell all my bones [none were broken, though the two thieves beside him had their legs broken]: they look and stare upon me. They part my garments among them, and cast lots upon my vesture.

¹⁸no money down, just worship me! . . . (or, buy *now*, pay later)

Matthew 4:8-9 Again, the devil taketh him up into an exceeding high mountain, and sheweth him all the kingdoms of the world, and the glory of them; and saith unto him, **All these things will I give thee,** if thou wilt fall down and worship me.

Luke 4:5-8 And the devil, taking him up into an high mountain, shewed unto him all the kingdoms of the world in a moment of time. And the devil said unto him, All this power will I give thee, and the glory of them: for that is delivered unto me; and to whomsoever I will I give it. If thou therefore wilt worship me, all shall be thine. And Jesus answered and said unto him, Get thee behind me, Satan: for it is written, Thou shalt worship the Lord thy God, and him only shalt thou serve.

¹⁹wait till you SEE IT!

This quote from Luke is not an isolated account, where perhaps he might have misheard or misread the proclamation of Messiah. Matthew and Mark both corroborate the declaration. Matthew put it in these words: "till they see the Son of man coming in his kingdom" (Matt.16:28); and Mark, "till they have seen the kingdom of God come with power." (Mark 9:1)

Unfortunately, what is known to psychologists as "selective listening" came into play here, i.e., hearing what one wants to hear. A sort of "tunnel vision" blinded them to the many other related teachings concerning the Kingdom. In terms of this particular teaching—that some, even standing in Yeshua's very presence at that time, were destined as not truly to taste of death, till they were to **see** the Kingdom come—Luke helps us understand: "There shall be weeping and gnashing of teeth, when ye shall see Abraham, and Isaac, and Jacob, and all the prophets, in the kingdom of God, and you yourselves thrust out." (Luke 13:28) In other words, a carnal death and cessation of existence and movement in the material realm of this world is really no big deal, in terms of eternal destinies and the incredible life of the World To Come. The true death, of real and lasting consequence, will consist in seeing the fabulous establishment of the everlasting joy of life in the Kingdom of God on Earth, but being barred and shut out from it into a place of perpetual torment, because of miserable choices and bad attitudes in the first life! There **shall be** weeping and gnashing of teeth at the knowledge that it was yours for the taking, but you opted for the iniquitous **here-and-now**, because all that Messiah and Bible "nonsense" didn't appeal to you, or required too much faith.

[20]**not the "1984" model of big brother**

John 15:12-15 This is my commandment, That ye love one another, as I have loved you. Greater love hath no man than this, that a man lay down his life for his friends. Ye are my friends, if ye do whatsoever I command you. Henceforth I call you not servants; for the servant knoweth not what his lord doeth: but I have called you friends; for all things that I have heard of my Father I have made known unto you.

[21]**the heart of the Kingdom**

Mark 10:13-15 And they brought young children to him, that he should touch them: and his disciples rebuked those that brought them. But when Jesus saw it, he was much displeased, and said unto them, Suffer the little children to come unto me, and forbid them not: for of such is the kingdom of God. Verily I say unto you, Whosoever shall not receive the kingdom of God as a little child, he shall not enter therein.

Matthew 18:2-4 And Jesus called a little child unto him, and set him in the midst of them, and said, Verily I say unto you, Except ye be converted, and become as little children, ye shall not enter into the kingdom of heaven. Whosoever therefore shall humble himself as this little child, the same is greatest in the kingdom of heaven.

[22]**the millennium of the child**

Zechariah 8:3-5 Thus saith the LORD; I am returned unto Zion, and will dwell in the midst of Jerusalem: and Jerusalem shall be called a city of truth; and the mountain of the LORD of hosts the holy mountain. Thus saith the LORD of hosts; There shall yet old men and old women dwell in the streets of Jerusalem, and every man with his staff in his hand for very age. And the streets of the city shall be **full of boys and girls playing** in the streets thereof.

Isaiah 9:6-7 For unto us a child is born, unto us a son is given: and the government shall be upon his shoulder: and his name shall be called Wonderful, Counsellor, The mighty God, The everlasting Father, The Prince of Peace. Of the increase of his government and peace there shall be no end, upon the throne of David, and upon his kingdom, to order it, and to establish it with judgment and with justice from henceforth even for ever. The zeal of the LORD of hosts will perform this.

Isaiah 11:5-9 And righteousness shall be the girdle of his loins, and faithfulness the girdle of his reins. The wolf also shall dwell with the lamb, and the leopard shall lie down with the kid; and the calf and the young lion and the fatling together; and **a little child shall lead them**. And the cow and the bear shall feed; their young ones shall lie down together: and the lion shall eat straw like the ox. And the sucking child shall play on the hole of the asp, and the weaned child shall put his hand on the cockatrice' den. They shall not hurt nor destroy in all my holy mountain: for the earth shall be full of the knowledge of the LORD, as the waters cover the sea.

Isaiah 65:20 There shall be no more thence an infant of days, nor an old man that hath not filled his days: for the **child shall die an hundred years old** [in the land of the "fountain of youth"]; but the sinner being an hundred years old shall be accursed.

Isaiah 49:25 Even the captives of the mighty shall be taken away, and the prey of the terrible shall be delivered: for I will contend with him that contendeth with thee, and **I will save thy children**.

Isaiah 54:13 And all thy children shall be taught of the LORD; and great shall be the peace of thy children.

Isaiah 66:8 Who hath heard such a thing? who hath seen such things? Shall the earth be made to bring forth in one day? or shall a nation be born at once? for as soon as Zion travailed, she brought forth her children.

Ezekiel 37:25 And they shall dwell in the land that I have given unto Jacob my servant, wherein your fathers have dwelt; and they shall dwell therein, even they, **and their children, and their children's children for ever**: and my servant David shall be their prince for ever.

Zechariah 10:9 And I will sow them among the people: and they shall remember me in far countries; and they shall live with their children, and turn again.

Malachi 4:5-6 Behold, I will send you Elijah the prophet before the coming of the great and dreadful day of the LORD: And he shall **turn the heart of the fathers to the children**, and the heart of the children to their fathers [reunited in joyful purpose], lest I come and smite the earth with a curse.

[23] **politics of convenience**

John 19:12-15 And from thenceforth Pilate sought to release him: but the Jews cried out, saying, If thou let this man go, thou art not Caesar's friend: whosoever maketh himself a king speaketh against Caesar. . . . But they cried out, Away with him, away with him, crucify him. Pilate saith unto them, Shall I crucify your King? The chief priests answered, We have no king but Caesar.

[24] **use your head—think twice!**

Revelation 20:4 And I saw thrones, and they sat upon them, and judgment was given unto them: and I saw the souls of them that were beheaded for the witness of Jesus, and for the word of God, and which had not worshipped the beast, neither his image, neither had received his mark upon their foreheads, or in their hands; and they lived and reigned with Christ a thousand years.

Lest we mistakenly assume that the archaic practice of beheading is no longer fashionable in the 20th century, or likely to ever make a comeback in our modern "civilized" world, consider a report by the Associated Press of October 27, 1996, entitled "Saudis holding Dhahran truck bombing suspect" in the Sunday edition of the local *Santa Fe New Mexican*. The report on the investigation of the Dhahran terrorist attack of June 25, 1996, which killed 23 (19 American) and injured 200, concludes with a paragraph on the investigation of the previous year's car bomb attack on a U.S. military facility in Riyadh, which killed 5 Americans and 2 Indians. Investigation of that incident by U.S. officials, according to the report, was short-circuited by the unavailability of the suspects—because the four Saudi men being held had in connection to that bombing had already supposedly confessed to Saudi officials and "were beheaded before U.S. officials could question them."

Contrary to the popular notion of the majority of Bible prophecy experts, the New World Order of Antichrist will not be European-based. According to the ancient prophecy of Isaac (approx. 2000 BCE) and recorded by Moses in Genesis 27:38-40, dominance roles will be reversed by the descendants of Esau (generally, father of the Arabs, conjoined with Ishmael by intermarriage, and consequently also of their sword-based culture and related religious evolution—Islam): "And by thy sword shalt thou [Esau] live, and shalt serve thy brother [Jacob]; and it shall come to pass **when thou shalt have the dominion**, that thou shalt break his yoke from off thy neck."—Gen.27:40 The Western World Order will soon see more than just its flags burning as it topples from 1st World status! Remember that the Antichrist Coalition of Revelation 17 will hate the Whore, make her desolate and naked, eat her "flesh," and burn her with fire. Beheading will be common in the "New World Order," not Western-style criminal "rehabilitation," nor the proscription of "cruel and unusual punishment."

[25]Christianity—fan club, spectator sport, or serious discipleship?

Luke 14:25-27, 33 And there went great multitudes with [Jesus]: and he turned, and said unto them, If any man come to me, and hate not his father, and mother, and wife, and children, and brethren, and sisters, yea, and his own life also, he cannot be my disciple. And whosoever doth not bear his cross, and come after me, cannot be my disciple. . . . So likewise, whosoever he be of you that forsaketh not all that he hath, he cannot be my disciple.

Acts 11:26 And *the disciples were called Christians* first in Antioch.

[26]tough love is wisely welcomed

Proverb 9:8 Reprove not a scorner, lest he hate thee: rebuke a wise man, and he will love thee.

Ecclesiastes 7:5 It is better to hear the rebuke of the wise, than for a man to hear the song of fools.

Proverb 27:5-6 Open rebuke is better than secret love. Faithful are the wounds of a friend; but the kisses of an enemy are deceitful.

Proverb 15:31-32 The ear that heareth the reproof of life abideth among the wise. He that refuseth instruction despiseth his own soul: but he that heareth reproof getteth understanding.

Proverb 6:23 For the commandment is a lamp; and the law is light; and reproofs of instruction are the way of life:

Proverb 10:17 He is in the way of life that keepeth instruction: but he that refuseth reproof erreth.

Proverb 15:10 Correction is grievous unto him that forsaketh the way: and he that hateth reproof shall die.

[27]it's simple

Revelation 14:6-7 And I saw another angel fly in the midst of heaven, having the everlasting gospel to preach unto them that dwell on the earth, and to every nation, and kindred, and tongue, and people, saying with a loud voice, Fear God, and give glory to him; for the hour of his judgment is come: and worship him that made heaven, and earth, and the sea, and the fountains of waters.

Ecclesiastes 12:13 Let us hear the conclusion of the whole matter: Fear God, and keep his commandments: for this is the whole duty of man.

[28]the city-building agenda

Isaiah 14:12 & 21 How art thou fallen from heaven, O Lucifer, son of the morning! how art thou cut down to the ground, which didst weaken the nations! . . . Prepare slaughter for his children for the iniquity of their fathers; that they do not rise, nor possess the land, nor fill the face of the world with cities.

[29]pass the collection plate for the building fund—a box for God?

Acts 17:24-25 God that made the world and all things therein, seeing that he is Lord of heaven and earth, dwelleth not in temples made with hands; neither is worshipped with men's hands, as though he needed any thing, seeing he giveth to all life, and breath, and all things . . .

Acts 7:48-50 Howbeit the most High dwelleth not in temples made with hands; as saith the prophet, Heaven is my throne, and earth is my footstool: what house will ye build me? saith the Lord: or what is the place of my rest? Hath not my hand made all these things?

Hosea 8:14 For Israel hath forgotten his Maker, and buildeth temples; and Judah hath multiplied fenced cities: but I will send a fire upon his cities, and it shall devour the palaces thereof.

[30]get the Spirit

John 2:19-21 Jesus answered and said unto them, Destroy this temple, and in three days I will raise it up. Then said the Jews, Forty and six years was this temple in building, and wilt thou rear it up in three days? But he spake of the temple of his body.

1 Corinthians 3:16 Know ye not that ye are the temple of God, and that the Spirit of God dwelleth in you?

2 Corinthians 6:16 And what agreement hath the temple of God with idols? for ye are the temple of the living God; as God hath said, I will dwell in them, and walk in them; and I will be their God, and they shall be my people.

1 Peter 2:5 Ye also, as lively stones, are built up a spiritual house, an holy priesthood, to offer up spiritual sacrifices, acceptable to God by Jesus Christ.

Revelation 3:12 Him that overcometh will I make a pillar in the temple of my God, and he shall go no more out: and I will write upon him the name of my God, and the name of the city of my God, which is new Jerusalem, which cometh down out of heaven from my God: and I will write upon him my new name.

[31]one or the other

Mark 16:15-16 And he said unto them, Go ye into all the world, and preach the gospel to every creature. He that believeth and is baptized [cleansed by immersion in total] shall be saved; but he that believeth not shall be damned.

Note: Considerable confusion surrounds the concept of baptism, and has been another of those bones of contention among various sects and denominations of squabbling Christians. The fact is that a ritual dipping in water can never cleanse the spirit, soul, or mind. As Apostle Peter put it, "baptism doth also now save us (not the putting away of the filth of the flesh, but the answer of a good conscience toward God,) by the resurrection of Jesus Christ." (1 Pet.3:21) That is, Jesus Christ proved by His resurrection from the dead that He is the Son of God, and thus that complete faith in His every word—by total immersion in it—will cleanse and save us by its effect on our hearts and minds (conscience). The key to this change of heart is *total immersion.*

Thayer's Bible Dictionary analyzes the meaning of the Greek word *"baptizo"* quite well, explaining that one of the most common connotations of the word is, *to overwhelm,* or *to be overwhelmed* by immersion or submersion. It reads, "The clearest example that shows the meaning of *baptizo* is a text from the Greek poet and physician Nicander, who lived about 200 BC. It is a recipe for making pickles. . . . Nicander says that in order to make a pickle, the vegetable should first be 'dipped' *(bapto)* into boiling water and then 'baptized' *(baptizo)* in the vinegar solution. Both verbs concern the immersing of vegetables in solution. But the first is temporary. The second, the act of baptizing the vegetable, produces a permanent change."

32His friends get it all

John 15:15 Henceforth I call you not servants; for the servant knoweth not what his lord doeth: but I have called you friends; for all things that I have heard of my Father I have made known unto you.

33the promise

John 14:25-26 These things have I spoken unto you, being yet present with you. But the Comforter, which is the Holy Ghost, whom the Father will send in my name, he shall teach you all things, and bring all things to your remembrance, whatsoever I have said unto you.

John 15:26-27 But when the Comforter is come, whom I will send unto you from the Father, even the Spirit of truth, which proceedeth from the Father, he shall testify of me: And ye also shall bear witness, because ye have been with me from the beginning.

John 16:7-15 Nevertheless I tell you the truth; It is expedient for you that I go away: for if I go not away, the Comforter will not come unto you; but if I depart, I will send him unto you. And when he is come, he will reprove the world of sin, and of righteousness, and of judgment: Of sin, because they believe not on me; of righteousness, because I go to my Father, and ye see me no more; of judgment, because the prince of this world is judged. I have yet many things to say unto you, but ye cannot bear them now. Howbeit when he, the Spirit of truth, is come, he will guide you into all truth: for he shall not speak of himself; but whatsoever he shall hear, that shall he speak: and he will shew you things to come. He shall glorify me: for he shall receive of mine, and shall shew it unto you. All things that the Father hath are mine: therefore said I, that he shall take of mine, and shall shew it unto you.

34the Daniel files—See Chapter 6 in this book for Daniel's corresponding (and corroborating) revelations providing the countdown to the end in specific numbers of days.

35save the planet from pride pollution

Revelation 11:18 And the nations were angry, and thy wrath is come, and the time of the dead, that they should be judged, and that thou shouldest give reward unto thy servants the prophets, and to the saints, and them that fear thy name, small and great; and shouldest destroy them which destroy the earth.

36mystery of seeds: life multiplies by death

John 12:24-25 Verily, verily, I say unto you, Except a corn of wheat fall into the ground and die, it abideth alone: but if it die, it bringeth forth much fruit. He that loveth his life shall lose it; and he that hateth his life in this world shall keep it unto life eternal.

37the everlasting covenant

Hebrews 13:20-21 Now the God of peace, that **brought again from the dead** our Lord Jesus, that great shepherd of the sheep, through the blood of the everlasting covenant, make you perfect in every good work to do his will, working in you that which is wellpleasing in his sight, through Jesus Christ; to whom be glory for ever and ever. Amen.

Matthew 26:28-29 For this is my blood of the new testament, which is shed for many for the remission of sins. But I say unto you, I will not drink henceforth of this fruit of the vine, until that day when I drink it new with you in my Father's kingdom.

Chapter 15—Ten Virgins

[1]**you have a lamp?—everybody has one of those!**

James 2:18-20 Yea, a man may say, Thou hast faith, and I have works: shew me thy faith without thy works, and I will shew thee my faith by my works. Thou believest that there is one God; thou doest well: the **devils also believe**, and tremble. But wilt thou know, O vain man, that faith without works is dead?

[2]**get ready!—this party is not just "come-as-you-are"**

Matthew 22:11-14 And when the king came in to see the guests, he saw there a man which had not on a wedding garment: And he saith unto him, Friend, how camest thou in hither not having a wedding garment? And he was speechless. Then said the king to the servants, Bind him hand and foot, and take him away, and cast him into outer darkness; there shall be weeping and gnashing of teeth. For many are called, but few are chosen.

[3]**what's it worth to you?**

Matthew 13:44-46 Again, the kingdom of heaven is like unto treasure hid in a field; the which when a man hath found, he hideth, and for joy thereof goeth and selleth all that he hath, and buyeth that field. Again, the kingdom of heaven is like unto a merchant man, seeking goodly pearls: Who, when he had found one pearl of great price, went and sold all that he had, and bought it.

[4]**fine linen for fine, well-prepared saints**

Revelation 19:7-9 Let us be glad and rejoice, and give honour to him: for the marriage of the Lamb is come, and his wife hath **made herself ready**. And to her was granted that she should be arrayed in fine linen, clean and white: for the fine linen is the righteousness of saints. And he saith unto me, Write, Blessed are they which are called unto the marriage supper of the Lamb. And he saith unto me, These are the true sayings of God.

[5]**pursuits and preoccupations of the "unbetrothed" heathen**

Luke 12:22-23, 29-34 And he said unto his disciples, Therefore I say unto you, Take no thought for your life, what ye shall eat; neither for the body, what ye shall put on. The life is more than meat, and the body is more than raiment. . . . And seek not ye what ye shall eat, or what ye shall drink, neither be ye of doubtful mind. For **all these things do the nations of the world seek after**: and your Father knoweth that ye have need of these things. But rather seek ye the kingdom of God; and all these things shall be added unto you. Fear not, little flock; for it is your Father's good pleasure to give you the kingdom. Sell that ye have, and give alms; provide yourselves bags which wax not old, a treasure in the heavens that faileth not, where no thief approacheth, neither moth corrupteth. For where your treasure is, there will your heart be also.

[6]**it's not the thought, but the effort that counts**

Philippians 3:7-15 But what things were gain to me, those I counted loss for Christ. Yea doubtless, and I count all things but loss for the excellency of the knowledge of Christ Jesus my Lord: for whom I have suffered the loss of all things, and do count them but dung, that I may win Christ, . . . That I may know him, and the power of his resurrection, and the fellowship of his sufferings, being made conformable unto his death; if by any means I might attain unto the resurrection of the dead. Not as though I had already attained, either were already perfect: but I follow after, if that I may apprehend that for which also I am apprehended of Christ Jesus. Brethren, I count not myself to have apprehended: but **this one thing I do**, forgetting those things which are behind, and **reaching forth** unto those things which are before, I **press toward the mark for the prize** of the high calling of God in Christ Jesus. Let us therefore, **as many as be perfect, be thus minded**: and if in any thing ye be otherwise minded, God shall reveal even this unto you.

[7]**despite what "they say"**—Please note that in the famous "Sermon on the Mount" when Yeshua several times says (in Matthew chapter 5), *"Ye have heard that it hath been said by them of old time . . ."* He was **not** referring (in the singular) to Moses in the Torah, nor to the LAW or Torah itself, but (plurally) to its interpreters, the ancient scribes and religious authorities. In their attempt to reduce the LAW of GOD to a narrow and less inclusive formula, they codified a minimized version of the Law given by Moses by interpreting it to mean only what suited them. Thus they succeeding in dismissing all of the logical and intended extensions of what the Spirit of that LAW really taught of itself. This, of course, excused huge volumes of unacceptable attitudes and behaviors that the LAW intended to prevent. It was precisely those atrocious attitudes and pernicious practices that Christ attempted reverse by clarifying what the LAW of GOD truly taught. After all, it was *"Jesus Christ, the same yesterday, and today, and forever"* who had given that LAW to Moses. (Search it out!)

[8]**the world system, or the promise?**

Psalm 106:24 Yea, they [having been miraculously delivered from oppressive Egypt, only to later lust for its delicacies] despised the pleasant land, they **believed not His word**...

Acts 7:39 To Whom our [doubting, double-minded] fathers would not obey, but **thrust Him from them**, and in their hearts turned back again into Egypt [the established order of that era].—Stephen the martyr

[9]**Dispensationalism**—Essentially, this notion distills into the "Christian" doctrine that different ages, or periods of history invoke different sets of commandments, rules, and provisions for ordering the affairs of believers during a specific epoch. It seems the definition of the particular age depends on whatever the "arbitrary" determination of the nature of the age may be by some consensus of "learned" opinion. Basically, it too often boils down to situational theology, where the circumstances are somehow deemed to dictate the pattern of faith and lifestyle of the believer, and where variant religious expectations are supposedly ordained by God (as per the religious "authorities") for certain periods. (They cite the Old and New Testaments as **the** classic example.) A valid example of this basic concept can be found in the era of sacrificial-blood worship involving ritual killing of animals to atone for sin up until the end of the Temple "dispensation." Now it is determined that Christ was the ultimate Passover Lamb, and all atonement has been forever accomplished, thus moving us into a new dispensation, which dispenses with the need for animal sacrifice (other than commemorative). Some point out that, since Christ, a new dispensation of (Messianic) grace has replaced an "outmoded" dispensation of (Mosaic) law. Arguments can be struck about the extremes of either view. However, the real problem with dispensational theology lies in the potential for arbitrary misapplication of the concept to rationalize a situationally oriented, plastic religious practice that can be variously molded to suit the convenience of the parties often sitting arbitrarily in authority with absolutely no Divine mandate. In very fact, Scriptural *absolutes* are often the prime targets for abolition; and disguised apostasy in the form of self-anointed authorities is the preying hunter.

[10]be sure you're sure—the Foundation surely is!

2 Timothy 2:19-21 Nevertheless the foundation of God standeth sure, having this seal, The Lord knoweth them that are his. And, Let every one that nameth the name of Christ depart from iniquity [see Rev. 18:4]. But in a great house there are not only vessels of gold and of silver, but also of wood and of earth; and some to honour, and some to dishonour. If a man therefore purge himself from these, he shall be a vessel unto honour, sanctified, and meet for the master's use, and prepared unto every good work.

2 Peter 1:10-12 Wherefore the rather, brethren, give diligence to make your calling and election sure: for if ye do these things, ye shall never fall: For so an entrance shall be ministered unto you abundantly into the everlasting kingdom of our Lord and Saviour Jesus Christ. Wherefore I will not be negligent to put you always in remembrance of these things, though ye know them, and be established in the present truth.

[11]the doctrine of Christ

John 12:25-26 He that loveth his life shall lose it; and he that hateth his life in this world shall keep it unto life eternal. If any man serve me, let him follow me; and where I am, there shall also my servant be: if any man serve me, him will my Father honour.— Jesus Christ

II John 1:8-11 Look to yourselves, that we lose not those things which we have wrought, but that we receive a full reward. Whosoever transgresseth, and abideth not in the doctrine of Christ, hath not God. He that abideth in the doctrine of Christ, he hath both the Father and the Son. If there come any unto you, and bring not this doctrine, receive him not into your house, neither bid him God speed: For he that biddeth him God speed is partaker of his evil deeds.

[12]many have lamps, few buy the oil

Matthew 22:14 For many are called, but few are chosen.

Matthew 7:14 Because strait is the gate, and narrow is the way, which leadeth unto life, and few there be that find it.

[13]"I know you not!"—or, "Enter thou into the joy of thy Lord!"??

Luke 9:25-27 For what is a man advantaged, if he gain the whole world, and lose himself, or be cast away? For whosoever shall be ashamed of me [Yeshua's example of faith and deferred reward] and of my words [renouncing the pride and joy of this world], of him shall the Son of man be ashamed, when he shall come in his own glory [power and wealth of the New World Estate of Messiah], and in his Father's, and of the holy angels. But I tell you of a truth, there be some standing here, which shall not taste of death [have no idea the great joy they shall lose], **till they see** the kingdom of God.

[14]faith or fortune: wanna take your chances?

Luke 18:18-25 And a certain ruler asked him, saying, Good Master, what shall I do to inherit eternal life? And Jesus said unto him, Why callest thou me good? none is good, save one, that is, God. Thou knowest the commandments, Do not commit adultery, Do not kill, Do not steal, Do not bear false witness, Honour thy father and thy mother. And he said, All these have I kept from my youth up [quite a moral fellow!]. Now when Jesus heard these things, he said unto him, Yet lackest thou one thing: sell all that thou hast, and distribute unto the poor, and thou shalt have treasure in heaven: and come, follow me. And when he heard this, he was very sorrowful: for he was very rich. And when Jesus saw that he was very sorrowful, he said, How hardly shall they that have riches enter into the kingdom of God! For it is easier for a camel to go through a needle's eye, than for a rich man to enter into the kingdom of God.

[15]**the tickets are not free**

Luke 14:25-28 And there went great multitudes with him: and he turned, and said unto them, If any man come to me, and hate not his father, and mother, and wife, and children, and brethren, and sisters, yea, and his own life also, he cannot be my disciple. And whosoever doth not bear his cross, and come after me, cannot be my disciple. For which of you, intending to build a tower, sitteth not down first, and counteth the cost, whether he have sufficient to finish it?

Matthew 13:44-46 Again, the kingdom of heaven is like unto treasure hid in a field; the which when a man hath found, he hideth, and for joy thereof goeth and selleth all that he hath, and buyeth that field. Again, the kingdom of heaven is like unto a merchant man, seeking goodly pearls: Who, when he had found one pearl of great price, went and sold all that he had, and bought it.

Revelation 3:15-19 I know thy works, that thou art neither cold nor hot: I would thou wert cold or hot. So then because thou art lukewarm, and neither cold nor hot, I will spue thee out of my mouth. Because thou sayest, I am rich, and increased with goods, and have need of nothing; and knowest not that thou art wretched, and miserable, and poor, and blind, and naked: **I counsel thee to buy of me** gold tried in the fire, that thou mayest be rich; and white raiment, that thou mayest be clothed, and that the shame of thy nakedness do not appear; and anoint thine eyes with eyesalve, that thou mayest see. As many as I love, I rebuke and chasten: be zealous therefore, and repent.

Psalm 11:5 The LORD trieth the righteous: but the wicked and him that loveth violence his soul hateth.

Psalm 34:19 Many are the afflictions of the righteous: but the LORD delivereth him out of them all.

[16]**interest and dividends—Christian financial strategy rationale**

Luke 19:23 Wherefore then gavest not thou my money into the bank, that at my coming I might have required mine own with usury?

Matthew 25:27 Thou oughtest therefore to have put my money to the exchangers, and then at my coming I should have received mine own with usury [interest].